IFIP Advances in Information and Communication Technology 402

IFIP – The International Federation for Information Processing

IFIP was founded in 1960 under the auspices of UNESCO, following the First World Computer Congress held in Paris the previous year. An umbrella organization for societies working in information processing, IFIP's aim is two-fold: to support information processing within its member countries and to encourage technology transfer to developing nations. As its mission statement clearly states,

> IFIP's mission is to be the leading, truly international, apolitical organization which encourages and assists in the development, exploitation and application of information technology for the benefit of all people.

IFIP is a non-profitmaking organization, run almost solely by 2500 volunteers. It operates through a number of technical committees, which organize events and publications. IFIP's events range from an international congress to local seminars, but the most important are:

- The IFIP World Computer Congress, held every second year;
- Open conferences;
- Working conferences.

The flagship event is the IFIP World Computer Congress, at which both invited and contributed papers are presented. Contributed papers are rigorously refereed and the rejection rate is high.

As with the Congress, participation in the open conferences is open to all and papers may be invited or submitted. Again, submitted papers are stringently refereed.

The working conferences are structured differently. They are usually run by a working group and attendance is small and by invitation only. Their purpose is to create an atmosphere conducive to innovation and development. Refereeing is also rigorous and papers are subjected to extensive group discussion.

Publications arising from IFIP events vary. The papers presented at the IFIP World Computer Congress and at open conferences are published as conference proceedings, while the results of the working conferences are often published as collections of selected and edited papers.

Any national society whose primary activity is about information processing may apply to become a full member of IFIP, although full membership is restricted to one society per country. Full members are entitled to vote at the annual General Assembly, National societies preferring a less committed involvement may apply for associate or corresponding membership. Associate members enjoy the same benefits as full members, but without voting rights. Corresponding members are not represented in IFIP bodies. Affiliated membership is open to non-national societies, and individual and honorary membership schemes are also offered.

Yogesh K. Dwivedi   Helle Zinner Henriksen
David Wastell   Rahul De' (Eds.)

Grand Successes and Failures in IT

Public and Private Sectors

IFIP WG 8.6 International Working Conference
on Transfer and Diffusion of IT, TDIT 2013
Bangalore, India, June 27-29, 2013
Proceedings

 Springer

Volume Editors

Yogesh K. Dwivedi
Swansea University Business School
Haldane Building, Singleton Park, Swansea, SA2 8PP, UK
E-mail: ykdwivedi@gmail.com

Helle Zinner Henriksen
Copenhagen Business School, Department of IT Management
Solbjerg Plads 3, 2000 Frederiksberg, Denmark
E-mail: hzh.itm@cbs.dk

David Wastell
Nottingham University Business School
Jubilee Campus, Nottingham, NG8 1BB, UK
E-mail: david.wastell@nottingham.ac.uk

Rahul De'
Indian Institute of Management Bangalore
Bannerghatta Road, Karnataka 560076, India
E-mail: rahul@iimb.ernet.in

ISSN 1868-4238   ISSN 1868-422X (electronic)
ISBN 978-3-642-43616-1   ISBN 978-3-642-38862-0 (eBook)
DOI 10.1007/978-3-642-38862-0
Springer Heidelberg Dordrecht London New York

CR Subject Classification (1998): K.4, K.6, H.4, J.1, J.7, D.2

Typesetting: Camera-ready by author, data conversion by Scientific Publishing Services, Chennai, India

Printed on acid-free paper

Springer is part of Springer Science+Business Media (www.springer.com)

Preface

This book presents the proceedings of the 2013 Conference of Working Group 8.6 of the International Federation for Information Processing (IFIP). The focus of WG8.6 is the diffusion, adoption, and implementation of information (and communication) technologies. This was the first time that the Group had met outside of its usual haunts, of North America and Europe, apart from one visit to Australia. We were delighted that the Indian Institute of Management in Bangalore agreed to host the conference. Not only is this an important step in broadening the international reach of the Group, but with Bangalore known as the Silicon Valley of India, reflecting the city's position as the nation's leading IT exporter, what better place in which to gather!

The central theme of the 2013 conference was the continuing difficulty of bringing information systems (IS) projects to successful fruition. Despite decades of research and the accumulation of a substantial knowledge-base, the failure rate of IS initiatives continues unabated. The recent abandonment of a multi-billion dollar project to computerize health records in the UK, the National Programme for Information Technology (NPfIT), provides just one spectacular recent example, and sadly it is not difficult to unearth more, as the papers in the book attest. Why is this so, we asked in our Call for Papers? Is the fault one of theory and inadequate understanding? Or is the problem one of knowledge transfer, the failure to embed research knowledge in the working practices of managers and policy-makers?

The primary aim of the conference was therefore to help advance our understanding of the success and failure of technology-based innovation. We asked a number of rhetorical questions to stimulate debate and reflection. Whether our theoretical base is too narrow was one such question. It is arguable that some theories, such as diffusion theory and the ubiquitous TAM (Technology Acceptance Model), have been over-represented in our research endeavors. Or maybe IS researchers have become too infatuated with theory, making our work inaccessible to practice? Papers addressing theory in a critical way were therefore very welcome, presenting and illustrating alternative conceptual lenses and standpoints.

While the conference theme explicitly invoked "grand successes and failures," the scope was not limited to large projects, and papers addressing smaller initiatives were explicitly encouraged. Indeed, we asked, perhaps there is much to be learned from considering questions of scale. Extending the variety of research methodologies was another area where we thought innovation could assist progress in the research community. Finally, we felt that there were organizational contexts that have also been relatively neglected. The bulk of IS research has tended to concentrate on commercial enterprises, yet the degree of contemporary IT-enabled change in the non-profit sectors is at least as great, and the challenges arguably stiffer.

The Call for Papers solicited submissions in two main categories: full-length journal style papers and short papers, which could be research in progress or polemical "position papers." In total, 65 submissions were received, representing a broad international cross-section of authors. While the majority were from the UK (29%), there was a strong local showing, with 19% of authors from India. This was our first meeting in a developing country, and we were very pleased with the high number of local submissions. A further 24% of authors were from western Europe, with The Netherlands and Scandinavia leading the way, followed by the US and Canada (13%). Australia and Singapore each represented 5% of the authorship, and other countries included Bangladesh, South Africa, New Zealand, and Namibia. The reviewing process was rigorous, with two independent reviews sought, and we are indebted to the international Program Committee for the sterling work they did, and the constructive feedback they provided, which enabled authors to improve their papers. Without their support, this conference would not have been possible. Although rigorous, the review process was nonetheless conducted in an inclusive, developmental spirit. Some full papers, for instance, which did not reach the acceptance threshold were felt to contain ideas of genuine merit. We wanted to give the authors an opportunity to share these with colleagues; authors were given the option of preparing a short paper and almost all took advantages of this.

The final set of 35 full papers appearing in these proceedings were clustered into five main groups, and appear in successive sections of the book. The majority (10) directly addressed the conference theme of IS success/failure; these papers are presented in Part I. Studies of the adoption of IT (typically using TAM like models) have been strongly represented in the work of WG8.6 since its inception, and five papers were assembled under this heading (Part II). Software development is another perennial theme of WG8.6, and four papers had this as their main focus (Part III). A large group of papers (nine in number) examined IT in the public sector; these are compiled in Part IV. The final set of seven papers addressed more general aspects of IS theory and methodology (Part V). In each part, note that papers are listed alphabetically according to the family name of the first author.

Papers in Part I, as noted, address the central issue of the conference, IS success, and its dark side of IS failure. *Bunker* et al. focus on multi-agency disaster management systems arguing for a greater focus on collaboration between organizations in their development. Using extensive survey data, *Coakes et al.* identify success factors for knowledge management projects, drawing on sociotechnical design principles. In the next paper, *Devos et al.* interrogate the failure of an outsourcing venture, particularly the role played by contractual factors. Based on a wide-ranging review of the literature on failure factors, *Dwivedi et al.* propose a taxonomy that takes into account project stages, failure type, and national context. *Elbanna and Linderoth* focus on motivations and drivers where IT adoption is voluntary, using a telemedicine case study to illustrate their argument. In a novel application of Bartel's theory of market separations, *Gunupudi and De* analyze the problematics of an agricultural market information system in India, while *Janssen et al.* focus attention on the special characteristics of large-scale transformation projects. *Papazafeiropoulou et al.* examine the reasons for improved supply chain performance in a supermarket chain through the implementation of its "green" logistics strategy. Failure factors in a developing country context are next investigated by *Vaidya et al.*, basing their fieldwork on an agricultural marketing project in India that was ultimately abandoned many years after inception. The final paper in Part I, by *Waring et al.*, reflects on the success of a local heath project in the UK focusing on stakeholder engagement.

Part II of the volume contains five papers on IT adoption. Examining the Australian livestock industry, *Hossain and Quaddus* identify market pressure, cognitive pressure, and government support as key drivers of RFID adoption. *Kapoor et al.* find low predictive value for some "innovation attributes," such as relative advantage, for an Indian interbank payment service, although cost did exhibit a strong link with adoption. In a literature study, supplemented by qualitative analysis, *Landeweerd et al.* present a theoretical analysis of user adoption for various Google products; they are pessimistic for Google Health, but positive for Google Search. *Rana et al.* develop an IS success model based on TAM that predicts positive outcomes for a "public grievance redress" system in India, highlighting the model's potential for enhancing the utility of the system. The final paper in this section, by *Srinivasan and Damsgaard*, discusses the tension between the individual orientation of traditional adoption models and "network adoption" in the context of social media.

Part III contains four papers focused on software development. The first two papers specifically examine agile methods. *Baskerville* and *Pries-Heje* analyze the way that agile methods are continuously adapted in practice, characterizing this as a process of fragmentation and "re-articulation," while *Michaelson* looks at the adoption of agile methods in the UK public sector. *Persson* then examines the effectiveness of collocation for collaboration in software development offshoring. Finally, *Thomas and Marath* address the relationship between risk, risk management and the outcome of software projects, using structural equation modeling to develop an integrated model.

Part IV contains a large group of papers addressing ICT developments in the public sector, many in a developing country context. *Bhat* deploys institutional theory, focusing on the way that eGovernment initiatives are legitimated using the example of India's Unique Identification (UID) project. *Brooks and Alam* describe a novel application of "Action Design Research" to develop an information system for land records in Bangladesh. In the next paper, *Haque and Mantode* discuss how information hubs can be created to support sustainable social development and the needs of vulnerable groups, framing their analysis in terms of Actor Network Theory. *Homburg and Dijkshoorn* provide an institutional analysis of the diffusion of personalized services at the municipal level in The Netherlands, emphasizing human agency and persuasion. *Kameswari* applies a "Common Pool of Resources" analysis to two agricultural projects in India, characterizing information as the "new commons." In an international survey of 187 countries, *Krishnan et al.* address the relationship between dimensions of e-participation and eGovernment maturity. *Molnar et al.* describe a framework for evaluating user experience with high-definition video in the delivery of public services. *Seror* analyzes issues of open source design and sustainability in the context of the Cuban national health care network. The final paper in this section, that of *Thomson and Akesson*, seeks to understand IS development and innovation complexity in governmental IS projects, proposing a novel metaphor, that of "fragmentation."

Part V gathers together a diverse set of papers that take IS theory and/or methodology as their main interest. *Gangadharan et al.* propose a methodology for deciding between the decommissioning of legacy systems and their continuation. *Larsen and Levine* consider the relationships between our discipline and cognate fields using the ideas of discourse communities and families of fields. *Madsen et al.* propose a novel framework for outsourcing decisions, with esthetic, symbolic, and instrumental dimensions; two projects are presented, in Denmark and Bangladesh. *Mkhomazi and Iyamu* examine factors that can guide the selection of theoretical frameworks for IS studies, with a particular interest in socio technically oriented theories. The paper by *Rao and De* then argues for the use of Stone's strong structuration theory (SST) as a lens for studying technology assimilation. *Vaziri and Ghadiri* present a novel neuroscientific model of human cognition for studying human-computer interaction, with specific applicability to problems of demographic transition. Finally, *Wastell* argues for a greater focus on individual variation in design science studies, as opposed to the search for universal principles.

The book is completed by Parts VI and VII that, respectively, compile the shorter papers (research in progress, practice papers, position papers) and poster papers.

In addition to the above papers, there were several invited academic presentations. We were delighted that *Geoff Walsham* accepted our invitation to address the opening plenary. His paper was entitled "Successes and Challenges in ICT-Based Projects: Some Evidence from India." Walsham discussed examples of successful ICT-based systems, going on to develop important implications for IS research. This preface concludes with a précis of his talk, quoting from the abstract he provided. The second academic keynote presentation was by *Karl Kautz*; a full copy of his paper opens the proceedings. The third academic keynote was provided by *Raghav Rao*, Editor of *Information Systems Frontiers*, on the subject of "Community Intelligence and Social Media." An invited essay by the Conference Chair (*David Wastell*) also appears in part V of the book.

In his address, Walsham began by highlighting examples of success in the Indian context, including "the business process and software outsourcing sectors... the phenomenal growth of the mobile phone across all strata of society... as well as specific IS initiatives such as the Indian Railways reservation system, and computerized land registration and bill payments systems in Andra Pradesh." While it is good to celebrate success, Walsham reminded us of the specter of failure highlighting "the failure of top-down projects to meet needs at lower levels, such as early attempts at the introduction of GIS for land management." He cautions that some of the successes he mentions "are not always easily sustainable over time, or do not benefit all sectors of society, particularly the poor," adding that "further challenges include the need to tackle major projects such as the provision of public health information systems ... where, in order to be effective, change needs to take place in a whole host of other areas such as human capacity building, attitudinal change, financing, and institution building."

In conclusion, Walsham pertinently asks what can IS academics contribute in this space of successes, failures, and complex challenges, making three cardinal points:

Firstly, I wish to argue that theory is a key contribution as a way of trying to generalize our experiences to be of relevance to wider contexts. But our theories of systems design and development do not seem up to the task of dealing with IS in a broader context of major institutional and societal change. We need to extend our theoretical scope and this brings me to a second implication, namely, the need to embrace multi-disciplinarity. I have argued elsewhere that the days of IS being the only player in the field of ICT implementation have gone. I believe that the IS field, with over 30 years of experience of IS diffusion, adoption and implementation, still has a lot to offer, but only if we actively engage with other disciplines with common interests: anthropology, computer science, organizational theory, science and technology studies, geography, sociology, development studies etc. My final point is to argue that the IS field needs to have a clear moral agenda to make the world a better place, rather than, for example, merely to make money. This is needed in order to inspire future generations of IS academics and practitioners that our field is a worthwhile focus for their working lives.

Socially relevant, multi-disciplinary research, guided by a strong moral compass: an inspiring vision for the Working Group and for the IS field in general. We hope that our gathering in Bangalore makes some small but important steps along the road ahead.

April 2013

Yogesh K. Dwivedi
Helle Zinner Henriksen
David Wastell
Rahul De'

Organization

General Chair

David Wastell   Nottingham University, UK

Program Chairs

Yogesh K. Dwivedi   Swansea University, UK
Helle Zinner Henriksen   Copenhagen Business School, Denmark

Doctoral Consortium Chair

Jan Pries-Heje   Roskilde University, Denmark

Organizing Chair

Rahul De'   Indian Institute of Management Bangalore,
                             India

Secretariat

Ravi Anand Rao   Indian Institute of Management Bangalore,
                             India

Doctoral Consortium Faculty

Atreyi Kankanahalli   National University of Singapore
Helle Zinner Henriksen   Copenhagen Business School, Denmark
Jan Devos   Ghent University, Belgium
Richard Baskerville   Georgia State University, USA
Yogesh K. Dwidedi   Swansea University, UK

Conference Sponsorship

The conference was supported by the generous help of:

- IBM
- InfoSYS

Program Committee

Dolphy Abraham	Alliance University, India
Md. Mahfuz Ashraf	University of Dhaka, Bangladesh
Michel Avital	Copenhagen Business School, Denmark
Jeff Baker	American University of Sharjah, UAE
Deborah Bunker	University of Sydney, Australia
Lemuria Carter	North Carolina A & T State University, USA
Hsin Chen	University of Bedfordshire, UK
Ioanna Constantiou	Copenhagen Business School, Denmark
Jan Damsgaard	Copenhagen Business School, Denmark
Jan Devos	University College West-Flanders, Belgium
Brian Fitzgerald	University of Limerick, Ireland
Bob Galliers	Bentley University, USA
Roya Gholami	Aston Business School, UK
Babita Gupta	California State University, Monterey Bay, USA
Arul Chib	Nanyang Technological University, Singapore
Andreas Eckhardt	Goethe University Frankfurt, Germany
Andreas Gadatsch	Bonn-Rhein-Sieg University, Germany
Åke Grönlund	Örebro University, Sweden
M.P. Gupta	Indian Institute of Technology Delhi, India
G Harindranath	Royal Holloway, UK
Richard Heeks	Manchester University, UK
Alfonso Durán Heras	Universidad Carlos III de Madrid, Spain
Vikas Jain	University of Tampa, USA
Marijn Janssen	Delft University of Technology, The Netherlands
Anand Jeyaraj	Wright State University, USA
Atreyi Kankanhalli	National University of Singapore, Singapore
Karlheinz Kautz	The University of Wollongong, Australia
Tor J. Larsen	Norwegian School of Management, Norway
Sven Laumer	University of Bamberg, Germany
Gonzalo Leon	Universidad Politécnica de Madrid, Spain
Linda Levine	Independent Researcher Consultant
Kalle Lyytinen	Case Western Reserve University
Lars Mathiassen	Georgia State University, USA
Ulf Melin	Linkoping University, Sweden
Amit Mitra	University of the West of England, UK
Michael D. Myers	University of Auckland Business School, New Zealand
Mike Newman	University of Manchester, UK
Peter Axel Nielsen	Aalborg University, Denmark

Table of Contents

Invited Paper

Sociomateriality and Information Systems Success and Failure   1
Karlheinz Kautz and Dubravka Cecez-Kecmanovic

Part I: IS Success and Failure

Repertoires of Collaboration for Disaster Management: Negotiating
Emergent and Dynamic Systems Success 21
Deborah Bunker, Linda Levine, and Carol Woody

Success or Failure in Knowledge Management Systems: A Universal
Issue 39
Elayne Coakes, A.D. Amar, and Maria L. Granados

Narratives of an Outsourced Information Systems Failure in a Small
Enterprise 57
Jan Devos, Hendrik Van Landeghem, and Dirk Deschoolmeester

IS/IT Project Failures: A Review of the Extant Literature for Deriving
a Taxonomy of Failure Factors 73
*Yogesh K. Dwivedi, Karthik Ravichandran, Michael D. Williams,
Siân Miller, Banita Lal, George V. Antony, and Muktha Kartik*

Tracing Success in the Voluntary Use of Open Technology in
Organisational Setting 89
Amany Elbanna and Henrik C.J. Linderoth

Market Separations Perspective of Agricultural Markets and Successful
AMIS: Beyond Technical Rationality 105
Laxmi Gunupudi and Rahul De'

Management and Failure of Large Transformation Projects: Factors
Affecting User Adoption 121
Marijn Janssen, Anne Fleur van Veenstra, and Haiko van der Voort

Green IT Logistics in a Greek Retailer: Grand Successes and Minor
Failures 136
*Anastasia Papazafeiropoulou, Georgios Gerostergioudis,
Hsin Chen, and Laurence Brooks*

Major Issues in the Successful Implementation of Information Systems
in Developing Countries 151
Ranjan Vaidya, Michael D. Myers, and Lesley Gardner

Bringing about Innovative Change: The Case of a Patient Flow
Management System in an NHS Trust 164
    Teresa Waring, Martin Alexander, and Rebecca Casey

Part II: Studies of IT Adoption

Does Mandatory Pressure Increase RFID Adoption? A Case Study
of Western Australian Livestock Industry 184
    Mohammad Alamgir Hossain and Mohammed Quaddus

Role of Innovation Attributes in Explaining the Adoption Intention
for the Interbank Mobile Payment Service in an Indian Context........ 203
    Kawaljeet Kapoor, Yogesh K. Dwivedi, and Michael D. Williams

The Success of Google Search, the Failure of Google Health and the
Future of Google Plus 221
    Marcel Landeweerd, Ton Spil, and Richard Klein

Examining the Factors Affecting Intention to Use of, and User
Satisfaction with Online Public Grievance Redressal System (OPGRS)
in India.. 240
    Nripendra P. Rana, Yogesh K. Dwivedi, and Michael D. Williams

Tensions between Individual Use and Network Adoption of Social
Media Platforms 261
    Nikhil Srinivasan and Jan Damsgaard

Part III: Software Development

Discursive Co-development of Agile Systems and Agile Methods 279
    Richard Baskerville and Jan Pries-Heje

Is Agile the Answer? The Case of UK Universal Credit 295
    Rosa Michaelson

The Cross-Cultural Knowledge Sharing Challenge: An Investigation
of the Collocation Strategy in Software Development Offshoring 310
    John Stouby Persson

An Integrative Model Linking Risk, Risk Management and Project
Performance: Support from Indian Software Projects 326
    Sam Thomas and Bhasi Marath

Part IV: IT in the Public Sector

Legitimation of E-Government Initiatives: A Study of India's Identity
Project 343
    Jyoti M. Bhat

Designing an Information System for Updating Land Records in
Bangladesh: Action Design Ethnographic Research (ADER) 359
    Laurence Brooks and M. Shahanoor Alam

Governance in the Technology Era: Implications of Actor Network
Theory for Social Empowerment in South Asia 375
    Akhlaque Haque and Kamna L. Mantode

Persuasive Pressures in the Adoption of E-Government 391
    Vincent Homburg and Andres Dijkshoorn

Information as "Commons": Applying Design Principles to ICTD
Projects 407
    V.L.V. Kameswari

E-Participation and E-Government Maturity: A Global Perspective 420
    Satish Krishnan, Thompson S.H. Teo, and John Lim

A Framework of Reference for Evaluating User Experience When Using
High Definition Video to Video to Facilitate Public Services 436
    Andreea Molnar, Vishanth Weerakkody, Ramzi El-Haddadeh,
    Habin Lee, and Zahir Irani

Designing Sustainable Open Source Systems: The Cuban National
Health Care Network and Portal (INFOMED) 451
    Ann Séror

Understanding ISD and Innovation through the Lens
of Fragmentation 467
    Michel Thomsen and Maria Åkesson

Part V: Theory and Methods

IT Innovation Squeeze: Propositions and a Methodology for Deciding
to Continue or Decommission Legacy Systems 481
    G.R. Gangadharan, Eleonora J. Kuiper, Marijn Janssen, and
    Paul Oude Luttighuis

Learning from Failure: Myths and Misguided Assumptions about IS
Disciplinary Knowledge 495
    Tor J. Larsen and Linda Levine

From Research to Practical Application: Knowledge Transfer Planning
and Execution in Outsourcing 510
    Sabine Madsen, Keld Bødker, and Thomas Tøth

A Guide to Selecting Theory to Underpin Information Systems
Studies 525
    Sharol Sibongile Mkhomazi and Tiko Iyamu

Organizational Assimilation of Technology in a Sunrise Industry –
A Story of Successes and Failures 538
    Ravi A. Rao and Rahul De'

Improving Human Cognitive Processing by Applying Accessibility
Standards for Information and Communication Technology 555
    Daryoush Daniel Vaziri and Argang Ghadiri

In Praise of Abundance: Why Individuals Matter in Design Science..... 566
    David Wastell

Part VI: Shorter Papers

Why Not Let IT Fail? The IT Project Success Paradox 579
    Paul J. Ambrose and David Munro

Social Software: Silver Bullet or an Enabler of Competitive
Advantage? 583
    Darshan Desai

A System of Systems Approach to Managing Emergence in Complex
Environments 587
    Igor Hawryszkiewycz

Curriculum Design and Delivery for E-Government Knowledge Transfer
in a Cross Cultural Environment: The Bangladesh Experience 596
    Ahmed Imran, Shirley Gregor, and Tim Turner

Actor Network Theory in Interpretative Research Approach 605
    Tiko Iyamu, Tefo Sekgweleo, and Sharol Sibongile Mkhomazi

Indian IT Industry Firms: Moving towards an Active Innovation
Strategy 611
    Rajeev Mukundan and Sam Thomas

Endless Bad Projects or Evidence-Based Practice? An Agenda
for Action... 619
    Briony J. Oates, David W. Wainwright, and Helen M. Edwards

Participatory Approach versus Bureaucratic 'Pressure': The Case of
Health Information Systems Programme 625
    C.R. Ranjini

Using the Lens of "Social Construction of Technology" to Understand
the Design and Implementation of Aadhaar (UID) Project 633
    Lewin Sivamalai

Quality Improvements for Ensuring e-Retailing Success in India:
Constructs and Frameworks   639
    Marya Wani, Vishnupriya Raghavan, Dolphy M. Abraham, and
    Madhumita G. Majumder

Innovation in Government Services: The Case of Open Data   644
    Zhenbin Yang and Atreyi Kankanhalli

Information Communication Technology (ICT) for Disabled Persons in
Bangladesh: Preliminary Study of Impact/Outcome   652
    Md. Jahangir Alam Zahid, Md. Mahfuz Ashraf,
    Bushra Tahseen Malik, and Md. Rakibul Hoque

Part VII: Poster Papers

Organization Culture Dimensions as Antecedents of Internet
Technology Adoption   658
    Subhasish Dasgupta and Babita Gupta

Facilitators and Inhibitors in the Assimilation of Complex Information
Systems   663
    Anand Jeyaraj

Virtual Worlds as Platforms for Digital Entrepreneurship: The Role
of Internal Governance and the Rule of Law   667
    Anuragini Shirish, Shalini Chandra, and Shirish C. Srivastava

Author Index   669

Sociomateriality and Information Systems Success and Failure[*]

Karlheinz Kautz[1] and Dubravka Cecez-Kecmanovic[2]

[1] University of Wollongong, School of Information Systems & Technology,
Wollongong NSW 2522, Australia
kautz@uow.edu.au
[2] University of New South Wales, School of Information Systems,
Technology & Management, Sydney NSW 2052, Australia
dubravka@unsw.edu.au

Abstract. The aim of this essay is to put forward a performative, sociomaterial perspective on Information Systems (IS) success and failure in organisations by focusing intently upon the discursive-material nature of IS development and use in practice. Through the application of Actor Network Theory (ANT) to the case of an IS that transacts insurance products we demonstrate the contribution of such a perspective to the understanding of how IS success and failure occur in practice. The manuscript puts our argument forward by first critiquing the existing perspectives on IS success and failure in the literature for their inadequate consideration of the materiality of IS, of its underling technologies and of the entanglement of the social and material aspects of IS development and use. From a sociomaterial perspective IS are not seen as objects that impact organisations one way or another, but instead as relational effects continually enacted in practice. As enactments in practice IS development and use produce realities of IS success and failure.

Keywords: IS success, IS failure, IS development, IS assessment, sociomateriality, actor-network-theory (ANT).

1 Introduction

IS success and failure has been a prominent research topic since the very inception of the field. The whole Information Technology (IT) industry, as Fincham (2002) notes, loudly trumpets its successes and failures and in particular "seems perversely captivated by its own failures" (p. 1). Some examples of high-profile IS project failures include the disastrous development of 'Socrate' by the French Railways (Mitev 1996), the dramatic failure of Taurus at the London Stock Exchange (Currie 1997), the failed patient administration system at NSW Health in Australia (Sauer et al.

---

[*] The argument presented in this keynote essay has subsequently been further developed in Cecez-Kecmanovic, D., Kautz, K. and Abrahall, R. "Reframing Success and Failure of Information Systems: A Performative Perspective", to appear in MIS Quarterly, 2013.

Y.K. Dwivedi et al. (Eds.): TDIT 2013, IFIP AICT 402, pp. 1–20, 2013.

1997), and the Internal Revenue Service's development of a new US Tax Modernisation System (Nelson and Ravichandran 2001). High failure rates of IS projects and our inability to understand and explain, let alone prevent, the failures suggest that perhaps existing assumptions and approaches to IS research have not served us too well.

In 2001, the Australian subsidiary of a large multinational insurance company dealing primarily in business and life insurance, which we call Olympia, undertook to become the first insurance provider in Australia of web-based e-business services to their brokers. In 2006, the web-based information system (IS), named 'Olympia-online' emerged as a sophisticated IS, eagerly adopted and highly praised by brokers. Olympia-online's success in the broker community created a competitive advantage for the company leading to an increase in their profit margins. However, being over time and over budget, and not delivering expected internal functionality the system was perceived as a big failure by the top business managers. That Olympia-online was considered simultaneously as a success and a failure, with both views firmly supported by evidence, is extraordinary and challenges the established understandings of IS success and failure. From a rationalist perspective IS success or failure are defined as discrete, objectively measured and definite states and outcomes contingent upon simple causation, e.g. certain technical characteristics and social factors or causally linked variables (DeLone and McLean 1992). The socio-technical and process oriented perspective assumes that there is no "objectively correct account of failure" (Sauer 1993, p. 24) or success, but it too assumes an objectified view resulting from politically and socially determined flaws and processes. Neither the rationalist nor the socio-technical process approach can explain the persisting co-existence of Olympia-online success and failure. From a social constructivist perspective (Fincham 2002), these co-existing perceptions can be explained by conflicting subjective interpretations and discourses of relevant social groups (Bijker 1993; Bartis and Mitev 2007). Assuming 'interpretive flexibility' of IS, this perspective helps understand how different social groups attribute different meanings and construct different assessments of an existing IS. This perspective has been critiqued for black-boxing IS and for putting too much emphasis on the interpretation and signification of IS while overlooking the ways in which IS' materiality is always already implicated in its social constructions (Orlikowski 2007).

In response we propose a sociomaterial perspective of IS success and failure informed by the works of Orlikowski and Scott (2008), Latour (2005), and Law (1992, 2004) among others. While social construction focuses on performativity of language and discourses, the sociomaterial perspective focuses on IS enactment in practice that implies performativity of both discourses and technologies. We suggest that an IS assessment is not only an interpretation or social construction, but a result of IS enactments in practice that produce realities (Law 2004). If an IS can be differently enacted in different practices we should expect a possibility that such enactments can produce different realities. It is this reality making capacity of IS enactment in different practices that we propose to understand the co-existing realities of IS success and failure. When different IS enactments create multiple realities, contradicting realities of IS assessments may emerge and coexist. To substantiate our claim we draw from sociology of science and technology studies and specifically actor-network theory (ANT) (Callon 1986; Latour 2005; Law 1992, 2004) as one prominent way of dealing with sociomateriality of IS (Orlikowski 2007). An ANT account of the Olympia-online grounds and illustrates the sociomaterial perspective on IS success and failure.

We first review different approaches to IS success and failure, then we introduce the key assumptions of the sociomaterial perspective. This is followed by a description of ANT in the research methodology section which leads to the ANT account of the Olympia-online development and use. The ensuing discussion focuses on the ways Olympia-online was enacted in the practices of the brokers, the developers, and the business managers, and how these different enactments created multiple, only partially overlapping realities. Finally we summarize the contributions of the socio-material perspective to understand the entangled, discursive-material production of IS success and failure.

2   Literature Review and Theoretical Background

We base our literature review on Fincham (2002) who distinguishes three perspectives on IS success and failure. The rationalist view explains success and failure as brought about by factors which primarily represent managerial and organizational features in system development and which are related through simple causation. DeLone and McLean's (1992) model of success and Lyttinen and Hirschheim's (1987) classification of the IS failure concept are well-known examples of this perspective. Numerous other studies found that social/organisational factors, rather than technical, had been dominant contributors to failure (e.g. Luna-Reyes et al. 2005; Lee and Xia 2005). Luna-Reyes et al. (2005) claim that as much as 90% of IS failures are attributed to these factors. Underlying the rationalist view is an assumption that IS success and failure are discrete states that can be identified and predicted by the presence/absence of certain factors. Although the lists of factors do not provide coherent explanations of why and how success and failure occur and rarely explain the phenomenon across different organizations, this is still the dominant view in the literature (DeLone and McLean 2003).

The process perspective addresses these shortcomings. It emphasizes organizational and social-political processes and explains success and failure as the result of a socio-technical interaction of different stakeholders with IS. Kautz and McMaster (1994) provide one example for this view; but Sauer's (1993) model of IS failure is the most comprehensive framework utilizing this perspective. Although it focuses on organizational and socio-technical processes, these are still seen to cause failure/success as discrete outcomes (Fincham 2002). The perspective remains anchored to some rational assumptions such as failure having a clear-cut impact and being objectivised as irreversible. Thus it does not cater for ambiguity in socio-political processes nor does it allow reflections on the relationship between success and failure, such as why success and failure are simultaneously attributed to the same IT artefact or how and why success is so often created out of failure.

Alternatively, Fincham (2002) puts forward a social constructivist, narrative perspective where the organizational and socio-political processes and the actions and stories accompanying it, are based on sense-making and interpretation and where IS success and failure are explained as a social construction. The social constructivist perspective draws attention to different viewpoints and interpretations of IS by relevant social groups thus resulting in interpretive flexibility of IT artefacts (Bijker 1993; Wilson and Howcroft 2005). Extending the social constructivist perspective with organizational power and culture, Bartis and Mitev (2008) explain how the dominant narrative of a more powerful relevant social group prevailed and disguised an IS failure as success. Mitev (2005) also proposes extending the social constructivist perspective by using ANT. Like McMaster et al. (1997) and McMaster and Wastell (2004), she utilizes ANT with its concepts of human and non-human actants interrelated in actor-networks going beyond simple explanations of technological determinism to explain success and failure. However, these accounts neglect a view of IT artefacts as more than social constructions, but less than reified physical entities (Quattrone and Hopper 2006).

This view emphasises the sociomaterial nature of an IT artefact: its agency resides neither in a technology nor in a human actor, but in a chain of relations between human and technological actants. With its rich theoretical background it inspired us to propose a fourth, sociomaterial perspective on IS success and failure which goes beyond social construction and the representational perspective where IS success and failure are represented either by objective measures or by subjective perceptions of social actors assuming that representations and the objects they represent are independently existing entities. The sociomaterial perspective assumes inherently inseparable sociality and materiality of IS (Orlikowski 2007; Orlikowski and Scott 2008). It introduces a way of seeing an IS development and use and its assessment not only discursively constructed but also materially produced and enacted in practice. Exemplified by ANT the sociomaterial perspective assumes a relational ontology involving human and non-human actors that take their form and acquire their attributes as a result of their mutual relations in actor-networks. Its relationality "means that major ontological categories (for instance, 'technology' and 'society', 'human' and 'non-human') are treated as effects or outcomes, rather than as explanatory resources" (Law, 2004, p. 157); IS development and use can thus be seen as relational effects performed within actor-networks. We focus on the performed relations and the phenomena of IS development, use and assessment as the primary units of analysis and not on a given object or entity. In following Barad (2003) we understand phenomena as ontologically primitive relations without pre-existing relata which exist only within phenomena; they "are the ontological inseparability of agentially intra-acting 'components'" (p. 815). The notion of intra-action constitutes an alteration of the traditional notion of causality. Intra-actions within a phenomenon enact local agential separability and agential cuts which effect and allow for local separation within a phenomenon. Hence, within inseparable phenomena agential separation is possible. Performativity then is understood as the iterative intra-activity within a phenomenon (Barad 2003). This perspective allows us to identify and to better understand IS-related phenomena by investigating them in their inseparability as well as in their local separability, intra-action and agency through agential cuts, both in the context of utilization and the development of IS. Table 1 summarizes the four perspectives on IS success and failure.

Table 1. IS success and failure Perspectives (extended from Fincham 2002)

Perspective	Form of organizational behavior and action	Methodological focus	IS success and failure seen as
Rationalist	Managerial and organizational structures and goals	Simple cause and effect	Objective and polarized states – outcomes of technological and social factors
Process	Organizational and socio-political processes	Socio-technical interaction	Socially and politically defined – outcomes of organizational processes and flaws
Constructivist, narrative	Organizational and socio-political processes; symbolic action, themes, plots, stories	Interpretation and sense-making of relevant social groups; narrative, rhetoric and persuasion	Social constructions, implying interpretive flexibility of IS
Sociomaterial, such as ANT	A relational view of organizations and IS as sociomaterial arrangements of human and non-human actors	Emergence and reconfiguration of IS development and use actor-networks; enactments of IS in practice	IS enactment and production of multiple realities in practice

The sociomaterial perspective helps us turn the epistemological question – how can we find out and predict whether an IS is 'true' success or failure? – into ontological ones: How does IS success or failure come about? How is an IS enacted in practice? How do these enactments produce different realities, including the coexisting assessments of IS success and failure? To answer these questions we do not take the social factors or processes or technology as given. Instead we investigate the actors and actants as they enrol and perform in heterogeneous actor-networks; we follow the emergence and reconfiguration of actor-networks and the ways IS enactments in practice are negotiated and realities are created. Within the sociomaterial perspective IS are seen as sociotechnical relational actants or actor-networks that come into being through enactment in practice. This enactment involves mutually intertwined discursive and material production. Different perceptions and interpretive flexibility of an IS, as advocated by social constructivists, reveal only one side of a coin – the discursive production of IS. The sociomaterial perspective broadens our gaze by attending to the ways in which IS are enacted and performed simultaneously and inseparably socially, discursively and materially, technologically in relations in practice.

We acknowledge that being performed and enacted in different practices IS are creating multiple realities and there are various possible reasons why an IS enactment creates one kind of reality rather than another.

3   Research Methodology

ANT embodies several key aspects of sociomateriality relevant to our examination of IS success and failure. ANT does not make a priori assumptions about the nature of actors or the ways they act to make up their worlds. Any human or non-human actor can be involved in relations, form alliances and pursue common interests in an actor-network. An IS development and implementation as well as utilization endeavour can be seen as emergent, entangled, sociomaterial actor-networks created by aligning interests of developers, users, documents, methodology and technologies. The alignment of interests within an actor-network is achieved through the enrolment of allies and translation of their interests in order to be congruent with those of the network (Walsham 1997). The actors enrolled in a network have "their own strategic preferences [and] the problem for the enroller therefore is to ensure that participants adhere to the enroller's interests rather than their own" (McLean and Hassard 2004, p. 495). Translation can be achieved through scripts, which influence actors to act in a particular way so as to achieve an actor-network's goals.

An actor-network does not imply existence of its constituting actors, but rather sees them constituted by the relations they are involved in. It is the morphology of relations which tells us what actors are and what they do (Callon 1999). The network changes through enrolment of new actors, creation of new alliances and changing relations among its actors. With an increasing alignment of interests and strengthening of relations an actor-network becomes more stabilized. This is what actor-networks strive for. However, they do not necessarily succeed; they may get weaker, break up and disappear. How they strengthen and stabilize or break up and dissolve is an interesting theoretical question with serious practical implications.

In line with other IS researchers who adopted ANT to provide robust accounts of the production and reconfiguration of relations in the development and implementation of IS seen as actor-networks (see e.g. Mitev 1996; Vidgen and McMasters 1997; Walsham and Sahay 1999; Holmström and Robey 2005) we develop an ANT account of the Olympia-online project. Without many prescriptions in the literature about how to do that we focused on practices of IS development and use and adopted the general advice 'follow the actors'. One member of the research team spent 6 months as staff on the Olympia-online development team. This was useful for gaining knowledge of the company, its management and IS development processes and for subsequent examination of actors and actor-networks. However the actual ANT study of the project started after her contract in the company had been concluded.

We initially focused on the development team, but then expanded our view as we traced enrolments, actors and their associations. The tracing of associations and identification and exploration of the creation and emergence of actor-networks led us to new human and non-human actors in the project team and beyond – to managers and brokers; the e-business platform, the insurance industry, etc. At some point following the actors and tracing further associations had to stop. We had to learn when and where to 'cut the network', in the words of Barad (2003) make agential cuts. "The trick is", says Miller (1996, p. 363), "to select the path you wish to follow, and those which you wish to ignore, and do so according to the assemblage you wish to chart".

During our study we encountered 46 human actors, engaged with technologies, important documents and other non-human actors, at different stages and locations. We had informal conversations with 21 human actors, traced additional 13 that played a role in the past but had left, and formally interviewed 12: 2 architects, 2 application developers, a data migration developer, a senior business analyst, a business project manager, a test team leader, a business expert underwriting, a business expert liaising with brokers, a senior IS executive and a senior General Insurance (GI) business manager. Documents that played an important role included a business plan, a business case and scope document, business information requirements, change requests, test plans, test cases, and project reports; important technology actants included the web-based e-business platform, a rule-based software engine, mainframe resources, application programs, interface designs and programs, and IT architecture.

The empirical data helped us reveal and reconstruct the trajectories of the actor-networks. They often exposed tensions and the political nature of the issues discussed. In the interviews as well as in the informal discussions we let the actors make sense of the project, their experiences and various events. Following the actors and their relations emerging in the project as well as executing, identifying and analysing agential cuts helped us map the creation and reconfiguration of several actor-networks. This was an iterative process that involved describing, analysing and revising these actor-networks, using ANT inquiry to reveal the inner workings of various actors and their networks e.g. enrolling actors into a network and ensuring that members of a network align with the enroller's interests; using delegates such as technology or documents to exert power and influence others. In this way we exposed different enactments of Olympia-online in practice and the ways in which they produced multiple realities including the coexisting and controversial assessments of its success and failure.

4   The Company Olympia and ITS Olympia-Online Project

Olympia-online was an industry-first e-business system in the Australian insurance market that transacted the company's insurance products directly to brokers over the web. Knowledge about building such systems was scarce in both the insurance and the IT industry. The final system was highly innovative in the way it represented the company's insurance products and enabled on-line engagement and interaction with brokers, who as intermediaries sell these products to customers. The withdrawal of the top management support for further Olympia-online development created a worrying situation for the company. Olympia-online was vital to the company since all its business was mediated through brokers; unlike other insurance companies, it had no direct contact with individual customers. System developers in particular were acutely aware that the lack of top managers' commitment to continue funding its further development would put the company at risk and seriously threaten its future competitiveness.

Prior to the development of Olympia-online Olympia was not seen as a major competitor in the Australian general insurance market. All e-business in the Australian Insurance Industry was conducted via 'BrokerLine', an outdated mainframe-based electronic platform, run by Telcom, an Australian telecommunications company. Early in 2001 Telcom announced that they were ceasing operation of BrokerLine and that all companies were required to move their business operations to a new web-based platform 'Horizon'.

Most insurance companies transacted their business both directly with individual businesses and via brokers, being reciprocally aligned with both; thus Olympia was particularly vulnerable to the platform change. Fearing loss of their business and simultaneously recognising opportunities of a new web-based platform, Olympia's GI Business Division and the Strategy & Planning Division went about putting together a business case for the development of a new web-based IS, Olympia-online. They inscribed Olympia's interest and its new strategy into the Olympia-online Business Plan, which became an effective instrument for enrolling the Information Services Department (ISD) into the new IS development actor-network. This inscription was strong enough to motivate ISD to attempt alignment with Horizon and the brokers. As a key actor in the new emerging actor-network ISD was charged with the responsibility to develop a concrete solution – a new IS that enabled transecting with brokers via Horizon's web-based platform as described in the Business Case documentation. With a prospect of becoming the only channel through which Olympia would interact with brokers to sell its products, Olympia-online development became a strategic IS project in the company.

Olympia-online was a new type of IS in the insurance industry. Without in-house experience or skills and resources, Olympia searched for a supplier with the capabilities to develop Olympia-online thus attempting to enrol an actor to ensure Olympia's alignment with Horizon. Based on the scripts expressed in the Business Case documentation, two companies bided for a contract with Olympia thus attempting to forge an alignment with the company. This process was mediated through Olympia's Senior ISD Architect. The company HighTech was successful as it did promise delivery within the desired timeframe and a fixed-price contract. Developers from HighTech succeeded in demonstrating that the Emperor, a proprietary rules engine of which HighTech was the sole reseller in Australia, was an appropriate technology upon which the new system could be built. By successfully aligning themselves with Olympia's strategy inscribed in the Business Plan, HighTech and Emperor became enrolled into the Olympia-online development actor-network. The signed contract marked the beginning of Phase 1 of the Olympia-online development. Phase 1 development began with initial requirements gathering sessions by the HighTech team.

4.1   Phase 1 Olympia-Online Development

The Hightech team had to understand the insurance business, the data and rules in insurance products, as they had no experience in insurance applications. Once development was underway, several problems emerged. It became clear to ISD staff that HighTech's developers had not grasped the breadth and depth of the problem, resulting in the project running seven months over schedule. In retrospect, the Senior ISD Architect involved in commissioning HighTech noted that the HighTech team "didn't understand the problem at hand" and underestimated its complexity, costs and the required development time. During this time, ISD staff realized that Emperor "was not the right engine for Olympia-online's purpose". When used to model insurance products and their complex business rules, Emperor exhibited severe limitations and rigidity. As a result the design of the application software was cumbersome and complex, requiring the development of extra software components to compensate for its insufficiency. Instead of working with a rule engine that had a "natural fit" with insurance products as HighTech developers initially claimed, the ISD team discovered a "dramatic misfit". Emperor was misaligned with Olympia-online's objectives.

In the initial Olympia-online development actor-network there were several attempts of alignment and many translations going on. The HighTech Project Manager attempted alignment with the Senior ISD Architect and at the same time exerted power over the Olympia team's work by making design decisions regarding the use of Emperor in the system's development based on his architect's advice. While he never fully disclosed Emperor's limitations for modelling insurance products, he successfully negotiated and established its key role in Olympia-online.

As the relations between the software components built on Emperor and those on the mainframe grew tighter the implications for the functionality and efficient operations of Olympia-online became more evident. The relations between the HighTech team and the Olympia team, Emperor and the mainframe system were highly contentious, yet critical for the development of Olympia-online. By insisting on Emperor as a platform for the application software the HighTech Project Manager by way of his Architect ensured that his company's interests were inscribed in the software. The more this software became dependent on Emperor the more this actor-network became irreversible[1].

During Phase 1 the development actor-network was continually reconfigured through a series of translation processes that strengthened some alignments but failed others, and thus prevented its stabilization. The two actors overseeing this work, the HighTech Project Manager and the Olympia Head Architect, had trouble ensuring the delivery of the system with the specified functionality on time. At the beginning of 2002, as Phase 1 was significantly delayed, the GI Business Division was anxious to announce to the brokers that the new system was ready for use. They publicly promised that full functionality would be available by mid 2002 which upset ISD staff. When finally delivered to the brokers, despite nine months delay, Olympia-online was a great success: brokers were delighted with the new technology. The web-based specification of insurance products enabled brokers' flexible interaction with Olympia while selling its products to customers. Able to focus on customer needs and tailor products to meet these needs brokers gradually changed their work processes. Their enactment of Olympia-online produced different practices in transacting business with Olympia and its customers.

This first implementation of Olympia-online however exposed numerous technical problems, slow performance, frequent crashes and defects. As a result ISD staff had

---

[1] Phase 1 was further complicated by yet another translation process going on in the development of the interface between Olympia-online and Horizon. This was carried out by another third party, that is, another actor-network which we did not dig further into as this was not relevant for answering our research question.

huge difficulties in maintaining it. Furthermore, its design was not modular and hence the system lacked the ability to be scaled to Olympia's future needs. ISD staff and their Senior Architect in particular, believed that Olympia-online's technical failures were caused primarily by the use of Emperor that "could not easily model complex insurance products". The Emperor's rule engine, they found out too late, was originally developed for specification of physical products such as machinery and had never been used before for products as complex as insurance. The enrolment of HighTech and Emperor into the Olympia-online development was, in their view, a wrong decision. In the meantime, the broker community strengthened their relation with Olympia and communicated its satisfaction with the system to the GI Business Division. Being first-to-market Olympia-online attracted new brokers and boosted business so GI revenue for business insurance grew significantly. Through their contacts with the HighTech Project Manager GI Business Managers believed that Emperor was the key contributor to the success. They were not aware of the problems experienced in the development nor did they realise the full extent of the system's technical failures and instability in operations. They thought the Olympia-online system was an unqualified success.

Based on this market success, GI Business Managers, in discussions with HighTech, made the decision to purchase $1 million worth of Emperor Licenses such that the existing system could be extended and more systems and products could be developed in the future. This decision was made without consulting ISD staff, as their mutual relations had deteriorated by that time. In the meantime, ISD staff were busy struggling to maintain an unstable system and respond to numerous defects. When Olympia-online became so unstable that its maintenance and use could no longer be sustained, ISD proposed Phase 2 of the Olympia-online development. Since GI managers had already spent $1 million on licensing it ISD had no other option but to continue the further development of Olympia-online with Emperor.

4.2   Phase 2 Olympia-Online Development

Phase 2 started mid 2003 and the system went live in April 2005 with one major goal being to bring the Olympia-online development and knowledge in house, since "it was the key to Olympia's overall strategy" to prevent expertise from leaving the company. This goal was not easily achievable since Olympia continued to be reliant on HighTech as the only resource provider for Emperor in Australia. The other goal was the delivery of the system on time and budget. Consequently Olympia-online was now developed under a stringent project governance and management regime. The emerging situation resulted in three partially overlapping actor-networks: a Steering Committee, a development, and a Brokers actor-network.

A Steering Committee consisting of stakeholders from the GI Business Division, the Strategy and Planning Division, as well as ISD, was created. The Steering Committee was financially responsible for the project and thus primarily concerned with timeframes and costs. According to a team member, Phase 2 "focused disproportionately on short-term issues and cost considerations, at the expense of long-term quality and functionality". This, in his view, stemmed from the Steering Committee via the Business Project Manager and the IS Project Manager, two new roles, who were responsible for short term goals – the system's delivery on time and on budget, but "seemed not concerned with the system's objectives in the long term".

The emerging Steering Committee actor-network grew more aligned with the commitment to impose tighter control over the Olympia-online project, keen not to repeat the mistakes from Phase 1. At the same time its relations with the development network deteriorated, leaving few options for interaction. In the meantime the development actor-network continuously reconfigured. Continued problems with Emperor and inadequate resources as requests for additional resources were rejected by the Steering Committee increased tensions and prevented its stabilization. In Phase 2 again the Olympia development team had not enough time and resources to design a modular architecture based on which all subsystems would be developed including future system expansion. The tight budget control and insistence on the planned timeline by the IS Project Manager increased tensions and did little to resolve the key problems in the development of the system.

A Brokers' actor-network emerged and grew strong throughout Phase 2. Major efforts and resources were allocated to redesigning Olympia-online to serve brokers due to the Business Experts' continued parallel engagement in the development actor-network and with the broker community. They successfully translated the project objectives to be aligned with their own and the broker community interests. Their involvement and influence ensured that the system was not implemented until a sufficient level of functionality and quality required by brokers had been delivered. While this caused tensions with the IS Project Manager "who was constantly pushing for fast delivery" the engagement of the Business Experts resulted in the inscription of the brokers' views and the translation of their interests in Olympia-online leading to a strong alignment between the system and the broker community and to a network stabilization. The quality of the resulting Olympia-online was, as the Business Expert liaising brokers confirmed, exceptional. This ensured that Olympia-online continued and enhanced its market success. This was acknowledged by a Senior GI Business Manager. However, he also said that the project overran, costed too much, and didn't deliver the expected internal functionality.

This view prevailed in the Steering Committee actor-network despite attempts of alignment by the two Business Experts to convince the Steering Committee about the system's market success. While they were initially enthusiastic about the Olympia-online development, the GI business managers did not engage with the Phase 2 development, as their enrolment in that actor-network became weaker rather than stronger. The reports to the Steering Committee by the IS Project Manager, providing the key relations with the development network, did not indicate early enough that Phase 2 would be delayed and over budget, nor did they indicate that the internal functionality would not be delivered. The managers' view was that they had pretty regular requirements for the system's core internal functionality, management and operational reporting, that "any IS would normally deliver". Their requests were not translated into the system. When the system at the end of Phase 2 did not deliver the requested functionality and when it became evident that it was again over time and over budget, there was no doubt in the Steering Committee network that the Phase 2 Olympia-online was an "obvious failure". The GI Business Division, ultimately responsible for funding, withdrew their support and the Steering Committee did not approve plans for building Olympia-online further. This decision might jeopardise Olympia's market position and a loss of competitive advantage.

5   How Olympia-Online became Both a Success and a Failure

The conflicting assessments of Olympia-online cannot be explained within existing perspectives. Taking the rationalist perspective (DeLone and McLean 1992, 2003) (see Table 1) one would expect that 'senior management support' evident in most part of the project is a good predictor of Olympia-online success. However this factor was probably more directly linked to system failure: GI managers support led to the decision to purchase the license that played a major role in the production of system failure. Another expected success factor, 'strict management control', evident in Phase 2, can also be associated more with the failure than the success. Circumstances and dynamics of organisational processes in any non-trivial IS development are so complex that a simple explanation of causally linked factors does not make much sense.

The process perspective would reveal organizational and socio-technical processes that led to successful innovation in selling insurance products and the brokers' interaction with the company, therefore leading to success. It would also reveal many technical flaws in designing Olympia-online that led to failure. The perspective however cannot deal with ambiguous and changing assessments nor with contradicting outcomes – Olympia-online is neither abandoned nor supported for future development. While the process perspective does not attempt to provide an objective account of IS success and failure it still sees them as discrete and irreversible 'outcomes', resulting from certain organisational and sociotechnical processes.

The social constructivist perspective would explain how both the success and failure of Olympia-online were socially constructed. From this perspective the stories and narratives of relevant social groups, GI managers, developers, and brokers, can be seen as producing the discourses of failure as well as the discourses of success. The Olympia-online system is perceived and interpreted differently by these relevant social groups, thereby implying its interpretive flexibility. Pluralist views and different Olympia-online assessments thus are perspectival in nature. The problem with social constructivism is that excessive power is attributed to representations and words and discourses of IS success and failure without recognising their material foundation.

5.1   Reonceputalizing the Success and Failure of IS

The sociomaterial perspective considers IS success and failure as relational effects, that do not exist by themselves but are endlessly generated in actor-networks (Law 2004). It directs attention to the different practices enacted by Olympia-online development and use and to the ways in which such enactments produced multiple realities of system success and failure. The sociomaterial perspective is premised on a conception of technology and IS as non-human actors which are constitutively entangled with human actors in webs of relations in situated practices (Orlikowski 2007). Instead of investigating how one impacts on the other, we experience these actors' worlds. This enables us to see how IS success and failure are produced by sociomaterial dynamics in actor-networks. Actor-networks are not clearly distinguishable entities, they are (parts of) sociomaterial entanglements and become visible through agential cuts.

The production of Olympia-online success in the Brokers' actor-network can be traced to the Business Experts' engagement to translate the brokers' needs and interests into the development of the Olympia-online software. Their engagement became even more prominent in Phase 2 as they forged close interaction and further alignment between brokers, the development team, the Olympia-online software and Horizon. Emerging through these processes was the brokers' network which had an evident overlap with the development network; they shared actors and relations that assisted their mutual alignment. Being heavily engaged in the system testing, the brokers expressed their high appreciation for the system quality. The new reality of Olympia-online enacted in the brokers' actor-network resulted from transformation of their work practices and their innovative ways of customizing products for customers and transacting business with Olympia. The wide adoption of these practices created market success and tangible benefits for Olympia. The production of success was not only the result of the brokers' attribution of meanings and discursive construction of Olympia-online in their practices. It was also material and technological; the development actor-network and the overlapping brokers' actor-network jointly created such a sociomaterial constellation that the development of Olympia-online and its enactment in the brokers' practices became closely connected, mutually triggering changes in each other. The brokers were part of and contributors to the sociomaterial constellation as they innovated their practices through the appropriation of Olympia-online and based on this experience suggested changes in the system.

A sociomaterial entanglement is a network arrangement, a mangle of practice, which implies inseparability of the social, discursive and the material, technological that are "mutually and emergently productive of one another" (Pickering 1993, p. 567). They are inseparable in the overall reconstruction of organisational reality, but become locally separable through agential cuts. It is in fact very difficult, sometimes impossible, to separate the social, discursive from the material, technological production of the Olympia-online reality in the brokers' practices. They are intimately fused in the brokers' situated experiences and their enactment of new and innovative practices in the sociomaterial constellation emerging in the brokers' actor-network. The sociomaterial constellation that fused together multiple meanings and material technologies of Olympia-online development, its software proper, and the brokers' practices, was created simultaneously in both networks. The two networks were porous enough to co-create such a sociomaterial constellation that in the brokers' network produced the reality of the Olympia-online success in the market.

The trajectory and dynamics of the Olympia-online development actor-network are even more complicated. The complexity of this network arose due to enrolment of numerous actants, complex translation processes and continuous building and reconfiguring of relations during both phases. The key enrolment in Phase 1 of the development network was that of the rule-engine Emperor. Due to Emperor's central role in modelling insurance products and related business rules the Olympia-online software became intimately dependent on it. With the purchase of the Emperor License, the actor-network further increased its dependence on Emperor with significant ramifications.

When the Olympia team engaged with Emperor's rule-based Engine – while designing and testing the software's structure, processes, user interface, security procedures, etc. – they experienced severe limitations in modelling insurance products. The built software was therefore cumbersome and complex. The sociomaterial constellation that emerged in the relations between the Olympia team, the HighTech team,

Emperor, the mainframe, and the business experts only allowed for a limited and ineffective translation of insurance products and business rules into the Olympia-online software. Emperor's agency in this translation process was not only a social construction. It was relationally and materially enacted through the project managers', the architects' and the developers' practices within this sociomaterial entanglement which did not leave them with much design alternatives, allowing only particular design practices, and leaving traces in the designed structures, application programs, and processes. This is congruent with Quattrone and Hopper's (2006) findings that agency of technology extends beyond human responses to it and that it resides in the chain of relations between the actants.

While after Phase 1, the general consensus amongst Olympia-online development team members was that Emperor should be abandoned this became politically unfeasible due to the money spent on Emperor licensing. Furthermore, the more code the development team developed based on Emperor the less likely they were to abandon it. Dependency on Emperor in the development network became thus more and more irreversible making it almost impossible to "go back to a point where alternative possibilities exist[ed]" (Walsham and Sahay 1999, p. 42). The increasing irreversibility of the development actor-network made its sociomaterial entanglement increasingly more critical and consequential for the final system.

Another important dynamics arose through this network's relations with the Steering committee network. During Phase 2 the Olympia team requested further resources arguing that the complexity of Olympia-online and the problems with Emperor necessitated much more than initially planned. However, no additional resources were approved by the Steering Committee. The very objective of creating this committee and the two new management roles in Phase 2 were to enforce strict budget control and the delivery deadline. This objective was firmly held by the committee and the network formed around it. Without additional resources the team was not able to deliver full functionality. Seeing the functionality for the brokers as a priority the team, to some extent influenced by the Business Experts, the development team allocated all their resources to develop this functionality first. It however meant delaying the development of functionality required by the GI managers. This was not known outside this network and was first reported by the IS Project Manager to the Steering Committee just before the end of Phase 2.

Although the Olympia-online development was not completed and its actor-network did not stabilize Phase 2 was concluded as the project was already over time and budget. At this point in time the developers were fully aware of the technical deficiency of the Olympia-online design. Highly limited resources and the complexity of the design had prevented a radical change of the architecture in Phase 2. It was a series of sociomaterial entanglements that we traced during this network reconfiguration in Phases 1 and 2, which produced the final Olympia-online system. But this did not happen in isolation. Relations emerging in the other two networks, partially overlapping with the development network, played their role as well.

The Steering Committee actor-network had a direct influence on the IS Project Manager and the Business Project Manager that were charged with the responsibility to impose stringent project and budget control. This was a major relation between the Steering Committee actor-network and the development network. By purchasing the Emperor license and thereby effectively enrolling it in the development actor-network the Steering Committee showed their commitment and support for the project. However, the relations between the two networks became weaker. Attempts by the Business Experts to strengthen the ties with the Steering Committee and align its network's objectives with that of the development network had not been doing well. In Phase 2 the two networks emerged less connected and less aligned than before. The market success of Olympia-online was acknowledged by the GI managers but this only confirmed their appreciation for Emperor. The sociomaterial entanglement within the Steering Committee actor-network was enacted by the managers' preoccupation with budget control and deadlines, sporadic relations with the HighTech team and reports by the IS Project Manager, including the final one informing them that the expected functionality requested by GI managers was not going to be delivered, and that the development was over time and budget. There were no relations with the development team or the application software. The resulting failure verdict seemed an inevitable outcome.

This analysis suggests the relevance of the emergence and reconfiguration of actor-networks understood as sociomaterial entanglements for the comprehension of different enactments and assessments of IS. The success and the failure of Olympia-online were more than different perceptions and social constructions by relevant social groups. Due to the assembling and reconfiguring of the actor-networks multiple sociomaterial constellations emerged. The sociomaterial entanglements involved inseparable and mutually constituting discursive and material constructions which we turned visible through agential cuts. The analysis shows it is not just humans who discursively construct the success or failure, nor is it only material resources, technology and material components of an IS such as internal and external functions, modular structures or platforms that exert influence on human actors thus causing the success or failure, it is the emergence of the(ir) sociomaterial relations within which they encounter each other and through which the discursive and the material technology are entangled and preformed, f. ex. through the purchase of licenses or resource constraints, and construct a success or a failure. Agential cuts turn these entanglements visible and render them locally separable. The success and failure of IS are made in and by multiple actor-networks.

5.2   Multiple IS Realities and IS Success and Failure

Olympia-online was continuously re-enacted in practices of different actor-networks, which produced multiple, alternative realities. The recognition of multiplicity of IS realities in practice is conceptually different from plurality implied by social constructivism (Law 2004; Mol 1999). Plurality assumes a single reality that is observed, perceived and interpreted differently by different social groups, hence plurality of views and assessments (Bartis and Mitev 2008; Wilson and Howcroft 2005). Multiplicity implies multiple realities that are "done and enacted rather than observed. Rather than being seen by a diversity of watching eyes while itself remaining untouched in the centre, reality is manipulated by means of various tools in the course of a diversity of practices" (Mol 1999, p. 77, emphasis in the original). Enactments of the Olympia-online development and use in different practices within the three different actor-networks produced multiple realities. The resulting co-existence of multiple

Olympia-online realities created a problem Olympia was incapable of resolving: it was stuck with contradicting assessments; unable to reconcile this multiplicity. The decision regarding investment into Olympia-online's further development was stalled. Beyond the project's fate Olympia's relationship with brokers, its market position, and ultimately the company's future are at stake. Such a situation raises the question: what could be done differently?

As conditions of creation and emergence of actor-networks are not given but created and re-created, realities might be done in other ways; different sociomaterial entanglements of an IS development "might make it possible to enact realities in different ways" (Law 2004, p. 66). Enacting an IS and performing a reality one way or another can thus be open for debate. Understanding the Olympia-online case may help both practitioners and researchers gain deeper insights into the production of the IS realities of success and failure, help undo some deeds, and perhaps prevent failure. The trajectories of the actor-networks in Phase 1 and 2 reveal the conditions for possible options at any point in time, with some actions and reconfigurations playing a more significant role than others.

The reality of Olympia-online's success in the market was produced by the brokers' network; key were the actions of the Business Experts who actively engaged in translating the brokers' needs into the IS and attracted brokers to engage in testing and who contributed to the resource allocation for testing Olympia-online's usability. This strengthened the relations between development and brokers networks thus producing success. However it hid the resource allocation to meet the brokers' needs. While it ensured high quality functionality for the brokers it withdrew resources from development of internal functionality relevant for the GI managers. On reflection, this could have been different, choosing perhaps a more balanced resource allocation.

The reality of Olympia-online enacted by the Steering Committee actor-network resulted in the assessment of failure. Neither the GI Managers nor other members of the committee ever questioned or revised the initial prediction of the project resources and duration for Phase 2 despite new evidence about the increasing complexity of the project and a need for larger resources to complete the project – contained in reports submitted to the Steering Committee. During Phase 2 the committee actor-network became more stabilized and at the same time more disconnected from the development actor-network. Consequently this network was narrowed and steadfast, leaving no options for alternative considerations. Despite the evidence of market success, Olympia-online for them was a failure. The failure verdict was natural and obvious: it was seen as "based on hard facts" as "the system was over time and over budget" and "its internal functionality was not delivered". However the use of these particular measures of project success/failure was never explicated. Options to discuss different assessment criteria and to question and revise initial estimates of required resources and time were not considered. A possibility of questioning assumptions regarding a stable and robust infrastructure had not been entertained. This might have led to opportunities for enactment of a different reality and for taking different action regarding Olympia-online's future development.

Finally, for the development actor-network the HighTech enrollment was highly consequential with Emperor playing a key role in the Olympia-online development. It was plagued by the developers' battle with Emperor and its integration with the mainframe. It engaged unexpectedly large resources thus contributing to prolonged delivery and missing functionality of the final system. Choosing an option to reject working with Emperor, even after the license was purchased, would have changed the network's trajectory; other options included contract termination with HighTech and the enrollment of other partner companies, fulfillment of the initial objectives to develop a modular architecture, and a more balanced resource allocation to deliver full system functionality.

The discussion reveals multiple and largely incoherent realities within the identified actor-networks. It reveals some possibilities and options to make different choices at particular points in time and enact realities in different ways. Some of these options still existed but were not seen by the actors when the decisions concerning Olympia-online's future were made. To see them actors needed to reflect on and understand the ways in which multiple Olympia-online realities were enacted in different practices. The more all stakeholder succeed in understanding the making of these multiple realities the more open they might become for re-negotiation and reconciliation of multiple assessments in the light of strategic objectives and market implications.

6   Conclusion

This essay proposes a sociomaterial perspective on IS success and failure. The investigation of the Olympia-online case, resulting in concurrently contradicting and unreconciled assessments, provided an opportunity to demonstrate a distinct theoretical and practical contribution of the sociomaterial perspective to the understanding of IS success and failure.

The sociomaterial perspective focuses on IS enactments in practices that are not only performed discursively but also and inevitably materially through sociomaterial relations involving material encounters which would be only partially understood by social constructivism. The sociomaterial perspective reveals how the success and the failure of IS are produced as relational effects in and by actor-networks. It draws attention to the contingently enacted realities of IS within emergent actor-networks of IS development and use in practice. Through the analysis of reconfigurations of the actor-networks, we illustrate how multiple realities of system success and failure have been produced concurrently. The lessons from the case teach us that there are options to make different choices along the way and to re-enact realities differently (Law 2004).

In addition, we examined how the networks could have been reconfigured differently. An actor-network "is not a network of connecting entities which are already there but a network which configures ontologies." (Callon 1999, pp.185). What an enrolment would do or change in an actor-network, is rarely known or well understood when it happens. This suggests further research. There are many open questions: How can multiple and contradicting realities be reconciled and and thus failure be prevented? How can premature stabilization of an actor-network be avoided and how can greater congruence between relevant actor-networks be enabled? How can alternative options for enacting IS reality differently be identified?

Finally, conducting and presenting an ANT study poses many challenges. Following the actors and investigating the relations within actor-networks by making agential cuts reveal complexities that resist clear and simplified presentations and a linear story typically expected of academic writing. An ANT study emphasises flow and change as key to understanding the being and doing of actors as well as the emergence and reconfiguration of actor-networks. As this is not easily communicated we produced snapshots and momentary outside views of actors' worlds at different points in the project timeline. These are inherently limited by the nature of the printed medium and a potential domain of future research might explore alternatives genres and new electronic media in presenting actor-networks and achieved research results.

Acknowledgements. We like to recognize Rebecca Abrahall who as a research student collected the data which build the empirical basis for our analysis.

References

Barad, K.: Posthumanist Performativity: Toward an Understanding of How Matter Comes to Matter. Signs: Journal of Women in Culture and Society 28(3), 801–831 (2003)

Bartis, E., Mitev, N.: A Multiple Narrative Approach to Information System Failure: A Successful System that Failed. European Journal of Information Systems (17), 112–124 (2007)

Bijker, W.E.: Do Not Despair: There Is Life after Constructivism. Science, Technology and Human Values 18(1), 113–138 (1993)

Callon, M.: Some Elements of a Sociology of Translation: Domestication of the Scallops and the Fisherman of St. Brieuc Bay. In: Law, J. (ed.) Power, Action and Belief: A New Sociology of Knowledge? Sociological Review Monograph, vol. 32, pp. 196–233. Routledge and Kegan Paul, London (1986)

Callon, M.: Actor-Network Theory: the Market Test. In: Law, J., Hassard, J. (eds.) Actor Network and After, pp. 181–195. Blackwell (1999)

Currie, W.: Computerizing the Stock Exchange: A Comparison of Two Information Systems. New Technology, Work and Employment 12(2), 9–36 (1997)

DeLone, W.H., McLean, E.R.: Information System Success: The Quest for the Dependent Variable. Information Systems Research 3(1), 60–95 (1992)

DeLone, W.H., McLean, E.R.: The DeLone and McLean Model of Information System Success: A Ten Year Update. Journal of Management Information System 19(4), 9–31 (2003)

Fincham, R.: Narratives of Success and Failure in Systems Development. British Journal of Management (13), 1–14 (2002)

Holmström, J., Robey, D.: Understanding IT's organizational consequences: An actor network theory approach. In: Czarniawska, B., Hernes, T. (eds.) Actor-Network Theory and Organizing, pp. 165–187. Liber, Stockholm (2005)

Kautz, K., McMaster, T.: Introducing Structured Methods: An Undelivered Promise? A Case Study. Scandinavian Journal of Information Systems 6(2), 59–78 (1994)

Latour, B.: Science in Action: How to Follow Scientists and Engineers through Society. Harvard University Press, Cambridge (1987)

Latour, B.: Technology is Society Made Durable. In: Law, J. (ed.) A Sociology of Monsters. Essays on Power, Technology and Domination, pp. 103–131. Routlegde (1991)

Latour, B.: Reassembling the Social: An Introduction to Actor-Network-Theory. Oxford University Press (2005)

Law, J.: The Anatomy of Socio-Technical Struggle: The Design of the TSR2. In: Elliot, B. (ed.) Technology and Social Processes. Edinburgh University Press, Edinburgh (1988)

Law, J.: Notes on the Theory of the Actor-Network: Ordering, Strategy and Heterogeneity. Systems Practice 5(4), 379–393 (1992)

Law, J.: After Method: Mess in Social Science Research. Routledge, London (2004)

Lee, G., Xia, W.: The Ability of Information Systems Development Project Teams to Respond to Business and Technology Changes: A Study of Flexibility Measures. European Journal of Information Systems (14), 75–92 (2005)

Luna-Reyes, L.F., Zhang, J., Gil-García, J.R., Cresswell, A.M.: Information Systems Development as Emergent Socio-Technical Change: A Practice Approach. European Journal of Information Systems (14), 93–105 (2005)

Lyytinen, K., Hirschheim, R.A.: Information Systems Failure: A Survey and Classification of The Empirical Literature. In: Zorkoczy, P.I. (ed.) Oxford Surveys in Information Technology, vol. 4, pp. 257–309. Oxford University Press, Oxford (1987)

McLean, C., Hassard, J.: Symmetrical Absence/Symmetrical Absurdity: Critical Notes on the Production of Actor-Network Accounts. Journal of Management Studies 41(3), 493–519 (2004)

McMaster, T., Wastell, D.: Success and Failure Revisited in the Implementation of New Technology: Some Reflections on the Capella Project. In: Innovation for Adaptability and Competitiveness, Proceedings of IFIP WG8.6 Working Conference, Leixlip, Ireland, Boston. Kluwer (2004)

McMaster, T., Vidgen, R.T., Wastell, D.G.: Technology Transfer – Diffusion or Translation? In: McMaster, T., Mumford, E., Swanson, E.B., Warboys, B., Wastell, D. (eds.) Facilitating Technology Transfer Through Partnership: Learning From Practice and Research, pp. 64–75. Chapman and Hall, London (1997)

Miller, P.: The Multiplying Machine. Accounting, Organisations and Society 21(7/8), 615–630 (1996)

Mitev, N.: More than a failure? The computerized reservation systems at French Railways. Information Technology and People 9(4), 8–19 (1996)

Mitev, N.: Are Social Constructivist Approaches Critical? The Case of IS Failure. In: Howcroft, D., Trauth, E. (eds.) Handbook of Critical Information System Research: Theory and Application, pp. 70–103. Edward Elgar, Cheltenham (2005)

Mol, A.: Ontological Politics: A Word and some Questions. In: Law, J., Hassard, J. (eds.) Actor Network Theory and After, Blackwell and the Sociological Review, Oxford and Keele, pp. 74–89 (1999)

Nelson, M.R., Ravichandran, T.: Understanding the Causes of IT Project Failures in Government Agencies. In: 7th Americas Conference on Information Systems, AMCIS, pp. 1451–1453 (2001)

Orlikowski, W.J.: Sociomaterial Practices: Exploring Technology at Work. Organization Studies 28(9), 1435–1448 (2007)

Orlikowski, W.J., Scott, S.V.: Sociomateriality: Challenging the Separation of Technology, Work and Organization. In: The Academy of Management Annals, vol. (2), ch. 10, pp. 433–474 (August 2008)

Pickering, A.: The Mangle of Practice, Agency and Emergence in the Sociology of Science. American Journal of Sociology 20(2), 241–261 (1993)

Quattrone, P., Hopper, T.: What Is IT? SAP, Accounting, and Visibility in a Multinational Organisation. Information and Organization (16), 212–250 (2006)

Sauer, C., Southon, G., Dampney, C.N.G.: Fit Failure and the House of Horrors: Toward a Configurational Theory of IS Project Failure. In: Proceedings of the 18th International Conference on Information Systems, ICIS, Atlanta, Georgia, pp. 349–366 (1997)

Sauer, C.: Why Information Systems Fail: A Case Study Approach. Alfred Waller, Henley-on-Thames (1993)

Vidgen, R., McMaster, T.: Black Boxes: Non-Human Stakeholders and the Translation of IT Through Mediation. In: Proceedings of the IFIP TC8 WG 8.2 International Conference on Information Systems and Qualitative Research, pp. 250–271 (1997)

Walsham, G.: Actor-Network Theory and IS Research: Current Status and Future Prospects. In: Proceedings of the IFIP TC8 WG 8.2 International Conference on Information Systems and Qualitative Research, pp. 466–480 (1997)

Walsham, G., Sahay, S.: GIS for District-Level Administration in India: Problems and Opportunities. MIS Quarterly 23(1), 39–65 (1999)

Wilson, M., Howcroft, D.: Power, Politics and Persuasion in IS Evaluation: A Focus on 'Relevant Social Groups'. Journal of Strategic Information Systems (14), 17–44 (2005)

Repertoires of Collaboration for Disaster Management: Negotiating Emergent and Dynamic Systems Success

Deborah Bunker[1], Linda Levine[2], and Carol Woody[3]

[1] Discipline of Business Information Systems, University of Sydney, Sydney, Australia
deborah.bunker@sydney.edu.au
[2] Independent Researcher Consultant & University of Sydney Pittsburgh, PA, U.S.A.
llherself@gmail.com
[3] Software Engineering Institute, Carnegie Mellon University Pittsburgh, PA, U.S.A.
cwoody@cert.org

Abstract. Disasters are emergent and dynamic scenarios involving diverse stakeholders in complex decision making and as such, disaster management systems must account for these conditions. In order to more effectively design, build and adopt these systems we suggest that emergency service agencies should consider supplementing their traditional "command and control" approaches and common operating pictures (CoP), with purposeful "collaborative" approaches. These would facilitate the generation of a dynamic operating picture (DoP), providing a range of systems options with which to better manage disasters. Collaborative management and negotiated integration of technology and information use as well as process development, represent a paradigmatic shift in our thinking about disaster management. We have utilized McCann's (1983) Negotiated Arrangements Theory (NAT) to highlight issues and problems with traditional command and control approaches and CoP, during three disaster scenarios. As a result of lessons learned from this analysis we suggest that developing a supplementary "repertoires of collaboration" approach to the negotiation of DoP for disaster management, would have a positive impact on disaster management outcomes.

Keywords: common operating pictures, dynamic operating pictures; disaster management; information systems management; collaboration, crisis response.

1   Introduction

When we speak of information systems (IS) for organisational purposes, there are many models and frameworks that deal with linear and cyclic patterns of IS design, construction, adoption and use, i.e. waterfall method, prototyping, agile design. Traditionally, practitioners and academics have focused on the construction of an IS as a systems artifact which assumes that the artifact can: firstly be successfully designed to a set of pre-determined specifications; and then be created using a set of pre-determined development principles that system builders can adhere to (Kroenke et al. 2012).

These assumptions are generally acceptable when organizational operations are; well-defined; highly structured; used and operated by the same people; built to

Y.K. Dwivedi et al. (Eds.): TDIT 2013, IFIP AICT 402, pp. 21–38, 2013.

specifications; and applied to cyclic and repetitive tasks (for example accounting, business analytics, HR etc).

Disaster management systems, however, are not characterized in this way. These systems are scenario driven and are generally ill-defined; ill-structured; self-organizing; self-reinforcing; used and operated by many different people (who often change each time the system is reconfigured); built in reaction to emerging situations; and therefore are generally applied to one-off courses of action. Disasters also move through many different phases (see Table 1) which require IS to be used in many different and flexible ways, i.e. preventing and preparing for a crisis as well as responding and recovering from it (Bunker & Smith 2009, Ehnis & Bunker 2012).

Traditional IS development, adoption and diffusion models, frameworks and theories, and information governance mechanisms, therefore, are not particularly effective in dealing with design, construction, adoption and use of disaster management systems. This is due to their limitations which focus on a traditional definition of complete and fixed requirements and a mechanized engineering approach to the development, adoption, diffusion and information and process compliance of such systems.

Table 1. Emergency Incident Types and Characteristics – derived in part from Blanchard-Boehm (1998) Greenberg et al. (2007), Kost & Moyer (2003), OEST (2006) and reproduced from (Bunker & Smith 2009)

	Medium	Agent	Elapsed Time Full Effect	Lead Time Warning	Amplitude	Magnitude	Area	Contm't Potential	Local/ Social Impact	Plan Effect
Bomb	Various	Explosive	Short	None	High	Various	Small	Good	Local/ social	Poor
Bushfire	Fire	Natural Activities	Various	Long	Various	Various	Various	Medium	Local	Good
Earthquake	Earth	Tectonic Activity	Short	Various	Various	Various	Various	Poor	Local	Medium
Fire,	Fire	Electrical/c hemical	Short	None	Various	Various	Small	Good	Local	Good
Floods,	Water	Natural Activities	Long	Long	Various	Various	Various	Poor	Local	Medium
Hazmat – land	Land	Chemical/ organic/ radiation	Various	None	Various	Various	Small	Good	Local	Good
Hazmat – sea	Water	Chemical/ organic/ radiation	Various	None	Various	Various	Small/ medium	Poor	Local/ social	Medium
Structural failure (transport, building etc)	Structure	Various	Short	Various	High	Various	Small	Medium	Local/ social	Good
Pandemic	Air/water	Biological	Medium/ Long	Medium	High	Various	Large	Poor	Social	Medium
Severe weather events	Air/water	Natural Activities	Various	Various	High	Various	Various	Poor	Local	Medium
Terrorist Act	Various	Various	Various	None	High	Various	Various	Poor	Local/ Social	Medium
Tsunami	Water	Natural Activities	Short	Short	Various	Various	Various	Poor	Local/ Social	Medium

What we do know is that during crises and disasters, traditional first responder command and control approaches to development of a common operating picture (CoP) for disaster management, are utilized with varying degrees of success and effectiveness (Bunker & Smith, 2009, Betts, 2003, Levine & Woody, 2010). Many governments and their emergency services agencies have adopted a Prevent, Prepare, Respond and Recover (PPRR) protocol (see Figure 1) which provides a common strategy for the development of this CoP but most emergency agencies use their own currently proven technologies and information systems that can be enhanced and scaled to optimize outcomes and value for money to deliver the CoP.

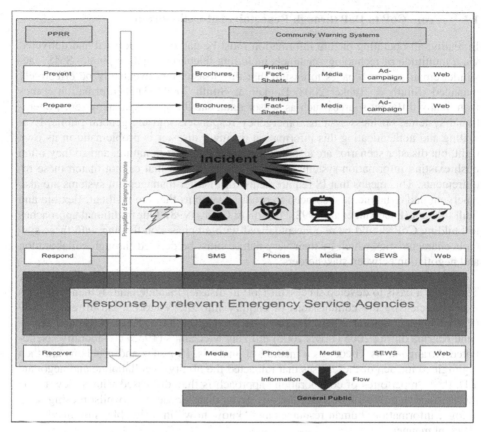

Fig. 1. Mapping of PPRR Approach to Community Warning Systems (CWS) - note changing requirements of CWS throughout an incident - diagram reproduced from (Bunker & Smith 2009)

The term "common operating picture" (CoP) is used by emergency services agencies and the military to describe "situational awareness, by enabling multiple organisations to view and share information in a timely manner across a single picture" (DIGO website <www.defence.gov.au/digo/geoint-palanterra.htm>). We would argue, however, that in the case of disasters or crises, agencies are presented with the need for a dynamic operating picture (DoP) where there is a requirement to view multiple representations of the same phenomenon and perhaps, other representations of related phenomena by many different stakeholders with many different objectives. In order to enable a DoP, technology/information/human resources must be supplied and managed by multiple stakeholders with different objectives, and this presents a different type of complexity to CoP that is problematic to deal with when negotiating systems outcomes.

A common operating picture view of a disaster, therefore, does not present the full range of representations of the disaster scenario nor deal fully with the emergent and dynamic nature of a disaster. It also does not take into account the need for multiple stakeholders to be able to collaborate in order to negotiate a relevant and applicable information systems outcome for their particular disaster management requirements.

1.1   From CoP to DoP through Repertoires of Collaboration

In reality, all operating picture information must be gathered, processed and delivered via a multitude of technology channels including telephone, mobile phone, SMS, facsimile, email and web pages to ensure that the disaster can eventually be effectively managed (Smith & Bunker 2008, Bunker & Smith 2009). This information comes from many different sources such as sensor data, satellites, geospatial systems, operational systems, business systems, emergency responders and the general public. Evaluating and authenticating this information during a disaster is problematic in its own right, but disaster scenarios are also emergent and dynamic in nature, and so they often push existing information systems and channels to failure that cannot match these requirements. This means that IS requirements for disaster management systems are also emergent and dynamic, and so need to produce systems that are resilient, flexible and fault tolerant (Pauchant et al., 1992, Pearson & Clair, 1998). Our traditional approaches to building CoP should be re-conceptualized with emphasis on dealing with these systems characteristics which by their very nature must be derived through collaboration and negotiation between stakeholders.

This paper firstly defines collaboration using McCann's (1983) Negotiated Order Theory as a basis to develop successful DoP in disaster management. It then examines data collected by the commissions of enquiry into the Victorian Bushfires of 2009 (Parliament of Victoria 2010), 911Terrorist Attacks in 2001 (Kean 2004) and Hurricane Katrina during 2005 (Davis 2006) utilizing McCann's (1983) collaborative Negotiated Arrangements Theory as a method of analysis. IS issues and problems are then highlighted in each of these cases that impacted the ability to collaborate and negotiate a DoP. A "repertoires of collaboration" approach is then discussed with a view to the more effective provision of a DoP for any given disaster scenario, whilst reusing technology, information, human resources and "know how" in a flexible, sustainable and efficient manner.

2   Collaboration and Negotiation for the Development of DoP for Disaster Management

Negotiation plays an important role in organizational collaboration "so when organizations agree on an issue, negotiation is used to find the best way or the best solution to address a task. If organizations 'agree to disagree' on an issue, however, negotiation then reflects an organization's willingness to compromise in order to find common ground" (Bunker & Smith 2009 – p 3). If an organization collaborates for a common strategy, well thought out business processes and ICT architecture can make a huge difference to this collaboration (Pang & Bunker 2005).

Bunker and Smith (2009) interviewed a number of key managers in multiple NSW government emergency services agencies (ESA) (Police, Rural Fire Service, Ambulance, State Emergency Service, State Emergency Management Committee) and utilized McCann's (1983) Negotiated Arrangements Theory to show that disaster management DoPs: 1) have different (but aligned) ESA stakeholder objectives which also add a layer of complexity to their specification; 2) encompass different types of emergency incidents of varying complexity and so must reflect and cope with incident complexity; 3) must not rely solely on any one information and communications technology (ICT) platform or delivery system for their economies of scale; 4) need to integrate ESA operational, community, communication and ICT requirements to legitimize and give them a sense of direction; 5) collaborative processes require further and more detailed studies into the psychology, content and action resulting from messaging and 6) need to be developed and deployed with a view to adaptation and change.

As part of a larger disaster management project based at the University of Sydney, and commissioned by the NSW Government, Emergency Information & Coordination Unit (EICU) a geospatial data reference architecture was produced (Qumer Gill 2012). This architecture outlines the collection, storage, processing and distribution of geospatial information to emergency services agencies that then use it to manage dynamic and emergent situations such as crowd control, crises and disasters. In the analysis of this architecture it was found that DoP are heavily reliant on:

- *Technological Flexibility and Connectivity* – as multiple systems produce a DoP the technological flexibility to build up information layers and differing and related perspectives is essential. As there is a requirement for different agencies and organizations to manipulate this information from different locations and in different forms, then technological connectivity through different channels e.g. online, offline and mobile is also an essential requirement;

- *Information Governance Mechanisms* - whatever the source, information authenticity; accuracy; reliability; and legality must be guaranteed in order to make effective decisions; and

- *Long Term Systems Sustainability and Resource Efficiency* – DoP require constantly updated information, flexible systems tools and skilled personnel to be available each time they are generated, to effectively view and interpret the picture and make appropriate decisions. As this is a resource intensive activity, and in light of government budget constraints, there is also a requirement for a better understanding of how to construct a DoP as efficiently as possible in order to ensure long term systems sustainability.

McCann (1983) maintains that negotiated arrangements (processes) are also needed by organizations in a shared problem domain to ensure a workable collaborative outcome. "The inability of stakeholders to negotiate needed roles and responsibilities and perform regulative functions will ultimately limit the viability of their problem domain" (McCann 1983– p 181).

Stakeholder collaboration and negotiating is the key, therefore, to the successful development of DoP and within this study McCann's (1983) five negotiated arrangements as they apply to DoP are as follows:

(a) *Diverse Stakeholder Involvement* - assure that benefits accruing to stakeholders as a result of their involvement are favorably balanced against their contributions over the long run;

(b) *Dealing with Uncertainty and Complexity* - manage uncertainty and complexity within the domain by developing coordination and control mechanisms for implementing policies and programs;

(c)   *Development of Economies of Scale* - generate economies of scale or otherwise facilitate the efficient procurement and allocation of resources among stakeholders;

(d)   *Development of a Sense of Shared Direction* - help maintain the sense of shared direction and legitimacy of that direction by creating and building a visible identity for those involved – e.g., a legally formed association or cooperation; and

(e)   *Development of an Orderly Process for Adapting to Change (More Suitable ICT Architectures)* - provide an orderly process for adapting to change by building the learning capacities and skills of stakeholders.

The Victorian "Black Saturday" bushfires (2009), Hurricane Katrina (2005) and 9/11 Terrorist Attacks (2001) are all typical of an emergent disaster scenario where traditional command and control CoP approaches to IS and supporting processes proved to be problematic due to lack of effective negotiated arrangements.

   As negotiated arrangements are critical to dealing with dynamic and emergent incidents the following section of this paper analyzes each of these disasters in turn, using McCann's 5 negotiated arrangements as a lens of analysis to determine evidence of negotiated arrangements or the impact of their absence.

3   Research Methods, Data Sources and Analysis

Negotiated Arrangements Theory had been used in a prior study of a major flood debrief (Bunker & Smith 2009) to show how various NSW Government emergency agencies collaborated to negotiate disaster management outcomes during a flood event. It was felt that this same approach would be a useful way to analyze and categorize data from a number of diverse disaster cases (bushfire, hurricane, terrorism) to understand how emergency organizations involved in these events collaborated (or not) and the resulting consequences.

3.1   Victorian "Black Saturday" Bushfires (2009)

Scenario

Australia is a dry and arid continent with only 5% of the land area suitable for habitation and cultivation. Bushfires occur regularly in the southern states of Australia from October to March when temperatures rise and humidity falls giving rise to perfect fire conditions. This combined with the Australian natural vegetation of Eucalyptus trees facilitates and accelerates fire events. The Victorian fires which started in January 2009, spread rapidly on 7th February 2009. At the time there were unprecedented and "extreme" fire conditions (high temperatures, low humidity, high volumes of forest "fuel") which were identified ahead of time by the Victorian Government and the relevant fire agencies, however, many long standing fire officers had no experience of such conditions (Parliament of Victoria 2010).

   Victorians were warned prior to these "extreme" conditions of the likelihood of fire outbreaks. Once the fires started the rate of their spread was uncontrollable and fire behavior was unique (never before experienced). As a result, of these fires 173 people died and many homes and businesses were lost at great personal and societal cost and impact.

Data Sources

Royal Commissions are major governmental enquiries into matters of public importance. They have quasi-judicial powers and the ability to compel witnesses to testify. Because of the circumstances and outcomes of these fires, including the tragic loss of so many lives, the Victorian government chose to hold a Royal Commission into these events. This commission ran from February 2009 and concluded its final report in June 2010 (Parliament of Victoria 2010) which is the primary input for the analysis in this paper.

Over 1200 public submissions were received and used to frame the investigation of the Commission. Those submissions that were ranked highest and that impacted the use of IS and supporting processes to form a common operating picture were; disaster warnings (430 submissions ranked 3rd highest) and emergency communications (140 submissions). It is these areas of the report which are the subject of our analysis.

The report classified its investigation and recommendations into: warnings (types and processes); information (how it is used); relocation; "Stay or go" policy; risk and refuge; incident management; emergency management; commonwealth response; and emergency calls and so the interpretation of the evidence also lends weight to the importance of IS and process issues in disaster management.

Data Analysis – Negotiated Order Theory

(a)   *Diverse Stakeholder Involvement*

Incident control centers (a shared resource) were not properly staffed and equipped to enable immediate operation in the case of these fires. State Emergency Response Plans (shared plans with input of resources from control agencies responsible for warnings) needed to be amended to focus on: "managing the message" i.e. "stay or go" policy. There was also no effective higher level emergency management and co-ordination arrangements during the bushfire season for example for police co-ordination of roadblocks with warnings "Evidence revealed a number of systemic problems with the way the roadblocks operated, among them inflexibility, poor communication and denying access to firefighters" (p. 9 – Summary).

Commonwealth resources also needed to be deployed more rapidly to assist State officers to detect, track and suppress bushfires; and provision of Emergency Management Australia briefings to states were also lacking.

(b)   *Dealing with Uncertainty and Complexity*

There was an absence of simpler and clearer language for impending disaster warning so that communication of warnings was unclear. "It became apparent during the Commission's hearings that a number of bushfire-related terms are cumbersome, have obscure meanings or are potentially confusing to the general public" (p. 20 – Summary).

There was also a lack of an orderly process for adapting to change as there was no mechanism to build on learning capacities and skills of all stakeholders from past incidents. When the situation became more complex and uncertain there was a difficulty in:

- posting of information by Incident Control Centers directly to ESA information portals;

- agreement of procedures by the Country Fire Authority (CFA) and Department of Sustainability and Environment (DSE) to create flexibility for officers of different designations to "give warnings" in the field (system of effective delegation and interagency warnings);

- placement of authority with Chief Officer... to issue warnings and manage risk information, co-ordination and centralization; close coordination among multiple organizations and roles for disaster response; and

- co–ordination and distribution of decision making so that information and communications dependencies were understood and managed e.g. the different organizations CFA and DSE were responsible for issuing various warnings but no entity (or shared standard) watched over the integrity of the whole system.

"The experience of 7 February also highlighted several areas in which high-level state arrangements need reform. On Black Saturday the roles of the most senior personnel were not clear, and there was no single agency or individual in charge of the emergency.......It recommends that the roles be clarified, including through organizational change" (p. 8 – Summary).

(c)   *Development of Economies of Scale*

The Emergency Services Telecommunications Authority and Telstra Triple Zero had little warning of high risk days (Office of the Emergency Services Commissioner responsibility) so that they could allocate resources and better prepare; and incident control centers (ICCs - a shared resource) had limited scope to prepare for and respond to the emergent disaster scenario. The report highlights that "..the state of readiness of ICCs and level 3 incident management teams that staffed them varied" (p. 8 Summary) – see point (a) previous.

(d)   *Development of a Sense of Shared Direction*

There appeared to be no utilization and learning from the wealth of reviews and reports to government on the topics of disaster management. "The Commission notes that the recommendations of previous enquiries have not always been implemented (p. 21 Summary)" and as a result there was no consensus approach to handling warnings (see point (b) previous) nor the development of a Memorandum of Understanding (MoU) for commercial operators on dissemination of warnings.

(e)   *Development of an Orderly Process for Adapting to Change (More Suitable ICT Architectures)*

Whilst government was working towards a common approach to warnings through development of Common Applications Protocol (CAP) and SEWS as PPRR approaches this was not in an advanced enough state to be useful in this case. As the report states "...various problems became evident with information technology at incident control centres, including because the CFA and DSE used different systems and incident management team staff sometimes had difficulty gaining access to both systems. This inhibited the use and transfer of information such as warnings, maps and situation reports" (p. 10 - Summary). There was also a shortfall in the resourcing and development of a multi ESA information warning portal and limited capacity to handle a greater information "surge" capacity for extreme events i.e. need to improve efficiency of internal information function (including additional work stations). There was also a need for Commonwealth (COAG) to promote more effective emergency call service arrangements in all States.

3.2   Hurricane Katrina (2005)

Scenario

Hurricane Katrina was the most destructive Atlantic hurricane of 2005 and one of the five deadliest in U.S. history._ More than 1,833 people perished during Katrina and the ensuing floods, making it the deadliest hurricane since the Okeechobee hurricane in 1928. Property damage for Katrina was estimated at $81 billion (in 2005 USD).

Katrina formed over the Bahamas and crossed south Florida as a moderate hurricane, before strengthening to a Category 5 hurricane over the Gulf. Then Katrina made her second landfall as a Category 3 hurricane on August 29 in southeast Louisiana. Much of the devastation was due to the storm surge; and the largest number of fatalities_occurred in New Orleans, Louisiana, which flooded when the levee system catastrophically failed. Eventually 80% of the city and large parts of neighboring parishes became flooded. The floodwaters lingered for weeks. The worst property damage occurred in coastal areas and towns, which were flooded over 90% within hours, with waters reaching 6–12 miles from the beach.

The failure of the levee system in New Orleans is considered the worst civil engineering disaster in U.S. history. A lawsuit was brought against the U.S. Army Corps of Engineers (USACE) and the designers and builders of the levee system as mandated by the Flood Control Act of 1965. Responsibility for the failures and flooding was laid directly on the Army Corps in January 2008. An investigation of the responses from federal, state and local governments also resulted in the resignation of Federal Emergency Management Agency (FEMA) director and New Orleans Police Department Superintendent.

The Coast Guard, National Hurricane Center, and National Weather Service were praised for their actions. They provided exact tracking forecasts with adequate lead time. Unfortunately, repeated and urgent appeals from national, state and local officials to residents to evacuate before the storm did not warn that the levees could break and fail.

Data Sources

The primary source for our analysis of Hurricane Katrina is the comprehensive special report, *A Failure of Initiative: Final Report of the Select Bipartisan Committee to Investigate the Preparation For and Response to Hurricane Katrina* (Davis 2006).

There is no shortage of examples of the failure of negotiated order and so we have selected a subset, covering topics including: Hurricane Pam exercise, levees, evacuation, and finally the National Framework, also specifically known as the National Response Plan (NRP) Catastrophe Incident Annex (CIA).

Data Analysis – Negotiated Order Theory

This analysis presents us with a number of negotiated arrangements that overlap.

(a)   Diverse Stakeholder Involvement AND (c) Development of Economies of Scale

The Hurricane Pam exercise of 2004 is a prime illustration of misunderstanding and a failure in these areas. This simulation, designed and run by private Baton Rouge based contractor, Innovative Emergency Management, Ltd., was sufficiently distorted so that it was unable to achieve its real objectives. The delivery of the results from the exercise was expedited so that these could be translated into operational plans. However, according to IEM President Beriwal, "the plan was not meant to provide operational detail but rather was designed to provide general guidance, a sort of "to do list" for state and localities. Beriwal characterized the exercise as a "work in progress," describing IEM's role as "facilitator and assessors of consequences" (p. 82).

The results from Pam were clearly misused and misaligned. "Some state and parish officials said they saw Pam as a "contract" of what the various parties were going to do, and the federal government did not do the things it had committed to doing. ... Beriwal said, however, the plan derived from the Pam exercise was intended as a "bridging document" designed to serve as a guide and roadmap to be used by emergency operational officials to take the Plan and turn it into more detailed individual operational plans" (p.83). The officials' viewed Pam as a contract.   IEM's stance reflects a view where the results of the exercise were intended to serve more loosely as guidance or a road map that would need to be operationalized and scaled up. These conflicting views are virtually a guarantee for difficulty and dissatisfaction on both sides.

(b)   Dealing with Uncertainty and Complexity

The response to Katrina was described by government officials and citizens alike as demonstrating poor leadership and poor coordination. The Katrina evacuation conveyed confusion and a lack of clarity. For example, the different parishes used a wide variety of terms to describe the level of evacuation imposed before declaring a mandatory evacuation. Jefferson Parish—the other major component of metropolitan New Orleans—never did declare a mandatory evacuation, except for the lower parts of the parish on the Gulf Coast. In a conference call among parish officials, Jefferson Parish President Aaron Broussard said he did not have the "resources to enforce" a mandatory evacuation (p. 110).

The wide variety of terms might suggest desired precision and accompanying rules to govern different conditions, but in this instance the effect was opposite, resulting in confusion and large parts of the population remaining in their home at great peril and not evacuating.   "Why would you get in the public media and ask a city, where 80 percent of its citizens ride public transit, to evacuate? What [were] they supposed to do? Fly? (p. 111).

The situation with the levees—flood walls which broke and flooded major portions of New Orleans—can be described as a "catch 22" around requirements and *dealing with uncertainty and complexity*. While federal regulations require monitoring levees during periods of potential flooding, the requirement is impractical to implement during a hurricane" (p. 87). In this circumstance, at once, there are requirements with no act of responsibility assigned at the same time as there are impractical requirements. The "standard project hurricane" was used nationwide for all hurricane protection projects where the loss of human life is possible. According to the US Army Corps of Engineers, the "standard project hurricane" was used to design the New Orleans levees and is roughly equivalent to a fast moving, or "moderate" category 3 hurricane. However, there is no direct comparison of the standard project hurricane" to a specific category on the Saffir-Simpson Hurricane Scale—which did not exist when the levees were designed. ...In addition, there is no "standard" hurricane—the actual forces that levees need to withstand are a function of several factors (p. 89).

This example is interesting in a number of ways. First, a "standard" by definition assumes structure, predictability and regularity. In Katrina, the hurricane was simultaneously treated as a standard and non standard event, and this incompatibility is an invitation for ambiguity and confusion at minimum and more likely chaos.

(d)   *Development of a Sense of Shared Direction*

In addition to the ambiguity and confusion that we see around a "standard hurricane," the response to Katrina revealed that local solutions were incompatible. A global perspective was missing and *shared direction* had not been negotiated. "The different local organizations involved had the effect of diffusing responsibility and creating potential weaknesses. For example levee breaches and distress were repeatedly noted at transition sections, where different organizations [primarily New Orleans parishes] were responsible for different pieces and thus two different levee or wall systems joined together" (pp. 91-92). One can envision a scenario where each local organization's use of rules and procedures might satisfy local needs; however, in conjunction their approaches are not interoperable. In disaster response, where the coordinated effort of many agents and agencies is vital, such errors have a critical impact.

(e)   *Development of an Orderly Process for Adapting to Change (More Suitable ICT Architectures)*

The failure of achieving of interoperability is succinctly expressed here: "The local sponsors—a patchwork quilt of levee and water and sewer boards—were responsible only for their own piece of levee. It seems no federal, state, or local entity watched over the integrity of the whole system, which might have mitigated to some degree the effects of the hurricane" (p. 97).

3.3   9/11 Terrorist Attacks (2001)

Scenario

9/11 was the first multiple hijacking in the United States, and the first in the world in more than thirty years. On September 11, 2001, nineteen terrorists boarded four commercial jetliners, all transcontinental flights, carrying a maximum load of 11,400 gallons of jet fuel. Their objective was to take control of the planes once they were airborne and turn them into flying weapons of destruction. This was a typical summer day in New York City and Washington, D.C. Before ordinary passenger jets became fiery menaces, people in the World Trade Center and Pentagon were working at computers, reading e-mail, speaking on the phone or processing paperwork. None of the civilians seemed to know what was to happen.

Four targets had been chosen, all iconic American buildings that would send a clear message of the depth of the terrorists' hatred for the United States. All four planes crashed, killing all on board—terrorists, crew members, and passengers, along with hundreds who were killed inside the structures, on the ground, and the men and women who ran into collapsing buildings in an effort to try and save others. Only one of the four planes did not find its target. Thanks to cellular phones, passengers heard of the other crashes and chose to sacrifice themselves rather than let another plane devastate a fourth target, killing even more innocent people.

Data Sources

The Complete Investigation: 9/11 Report with Commentary by The New York Times. (Kean, 2004) was used as the primary source of information about the terrorist attack on September 11, 2001. This document provided a detailed description of the steps leading up to the attack, the actions taken by responders, victims, and government bodies tied to the scenes of the attacks, and an analysis of actions taken after the attack to address problems. The commission interviewed over 1,200 people in 10 countries and reviewed over two and a half million pages of documents, including some closely guarded classified national security documents. Before it was released by the commission, the final public report was screened for any potentially classified information and edited as necessary.

There is a wealth of relevant material to use for this analysis. We have selected examples pertaining to recognizing the threat, preparation for a possible attack, and managing first responders.

Data Analysis – Negotiated Order Theory

(a)   *Diverse Stakeholder Involvement AND* (b) *Dealing with Uncertainty and Complexity*

Information sharing among stakeholder groups was identified as a critical gap in the identification and possible deterrence of terrorists in advance of the attack. Many lost opportunities for stopping the attack were identified in hindsight (p. 549). It was found that 15 of the 19 hijackers were potentially vulnerable to interception by border authorities. Analyzing their characteristic travel documents and travel patterns could have allowed authorities to intercept 4 to 15 and more effective use of information available in the US government databases could have identified up to 3 hijackers.

However, recognizing and acting on these pieces of critical information was extremely difficult to do in advance, and technology sources were not directly linked to the screening roles where interception could have occurred.

With respect to handling complexity, frequently a significant element of information was not recognized and shared because it comes bundled with thousands of other pieces of information and is lost in the volume. Also, identification of issues within the noise of constant day to day chatter requires someone to be listening for the message. There was a continual focus on rules of engagement without consideration of the desired results of the interactions.

Information may not be shared because those needing the information view it differently. The FBI focuses only on investigations and not on intelligence. Information not tied to a criminal investigation is not viewed as important. Hence content related to terrorist monitoring by the CIA was not readily useful to the FBI and not valued. Current rules governing information sharing require a clearly demonstrated "need to know" before sharing occurs. This approach assumes it is possible to know in advance what information is needed and why and assumes risk of exposure inappropriately outweighs the value of wider sharing.

(c)   *Development of Economies of Scale AND* (d) *Development of a Sense of Shared Direction*

A heightened terrorist threat resulted in tightened security in U.S. foreign facilities such as embassies and consulates, but precipitated no domestic response to negotiating economies of scale and efficient procurement and allocation of resources. U.S. foreign facilities have clear actions to be taken in case of threats (playbooks). No sense of shared direction was developed and domestic agencies had no game plan. Moreover, none of the organizations issuing the warnings instructed domestic agencies to develop a playbook. Even when specific threat concerns related to airlines were identified and communicated to the FAA, the responses mirrored actions taken to address hijacking and did not include consideration of a new type of terrorist (p. 379).

(e)   *Development of an Orderly Process for Adapting to Change (More Suitable ICT Architectures)*

Responders at the WTC included members of the Port Authority, the fire department (FDNY) and the police (NYPD). Each of these groups had their own chain of command, their own communication protocols, and their own procedures and practices. Consequently, the groups did not have *shared and orderly meta-processes for coordinated response.* FDNY took over control of the towers to address the fire and the police worked in the surrounding areas to cover traffic flow and cordon off the area. Helicopter surveillance was provided by NYPD (p. 405). In a 17-minute period NYC and Port Authority of NY and NJ had mobilized the largest rescue operation in the city's history (over 1000 first responders), evacuation of the first tower had begun, and a decision was made that the fire in the first tower could not be fought. Then the second plane hit the World Trade Center. As the crises unfolded, the inability of various responder groups to share situational awareness information began to impact operational effectiveness (p. 422).

Victims trapped in the building were calling the 911 emergency response resources asking what to do. Although the offices in the WTC had gone through practice drills, when these were carried out the occupants were left gathering on the floor and awaiting instructions. When no instructions came due to communication failures, the occupants did not know what to do (p. 420). People from upper floors of the WTC went to the roof; helicopter evacuations were used successfully in the previous bombing. The helicopters were operated by NYPD and no FDNY personnel were placed in them during monitoring and decision making to determine if such a rescue option was feasible this time. The 911 operators did not receive any communication from site sources and did not know the location of the fire (floors) and could not tell people if it was possible for them to descend. They told victims to remain in place (standard response protocol) leaving the individuals trapped when many could have left safely.

The established procedures worked well as far as they went: police cleared the area and blocked further entrée; fire personnel identified what could be done to address fire and organized an orderly evacuation; port authority rescued people from PATH trains and metro below WTC; and an evacuation path was developed by fire personnel from the site directing people away from falling debris (p. 427). Each of these effective responses was handled by a single responder organization under a single command.

The limitations of the communication capabilities of FDNY with police and port authority personnel resulted in limited situational awareness being shared within the buildings. The occupants in building 2 did not know when building 1 had collapsed and did not recognize the significance of this event to their survival (many ignored the notification to evacuate when it came from another command).

In contrast, the Pentagon had rehearsed joint exercises among a range of first responders and had a clear command structure for blended response – all commands had a clear view of the site and could monitor the situation and communicate with their units. This allowed them to respond jointly to the changing situation. The circumstances of the attacked zone at the Pentagon were very different from NYC. The site was isolated physically from normal pedestrian and vehicle travel routes and under the control of a military organization with a structured military chain of command. The victims were not totally reliant on general first responder support (p. 451).

4   Discussion

The review of issues in collaboration and negotiation of outcomes across all three disasters show that there are many inter-dependent information, warning and communications connections that are critical, for effective disaster management. When these connections fail, generally as a result of staying with traditional command and control CoP approaches, there appears to be no acceptable alternative, i.e. there was no ability to negotiate a substitute disaster management picture. For example, in all three disasters there was a lack of a holistic view of the incident, i.e. lack of shared protocols (communications and procedures) and lack of ability to cope with the resulting information surge, which resulted in poor shared situational awareness of what was unfolding and the most appropriate response to it.

In the case of each disaster we see:

• Incompatibility of local responses and a lack of global management of the emerging disaster;

• Imprecise and ambiguous warnings and a lack of urgency to react/evacuate being communicated;

• A lack of oversight and sense of common purpose resulting in poor information/technical/human resource management;

- "Paralysis" of government agencies as they did not want to be seen to be complicating disaster response by over-reacting or wasting resources;

- Poor recognition of threats (in all 3 incidents) due to lack of sharing and ownership of different views of information, which was a critical gap in recognizing the threats posed by these incidents in the first place; and

- Little coordinated oversight of the "command and control" structures between emergency agencies and their inability to flexibly and effectively share changing situational awareness.

The necessity is growing for the development of approaches to collaboration for, and negotiation of, dynamic operating pictures for disaster management. As we know, DoP rely heavily on: technological flexibility and connectivity; information governance mechanisms; long term systems sustainability and resource efficiency (Qumer-Gill 2012), while disaster management stakeholders are required to negotiate roles and responsibilities to perform regulative functions, otherwise the viability of satisfactory disaster management outcomes are at stake (McCann 1983).

McCann (1983) gives us a useful starting point by which to formulate approaches for DoP development as negotiated arrangements theory attempts to address differences in socio-organisational factors by focusing on: (a) diverse stakeholder involvement; (b) dealing with uncertainty and complexity; (c) development of economies of scale; (d) development of a sense of shared direction and (e) development of an orderly process for adapting to change (more suitable ICT architectures) in order to facilitate collaboration between organizations. By combining negotiated arrangements characteristics with DoP requirements we are able to generate a collaborative focus for disaster management, what we call "repertoires of collaboration" for governments, agencies, businesses and the community when negotiating a DoP for any given disaster scenario (see Table 2). In asking these questions of all stakeholders in each instance of a disaster, a new DoP is generated to suit the emergent and dynamic characteristics of that scenario while reusing technological/informational/human resources and process knowledge that is available to hand and which suits the new circumstances. This is a departure from the current "command and control" approach to disaster management where agencies establish a command centre to assemble a common operating picture. Our approach facilitates collaboration of decentralized stakeholders and resources for the management of dynamic and emerging scenarios.

The initially developed questions could be used to make improvements to scenario dependent technology, information and process management. In time, appropriate metrics might also be developed and trialed in order to measure costs and benefits of improvements to the use of these resources.

Further incorporation of "lessons learned" from the analysis of other disaster scenarios would give the global research community a more holistic view of the types of disaster that may occur, the various environments in which governments, agencies, business and communities operate, as well as a direction to more effectively harness and manage technical/information/human resources. This is particularly important for areas of the world where resources are scare and where a response may rely on foreign aid and personnel. Disaster scenarios in these situations, are often more complex

Table 2. Negotiated Arrangements for a Dynamic Operating Picture

DoP REQUIREMENTS ➡ Negotiated Arrangements CHARACTERISTICS ⬇	Technological flexibility and connectivity	Information governance mechanisms	Long term systems sustainability and resource efficiency
Diverse stakeholder involvement	What technology can we supply to design and deliver (enable) the DoP ?	How can we supply authentic, accurate, reliable and legal information (quality) to the DoP ?	How do we sustain a DoP architectural focus over the long term while minimizing organizational (process) requirements?
Dealing with uncertainty and complexity	How do we identify the most successful and simplest way to technically enable the DoP ?	How can we reduce information complexity while increasing its quality in the DoP?	How to we sustain a DoP while minimizing process complexity?
Development of economies of scale	How do we collaborate with other stakeholders to procure, allocate and manage technologies for the DoP?	How do we collaborate with other stakeholders to procure, allocate and manage information in the DoP?	How do we collaborate with other stakeholders to ensure long term systems sustainability and resource efficiency of the DoP?
Development of a sense of shared direction	How do we organize stakeholders to identify with and enable the DoP architecture?	How do we organize to ensure that all stakeholders are managing information in a way that enables the DoP?	How do we organize to combine architectural and informational components supplied by stakeholders in a sustainable and efficient manner (multi-stakeholder processes)
Development of an orderly process for adapting to change	How do we retain the knowledge and experience of DoP design and delivery for the next disaster scenario?	How do we retain the knowledge and experience of DoP information sourcing and supply for the next disaster scenario?	How do we retain the knowledge and experience of DoP multi stakeholder processes for the next disaster scenario?

to manage due to perceived lack of control over resource management and allocation as well as cultural conflicts between domestic and foreign personnel. Inter-regional disaster management and response is also more complex for similar reasons. Disaster management systems, information and processes could be managed to reduce complexity and conflict if we develop sufficient knowledge about these scenarios and what are appropriate responses to them.

5   Conclusion

Disasters are emergent and dynamic scenarios involving diverse stakeholders. To improve disaster response, we suggest that emergency service agencies should consider supplementing their "command and control" approaches and common operating pictures (CoP), to better account for these conditions.

This paper focuses on collaboration as a means to supplement current practice, and uses McCann's (1983) Negotiated Order Theory as an analytical lens and as a basis to develop successful DoP in disaster management. We then examined data collected by the commissions of enquiry into the Victorian Bushfires of 2009 (Parliament of Victoria 2010), Hurricane Katrina during 2005 (Davis 2006) and 911 Terrorist Attacks in 2001 (Kean 2004).

Our analysis demonstrates that these three quite different disasters share common command and control CoP systems failings. This suggests that development of a negotiated DoP, rather than the usual CoP "command centre" approaches to domain specific disasters such as bushfires, hurricanes or terrorist acts, may be more appropriate for disaster management in general. The analysis provided in this paper could equally be applied to other disaster scenarios, such as the Fukoshima Tsunami (2011),

Haiti Earthquake (2010), Gulf Oil Spill (2010) or Queensland Floods (2010/11) to highlight similarities and differences between them and then derive where CoP approaches can be best supplemented with collaboration and negotiated DoP.

Our analysis of these cases also highlights the unique socio-organizational aspects of federal, state and local governments and community groups and the resulting structural, policy and cultural roadblocks to effective disaster management. Socio-organizational factors and their impact on collaborative negotiated outcomes often literally mean the difference between life and death in a disaster scenario.

Building on the creation of a disaster scenario "bank" as well as repertoires of collaboration for the negotiation of DoP, the longer term objective of this project is the development and introduction of unique, easily understood, collaborative disaster management information and process modeling methods, organizational structures and metrics to complement the "repertoires" approach to enabling DoP. These would be useful to accelerate the maturity of government inter-agency information and process improvement approaches, as well as translating successful process improvements to other agencies, by enabling collaborative communication and adaptation of information, process and organizational change. By incorporating tools and metrics to model, compare and evaluate disaster management information and process approaches, their organization and management, government, community groups and ICT providers will be able to utilize this knowledge to facilitate optimal outcomes in disaster management regardless of scenario.

References

Betts, R.: The missing links in community warning systems: findings from two Victorian community warning information systems projects. The Australian Journal of Emergency Management 18(3), 37–45 (2003)

Blanchard-Boehm, R.D.: Understanding public response to increased risk from natural hazards: Application of the hazards risk communication framework. International Journal of Mass Emergencies and Disasters 16(3), 247–248 (1998)

Bunker, D.J., Kautz, K., Nguyen, A.: The Role of Value Compatibility in IT Adoption. Journal of Information Technology 22, 69–78 (2007)

Bunker, D., Smith, S.: Disaster Management and Community Warning (CW) Systems: Inter-Organisational Collaboration and ICT Innovation. In: Pacific Asia Conference on Information Systems, Hyderabad, India, July 12 (2009)

Council of Europe, Early Warning: The Key Requests to Early Warning System (Community Awareness) – submitted by Victor Poyarkov, AP/CAT, 9 rev Or.E (2005)

Davis, T.: A Failure of Initiative: Final Report of the Select Bipartisan Committee to Investigate the Preparation For and Response to Hurricane Katrina, U.S. House of Representatives, US Government Printing Office (2006)

Ehnis, C., Bunker, D.: Social Media in Disaster Response: Queensland Police Service - Public Engagement During the 2011 Floods. In: Australasian Conference on Information Systems ACIS 2012, Geelong, Australia, December 5 (2012)

Gray, B.: Conditions facilitating interorganizational collaboration. Human Relations 38(10), 911–936 (1985)

Gray, B., Wood, D.J.: Collaborative alliances: Moving from practice to theory. Journal of Applied Behavioral Science 27(1), 3–22 (1991)

Greenberg, M.R., Lahr, M., Mantell, N.: Understanding the Economic Costs and Benefits of Catastrophes and their Aftermath: A Review and Suggestions for the U.S. Federal Government. Risk Analysis 27(1), 83–96 (2007)

Kean, T.: The Complete Investigation: 9/11 Report with Commentary by The New York Times. National Commission on Terrorist Attacks Upon the United States. St. Martin's Press, New York (2004), http://www.9-11commission.gov

Kost, J., Moyer, K.: Real time warnings to citizens. Gartner Advisory Group, February 13 (2003), http://intranet.vic.gov.au/xgov/gartner/GGV4.nsf

Kroenke, D., Bunker, D., Wilson, D.: Experiencing MIS, 2nd edn. Pearson Australia, Sydney, Australia (2012)

Levine, L., Woody, C.: System of Systems Analysis of Catastrophic Events: A Preliminary Investigation of Unprecedented Scenarios. IEEE HST 2010, Waltham MA, USA (2010)

McCann, J.E.: Design guidelines for social problem-solving interventions. Journal of Applied Behavioral Science 19(2), 177–189 (1983)

Nathan, M.L., Mitroff, I.I.: The use of negotiated order theory as a tool for the analysis and development of an interorganizational field. Journal of Applied Behavioral Science 27(2), 163–180 (1991)

Office of the Emergency Services Commissioner (OESC 2006) Community Information and Warning System, Department of Justice, Victorian Government (2006)

Pang, V., Bunker, D.J.: Development of a Framework to Examine the Collaborative Process in Inter-Organisational System Adoption. In: 2nd Annual Conference on IS/IT issues in Asia Pacific (ISAP) Las Vegas, pp. 13–23 (December 2005)

Parliament of Victoria, Victorian Bushfires Royal Commission Report (July 2010)

Pauchant, T.C., Mitroff, I.I., Ventolo, G.F.: The Dial Tone Does Not Come from God! How a Crisis Can Challenge Dangerous Strategic Assumptions Made About High Technologies: The Case of the Hinsdale Telecommunication Outage. The Executive 6(3), 66–79 (1992)

Pearson, C.M., Clair, J.A.: Reframing Crisis Management. The Academy of Management Review 23(1), 59–76 (1998)

Pearson, C.M., Mitroff, I.I.: From Crisis Prone to Crisis Prepared: A Framework for Crisis Management. The Academy of Management Review 7(1), 48–59 (1993)

Qumer Gill, A.: NSW Land and Property Information EICU Reference Architecture 1.0. (October 2012)

Sikich, G.W.: Hurricane Katrina: Nature's dirty bomb incident (2005), http://www.continuetycentral.com/featured0247.html

Smith, S., Bunker, D.: Community Warning Systems: An Information Process and ICT Architecture Approach for Emergency Incident Response. – Issues Paper prepared for the NSW Department of Commerce (2008)

Tarrant, M.: Hurricane Katrina. The Australian Journal of Emergency Management 20(4), 32 (2005)

Success or Failure in Knowledge Management Systems: A Universal Issue[*][**]

Elayne Coakes[1], A.D. Amar[2], and Maria L. Granados[1]

[1] Westminster Business School, University of Westminster, 35 Marylebone Road
London, NW1 5LS, UK
{coakese,m.granados}@westminster.ac.uk
[2] Stillman School of Business, Seton Hall University, South Orange, NJ 07079, USA
Ad.amar@shu.edu

Abstract. This paper takes a sociotechnical viewpoint of knowledge management system (KMS) implementation in organizations considering issues such as stakeholder disenfranchisement, lack of communication, and the low involvement of key personnel in system design asking whether KMS designers could learn from applying sociotechnical principles to their systems. The paper discusses design elements drawn from the sociotechnical principles essential for the success of IS and makes recommendations to increase the success of KMS in organizations. It also provides guidelines derived from Clegg's Principles (2000) for KMS designers to enhance their designs. Our data comes from the application of a plurality of analysis methods on a large comprehensive global survey conducted from 2007 to 2011 of 1034 participants from 76 countries. The survey covers a variety of organizations of all types and sizes from a comprehensive selection of economic sectors and industries. Our results showed that users were not satisfied with the information and knowledge systems that they were being offered. In addition to multiple technology and usability issues, there were human and organisational barriers that prevented the systems from being used to their full potential. We recommend that users of KMS are integrated into the design team so that these usability and other barriers can be addressed during the feasibility stage as well as the actual design and implementation phases.

1 Introduction

Despite much theoretical (e.g., DeLone and McLean (1992; 2003)) and some practical works within organisations that study measures of organizational support such as

---

[*] To maintain the page limit imposed by IFIP 8.6, we eliminated a number of tables, literature, and other information from this paper. Interested readers may contact authors for them.

[**] With acknowledgements to the researchers who prepared much of the TAM literature review for the TWOLER project at the University of Westminster. The authors wish to thank JISC and the Promoting Student Web 2.0 Contributions with Lightweight Enterprise RSS project who provided grant support for the sociotechnical evaluation study. Thanks to Institute for International Business at Seton Hall University for the travel related grants pertaining to this project.

Y.K. Dwivedi et al. (Eds.): TDIT 2013, IFIP AICT 402, pp. 39–56, 2013.
© IFIP International Federation for Information Processing 2013

leadership, incentives, co-worker and supervisor (e.g., Kulkarni, Ravindran, and Freeze (2006)), we still find that many systems fail on their first implementation, or even fail altogether. These failures appear to refer to all types of information systems (IS) in all fields of organisational life. Not enough attention has been paid to understand the failures especially through a broad-based study of all stakeholders in design, implementation and use of knowledge management systems (KMS). The few studies undertaken about knowledge management systems failures seem to indicate that knowledge management systems fail at least as often, if not more often, than any other information system. User experience builds their beliefs about system quality and knowledge/information quality which determines KMS use (Wu and Wang, 2006).

While DeLone and McLean (2002) did modify their original IS success model by converting Individual Impact and Organizational Impact to Net Impact (DeLone and McLean, 1992), KMS specific quantitative impacts could not be measured either at individual or organizational level (Jennex and Olfman, 2003). Davenport, DeLone, and Beers (1998), in the context of KM projects, consider senior management support, motivational incentives, and knowledge friendly culture among their eight factors for success. In their KM success model, Massey, Montoya-Weiss, and O'Driscoll (2002) consider three key managerial influences: coordination, control, and measurement; disciplined project management; and leadership. However, no study considered detailed sociotechnical factors in a wide population of KMS users, managers, and knowledge workers. The question, therefore, this paper addresses is: what can KMS designers learn from sociotechnical principles to improve the success rate, and avoid the failure rates of these systems, and reduce user experiences and beliefs about system quality and knowledge/information quality that then discourage KMS use? In particular, the paper addresses the underlying factors that cause failure in three specific sociotechnical areas: technology; human; and organisational. Additionally, it investigates the underlying organisational, human and technical conditions that should be put in place as part of the overall knowledge management system design.

The reasons for KMS failure are multi-faceted and both social and technical factors are involved as well as organisational factors. For instance; authors such as Hurley (2010) argue that hierarchical organisations are not conducive to knowledge sharing and that additionally, unless it is a cultural norm that knowledge is shared, systems will not work. Technology, they state, cannot be the driver, but can facilitate when the culture is appropriate. Akhavan, Jafari, and Fathian (2005) agree. In their list of the 10 most important failure factors not only do they mention organisational culture but additionally they echo a number of points which we saw identified in our survey (details given below) such as the lack of budget; lack of top management support; resistance to change; and current and new systems being unable to link. Many of these factors are also to be found in all information systems failures and thus we would argue that considering the sociotechnical factors of knowledge management systems is equally appropriate for considering how KMS might achieve success as for any other information system (IS).

This paper therefore takes a sociotechnical viewpoint of knowledge management system implementation in organisations and evaluates their success and failure across a variety of organisations and industrial sectors with data taken from a worldwide study.

The data which is presented is derived from what we assert is the largest global knowledge management survey of knowledge workers ever undertaken with 1034 participants across 76 countries coming from a balanced sample of organisations in terms of sector, size and status. Additionally, 15 in-depth interviews with company directors and CEOs were conducted. This data was analysed through both qualitatively and quantitatively as appropriate and the statistical results were valid to the 95% of significance. Content analysis was used on the qualitative data and multi-rating was utilised to ensure its validity.

Our results showed that users were not satisfied with the information and knowledge systems that they were being offered. In addition to multiple technology and usability issues, there were additionally human and organisational barriers that prevented the systems from being used to their full potential. A sociotechnical evaluation would indicate that this was not unexpected considering the ways in which these systems had been implemented. A high failure rate is to be expected when stakeholders are not consulted in how they undertake their work and which technologies are best fit for the purpose.

The paper begins with a discussion of sociotechnical evaluation methods for organisational projects emphasising the design elements considered essential for project success. This is followed by a brief discussion of the sixteen major models used for system evaluations and their linkage into the sociotechnical principles which permitted us to derive our propositions for likely knowledge management system success. We then discuss our empirical data and the research methodology utilised.

Finally we link our data to the propositions and discuss the validity of theory against practice. We suggest the major implications of this study for future knowledge management system design and implementation, providing advice for knowledge management managers and system designers of better ways to design such systems.

2   Sociotechnical Considerations

Coakes and Coakes (2005) said that sociotechnical thinking is important to the design, development, implementation, and use of information technology systems in organisations. It addresses vital issues in combining the use of powerful information and communication technologies with effective and humanistic use of people. Sociotechnical perspectives can be characterised as being holistic and will take a more encompassing view of the organisation, its stakeholders in knowledge, and the environment in which it operates.

Coiera (2007) argues that sociotechnical design and evaluation are inter-related processes where one affects the other. Evaluation can be of two types: summative – whereby there is a test of hypotheses as to whether the system met the user needs; or formative – where there is an analysis of needs. Some sociotechnical designs can be provocative when finding out about user needs. Coiera (2007) is critical of the Technology Acceptance Model (TAM) concepts as they focus on individuals and the *fit* between task, technology, and individuals but ignore the organisational or task context. Many articles in the 1990s used the TAM model, or its extensions, as a substitute for sociotechnical models (Whitworth et al, 2008), thus concentrating closely on the software interaction with the organisational users. This limited view of the sociotechnical mindset is followed by Dixon (1999) using the ITAM framework (Information Technology Acceptance Model); Tsinakis, Kouroubali (2009) using the FITT (fit between individuals, task and technology) framework; and Peute et al (2010), who use the UIS (User Interaction Satisfaction) concept. Berg (1999) also follows the 'herd' through discussing sociotechnical evaluation solely in the context of an information technology system and the existing work practices that it will impact.

A contrasting view to more modest evaluation concepts in regard to success and failure is that of Clegg (2000) who considers the entirety of the organisation and not just the system under consideration. This viewpoint is more aligned with the original sociotechnical principles as laid out by Cherns (1976) for organisational design. Reading his paper of 2000 (Clegg, 2000) and also Cherns (1976; 1987), we can derive some evaluation questions that need to be asked of any system whether or not it is a knowledge management system or a more standard information system. These principles and evaluation questions will equally apply.

Having derived post-hoc evaluation questions we can then say that these questions can also be used as questions to be asked during the design and implementation process by changing the tense of the question to the present and/or future. Thus 'was' would become 'is' and so on. These questions then become ones that should underpin all new knowledge management system design projects.

2.1   Clegg's 19 Sociotechnical Design Principles

Clegg's (2000) 19 principles are divided into 3 sections: Meta Principles; Content Principles; and Process Principles; and each Principle 'acquires' a set of questions that needs to be answered when designing according to these sociotechnical principles. Clegg's work is drawn from the seminal set of principles outlined by Cherns (1976; 1987).

In Table 1, we look at these principles and identify the questions that they must raise in terms of not just past evaluation of the success or failure of any information systems including that of KMS, but also how to design new systems that can succeed.

Table 1. Clegg's Principles and the Related Evaluation Questions

	Clegg's Principle	Design and Implementation Questions: Use also for post-hoc Evaluation
	Meta principles	
1	Systemic Design	Is there a built in capacity to / or a built in process to review the impacts of current design and make amends accordingly? Reflexivity leading to action and re-action.
2	Centrality of Values and Mindset	Do the technical design / technologies support the human [resources] to meet their goals? Do their goals meet / complement the needs of the systems/s?

Table 1. (*continued*)

3	Design involves making choices Design should be business reflected	Can stakeholders influence the design? Whose needs could be met?
4	Design should be user reflected Design should be manager reflected	Does the technical design reflect the result of a fad?
5	Design is a social process	Do the structures permit of evolution after stakeholder views are aired? Can stakeholders influence the design?
6	Design is socially shaped	Is the design / technology the result of movements in the external world? What social movements impact this design?
7	Design is contingent	Are the choices contingent on decisions and the satisficing[1] of goals?
	Content principles	
8	Core processes should be integrated	Are the systems integrated?
9	Design entails multiple task allocations between and amongst humans and machines	Are the possible tasks explicitly allocated to either technology or humans?
10	System components should be congruent	Are the systems consistent? Can those who need to take the necessary action? Can they obtain the information they need?
11	Systems should be simple in design and make problems visible	Is it easy to identify problem areas and allocate resources?
12	Problems should be controlled at source	Can problem areas be easily identified?
13	The means of undertaking tasks should be flexibly specified	Can users have choices in using the systems? Are there alternatives in how tasks are performed?
	Process principles	
14	Design practice is itself a socio-technical system	Does the process of design follow the meta principles?
15	Systems and their designers should be owned by their managers and users	Who owns the system design? And the systems that are designed?
16	Evaluation is an essential aspect of design	Is there reflective action? Who influences the design? What are the goals against which this reflection could be measured?

---

[1] **Satisficing is a** term used to describe how people make rational choices between options open to them and within prevailing constraints. Herbert Simon (*Administrative Behaviour,* 1957) argued that decision-makers can rarely obtain and evaluate all the information which could be relevant to the making of a decision. Instead, they work with limited and simplified knowledge, to reach acceptable, compromise choices.

Table 1. (*continued*)

17	Design involves multidisciplinary education.	What disciplines do the designers come from?
18	Sufficient resources and support are required for design	Is this true?
19	System design involves political processes	Is there a diversity of views? Who influences the change process? Do organisational politics play a part in the design process?

The comprehensive literature review we undertook permitted us to formulate the following propositions about stakeholder behaviour towards systems. These propositions were derived from the operationalism of the models as applied to users of the systems, i.e., what the users thought and how they intended to behave, or did behave, towards the system as identified in these models. Additionally the variables and meaning identified were used to refine these propositions.

2.2   Propositions

P1.   *System performance has an influence on intention to use the system;*
P2.   *Effort required to be expended has an influence on intention to use the system;*
P3.   *Attitude toward using technology (now or prior to using) has an influence on intention to use the system;*
P4.   *Attitude toward using technology will not have significant influence on intention to use the system;*
P5.   *Social Influence has an influence on intention to use the system;*
P6.   *Facilitating conditions have an influence on behavioural intention to use the system;*
P7.   *Self-efficacy (ability to influence, affect, or time required to affect) has an influence on intention to use the system;*
P8.   *Computer self-efficacy will not have a significant influence on intention;*
P9.   *Anxiety has an influence on intention to use the system;*
P10.   *Computer anxiety will not have a significant influence on intention to use the system;*
P11.   *Facilitating conditions have an influence on usage of the system;*
P12.   *Facilitating conditions will not have a significant influence on intention to use the system;*
P13.   *Behavioural intention will have a significant positive influence on usage of the system;*
P14.   *The influence of performance on intentions will be moderated by social influence;*
P15.   *Social Influence on intentions will be moderated in mandatory settings (i.e. where usage is compulsory).*

The above inferences related to the causal factors of KMS usage were used as propositions when designing and analysing our research data.

In the following section, we describe our research methods and how our primary data was collected. We then demonstrate our analysis methods, and in our Findings, we discuss what we have discovered and the veracity or not of our propositions. Finally, we discuss the implications from our research both theoretical and empirical, for organisations in implementing more successful knowledge management systems.

3   Research Methods

3.1   Content Analysis

We utilised content analysis to discover the theming of the open-ended responses to our questions. Content analysis is used in qualitative and inductive research for *thematic* purposes: for the analysis of words and phrases. It provides an objective, systematic description of the content of text and determines the presence of certain textual items such as words, phrases, etc. that are repeated and thus can be quantified or 'themed'.

The text is assigned a code – and broken down into 'chunks'. Each piece of text is coded to assign it a value type – and to identify whether it is related to other pieces of text. Thus, typically the researcher is looking for key phrases that are repeated across texts. It also permits relational analysis so as to make the connections from the concept and identify which concepts are related to which others (Stemler, 2001).

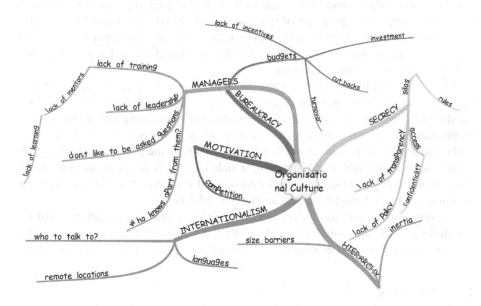

Fig. 1. Mindmap of Organizational Barriers

Content analysis is a reliable technique that enables researchers to sift and categorise large volumes of data in a systematic fashion. It permits inferences that can be later triangulated with other methods of data collection. In particular it examines patterns and trends in documents and establishes themes and concepts that are repeated.

The results are then an objective assessment of inferences about the data messages and can identify intentions, biases, prejudices and oversights amongst other themes (Berelson, 1952).

We have mapped the content into mindmaps (see Figure 1 as an example of these maps) for a pictorial representation of the main issues identified by our participants.

3.2   Sampling

Our sample for this survey was a convenience sample of knowledge workers, whereby people were invited by email, mailing lists and websites to complete the survey, and additionally, word of mouth was used to complete the survey. Whilst the complete survey received 1034 participants, the open-ended responses were from just over 100 participants. However, this is still a very high number of responses for analysis and to suggest a qualitative validity of the outcomes.

We argue that in undertaking the analysis of our research we should take a realist, positivist, and nomothetic approach. Thus contradictions can be seen but by using multi-methods and approaches, triangulation occurs, and the research approaches both the social element through subjectivism and the technical element through a deterministic method, such as a survey.

Triangulation is used to counter the criticisms that are usually levelled at social researchers—the subjectivism of their approach. It is also used to provide the means by which the interpretivist principle of suspicion is addressed (Klein and Myers, 1999) which requires sensitivity to possible biases in the minds and assumptions of both the researchers and the participants and to alleviate any distortions in the narratives collected through, for instance, interviews.

When designing this research it was vital to be aware of the following five things: (a) the questions; (b) the propositions; (c) the unit of analysis; (d) the logic that links the data to the propositions; and (e) the criteria for interpreting the findings. Each proposition must direct attention to something to be examined within the scope of study. Each piece of data collected should also match to the propositions taking into consideration that a real-world situation, which is what is being considered in this study, is inevitably complex and multi-dimensional and, thus, any proposition, it can be argued, can be matched to more than one type of data.

It is important to note that we piloted the survey pre-general circulation to test understanding of the questions and to ensure that the answers that we were receiving were as expected. A small number of adjustments were made as a result of this pilot.

4   Findings

The content analysis of the free-form text inputted into the survey demonstrated that there were significant issues in all three of the identified areas: human, organisational and technological. Clearly, as some of our participants were not from either the UK or the US you might expect that, for some countries, the technology might not be sophisticated or that there might be other technical issues related to the country's infrastructure, however there were far more comments about technological issues than one might therefore have expected (See Table 2). We rationalize that people tolerate, accept, and adapt to the flaws in technology and work with these flaws and still gain success by gaining control over it. However, when it comes to people and organization, the respondents believe that these are as much a barrier as technology. They feel helpless about their expected behaviour and experience barriers that will not permit them to bring success to KMS in their organization.

Table 3 presents the type of responses obtained for the three areas, including the number and percentage of participants that did not identify those barriers in their organisations. Of the 108 participants that answered the open questions, 18% did not encounter technology barriers in locating this knowledge in their organisations; 17.6% did not encounter organisational barriers; but only 5.6% did not encounter human barriers.

Table 2. Number and Percentage of Responses to Technology, Human and Organisational Barriers per Country

	Human barriers		Technology barriers		Organisational barriers	
	Freq.	%	Freq.	%	Freq.	%
United States	49	60.5%	43	59.7%	39	55.7%
United Kingdom	10	12.3%	9	12.5%	10	14.3%
Australia	6	7.4%	6	8.3%	6	8.6%
India	5	6.2%	5	6.9%	4	5.7%
Canada	3	3.7%	2	2.8%	3	4.3%
Brazil	1	1.2%	1	1.4%	1	1.4%
Bulgaria	1	1.2%	0	0.0%	0	0.0%
France	1	1.2%	1	1.4%	1	1.4%
Latvia	1	1.2%	1	1.4%	1	1.4%
Netherlands	1	1.2%	2	2.8%	2	2.9%
Pakistan	1	1.2%	1	1.4%	1	1.4%
Philippines	1	1.2%	1	1.4%	1	1.4%
Sweden	1	1.2%	0	0.0%	1	1.4%
Grand Total	**81**		**72**		**70**	

Table 3. Responses to Organisational, Technical and Human Barriers

	Technology barriers		Human barriers		Organisational barriers	
Open responses	82	75.9%	97	89.8%	77	71.3%
No barriers	20	18.5%	6	5.6%	19	17.6%
No valid responses	6	5.6%	5	4.6%	12	11.1%
Grand Total	**108**		**108**		**108**	

So we can clearly see from this result that human barriers remain the major issue with knowledge sharing wherever people are located. Comments such as:

People are busy with what they think is their "own work."
Sometimes, it is difficult to find the time to help others.
Or *silos and turf*

were common complaints from all participants - we saw this issue also in the main survey - see Figure 2.

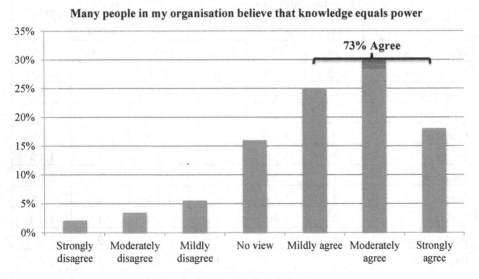

Fig. 2. Knowledge Equals Power

We saw during our interviews that the additional issues were raised as reasons why their knowledge management initiative was failing - see Figure 3. Silos were the central issue but we also saw that the constantly changing organisational environment made it difficult to identify and ensure that relevant knowledge was shared; and that there were many delays in implementing such knowledge sharing programmes from management levels, who may not think it a high enough priority to counter delays from service or technology providers.

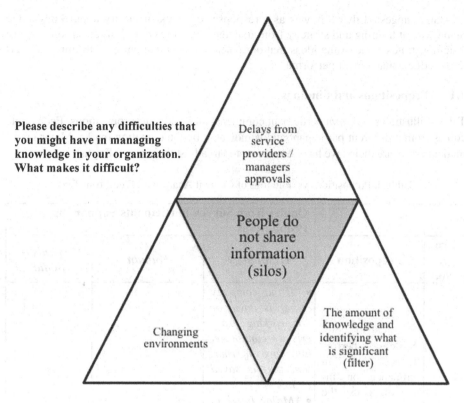

Please describe any difficulties that you might have in managing knowledge in your organization. What makes it difficult?

Delays from service providers / managers approvals

People do not share information (silos)

Changing environments

The amount of knowledge and identifying what is significant (filter)

Fig. 3. Difficulties in Managing Knowledge

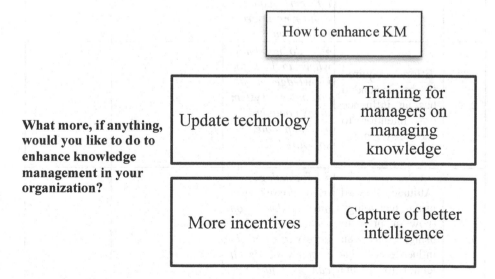

How to enhance KM

What more, if anything, would you like to do to enhance knowledge management in your organization?

Update technology

Training for managers on managing knowledge

More incentives

Capture of better intelligence

Fig. 4. Enhancing Knowledge Management

Many suggested that this was as a response to a lack of clarity about knowledge management training and strategy from managers and the central organisation. Figure 4 demonstrates some of the ideas that our participants had about how to improve their knowledge management performance.

4.1   Propositions and Findings

Table 4 illustrates *verbatim* participant comments alongside our propositions. Each quote comes from a different participant and is indicated by the quotation marks. Major grammatical errors are theirs; we have not attempted to adjust their use of English too much.

Table 4. Propositions vs. Findings of Content Analysis of Free-Form Text

Prop. No.	Proposition	Quotes from Survey Participants Supporting Propositions		
		Technology	*Human*	*Organisational*
1.	System performance has an influence on intention to use the system	• *"If our company server is down or not working properly we cannot get into any information that is saved on it."* • *"Major barriers would be slow internet connection or no internet connection."*		
2.	Effort required to be expended has an influence on intention to use the system	• *"I do not know where to look for knowledge on the computer system in my company."* • *"complicated software"*		
3.	Attitude toward using technology (now or prior to using) has an influence on intention to use the system	• *"Technology itself doesn't give any guidance on the contents of or access to what's in people's heads. It can facilitate tracking down information or*		

		knowledge howev-er, by making information ac-cessible electroni-cally".		
4.	Attitude toward using technology will not have significant influ-ence on intention.	• *"None really"*		
5.	Social Influence has an influence on intention to use the system			• *"Silo mentality"*
6.	Facilitating con-ditions have an influence on behavioural in-tention to use the system			• *"Stove-piped report-ing"*
7.	Self-efficacy (ability to influ-ence, affect, or time required to affect) has an influence on intention to use the system			• *"Meeting cancellations, less though-tful data entry."* • *"Available time and distance of knowledge holders."*
8.	Computer self-efficacy will not have a significant influence on intention.			• *"None. It is there for the taking. It is just getting the time."*
9.	Anxiety has an influence on intention to use the system		• *"People don't like change."* • *"Negative beha-viours"* • *"None. My manager is very helpful when I go to her to ask for knowledge"*	

10.	Computer anxiety will not have a significant influence on intention.		
11.	Facilitating conditions have an influence on Usage		• *"Not enough people know the process or who to contact"*
12.	Facilitating conditions will not have a significant influence on intention.		• *"In general, people are happy to share knowledge within our firm -it's all about the time needed to actually get together to accomplish."*
13.	Behavioural intention will have a significant positive influence on usage.		• *"Protectionist attitudes/behaviours"* • *"Making sure people upload new content to the KMS"*
14.	The influence of performance on intentions will be moderated by social influence;		• *"Unwillingness of others to share information or lack of knowledge from people who should have it"* • *"Significant paternalistic, hierarchic organization"*
15.	Social Influence on intentions will be moderated in mandatory settings (i.e. where usage is compulsory)		• *""Rice Bowl" Mentality - This is my area and no one should intrude in my empire."* • *"If you don't ask the correct questions, in the correct format, to the*

			correct person you won't get the answers you need." • *"Complete lack of people offering information, it has to be pulled from them."*	

In Table 4, we see that, in fact, all our propositions have been validated.

Our initial subset of propositions involved the use of technology, and our first proposition (*P1*) related to system performance: if the system is not working well, then users cannot or will not use the system. Our second proposition (*P2*) related to how much effort was then needed to use the system and our respondents strongly believed that their KMS were too complicated and had very poor search facilities, thus meaning that they have to expend a great deal of effort to find what was needed, and thus they were not inclined to use the system. We then proposed that any current or prior attitudes towards technology (and knowledge) would influence whether or not people would use a KMS (*P3*). Clearly many of our participants believed strongly that knowledge was in people's heads and thus using technology would not help them find it (*P4*). They did agree however, that some explicit information could be found through the use of technology.

In relation to the organisational factors that affect people's intention to use a KMS, we first proposed that there would be a social influence on whether or not the system would be used (*P5*). Our respondents agreed that there was an inbuilt resistance to change in their organisations, including many negative behaviours that would prevent people from using a KMS. People were concerned only with their own section or department and were anxious to ensure that this knowledge stayed within their 'silo'. This could be negativity enhanced or alleviated by the facilitating conditions in these organisations (*P6*). But as many organisations still operate within a strict hierarchy or bureaucratic structure, then reporting will always go upwards for them thus knowledge sharing and knowledge acquisition will be limited to what is the minimum required for a report rather than an expansion of knowledge and encouragement to include others in the activity. Many of our respondents were critical of others and their use of the system which meant that they could not impact what knowledge was inputted (*P7, P8*). Again behavioural conditions in organisations will dictate what is considered important and clearly knowledge sharing and the inputting of explicit or tacit knowledge into a KMS were not considered important for many. If they had the time, they would consider using it but this time was not available to them.

In relation to the human factors, we see that resistance to change was cited as a main reason why KMSs were not used in some organisations. Resistance is often caused by anxiety about personal performance in relation to technology and is cited by many authors as a key reason for difficulties in implementing any information system (IS), such as Akhavan, Jafari, Fathian (2005) discussed above. This would also apply to our proposition about anxiety (*P9, P10*), where people would prefer to go to a manager rather than use a system even though they say that they have issues with such a system. People know who to ask when they want verbal knowledge, or at least who to ask in order to find out whom to ask... but with new systems they don't know the processes well enough or who they should ask when they have an issue, or need to find something that is not evident on the system. Facilitating conditions, such as organisational structure and training, and knowing people outside of their departmental silo come into effect, and, for many, these are not known or well understood (*P11, P12*). Even where people are willing to share, if the conditions in which they have the time to share, and the managerial willingness for them to attend such things as communities of practice and share across these departmental silo walls, are not there, then knowledge sharing will not, and does not, take place.

If we then look again at people's behaviour, we can see that if they feel negatively towards a KMS, in that it is taking away their knowledge power, they will not upload their tacit knowledge into it, and will find reasons not to upload their explicit knowledge citing the lack of time more often than not (*P13, P14, P15*). If senior managers do not 'walk the talk' but continue to operate in a paternalistic and hierarchical manner then the social influence will be against usage of the KMS. However, mandatory use will ensure that some information is uploaded but not necessarily the right knowledge or all that you need to know. Some knowledge will be retained and may be very difficult to obtain as people protect their power and influence.

None of these above observations will be unexpected to those who read the theory about organisational behaviour and how it impacts on human behaviour in an organisation. But here we have proof of it happening in all cultures across the world. This is new information as we can compare our results across countries and organisational type. Over half our respondents from the United States for instance have issues in all three areas of KMS: technological, human, and organisational; across all sectors and sizes of organisations.

5   Discussion, Conclusion and Directions for Future Research

We studied the causes of success and failure and report the results from a survey which is not only the largest KM survey of knowledge workers, KM managers, and senior managers undertaken covering the whole world, but also represents all industrial sectors, and envelops all types of organisations. The size and scope of coverage of our study combined with qualitative and quantitative analyses of the data give a strong validity to our findings, and a wide applicability. We believe that all organizations can make some use of our recommendations in enhancing the success, and avoiding the failure, of their KMS. We summarize some of these results and their implications for the practice of managing knowledge in the paragraphs below.

Looking specifically at the subset of results taken from our open-ended questions answered by 108 participants from across many countries and cultures, we find that a number of conditions in three areas—Human Behaviour, Technical Issues, and Organizational Issues— need to be met before a KMS can be successful. There are 15 conditions that we have tested through content analysing the results of the free-form input from the 108 participants as formulated in fifteen propositions. Based on our analyses, we find that all our propositions are validated. We can therefore suggest that unless the conditions suggested by these 15 propositions are in place in any organisation, a KMS will not be fully successful.

We therefore recommend that, firstly, the 19 questions we have designed to ensure adherence to Clegg's 19 Sociotechnical Principles (2000) are used to help design the technical system; and secondly, that the 15 technology, human and organisational conditions validated by our research are put in place before and during the implementation of KMS. This implies that the organisational structure and silos will need to be flattened, and communication established between all departments at all levels. This will require a reduction in hierarchy in organizations where the KMS function is important. It also requires encouraging and rewarding the sharing of information through organizational policies, since we find that people do not share information because they do not want to part with their knowledge, or they do not feel that it is one of their tasks or job role. Our survey reveals that there is much negative behaviour in organizations that gives employees a sense of insecurity and which causes an inbuilt resistance to change. Since people who feel secure do not resist change, organizations should develop a culture, policy and structure that make employees feel secure. This will set behavioural conditions that emphasize the importance of not resisting change and encourage the sharing of knowledge. A system that promotes and rewards knowledge sharing behaviour rather than the one that results in the hoarding of knowledge, will need to be put in place. Training about the importance of knowledge sharing and the use of the new system will need to begin at the design stage when stakeholders will need to be involved to ensure that searching in particular, is easy and relevant. A simple system with simple interfaces that are easy to use will be required and participation of the major stakeholders in design and development prototyping will help ensure that the system better meets their needs.

Finally, time will need to be built into daily and weekly tasks for knowledge sharing including regular meetings of communities of practice when best practice can be shared and innovatory knowledge can be developed. The start of knowledge sharing will have to begin with management. And, that will also be the start of building factors for the success of a KMS, and for avoiding factors that will cause a KMS to fail.

Our analysis of the underlying factors relating to KMS success and failure provides a number of limitations that suggest that further research on this theory would be valuable. Firstly, while our survey sample of 1034 participants is very extensive and fully represents all economic sectors, industries, and regions of the world, the sample of open-ended question participants is biased in favour of the UK and USA. Future research may be directed by expanding the sample to include non-Western cultures and other regions of the world. Although intuitively we do not believe that that would make any new revelations contradicting ours, it would hopefully reaffirm what we found or may help update it.

Secondly, a few in-depth case studies from several economic sectors, global regions, and industries, and several organisations would validate the design principles and underlying failure factors given in this paper. One could propose that some variations coming from such diverse case studies may help expand or, more specifically, sharpen the application of these principles and factors to specific cases.

Thirdly, whilst the survey was completed by 1034 participants, the KMS success and failure theory was tested at a very general level. The future research can better tie all aspects of this general theory by revalidating them more specifically; therefore, a comprehensive survey testing specifically these 15 propositions would help apply the new theory at a more practical level.

References

Akhavan, P., Jafari, M., Fathian, M.: Exploring Failure-Factors Of Implementing Knowledge Management Systems In Organisations. Journal Of Knowledge Management Practice 6 (2005), http://www.tlainc.com/articl85.htm (accessed October 19, 2012)

Berelson, B.: Content analysis in communication research. The Free Press, Glencoe (1952)

Cherns, A.: The principles of sociotechnical design. Human Relations 29(8), 783–792 (1976)

Cherns, A.: The principles of sociotechnical design revisited. Human Relations 40(3), 153–162 (1987)

Clegg, S.: Sociotechnical Principles for System Design. Applied Ergonomics 31(5), 463–477 (2000)

Coakes, J., Coakes, E.: Sociotechnical Concepts applied to Information Systems. In: Cooper, C.L., Argyris, C., Starbuck, W. (eds.) Management Information Systems. Encyclopaedia of Management (7), pp. 1024–1029. Jaico Publishing House (2005)

Coiera, E.: Putting the technical back into socio-technical systems research. International Journal of Medical Informatics. 76(1), S98–S103 (2007)

Davenport, T.H., DeLone, D.W., Beers, M.C.: Successful knowledge management projects. Sloan Management Review 39(2), 43–57 (1998)

DeLone, W.H., McLean, E.R.: Information systems success: The quest for dependent variable. Information Systems Research 3(1), 60–95 (1992)

DeLone, W.H., McLean, E.R.: Information systems research revisited. In: Proceedings of 35th Hawaii International Conference on System Sciences. IEEE Computer Society (January 2002)

Dixon, N.M.: The Organizational Learning Cycle: How we can learn collectively. Gower Publishing, New York (1999)

Hurley, L.: Reasons why knowledge management systems fail, Helium (April 27, 2010), http://www.helium.com/items/1816248-why-do-knowledge-management-information-systems-fail (accessed November 22, 2012)

Jennex, M., Olfman, L.: A knowledge management success model: An extension of DeLone and McLean's IS success model. In: AMCIS 2003 Proceedings. Paper 330 (2003), http://aisel.aisnet.org/amcis2003/330

Klein, H.K., Myers, M.D.: A Set of Principles for Conducting and Evaluating Interpretive Field Studies in Information Systems. MIS Quarterly 23(1), 67–93 (1999)

Kulkarni, U.R., Ravindran, S., Freeze, R.: A knowledge management system success model: Theoretical development and empirical validation. Journal of Management Information System 23(3), 309–347 (2006)

Massey, A.P., Montoya-Weiss, O'Driscoll, T.M.: Knowledge management in pursuit of performance: Insights from Nortel Networks. MIS Quarterly 26(3), 269–289 (2002)

Peute, L., Aartsb, J., Bakkerc, P.J.M., Jaspers, M.W.M.: Anatomy of a failure: A sociotechnical evaluation of a laboratory physician order entry system implementation. International Journal of Medical Informatics 79(4), e58–e70 (2010)

Stemler, S.: An overview of content analysis. Practical Assessment, Research & Evaluation 7(17) (2001)

Tsinakis, M., Kouroubali, A.: Organizational factors affecting successful adoption of innovative eHealth services: a case study employing the FITT framework. International Journal Medicine Information 78(1), 39–52 (2009)

Whitworth, V., Bañuls, C., Cheickna, S., Mahinda, E.: Expanding the criteria for evaluating socio–technical software. IEEE Transactions On Systems, Man, And Cybernetics—Part A: Systems And Humans 38(4), 777–790 (2008)

Wu, J.-H., Wang, Y.-M.: Measuring KMS success: A respecification of the DeLone and McLean's model. Information & Management 43(6), 728–739 (2006)

Narratives of an Outsourced Information Systems Failure in a Small Enterprise

Jan Devos, Hendrik Van Landeghem, and Dirk Deschoolmeester

Ghent University, Belgium
{jang.devos,hendrik.vanlandeghem,
dirk.deschoolmeester}@UGent.be

Abstract. In this study we investigate a case of an outsourced information systems (IS) failure (OISF) within the collaborative partnership among asymmetric partners. A small and medium-sized enterprise (SME) is dealing with an independent software vendor (ISV) conducting a project of implementing an IS that fails. We used a narrative research methodology for our enquiry. In the construction of our narrative we followed the OISF framework as a theoretical touchstone. As a major conclusion we found that asymmetric collaborations with partners with inadequate managerial and technical IT capabilities are extremely prone to OISF's. We showed that an outcome-based and fixed price contract is not an adequate instrument to conduct such a partnership and to avoid a failure.

Keywords: IT/IS, failures, OISF framework, case study, narrative methodology, trust, contracts, principal-agent.

1   Introduction

Although the phenomenon of IS failures is well known in both IT practitioners and scholar communities, there is still little known that helps to decrease the associated concerns (Group 2004; Verner et al. 2012). To our best knowledge research on IS failures tend to be scattered and too much focused on projects conducted in mature and large organizations and too little on a deep understanding of what small and medium-sized enterprises (SMEs) with lower managerial and technical IT capabilities drive to adopt information systems (Avison et al. 2006; Bartis et al. 2008; Conboy 2010; Kreps et al. 2007). We focus here on an IS failure in an SME.

Although SMEs do not constitute a homogenous group of (smaller) organizations, when it comes to implementing information systems, most of them depend on an ISV (Devos et al. 2012). SMEs do not have as much resources (e.g. financial, material and knowledge) than large organizations (Welsh et al. 1981). This can be noticed in the absence of an IS function in SMEs, but also in the lower level of IT adoption (Antlova 2009; Bruque et al. 2007). Nor is there a clear and comprehensive vision on what information systems could mean within these organizations (Cragg et al. 1993; Huang et al. 2010). Most of the decision making in SMEs is centred around the CEO, which is often an entrepreneur who does not make a separation between ownership (governance)

Y.K. Dwivedi et al. (Eds.): TDIT 2013, IFIP AICT 402, pp. 57–72, 2013.

and control (management) in his organization (Lefebvre et al. 1997; Levy et al. 2005; Thong et al. 1995). This can be good or bad. Well committed CEOs can establish the critical success factors for avoiding IS failures (Admiraal et al. 2009). However there are still IS failures with committed CEOs to be noticed, mainly due to poor managerial and technical IT skills (Devos et al. 2012). Within the large set of IS failures we focus here on the outsourced IS failure (OISF). An OISF is a failure that arises during an IS project in an outsourced environment (Devos et al. 2008).

This paper is structured as follows: in section 2, we elaborate on the concept and framework of OISFs. In section 3 we bring a summary of our research method is presented. Section 4 bring the narrative of an OISF. Finally in section 5 we bring our conclusions.

2   Outsourced IS Failures

IS failures can be divided in *expectation* (Lyytinen et al. 1987) and *termination* (Sauer 1993) failures. Expectation failures can be categorised in *correspondence*, *process* and *interaction* failures. *Correspondence failures* happen when IT artefacts are evaluated towards previous defined design objectives. A lack of correspondence between design objectives and evaluation is seen as a failure. *Process failures* arise when there is unsatisfactory development performance, i.e., one fails to produce a workable system or to deliver within the budget constraints of time and costs. Process failures are sometimes becoming 'runaways' or escalating projects (Iacovou et al. 2005; Keil 1995). *Interaction failures* are situated within the mismatch between requirements and user acceptance. An interaction failure appears when an IT artefact is not used.

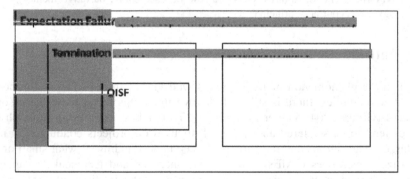

Fig. 1. A classification of IS failures

In summary, an IS expectation failure is the inability of an IS to meet the expectations of the stakeholders. Sauer brought up the more pragmatic concept of the termination failure (Sauer 1993). According to Sauer an IS failure can only occur when the development process or operation of an IS causes dissatisfied stakeholders to abandon the project. There is an extra dimension to IS failures that is not covered by those descriptive models, which is called the Outsourced IS Failure (OISF). An OISF is a failure that arises during an IS project in an outsourced environment. We use the taxonomy of Lacity and Hirschheim of outsourcing options and focus on Project Management

(Dibbern et al. 2004). So OISF's are a subset of process failures within the expectation failures category of Lyytinen & Hirschheim (Lyytinen et al. 1987). In figure 1 we give a illustrative overview of the classification of IS failures.

When two parties find each other in a outsourced IS project governed by a principal-agent setting some dynamics must be taken into account (Eisenhardt 1989; Jensen et al. 1976). We consider here an SME-principal, represented by the CEO and an ISV-agent represented by the CEO in the role of the sales representative. The SME-principal is in search for an ISV who can implement a strategic information system (e.g. ERP, CRM, SCM) in his organization. This is a typical case of a bidirectional asymmetric relationship which should move into an asymmetric collaboration. With a decision of this kind and magnitude serious risks are involved that most likely will affect the outcome of the project. Some academics have pointed out that outsourcing increases risks leading to IS failures (Aubert et al. 2003; Natovich 2003). These risks are related to human behaviour, organizational and project management issues (Schmidt et al. 2001). Devos et al (2009) have developed a framework to describe the OISF (Devos et al. 2009a). This framework is presented in figure 2.

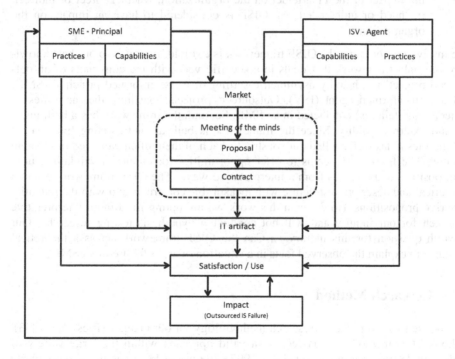

Fig. 2. The Outsourced IS Failure framework

The OISF elaborates on the findings of Lyytinen and Hirschheim on IS failures and is based on the construct of IS use and IS development as the foci of organisational action (Lyytinen et al. 1987). These concepts were partly recycled in the concept of the IT artefact and its immediate nomological net or IS-net developed by Benbasat et al. (Benbasat et al. 2003). Consecutively, the nomological net was further refined by Gable et al. by bringing in constructs from the Delone and McLean IS Success model (DeLone et al. 2003; Gable et al. 2008). The interrelated constructs of the OISF framework are:

- a risk-neutral SME-principal with managerial, methodological and technological capabilities and practices for planning, designing, and implementing IT artefacts;
- a risk-averse ISV-agent with managerial, methodological and technological capabilities and practices for planning, designing, and implementing IT artefacts;
- a market where SME-principals and ISV-agents meet each other;
- a meeting-of-the-minds where SME-principals and ISV-agents establish a contract;
- an IT artefact, which is a human construction, utilitarian and not neutral;
- the use of the IT artefact, including a development and implementation trajectory;
- the impact of the IT artefact on the organization, whether direct or indirect, intended or unintended. An OISF is considered to have an impact on the organization.

The motivation for using the OISF framework is twofold. First it is to our best knowledge the only framework that deals in a specific way with the constructs of an outsourced project in a heavily asymmetric setting of a less informed principal (SME) and a well-informed agent (ISV). Outsourced projects constitute the majorities of projects (and failures) conducted in an SME. Second, the framework has a high internal and external validity. Since the framework is built around existing frameworks and theories it has well spelled out constructs, each of them often validated in separate settings. The framework seems to offer opportunities for empirical validating, both from positivistic as well as from a interpretative way. The OISF framework offers a theoretical and descriptive structure with measurable constructs and with the potential to derive propositions. However in this work we are opting for a more interpretative approach for our inquiry and will not conduct a hypothesis testing research. Our research question for this inquiry is: Can the OISF framework act as a theoretical guidance to explain the observed facts in a situation of an IS failure in an SME?

3   Research Method

We choose to use a narrative research methodology for our enquiry (Riessman 1993). Although this methodology is seen as a valid approach within the large variety of qualitative IS research methods (Myers 1997), the use in IS research and particularly on IS failures is rather limited (Bartis et al. 2008; Brown et al. 1998; Davidson 1997; Fincham 2002; Wagner 2003; Webb et al. 2007). According to Webb and Mallon (2003) narrative analysis is becoming more important to IS research. We argue that the method of telling stories is indeed underestimated and largely suitable for research on IS failures. The phenomenon of an IS failure is complex, multifaceted and constitutes an amalgam of technological, methodical, and social constructs which are not easy if possible at all, to be analysed separately (Lyytinen et al. 1987). We argue that an IS failure is largely the outcome of the human mind. Narratives provide us a way to create a shareable understanding of social-technical phenomena. We organize our experience of human happenings mainly in the form of narratives – stories, excuses, myths, and reasons for doing and not doing (Bruner 1991). Positivistic assumptions from natural sciences alone prove little to understand socio-technical systems. Many IS researchers pleaded therefore already for a pluralist approach in our field (Lee 1999; Mingers 2001; Weber 2004). However al lot of research on IS failures has concentrated on deficits in the process of developing and implementing information systems or on the root causes of failure but less on meaning or sense making of the concept of an IS failure (Barker et al. 2003; Beynon-Davies 1999; Cerpa et al. 2009; Chen et al. 2009; Cule et al. 2000; Ewusi-Mensah 2003; Sauer 1993). Therefore we need a research approach that offers us the possibility to deal with the complexity of the phenomenon as a whole, instead of working by means of a reduction of reality.

A narrative is an interpretation of events that constitutes the core of organizational knowledge and reflects the significance organizational issues that actors seek to dramatize (Czarniawska 1997). In its essence a narrative is defined as a 'tale, story, and recital of facts especially a story told in the first person' (Myers 1997). Narratives or story telling is to be seen as a metaphor for creating order and to construct text that brings a rich description for a complex phenomenon in a particular context (Riessman 1993). The narrative is idiographic in nature and therefore generalizability is difficult to obtain. We are inspired by the same challenges of generalizability of IS research in general and within the case study research in particular (Eisenhardt 1991; Lee et al. 2003; Yin 2003). We apply the case study research and try to bring as much as possible empirical (primary) data into the narrative. This implies that we have used multiple sources of data. To build up the narrative we used a real case of an outsourced IS failure in an SME. The case was well documented since it was subject to litigation. It is an typical example of a termination failure (Sauer 1993).The SME-principal ordered an information system with an ISV-agent and his expectations are not fulfilled. Therefor a court order was requested to obtain a contract dissolution. We collected all the primary data from the expert witness who was assigned to give advice on the failure to the court. Litigation files are most useful for scientific research, since they are well documented and they come from multiples sources (e.g. plaintiff and defender) which constitutes already a triangulation of the empirical data. We also had several interviews with the expert witness, which was an extra source of data. Although the expert opinion itself was a well-used source as an official document brought before court, we did not strive for alignment with the findings of the expert witness. The expert opinion offers only answers to questions raised by the court. Our purpose was pure academic within a quest for knowledge on IS failures. Although we maintained the same rigor of the positivistic case study research (Dube et al. 2003), our method is not positivistic in nature, but tend to be more interpretive (Walsham 1995). Our work is inspired by the work of Wagner et al. (2004) (Wagner et al. 2004). So we kept a theoretical stance in mind. During the building of the narrative, we investigated the validity of the OISF framework as a guidance to reveal a meaning of the OISF. Although we build the narrative with the guidance of a theoretical concept our conclusions in terms of generalization of the findings can go no further than the case itself.

4   The Narrative of an OISF

SME Principal: Blackbird Inc.

Blackbird Inc. is a small enterprise selling and servicing brown and white goods mainly on a domestic market. Being a small company Blackbird is also selling products which are all closely related with brown and white goods, like electrical installation kits, tools, and even computers. The company is also offering services like installation projects, repairs and maintenance. The company has an inventory of spare parts of the products they sell. Sales goes directly through their stores. There is one main store and one outlet store a few tens of kilometres from the main store to service a local market over there. The customers are local residents, do-it-yourselves and small companies. So there is a wide variety in the sales administration. Direct sales goes over the counter desk with direct payments, cash or by wire. But there is also more indirect sales through sales orders received by telephone, fax or e-mail and delivered by own firm vans on regulars schedules.

Blackbird was founded by Mr & Mrs Vanderbilt, husband and wife, both are playing an active and important role in their company. Mrs Vanderbilt takes care of the (direct) sales and the purchase. Mr Vanderbilt conducts the projects, the indirect sales and the service operations (repair, maintenance). The staff is very limited and is working in the stores. But there are three people working in the order department and there is an internal accountant. There is also a part-time IT manager, who is mainly doing technical tasks and duties as installing routers, PC and printers.

ISV Agent: Andreas Inc.

Andreas is a small local ISV. The company is not a business partner of a larger software supplier (e.g. Microsoft, Oracle, SAP) but develops bespoke applications. Their mission is to develop software for complex business processes. Although Andreas asserts that a Scrum methodology (Schwaber 2009) is applied for customer projects, a more waterfall development method is more be noticeable in their practices. According to their website Andreas offers also advice, support and training as separate service offerings. The company is young (founded in 2004) and has a staff of only four people which included the two founders at the time they met Blackbird. Andreas is steadily growing in staff and turnover and collected some nice sales references of realized software projects. These projects all seems to be very small and rather isolated and not within the core of what typical constitutes an ERP system. Examples of realized projects are: reporting projects, interfacing projects, and standalone web applications. There is no indication that Andreas has a lot of experience with the development and implementation of ERP-like applications, nor do they have an experienced staff in business processes and project management aside from the CEO's.

Meeting of the Minds

At a certain moment the principal and the agent will have a meeting of the minds. This is the moment where both parties are willing to contract. Both parties are now arrived at a mutual level of understanding and trust.

Blackbird was in search for a new information system to support their growing business needs. The current Unix system has run out of his limits and it was time for a modern Windows-based computer system. Mr and Mrs Vanderbilt spoke about a Windows-based computer system as the archetype of a contemporary graphical user interface, with mouse and rich features on the clients workstation.

First Mr & Mrs Vanderbilt consulted with the help of the IT manager, a major ERP vendor distributing and implementing Microsoft software. However they soon found out that the price for such a system was far above their planned budget. At that time Mrs Vanderbilt remembered a nice gentlemen in IT that she met and talked to on a reception of the local society of entrepreneurs. For her this looked as a trustful and skilled person. She got his business card and made a phone call to … Andreas.

Both parties met and problems were discussed. Andreas accepted the challenge to go for a tender offering a good and cheap solution for Blackbird.

Proposal

The tender of Andreas was a document of five pages containing: 1) the context, 2) the architecture, 3) a project plan, 4) a fixed price and 5) some concluding remarks. The proposal reflects largely the sphere of trust that exist between the two parties. The proposal was edited in very positive way and revealed no possible risks that could arise during a collaboration between the parties. It was framed in a way that Blackbird could be at ease while Andreas would take care of almost everything going from re-quirements analysis to training and delivery. At this embryonic moment of the project trajectory trust between the collaborating parties was of major importance. Trust is the only mechanism that Blackbird as the unformed principal had at its disposal. This was well understood by Andreas. It was also clear that Blackbird was not willing to make the cost of reduce the information asymmetry with Andreas.

In the context section of the tender, Andreas states that the existing system was only briefly evaluated and that only two elements came out to motivate the acquisition of a new information system. The first element was the lack of support for the current system platform and continuity of the used technology (Unix). The second element was the poor and expensive support for the existing application. Andreas choose for a bespoke application for Blackbird. Although Andreas explicitly mentioned the limited information on the functional requirements, they take the risk for the assignment, stating that extra analysis will be needed during the course of the project. This pro-posed solution fulfil the first motivational element for a new information systems. To achieve the second element, the lack of platform support, Andreas called in the help of a third party with necessary skills and expertise on the chosen Microsoft platform.

The software architecture in the proposal of Andreas is described in half a page and refers only to two components: a client administration application (CAA) and a server application (SA). The CAA has six functional domains: client administration, supplier administration, product administration, purchase orders, sales orders and system ad-ministration. None of these functional domain is spelled out in more detail except for their title identification. The SA paragraph is even shorter: only two sentences. The first sentence is describing a procedure of servicing maintenance orders and a very short sentence describing the actions needed for material handling in the warehouse.

The project plan is a one page sheet containing the project start date (16-06-2008), the project end date, being also the final delivery date (9-9-2008), the total number of programming, analysing, testing and implementation days (90 men days), the allocated staff (4 persons: A, B, C and D). The project has a work breakdown structure of 45 detailed tasks, each of them having a start and end date and an amount of budgeted work expressed in hours or days. None of the detailed tasks has a description in depth of the work or actions to be done.

The fourth part of the proposal is a fixed price of €55.000 for the complete project. Although this is not mentioned in the proposal, it could be derived that Andreas has an average tariff of €611.11 for one day of work. The proposal also states that hardware, manuals and extra training is not included in the price. Manuals are not necessary according to Andreas and a basic training is incorporated in the initial project offering.

Finally there are some concluding remarks in the proposal. First of all, Andreas repeats its offer that hardware is not included in the price. there are also three statements concerning the application. First is a statement concerning the property rights of the software (source code) that goes entirely to Blackbird. Secondly there is a statement on the unlimited number of users and servers that can be applied to the application. And finally a maintenance contract on the software is possible but not obligatory. Andreas closed the document with the remark that some explanation is needed with the offerings.

Contract

Both parties did not take too much time to contract. The initial proposal was entirely kept as the basis for the contract negotiations. So an agreement based on the proposal and on the oral explanation of the sales representative (the CEO) was settled and the contract was signed. The contract specifies a fixed price of €55.000, as mentioned in the proposal. Both parties felt quite optimistic about the endeavour that was to take off.

IT Artefact

According to Andreas the IT artefact was developed with the use of a Scrum approached (Schwaber 2009). There were seven sprint cycles, all equally having a planned timeframe of one month. In table 1 the initially contracted and planned sprint cycles (first column) and the ex post executed sprint cycles (second column) are shown. The third columns shows the deviation in days between what was planned and what actually happened.

After each sprint cycle an invoice was made by Andreas, send to Blackbird and almost immediately paid, as agreed in the contract.

Table 1. Overview of the Scrum Sprint Cycles

Planned Sprint Cycle	Executed Sprint Cycle	Deviation (days)
31/05/2008	31/05/2008	0
30/06/2008	30/06/2008	0
31/07/2008	25/07/2008	0
31/08/2008	3/10/2008	33
30/09/2008	30/04/2009	210
31/10/2008	30/11/2009	390
30/11/2008	30/06/2010	578

Satisfaction / Use

The satisfaction and use constructs were heavily challenged during the project. The users became very agitated and nervous when more and more errors and bugs cropped up while using the software. The user satisfaction dropped to a freezing cold when data inquiries took long execution times affecting also the response times, leaving the users with an enormous frustration towards the system. Sales invoices were not correctly assembled and printed which aggravated the users even more.

Usage of the inventory and the direct sales modules was not possible because of the software being not yet complete. Also the link with the accounting system was missing which led to a lot of manual work. Finally after more than a year since the last delivery and a standstill for several months, Blackbird lost all confidence in a good and final ending of the project. Blackbird edited a list with complaints, bugs and change requests, 45 in total and handed it over to Andreas. Some of the items on the list give some more information on the real situation of the IT artefact. Some of the most compelling items from the list are:

- *We (Blackbird) have to propose everything to Andreas, even these things that we consider as evidently present in a business software...*
- *If we enter new a product in the system, we cannot see if the product is already created. So every now and then we create doubles...*
- *The system is halted for unknown reasons sometimes up to four or five times within a day. After each halt we have to reboot the system which takes a lot of time.*

All items in the list where qualified by Andreas as change requests. The straw that broke the camel's back was the reaction of Andreas that the budget was spent and that from now on programming and debugging had to be paid extra.

There was also a very intense email communication between then users of Blackbird and the programmers of Andreas. The oldest emails were rather politely written and accordingly exchanged. However when the number of problems with the software increased, the style of the emails became more aggressive and fierce.

OISF

By the middle of 2011, Blackbird ran out of patience and asked for a court order to obtain a contract dissolution with Andreas. They also requested a complete refund of the investment money that was contractually agreed and already paid to Andreas, an indemnity for losses due to the failure of the information system and the payment of all supplementary costs for the litigation. An extra damage of €30.000 was also asked because Blackbird had to pay a fine to the tax collector due to uncompleted annual reports from the information system. In their court order, the judges made the following assessment:

It is beyond reasonable doubt that the software that Blackbird has ordered from Andreas, is not fully operational, despite the numerous interventions between parties and specially these of Andreas. Although Blackbird claims that Andreas does not fulfil their contractual obligations and duties, this not proven, even more, Andreas makes in their defence the same claims, saying that Blackbird is neglecting the agreements made between the two parties. Although the court sees that a dispute has risen between the two parties, it does not known yet if there is enough evidence for a contract dissolution.

However the court took notice of the fact that Blackbird made a lot of complaints, sent by email, towards Andreas. Also the court sees that Blackbird has paid the price agreed in the contract. So the complaints cannot be ignored. Therefore the current situation with the information system needs some further investigation. An expert witness is needed to make the necessary observations.

The duty of the expert witness is to investigate if the complaints made by Blackbird have merit when an investigation of the information system is done. Therefore an expert witness will be ordered to conduct an Expert Assessment. The expert witness should give an answer to the following questions:

1. *Invite all parties and take notices of their statements, oral as well as written.*
2. *Describe the information system*
3. *Describe all the performed work*
4. *Investigate if the performed work by Andreas is done according to 'art and best practices'*
5. *Describe the shortcomings and flaws and assign the accountabilities*
6. *Assess the damage*

The expert witness is currently conducting his investigation and is also trying to reconcile the parties.

5   Conclusions

We used a narrative to understand the OISF that occurs between an SME-principal and an ISV-agent. In the building of our narrative we followed the OISF framework of Devos et al. (Devos et al. 2009a). The OISF framework was used as a theoretical guidance for making reflections and for structuring a chronology in the narrative. The case is taken from a litigation file of an OISF the was brought before court.

As an overall observation we could see that the court (and the legal councillors of both parties) implicitly and a priori qualifies the collaboration between parties as a principal-agent agreement. This implies that already a mind-set is established with the stakeholders before the process of the OISF evaluation took place. As a researcher it is paramount to avoid that pitfall. Within a principal-agent setting an intense collaboration between parties is not always expected nor is a bi-directional information asymmetry assumed. On the contrary, the principal is primarily assumed to be the less informed party and the agent the most informed party. This is a biased assumption grounded in a belief that IS projects are mainly technological projects. The similarity in the terminology with construction projects is remarkable. However this is not entirely true for IS projects, which suggest a strong collaboration of the parties involved and where both parties also have to exchange hidden information before and during the project. The principal has to reveal as much as possible information on the actual flow of the current (and future) business processes. In this case we could observe that there was certainly not enough information available for Andreas to build a complete, ERP-like information system within the planned time and budget. On the other hand it was not clear if Blackbird was fully aware of their duty to describe as much as possible of the current requirements. However Andreas, as the most informed party on the techniques of conducting IS projects, had the obligation to perform a requirements elicitation and analysis study and should have forced Blackbird to participate in this. It looks as if both parties where unaware of the complexity and the granularity of all functions within the system. For Andreas it was one of their first ERP-like projects. Towards Blackbird they only send signals that indicate that they had control over the full project.

We could observe that the initial trust between the two actors gradual deteriorates when the project evolves. The selection of the ISV was almost entirely based on trust. In the principal-agent literature trust is not considered, only control is at stake (Devos et al. 2008). However it is shown that trust is major importance to avoid an OISF in SMEs (Devos et al. 2009b). Trust has been identified as an major construct in the success of partnerships, strategic alliances, and networks of firms (Das et al. 1998). The ISV, acting as the project leader seems to gradual lose control over the project and was captured within the strict boundaries of the fixed price contract. Andreas did not wanted to spend too much time on unclear requirements and focused more on clear and well written out ones. However it became more and more clear for both parties during the course of the project that the hope for frozen requirements was idle. This phenomenon was already discovered in electronic auctions and in IT outsourcing projects where a bidden party can make a too low bid so the entire project is jeopardized leading to relational problems (Kern et al. 2002).

First idle promises made by the agent towards the principal, to calm down and to hide the rudderless the project. But when the number of reported problems increase, the style revers and the communication became more and more accusatory. Although the principal sticks to the notion of trust, gradually the focus shifts to the fixed price contract as the ultimate and sole control measure.

The multi-voiced answers to the questions of the expert witness show not only the conflicts between the actors, but point to a deep gap between the perceptions and understandings of what constitutes an information system in an (SME) organization. The principal had a profound lack of IS/IT capabilities. We expressly make here a difference between IT (Information Technology) and IS (Information Systems). It can be assumed that profound knowledge of IT is not always needed for SMEs implementing an information system. But the IS managerial capabilities were not what could be expected from a CEO even of an SME. Although the CEO runs a small business, some understanding of the impact of an IS in an organization is paramount. On the other hand, the ISV had an obsession with IT and the conviction that the development and implementation of an IT artefact is purely based on positivist assumptions. The development method (Scrum) and the programs (code) got all the attention, but there no efforts were made to invest in the relation with the (unskilled) principal. A striking example of this gap was the enthusiasm shown by the ISV and his belief that he convinced the principal of using the Scrum method. Although the SME acknowledges the fact that Scrum was mentioned by the ISV he never understood what it was all about.

As compared with a strategic IT project conducted in a large organization, an IT project in an SME does not have so many stakeholders. This was also noticeable here. There were no groups of stakeholders with hidden expectations that could jeopardize the success of the project. As a consequence an in-depth stakeholders analysis with identification and evaluation of stakeholders and their expectations was easily made and done. The CEOs of both parties, as the major stakeholders were actively engaged in the project. Both CEO's had several roles in the project. The CEO of Blackbird took the roles of project leader and key user. The CEO of Andreas took the roles a project leader, business analysis, software architect and developer. This case shows that even with a limited amount of committed stakeholders an IT project can deteriorate quickly.

Another remarkable finding in this case is the very scarce documentation on the project proceedings. Even the contract and the proposal were not very elaborate on the project scope and objectives. The only written project documentation were printed emails exchanged between parties. It is clear that this kind of communication is extremely informal and offers not a good way to streamline a project. It looks like IT people have a profound problem with building up project documentation. Although there are methods available like PMBOK or Prince2 none of these method were even considered to be of use during the project. This is to our opinion a critical failure of most educational curricula in computer science. All too often the focus in graduate and undergraduate courses on IT/IS goes too much to the technological features of IS projects. The perspective of a socio-technical system is sometimes forgotten if not completely ignored. The multifaceted nature of human interaction suggests that straightforward application of empirical methods of natural science in organizations is problematic (Stowell 2008). The people from Andreas, all having a graduate degree in computer science, had a strong belief in the neutrality of technology and underestimated clearly the impact of the human factor. Moreover, people from Andreas tend to forget what Ciborra stated: 'that the real world has vague and murky contours' (Ciborra 2002). It is however not easy to understand organizations and the relation with IS since it is not possible to make laboratory replicates or simulations. Although the Scrum method claims to cope with these shortcomings in an innovative approach of the IS development process, the method implies a paradigm shift away from the more traditional 'waterfall' approaches. This is much harder to do then to learn the features of the method. The paradigm shift also implies that we incorporate failure into our methods and processes. According to Edmondson: "We are programmed at an early age to think that failure is bad. That belief prevents organizations from effectively learning from their missteps" (Edmondson 2011). However, we also belief that these more novel and iterative ways of building information systems are not so easily reconciled with a fixed price and time contract.

We may conclude that the OISF framework indeed shows a theoretical guidance for explaining an IT failure in an SME. The framework offers more than likely also such guidance for larger organization, however this has to be researched. We believe that in these cases the adjective 'larger' is better replace by 'more mature' organisations.

Finally, our study has some limitations. The generalization and replicability of the present study is constrained by the use of the single case study method. Since every case is unique we can only use theories to verify if data coming from a real-world case is consistent with the assumptions of these theories. In this study we used the framework for OISFs. Although the OISF framework is more a descriptive theory with less explaining and predicting power, we hope that the chronological sequence of events revealed by this narrative is helping in preventing future IS failures.

References

Admiraal, W., Lockhorst, D.: E-Learning in Small and Medium-sized Enterprises across Europe Attitudes towards Technology, Learning and Training. International Small Business Journal 27(6), 743–767 (2009)

Antlova, K.: Motivation and Barriers Of ICT Adoption In Small And Medium-Sized Enterprises. E & M Ekonomie a Management 12(2), 140–155 (2009)

Aubert, B.A., Patry, M., Rivard, S.: A tale of two outsourcing contracts - An agency-theoretical perspective. Wirtschaftsinformatik 45(2), 181–190 (2003)

Avison, D., Gregor, S., Wilson, D.: "Managerial IT unconsciousness. Communications of the ACM 49(7), 89–93 (2006)

Barker, T., Frolick, M.N.: ERP implementation failure: A case study. Information Systems Management 20(4), 43–49 (2003)

Bartis, E., Mitev, N.: A multiple narrative approach to information systems failure: a successful system that failed. European Journal of Information Systems 17(2), 112–124 (2008)

Benbasat, I., Zmud, R.W.: The identity crisis within the is discipline: Defining and communicating the discipline's core properties. Mis Quarterly 27(2), 183–194 (2003)

Beynon-Davies, P.: Human error and information systems failure: the case of the London ambulance service computer-aided despatch system project. Interacting with Computers 11(6), 699–720 (1999)

Brown, A.D., Jones, M.R.: Doomed to failure: Narratives of inevitability and conspiracy in a failed IS project. Organization Studies 19(1), 73–88 (1998)

Bruner, J.: The Narrative Construction Of Reality. Critical Inquiry 18(1), 1–21 (1991)

Bruque, S., Moyano, J.: Organisational determinants of information technology adoption and implementation in SMEs: The case of family and cooperative firms. Technovation 27(5), 241–253 (2007)

Cerpa, N., Verner, J.M.: Why Did Your Project Fail? Communications of the ACM 52(12), 130–134 (2009)

Chen, C.C., Law, C.C.H., Yang, S.C.: Managing ERP Implementation Failure: A Project Management Perspective. IEEE Transactions on Engineering Management 56(1), 157–170 (2009)

Ciborra, C.: The Labyrinths of Information: Challenging the Wisdom of Systems. Oxford University Press, USA (2002)

Conboy, K.: Project failure en masse: a study of loose budgetary control in ISD projects. European Journal of Information Systems 19(3), 273–287 (2010)

Cragg, P.B., King, M.: Small-Firm Computing - Motivators and Inhibitors. Mis Quarterly 17(1), 47–60 (1993)

Cule, P., Schmidt, R., Lyytinen, K., Keil, M.: Strategies for heading off is project failure. Information Systems Management 17(2), 65–73 (2000)

Czarniawska, B.: Narrating the Organization. Chicago University Press, Chicago (1997)

Das, T.K., Teng, B.S.: Between trust and control: Developing confidence in partner cooperation in alliances. Academy of Management Review 23(3), 491–512 (1998)

Davidson, E.J.Y.: Examining Project History Narratives: An Analytic Approach. In: IFIP TC8 WG 8.2 International Conference on Information Systems and Qualitative Research, pp. 123–148. Chapman & Hall, Ltd., Philadelphia (1997)

DeLone, W.H., McLean, E.R.: The DeLone and McLean model of information systems success: a ten-year update. Journal of Management Information Systems 19(4), 9–30 (2003)

Devos, J., Van Landeghem, H., Deschoolmeester, D.: Outsourced Information Systems Failures in SMEs: a Multiple Case Study. Electronic Journal of Information Systems Evaluation 11(2), 73–84 (2008)

Devos, J., Van Landeghem, H., Deschoolmeester, D.: IT Governance in SMEs: A Theoretical Framework Based on the Outsourced Information System Failure (2009a)

Devos, J., Van Landeghem, H., Deschoolmeester, D.: IT Governance in SMEs: Trust or Control? In: Dhillon, G., Stahl, B.C., Baskerville, R. (eds.) Information Systems - Creativity and Innovation in Small and Medium-Sized Enterprises, pp. 135–149 (2009b)

Devos, J., Van Landeghem, H., Deschoolmeester, D.: Rethinking IT governance for SMEs. Industrial Management & Data Systems 112(1-2), 206–223 (2012)

Dibbern, J., Goles, T., Hirschheim, R.: Information Systems Outsourcing: A Survey and Analysis of the Literature. The DATA BASE for Advances in Information Systems 35(4), 6–102 (2004)

Dube, L., Pare, G.: Rigor in information systems positivist case research: Current practices, trends, and recommendations. Mis Quarterly 27(4), 597–635 (2003)

Edmondson, A.C.: Strategies for Learning from Failure. Harvard Business Review 89(4), 48 (2011)

Eisenhardt, K.M.: Agency Theory: An Assessment and Review. Academie of Management Review 14(1), 57–74 (1989)

Eisenhardt, K.M.: Better Stories and Better Constructs - The Case For Rigor and Comparative Logic. Academy of Management Review 16(3), 620–627 (1991)

Ewusi-Mensah, K.: Software Development Failures. MIT Press, Cambridge (2003)

Fincham, R.: Narratives of success and failure in systems development. British Journal of Management 13(1), 1–14 (2002)

Gable, G.G., Sedera, D., Chan, T.Z.: Re-conceptualizing information system success: The IS-Impact measurement model. Journal of the Association for Information Systems 9(7), 377–408 (2008)

Group, S.: Third Quarter Research Report. The Standish Group International (2004)

Huang, R., Zmud, R.W., Price, R.L.: Influencing the effectiveness of IT governance practices through steering committees and communication policies. European Journal of Information Systems 19(3), 288–302 (2010)

Iacovou, C.L., Dexter, A.: Surviving IT project cancellations. Communications of the ACM 48(4), 83–86 (2005)

Jensen, M.C., Meckling, W.H.: Theory of Firm - Managerial Behavior, Agency Costs and Ownership Structure. Journal of Financial Economics 3(4), 305–360 (1976)

Keil, M.: Pulling the plug: Software project management and the problem of project escalation. Mis Quarterly 19(4), 421–447 (1995)

Kern, T., Willcocks, L.P., van Heck, E.: The winner's curse in IT outsourcing: Strategies for avoiding relational trauma. California Management Review 44(2), 47 (2002)

Kreps, D., Richardson, H.: IS success and failure-the problem of scale. Political Quarterly 78(3), 439–446 (2007)

Lee, A.S.: Rigor and relevance in MIS research: Beyond the approach of positivism alone. Mis Quarterly 23(1), 29–33 (1999)

Lee, A.S., Baskerville, R.L.: Generalizing generalizability in information systems research. Information Systems Research 14(3), 221–243 (2003)

Lefebvre, L.A., Mason, R., Lefebvre, E.: The influence prism in SMEs: The power of CEOs' perceptions on technology policy and its organizational impacts. Management Science 43(6), 856–878 (1997)

Levy, M., Powell, P.: Strategies for Growth in SMEs: The Role of Information and Information Systems. Elsevier, Oxford (2005)

Lyytinen, K., Hirschheim, R.: Information-Systems Failures - A Survey and Classification of the Empirical Literature. Oxford Surveys in Information Technology (4), 257–309 (1987)

Mingers, J.: Combining IS research methods: Towards a pluralist methodology. Information Systems Research 12(3), 240–259 (2001)

Myers, M.D.: Qualitative research in information systems. Mis Quarterly 21(2), 241–242 (1997)

Natovich, J.: Vendor related risks in IT development: A chronology of an outsourced project failure. Technology Analysis & Strategic Management 15(4), 409–419 (2003)

Riessman, C.K.: Narrative Analysis. SAGE Publications (1993)

Sauer, C.: Why Information Systems Fail: A Case Study Approach. Alfred Wailer, Henley-on-Thames (1993)

Schmidt, R., Lyytinen, K., Keil, M., Cule, P.: Identifying software project risks: An international Delphi study. Journal of Management Information Systems 17(4), 5–36 (2001)

Schwaber, K.: Agile Project Management with Scrum. Microsoft Press (2009)

Stowell, F.: Do We Mean Information Systems or Systems of Information? International Journal of Information Technologies and the Systems Approach 1(1), 25–36 (2008)

Thong, J.Y.L., Yap, C.S.: CEO Characteristics, Organizational Characteristics And Information Technology Adoption in Small Businesses. Omega-International Journal of Management Science 23(4), 429–442 (1995)

Verner, J.M., Abdullah, L.M.: Exploratory case study research: Outsourced project failure. Information and Software Technology 54(8), 866–886 (2012)

Wagner, E.L.: Interconnecting Information Systems Narrative Research: Current Status and Future Opportunities for Process-Oriended Field Studies. In: Wynn, E.A., Whitley, M., Myers, M., DeGross, J.I. (eds.) Global and Organizational Discourse About Information Technology, pp. 419–436. Kluwer Academic Publishers, Boston (2003)

Wagner, E.L., Galliers, R.D., Scott, S.V.: Exposing Best Practices Through Narrative: The ERP Example. In: Kaplan, B., Truex, D., Wastell, D., Wood-Harper, T., D.J.I. (eds.) Information Systems Research: relevant Theory and Informed Practice, pp. 443–451. Kluwer Academic Publishers, Boston (2004)

Walsham, G.: Interpretive Case-Studies in is research - Nature and Method. European Journal of Information Systems 4(2), 74–81 (1995)

Webb, B., Mallon, B.: A method to bridge the gap between breadth and depth in IS narrative analysis. Journal of the Association for Information Systems 8(7), 368–381 (2007)

Weber, R.: The rhetoric of positivism versus interpretivism: A personal view. Mis Quarterly 28(1), III–XII (2004)

Welsh, J.A., White, J.F.: A Small Business Is Not A Little Big Business. Harvard Business Review 59(4), 18 (1981)

Yin, R.K.: Case Study Research: Design and Methods, 3rd edn. Sage Publications, Inc., Thousand Oaks (2003)

IS/IT Project Failures: A Review of the Extant Literature for Deriving a Taxonomy of Failure Factors

Yogesh K. Dwivedi[1], Karthik Ravichandran[2], Michael D. Williams[1], Siân Miller[1], Banita Lal[3], George V. Antony[4], and Muktha Kartik[5]

[1] The School of Business, Swansea University, Swansea, UK
ykdwivedi@gmail.com, {m.d.williams,669196}@swansea.ac.uk
[2] Tractors and Farm Equipment Ltd., Bangalore, India
karthik_19@hotmail.com
[3] Nottingham Business School, Nottingham Trent University, Nottingham, UK
banita.lal@ntu.ac.uk
[4] Post Doctoral Fellow, School of Management Studies,
Cochin University of Science & Technology, Cochin
drgeorgevantony@gmail.com
[5] Mahindra Satyam, Bangalore, India
Muktha.kartik@gmail.com

Abstract. The majority of the existing literature is based upon the assumption that, by paying attention to success factors, failure will be avoided. In the case of challenged projects, where failure factors are overcome the projects go on to be delivered successfully. Hence, it is worthwhile to explore the key factors that determine failure, since this information may be useful in averting future project failures. This research aims to collate and classify existing research in order to: (1) understand the common failure factors; and (2) categorise identified factors pertaining to country, project stage and failure categories. In so doing, this research work goes beyond the identification of traditional factors since it further classifies them according to project stages, failure types and geographical regions. This research contributes to knowledge by identifying and synthesising existing understanding of the failure of IS/IT projects.

Keywords: IS/IT Project, Failure, Literature Review, Taxonomy of Factors.

1   Introduction

Failure is a common phenomenon in projects. Bignell and Fortune (1984) defined failure broadly as the shortfall between performance and standards. In context of IS/IT, Ewusi-Mensah (2003, p.7) defined failure as is "either the implemented system not meeting the user expectations or inability of creating working or a functioning system". According to Sauer (1993), if a project organization loses support and fails to manage the service, then ultimately the project will fail.

IS projects have been renowned for failures since before the 1990s, more than 75% of all projects were considered failures (Beynon-Davies, 1995, p. 171). Although the percentage of successful projects seems to have increased in the recent past, challenged projects remain constant at around 50% (Standish Group report, 2006 as cited

Y.K. Dwivedi et al. (Eds.): TDIT 2013, IFIP AICT 402, pp. 73–88, 2013.

in Nasir & Sahibuddin, 2011). The lack of improvement may be attributed to complexity in projects, size, movement of the project team and the organizations failure to look back at the past projects (Nelson, 2007). Project Management (PM) is the most efficient way of delivering projects (Avots, 1969). However, Lyytinen and Robey (1999) found that traditional PM practices and advancement in tools and methods has had little impact on failure and failure factors. Thus if tools cannot prevent failures, a careful understanding of failure factors is imperative. Analysis of project failures is still ambiguous since it is often reported post hoc. Proactive diagnosis remains primitive. Migration to leading rather than lagging indicators in PM would promote this (Stewart & Mohamed, 2004). Project Managers are further handicapped by the lack of commonality in reported failure factors. Focus on an understanding of common failure factors is essential to aid project managers in avoiding those mistakes which lead to failure.

The overall aim of this paper is to collate and classify existing research in order to: (1) understand the common failure factors; and (2) categorize identified factors by country, project stage and project category. This paper is structured into the following sections: categorization of failure; taxonomy of failure factors; failure factors according to project lifecycle stages; failure factors according to geography; types of failure, discussion; and conclusions outlining theoretical contributions and implications.

2   Categorising Failure

Existing literature has categorized IS failure using various approaches. For example, Ewusi-Mensah (2003, p.8) characterized failure as "Software Runaways" from original plans in cost and delivery. Another common approach classifies failed projects as challenged and impaired projects (Dalcher, 2003; Standish group, 1995; Yeo, 2002). Projects that were cancelled or abandoned during the project life cycle were considered 'impaired'. 'Challenged' projects are those which have suffered the impact of failure but have survived (Standish group, 1995). Lyytinen and Hirschheim (1987) suggested four types of failure: correspondence failure, process failure, interaction failure and expectation failure. Correspondence failure refers to system's inability to correspond to what is required. Process failure (similar to software runaways) leads to shortfalls in time and budget constraint is associated with poor Project Management. Interaction failure refers to where the developed system is unsatisfactory to the user (Lyytinen and Hirschheim, 1987). Sauer (1993) criticized these categories of failures for their limited scope. In response, Lyytinen and Hirschheim (1987) introduced the concept of expectation failure encompassing the three preceding categories where the project fails to meet stakeholder expectations in terms of correspondence, process and interaction. Expectation failure was further divided into development failure and use failure (Lyytinen and Hirschheim, 1987).

A drawback of expectation failure is that it does not consider differences in situation. Both impaired and challenged projects (Standish group, 1995) can be categorized as expectation failure. Sauer (1993) offered the following criticisms of expectation failure: (1) Defining expectations and its relative importance to stakeholders is unclear. Factors beyond cost, time and quality need to be considered; (2) Intentional issues are missed in the scope of expectation failure. What the project is intended to do may be different from expectation; and (3) Differential capacities can manifest themselves as failure, for example the failed London ambulance project where users did not have the capacity to use the system (Sauer, 1993). Sauer (1993) argued that the interest of the most important stakeholder should be considered in defining project requirements and developed an alternative classification of failure to bring out the exchange between the organization and the project supporters. Sauer (1993) described termination failure which occurs when development or operation and maintenance ceases and all interests in the project have ceased with no continuing supporters. Ewusi-Mensah (2003) describes this as abandonment and termination failure is total abandonment, with substantial and partial being other classifications of failed projects. Total abandonment can be seen as an extreme example of an impaired project. Substantial abandonment is similar to the status of a challenged project where major stoppages occur and, at times, the changes to the original specification finally overcome the failure factors. Partial abandonment refers to a reduction in the original scope without modifying the original project specifications (Ewusi-Mensah, 2003). Escalation failure is introduced by Newman and Sabherwal (1996) where overshooting time and budget leads to failure.

Further classification is based on Project and PM levels. The project level will focus on failure factors that can occur after delivery of the project such as usability, maintenance and user feedback. The failure factor pertaining to PM occurs during the development and implementation of project and can be further classified as either within the PM scope covering limited and complete control and finally wholly outside the purview of PM (Schmidt et al., 2001). Atkinson (1999) classifies PM failures as 'Type I and II' errors. Type I relates to carrying out an activity wrongly, for example, planning, estimating or project control. Type II relates to ignorance, forgetting or not carrying out an intended activity resulting in a failure factor (Atkinson, 1999). This literature examining different criteria for failure will be used to classify and group the failure factors according to the above discussed classification and terminologies of failure.

3   Taxonomy of Failure Factors

This section identifies and classifies factors that contribute to a failure of project management (PM) and projects.

3.1   Project Management Factors

Verner et al. (2008) reveals that the majority of projects suffer failure factors arising from poor PM and organizational factors outside the project managers control. Avots (1969) revealed that PM techniques where used as a general tool may lead to more failure factors than where used towards specific objectives and with greater discipline such as in the aerospace sector. Many symptoms can indicate PM failures the most common being cost and/or time overruns and erosion of quality (Avots, 1969). Atkinson (1999) suggests that, in many cases it is difficult to achieve more than two out of the three familiar success criteria of time, cost and quality. Most PM failures occur due to a commonly occurring set of factors (Avots, 1969). The basis for undertaking a project is a complete understanding of the need for the project. The capability of the project manager is crucial since they are responsible for organizing and leadership throughout the PM life cycle. Even with the right project manager the failure can still arise from a lack of management support especially when management is unclear about the objectives. Projects can quickly descend into failure if the tasks and activities are not clearly defined and allocated. Management needs to understand the need for tools and techniques and to support the PM team to avoid failure caused by the misuse of tools and techniques. Project termination in the case of success or failure should be smooth with the full support of stakeholders, otherwise an apparently successful project can be deemed a failure. Atkinson (1999) argued that even after 50 years of research into Project Management, failure factors are still limited to the Iron Triangle elements of cost, time and quality. Furthermore, failure factors may commonly be seen as the Type I and II errors discussed above. However, errors of omission (Type II) remain a strong contender towards failure in Project Management (Atkinson, 1999).

More recently, Jones (2004) introduced the following factors relating to the failure of PM. Planning arise from inadequate time allocated for a detailed requirement analysis, ineffective change management, inappropriate human resource management and, finally, insufficient time for inspection, testing and defect repairs. A lack of correct sizing approaches and tools, projects tend to understate the scale of work resulting in failure (Jones, 2004). Inadequate milestone tracking and reporting are causes of PM failure. Change management and quality control are the final factors that are important in any kind of projects and omission of these activities will end up as failure (Jones, 2004).

3.2 Project Factors

There are many factors which affect project goals and objectives and emerge as factors leading to failure. Many studies give a wide range of failure factors. Failure factors are listed in Table 1 showing common and exclusive factors applicable to Project ('P') and Project Management ('PM'). According to Pinto and Mantel (1990) project failures are vague and observation-based the failure factor varies from initial stages of the lifecycle to final implementation. The first major group factors that contributes to failure are classified as 'project' covering size, value, span, uniqueness, urgency and density of the project (Al-Ahmad et al., 2009; Belassi and Tukel, 1996; Schmidt et al., 2001; Tukel and Rom, 1998).

The size of the project is an important factor in planning resources and estimating the time. The chance of this becoming failure factor is high if not taken into account during estimation and planning (Tukel and Rom, 1998). The size of the project will have a direct impact on the complexity of the problem (Ewusi-Mensah, 2003). The project size factor is demonstrated through "scope creep", in the number of suppliers and organizations involved in the project and it may be correlated with the team size (Schmidt et al., 2001).

Value can contribute to failure, with larger value projects being more likely to fail (Wallace et al., 2004). Closely associated with value is loose budgetary control that is often the reason for project failure. Although this is closely associated with PM failure, sub factors related to budget overrun fare worthy of mention. Three critical sub factors are: detailed line item follow-up, emphasis of short-term budget targets and the level of tolerance for budget revision (Conboy, 2008).

Table 1. Failure factors for project (P) and project management (PM) identified in existing studies

Failure Factors	P	PM	Reference
Project: Size and Value; Uniqueness; Density of Project; Life cycle; Urgency	*		Al-Ahmad et al. (2009); Belassi and Tukel (1996); Schmidt et al. (2001)
Team (Covers Project team and Project manager Characteristics): Turnover; Staffing build-up; Knowledge; Motivation Levels	*		Wallace et al. (2004)
Project Team: Technical background; Communication Skills; Commitment	*		Belassi and Tukel (1996)
Absence of an influential champion and Change agent	*		Yeo (2002)
Improper definitions of roles and responsibilities		*	Al-Ahmad et al. (2009); Schmidt et al. (2001)
User: User conflicts	*		Wallace et al.(2004).
User involvement and Commitment	*	*	Attarzadeh and Ow (2008); Al-Ahmad et al. (2009); Brown and Jones (1998); Jiang et al. (1998); Johnson et al. (2001); Hartwick and Barki (1994); Schmidt et al. (2001)
User Resistance: Lack of Felt Need; Uncertainty; Lack of involvement in Change; Personal Characteristics	*		Field (1997); Hirschheim and Newman (1988); Jiang et al. (1998); Markus (1984); Yeo (2002)
Lack of user input: Did not Need It Any Longer		*	Attarzadeh and Ow (2008)
Conflict between user department: Failure to manage end-user expectations	*		Al-Ahmad et al.(2009);Schmidt et al. (2001)
Goal: Goals are ambiguous, too narrow and Conflicting		*	Dickson et al. (1978); Johnson et al. (2001); Lyytinen (1987)
Objectives and Value gap	*		Attarzadeh and Ow (2008); Heeks (2006); Munns and Bjeirmi (1996)
Ambiguous business needs and unclear vision	*		Yeo (2002)
Resources (Economic): Staffing and Skill gap; Time and Money gap	*	*	Attarzadeh and Ow (2008); Heeks (2006)
Unrealistic Time Frame		*	Attarzadeh and Ow (2008); Yeo (2002)
Requirement: Conflicting system requirement; Difficulty in defining input and output	*		Wallace et al. (2004)
Weak definitions of requirements and scope; Incomplete specifications when project started; Consultant/vendor underestimated the project scope and complexity	*	*	Attarzadeh and Ow (2008); Yeo (2002)
Misunderstanding the user requirements; Lack of frozen requirements; Changing scope and objectives	*		Al-Ahmad et al. (2009); Schmidt et al. (2001)
Planning and Control	*		Wallace et al. (2004)

Failure Factors	P	PM	Reference
Incomplete Requirements and Specifications; Changing Requirements and Specifications		*	Attarzadeh and Ow (2008)
Failure to apply essential PM practices		*	Dalcher and Drevin (2003); Evans et al. (2001)
Lack of effective PM methodology Lack of effective PM skills		*	Al-Ahmad et al. (2009); Schmidt et al. (2001); Verner et al. (2008)
Preoccupation with Technology in project planning	*		Flower (1996);Yeo (2002)
Reactive and not pro-active in dealing with problems; Inadequate project risk analysis; Incorrect assumptions regarding risk analysis	*		Yeo (2002)
Technology and Technological High risk restricts choices		*	Ewusi-Mensah (2003); Lyytinen (1987)
Technology Gap	*		Field (1997); Heeks (2006)
Inappropriate Technology; Ignorance of IT		*	Mitev (1996)
Technology Focus over human relations	*		Flower (1996); Yeo (2002)
Technology Illiteracy; Chosen technology changes		*	Attarzadeh and Ow (2008)
New Technology failure	*		Al-Ahmad et al.(2009); Schmidt et al. (2001)
External Environment: Economy		*	Lyytinen (1987)
Political; Social; Nature Client Competitor	*		Belassi and Tukel (1996); Munns and Bjeirmi (1996); Pinto and Mantel (1990)
Process Features		*	Lyytinen (1987); Dickson et al. (1978)
Changes in design specifications late the project; Involve high degree of customization	*		Yeo (2002)
Organisation		*	Heeks (2006); Lyytinen (1987)
Organisational Environment	*		Verner et al. (2008); Wallace et al. (2004)
Top management support; Project organizational structure; Functional managers' support	*		Al-Ahmad et al. (2009); Belassi and Tukel (1996); Flower (1996); Heeks (2006); Schmidt et al. (2001); Yeo (2002)
Management Development; Motivation; Culture and Feedback	*		Irani et al. (2001)
Unrealistic management expectations and unwarranted optimism; Lack of proactive risk management; Untimely decision making; Lack of program management leadership		*	Dalcher and Drevin (2003); Evans et al. (2001)
Poor Management		*	Mitev (1996)
Hostile Company culture	*		Flower (1996); Yeo(2002).
Top down management style	*		Yeo (2002).
Managerial Influence; Poor stakeholder management	*		Flower (1996) ;Yeo (2002)

Failure Factors	P	PM	Reference
Organisational Consequences	*		Brown and Jones (1998)
Self Image		*	Lyytinen (1987).
Learning: Educational Barriers; Organisational Intelligence; Disincentives for Learning		*	Lyytinen and Robey (1999)
Managers ignore best practices and lessons learned	*		Field (1997)
IS related: IS operations Problem; IS Failure; IS implementation; Data Problems; Process gap	*		Davis et al.(1992); Heeks (2006); Jiang et al.(1998); Lyytinen (1987); Thong et al. (1994); Heeks (2006).
Not managing change properly	*		Al-Ahmad et al.(2009); Schmidt et al. (2001)
Conceptual Problem	*		Lyytinen (1987)
Complexity Problem	*		Lyytinen (1987); Wallace et al. (2004)
People Problem	*		Lyytinen (1987)
Factors related to the Project Manager	*		Belassi and Tukel (1996)
Communication; Workforce management conflicts	*		Yeo (2002); Irani et al. (2001)
Human Error		*	Mitev (1996)
Vested Interest	*		Flower (1996); Yeo (2002)
Outsourcing: More than one supplier; Poor Selection decision	*		Belassi and Tukel (1996); Flowers (1996); Schmidt et al. (2001); Wallace et al. (2004); Yeo (2002)
Weak management of Suppliers	*		Brown and Jones (1998)
Legal Issues	*		Munns and Bjeirmi (1996); Pinto and Mantel (1990)

Span covers the period during which the project must be executed and is closely related to failures related to overshooting time and delivery, coupled with urgency. Uniqueness is important when compared with standard activities. More unique activities require more planning by the Project Manager (Belassi & Tukel, 1996). Density is the number of predecessor activities which need to be completed before beginning a new activity (Tukel & Rom, 1998). This is related to escalation which is a key Project Manager activity when they encounter problems with density which may impact resources planning.

The factor in the second category is the part played by the team involving the skills and attributes of the project team and project manager which are key in the planning and termination stages where commitment and energy play a major role (Belassi & Tukel, 1996). Team turnover, staffing build-up, communication and motivation are additional sub factors (Wallace et al., 2004). The project manager should be an influential change agent (Yeo, 2002). According to Johnson (2001) 97 % of project which are successful are managed by skilled and experienced project managers (Johnson, 2001). Poor leadership is a failure factor especially affecting the early stages of a project (Morris and Hough, 1987).

User failure falls within the top three project failure factors (Attarzadeh & Ow, 2008). Users need to be carefully involved and become a part of quality assurance.

Misunderstanding user requirements is one of the 17 failure factors identified by Schmidt et al. (2001). Further issues like conflict between user departments and lack of user responsibilities also contribute to failure (Wallace et al., 2004). Jiang et al. (1998) looks at failure through expectation failure theory and observes that failure can occur during development or during system use and is viewed differently by different stakeholders. The research discusses four types of failure namely IS failure, user involvement, user resistance and implementation failure. The research revealed that the failure factors are more common and frequent later in the development life cycle. The failure factor varies according to the IS users and IS professionals. User assistance, interviewing and resource commitment factors tend to have less impact on failure factors.

Unclear goals and business objectives lead to failure (See Table 1). Ambiguous business goals and unclear vision constitute significant factors in failure (Yeo, 2002) leading to failure in time, cost and quality (Al-Ahmad et al., 2009; Field, 1997; Johnson, 2001). Project creep and changes in goals and objectives during implementation affects many projects (Al-Ahmad et al., 2009; Schmidt et al., 2001). Narrow and conflicting goals can become failure factor (Lyytinen, 1987). Many projects fail due to the lack of stakeholder consensus (Ewusi-Mensah, 2003).

The requirement factor is closely associated with goals. Many projects suffer failure due to changing requirements, unclear, ambiguous and unusable requirements (Wallace et al., 2004) and misunderstood user requirements and the failure to freeze requirements (Al-Ahmad et al., 2009; Schmidt et al., 2001). Cost and delivery overruns are resource or economic factors. Cost overruns and missed delivery can result in project termination. Ewusi-Mensah (2003) includes escalation of costs and completion schedules, actual project expenditures and delivery below the estimates and finally lack of funds. These indirect factors may be the reason for the overrun. Failure can also be due to time and delivery below the estimates related to estimation issues in project management. Finally the depletion of funds can result in project termination

Content driven failure or the technology factor (Yeo, 2002) brings a high risk of failure since technology affects operational processes at a group or personal level (Lyytinen, 1987). Technology complexity refers to technology that is new to the project, technology linked to many other systems, immature technology and automation (Wallace et al., 2004). Technology incompetence and new technology may lead to a challenge which may be overcome whereas technology illiteracy will lead to an impaired project (Attarzadeh and Ow, 2008). Technological factors include inadequate process, high degrees of customization, computer hardware availability and correct infrastructure and compatibility with the existing system (Ewusi-Mensah, 2003). Complexity is closely allied to the technology factor. This can be in the form of new technology and to which the organization has not been previously exposed (Wallace et al., 2004). By contrast, Kappelman et al. (2008) argues that no IS project fails due to the technology factor, but rather due to people and process which manifests as a technical issue. This is supported by Nelson (2007) who reveals that only 4 percent of the top ten failures listed technology as a factor compared with process and people.

External failure factors include economic, political, social and competitor factors. Frequently the project manager cannot control these factors since they are outside the organization (Belassi & Tukel, 1996). These factors are evident in the planning stage, although Pinto and Mantel (1990) find that some of these factors may affect all stages of the project. Organizational factors include top management support, management decision making, organization structure, motivational factors and organizational culture. Top management support is critical, especially where a champion support the project manager in meeting the project goals. A functional organizational structure, rather than a pure project or matrix structure, facilitates better resource sharing (Belassi and Tukel, 1996). Wallace et al. (2004) add organizational politics, lack of stability and resource redirection. Unrealistic management expectations and the absence of leadership are identified by Evans et al. (2002).

Of the studies that have looked at failure, only few (for example, Lyytinen and Robey, 1999) identified a lack of learning from previous failures as a major failure factor in IS projects. Failures in hospital and health care projects can derive from organisational consequences such as redundancy and loss of status, complex bureaucratic procedures, unrealistic expectations, lack of resource, uncooperative customers and weak supplier management (Brown and Jones, 1998; Sauer et al. 1997). Gauld (2007) suggests that discontinuity of key management staff, ill-defined needs and objectives and no appointed chief information officer all contribute to failure. People factors relate closely to the team factor and is ranked in the top three IS failure factors (Lyytinen, 1987). Human error, conflicts and communication inside and outside the organization contribute to failure. A lack of education and user training were found by Irani et al. (2001, p.58) to lead to "noise" in the system, impacting other factors like cost, delivery times and productivity.

With outsourcing, risk factors multiply with more suppliers (Wallace et al., 2004). Multi-supplier projects encounter coordination and integration issues (Schmidt, 2001) stemming from unclarity in objectives and scope, coupled with control and progress monitoring of suppliers. Near shore and local outsourcing face fewer failure factors compared to offshore outsourcing (Miller, 2008). Chen et al. (2009) discussed the impact of poor buyer preparation including inadequate supplier information and a lack of understanding of procurement. Legal issues, which can be categorized as a part of the external environment can hinder projects (Munns and Bjeirmi, 1996; Pinto and Mantel, 1990).

Using four major reports on project failure (Chaos Report, KPMG survey, Computer Weekly programme survey and Align IT group), Miller (2008) suggested the following top failure factors: (1) Incomplete Requirements; (2) User Factor; (3) Planning failure; (4) Lack of management support/ involvement; (5) Lack of resources; (6) Weak business case; and (7) Unclear Objectives.

4   Failure Factors According to Project Life Cycle

Most projects are developed using a life cycle model coupled with a PM methodology. This provides stability and predictability and controls the development stages (Lyytinen, 1987). Based on the project stages a comparison has been drawn against the failure factors (see Table 2) to illustrate the relative importance of selected factors according to the stages of a project.

Table 2. Failure Factors (as derived from Table 1) across Project Life Cycle Stages that are adopted from the PRINCE2 Methodology [**Legend: C = Critical; LC=Less Critical; MC=Mildly Critical**]

Failure Factors	Conception	Planning	Production	Handover	Utilisation	Close down
Project	C	C	C	C	MC	MC
Team	LC	C	C	C	LC	LC
User	C	LC	C	C	C	LC
Goal	C	C	MC	MC	LC	LC
Resources (People, Time and Money)	MC	C	C	C	LC	LC
Requirement	C	C	C	C	LC	LC
Planning and Control	LC	C	C	C	LC	LC
PM	LC	C	C	C	LC	LC
Technology	LC	C	C	C	C	MC
External Environment	LC	C	C	C	C	C
Process Features	LC	C	C	C	C	LC
Organisation	C	C	C	LC	LC	LC
Learning	LC	C	C	C	C	MC
IS	LC	C	C	C	C	LC
Conceptual	C	C	LC	LC	LC	LC
People	LC	C	C	C	C	LC
Complexity	C	C	C	LC	LC	LC
Outsourcing	LC	C	C	C	MC	MC

5   Failure Factors According to Geography

The cultural perspective has been examined as a contributor to project failure (Camprieu, et al., 2007; Rees-Caldwell and Pinnington, 2012). Hofstede's framework looks at national preferences along the dimensions of Power-Distance, Individualism, Uncertainty-avoidance and Long term orientation (Hofstede, 1991). Uncertainty-Avoidance (U-A) may be predictor of failure in some geography. Hofstede (2012) found that with a greater acceptance of uncertainty in the West, there may be more user related failures. A high score on the U-A index, demonstrates a willingness to accept that some things may need to be agreed later but the project can proceed without these being made explicit. If this is not dealt with until later in the project, then there may be a failure due to this uncertainty having not been resolved. However, where there is a low U-A score, the project is unlikely to proceed until these have been agreed.

Cultural factors impact technological, environmental and social failure factors. The UK and USA both tend to be more individualistic in comparison with Singapore and other eastern countries. Where the PM is individualistic the temporary task becomes the main focus and a collectivist culture may experience problems created by cultural incompatibility and 'lose their work identity' (Rees-Caldwell & Pinnington, 2012). The table below shows results from the literature survey comparing failure factors by country. It is interesting to note, irrespective of geography, organization ranks as a top failure factor, followed by user, goal, requirement and PM control factors (Table 3).

Table 3. Failure factors significance ranking country wise (Source: See Table 1 for sources) Note: Number in cells represent number of studies that reported a particular factor in context of a particular country

Failure Factors	US	UK	FINL AND	SINGA PORE	HONG KONG	CAN ADA	MALA YSIA
Project	-	-	11	-	-	-	-
Team	7	-	3	-	7	-	-
User	3	1	5	7	2	-	7
Goal	6	6	12	-	3	1	-
Resources (People, Time and Money)	2	7	6	-	5	-	-
Requirement	5	4	7	-	4	-	-
Planning and Control	-	-	4	1	8	-	2
PM	4	-	1	3	-	2	1
Technology	8	5	10	6	6	-	4
External Environment	-	-	-	8	-	-	6
Process Features	-	-	-	-	-	-	-
Organisation	1	3	2	2	1	3	3
Learning	-	-	-	-	-	-	-
IS	-	-	-	-	-	-	-
Conceptual Problem	-	-	-	4	-	-	-
People Problem	-	2	8	5	-	-	-
Complexity Problem	-	-	-	-	-	-	5
Outsourcing	-	8	9	-	-	-	-

6   Failure Factors According to Types of Failure

Failure factors are complex, layered and interdependent. External factors as well as internal issues play a major role in impacting failure. The literature analysis demonstrated that failure in most impaired projects is due to more than one factor which are often interrelated. In order to prevent these factors or to detect them before they become catastrophic it is important to understand the classification and measure the failure factors. Type of Failure vs. Failure Factors from the literature is presented in Table 4.

Table 4. Type of Failure vs. Failure Factors (Source: Factors Adopted from Munns and Bjeirmi,1996; Types of Failures from Ewusi-Mensah, 2003) [Legend '*' Significant '-' No significant relation from literature]

Failure Factors	Challenged Project	Impaired Project	Correspondence Failure	Process Failure	Interaction Failure	Expectation Failure	Escalation Failure	Termination Failure
Project	*	-	-	-	-	-	-	-
Team	*	-	-	-	-	*	-	-
User	*	-	-	-	*	-	-	*
Goal		*	*	-	-	-	-	-
Resources (People, Time and Money)	*	-	-	*	-	-	*	-
Requirement	-	*	*	-	-	-	-	-
Planning and Control	-	*	-	*	-	-	-	-
PM	-	*	-	*	-	-	-	-
Technology	-	*	-	-	-	-	-	*
External Environment	*	-	-	-	-	-	-	-
Process Features	*	-	-	-	-	-	-	-
Organisation	-	*	-	-	-	-	-	*
Learning	*	-	-	-	-	-	-	
IS	-	*	-	-	-	-	-	*
Conceptual Problem	-	*	-	-	-	-	-	-
People Problem	*	-	-	-	-	*	-	-
Complexity Problem	*	-	-	-	-	-	-	-
Outsourcing	-	*	-	-	-	*	-	-

7   Discussion

Early warning signals are critical in identifying potential project failures. The failure of IS can be classified into development and user level failures (Lyytinen, 1988). This classification is helpful in categorizing failure factors and understanding the commonality of factors between users and other stakeholders involved in the development. An important distinction is the difference between the Project and PM since the scope of involvement between the project team and the users differ. Munns and Bjeirmi (1996) define project team involvement in planning, development and handover stages, whereas the user or client is involved in all stages of the project.

The iron triangle measures of cost, time and quality has been a powerful influence on project management in all sectors. Cost and time are difficult to measure during the early stages of a project and may continue to shift over the project life cycle.

Quality measurement is highly dependent on perception, and will also change during the lifecycle (Atkinson, 1999). When these measures are mapped against the classification criteria, cost, quality and time factors are related mostly with PM. The PM falls into the subset of project factors and it is important to capture failure factors at the PM stage since they may provide an early warning for factors that might arise later. PM might be successful without any apparent failures, but nonetheless, a project can be deemed a failure, with failure factors emerging at a later stage (Munns & Bjeirmi, 1996). Many studies have focussed on Project failures but few studies specific to PM failures. Common failures are missed budgets, time and user expectations. With difficulty in defining failure or success the project may avert failure by grouping the factors based on the Project Life cycle stages.

Many studies have focused on the identification of the factors leading to IT failures. Early studies focused on individual explanations, with later studies finding behavioural and social factors. Later research focuses on success and failure factors in PM, organisation and process (Attarzadeh & Ow, 2008; Sauer et al., 1997). An additional factor is the role of cultural differences. Hofstede's dimensions are valuable but are the subject of few studies (for example, Schmidt et al., 2001; Shore and Cross, 2005). This paper attempted to classify the cultural element mapped across the project life cycle stages.

Many works have analysed and listed failure factors from impaired projects, stating what may have gone wrong pointing to the "Lesson Learnt" registers which exist to prevent such failures in the future. However, further focus on early warning indicators of failure factors would be beneficial. Charette (2006) sees a metaphor with an airplane crash where there are many levels of safety warnings, and after a crash, extensive investigation seeks to identify the failure factors. Similarly, in IT failure, greater focus on early warning indicators and the learning from failure need to be incorporated into the PM process (Charette, 2006).

8   Conclusion

This paper sought to identify factors contributing to IS/IT project failure by reviewing relevant literature. These are the conclusions drawn from the literature analysis and categorisation of IS/IT project failure literature: (1) It is important to distinguish between factors impacting the project and PM. The project involves a longer time whereas PM is only until project handover; (2) The majority of project failure factors occur in combination rather than in isolation; (3) Failure factors are complex and interdependent; (4) External factors play a major role in impacting failure. Recent studies focus on behavioural and social factors and project management, organisation and process framework covering success and failure factors; (5) Failure factors in the West differ in prioritisation compared with the East, with more focus on failures of PM and planning factors in the East compared organisation and user related factors which are more prevalent in the West; and (5) Early warning signals have taken on a new importance to prevent the major failures from occurring.

8.1   Theoretical Contributions and Implications

This research contributes by identifying, collating, analysing and synthesising existing research on the failure of IS/IT project and project management. It provides a list of large number of factors highlighting those that are reported in more than one study. This study also attempts to identify failure factors by a particular geographical location. In brief, this paper offers a one-stop source for literature on failure of IS/IT project for both researchers and practitioners. Based on synthesis of findings from existing literature, the following recommendations can be formed: (1) Training and usage of standard Project Management tools can be the key to avoiding failure factors; (2) Dedicated focus on requirements, project management and learning and knowledge management is required to avoid failures with requirement aspect being most critical; (3) User experience and feedback should be sought throughout the Project Lifecycle; (4) Supplier selection, evaluation and management can be critical to avert failures and ensure success in outsourced projects; and (5) Project Managers should focus on governance, risk management and regulatory factors to stay ahead of competition.

References

Al-Ahmad, W., Al-Fagih, K., Khanfar, K., Alsamara, K., Abuleil, S., Abu-Salem, H.: A Taxonomy of an IT Project Failure: Root Causes. International Management Review 5(1), 93–104 (2009)

Atkinson, R.: Project management: cost, time and quality, two best guesses and a phenomenon, its time to accept other success criteria. International Journal of Project Management 17(6), 337–342 (1999)

Attarzadeh, I., Ow, S.H.: Project Management Practices: The Criteria for Success or Failure. Communications of the IBIMA 1, 234–241 (2008)

Avots, I.: Why Does Project Management Fail? California Management Review 12 (1), 77–82 (1969)

Belassi, W., Tukel, O.I.: A new framework for determining critical success/failure factors in projects. International Journal of Project Management 14(3), 141–151 (1996)

Beynon-Davies, P.: Information systems 'failure': the case of the London Ambulance Service's Computer Aided Despatch project. European Journal of Information Systems 4, 171–184 (1995)

Bignell, V., Fortune, J.: Understanding Systems Failures. Manchester University Press, Manchester (1984)

Brown, A.D., Jones, M.R.: Doomed to Failure: Narratives of inevitability and conspiracy in a Failed IS Project. Organisation Studies 19(1), 73–88 (1998)

Camprieu, R., Desbiens, J., Feixue, Y.: 'Cultural' differences in project risk perception: An empirical comparison of China and Canada. International Journal of Project Management 25, 683–693 (2007)

Charette, R.N.: Why Software Fail (August 29, 2006), http://www.spectrum.ieee.org/print/1685 (retrieved July 02, 2012) from IEEE Spectrum

Chen, J., Xu, L., Whinston, A.: Managing Project Failure Risk Through Contingent Contracts in Procurement Auctions. Advance, 1–17 (2009)

Conboy, K.: Project Failure en Mass: A Study of Loose Budgetary Control in ISD Projects. Sprouts: Working Papers on Information Systems 8(40), 1–14 (2008)

Dalcher, D.: Understanding Stories of Information Systems Failures, Sweeden. Action in Language, Organisations and Information, pp. 221–236 (2003)

Dalcher, D., Drevin, L.: Learning from Information Systems failures by using narrative and ante-narrative methods. In: Proceedings of SAICSIT, UK, pp. 137–142 (2003)

Davis, G., Lee, A., Nickles, K., Chatterjee, S., Hartung, R., Wu, Y.: Diagnosis of an information system failure: a framework and interpretive process. Information and Management 23, 293–318 (1992)

Dickson, G.W., Senn, J.A., Cherv, N.L.: Research in Management Information Systems: The Minnesota Experiments. Management Science 23, 913–934 (1977)

Evans, M.W., Abela, A.M., Beltz, T.: Seven Characteristics of Dysfunctional Software Projects. The Journal of Defense Software Engineering, 16–20 (April 2002)

Ewusi-Mensah, K.: Software Development Failures: Anatomy of Abandoned Projects. The MIT Press, London (2003)

Flowers, S.: Software failure: management failure. John Wiley, Chichester (1996)

Field, J.: Passive or Proactive? Adults Learning 8(6), 160 (1997)

Gauld, R.: Public sector information system project failures: Lessons from a NewZealand hospital organization. Government Information Quarterly 24, 102–114 (2007)

Hartwick, J., Barki, H.: Explaining the role of user participation in information system use. Management Science 40(4), 440–465 (1994)

Heeks, R.: Health information systems: Failure, success and improvisation. International Journal of Medical Informatics 75, 125–137 (2006)

Hirschheim, R., Newman, M.: Information Systems and User Resistance: Theory and Practice. The Computer Journal 31(5), 398–408 (1988)

Hofstede, G.: Cultures and Organisations Software of the Mind. McGraw Hill Book Company, UK (1991)

Hofstede, G.: National Culture (April 2012) http://geert-hofstede.com (retrieved April 20, 2012), from Geert Hofstede

Irani, Z., Sharif, A., Love: Transforming failure into success through organisational learning: an analysis of a manufacturing information system. European Journal of Information Systems 10, 55–66 (2001)

Jiang, J.J., Klein, G., Balloun, J.: Perceptions of system development failures. Information and Software Technology 39, 933–937 (1998)

Johnson, J., Boucher, K.D., Connors, K., Robinson, J.: Collaboration: Development & Management Collaborating on Project Success (February/March 2001)

Jones, C.: Software Project Management Practices: Failure Versus Success. The Journal of Defense Software Engineering, 5–9 (October 2004)

Kappelman, L. A., McKeeman, R., & Zhang, L. (2008, Fall). Early Warning Signs Of IT Project Failure : The Dominant Dozen. Information Systems Management, 31-36.

Lyytinen, K.: Different Perspectives on Information Systems: Problems and Solutions. ACM Computing Surveys 19(1), 1–46 (1987)

Lyytinen, K., Hirschheim, R.: Information systems failures: a survey and classification of the empirical literature. Oxford Surveys in Information Technology 4(1), 257–309 (1987)

Lyytinen, K., Robey, D.: Learning Failures in Information Systems Development. Journal of Information Systems 9, 85–101 (1999)

Markus, M.: Power, politics, and MIS implementation. Communications of the ACM 26(6), 430–444 (1984)

Miller, J.: A total benefits strategy is a valuable approach in HR outsourcing. Employment Relations Today 34(4), 55–61 (2008)

Mitev, N.N.: More than a failure? The computerized reservation systems at French Railways. Information Technology &People 9(4), 8–19 (1996)

Morris, Hough, G.: The Anatomy of Major Projects. John Wiley and Sons, New York (1987)

Munns, A.K., Bjeirmi, B.F.: The role of project management in achieving project success. International Journal of Project Management 14(2), 81–87 (1996)

Nasir, M.H.N.M., Sahibuddin, S.: Addressing a critical success factor for software projects: A multi-round Delphi study of TSP. International Journal of Physical Sciences 6(5), 1213–1232 (2011)

Nelson, R.R.: IT Project Management: Infamous Failures, Classic Mistakes, and Best Practices. MIS Quarterly Executive 6(2), 67–78 (2007)

Newman, M., Sabherwal, R.: Determinants of Commitment to Information Systems Development: A Longitudinal Investigation. MIS Quarterly, 23–54 (March 1996)

Pinto, J.K., Mantel, J.S.: The Causes of Project Failure. IEEE Transactions On Engineering Management 37(4), 269–275 (1990)

Rees-Caldwell, K., Pinnington, A.H.: National culture differences in project management: Comparing British and Arab project managers' perceptions of different planning areas. International Journal of Project Management 20, 1–16 (2012)

Sauer, C.: Why information systems fail: A case study approach. Alfred Waller, Oxfordshire (1993)

Sauer, C., Southon, G., Dampney, C.N.: Fit, failure, and the house of horrors: toward a configurational theory of is project failure. In: Proceedings of the Eighteenth International Conference on Information Systems, pp. 349–366. ICIS, Atlanta (1997)

Schmidt, R., Lyytinen, K., Keil, M., Cule, P.: Identifying Software Project Risks: An International Delphi Study. Journal of Management Information Systems 17(4), 5–36 (2001)

Shore, B., Cross, B.J.: Exploring the role of national culture in the management of largescale International Science Project. International Journal of Project Management 23, 55–64 (2005)

Standish Group Report. Chaos Report. Boston, Massachusetts, USA: Standish Group (July 01, 1995), http://www.standishgroup.com (retrieved)

Stewart, R.A., Mohamed, S.: Evaluating web-based project information management in construction: capturing the long-term value creation process. Automation in Construction 13(4), 469–479 (2004)

Thong, J.Y., Yap, C.-S., Raman, K.S.: Engagement of External Expertise in Information Systems Implementation. Journal of Management Information Systems 11(2), 209–231 (1994)

Tukel, O.I., Rom, W.O.: Analysis of the characteristics of projects in diverse industries. Journal of Operations Management 16, 43–61 (1998)

Verner, J., Sampson, J., Cerpa, N.: What factors lead to software project failure? In: Second International Conference on Research Challenges in Information Science, pp. 71–79. RCIS, Marrakech (2008)

Wallace, L., Keil, M., Rai, A.: Understanding software project risk: a cluster analysis. Information &Management 42, 115–125 (2004)

Yeo, K.: Critical failure factors in information system projects. International Journal of Project Management 20, 241–246 (2002)

Tracing Success in the Voluntary Use
of Open Technology in Organisational Setting

Amany Elbanna[1] and Henrik C.J. Linderoth[2,*]

[1] Royal Holloway University of London, School of Management, United Kingdom
Amany.Elbanna@rhul.ac.uk
[2] University of Skövde, School of Technology and Society, Sweden
henrik.linderoth@his.se

Abstract. Explaining success and failure of IT initiatives is a subject with long tradition in the information system field. However, users' drivers and motivation of the adoption of voluntary open-ended technology has been understudied. It is not clear why users would choose to adopt a new voluntary technology and how and why its use options and possibility unfold. In this paper these questions are examined through the analysis of a longitudinal case study (1994-2012) of telemedicine adoption in a northern Swedish county. The findings reveal that it is not sufficient to make an open voluntary technology available for its users, or passively demand them to use the technology. Successful use would occur through a continuous interplay between users' technology mental models and their organisational setting and work practices. When in contradiction with the latter, users would not consider the system and hence its use could fade away. Institutional entrepreneurs who have the ability to imagine new and different possibilities and encourage organisational members to experiment and explore possible use and benefit from the technology could influence the initial mental model.

Keywords: IS-success, IS-use, open technology, mental models, institutional setting, voluntary use, telemedicine.

1 Introduction

The use of information systems in organisations presents one of the early signs of success. Most studies examined the use of systems in organisational setting where this use is mandatory. Mandatory use of systems means the practice of institutional pressure to channel employees to use the system. This could be done through consistently urging employees to use the system (Orlikowski, 1996), do not accept work done outside the system, and/or penalise employees for not using the system (Elbanna, 2010). Examples of mandatory systems are ERP, CRM, Lotus Notes, and e-procurement. Little is known about the use of voluntary systems in organisational setting. Voluntary use of systems in organisational setting means that there is institutional acceptance that a new system provides an alternative way to do the work and it is

---

* Corresponding author.

Y.K. Dwivedi et al. (Eds.): TDIT 2013, IFIP AICT 402, pp. 89–104, 2013.

up to the employee to choose between alternatives. It is not clear why employees would voluntarily choose to use the new system over alternative ways of working.

Information systems research has identified information systems along a continuum from closed systems to open systems (Petter, DeLone and McLean, 2008). Closed systems are systems that are presented to users with prescribed business processes and use cases such as functional systems (finance, marketing, accounting), Enterprise systems (ERP, CRM), and e-commerce systems. Users of closed systems cannot change the system configuration and use cases from their end as they require significant systems re-configuration and programming. On the other hand, open systems come with generic technology in need of use cases and applications development, it is up to users to find use cases and follow them. Examples of open systems in organisational setting include teleconferencing, Lotus Notes, Intranet, Internet. Most of the studies that examined open systems did so in mandatory use organisational setting where users are constantly urged to use the system and standardisation between use cases are considered and required by the organisation (Bhattacherjee, 1998; Damsgaard and Scheepers, 2000). The use of open systems in voluntary use organisational setting has received less attention however it presents an interesting case of organisational investment waiting for possible development of application and use cases. Users' drivers and motivation of the adoption of open technology in voluntary organisational setting along with the adoption process have been understudied.

This study questions how and why users would choose to adopt a new voluntary technology and how and why its use options and possibility unfold. It examines these questions through a longitudinal case study (1994-2012) of telemedicine adoption in a Swedish county that over the years became one of the most successful cases of telemedicine application in a Swedish county. Telemedicine presents an example of an open technology in a voluntary organisational setting. It comprises a video conferencing system to which different optical equipments could be connected. The applications of telemedicine for the daily practices of medical staff and administration are not pre-defined but rather depend on users and their local settings (Linderoth, 2002). Indeed, telemedicine can be regarded as a service in need of use cases (Ekeland, 2007). The study adapt Porac et al (1989) framework of the interaction between the cognitive and material elements.

The following sections of the paper are organized as follows. The second section - after the introduction- provides a brief review of literature. The third section presents the theoretical grounding of the paper and adapted framework. The fourth section outlines the research methods and case description. The fifth section presents the research findings and the final section offers a discussion and conclusion of the study.

2   The Voluntary Use of Technology

Researchers have developed a number of models to explain IS success. Technology Acceptance Model stands as one of the well known models in this regard however it is argued that acceptance is not equivalent to success but a pre-condition of success (Petter, DeLone and McLean, 2006). Delone and Mclean's IS success model and its expansion stand as other well known models in this regard (DeLone and McLean, 1992) (DeLone and McLean, 2003). In these models, DeLone and McLean identified "use" as one of the factors that determine success. It should be noted that information systems use is considered a measure of success only "where use is voluntary" (Lucas, 1981, p. 14).

However, most information systems use studies focus on the mandatory use of systems in organisational setting. Mandatory use is typically assumed to be in organisational setting where institutional power, enforcement, and user resistance exist. In this mandatory use setting, employees do not have the privilege of choosing whether to use the information systems available or not and rarely have the opportunity to select the information systems applications they use (Karahanna and Straub, 1999). When voluntary use is considered, the majority of studies focus nearly exclusively on the individual use of systems as a recent literature survey on the state of ICT research shows (Tscherning and Damsgaard, 2008). The study of the voluntarily use of systems in organisational setting has been overlooked as research has implicitly or explicitly assumed that voluntarily use exists on personal and individual levels and rarely on organisational setting.

As figure 1 shows, there is a spectrum of systems that could be classified under the mandatory-voluntary and open-closed categories. In mandatory open systems, users are required to use the system to conduct business processes and their adoption is monitored. Non-adopters are warned against conducting business processes outside the system and strongly channelled to use the system. Orlikowski (1996) for example observed that the introduction of an open system –in this case a call tracking system for the customer support department at Zeta Corporation - was surrounded by "ongoing urging by managers" for users to use the system (Orlikowski, 1996, p.72). She also reported that the use of the systems was monitored by managers who emphasised to users that "keeping process documentation up to date [through the use of the system] was ...as just as critical or even more important than problem solving [which was the employees' daily tasks in answering clients calls and dealing with their technical problems or enquiries]" (ibid, p.75). On the contrary, in voluntary open systems, the organisation installs the generic system/technology in the hope that users will find applications and use cases for it and use them. There is no particular blue print or prescription for use and there is less urging and monitoring of use since use itself is based on users developing use cases and applications.

Regarding the use of open systems in mandatory organisational setting, research has shown that open-ended technology such as Intranet, e-mail, Lotus Notes, and other groupware technology are malleable at the users' end. Its use in the organisation is characterised by high degree of improvisation and sense-making that challenges the traditional rational and planned technology adoption frameworks (Ciborra, 1996; Orlikowski, 1996; Orlikowski and Hofman, 1995). The study of mandatory open systems provided a fresh look at what has been then new types of technology. Today, newer understanding of use of technology emerged in organisation where organisations are willing to offer open technology to users in order to explore, develop applications, and use cases on voluntary basis. This new type of use should be of interest to IS research if the IT and its use are to be taken seriously (Orlikowski and Iacono, 2001).

In the following section, we argue that in open technology use in voluntary organisational setting, a cognitive sense making approach needs to be complemented by an explicit account of the organisational context.

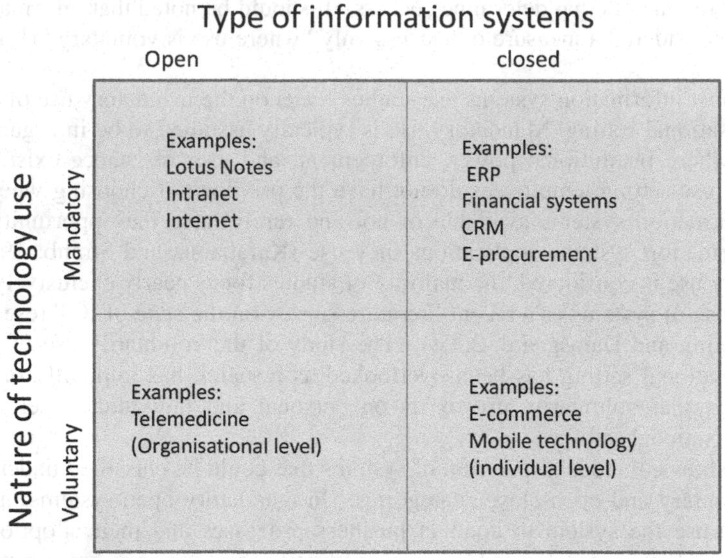

Type of information systems

	Open	closed
Mandatory	Examples: Lotus Notes Intranet Internet	Examples: ERP Financial systems CRM E-procurement
Voluntary	Examples: Telemedicine (Organisational level)	Examples: E-commerce Mobile technology (individual level)

Nature of technology use

Fig. 1. Types of information systems and nature of use

3   Theoretical Grounding: Technology Enactment

Studies of organisational evolvement and learning have highlighted the importance of cognition and action in organisational change (Weick, 1982; Weick, 1995). The concept of enactment was developed in an attempt to understand how shared perceptions come to being through constant feedback loop between the cognition and action where both impact each other. It follows an interpretive approach to understand organisational activities. Porac et. al. (1989) succinctly summarise the four assumptions upon which this interpretive approach rests as: (1) activities and structures of organisations are assumed to be determined in part by the micro-momentary actions of their members; (2) this action is based on an information-processing sequence where individuals attend to cues in the environment, interpret the meaning of these cues, then externalise these interpretations via concrete activities; (3) that individuals construct actively an interpretation by linking received cues with well-learned and/or developing cognitive structures; (4) individuals are assumed to have a reflective capability and ability to verbalise their interpretations (Porac, Thomas and Baden-Fuller, 1989, p.398). Porac et al (1989) study the community of Scottish knitwear makers in Hawek and how they enact their strategic competitive position. They showed that decision-makers construct a mental model of the competitive environment through processes of induction, problem-solving, and reasoning, which consists minimally of two types of beliefs: beliefs about the identity of the firm, its competitors, suppliers and customers, and causal beliefs about what it takes to compete successfully within the environment which has been identified. Figure 2 exhibits this framework.

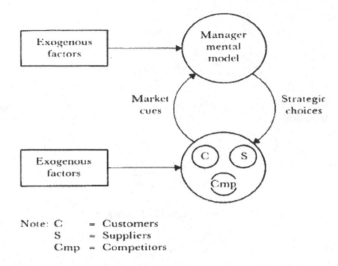

Note: C   = Customers
       S   = Suppliers
       Cmp = Competitors

Fig. 2. Reciprocal influence of the technical and cognitive levels of analysis [Source: Porac et al., 1989, p.399]

While shows that cognition and action reinforces each other, it also shows that mental models are influenced by information exogenous to this transactional network. Just as mental models are determined by cues from transactions within the value chain, such transactions are also determined by the cognitive construction of organisational decision-makers. This figure shows that the material and cognitive aspects of an organisation are linked together in a loosely coupled 'enactment' process where each is determined partly by the other. In this sense, "what human perceivers do is to take whatever scraps they can extract from the stimulus input and if those conform to expectancy, to read the rest from the model in the head" (Bruner, 1986, p.146).

As social theorists invite a view of structure and institutional practices as both process and form (Giddens, 1976; Strauss, 1978), the existing institutional practices as forms could be explicitly included in this framework. Figure 3 shows the study adapted framework that explicitly account for both the users mental models and their institutional setting. This is in line with Jensen et al. (2009) argument of the need to complement sensemaking with elements of the institutional theory to better account for people in their organisation setting.

The concept of enactment has been applied in information systems research (Fountain, 2001; Orlikowski, 1996; Orlikowski, 2000). These studies showed that the organisational push of compulsory information systems could cut through the existing institutional arrangement and urge users to act –positively or negatively- which is a necessary component for the enactment process. However, the question remains why users would change their mental models and enact a different institutional arrangement on a voluntarily basis?

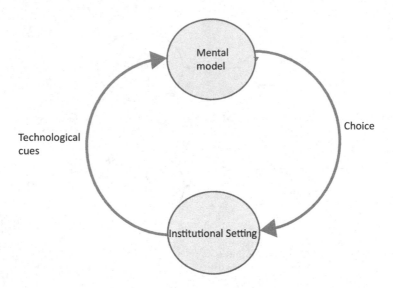

Fig. 3. Technology enactment in organisational setting

4   Research Methods and Setting

4.1   Research Methods

This research belongs to the interpretive tradition of information systems research (Lee and Baskerville, 2003; Walsham, 1995a; Walsham, 1995b). It applies a case study approach to understand the use of telemedicine application over time (Eisenhardt, 1989). Longitudinal data was collected by the corresponding author over a period of 18 years between 1994 and 2012 over three phases. It was based on formal and informal semi-structured interviews, participant observation of project meetings and meetings between project management and equipment suppliers, examination of use records, documents review, and collection of news items. The phases of data collection and methods used are as follows.

The *first phase* took place between 1994 and 1999. In this phase, 62 interviews were carried out with 32 respondents namely; physicians, politicians and managing directors of hospitals. Interviews were carried out on four occasions: in 1996, 1997, 1998 and 1999. Observations of project meetings and also meetings between project management and suppliers started in 1994 before the equipments were purchased and installed in August 1996 and continued throughout this phase. The aim of data collection at this phase was to understand the different expectations of the involved actors' regarding the future deployment of telemedicine technology and how the technology was deployed.

The *Second phase* took place between 2003 and 2006. In this phase, seven formal follow up interviews with physicians and the managers for the telemedicine support unit were undertaken in addition to a number of informal interviews and conversations with teams. In addition, an access to telemedicine use records was obtained and records were examined. The use records contained data from 1650 occasions between June 2003 and January 2006 of telemedicine use. Each time the system was used, the party initiating the interaction needed to fill in some data before s/he could log off the system. Data registered encompassed: date, time, host (who initiate the interaction), connected (who has been contacted), duration of contact, comments and person initiating the contact.

The third phase of data collection took place between 2006 and 2012. It consists of follow up conversations and informal visits in addition to the collection of news items regarding the progress of the use of telemedicine in the County.

4.2   Research Setting

The studied case presents one of the most successful cases of telemedicine application in a Sweden county. It began in the early 1990 when few physicians in the county became interested in the telemedicine technology and in 1994 a group consisting of physicians and a technical director started to identify medical specialties that could be suitable for telemedicine. In autumn 1994, they identified dermatology (skin diseases), orthopaedics, otorhinolaryngology (ear, nose and throat diseases), radiology, pathology, cytology, surgery and gynaecology as appropriate specialties. However, in spring 1995 radiology was dropped out because another project regarding the digitalization of the radiology departments in the county started. During 1995 it was decided that telemedicine equipments should be installed at two remote health centres, at the departments in the university hospital and at two county hospitals and the funding was approved by the county board.

The chosen technical platform was a standalone video conferencing system that could be connected with optical medical equipments. By the connection of optical equipments to the video conferencing system, it was possible for general practitioners to examine patients and transmit pictures, e.g. the ear, or the skin of patients, live or frozen to the specialists. It was also possible to connect a microscope to the equipments for the examination of frozen sections. For example, the microscope that was located at a county hospital could be remotely operated and maneuvered by a pathologist at the university hospital.

Two groups were formed in the implementation phase; general telemedicine group and tele-pathology group. The general telemedicine group (GTE) aimed to develop and test communication between general practitioners at two health centres and specialists at the county hospital, and at the university hospital. The specialties involved were dermatology, orthopaedic, and ENT (ear, nose and throat). The specialists were located at the university hospital, except for the orthopaedists who were located both at the university and a county hospital. The tele-pathology group (PAT) identified two applications namely video conferencing and remote analysis of specimen and aimed to develop and test equipments between health centres, county hospital and university hospital. However project's participants had expected a higher number of consultations, the project was considered successful by the County as it continued to invest in telemedicine equipments. As a result, 40 units of telemedicine equipment were installed at hospital clinics and health centres. As the telemedicine infrastructure was expanded, a support department, named the TeleMedLab, was established in 1999. In January 2006 the telemedicine infrastructure installed in the counties health centres and hospitals has expanded to approximately 70 units and in September 2007 this number went up to over 100 units. In 2012, the county was considered to be the Swedish county with the most developed use of telemedicine by representative from other Swedish counties.

5   Research Findings

In this section a few different applications will be described. The purpose of choosing these applications is to illustrate how the established institutional logic and technology mental models were challenged and how new technology mental models found its way through and were later institutionalised.

5.1   The Need for Institutional Entrepreneurs

The core team of medical specialists who was enthusiastic to implement telemedicine technology was involved with the technical team during the implementation. However once the system went live, it became down to departments to decide whether they can use it and in which cases. The implementation team view was that departments should identify some ideas of initial use in order to get the equipment installed in their clinics. This view was expressed as:

> "...if this [telemedicine] should function, there need to be a demand from the organization, we need to feel that we get something out of it"

The GTE group members realised that telemedicine is not a technology that comes with a prescribed use. It is down to users to either use it or not. Even if they decide to use it, users still need to define and construct their use cases. A general practitioner, who was one of the enthusiasts of telemedicine implementation, expressed this view as follows:

> "You must have fantasy and power of imagination in order to see how this [telemedicine] can be used. If you do everything as before, you do not see any advantage"

The need to find people with imagination and spirit to experiment was, implicitly, recognized by politicians and the managing directors at the hospitals. The managing director at the university hospital stated that development of applications and how to organise the daily activities were matters for the users.

5.2   Institutional Entrepreneur and the Evolvement of Technology Mental Model

In the dermatology department, there was initially no demand for the system as users could not see a reason for using it, but some dermatologist had to use it due to their involvement in the project. Hence, Dermatology did not initially have a telemedicine unit at their clinic. Instead, if they decided to use it, they had to walk through the hospital to the video conferencing studio.

Dermatologist considered their direct contact with patients to be an integral part of their professional identity (Chreim, Williams and Hinings, 2007). This enacted view was expressed by a dermatologist as follows:

> *"We should not be like a radiologist, just looking at a flat picture....you need to touch, feel and smell".*

The necessity of interacting with patients was supported and enforced by the existing institutional financial arrangement that compensate specialists on the basis of the number of patients visiting the practice. The concern of the possible financial loss contributed to the enforcement of the existing mental model that advocates direct interaction with patients. Also the career path including performance evaluation and promotion of physicians were dependant on their research output. Dermatologists viewed research to be dependent on the continuous flow of patients visiting the clinic. Hence they feared that if the numbers of visiting patients drop as a result of using telemedicine, their research will be negatively impacted and hence their performance evaluation and career.

The existing institutional arrangement supported the view that patients had to be seen face-to-face. Hence the initial mental model of most Dermatologist towards telemedicine was that there is no use of such technology. Another medical specialist claimed that the importance of the presence of patients in consultations is overestimated, but preferred not to express this opinion in public. Thus, he was not willing to risk contradicting the institutional professional identity and arrangement.

The understanding of how the technology could be used at the department of dermatology changed slowly as a new dermatologist joined the team. She saw the available telemedicine equipment and became interested in exploring how they could benefit the department. So she started an initiative to experiment with finding possible use cases for the telemedicine equipments. The initiated experiment identified classes of patients and consultations that could be done through the system.

At that time, there was a shortage of staff at the dermatology clinic at a district hospital 140 km away from the university hospital. This shortage of staff required that university hospital staff had to rotate between them a weekly visit to the district hospital. This weekly visit was considered to be a tiring trip and undesired task. It required a member of staff from the university hospital dermatology department to take the bus at the very early morning for a two-hours journey to the district hospital once a week to meet and examine patients the whole day and in the late afternoon spend another two hours by the bus in his/her way back journey. However this duty was rotating among dermatologists and was also compensated with one day off, it was not a popular task. The dermatologist who soon became the head of the department presented the findings of the experiment to other dermatologists as a possible solution that could save them the long bus journey to the district hospital. This solution was then welcomed by dermatologists as it could ease the burden of waking up at 4.30 in the morning to take the bus. Dermatologists became involved in the discussion regarding what kind of patients were appropriate for telemedicine examinations and the possible procedures to be followed when using the equipments. It was agreed that the nurse at the district hospital could take photos of the patients' skin, send them to the university hospital where the dermatologist examines the photos while the nurse is with the patient.

The remote examination of dermatology patients was successful as dermatologist in the university hospital announced that they will never commute again to the district hospital. As the nurse at the district hospital who was involved at the experiment retired few years later, the new nurse considered telemedicine consultations to be part of the definition of her role and the routine regarding how patients should be treated. Thus, the mental model regarding telemedicine use changed at the dermatology clinic from being very sceptical of telemedicine consultations in the first few years to be one of the enthusiasts of using the technology. Dermatology became one of the heaviest users 10 years later.

5.3   Contradiction between the Technology Mental Model and the Institutional Practices

In the GTE group, there was low number of ad hoc consultations from health centres to university hospitals. Initially the health centre saw telemedicine as an opportunity to get hold of university specialists on ad hoc basis. However soon, GPs at the health centres found out that despite the technical possibility of telemedicine to connect with university hospital, the institutional arrangements at the university hospitals made it difficult to find specialists on ad hoc basis. They also found out that ad hoc consultation does not mean instant consultation as university hospitals' specialists still need time to operate the equipments.

This view was expressed by a general practitioner at the health centre as follows:

> "It is the accessibility [of clinical specialists] that makes it complicated, the system is not complicated....If I should try to reach someone who is not accessible, s/he should be searched for, and then they cannot handle the equipment and do not know what to, suddenly an hour is gone"

The health centres mental model regarding using telemedicine as a mean for immediate access to medical specialists contradicted the institutional barriers between university hospitals and health centres and the professional status of university hospitals specialists and hence was met with cynicism from university hospitals specialists. This view was expressed by a general practitioner as follows:

> "Suddenly is the primary care is coming and putting demands on the hospital care, to for example develop routines for managing incoming consultations from the primary care....or to develop services for the primary care"

5.4   Enacting Existing Organizational Routines

Contrary to the GTE-project, laboratory specialists involved in the PAT project had in mind from the beginning one application which was to organise clinical conferences via telemedicine between the clinic of gynaecology at the district hospitals and pathologists and oncologists at the university hospital. The clinical conferences application became - over the years - the major application of telemedicine in the county.

The practice of having a weekly professional meeting for specialists at university hospitals is a well established professional and institutional practice. It aims to provide weekly encounters for all levels of specialist doctors and students to discuss and learn from different cases. The organisational routines of university hospitals provided mechanisms for these meetings to take place on regular basis as they are considered important weekly events for mentorship and competency development and part of what makes a university hospital. So when introduced to telemedicine, Pathologists at the university hospital immediately found a use case that is in line with the existing practices, professional convention and organisational routine –namely clinical conferences. They approached the use of telemedicine clinical conferences as an extension of the current practices and routine that ensure providing quality learning environment. This provided the participating gynaecologists at the district hospitals with perceived value of participating in these conferences.

While Pathologists at the university hospital used the conferences as competencies development opportunity for gynaecologists, gynaecologists' mental model of pathology conferences evolved from being a mean for competence development to an integrated part of their operations and decision making. Gynaecologists' mental model evolved to consider it an opportunity to discuss patients' cases with pathologists and take decisions accordingly. It became common to hear gynaecologists discussing a patient case saying: "*Let's wait to the conference until we decide on further treatment*", the head of the gynaecology department said. Specialist found these conferences as a way to diagnose difficult cases where a patient diagnosis could be changed during a conference due to additional information that was coming up.

Telemedicine clinical conferences soon became part of the routine activities, and the application was adopted at another county hospital. The organisational routine and arrangement for preparing and conducting clinical conferences was adopted and extended to telemedicine application. For example, conferences were held at the same time and same day every week, and detailed routines were set up for how to report a case that should be discussed at the conference.

5.5   Contesting the Existing Mental Model of Time

The PAT project management suggested from the beginning another application for telemedicine which was tele-pathology meaning the immediate analysis and reply on frozen specimen/sections. In this application, a microscope for the examination of the frozen sections was located at the county hospital but was manoeuvred by the pathologists and cytologists at the university hospital. The aim of the application is to speed up the analysis and give surgeons a reply within few minutes regarding the nature of the sample. This application was not put in any significant use and soon faded away.

Surgeons at the county hospital who should use the technology for urgent answers on frozen section were sceptical if they could trust the results because the method was not scientifically validated. The method was later scientifically validated by the management of the PAT-project and the findings showed that there were no significant differences between the traditional way of diagnosing frozen sections and diagnosing via tele-pathology. However, surgeons continued to be disinterested in this application. The speed of receiving the reply back was in sharp contrast with the previous routine of sending a sample of suspicious tumour while operating to the lab and receiving the results days after the operation. Surgeons found it difficult to mentally prepare in such a short period to convey a serious message to a patient that could confirm the existence of cancer in his/her body. They also found it inconvenient to know the results of analysis while operating and preferred to continue to leave the results to a later stage following the current professional practices. Concerns were also raised about how the patients would react if they were given the answer "cancer" half an hour after a section had been taken. The surgeons felt ambivalent towards the speed of results that this application provided which was in sharp contradiction with professional practices and also the procedures of giving patients feedback.

6   Discussion and Conclusion

This paper questioned why would users choose to adopt a new voluntary technology and how and why does its use options and possibility unfolds? To answer these question a longitudinal case study (1994-2012) of one of the most successful counties' in Sweden in its use of telemedicine systems was examined.

The findings show that in the voluntary use of open technology, users' initial mental model develops based on the existing institutional arrangements, routines, and definition of professional identity (institutional logic for short). This is in line with other studies on technology frames, sense making and mental models (Davidson, 2002; Davidson and Pai, 2004; Orlikowski and Gash, 1994). If the technology is found to be in line with the latter users will be likely to develop a positive mental model regarding the technology. They would readily incorporate it into the current organisational fabric and include it in the existing organisational routine. This was the case with clinical conferences. The practice of clinical conferences and providing weekly opportunity for professional development constituted part of the existing professional identity of specialists at university hospitals. They were also aligned to the existing routine of scheduling and preparing for these events. So university staff readily developed a positive technology mental model and used it to conduct clinical conferences with the health centres following the existing institutional arrangement and routine. For district hospital staff, this was considered a good learning opportunity that brought them up to the university hospital practices and hence developed a positive mental model and were eager to adopt similar organisational routine and arrangement.

In addition, the study shows that on a voluntary use basis when the technology is perceived to be in contradiction with the institutional arrangements, routines, and existing definition of professional identity, users would not show much interest in the technology and might exclude it from the outset as an alternative to do their work. The use of technology could then fade away. In this case, the existence of an institutional entrepreneur could help users to imagine new possibilities and other ways of working. Institutional entrepreneurs can also contextualise the use of the new technology and help users to find use cases.

The study also shows that institutional entrepreneurs present an exogenous factor that could influence the users' technology mental model through imagining, suggesting, and inviting the thinking of new possibilities and ways of working. This is in line with previous research on organisation studies that suggest that institutional entrepreneurs have the capacity to imagine alternative possibilities and the ability to contextualise past habits with the contingencies of the moment (Emirbayer and Mische, 1998; Garud, Hardy and Maguire, 2007). This was the case with the dermatologists. The new dermatologist acted as institutional entrepreneur and initiated an experiment to explore the possibility to diagnose patients of the district hospitals. As users became involved, they identified patients with chronic disease to be suitable for telemedicine interaction. Organizational routine and new procedures had to be developed to align with the shift of dermatologists' mental model. With the change in staff, the new mental model became an organizational reality and an established way of dealing with patients with chronic disease.

While Porac et al. (1989) framework has been used in another research (Elbanna, 2012), it is the explicit consideration of the role of institutional elements in the development and enactment of users' technology mental models that presents one of the contributions of this study. Figure 4 shows that in the use of open technology in voluntary organisational setting, the technology mental model and organisations routines feed into each other; a change in one would trigger changes in the other. By drawing on the perceived current problems and what is done in other use cases, the institutional entrepreneur provides initial possibilities to apply the technology in the organisational context and infuse an experimentation spirit around it. The choice of applying the technology is then tested against other mental models originating from institutional logics and routines in the users' contexts. In case where chosen applications of the technology are well aligned with the institutional logic and routines in the user's context, technology use becomes an integrated part of the mental model. i.e. prevailing mental models are challenged to a very low degree. If the chosen application challenges the mental models and interfere with an established institutional logic, technology use will be seen as something that is causing problems more than solving problems in the users' context. However the existence of other use cases and peers approval could send cues that change the mental model.

As users perceive that the use of the new technology is solving a problem or improving practices, users will shift to a new mental model where technology becomes an integral part of what they do. Therefore, managers and practitioners need to chase the changes in perception through changes in organisational routine and procedures. As the medical profession is highly regulated by strict code of practice and protocols, new procedures need to be developed and written once changes of understanding occur (Linderoth, 2002).

In mandatory use organisational setting, users could be under pressure and significant stress (Wastell and Newman, 1993). In contrast, in voluntary use organisational setting, users are invited to explore and experiment without pre-conceived ideas or blueprint for use. Users need to imagine new possibilities for doing the work and ways to use the technology is particularly important in open voluntary technology. Urquhart (1997) in her study regarding users-developer interactions during requirements determination had also identified imagination as a pattern of interaction tactics (Urquhart, 1997). The role of imagination and how it could be infused is in need of further investigation. Researchers are invited to follow up from this study to examine it in-depth.

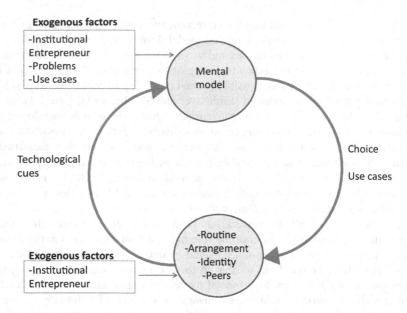

Fig. 4. The cycle of enacting open technology in voluntary organisational setting

Contrary to the existence of a window of opportunity for users to change the implemented systems after which the system will be stabilised (Tyre and Orlikowski, 1991), in the voluntary use organisational setting, finding use cases and applications is an on-going process of innovation. It requires imagination and thinking of possibilities and is triggered by the availability of equipments.

The nature of systems use in their organisational setting and where its use could be located in the possible voluntary - mandatory continuum has been largely overlooked (Petter et al., 2008). Indeed, studies that examined voluntary use did so through studying university students or making the participation of the study itself voluntary (Moez, Hirt and Cheung, 2007; Weill and Olson, 1989). This study presented a case study of voluntary use in its organisational setting. In doing so, it contributes to the understanding of voluntary technology in organisational setting.

In conclusion, it is not sufficient to make an open-ended voluntary technology available for its users, or passively demand them to use the technology. Successful use would occur through a continuous interplay between mental models, actions and organisational elements. Hence ideas of use could be suggested to understand initial impediments that management need to reduce, institutional entrepreneurs need to actively find use cases, compare experiences, and initiate debate while experimentation and exploration are invited and encouraged.

References

Bhattacherjee, A.: Management of Emerging Technologies Experiences and Lessons Learned at US West. Information and Management 33, 263–272 (1998)

Bruner, J.S.: Actual Minds, Possible Worlds. Harvard University Press, Cambridge (1986)

Chreim, S., Williams, B.E.B., Hinings, C.R.B.: Interlevel Influences on the Recon-struction of Professional Role Identity. Academy of Management Journal 50(6), 1515–1539 (2007)

Ciborra, C.U.: What Does Groupware Mean for the organizations hosting it? In: Ciborra, C.U. (ed.) Groupware and Team Work: Invisible Aid or Technical Hindrance. John Wiey, Chichester (1996)

Damsgaard, J., Scheepers, R.: Managing the Crises in Intranet Implementation: a stage model. Information Systems Journal 10(2), 131–149 (2000)

Davidson, E.J.: Technology frames and framing: A socio-cognitive investigation of require-ments determination. MIS Quarterly, 329–358 (2002)

Davidson, E.J., Pai, D.: Making sense of technological frames: Promise, progress, and poten-tial. Information Systems Research, 473–491 (2004)

DeLone, W.D., McLean, E.R.: The DeLone and McLean Model of Information Systems Suc-cess: A Ten-Year Update. Journal of Management Information Systems 19(4), 9–30 (2003)

DeLone, W.H., McLean, E.R.: Information Systems Success: The quest for the dependent variable. Information Systems Research 3(1), 60–95 (1992)

Elbanna, A.: Making Business Sense Of Ambiguous Technology: The Case Of Second Life. In: European Conference of Information Systems Barcelona, Barcelona (2012), http://aisel.aisnet.org/ecis2012/52

Elbanna, A.R.: From intention to use to actual rejection: the journey of an e-procurement sys-tem. Journal of Enterprise Information Management 23(1), 81–99 (2010)

Emirbayer, M., Mische, A.: What Is Agency? American Journal of Sociology 103(4), 962–1023 (1998)

Fountain, J.E.: Building the Virtual State - InformationTechnology and Institutional Change. The Brookings Institution, Washinghton (2001)

Garud, R., Hardy, C., Maguire, S.: Institutional entrepreneurship as embedded agency. Organi-zation Studies 28(7), 957 (2007)

Giddens, A.: New Rules of Sociological Method. Hutchinson, London (1976)

Jensen, T.B., Kjærgaard, A., Svejvig, P.: Using institutional theory with sensemaking theory: a case study of information system implementation in healthcare. Journal of Information Technology 24(4), 343–353 (2009)

Karahanna, E., Straub, D.W.: The Psychological Origins of Perceived Usefulness and Ease of Use. Information & Management 35, 237–250 (1999)

Lee, A.S., Baskerville, R.L.: Generalizing Generalizability in Information Systems Research. Information Systems Research 14(3), 221–243 (2003)

Linderoth, H.C.: Fiery spirits and supporting programs of action - Keys to exploration and exploitation of open technologies. International Journal of Healthcare Technology and Man-agement 4(3/4), 319–332 (2002)

Lucas, H.C.J.: Implementation: the key to successful information systems. Columbia University Press, New York (1981)

Moez, L., Hirt, S.G., Cheung, C.M.: How habit limits the predictive power of inten-tion: The case of information systems continuance. MIS Quarterly 31(4), 705–737 (2007)

Orlikowski, W.J.: Improvising Organisational Transformation Over Time: a situated change perspective. Information Systems Research 7(1), 63–92 (1996)

Orlikowski, W.J.: Using Technology and Constituting Structures: A practice lens for studying technology in organisations. Organization Science 11(4), 404–428 (2000)

Orlikowski, W.J., Gash, D.C.: Technological frames: making sense of information technology in organizations. ACM Transactions on Information Systems 12(2), 174–207 (1994)

Orlikowski, W.J., Hofman, J.D.: Realizing The Potential of Groupware Technologies: An improvisational strategy for change management. Massachusetts Institute of Technology, Cambridge (1995)

Orlikowski, W.J., Iacono, C.S.: Research commentary: Desperately seeking the "it" in it research-a call to theorizing the it artifact. Information Systems Research 12 (2), 121–134 (2001)

Petter, S., DeLone, W., McLean, E.: Measuring Information Systems Success: Models, dimensions, measures, and interrelationships. European Journal of Information Systems 17, 236–263 (2006)

Petter, S., DeLone, W., McLean, E.: Measuring information systems success: models, dimensions, measures, and interrelationships. European Journal of Information Systems 17(3), 236–263 (2008)

Porac, J.F., Thomas, H., Baden-Fuller, C.: Competitive Groups as Cognitive Com-munities: The case of Scottish knitwear manufacturers. Journal of Management Studies 26(4), 397–416 (1989)

Strauss, A.: Negotiations. Jossey-Bass, San Francisco (1978)

Tscherning, H., Damsgaard, J.: Understanding the Diffusion and Adoption of Telecommunication Innovations: What we know and what we don't know. In: Leon, G., Bernados, A.M., Casar, J.R., Kautz, K., DeGross, J.I. (eds.) Open IT-Based Inno-vation: Moving Towards Cooperative IT Transfer and Knowledge Diffusion. IFIP AICT, vol. 287, pp. 39–60. Springer, Boston (2008)

Tyre, M.J., Orlikowski, W.J.: Windows of Opportunity: Creating occasions for technological adaptation in organizations, Center for Information Systems Research, Sloan School of Management, pp. 1–42. MIT (1991)

Urquhart, C.: Exploring Analyst-Client Interaction Communication: Using Grounded Theory techniques to Investigate Interaction in Informal Requirements Gathering. In: Lee, A.S., Liebenau, J., DeGross, J. (eds.) Information Systems and Qualitative Research, pp. 149–181. Chapman & Hall, London (1997)

Walsham, G.: The Emergence of Interpretivism in IS Research. Information Systems Research 6(4), 376–394 (1995a)

Walsham, G.: Interpretive Case Studies in IS research: Nature and method. European Journal of Information Systems (4), 74–81 (1995b)

Wastell, D., Newman, M.: The behavioral dynamics of information system develop-ment: A stress perspective. Accounting, Management and Information Technologies 3(2), 121–148 (1993)

Weick, K.E.: Enactment Processes in Organizations. In: Staw, B.S., GR (eds.) New Directions in Organizational Behavior, Robert E. Krieger, Malabar (1982)

Weick, K.E.: Sensemaking in Organizations. Sage, Thousand Oaks (1995)

Weill, P., Olson, M.H.: An assessment of the contingency theory of management information systems. Journal of Management Information Systems 6(1), 59–85 (1989)

Market Separations Perspective of Agricultural Markets and Successful AMIS: Beyond Technical Rationality

Laxmi Gunupudi and Rahul De'

Indian Institute of Management Bangalore
Bannerghatta Road, Bangalore - 560076
{gunupudi.laxmi10,rahul}@iimb.ernet.in

Abstract. Agriculture is an important economic activity and is a primary driver of economic growth of many developing countries. Improving the performance and profitability of agricultural markets will lead to the growth of the agricultural sector. Information and Communication Technologies (ICT) based Agricultural Market Information Systems (AMIS) is a development initiative which promises to empower the stakeholders of the agricultural supply chain with information and aid the development of the agricultural sector. Many attempts have been made by governments in a number of developing countries to provide AMIS, with a poor success rate. It is important to understand the factors that determine the success or failure of these systems. In this paper we take the theoretical lens provided by Bartels' theory of market separations in order to define the success of AMIS. Using a technical/rational view, we conduct a two level analysis of market separations – those in agricultural markets and those in AMIS services markets. We find that information separation is a strong feature that exists in agricultural markets and AMIS provide good means of reducing this separation. Success of AMIS is defined by the reduction of market separations at both these levels. Later we go beyond technical rationality and note that socio-political issues limit the utilization of market information provided by AMIS. Thus we state that socio-political separation of agricultural markets must also be tackled in order to successfully implement AMIS. A comprehensive policy environment in a region can help reduce these separations.

Keywords: Market Separations, AMIS, ICT.

1 Introduction

Socio-economic and industrial development of any nation depends upon the growth in its agricultural sector. It is particularly true in the case of developing countries, where a large percentage of the population lives in rural areas and agriculture is their primary occupation (Ogen, 2007). This sector drives the growth of the economy by meeting food requirements and providing raw materials to industries and by generating employment and earning foreign exchange.

Agricultural produce is traded in agricultural markets. Agricultural marketing spans across numerous activities covering all the services involved in moving an

Y.K. Dwivedi et al. (Eds.): TDIT 2013, IFIP AICT 402, pp. 105–120, 2013.

agricultural produce from the farm to the consumer such as planning production, growing and harvesting, grading, packing, transport, storage, agro- and food processing, distribution, advertising and sale. In developing countries, traditional agricultural markets function poorly. Market information systems can provide a means to reduce the inefficiencies and power inequalities that exist in these markets(Shepherd, 1997; Gunupudi & De, 2011). Proliferations of ICT-based AMIS can help in achieving economic efficiency, performance and equity in these markets. They empower various stakeholders in the agricultural supply chain with information about different markets. This can help in correcting large scale imperfections that exist in rural and unorganized markets, thereby making them more efficient and productive (Abraham & Rueben, 2008). Information from these systems has been posited to benefit all the stakeholders of the sector. Farmers take better decisions with regards to choice of markets, arbitrage, and production planning. Traders benefit from lower costs of gathering information. Government and policy makers take informed decisions about food security planning and policy (Islam & Gronlund, 2010).

Though many attempts have been made by a number of governments to provide Agricultural Market Information Services (AMIS), the success rate is poor. In this paper, we take both development and Information Systems (IS) perspectives to understand the factors that determine the success of AMIS. The focus of the development perspective is on improving the efficiency and performance of agricultural markets. The IS perspective deals with implementing an efficient and usable system that provides useful and reliable information to the stakeholders. Diversity has been an implicit and dominant theme in IS research and theories from several reference disciplines have contributed to theoretical foundations of IS discipline (Benbasat & Weber, 1996). Given the context of markets, we borrow the theory of market separations from the marketing discipline to understand the functioning of agricultural markets. We take the developmental perspective to understand the separations in agricultural markets and the IS perspective to understand the separations in AMIS services markets. In the following section we take a look at the functioning of agricultural markets in developing countries.

2   Agricultural Markets in Developing Countries

Markets represent the meeting space for demand and supply of commodities. In economic terms it is any structure meant for exchange of goods, services and information between buyers and sellers. Market prices are a reflection of demand-supply equations, production costs and marketing costs.

Economies of many developing countries are heavily dependent on agricultural sector and allied activities (Ogen, 2007) (in India, for instance, agriculture and allied activities contribute about 30% of Gross Domestic Product). Agricultural produce is traded in agricultural markets. In developing countries, traditional agricultural markets function poorly and homogeneous goods sold at different locations do not have the same prices (net of transportation costs) (Shepherd, 1997). In 2007, World Bank has given top priority for improving market efficiency as a part of the agriculture-for-development agenda. They believe that the context of failed markets determines the livelihood of people in rural areas in developing countries and that secured and sustained agricultural growth is only possible when markets function properly (WorldBank, 2008). To understand the functioning of agricultural markets in developing countries, we look at the situation in India in the next section.

2.1 Functioning of Agricultural Markets in India

Agricultural marketing is primarily concerned with buying and selling of agricultural products. Let us consider the case of Indian agricultural markets. In the earlier days when the village economy was more or less self-sufficient, each neighbourhood had its own designated location where buyers and sellers engaged in trade, without the presence of a strong institution and the farmer sold his produce to the consumer on a cash or barter basis. Today's agricultural marketing has to undergo several exchanges before it reaches the consumer in the form of assembling, preparation for consumption and distribution. Sale of agricultural produce depends upon the demand for the product at that time, availability of storage etc. The products may be sold directly in the market or it may be stored locally for the time being. Moreover, it may be sold as it is gathered from the field or it may be cleaned, graded and processed by the farmer or the merchant of the village. Distribution system must ensure the balance between the supply with the existing demand by wholesaling and retailing in various points of different markets like primary, secondary or terminal (Biswas, 2011).

Farmers, small and large traders, Government and policy makers are the major stakeholders of these agricultural markets. Farmers sell their produce to traders in the markets. Small traders trade in few mandis and they buy products from farmers and sell them to the wholesaler. Large traders trade at a number of markets. They have their own information networks. These traders invest in storage and transportation facilities and take advantage of both spatial and temporal arbitrage. This prevents the entry of small traders to the markets. Government has an important role to monitor differences in prices at which famers and retailers sell their products in various markets to check for inefficiencies. Policy makers are responsible for making policies with regard to food security. They have to identify early warnings of food shortages and manage food security reserves (Helder & Nyhoff, 1994). They also have to be alert to the traders' association's lobbying activities.

Indian Government has framed some salient policies for efficient functioning of agricultural markets (Thomas, 2003). "Primary commodities" were defined, for which the government sets a minimum support price (MSP). A farmer can sell his produce to the government if the market price falls much below the MSP. Formal agricultural commodities markets are restricted to localized wholesale markets called *mandis* where the price of these commodities is determined. In mandis traders purchase commodities from farmers and then auction and sell these commodities to wholesalers. If the prices of these commodities go below MSP, traders have to purchase the commodities at MSP and they are later compensated by the mandis for the price differential. Only those traders with a license from the mandi can buy and sell commodities at the mandi. Mandis collect a market fee from the traders. Commodity prices are determined by a process of auction which happens at a fixed time at each mandi. As each lot is auctioned, a new price is set.

2.2   Agricultural Market Information Systems (AMIS)

Agricultural Market Information System (AMIS) is defined as "*A service, usually operated by the public sector, which involves the collection on a regular basis of information on prices and in some cases, quantities of widely traded agricultural products from rural assembly markets, wholesale and retail markets, as appropriate, and dissemination of this information on a timely and regular basis through various media to farmers, traders, government officials, policy makers and others including customers.*"(Shepherd, 1997)

It is a system that links information from various agricultural markets across the country and provides the same to the various stakeholders. It involves the usage of ICT, such as the internet and mobile phones, in co-ordination with mass media like radio, newspaper and television along with blackboard displays and public addressing systems at the market place. The idea is to provide a reliable information network for data collection and information dissemination. Prior research has investigated the spread and use of AMIS in least developed countries in terms of users, management, funding, infrastructure and data (Islam & Gronlund, 2010). Their findings show that data collection and information dissemination are two major activities involved in providing AMIS.

The systems provide current and up-to-date information on prices and market conditions such as transportation details and weather conditions based on raw data collected. They also gathers data over time and provide useful analysis regarding seasonal price trends, market trends, forecasts and comparative analysis of prices across markets.

These systems can be classified based on the ownership, technology used and coverage. Ownership of these systems varies from state-run market information systems to privately managed ones and also public-private ownership arrangements where the initiative is taken up by semi-government organizations or by partnership between government and private agencies. Technology used can be traditional like the newspapers, bulletin boards or price boards at the markets; semi-modern like television and radio; modern like internet and mobile phones. Coverage varies from being local which is restricted to a particular region or state to national where the information dissemination happens across the country.

AMIS provides numerous benefits to its stakeholders. *Spatial arbitrage* is the process of exchange of commodities taking advantage of price differences across markets which exceed the transaction costs (of operating in those markets) and *temporal arbitrage* is the process of exchange of commodities taking advantage of price differences over time. Current information is generally useful for spatial arbitrage and historic information is useful for temporal arbitrage. With the availability of information, farmers can take advantage of both spatial and temporal arbitrage. Analysis of this current and historic data helps in identifying trends which can further help farmers in taking decisions on production planning (Shepherd, 1997). Knowledge of prevailing market prices can help farmers negotiate with the traders from a position of relative strength. Depending on customer preferences and demand (reflected in price information), they may even improve the quality and presentation of their product. Analysis of market and price trends from AMIS can help them make informed decisions on the quality and quantity of their produce. They may change their marketing plans and may even take advantage of group marketing (Holtzman & al., 1993). Large traders can reduce their investment on private information networks and make use of their storage capacities to benefit from temporal arbitrage. Many new small traders may enter the markets with the availability of market information (Shepherd, 1997). Government can make use of reliable market information to evaluate market performance and to identify macro economic constraints (Evans & Lynton, 1997). Policy makers can get early warnings of food shortages and use forecast data for production planning and for managing food security reserves (Evans & Lynton, 1997). Customers can also negotiate with traders better with the available information.

3   Theory of Market Separations

Bartels' theory of market separations (Bartels, 1968) describes four kinds of separations between the consumers and producers that impact exchange and consumption of agricultural products. Markets can function efficiently when these separations are reduced. The four kinds of separations are described as follows:

- **Spatial** – Consumers and producers are separated by physical distances.
- **Temporal** – Consumers and producers are separated by time difference between the production and consumption of goods.
- **Informational** – Consumers and producers are separated by knowledge of products and market conditions.
- **Financial** – Consumers and producers are separated by lack of purchasing power at the time of need.

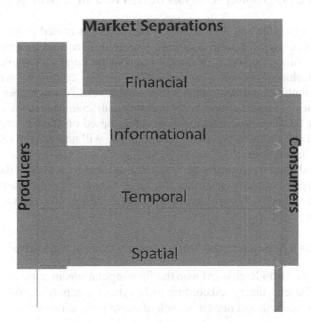

Fig. 1. Market Separations from Bartels' Theory

These separations (as illustrated in Figure 1) prevent successful market transactions between the producers and consumers. The strength and impact of each of these separations depends upon the social context of the markets (Bartels, 1968). This theory has been used in IS research earlier to analyze the role of Information and Communication Technologies (ICTs) in development at the Bottom of the Pyramid (BOP) (Tarafdar & Singh, 2011). In the next section we will briefly explain the research objective and methodology.

4   Research Question and Methodology

In this paper, we would like to take the market separations perspective to understand the functioning of agricultural markets in developing countries and the role of ICTs in bridging these separations. Given the context, this theory is appropriate in understanding the inefficiencies of agricultural markets. We would like to address the research question: *How can AMIS systems be designed to close the separations in markets for agricultural commodities in developing countries?*

We primarily rely on published literature on agricultural markets and design of AMIS. This is a conceptual paper based on prior research, where we provide a new theoretical lens for evaluating market information systems from both a developmental and IS perspective. We also look at some field studies to support our argument.

In the following sections we take up a detailed analysis of these markets and associated IS using the theoretical lens of market separations theory.

5   Technical/Rational Analysis of Agricultural Markets and AMIS

The body of knowledge based on technical rationality is rooted in the normative research paradigm concerned with systematic reasoning, decision making, and governing of practice through methods, techniques and technologies (Avgerou & McGrath, 2007). Using technical rationality as our driver, in this section, we will take up the analysis of agricultural markets and AMIS at two levels. At the higher level we map the inefficiencies of agricultural markets in developing countries to the market separations that exist between producers and consumers based on Bartels' theory. Here the goods of exchange are the agricultural products. We will analyze the role of AMIS in reducing these separations.

At the second level we consider the services provided by AMIS as the goods of exchange and map the market separations that exist between the providers of these services and the consumers. We will look at the AMIS design process which can reduce these separations.

5.1   AMIS as a Solution to the Market Separations in Agricultural Markets

In this section we will identify and map the four separations in agricultural markets as identified by Bartels' theory. According to his theory, depending on the context of application, the strength and impact of each of these separations vary.

In the context of agricultural markets, the producers are farmers who want to sell their agricultural products in the markets. They represent the supply side in the equation. Consumers are those people who are in need of and are willing to purchase the agricultural produce for consumption. They represent the demand side. Market prices of the products are reflective of the demand and supply.

The following is the analysis of agricultural markets on the basis of FAO's bulletin (Food and Agricultural Organization of the United Nations (Shepherd, 1997)) along the lines of market separations theory:

- **Spatial:** This separation occurs when producers are unaware of the demand for their produce in markets other than their regular trading market and consumers are unaware of the availability of the product of their choice in other markets. Market prices are indicative of demand and supply. Market price information from various markets and availability of transportation facilities can help reduce this separation. Farmers can transport their produce to the markets where there is demand and take advantage of spatial arbitrage.

- **Temporal:** This separation occurs when the producers are unaware of the demand and price trends for their produce. This happens under certain conditions when demand and supply are out of phase and demand lags supply. Availability of information on historical price and demand trends and their analysis to forecast demand can help farmers take decisions about storage of their produce to take advantage of temporal arbitrage and thereby reduce temporal market separation.

- **Financial:** This separation occurs when buyers do not have purchasing power at the time when they have willingness or need to buy. This happens when producers do not have the information on demand for their produce at the time of sale. Again, information on demand cycles for their produce and forecasts about the same can help farmers plan their production and reduce financial market separation.

- **Informational:** This separation occurs as a result of differential information held by producers and consumers on product prices and market conditions. This can be considered as an outcome of information asymmetries that exist in agricultural markets. Information asymmetry is defined *"as a situation where some party in a transaction benefits from having preferential access to information"* (Stiglitz, 2002). George Akerlof, Michael Spence and Joseph E. Stiglitz were awarded the Nobel Prize in the year 2001 in Economics for their study of markets with information asymmetry. Traders have preferential access to information in this context and they benefit from this advantage. They manipulate the information that both producers and consumers have in order to gain this advantage.

The following table summarizes the four market separations in agricultural markets and their possible solutions.

Table 1. Market Separations in Agricultural Markets

Market Separations in Agricultural Markets		
Market Separation	**Underlying Cause**	**Possible Solution**
Spatial	Producers unaware of demand and consumers unaware of supply in different markets	Provision of Market price information and transportation facilities.
Temporal	Demand and suppply out of phase and demand lags supply	Provision of information on price trends and access to storage facilities.
Financial	Demand supply mismacth resulting from improper production planning	Provision of information on demand and price trends for production planning
Informational	Lack of information on market prices and market conditions	Provision of information on market prices and market conditions

From the analysis of the above separations, we can easily conclude that solving the problem of informational separation will also reduce the other separations in the context of agricultural markets. Availability of information on market conditions and prices across the region or state will help producers plan their production and take advantage of spatial and temporal arbitrage.

This can be illustrated as shown in Figure 2.

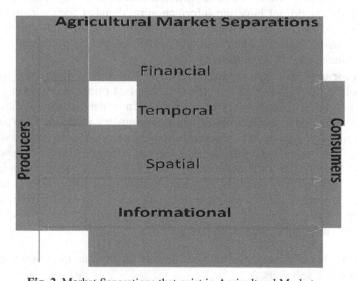

Fig. 2. Market Separations that exist in Agricultural Markets

AMIS provides both current information and analysis of historic data. Current information will help producers and consumers in reducing the spatial and informational separations. Demand and price trends and forecasts from the analysis of historic data will help producers plan their production or store their produce thereby reducing temporal and financial separations.

5.2   Market Separations Perspective of AMIS Services and AMIS Design

Considering the services provided by AMIS as the goods of exchange, in this section we map the market separations that exist between the providers of these services and the consumers.

In this case, providers of these services who are responsible for collection of raw data from markets and dissemination of information are the producers. They represent the supply side. Stakeholders of agricultural markets who are interested in the information being provided by these services are the consumers and they represent the demand side.

Prior work on AMIS (Gunupudi & De, 2011) has come up with some guidelines for designing AMIS for economic sustainability and effectiveness. Their guidelines define the processes for data collection and information dissemination. Following is the analysis of AMIS service market separations and possible design solutions for reducing these separations based on the above guidelines.

- **Spatial** – This market separation occurs when consumers are not able to access information from AMIS. In order to reduce this separation, AMIS must aim to reach target audience through locally available and accessible modes of information dissemination. Full-time, trained, data collectors must ensure that up-to-date and reliable data is collected. The focus must not be on technological sophistication of medium of information dissemination, but on provision of accurate and consistent information to a wide target audience (Shepherd, 1997).

- **Temporal** – This market separation occurs when consumers do not have information on historical prices or demand trends and are unable to forecast prices and demand. This separation can be reduced by providing extension services where one can obtain information on demand and price trends, price forecasts, crop patterns and other related aspects. Information from these services must help target audience take important decisions. Mobile phone services have been identified in prior research as a good means of providing these extension services(Davis, 2008).

- **Financial** – This market separation occurs when consumers are not in a position to afford the services provided by AMIS. To reduce this separation, during the design phase, broadcasting charges and sponsors should be identified and economically sustainable modes of dissemination must be chosen. Basic information such as market prices and market conditions which constitute current information must be provided free to all the target audience and extension services which provide information on price trends and forecasts must be provided on a pay-per-use basis. This will ensure that the services provided are equitable and at the same time ensure the economic sustainability of the system, thus reducing financial market separations in this context (Dinar, 1996).

- **Informational** – This market separation is a result of consumers' ignorance of available AMIS services and their access procedures. AMIS design must ensure that consumers are aware of all the available services on AMIS. Design must aim to increase the perceived value of these services. Offering training courses to farmers on the usage of these services (Singh, 2006) is a good way of reducing this markets separation. Field workers can also help people interpret the information received from these services.

These separations in AMIS services markets are summarized in the following table (Table 2).

Table 2. Market Separations in AMIS Markets

Market Separations in AMIS Markets		
Market Separation	**Underlying Cause**	**Possible AMIS Design Solution**
Spatial	Consumers unable to access information from AMIS	Locally available and accessible medium of information dissemination must be chosen. Trained and full-time data collectors must ensure up-to-date reliable information.
Temporal	Consumers do not have information on price and demand trends and forecasts	Extension services of the system can provide specific information on price and demand trends in markets. This information can be disseminated through mobile phones.
Financial	Consumers cannot afford AMIS services	Revenue model must be designed to ensure both financially sustainability and equitability of the system.
Informational	Consumers are not aware of AMIS services and their access procedures	Marketing of these services must also train the users on the usage of the services and interpretation of information received

From the analysis of above separations, we understand that following design guidelines for effective and reliable AMIS, providers can ensure that market separations are reduced and services are utilized by the stakeholders of agricultural markets. Choice of an appropriate information dissemination medium reduces spatial separations and provision of extension services reduces temporal separations. Suitable revenue model ensures that financial separation is reduced and marketing of services and training on usage of these services and interpretation of information received reduces informational separation.

In the following section we integrate the two levels of analysis to define successful implementation of AMIS in developing countries.

6   Beyond Technical Rationality: Fifth Dimension of Market Separations in Agricultural Markets (Socio-Political Separations)

AMIS is one of the initiatives that stems from active innovation perspective of technology and development. According to this perspective, markets will not deliver to the poor and interventions in the form of innovations are imperative to meet development goals (Heeks, 2008).

As stated by Heek's (2008) it is important to evaluate the ICT for Development initiatives for success. In order to define success for an AMIS implementation, we need to take two perspectives. One is the developmental perspective and the other is the IS perspective.

The primary developmental objective behind providing AMIS is to make the agricultural markets in developing countries more efficient and profitable. This will lead to the growth of the agricultural sector, which is a primary driver of GDP for these countries, there by contributing to the development of the country as a whole. Simon defined human development *"as the process of enhancing individual and collective quality of life in a manner that satisfies basic needs (as a minimum), is environmentally, socially and economically sustainable and is empowering in the sense that people concerned have a substantial degree of control over the process through access to the means of accumulating social power"* (Simon, 1997). Therefore AMIS supported by ICTs can be defined as a development initiative that empowers the stakeholders in the agricultural value chain with information.

From an IS perspective, AMIS has to be a usable system providing reliable information which is useful to the stakeholders. Scalability and sustainability are some of the measures of success of ICT for Development initiatives (Heeks, 2008).

In this paper, taking the theoretical lens of Bartels' market separations, we have analyzed market separations of AMIS at two levels. The first level deals with the market separations in agricultural markets corresponding to the developmental perspective. We identified informational separation as a strong separation in agricultural markets which can be reduced by the provision of AMIS. In the second level, we analyzed the market separations of the AMIS services markets, which correspond to the IS perspective. From the above analysis we can successfully conclude that success of any AMIS can be determined by its ability to reduce market separations at both these levels.

The above analysis involves a technical/rational view of agricultural markets. Primary assumption underlying this analysis is that, information provided by AMIS services will definitely be utilized in reducing these market separations. In the case of developmental initiatives like this, it is important to understand the socio-political context of implementations (Avgerou & McGrath, 2007).

When we look at the socio-political context of AMIS implementation, we come upon many situations that limit the effective utilization of information provided by AMIS services. In the case of rural India, many farmers have limited outlets for their produce. They are constrained by traditional trading relationships with middlemen.

These relationships can be attributed to many reasons. An obvious rational explanation is their dependence on these middlemen for credit which binds them in these relationships. Other socio-political barriers to utilization of information by farmers and other stakeholders are local power politics. Prior research has identified the following factors that cause socio-political separations:

- **Caste** – Caste shapes the outcomes of ICT implementations because of its influence on both the social and political contours of village life (Nicholas, 1968). Prior research findings on the outcomes of implementation of kiosks in India state that caste manifests itself *"in everyday practices of access to, mobility around, sharing of knowledge about, and use of the kiosks"* (De', 2009) (in the case of Bhoomi Kiosks for land records). Caste can act as a barrier in this context of AMIS with regards to access to both technology and agricultural markets.

- **Community Membership** – Similar to caste, membership to various communities creates barriers to utilization of information from AMIS. Prior research suggests that members of certain communities do not usually cross the boundaries that are created as a result of social structures that have been dominant over years. These boundaries prevent the movement of agricultural produce to markets that are in other regions or domains. This phenomenon has been observed in a study in Kuppam town (in the state of Andhra Pradesh in India), where the access to dealers in a market was driven by community membership. Members of certain communities did not access these dealers as they were from groups outside the 'boundary' of their community.

- **Community Leader** – In many areas, community leaders take a decision on the agricultural markets to trade for the entire community. Members of the community have to abide by the decision taken by the leader. This prevents the members of the community from trading in other markets.

- **Gender** – Prior studies by FAO in 2011 have noted that women in agricultural sector in developing countries have lower education and are lesser likely to have access to technology extension services compared to men. Gender roles within a specific geographic and cultural context determine the access to these services (FAO, 2010-2011). Also in some regions, access to agricultural markets is based on gender. Hence we consider gender as one of the barriers that contributes to socio-political separations in agricultural markets.

The following table (Table 3) highlights the underlying causes that contribute to socio-political separations.

Table 3. Socio-Political Separations

Socio-Political Separations	
Causes	**Underlying Reasons**
Caste	Caste influences the access to agricultural markets.
Community Membership	Membership to a community plays a crucial in deciding the target agricultural markets for sale.
Community Leader	Community leaders determine and decide the target markets for agricultural produce.
Gender	Women have lesser access to technology compared to men. Women's access to agricultural markets is restricted in some areas.

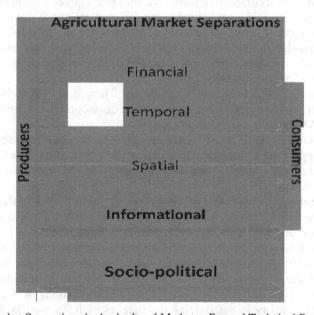

Fig. 3. Market Separations in Agricultural Markets - Beyond Technical Rationality

Taking this view, we find that, socio-political separations have a very strong impact in agricultural markets. In our view, this market separation is most difficult to tackle. Effective and efficient design of AMIS might reduce the market separations defined by Bartels' in this theory. But success of AMIS depends on reducing the socio-political separation that exists. It is important for policy makers to make appropriate policy changes to remove these socio-political barriers along with implementation of a system like AMIS. Thus wider policy environment in the country determines the success of AMIS to a large extent.

7   Conclusion

In this paper we make use of Bartels' theory of market separations to define success for the implementation of AMIS. The objective of the paper is to understand how AMIS systems can be designed to close the separations in markets for agricultural commodities in developing countries. From technical/rational analysis of separations in agricultural markets and markets for AMIS services, we find that informational separation is a strong factor in agricultural markets. Reduction in informational separation will eventually reduce other separations. AMIS empowers players in agricultural markets with the requisite information, thereby reducing the market separations. Effective design of AMIS can ensure reduction of separations in AMIS services markets. From a developmental perspective it is important to reduce separations in agricultural markets and from an IS perspective we need to reduce separations in AMIS service markets. Thus we define success of AMIS by the reduction of market separations at both these levels.

Going beyond the technical rationality, we find that market separations in the context agricultural markets are not limited to the four separations as defined by Bartels'. Socio-political context creates a number of barriers for the effective utilization of information provided and the impact of AMIS in reducing these separations is limited. Thus we identify the fifth dimension – socio-political separation in the context of these markets. Caste, community membership, community leaders and gender are some of the barriers that lead to this separation. Thus, it is extremely important to recognize diversity in contexts in order to achieve development outcomes from initiatives such as AMIS.

Implementation of AMIS must be accompanied by changes in wider policy environment to support the stakeholders in utilizing the information effectively. Policies related to credit, public-distribution, financial inclusion etc. will have an impact on the success of AMIS.

We believe that it is important to identify an appropriate theoretical lens to evaluate the success of IS in developmental contexts. Imperfections and separations in agricultural markets have been implicitly studied in prior research. This is a conceptual paper based on prior research on agricultural markets and AMIS, where we provide a new theoretical lens for evaluating market information systems from both a developmental and IS perspective. We also extend this theory to make sense of the socio-political factors that greatly impact such implementations. It demonstrates the suitability of this theory in determining the success of ICTs used in developmental contexts. We intend to empirically validate the concept put forward in this paper.

References

Abraham, Rueben: Mobile Phones and Economic Development:Evidence from the fishing industry in India, vol. 4(1), pp. 5–17. The MIT Press (2008)

Avgerou, C., McGrath, K.: Power, rationality, and the art of living through socio-technical change. MIS Quarterly 31(2), 293–315 (2007)

Bartels, R.: The General Theory of Marketing. Journal of Marketing 32(1), 29–33 (1968)

Benbasat, I., Weber, R.: Research Commentary: Rethinking "Diversity" in Information Systems Research. Information Systems Research 7(4), 389–399 (1996)

Biswas, A.: Agricultural Marketing in India (July 4, 2011),
http://www.domain-b.com/economy/agriculture/
20040713_marketing.html (retrieved from TNAU Agritech PPortal)

Davis, K.E.: Extension in Sub-Saharan Africa: Overview and Assessment of Past and Current Models, and Future Prospects. Journal of International Agricultural and Extension Education 15(3), 15–28 (2008)

De', R.: Caste Structures and E-Governance in a Developing Country. In: Wimmer, M.A., Scholl, H.J., Janssen, M., Traunmüller, R. (eds.) EGOV 2009. LNCS, vol. 5693, pp. 40–53. Springer, Heidelberg (2009)

Dinar, A.: Extension Commercialization: How much to charge for extension services. American Journal of Agricultural Economics 78(1), 1–12 (1996)

Evans, Lynton, J.: Strategic Grain Reserves - Guidelines for their establishment Management and Operation. FAO Agricultural Services Bulletin 126

FAO. The State of Food and Agriculture (2010-2011),
http://www.fao.org/docrep/013/i2050e/i2050e.pdf (retrieved from FAO)

Gunupudi, L., De, R.: Role of AMIS in Resolving Information Asymmetries in Agricultural Markets: Guidelines for AMIS Design. CPR South 6. Bangkok: Available at SSRN 1976188 (2011)

Heeks, R.: ICT4D 2.0: The next phase of applying ICT for international development. Computer 41(6), 26–33 (2008)

Helder, J., Nyhoff, J.-J.: Market Information for Early Warning. In: Document Presented to the SADC Early Warning System for Food Security Training Workshop, Harare (1994)

Holtzman, J., et al.: Market Information Systems and Services: Lessons from the AMIS Project Experience. Abt Associates, Bethesta (1993)

Islam, M.S., Grönlund, Å.: Agriculture market information services (AMIS) in the least developed countries (LDCs): Nature, scopes, and challenges. In: Wimmer, M.A., Chappelet, J.-L., Janssen, M., Scholl, H.J. (eds.) EGOV 2010. LNCS, vol. 6228, pp. 109–120. Springer, Heidelberg (2010)

Nicholas, R.W.: Structures of politics in the villages of Southern Asia. In: Singer, M., Cohn, B.S. (eds.) Structure and Change in Indian Society pp. 234–284. Aldine Transaction (1968)

Ogen, O.: The Agricultural Sector and Nigeria's Development: Comparitive Perspective from the Brazilian Agro-Industrial Economy. Nebula 4.1, 184–194 (2007)

Shepherd, A.W.: Market information Services: Theory and Practice. Agricultural Services Bulletin No.125 FAO - The UN (1997)

Simon, D.: Development Reconsidered: New Directions in Development Thinking. Geografiska Annaler 79B(4), 183-201 (1997)

Singh, S.: Selected Success Stories on Agricultural Information Systems. Asia-Pacific Association of Agricultural Research Institutions (2006)

Stiglitz, J.E.: Information and the change in the Paradigm in Economics. The American Economic Review 92(3), 460–529 (2002)

Tarafdar, M., Singh, R.: A Market Separations Perspective to Analyze the Role of ICT in Development at the Bottom of the Pyramid. In: Proceedings of SIG GlobDev Fourth Annual Workshop, Shanghai, China, December 03 (2011)

Thomas, S.: Agricultural commodity markets in India: Policy Issues for Growth. Indira Gandhi Institute for development Research, Goregaon (2003)

WorldBank, World Development Report, Retrieved from The International Bank for Reconstruction and Developmet/ The World Bank, The Washington DC, USA (2008), http://siteresources.worldbank.org/INTWDR2008/Resources/ WDR_00_book.pdf

Management and Failure of Large Transformation Projects: Factors Affecting User Adoption

Marijn Janssen, Anne Fleur van Veenstra, and Haiko van der Voort

Delft University of Technology, Jaffalaan 5, 2628 BX Delft, The Netherlands
{m.f.w.h.a.janssen,a.f.e.vanveenstra,
h.g.vandervoort}@tudelft.nl

Abstract. Transformational e-government (t-government) aims to realize public sector reform. Yet many of the large transformation projects have not resulted in the desired outcomes, as stakeholders did not adopt the results of the projects. These projects are characterized by a large number of stakeholders, many uncertainties and complexities. Although there is a vast amount of literature available on project failure and despite its importance of this topic, little is known about factors influencing the adoption of large transformation projects by stakeholders. In this paper factors influencing and delaying the adoption of a large transformation project are identified. Adoption is hindered by a combination of factors originating from the complexity and uncertainties in combination with too high ambition levels and the neglecting existing realities. During the transformation process the focus on the users was lost and shifted towards an internal orientation.

Keywords: Transformational government, e-government, failure, project failure, adoption, diffusion, XBRL.

1   Introduction

Transformational e-government (t-government) efforts aim to move beyond creating better service delivery for citizens and businesses and realize public sector reform (Beynon-Davies, 2007; Cordella & Iannacci, 2010; Dawes, 2008; Morgeson III & Mithas, 2009). Transforming government in a complex endeavor, as it requires radical change trajectories resulting in permanent organizational change (Irani, Elliman, & Jackson, 2007; Weerakkody & Dhillon, 2008). T-Government can be defined as the "ICT-enabled and organization-led transformation of government operations, internal and external processes and structures to enable the realization of services that meet public-sector objectives such as efficiency, transparency, accountability and citizen centricity" (Weerakkody, Janssen, & Dwivedi, 2011, p. 321 p. 321). Many transformation projects do not live up to expectations (McAfee & Andrew, 2003) and e-government projects are subject to failure (Loukis & Charalabidis, 2011). Transformation projects run often over budget, over time, do not deliver functionalities and other requirements.

The cost of failure are tremendous and have been estimated in terms of billions of Euros. Project might completely fail and have to do over again or are only delayed

Y.K. Dwivedi et al. (Eds.): TDIT 2013, IFIP AICT 402, pp. 121–135, 2013.
© IFIP International Federation for Information Processing 2013

and are more expensive and providing less functionalities. Yet what constitutes a failure is often open to discussion. Different stakeholders might have their own metrics for determining success or failure. Transformation projects can be deemed failures due to the inability to meet requirements, or might be viewed as successful when only exceeding time and/or budget. Project failure can be ranked on a scale ranging from not delivering required functionalities to complete failure in which almost all efforts and money is wasted. Often projects are evaluated based on the delivered functionalities, budget used and time used to finish the project. In this paper we take another perspective by adopting the user view. The basic idea is that user adoption determines the success or failure of a project.

Project failure has been extensively studied in ICT projects (Daniels & LaMarsh, 2007; Lu, Liu, & Ye, 2010; Pinto & Mantel, 1990; Yeo, 2002). There are several categories of project failure, including people, process, product and technology (McConnell, 1996). Nelson (2007) uses this categorization to list classical project management mistakes. Factors like complexity, uncertainty, scope creep, opposing stakeholders requirements, lack of top-management support and resistance are frequently mentioned in the literature as project failure factors. In this paper we will study factors influencing the adoption by users.

The user perspective is often taken when discussing the adoption of technology. Well established theories such as the technology acceptance model (TAM) (Davis, 1989) diffusion of innovation (Rogers, 2003) and unified theory of acceptance and use of technology (UTAUT) (Venkatesh, Morris, Davis, & Davis, 2003) provides factors influencing user adoption. UTAUT aims to explain user intentions to use a system and subsequent usage behavior. Performance expectancy, effort expectancy, social influence, and facilitating conditions are direct determinants of usage intention and behavior. Important facilitating adoption factor are investment, support and social relationships (Venkatesh, et al., 2003). More specific adoption theories argue for the need to take into account the context and specific conditions (Orlikowski, 2000). These models look at the adoption of technology and systems once they are in place. In contrast to this literature we will analyze factors that influence adoption during a project.

We investigated a transformation project running over 6 years and which did not gain high levels of user acceptance. Based on interviews we gained in-depth knowledge of the factors influencing the adoption by users. This paper is structured as follows. In the next section the research methodology is presented followed by the case study description in section 3. From the case study we derive factors affecting the adoption which are discussed in section 4. This is followed by a discussion and overview of the factors. Finally we will draw conclusions and provide recommendations for further research.

2   Research Approach

Transformation is expected to have an enduring and long-term impact and influence organizational and technical aspects. Transformation differs from ICT project failures and private sectors projects. Gauld (2007) found that in public administration much more complex project commissioning and development is necessary due to political and organizational elements. As such in-depth insight is necessary to understand the factors. Due to the complex nature and the need to gain a deep understanding of the factors influencing user adoption, a qualitative approach based on case study research was adopted for this research (Yin, 2009).

The case study was selected as it concerned a large transformation project in the Dutch government. A large amount of information and reports was available over the past which helped to understand the project history. We conducted a search on the Internet and search two major Dutch ICT-magazines. This helped to create a retrospective picture of the transformation project. This picture provided us the content and the scope of the project. In addition a first list of important adoption factors were derived.

Our next analyses used project failure and adoption and diffusion factors as a basis. Both literature as well as the first list of factors were used to derived an interview protocol. The interview protocol should ensure that the relevant elements were taken into account. The interview protocol contain factors like stakeholders, processes, information sharing, technology, performance expectancy, effort expectancy, social influence, and facilitating conditions investment, support and social relationships.

In the next step fifteen semi-structured interviews were carried out over the course of a three months period (Janssen et al., 2010). Publicly available documents were systematically analyzed. Such a perspective allowed us to understand the forces and factors influencing user adoption as well as how the process of change took place. The fifteen interviewees included project managers, software developers, user associations and various types of users. Representatives from both small and medium-sized enterprise (SME) and large user organizations were interviewed. This allowed us to understand the diversity of users. All interviews lasted between one hour and an hour and half. Most interviews were conducted by two researchers comparing results afterwards; some interviews were conducted by one interviewer. Transcripts of the interviews were made and all interviews were given the resulting report.

3   Case Study Description

The introduction of the international Extensible Business Reporting Language (XBRL) standard in the Netherlands was set out to transform the process of legally required financial reporting by companies. Whereas in the past a large number of documents should be submitted on paper, the vision behind this transformation project was that reports required by government could be submitted as a single report by making use of the XBRL format. XBRL was originally developed as a XML-based standard for external financial reporting. Nowadays it is also used for internal financial and non-financial reporting which makes it possible to use this for a broader range of reporting functions including the reporting of statistical, tax, and inspection data.

In the old situation business had to report all kinds of report to various governmental organizations who acted relatively independently. They all posed their own reporting standards and requirements on the companies. Figure 1 gives an overview of the desired situation in which reports are based on a shared taxonomy and submitted over a common gateway. Instead of all government agencies defining their own requirements for these financial reports, a taxonomy was created to harmonize definitions used by the Dutch government in the financial domain. Furthermore, a common process infra-structure is under development to be used for submitting all financial reports. Al-though the XBRL standard can be used for financial reporting across many sectors, the current project set-up includes only a few reports; tax reporting to the Inland Rev-enue Service (IRS), the submission of financial year reports to the Chambers of Commerce and the submission of data to the national bureau for statistics (CBS) (Bharosa et al., 2013). The process infrastructure developed to facilitate data ex-change consists of a unified gateway for transferring bulk data to various government. For the delivery of financial information the companies report financial and other information to the government and are the *end-users*. Companies use often software or Software-as-a-Service (SaaS) solutions to submit their information to the govern-ment. Furthermore, most businesses us financial intermediaries for preparing and auditing of their reports. Software provides and financial intermediaries also use the gateway and are named *users*.

As generating financial reports will be done using an open standard, organizations are able to innovate and new applications may emerge as well as new organizations developing new services. This likely results in a transformation of the situation in the traditional value chains will be changed. Especially it is expected that the role of fi-nancial intermediaries will change. Another example of this is that banks might also receive the information in the future using XBRL (See figure), although this probably will be done using a different infrastructure and accompanying gateway.

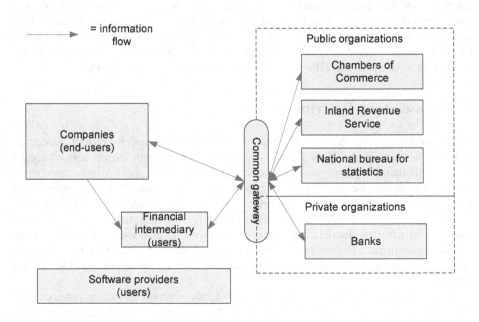

Fig. 1. The scope and the main actors involved in the architecture

The project was aimed at contributing to the central government agenda to achieve a decrease of the administrative burden of businesses. In 2007, the central government estimated that around 350 million euro's worth of administrative tasks of businesses could be cut and around a million tax filings using XBRL could be achieved yearly by 2008. Also it was expected that in 2007 the first version of the process infrastructure developed for exchanging data based on XBRL would be ready. However, it was not expected that an authentication mechanisms needed to be developed. In 2009, however, it appeared that none of the above mentioned goals were met or will be met within a short time frame. Users and end-users did not adopt the system yet. Generally, businesses and government agencies claim that they were not yet ready for implementing the XBRL standard and for submitting their reports. They often stated that they were waiting for the central government to make decisions before they will invest. A set of factors affected the adoption by users and end-users which will be discussed next.

4   Factors Affecting Adoption

Based on our understanding of the literature and the analysis of the case study we identified the following factors which contributed to the slow adoption of the transformation project. We clustered the factors in a number of categories to make them more manageable and as they depict towards a similar causes of slow adoption. The factors are related to and dependent on each other and not mutually exclusive.

4.1   Amount and Diversity of Stakeholders

In the project a large number of stakeholders were involved, who had their own interests and concerns. First of all, the public organizations that receive the reporting have a variety of interest and requirements. Smaller public organizations can gain less benefits, whereas large organization can gain many efficiency gains. Requirements differ from yearly to more frequent reporting. On the receiving side also banks are involved as they potentially can receive information from companies in the XBRL format. Although Banks are interested in different information, they share the concern of having high information quality.

Financial intermediaries, mainly comprising accountants, are a crucial stakeholder group. This stakeholder group is quite diverse, as there are a few large international accountancies and many smaller companies operating locally. In the old information they often collected and aggregated information from a business, whereas in the new situation report can be directly created from the information systems. They are affected as they can be bypassed easily by automating the process and there traditional revenue model is challenged. As they are afraid that the landscape might diminish their revenue model, they have no sense-of-urgency to collaborate. On the other hand using XBRL can make the work of accountants more efficient as they need to carry out fewer tasks and create fewer reports. There are some smaller and innovative intermediaries that see this as a source of competitive advantage and are interested in adoption.

The software companies developing (financial) software for businesses and intermediaries supporting XBRL data form another stakeholder group. They have to invest in the technology and integrate it in their software to ensure easy adoption by businesses. As all software vendors can do this, they see it hardly as a means for gaining competitive advantage and therefore want to minimize their adoption costs.

Business that are obliged to report their financial situation to the government are the actual end-users who need to provide their information to the government to comply with the law. These business constitute organizations covering all kind of industries and sectors and having different sizes. Small and Medium Enterprises (SMEs) are often not aware of XBRL and are not interested as they are primarily users of software, but are not interested how it works. They have no time and no interest to understand the benefits of the transformation. They completely rely on their software providers and financial intermediaries to adopt. Large organization can have often different reporting obligations and are aware of the need to adopt. They have the capabilities and expertise and often view a lot of advantages. In order to make advantage of this development they have to adopt their systems and processes.

Striking is that most of the end-users are often not aware of the project, its technologies and its potential impact. They are dependent on financial intermediaries and software providers to innovate. The latter have hardly any interest to change the status quo, as they are afraid that they have to make the investments, but that they will not directly benefit from it. Although there are exceptions.

4.2   Organic Approach

In the project a large number of stakeholders coming from both the public as private sector were involved. The project was initiated at the ministerial level and a large-scale approach was taken involving as many stakeholders as possible. One reason for this large-scale involvement was to ensure commitment of all organizations and that all possible requirements would be identified and voices were heard. By involving all stakeholders, the idea is that less resistance would be created and the transformation would become more easily. What happened was the contrary. By involving a large number of various players the progress was delayed, there were struggles concerning the requirements and instead of becoming supporters of the project the resistance grew. Whereas there were supporters at the start users got disillusioned by the limited progress. The direct visible results took a long time to realize. Over time the disadvantages and risks were more and more discussed and emphasized rather than the possible benefits.

The involvement of a large and diverse set of stakeholders requires that an incremental and piecemeal approach is taken. The project is developed organically and influenced by the many stakeholders pushing and promoting certain issues. The initial project focus was not on developing and making a system work but on identifying all possible conflicting views. Consequently, the project grew of its own accord and all kinds of opinions were presented and communicated. Stakeholders were pursuing other directions and ventilate their opinions in online discussion groups and newspapers undermining the project credibility (one reason for doing this is that their core value are affected, see below).

Due to the complexity and the many stakeholders the time horizon of the project was extended and the initial IT was caught up by new technologies. The project chased the new technology, whereas the old technology was not under control yet and became legacy. Their hope was that the new technology would solve the problem. Instead of solving the problem it was unproven and even created more delay. The focus remained on innovation instead of on implementation and ensuring for a stable and sustainable platform.

Overall, an organic and piecemeal growth resulted in muddling through, delaying and frustrating the project instead of realizing the intention of ensuring commitment and overcoming resistance.

4.3   Technology and Law Are Intertwined

The project under study shows a dependency between law and technology development. During the project the questions were raised if electronic reporting is allowed by laws and about the degree to which these financial reports created have sufficient quality to comply with the law. The conformity with law was contested several time resulting in delay. A tension is whether technology innovation is necessary before law can be changed or if law needs to be changed before a technology innovation can materialize.

In the project a main question was when legislation about reporting using XBRL-based technology would be introduced. Several interviewees indicated that they would be reluctant to adopt new technology without a clear obligation determined by law. In the case study it was chosen to develop a gateway and other facilities first. Only after the infrastructure was in place it was decided to make a change in law which state that in 2013 the use of XBRL will be obliged. This approach resulted in a project delay as the development and change in law was done in sequential instead in parallel. Having no change of law resulted in uncertainty in whether or not XBRL would be adopted. This in turn resulted in in a wait and see attitude of many stakeholders. Only after a law was introduced stating that XBRL would be mandatory by government the stakeholder gained a sense of urgency to be ready for the adoption.

The intertwinement of law and technology, makes it unclear what should be done first, a change in law or the development of a working infrastructure. Not having both in place resulted in the not making of any critical decisions by many stakeholders and resulted in ambiguity and expectations that could not be met. Ideally both should be done in parallel, however, there was a deadlock in the project. The project technology development was waiting for a change in law, whereas, a change of law was waiting for the technology innovation to be ready. Resulting in a kind of catch-22 situation.

4.4   Scope Creep and Ambition Level

The many changes during the project resulted in uncertainties by the stakeholders about the direction of the project, what it will deliver and how it will help them. The scope and size of the project changed several times. Changes in the scope influenced the business case for adopters. This influence was even strengthened by the unrealistic ambition level. The project was announced as providing a solution for companies that would enable companies to provide all required information by the government by pressing a single button. The other activities needed such as collecting and processing information by companies were not mentioned. This caused resistance as expectations were not met. Furthermore, instead of making the system work within one area (financial reporting) the project focussed on broadening the scope and involving more companies coming from other sectors. The project tried to involve the banking sectors as these were also interested in the financial reporting. Instead of lowering the resistance and gaining of acceptance, this resulted in new requirements on the system and companies providing the information. Ultimately this scope creep resulted in more delay and resistance.

New opportunities arise through standardization of financial reporting and the implementation of a common gateway. When more and more businesses and government organizations start using XBRL for their information exchange processes business models and processes are likely to change. This is likely to result in new opportunities. For example, in the future it will also be possible to report non-financial data using XBRL, such as data on insurances or inventory systems, and to allow for process integration crossing boundaries of individual companies. This will results in benefits in other areas than initially expected. The awareness of these new opportunities resulted a scope creep.

Possible users were lured in with a very promising business case and they make often the initial arrangement to adopt. After some time it was clear that new elements were added and there was no working system that they could adopt. In order to adopt the system they would need to change their processes and systems again requiring the making of adoption investments another time. Due to the uncertainty of continuity and a lack of a working system, most users would opt for not adopting and wait for a full swing version to arrive. As a result the enthusiasm of the initial early adopters was lost.

Some development problems were tacked by adding new elements to solve the initial problems. Although this might solve the actual problem, it also results in additional complexities that need to be managed and introduces new risks. The way these risks were handled was the same way as the risks were created, by adding new elements, which again added to the complexities. This continues till the complexity reaches a level that it cannot be managed anymore.

Overall, the scope creep resulted in an increased complexity, further delay, and a blurred picture concerning the ambition level. This influenced the adoption of stakeholders, as the initial enthusiasms of most of the early-adopters was lost.

4.5   Continuous Changes and Uncertainty

In the project there were continuous changes resulting in uncertainties about outcomes and a focus on dealing with incidents. Realizing process transformation is time consuming and requires a clear vision. One interviewee expressed the project volatilely as *"I was lost in the landscape, one day it seemed to be perfectly all right, the next day the landscape look different"*. The many uncertainties and incident management are expressed by the many news items that were published in magazines during the project. These news items found in the magazines was a way for stakeholders to express their opinions. This often included a lot of criticism on the project. The news items influenced not only the direction of the project, but had also a negative effect on the adoption by users.

During the project, new applications of the technology were found which could contribute to the further reducing of administrative burden. Initially these kinds of features were added and included. After a while there was awareness that this would not progress the project. A clear scope was defined to ensure that part of the system could be developed, however, this scope would result in the need for users to have multiple processes as the system would not have all needed functionality to deal with all processes. Finalizing one component does not contribute to creating value as all components are necessary to make it work. The potential efficiency gains, however, are tightly intertwined with the implementation of the complete process infrastructure. *"XBRL as such does not realize a decrease of the administrative burden, as it is about the way in which it is applied"*. In conclusion, there is a continuous tension between expanding the project or limiting the functionalities. The first would result in a delay, whereas the second would result in less benefits for the users.

An factor contributing to the delay was the combination of innovation and system development. The innovation about how the new infrastructure would look like was never completed. Instead when new developments and technologies entered the project, they tried to include them in the system development. The mixing up of system innovation and system development resulted in unclear goals, uncertainty about what would be delivered and negatively influenced adoption decisions. One interview concluded that *"the changes contribute to less adoption ... due to the many changes the project will be in the news again resulting in yet another uncertainty to adopt"*.

During the project there was the uncertainty about the control and maintenance once the project would be finished. The project concerned the development of a new system, but no budget was reserved for maintaining the system. Stakeholders were reluctant to adopt as there was no certainty about its continuity. Users would have to change their processes and systems at the risk that once the project ended they could not use the system anymore. Only at a later stage long term sustainability was created by involving the control and maintenance organizations of the government, who would ensure control and maintenance to keep the system work.

Finally, due to the long-time of the project key personnel moved away and with them the knowledge they possessed. This blocked organizational learning as new staff needs first to understand what is going on. Furthermore organization memory disappeared resulting in the making of the same failure several times.

4.6   Technology Is Leading Instead of the Business Case

The project was launched with the promise that all information could be delivered by pressing one button without bringing to the attention the need to have suitable software and other facilities. The presentation of this simple business case resulted in exaggerated and unrealistic expectation.

Although the project impacts the way information is reported and needed considerable transformation from both business and companies, the project was primarily viewed as a technology project. The transformation process was only given limited attention. Instead the collaboration with software developers and vendors was given a lot of attention which reinforced the focus on technology aspects. By focussing on these types of stakeholders most attention was given to the technology, instead of on realizing the business case and creating value for the users.

Another reason for focussing on the technology was the immaturity of the technology at the start of the project. It was not proven that the technology could realize the intended solution. The focus was on making the technology work instead of on the reduction of the administrative burden for companies.

Due to the scope creep there was a shift in the reduction of the administrative burden. Initially the anticipated reduction of the administrative burden due to the technology innovation was higher, however, due to the simplification of the requirements on reporting the benefits that could be gained were lower. This impacted the business case, however, no new business case was made. Users more and more expected that efficiency gains could not be accomplished on their side. Nevertheless they were willing to collaborate if this would result in efficiency gains on the government side. Large-scale standardized tax filing can be used to accomplish large efficiency gains for the Dutch tax organization. However, also the tax organization claimed that their investments are higher than their gains. They argued that they switched to digital tax filing for businesses already in 2005, based on a different data standard. Only switching to another standard (XBRL) will not result a large efficiency gain. As such the whole business case that was made for both companies and the government was challenged and no new business case was made. The project concentrated on the technology instead of making the system work. In short, there was a focus on the technology instead on users and transformation.

4.7   Violating Core Values

The impact of the transformation goes beyond a single organization. Some organizations might see that there existing business models are violated and there profit margin might vaporize. The changes affect the fundamental core values of organization. In the case study some accountants feared running out of business when financial reporting can be done in a standardized and digitized manner. They make their money by entering data and checking if the data is correct, which will be an automated task by introducing XBRL. The companies felt that their revenue model will change and fundamental changes in their value-adding roles and processes are necessary. Like in other industries, for example tourism, the role of intermediaries will change due to the ability to directly connect using lower transaction costs. Traditional roles vanish due to increased direct contact and new roles become into place. As there is uncertainty about the new roles and services and no clear vision how the new business model of financial intermediaries would look like, they often preferred the status quo and would avoid adoption. One interviewee commented "*the project was not able to communicate the vision .. it remained vague'*. As financial intermediaries play a pivotal role in the adoption companies often did not adopt.

This problem is further complicated as this is often not part of the rationality in which communication is done. Instead of clarifying the problem and starting the discussion about the changes and new possible roles, the changing business model of financial intermediaries was not addressed. This became visible in resistance and other motivations for not adopting. It was only found afterwards that violating of core values was a root cause of the resistance.

A factor contributing to his is how the financial intermediaries are represented. The interactions with user groups and intermediaries was limited, "*users were not sufficiently involved in the project management*". This also resulted in the focus on the technology instead on the business case. In government initiated projects a high level of involvement and participation of stakeholders is a common approach. The case show high level of participation of organizations defending their own stakes and hardly any involvement of the users who should gain the benefits of the reduction of the administrative burden. The political influence is substantial. The government defines the problem of the users, whereas essential aspects such as violating the core values are neglected. The user problem is defined without involving users and knowing the real problems. This is one of the reasons why some stakeholders used magazines and other outlet to express their concerns and interests.

4.8   Project Governance

Governance is necessary to steer the project in the right directions. The principal is in charge of major decisions, should have a clear vision which serves as a guideline for directing progress. Project commissioning is the process of assuring that all systems and components will be developed, tested, operated, and maintained according to the desired requirements of the owner or final client. Various Ministries were involved in the project and commissioned the project by providing funding.

In the project the principals lacked expertise and had no shared vision. the system development was outsourced to external parties. Multiple sourcing parties were involved as the management and the software developments was separated and the project team was made up of individuals from various external organizations. Some public servants were added to the project team to ensure the specification of requirements and gaining the necessary input. Governance was based on high-level agreements (meeting deadline and staying in budget) and there were limited possibilities to know what is really going on and what the crucial decisions were that should be taken. In several cases the board was involved in crucial decisions making, but sometimes in a stage that was too late, i.e. stakeholders were already complaining or stepped out. If the board was involved in the decision-making there was no feedback mechanisms to understand and evaluate the impact of their decisions. Furthermore users and user associations were hardly involved which resulted that the governance was often not aware of early-warning indicators and other small signals and were only confronted with this once it hits the news. Hence they were not able to take any actions on this.

5   Discussion

The analyses of the case study shows a large number of factors which are often interrelated and affect the adoption decision. Some factors resulted in a project delay which ultimately influenced the decision whether to adopt by users. From the interviews it appeared that there is no dominating factor, but that the multitude of factors contributed to the slow adoption. One interviewee summarized this "*it is the interplay between events that resulted in our decision to postpone adoption*". The interviewee was referring to a combination of the factors that are summarized for each of the categories in table 1.

Table 1. Overview of categories and factors influencing adoption (continued on next page)

Categories	Factors affecting adoption
1. Amount and diversity of stakeholders	• Different and opposing interests of stakeholders • Homogenous approach to a diverse group • Lack of interest in XBRL by users • End-users are not aware of the impact • No sense of urgency
2. Organic approach	• Involvement of large number of players • Shifting requirements • Delay resulted in disillusionment of stakeholders • Emphasize on disadvantages and risks instead of benefits • Stakeholders expressing their concerns publicly • Focus on satisfying all stakeholder instead of ensuring for a stable and sustainable platform
3. Technology and law are intertwined	• Law blocks system development and adoption • Lack of a system creates no urgency to change the law
4. Scope creep and ambition level	• Scope and size of the project changed several times • Extending to other domains without ensuring that it works within the initial domain • New opportunities arise during the project • Users had to adopt their processes and systems multiple times • Problems were solved by expanding and extending the project
5. Continuous changes and uncertainty	• Negative publicity • Broadening and narrowing functionalities • Intertwinement of system development and innovation • Continuity is not covered • Move away of key staff (knowledge retention)
6. Technology is leading instead of the business case	• Exaggerated expectations • No attention for transformation • Focus on software development and software vendors • Immature technology • Reduction of functionality resulting in less benefits
7. Violating core values	• No insight in changes of the business models of users • No transparency of changes required for adoption • Lack of vision • Insufficient contact with users
8. Project governance	• Inability to fulfill the project commissioner role by the government • Lack of knowledge of technology and practice to proactively steer the project • Lack of leadership • No insight in users' needs and requirements • Management by focussing on deadlines and budget • No clear governance structure

The lack of adoption or delay in adoption is caused by a mix of technical, organizational and political complexity in combination with too high ambition levels and neglecting existing realities. During the project the transformation purposes were lost, the focus was shifted from transformation towards a focus on technology in which users were hardly given any attention. Some of the user who were prepared to be early adopters were disappointed by the limited progress and the many changes during the project. The many changes made it difficult for them to prepare their organization. Furthermore due to changes the initial investment in adopting their systems to submit XBRL-based reporting did not pay off and they had to make another investment. Having a working system and clear vision on how further releases would look like and how continuity can be guaranteed are key factors that should be met before users will adopt.

The initiation of the project was based on a view on the desired situation which proved to be more complicated. During the project decisions could not be made based on a sound business case. Despite the many changes the business case was not updated and could not be used as a basis for the guiding decisions. The many complexities and uncertainties resulted in a focus on managing incidents in which the focus on the user is lost. Scope creep, negative news, changes, unclear vision and other factors had a devastating effect on the entire project. Users who initially had high expectations became disappointed. For user adoption a reliable and working system should be available as a number of organizational changes are necessary and stakeholders have to agree on the necessity of this change. Furthermore continuity should be guaranteed. If users expect a short project lifetime, they will not be prepared to make any decisions favouring the adoption. The initiating stakeholders did not realize that system adoption would require a substantial transformation process. Much of the attention was focussed on making the project work, instead of on the user adoption.

6   Conclusions and Further Research

A main objective of transformational (t-government) is to realize public sector reform. Large transformation projects will likely fail due to the multiple complexities, uncertainties and amounts of stakeholders that need to be dealt with at the same time. To understand the impact on user adoption we analyzed a large transformation project. We identified 8 categories containing 38 factors affecting the adoption by users. The combination of factors resulted in neglecting the user. This had a devastating effect on the entire project, resulting in delays and disappointed users. The user should be carefully managed in such projects as adoption is necessary for making the transformation work.

When comparing the factors influencing adoption with project management failure factors (e.g. Daniels & LaMarsh, 2007; Lu, et al., 2010; Pinto & Mantel, 1990; Yeo, 2002) it shows similarities and differences. Factors like lack of leadership and vision, insufficient contact and so on are well-known in the project management literature contributing to project failure, whereas delay, intertwinement of law and technology, continuity after the project and violating core value is hardly found in this literature. These might be typical for user adoption in large transformation projects. We recommend to compare project management failure factors and adoption factors in further research, as combining both streams can contribute to more insight.

After our research ended the project continued and many of these factors are addressed in the next stage of this project. Based on the analysis a plan has been made to progress the project and ensure adoption by the users. We recommend to analyze the actions taken and the effect of user adoption in further research, as effective actions can serve as a guidance for other projects. This might result in a list of success factors that can improve user adoption, which can be tested in further research.

References

Beynon-Davies, P.: Models for e-government. Transforming Government: People, Process and Policy 1(1), 7–28 (2007)

Bharosa, N., Janssen, M., Wijk, R.V., Winne, N.D., Voort, H.V.D., Hulstijn, J., et al.: Tapping into existing information flows: The transformation to compliance by design in business-to-government information exchange. Government Information Quarterly 30(supplement), s9–s18 (2013)

Cordella, A., Iannacci, F.: Information systems in the public sector: The e-Government enactment framework. Journal of Strategic Information Systems 19, 52–66 (2010)

Daniels, C.B., LaMarsh, W.J.: Complexity as a Cause of Failure in Information Technology Project Management. Paper Presented at the IEEE International Conference on System of Systems Engineering, SoSE 2007 (2007)

Davis, F.D.: Perceived Usefulness, Perceived Ease of Use, and User Acceptance of Information Technology. MIS Quarterly 13(3), 319–340 (1989)

Dawes, S.S.: The Evolution and Continuing Challenges of E-Governance. Public Administration Review (Special issue on The Quest for High-Performance Administration) 68(4), S86–S102 (2008)

Gauld, R.: Public sector information system project failures: Lessons from a New Zealand hospital organization. Government Information Quarterly 24, 102–114 (2007)

Irani, Z., Elliman, T., Jackson, P.: Electronic transformation of government in the UK: a research agenda. European Journal of Information Systems 16(4), 327–335 (2007)

Janssen, M., Veenstra, A.F.V., Groenleer, M., Voort, H.V.D., Bruijn, H.D., Bastiaansen, C.: Uit het Zicht: Beleidsmaatregelen voor het versnellen van het gebruik van ICT-toepassingen voor administratieve latenverlichting Delft: ACTAL (2010)

Loukis, E., Charalabidis, Y.: Why do eGovernment Projects Fail? Risk Factors of Large Information Systems Projects in the Greek Public Sector: An International Comparison 7, 2(59-77) (2011)

Lu, X., Liu, H., Ye, W.: Analysis failure factors for small & medium software projects based on PLS method. Paper Presented at the The 2nd IEEE International Conference on Information Management and Engineering, ICIME (2010)

McAfee, Andrew: When too much IT knowledge is a dangerous thing. MIT Sloan Management Review, 83–89 (2003)

McConnell, S.: Rapid Development. Microsoft Press (1996)

Morgeson III, F.V., Mithas, S.: Does E-Government Measure Up to E-Business? Comparing End User Perceptions of U.S. Federal Government and E-Business Web Sites. Public Administration Review 69(4), 740–752 (2009)

Nelson, R.R.: IT project Management: Infamous failures, classic mistakes and best practices. MISQ Executive 6(2), 67–78 (2007)

Orlikowski, J.W.: Using Technology and Constituting Structures: A practice Lens for Studying Technology in Organizations. Organization Science 11(4), 404–428 (2000)

Pinto, J.K., Mantel Jr., S.J.: The causes of project failure. IEEE Transactions on Engineering Management 37(4), 269–276 (1990)

Rogers, E.M.: Diffusion of innovations. Free Press, New York (2003)

Venkatesh, V., Morris, M., Davis, G., Davis, F.: User Acceptance of Information Technology: Toward a Unified View. MIS Quarterly 27(3), 425–478 (2003)

Weerakkody, V., Dhillon, G.: Moving from E-Government to T-Government: A Study of Process Re-engineering Challenges in a UK Local Authority Perspective. International Journal of Electronic Government Research 4(4), 1–16 (2008)

Weerakkody, V., Janssen, M., Dwivedi, Y.: Transformational Change and Business Process Reengineering (BPR): Lessons from the British and Dutch Public Sector. Government Information Quarterly 28(3), 320–328 (2011)

Yeo, K.T.: Critical failure factors in information systems projects. International Journal of Project management 20(3), 241–246 (2002)

Yin, R.: Case Study Research: Design and Methods, 4th edn. SAGE Publications, California (2009)

Green IT Logistics in a Greek Retailer: Grand Successes and Minor Failures

Anastasia Papazafeiropoulou[1], Georgios Gerostergioudis[1],
Hsin Chen[2], and Laurence Brooks[1]

[1] Brunel University, UK
[2] University of Bedfordshire, UK
{anastasia.papazafeiropoulou,
georgios.gerostergioudis,laurence.brooks}@brunel.ac.uk,
hsin.chen@beds.ac.uk

Abstract. Environmental sustainability is one of the issues that organizations need to face today. Nevertheless, Green IT practices have their disadvantages, especially financial ones, which make the green logistic topic controversial to organizations. Achieving zero emissions while receiving financial benefits is idealistic thus companies need to adapt specific green strategies according to their particular needs. This study analyzes a specific company in terms of its green logistics strategy in order to discover any shortcomings and to depict how issues from literature review can influence the operation of the organization. This company is a super market chain dominant in the market of northern Greece. Focusing on the e-logistics of the firm, issues such as warehouse management system, inventory control, transportation, distribution and reverse logistics are examined in combination with the environmental consciousness. Our results could be useful to companies looking to exploit Green IT logistics.

Keywords: Green Logistics, environment, retailing.

1 Introduction

Logistics used to depict the transport, storage and handling of products as they move from raw materials source to their point of consumption. Over the past few years, in a background where public and government concern for the environment increases, firms are "forced" to reduce their environmental impacts of their logistics processes and turn them to green (McKinnon, et al., 2011). In response to this pressure, a new approach to logistics emerged in the early 1990s, which focused not only on the standard logistical objectives for efficient, effective, and fast handling and movement of goods, but also took into account measures for protecting the earth's environment: the "green logistics" approach (Aronsson & Brodin, 2006). Freight transport is responsible for 8% of CO2 emissions worldwide. Warehousing and package of products account for 2-3% (Ribeiro & Kobayashi, 2007). The pressure for the firms to transform their logistics operation to environmental friendlier is becoming very intense. Making Logistics 'green' will involve more than reducing carbon emissions. It consists also

Y.K. Dwivedi et al. (Eds.): TDIT 2013, IFIP AICT 402, pp. 136–150, 2013.

the endeavors to cut other environmental costs of logistics and reconcile the economic, environmental and social objectives in logistics (Brundtland Commission, 1987) (Fiksel, 2010). By Green Logistics the companies not only pose an environmental friendly image to the public view, but also support and improve their general performance. Painting logistics "green" is not easy. The cost-saving strategies related with logistic operators are often in contrast with the environment, since they usually maximize the environmental costs. Moreover, logistics do not usually pay back the full costs of using the infrastructures. As a result, logistical operators use the most polluting and least energy efficient transportation modes to increase the velocity of distribution (Rodrigue, et al., 2001). Green design and operations, reverse logistics, waste management and green manufacturing in the firms are included in the Green Supply Chain Management, focusing on a better relation with the environment. The main aim of green logistics is to reduce the environmental harmful procedures in supply chain such as the diminishing of material resources, overflowing waste and other kinds of environmental pollution. Existing research on the adoption and application of Green logistics today is limited thus this paper aims to examine the green logistics and e-logistics strategy of a Greek super market chain. The objectives are the in-depth examination of the practices followed by the specific company and the determination of the trade-offs between the Green IT investment and actual benefits for the organization.

2   Green Logistics

Green logistics is a concept that is gaining popularity all over the world. More organizations are trying to make their logistics green in order to present a more environmentally friendly face (Rao & Holt, 2005). 1989 marked the advent of Green Supply Chain Management, based on an idea of reused products and recycling (Fortes, 2009). Green Logistics emprise the connection of ecological operation in the supply chain, including the product design, choice and shipment of raw materials, the products elaboration, its delivery to the customer and the product's life cycle after the usage (Srivastava, 2007). The main purpose of Green Logistics is to minimize the environmental harmful effect of a product or a service covering the phases of extraction of raw materials and sourcing, manufacturing, distribution and product recovery (McKinnon, et al., 2011). According to Boks and Stevels (2007) the meaning of the word Green divided to three different perspectives: *the Green Science, Green Government* and *Green Customer*. The first of them refers to these procedures by which the effect of a product or a service in the environment is measured and the product's life cycle is analyzed. Green Government mostly worries about emissions of each process in the supply chain, as well as with the availability of the energy sources, population and geographical location. Responsible for this is the European Commission with guidelines and legislations (Sarkis, 2003). Finally, the third of the above perspectives is trying to interpret the customer's perspective towards the environment, if it is friendly or not (Boks & Stevels, 2007).

2.1   Why Green Logistics

Unarguable, the reasons which force organisations to make on investment of Green logistics are different in each country, sector and organization (Scot & Fischer, 1993). Furthermore, governmental allowances can help the increase of more green supply chains, although the firms need to strategically decide to become friendlier with the environment because this is the "right thing to do" (Wang, et al., 2011). The three basic benefits of green logistics are the competitive advantage, because the customers prefer the more ecological firms, motivating aspects, from the workers and employees to help the environment and obviously financial benefits, through reduction of the use of resources (Rao & Holt, 2005). Good will towards the environment is not the only reason why companies choose to transform their logistics systems. Profitability, cost reduction, waste reduction, advertising and other financial and marketing issues have driven the implementation of Green Logistics (McKinnon, et al., 2011). Also, one of the most significant reasons of Green Logistics existence is the environmental laws the governments instituted (Paulraj, 2008). For example the Environmental Protection Agency (EPA) protects the human health of each potential danger the environment can pose. In addition, laws and rules such as the Restriction of Hazardous Substances refer not only to the manufactures, but also to the suppliers, retailers even to the customers (Trunick, 2006). Another important motive of Green Logistics is the intense competition between the firms. Every organization aims to impress the customer about their ecological profile and stand out of the competition. Green Supply chain is one of the best ways of marketing and advertisement regardless if the competitors use it or not (Clark, 1999).

2.2   IT and Green Logistics

Information Systems (IS) can provide great help in Green Logistics management. By the efficient use of information technology, the appropriate function of the network will occur, aiming towards faster and more effective green supply chain management. Cutting edge technologies in logistics cannot only improve the business performance, but can reduce the ecological impacts as well. For instance, information sharing techniques create an efficient and green supply chain (Heying & Sanzero, 2009). Techniques like information sharing can facilitate the environmental performance of a firm through a better cooperation between the partners or the sectors of the firm, in order to recycle and reuse the products (Bernon, et al., 2011). Internal cross-departmental integration can also contribute to greener logistics. For instance the better anticipation of customers' demand can reduce the returns of unsold products which harm the environment (James, et al., 2004). IT practices such electronic data interchange (EDI) can improve environmental consciousness. For instance, by using EDI organizations diminish the paper consumption, e.g. prints of invoices. However, it is important to note that these techniques could cause an increase in energy consumption, which could harm the environment (Sarkis, et al., 2004).

IS can provide management tools for the supply chain of a firm and its logistics transport them (Hoek, 2004). Moreover, Warehouse Management System software can also facilitate to overcome the problems related with returns. These systems can produce a competitive advantage, allure new suppliers and manage the returns process (Parvenov, 2005). Although, studies have shown that there is not the perfect information system that can anticipate the amount of returns and provide the best solution to become more ecological (Mortensen & Lemoine, 2005). In conclusion, there are a number of issues related to Green IT but in this study we emphasise in the use of IT to support green logistics.

2.3   Rationale for Implementing a Green Logistics Strategy

Green Logistics not only improve the ecological performance of companies, but also can raise sales, improve market share and promote new opportunities for the green organisations which sequentially bring financial profits (Rao & Holt, 2005). Moreover, Green Logistics can enforce the economic performance and provide competitive advantage because, through them raw materials and energy are saved. Apart from cost reduction through the green performance, there is also a reduction of the risk for any potential fines from the government for not following the green laws (Klassen & McLaughlin, 1996). Nevertheless, there are still a number of sceptics on this subject, claiming that Green Logistics can harm the financial performance of the firm. As a result in many cases the meaning of Green Logistics either is overseen or avoided (Klassen & McLaughlin, 1996). The cost of the Green equipment, the lack of commitment from senior managers, the lack of green standards can influence the implementation of Green Logistics in a specific industry sector (Min & Galle, 1997). The change into greener logistics sounds easy and profitable but in reality is a complicated strategy which can involve a lot of risks. (Rodrigue, et al., 2001). Cost could be the major impediment as ecological functions can cost more than the less green ones. Also, in terms of time-delivery, the more ecological modes seem to be the less reliable. As far as the warehouses' function is concerned, the reduction of the inventory provokes more emissions because the products are moving all the time trying not to be stored in one warehouse (Rodrigue, et al., 2001). Furthermore, the high cost of environmental programs, lack of buyers, supplier awareness or national regulations are issues which need to be dealt with by firms in order to improve their environmental performance (Rao & Holt, 2005).

The above literature review has revised a number of under-examined areas which will be the focus on this study. All these area are depicted in figure 1. The selections of these themes have been based on the literature in relation to the specific context of the case study, which is a Greek retailer. Retailers are responsible for the collection, storage, distribution and disposal of products. They have the role of the receiver of customers recycling. For the aforementioned reasons they commonly act as pioneers in reducing waste and preserving the quality of product life and natural resources (Triantafyllou & Cherrett, 2010). The company under consideration is a retailer who having all these concerns in mind has embarked in a green logistics operation as described in the next sections. Our purpose is the study the company's efforts as a way to determine the trade-off between being green and investments needed.

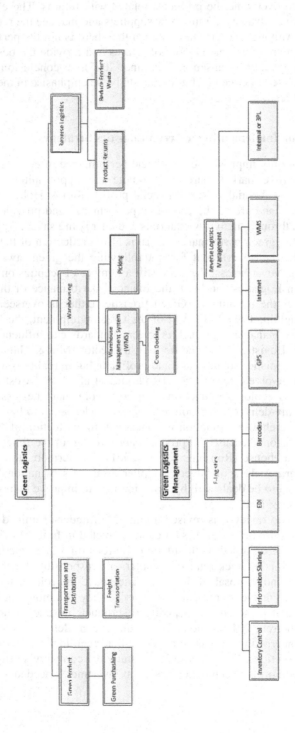

Fig. 1. Key issues to be examined

3   Research Methodology

This study was designed as a qualitative single case study. Case study research is an approach of researches in real life, especially in management topics. When a holistic study is needed this kind of research is one of the best which can be used. By asking comprehensive questions, the organization's culture is investigated, and the findings refer mostly to the specific firm (Boyatzis, 1998). As it is referred this paper focuses only on one firm, a super market chain, by providing information and a clear picture to the reader about the specific company and its green logistics. Masoutis is a super-market chain in Greece. Its headquarters are located in Thessaloniki. The company was established in 1976 by Diamantis Masoutis - who still owns the company. Masoutis is by far the biggest regional grocery retail chain in Greece. As of 2012, the company has a total of 234 retail stores. All of them are located in Northern Greece. The main warehouse is located in Thessaloniki at the area called Kavalari. The warehouse, 57.400 m^2, was a 75 million investment aiming to cover the logistic needs for each super market. All the stores are provided the products either from the main warehouse of the company or directly from the supplier, according to their specific contracts. The warehouse is operated by 400 warehouse employees. Masoutis has its own trucks to distribute the products but also cooperates with three 3PL companies. There are 80 different exits in the warehouse, providing the opportunity to load 80 different trucks at the same time. In addition, they adopted a new technology, which is based on automations and RFIDs. Moreover, there is a specific place for the destroyed, or unable for reuse products where their landfill occurs. The ecologic standards are followed during the warehouse's construction and operation. The company does not manufacture any product but it cooperates with partners in order to produce its own label products which are recyclable and almost all of them reusable. As far as the data collection is concerned, interviews and documents were occurred to collect the data. Semi-unstructured interviews were the main body of the data collection in the case study, asking flexible questions applicable to any change maybe was needed (Saunders, et al., 2003). The anonymous interviews were based on records alongside note taking techniques (Bernon, et al., 2011). Documentation such as blueprints of any innovation or change in the firm, personal notes of the employees, personnel records, stakeholders' reports etc. were also used. The interviewees belong in 4 different groups representing diverse views within the organization. The 4 main groups for the interviews were:

- Top management executives (3 people)
- Procurement managers (4 people)
- Supply chain assistants (10 people)
- Warehouse employees (10 people)

The sample for interviewees was selected randomly in order to have a holistic and impartial point of view (Saunders, et al., 2003).

Moreover, observation was another means used to gather the data. Observation is way of data collection by watching behaviors, events, or noting physical characteristics in their natural setting (Lofland, 1994). The observations took place within 3 weeks in May 2012. Qualitative data analysis (Silverman, 2006) has been used to analyze the collected data. Thematic analysis (Boyatzis, 1998) was the specific technique used to analyze the key issues depicted in figure 1. Additionally, describe-compare-relate was the main way of data analysis. Comparisons and exemplar analysis were used to filter and correlate categories or themes from the literature review in light of the case study (Bazeley, 2009).

4   Findings

According to top management executive 1 from the company, over the years have embodied and reinforced Green Logistics in their culture, and ecological consciousness in their strategy. They are also committed to follow loyally the regulations towards the environment proved by their effort to obtain any required certification related to the environment. According to the same manager, they have decided to become even more ecological in their logistic procedures, because they believe this brings better functionality as well as financial benefits. They aspire to become one of the greenest retailers in Greece by rating Green Logistics among their top three supply chain priorities. In line with this strategy, senior managers have already mapped their supply chain in three main sectors receipt, inventory and distribution and separately they are trying to make all of them more ecological. In the next sections we examine the company's actions in relation to Green logistics themes presented in figure 1.

4.1   Green Product

As the company is not a manufacturer their effort in using green products is focused on using ecologically responsible suppliers. Due to company's dominant position in the market they can even force their existing suppliers to become ecological in order to increase their orders. For instance, top management executive 1 declared: "*As much as our suppliers care about the environment, we care about them*". The company has initiated the development of a scorecard in order to collect data according to the environmental performance of some products. By that they have developed the eco-labeling technique. They use eco-labeling on some products, informing the costumers which products are the most ecological and how many emissions were exposed during their production. Procurement manager 2 declared, "*It was tough to convince our suppliers to use ecol-labels on their products, because they feel unsure about people's reaction. Eventually almost everybody comforted in this situation by giving to them better offers from our side*". In addition, the company has made sure that their own label products, which are manufactured by outsourcing plants, are ecological and recyclable as well as economical. Their strategy in this area was to provide cheap but green products to customers. The interviewees reported that even the consumables that the company uses in a daily basis, are environment-friendly, despite the facts that sometimes they are more expensive.

4.2   Transportation and Distribution

This company uses mostly road freight. The distribution in three islands occurs by ferries. They mainly distribute the products by their own trucks and they are cooperating with three 3PL (third party logistics) company, which fulfill the environmental needs by the terms of gas emissions, noise, congestion etc. Moreover, under negotiations with the suppliers, they deliver their products by themselves at the stores. In addition, there are occasions where the supplier is allocated to a place near to a store, so the company's truck visit them at the end of its route and load the products which are needed in the central warehouse. By that, less transportation is occurredIn addition, one of the main aims of the firm is to diminish the return products. In order to succeed that they don't accept returns from the stores by reasons, such as warehouse stock, wrong anticipation or other unimportant reasons. By doing that, they reduced the routes and the fuels consumption (Ubeda, et al., 2011). As a result, they have transformed the firm to a greener one. Procurement manager 1 stated: *"unreasonable returns is like the worm which parasites in the apple, and we want our warehouse to be a healthy apple"*. The distribution routes are determined by the place of the store, the freight of each truck, the capacity of each truck, the congestion and the less fuel consumption, in order to reduce the costs and increase their green performance as a company. After 3 interviews with the distribution managers we concluded that the busiest period of delivery is between 8 to 12 am. Because of the regular checking and servicing of each trunk, it is rare for a truck to break down and cause environmental harms. The use of Information Communication Technology (ICT) in the form of on line stores has also contributed to the company's green strategy. The online buying is operating in some areas according to the workload and the demand they have in the specific area. By that they urge the customers not to use their cars so as to decrease the CO_2 emissions. By delivering the products at the customer's door they can save money and fuel consumption. They found that by operating online shopping they can lower the carbon and the environmental footprint (Edwards, et al., 2009). Many retailers declared that there are environmental benefits of online grocery distribution. One of the long-term goals of the firm is to evaluate the CO_2 emissions of online and ordinary shopping through an analysis of customers' shopping habits, alongside with an analysis of the related freight movements countrywide.

4.3   Green Warehousing

Recently, the firm moved to a larger and more innovative and eco-friendly warehouse. They are also trying to perform less storage for the products and increase the cross-docking procedure. After negotiation with the supplier, they know when to deliver the products in the warehouse, at the right time when the other trucks are going to be loaded. As a result, the received products are distributed on the spot. By that, the emissions caused by the storage products are almost reduced to zero.

As far as the function inside the warehouse is concerned, the greenest functionality is the one with the least movements of both equipment and working staff. The company made enormous efforts to lower these movements by using Enterprise Resource Planning (ERP) systems. The picking occurs through the RFID technology by which each product has a barcode and by scanning it you can give some orders to the system such like delete, load, sent, move to a new place etc. At the moment, they are considering two new technologies of picking in a warehouse, the Voice technology and the Pick to Light. Furthermore, they set the warehouse in order to diminish the movements from the other side as well, at the store where the products are delivered. The structure of the warehouse and the racks inside it actually force the warehouse employee to pile up the products in a trolley for a specific store at the opposite order of the store's racks. Therefore, when the employee at the store receives the products it is easy to unpack them and place them at the racks avoiding any backwards or extra movement.

4.4   Reverse Logistics

Regarding the reverse logistics, the company defying cost, adopted green reverse logistics practices which provides the opportunity for their customers to dispose his/her garbage in recycling bin next to every store of the firm. The decision of following a green policy in reverse logistic was taken not only for the financial gains but also to improve the living standard of their customers. As it is already mentioned the firm trying to reduce the fuel consumption they cancel the returns from the stores to the main warehouse. They accept them only if there is a customer's request, the product can be used again, it needs to be allocated somewhere else, repair, refurbishing, remanufacturing and cannibalization. Setting recycling bins next to each store make the above decision of products' returns cancellation even more feasible. The company's trucks when they finish their routes in order not to cover distances without load, they collect the returns from the stores to the warehouse. In addition the firm deals with the suppliers who distribute some products by themselves at the stores, to collect any return of their product the store has and reuse them somewhere else. All of the return products in the warehouse proceed to reuse, recycle or landfill.

4.5   Green Logistic Management

E-logistics: A number of IS and technologies are used by the company to apply their Green Logistics Management. The top management executive 2 denoted, *"We are trying to set some benchmarks in order to measure our green performance in order to make it greener as the time goes by"*. Below, the IS that the company uses will be described and the way that IS improve the ecological image of the firm will be analyzed. The most reliable way to capture the e-logistics implications on the environment is to investigate them from the perspective of the movement of materials and information through the supply chain (Sarkis, et al., 2004).

EDI: The company uses EDI to cooperate with suppliers in payments and to provide them statistical data for their products (sales, demand, stock etc.). By that, they save a lot of paper work, which has a positive impact on the environment. Moreover, by the statistics of each product, another paper-free procedure, the supplier can anticipate better the product demand and decrease the overproduction and the warehouse stock. By these actions the overall logistics footprint is minimised.

Information Sharing (over the Supply Chain): Masoutis has adopted cross-company information sharing. By that, two or more companies can access data of another company and vice-versa. The company shares its data only with big suppliers, such as Procter & Gamble, Unilever, in order to avoid the "bullwhip effect". Bullwhip effect describes the big fluctuations of a product stock in the warehouse (Lee, et al., 2000). Our company by providing data according to the supplier's products only succeed to minimise the stock in the warehouse and meet environmental standards by reducing warehouse emissions. Thus, the supplier knows the location, time and the quantity of the products that he has to deliver which avoided complimentary actions such as a second route. As a result, the fuel emissions are lower. In addition as the supply chain assistant 8 denoted, *"donot forget the fact that we share our information not our profits"*.

Inventory Control: Being one of the largest and more innovative warehouses in Greece, the company implemented an IS to control their inventory. By that, time is saved in picking while the distances which are covered by the electric forklifts are reduced. Consequently they save huge amounts of energy and fuels. Moreover, when a senior manager has to order another load from a supplier, they are advised the inventory control system to check the remainder stock and the weekly and monthly flow of each product. As a result, they can easily forecast the product demand and order the exact needed amount of products, hence reduced the stock in warehouse and improved the green warehouse performance. They can also perform monthly checks in the inventory and correct any potential mistakes. Keeping under control their inventory, they know exactly the volume of the emissions they produce and what actions need to take to reduce the emissions. As the warehouse employee 3 declared, *"By following the instructions from the product, it not only saves the environment but also saves our times, which make us much happier"*.

Internet and Barcodes: By using the Internet, paper works were minimized, i.e. they replaced faxes with emails. Internet also provides the firm with new solutions or options to become even greener in its functionality. Moreover, the company is not a small super market chain but covers every corner of northern Greece. As a result, they sell services as well as papers, books and magazines. Concerning the environment they are planning to provide these products online in order to improve their ecological face. As for barcodes, maybe barcode does not have a direct positive impact to the environment but it is the driving force for IS which actually provide greener solutions and functions..

Global Positioning Systems (GPS): In the case study company, they use GPS to locate their trucks and any traffic congestion. By checking the traffic daily in cities they can set a better route in order to save fuels and to present more environmentally friendly face. The warehouse employee 2 (the driver) stated, *"GPS is one of the best inventions I have even seen during the 20 years of driving. It keeps me always posted and helps my vehicle to consume fewer fuels"*.

4.5.1 Warehouse Management System

All the above and some other IS provide data in a general Warehouse Management System (WMS), which only the senior managers can access. According to that they can prevent discrepancies in the operations, which can cause a negative impact on the environment. For instance, a senior manager reported that 2 months ago through the system they managed to predict the meat production for the next 2 months. Thus, they closed down one of the three massive refrigerators in order to gain money and energy. By that the warehouse emissions decreased substantially comparing to the previous years. The WMS also includes the reverse logistics operation. They provide the optimum route to collect the returns from customers or stores. In doing so, they are trying to minimize the returns and the product's waste. Reverse logistics is a significant part in logistics and the case study firm pays a lot of attention to keep its supply chain green, both ways.

5   Discussion on Benefits vs. Costs for the Company

The retail sector has made considerable effort to become greener in their supply chain, but with the rising cost they reached to a point that becoming green is expensive and futile. For instance, the case study company is spending huge amount of money trying to build greener stores and a greener warehouse. The top management executive commented: *"Since we decided to build a green warehouse the costs have raised almost double as we anticipated. However, we proceeded and eventually we did not regret at all"*. According to the same manager, they could have spent almost half amount of money if they have chosen un-ecological ways of infrastructure and operation. This verified by the literature as Green products and services are often more expensive than ordinary ones (Philipp & Militaru, 2011). It is difficult to quantify the cost of going green. However, in this case the cost savings increased since the adoption of green techniques in their logistics. Moreover, they can measure the Return on Investment (ROI) of green logistics in sales, market share, happier customers and employees and enhancement of the brand. In addition, as the procurement manager 1 claimed, *"A better future for our kids is a benefit as well"*.

By distributing **green products** the company has broadened the market share by adding another portion of people in their target group, the environmental friendly consumers. After some months it was discovered that the profits from this part of people overtake the cost of manufacturing and distributing green products. As for **transportation and distribution** is concerned, the decision of buying ecological vehicles was taken under serious consideration. So far, the board is pleased by that decision because they spend less money in fuels and services. By developing the optimum route of product distribution for every day according the day's needs they save money in fuels and pointless trips. For implementing **green warehousing** they went to great lengths to establish a fully innovative and contemporary environmental friendly warehouse. However, as the time goes by, their profits overcome the cost by the reduction on the energy bills of the warehouse. Moreover, following green procedures to storage and distribute products they save much space in the warehouse, providing them the opportunity to store other kinds of products. By that they can storage every single product which circulates in the Greek retail market, addressing by that to a bigger target group which can provide financial benefits.

As mentioned in the analysis section, the company, by using green **reverse logistics** saves big amounts of money, reducing the products waste and increasing their usability.

Use of **IT and e-logistics** the company believes that they have achieved major financial benefits. As the top management executive 3 claimed: *"We have been trying for years to bridge the gap between environment and financial profits in our supply chain. By using e-logistics, we have built this bridge much faster"*. This is achieved by using **EDI, information sharing over the supply chain, electronic inventory control, Internet and barcodes** and **GPS technology.** Last but not least, the company decided to implement a **green warehouse management** which produces financial benefits by helping and supporting all of the above techniques.

After the analysis in section 4 as well as this discussion it is apparent that the combination of logistics, environment and IT not only protects the environment but also offers financial benefits for the case company. Warehouse employee 1 claimed, *"Since we have applied the IT in our logistic plan, it is easily noticeable the financial benefits especially in reduced workload and reduced products' waste"*.

Moreover, the **government's pressure** towards green logistics has also been a major driver for the adoption of green practices. A green supply chain can cost money to build but it can save you money from government's fines. As the top management executive 1 stated, *"do not neglect the fact that, we are getting a lot of pressure to become friendlier with the environment by the government. So, the WMS besides everything else helps as to absorb this pressure and become green and legal at the same time"*. In summary, the company's profit has risen since they adopt the green supply chain strategy. The return of the green investment came quickly and there was no time that they regretted this action. Also, by promoting even more ecological products they managed to broaden their market target and obviously their market share. As a result, the company strongly believed that green logistic techniques provided not only financial gains but also competitive advantage. This is in line with the literature that Green logistics can provide financial gains and competitive advantage in the firm (Rao & Holt, 2005).

6   Conclusions

Customer's consciousness and *governmental pressures* are two of the main reasons that urged firms to become greener in the supply chain. Nowadays, the embodiment of green logistics in company's strategy is common worldwide. Although, the above company does not manufacture products but only distributes them, contributes in a greener supply chain between partners and suppliers by encouraging their suppliers to create ecological products. Moreover, they have already adopted the Just in Time technique with some suppliers and they are trying to apply it in every supplier. By that, they decrease the time of storage and the warehouse emissions According to the green warehousing the above company uses renewable sources of energies such as solar energy (Preuss, 2005). Many interviewees noticed that the customers are not always ecologically-conscious thus, they are not willing to pay more for a greener product. As a result, companies face the challenge to make the products and the entire supply chain process more ecological by keeping the same product's price (Braithwaite & Knivett, 2008). E-logistics can facilitate and improve the firm's image towards the environment in the inventory management through information sharing as the case study company does by sharing records and reduce the delays and the paperwork. In addition, e-logistics can help through postponement by delaying the manufacturing of the product until the customer orders it by reducing the inventory in warehouses (Park & Roome, 2002). Furthermore, through these systems companies can manage more than one warehouse at the time reducing the general stock and inventory and helping the warehouse management through disaggregation (Sarkis, et al., 2004). With the right guidance and operation E-logistics can provide environmental protection. IS which measure the performance is useful in supply chain. The traditional IS in supply chain are focus-oriented around accuracy, cost and time. Nowadays, firms must implement the environmental responsibility as another core subject into their IS (Bhagwat & Sharma, 2007). Software suppliers are trying to help firms out to measure their emissions in economical terms and to capture the CO_2 emissions from their supply chains. They even provide models to describe the ecological performance of the firm (Braithwaite & Knivett, 2008). Companies can adopt a green model which actually measures the green performance of the firm according to some indicators or standards and provide solutions in order to become greener. Moreover, through this model they can compare themselves with other companies in the same sector (Consulting, 2003). Also, companies in retail sector can convince their suppliers to adopt a green strategy and restrict them to use some chemical elements which are harmful to the environment. In addition, constant training and feedback to the workforce about green procedures are needed. Creating awareness of green logistics' benefits could produce a greener culture and more ecological operation. Although our results show that the overall benefits of adopting green logistics are visible, implementing green logistics might result in increased bills and extra expenses especially at the induction period.

To conclude, it is difficult to become green. There are plenty of tools which can facilitate the procedure and make it less time consuming to implement. Each firm has to measure their performance, to set a benchmark in order to establish and find out more movements and changes which can provide benefits towards the environment. According to the green techniques that have to be part of the supply chain, each of them has its own strategic and management requirements. This paper provides some recommendations and useful information to other companies looking to exploit green IT logistics. This paper however has not covered the entire green logistics field. Thus, further investigation is recommended to cover other green logistics aspects especially for firms under specific circumstances of operation.

References

Aronsson, H., Brodin, H.: The Environmental Impact Of Changing Logistics Structures. The International Journal of Logistics Management 17(3), 394–415 (2006)

Bazeley, P.: Analysing Qualitative Data: More Than 'Identifying Themes'. Malaysian Journal of Qualitative Research 2(1), 6–22 (2009)

Bernon, M., Rossi, S., Cullen, J.: Retail reverse logistics: a call and grounding framework for research. International Journal of Physical Distribution & Logistics Management 41(5), 484–510 (2011)

Bhagwat, R., Sharma, M.K.: Performance measurement of supply chain manage-ment:A balanced scorecard approach. Computers & Industrial Engineering 53(1), 43–62 (2007)

Boks, C., Stevels, A.: Essensial Perspectives for Design for Environment. Experiences from the Electronic Industry. Production Research 45(18), 4021–4039 (2007)

Boyatzis, R.: Transforming Qualitative Information: Thematic Analysis and Code Development, 1st edn. SAGE, United States of America (1998)

Braithwaite, A., Knivett, D.: Evaluating A Supply Chain'S Carbon Footprint – A Methodology and Case Example of Carbon-to-Serve. In: Lyon: Logistics Research Network 2008: Conference Proceedings (2008)

Brundtland Commission: Our Common Future, 1st edn. Oxford University, Oxford (1987)

Clark, D.: What Drives Companies to Seek ISO 14000 Certification. Pollution Engineering Summer, pp. 14–18 (1999)

Consulting, L.G.: Postconflict (2003),
http://postconflict.unep.ch/humanitarianaction/documents/02_08-04_05-11.pdf (accessed June 21, 2012)

Edwards, J., Cullinane, S., McKinnon, A.: GreenLogistics (2009),
http://www.greenlogistics.org/SiteResources/7ffc66c2-4e53-4c3d-a29d-f62f49458dfa_J.Edwards%20-%20Carbon%20auditign%20conventional%20and%20online%20book%20supply%20chains.pdf (accessed September 2, 2012)

Fiksel, J.: Design for Environment, Second Edition: A Guide to Sustainable Product Development: Eco-Efficient Product Development, 2nd edn. McGraw-Hill Professional, London (2010)

Fortes, J.: Green Supply Chain Management: A Literature. Otago Management Graduate Review 7(1), 51–62 (2009)

Heying, A., Sanzero, W.: A Case Study of Wal-Mart ' s " Green " Supply Chain Management. Operations Management, 1–10 (May 4, 2009)

Hoek, R.: Using information technology to leverage transport and logistics service op-erations in the supply chain: an empirical assessment of the interrelation between technology and operations management. International Journal of Technology Management 23(1), 207–222 (2004)

James, M., Grosvenor, R., Prickett, P.: e-Distribution: Internet-based management of a merchandiser supply chain. Supply Chain Management: An International Journal 9(1), 7–15 (2004)

Klassen, R., McLaughlin, C.: The Impact Of Environmental Management On Firm Performance. Management Science 42(8), 1199–1213 (1996)

Lee, H., So, K., Tang, C.: The Value of Information Sharing in a Two-Level Supply Chain. Management Science 46(5), 626–643 (2000)

Lofland, J.: Analyzing social settings: a guide to qualitative observation and analysis, 1st edn. Thomson Wadsworth, London (1994)

McKinnon, A., Cullinane, S., Browne, M., Whiteing, A.: Green Logistics: Improving the environmental sustainability of logistics, 1st edn. KoganPage, London (2011)

Mortensen, O., Lemoine, W.: Information Technologies and Supply Chain Integration. A study among manufacturers and transport and logistics service providers. In: Netherlands, Workshop Supply Chain Management and Communication Technology. University of Groningen (2005)

Park, J., Roome, N.: The Ecology of the New Economy: Sustainable Transformation of Global Information, Communications and Electronic Industries, 1st edn. Greenleaf, Midsomer Norton (2002)

Parvenov, A.: SupplyChainDigest (2005),
http://www.scdigest.com/assets/Reps/SCDigest_Best_Practices_Warehouse_Returns.pdf (accessed June 6, 2012)

Paulraj, A.: Environmental Motivations: a Classification Scheme and its Impact on Environmental Strategies and Practices. Business Strategy and the Environment 18, 453–468 (2008)

Philipp, B., Militaru, D.: Key Factors for Environmentally Friendly Logistics Services in the French Region of Picardy. International Journal of Logistics Research and Applications: A Leading Journal of Supply Chain Management 14(6), 413–426 (2011)

Preuss, L.: The Green Multiplier: A study of Environmentla Protection and the Supply Chain, 1st edn. Palgrave MacMillan, New York (2005)

Rao, P., Holt, D.: Do green supply chains lead to competitiveness and economic performance? International Journal of Operations & Production Management 25(9), 898–916 (2005)

Ribeiro, S.K., Kobayashi, S.: In Climate Change 2007: Mitigation. Contribution of Working Group III to the Fourth Assessment Report of the Intergovernmental Panel on Climate Change. In: Bose, R., Kheshgi, H. (eds.) Transport and its Infrastructure, pp. 325–380. Cambridge University Press, Cambridge (2007)

Rodrigue, J.-P., Slack, B., Comtois, C.: Green Logistics (The Paradoxes of). Business Administration Production, Operations and Manufacturing Management Papers, pp. 1–11 (2001)

Sarkis, J.: A strategic decision framework for green supplychain management. Journal of Cleaner Production 11(4), 397–409 (2003)

Sarkis, J., Meade, L.M., Talluri, S.: E-logistics and the natural environment. Supply Chain Management: An International Journal 9(4), 303–312 (2004)

Saunders, M., Lewis, P., Thornhill, A.: Research Methods for Business Students, 3rd edn. Prentice Hall, England (2003)

Scot, J., Fischer, K.: Introduction: The Greening of the Industrial Firm, 1st edn. Island Press, Washington (1993)

Silverman, D.: Interpreting Qualitative Data, 3rd edn. SAGE Publications Ltd., London (2006)

Srivastava, S.K.: Green supply-chain management: A state-of the-art literature review. International Journal of Management Reviews 9(1), 53–80 (2007)

Triantafyllou, M.K., Cherrett, T.J.: The logistics of managing hazardous waste: a case study analysis in the UK retail sector. International Journal of Logistics Research and Applications 13(5), 373–394 (2010)

Trunick, P.: A Green Role for Logistics. Logistics Today 47(6), 26–28 (2006)

Ubeda, S., Faulin, J., Arcelus, F.: Green logistics at Eroski: A case study. Int. J. Production Economics 131(1), 44–51 (2011)

Wang, C., J, V., Mercer, J., Zhao, Y.: A case-based model facilitating retailing op-erations going "green": A proposed research agenda with a consideration of recession. Dalian, Asia Pacific, s.n., pp. 1–4 (2011)

Major Issues in the Successful Implementation of Information Systems in Developing Countries

Ranjan Vaidya, Michael D. Myers, and Lesley Gardner

Department of Information Systems & Operations Management,
University of Auckland Business School,
OGGB, 12 Grafton Road, Auckland, New Zealand 1010
{r.vaidya,m.myers,l.gardner}@auckland.ac.nz

Abstract. Information systems projects in developing countries continue to fail. Our research aims to understand some of the major issues that negatively impact the success of public sector information systems projects in developing countries. For this, we conducted a qualitative study of a state agricultural marketing board in India. The board initiated an information systems project in 2003. The objective of the project was to connect the various agricultural markets spread across the state by deploying hi-tech information and communication technologies. Unfortunately, the project was abandoned because of the growing conflicts between the government and private vendors implementing the project. The major stakeholders in the project included the government, private vendors, farmers and traders. The data for this critical case study were collected over a period of eight months from 2009 to 2012 using semi structured interviews, field visits and observations. The findings suggest that the *lack of trust* and *resignation* (to certain unfair practices being virtually impossible to change) are the core issues that impede success of information systems implementation in developing countries.

Keywords: information systems failure, developing countries, critical case study, agricultural marketing.

1 Introduction

The UN millennium development goals have changed the emphasis of *development* from economic growth to poverty reduction (Christiaensen, Demery, & Kuhl, 2010). As almost three fourths of the world's poor live in rural areas and depend on agriculture for their livelihood (Giovannucci et al., 2012), many international developmental institutions are focusing their efforts on improving agriculture in these areas. Poverty reduction can be achieved in a variety of ways e.g. improving agricultural productivity by increasing crop yields, or by improving the supply chain and marketing of agricultural produce.

In this article we focus on how Information and Communication Technology (ICT) can play a decisive role in agricultural marketing. Information about weather forecasts, market prices, and the demand-supply status can be readily accessed and distributed through ICT. In the last two decades many government organisations, non-government

Y.K. Dwivedi et al. (Eds.): TDIT 2013, IFIP AICT 402, pp. 151–163, 2013.

organisations, and corporate and funding agencies across the developing countries have initiated ICT projects that exclusively deal with agricultural marketing (Banker, Mitra, & Sambamurthy, 2011; Kamala, 2008).

However, empirical evidence indicates that there are various kinds of problems in the conceptualisation, design and implementation of these projects. In most cases, these projects are conceptualised as *price information systems* that do not address the *marketing* asymmetries in the supply chain (Islam & Grönlund, 2010). They suffer due to various contextual problems such as lack of education and the illiteracy of the farmers (Lokanathan & De Silva, 2010), lack of supporting policies (Rao, 2007) and intermittent political interference (FAO, 1997). Economically, these projects often do not have proper funding support (Tollens, 2006). The government organisations implementing these tend to be ridden with rigid bureaucracies, corruption and inefficient project management (Islam & Grönlund, 2010). The situation is further acerbated because agricultural technology adoption is difficult in these developing countries, both because of geographical and cultural reasons (Aker, 2011; Batt, 2001a).

Given these various kinds of problems and issues related to agricultural marketing information systems (AMIS) implementation, this research project seeks to understand the major issues in the successful implementation of AMIS in developing countries. Consequently the research question that it addresses is: What are the major issues in the successful implementation of agricultural marketing information systems in developing countries?

To try to answer this question, the research undertakes a critical case study of the implementation and adoption of an agricultural marketing information system in India. The AMIS was designed to improve the lives of the poor farmers by streamlining the entire auction process, giving them access to price information, and generally improving transparency. The AMIS was implemented in over two hundred market yards (popularly called as Mandi) in one state of India beginning in 2003. Unfortunately however, by 2011-2012 the project was abandoned. This case study provides a good opportunity to understand the major issues in the implementation of AMIS in developing countries.

The paper is structured as follows. In the next section we present a literature review on agricultural marketing information systems. This is followed by the description of our research method. Section four presents the case study of the agricultural marketing board. In section five we present our analysis of the case. Finally, we present our conclusions.

2   Literature Review

A literature review of seventy six research articles covering the period of thirty five years from 1967 (Abbott, 1967) to 2011 (Ghadiyali, Lad, & Patel, 2011) indicated three major themes namely; conceptual challenges to AMIS implementation, empirical challenges to AMIS implementation and trust issues in AMIS implementation. Ontologically, the conceptual and empirical challenges together represent the design-reality gap (Heeks, 2002). Trust issues, on the other hand, represent the human issues of implementation. Together these three conceptual elements provide a good picture of the implementation challenges. Each of these is briefly discussed here.

2.1   Conceptualization Challenges to AMIS

Information systems researchers have identified four types of agriculture related information systems. These are knowledge management systems, inspection and certification systems, market information systems and procurement and traceability systems (Parikh, Patel, & Schwartzman, 2007). A "marketing information system" fails to fall in any of these categories because of the conceptual differences between the terms *market* and *marketing* in agriculture. Park (1989) conceptualises agricultural activities as complex business activities rather than a simple means of subsistence. The author sees *agricultural marketing* as a coordinated activity of farm supplies, harvesting and production, logistics and commodity processing. The author mentions that while price information systems are well conceived, the 'marketing' component has not received adequate attention from developers. Shepherd and Schalke (1995) suggest that *marketing* is a broader concept that includes "details on potential market channels, payment requirements, packaging, quality and a whole range of other information, including market information." According to Van Crowder (1997), *market information* alone limits the farmers to react to changes in prices. *Marketing information,* on the other hand, provides them an opportunity to manoeuvre according to the market dynamics. By and large AMIS have been wrongly conceptualised as price information systems and hence the majority of AMIS projects in developing countries merely capture the price or quantity of agricultural commodities in various retail or wholesale markets (Tollens, 2006).

2.2   Empirical Challenges in AMIS Implementation

Researchers have identified various implementation challenges of AMIS. Often organisations implementing AMIS deploy their own staff for collection of data. This results in overhead expenses that cannot be sustained over a long period. Second, there are issues related to public sector organisational culture in developing countries. Researchers have suggested that rigid bureaucracy, corruption and the attitude of government officers in developing countries pose a challenge to information systems implementation generally, and AMIS implementation in particular (Krishna & Walsham, 2010; Walsham, 2010). AMIS are sometimes deployed to serve the information needs of the government officers rather than the farmers who are meant to be the intended beneficiaries in AMIS (Tollens, 2006). Third, researchers have identified issues with data collection and their accuracy (Islam & Grönlund, 2010). Fourth, there are contextual challenges to AMIS implementation. AMIS implementation might not be accompanied with changes in the statutory laws as is demonstrated in the e-choupal case (Rao, 2007). There are also frequent interventions from the powerful stakeholder groups such as traders and politicians (Shepherd, 1997).

2.3   Trust Issues in Agricultural Marketing

Some researchers have highlighted the importance of trust in agricultural marketing. Researchers have suggested that trust is paramount in agricultural marketing as it reduces uncertainty across the agricultural supply chain and trustful relationships are essential for agricultural development (Ballantyne, 2009). Some factors or conditions have a negative impact on trust formation in agriculture marketing in developing countries, for example, use of coercive power by stakeholders, opportunistic behaviour and trader collusion.

On the other hand, relationship investments, satisfaction with past services, information sharing attitudes and humbleness have a positive impact on trust formation (Banerji & Meenakshi, 2004; Batt, 2001a; Best, Ferris, & Schiavone, 2005). Some researchers have suggested that trust formation in agricultural marketing is a long term process (Batt, 2001a, 2001b; Molony, 2008).

Certain behavioural patterns of the stakeholders in agricultural marketing can have an impact on stakeholder trust (Drafor & Atta-Agyepong, 2005; Jensen, 2010; Mittal, Gandhi, & Tripathi, 2010). Based on our analysis of seventy six research articles, we were able to identify those agricultural marketing related practices of farmers and traders that have an impact on trust levels between the stakeholders. These are presented in the Table 1.

Table 1. Stakeholders' patterns of behaviour cited by researchers

Practices of stakeholders	Citation Source
Farmers do not abide by their auction contracts.	(Best et al., 2005)
Farmers do not pack their agricultural commodities properly.	(Batt, 2004)
Farmers do not show a true representative sample of their commodity to the traders.	
Traders exaggerate their purchase prices and under-quote their selling prices.	
Traders make less payment to farmers than the agreed prices.	(Pokhrel & Thapa, 2007)
Traders do not divulge their purchase information for fear of being taxed.	(Tollens, 2006)
Traders do not weigh the commodity correctly.	(Chengappa, 2003; Kydd & Dorward, 2004)
Traders form cartels to control commodity prices.	(Meenakshi & Banerji, 2005)
Traders control the harvesting of commodities.	(Pokhrel & Thapa, 2007)
Traders are inclined to offer the lowest possible prices to farmers.	(Goyal, 2010 ; Muto & Yamano, 2009)
Traders provide seed loans to the farmers on the condition that the produce will be sold to the traders at pre fixed prices.	(Batt & Rexha, 1999)
Traders provide credits to the farmers.	(Anupindi & Sivakumar, 2007; Blattman, Jensen, & Roman, 2003; Molony, 2008; Shepherd, 1997)

Amongst the three themes discussed above, we focus on trust issues in AMIS implementation from now on. This is for two reasons. First, researchers have suggested that trust formation is critical for the success of agriculture marketing (Almond & Hainsworth, 2005) and yet trust issues are usually not given adequate importance in AMIS design and implementation(Islam & Grönlund, 2010). Second, trust (or rather, the lack of trust) was the major issue leading to the failure of the AMIS in our particular case.

3   Research Method

We used qualitative case study research, since qualitative research helps the researchers to understand the behaviour of people in the light of their context and values (Myers, 2009). Specifically, we used critical case study research, since critical research in IS "is concerned with social issues such as freedom, power, social control, and values with respect to the development, use, and impact of information technology" (Myers & Klein, 2011 p.17). The data for the study was collected by one of the authors for a nine month period between 2009 and 2012. The data was collected from 23 semi structured interviews with the stakeholder groups namely farmers, traders, government officers and private partners. The interviews with the government officers and private partners were undertaken at different levels of hierarchy. The interviews with the farmers and traders were undertaken at market yards as well as their villages. These interviews and field visits were carried out at four different yards in the state. At the micro level, the constant comparison method (CCM) proposed by Boeije (2002) was followed to identify the main themes. Thematic analysis was then undertaken as per the guidelines proposed by Braun & Clarke (2006) leading to the identification of our main findings.

4   Case Description

The case study is of a government owned agricultural marketing board in India. The board controls over 200 hundred market yards of the state which are commonly called as *Mandi*. The farmers bring their produce to these yards where it is auctioned.

Studies indicate that there are large price discrepancies across these market yards and often the farmers are not able to realize the best available prices (Goyal, 2010). Past studies also indicate that farmers face various kinds of problems in the yards such as cheating in commodity weighing, bearing the cost of commodity bags, delays in the payments, etc. These problems have an impact on the socio-psychological well-being of the farmers (Anupindi & Sivakumar, 2007). It is against this background that the board initiated the project to computerize its operations in 2003. The project intended to make the yard operations transparent and help the decision making of the stakeholders, particularly the farmers (Vaidya, Myers, & Gardner, 2011).

In this project, sixty four yards were selected from the over two hundred yards of the state. The data on auctions and weighing was to be collected through hand held electronic machines. A software application was developed to upload the data to a central server. The collated data on commodity prices and volumes was redistributed to the market yards. In the yards, this data was displayed on computers as well as television sets. This helped the farmers and traders to know the rates prevalent in other neighbouring yards. Also, the website of the board displayed the latest commodity data. The private vendor installed the hardware and also deployed manpower to conduct these tasks on built-own-operate basis. The vendor charged a fee for their services, which was based on the yard type and ranged between thirteen to seventeen per cent (MAPIT, 2006; Vaidya, 2009).

A 2008 evaluation by the Department of Information Technology, Ministry of Information and Communication Technology, Government of India indicated that the project was a success (DIT, 2008 p.92). However, our visits to the yard in 2010 revealed that conflicts had developed between the private partners and the government on various issues. The government blamed the private partners for not being sincere, whereas the government officers complained that the private partners were not sincere. The private partners, on the other hand, blamed the government for lacking the appropriate organisational culture for computerisation. In 2011 the equipment of the private partners was seized by the respective yards. Following this the private partners appealed in the state high court where they lost the case. The reasons for the failure of the project are presented in the next section.

5   Case Analysis

Our analysis of the stakeholder interviews revealed that lack of trust was the most important issue in the unsuccessful implementation of the agricultural marketing information systems project. Each stakeholder group regarded the other stakeholder group as dishonest, lacking sincerity and also hegemonic. Nearly all the stakeholders blamed the farmers for not showing the true sample of commodities to the traders. For example, one government officer described this as follows:

> "The farmers have different qualities of the commodity. What is shown as the sample is different from the actual commodity. For example on the top of the bag, they keep good quality while in the bottom, they keep the poor quality. The trader cannot inspect the full commodity as the bags and trolleys are too large to be fully opened...so if you go to the yard premises, you will observe that these conflicts are occurring continuously".

All the stakeholders blamed the traders for doing unregistered trade transactions. According to the other stakeholders, traders under reported their commodities in order to save their service charge payments to the yards. One of the private partner employees described this as follows:

> "The two per cent service charge that the traders are required to pay brings a lot of difference to them as their transaction gets documented. If documented, they have to pay other taxes such as value added tax or sales tax. Sometimes such taxes may reach as high as twenty per cent of the purchased commodity. Obviously the traders try to avoid it".

The private vendors blamed the government officers for lacking the organizational culture that was necessary for the successful implementation of information systems projects. For example one private partner employee mentioned as follows:

> "If any senior officer from the head office comes for a visit to the yard, then all his expenses are borne by the junior government officers. However, I have never seen a junior claiming these expenses from the yard. I fail to understand this, why the junior does not claim these expenses. Is it not his right, is he not entitled to claim these expenses? What is the reason? Why he does not claim these expenses? Sometimes the juniors also ask the private partner to pay for these expenses. Why should the private partner pay for these expenses?"

The government officers blamed the private partners for manipulating their reports in order to prove that computerization was yielding benefits to the yards. This was explained by one government officer as follows:

"I will give you one more example of the...tricks that private partners play to prove the effectiveness of the IS. The traders submit their records of the transaction usually after ten days. For instance, for the trade done between the 1st and 10th of a month, the trader submits the record on 11th. Similarly for the next 10 days, the records are submitted after 20th. Obviously, if you check the computerized records on the fifteenth, it will show that some traders have not paid their service charges. So the private partner reports a recovery from the trader, when in effect the truth is that the trader has not yet submitted the records. So the private partners do such false reporting to show that the IS has been successful in recovering the service charge payments. I can say this thing on behalf of the entire board that just to prove that they have made a positive impact on the yard revenue they present wrong information and do all kinds of manipulations".

The government officers also felt that the private partners often emulated the bureaucratic style of functioning of the government. A government officer revealed this as follows:

"If we ask for any new information or any new module, they say that the required information or module can be generated only after the approval or sanction from the Mandi board".

The same officer presented another example that revealed the working of the private partner:

"I will give an example of the things that they (private partner) do. There is a module in their software for the salary records of the Mandi employees. We were instructed by the authorities in the board that we should help them in the computerisation of the salary records. So we were asked by the establishment section to help this process. The private partners wrote us a letter asking that we should provide them the required information related to employees and their salary records. This meant that we should provide them the data in a format. Obviously this implied that we first do the data entry ourselves and then provide them the data. After some time when we asked them as to why they have not started with the data entry of the salary records? Their site in-charge replied that they had already written a letter to us asking for the required information. Now it is their responsibility to enter the data for the 300 staff employed here. If we are asked to provide the data to them, obviously we will need to do the data entry ourselves. So then what's the work of the private partner? We do not have staff for our own works, and they expect that we will have the staff to enter the data of 300 employees. So we told them clearly that our responsibility is to provide you with the records and not the data and so we will provide you the records and you are supposed to feed these records in your system".

An integrated model of trust formation, based on each stakeholder group's perception about the other stakeholder group, is presented in figure 1. The model presents four key constructs that contribute to trust formation. These include *stakeholder attitude, stakeholder sincerity, stakeholder honesty* and *stakeholder efficiency*. Within *stakeholder attitude,* it suggests that *hegemonic attitude* has negative implications on trust formation.

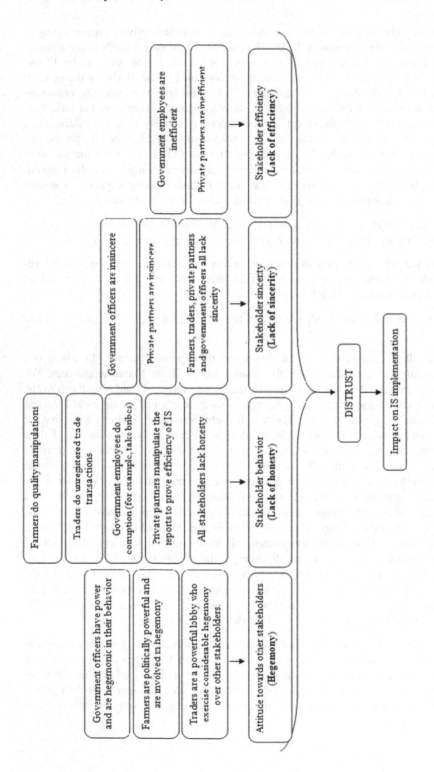

Fig. 1. Integrated model of trust formation

The discussion above demonstrates that *stakeholder trust* was a key issue *in the unsuccessful* implementation of this agricultural marketing information system. Our evidence suggests that indeed yard stakeholders did not trust each other and that they blamed the other stakeholder group for various problems present in the yard. But at the same time our empirical evidence indicated that yard stakeholders were aware about their own behaviour that had a negative impact on functioning of the yards. For instance, farmers were aware of their involvement in the acts of quality manipulations. The traders accepted that it was common for them to under-report their trade transactions; and the government officer readily agreed to the fact that they did "corruption". Table 2 presents some excerpts, in which the stakeholder groups indicated that they were well aware of their own behaviour.

Table 2. Stakeholder excerpts on behavioural self-awareness

Trader	Some companies do not register their purchase of the soya. Then they sell the processed soya products such as de-oiled cakes, oil, etc.
Government Officer	See I am not a puritan...even I do a little (corruption)...but only as per my requirement...
Farmers	...farmers did not provide the promised quality to the companies...instead they mixed the lower varieties with the higher ones...

This indicates that each stakeholder group was involved in certain activities that had a negative impact on *trust*, but at the same time, the stakeholders were also aware of their behaviour. This suggests that everyone knew what the others were doing. It seems as if each stakeholder accepted the *untrustworthy behaviour* of the other stakeholder, including themselves, in spite of being aware that such behaviour had a negative impact on the overall functioning of the yard. This can be understood from the following excerpt by a government officer:

> "It is the weighing process that is the most problematic because those who weigh the commodity, they harass the farmers a lot. They will not weigh the commodity timely; they will not weigh the commodity properly. The weighing labourers are very rude and rash, some of them are not worth talking to. But the farmer keeps his patience, he tolerates everything...he has to tolerate everything...he cannot help it...if he fights or opposes, his payment is delayed...so he tolerates everything..."

Observe here that the government officer mentions that the labourers who weigh the commodity are hegemonic, dishonest and insincere in fulfilling their responsibilities. However, the officer also mentions that the farmers *tolerate* such behaviour of the labourers. This suggests that stakeholders have a high sense of *resignation* as they have no other alternatives to the yard.

Another excerpt from a farmer will further establish that *resignation* along with *mistrust* presents a major challenge for the functioning of the yards. This excerpt relates to a discussion with a farmer who had just completed the weighing of the commodity. There was some conflict between the labourers and farmers while the weighing was still in progress. After the conflict de-escalated, one of the authors approached the farmers and asked them about the conflict. The farmer described the conflict as follows:

> "Actually it is the duty of the labourer to weigh the commodity. He is required to lift the commodity from the vehicle and put it on the weight balance. He is also required to remove it from the weigh balance but they do not do the entire work. So the labour did not come to do this work yet we had to pay to the labourer. So that is what happens here…so they got their labour charges even when they had not done the labour…the rule of the Mandi is that the labourer will weigh the commodity and then will take the charges from us…but here as you may have seen we paid the labourer charges even when they did not do any labour…see if there is a big lot…say in a truck …then the labours take interest in unloading it…else they do not take interest…and suppose we tell them that we need no labour…then they will weigh our commodity late in the evening…and hence we will be relieved later…so we gave them 50 rupees and also did the labour on our own…so that we may be relieved quickly from the yard…see one of us has come from 20 kilometres and another has come from 30 kilometres…"

The foregoing statement clearly suggests that the farmers agreed to pay the labour charges in spite of the fact that the labourers did not do any labour. The farmer also describes the repercussions of not paying to the labourer - "so that we may be relieved quickly from the yard". The farmer was fearful that if he will not pay to the labourers, it will have certain consequences i.e., he will not be relieved from the yards timely or that his payments will be delayed. This fear of further delay in the yards, to the already exhausted farmer, forces him to *succumb* to the whims of the labourers. Of course, farmers *mistrust* the labourers, but the economic circumstances are such that, in spite of this *mistrust,* the farmers resign themselves to participating in transactions with them.

Let us look at another example. The government officers, both senior level and junior level, are well aware that the farmers are involved in quality manipulations, yet they are not willing to install quality checking mechanisms in the yards. For example, one government officer mentioned that quality problems are a prime source of conflicts in the yards and that there were no facilities in the yards to grade the commodity quality. For example, one government officer mentioned this as follows:

> "The farmer does not have grading equipment for these different commodities. So if we can install these different grading machines in the yard such conflicts will be reduced. So computerisation should look into these aspects also".

In spite of awareness about this issue – an issue that is prevalent for a long time – the government officers ignored the problem and made no effort to resolve it. On another occasion, the same government officer mentioned that he was not promoted for years and the first promotion that he received was after twenty seven years of service. His concluding remarks are as follows:

> "why should I be any more interested so, slowly, I have now become disinterested in the affairs of the yard…let it go…who cares…"

This attitude clearly suggests that the yard officer had become disinterested in resolving the problems in the yards. This again suggests that stakeholders are well aware of the precise nature of yard issues, but they become reluctant to resolve them for various reasons. Clearly there are two issues here: *reluctance to confront the issues in appropriate forums* and *mistrust*. The former is *resignation*. Our analysis reveals that mistrust and resignation were the two major issues that had a negative impact on the implementation of this agricultural marketing information system.

6   Discussion and Conclusions

Our findings have revealed that *mistrust* and *stakeholder resignation* were the major issues that negatively impacted the successful implementation of this agricultural marketing information systems. We believe that our findings may be applicable to similar projects in other developing countries. Researchers studying agricultural ICT implementation in developing countries such as Tanzania and Dar es Salaam have argued that trust relationships between the farmers and traders are important for the successful implementation of ICT projects (Molony, 2008). Trust is an important success factor in situations characterised by uncertainty, risks and incomplete buyer information (Batt, 2001a, 2003; Batt & Rexha, 1999).

However, overcoming lack of trust is difficult in developing countries, given that they are characterised by poverty, exploitation and corruption. Our findings clearly demonstrate that honesty, efficiency and sincerity were missing amongst all the stakeholders. To counter exploitation and corruption, stakeholders adopt practices of dishonesty and hegemony themselves: it is a cycle that keeps repeating itself.

We have suggested that low levels of trust and helplessness result in the *resignation* of stakeholders. Past studies have also suggested that *mistrust* becomes a chosen strategy of stakeholders when there is an expectation of selfish behaviour from other stakeholders (Baba, 1999). Hence we conclude that *trust* and *resignation* are the core issues in the successful implementation of information systems in developing countries.

References

Aronsson, H., Brodin, H.: The Environmental Impact Of Changing Logistics Structures. The International Journal of Logistics Management 17(3), 394–415 (2006)

Bazeley, P.: Analysing Qualitative Data: More Than 'Identifying Themes'. Malaysian Journal of Qualitative Research 2(1), 6–22 (2009)

Bernon, M., Rossi, S., Cullen, J.: Retail reverse logistics: a call and grounding framework for research. International Journal of Physical Distribution & Logistics Management 41(5), 484–510 (2011)

Bhagwat, R., Sharma, M.K.: Performance measurement of supply chain manage-ment:A balanced scorecard approach. Computers & Industrial Engineering 53(1), 43–62 (2007)

Boks, C., Stevels, A.: Essensial Perspectives for Design for Environment. Experiences from the Electronic Industry. Production Research 45(18), 4021–4039 (2007)

Boyatzis, R.: Transforming Qualitative Information: Thematic Analysis and Code Development, 1st edn. SAGE, United States of America (1998)

Braithwaite, A., Knivett, D.: Evaluating A Supply Chain'S Carbon Footprint – A Methodology and Case Example of Carbon-to-Serve. In: Lyon: Logistics Research Network 2008: Conference Proceedings (2008)

Brundtland Commission: Our Common Future, 1st edn. Oxford University, Oxford (1987)

Clark, D.: What Drives Companies to Seek ISO 14000 Certification. Pollution Engineering Summer, pp. 14–18 (1999)

Consulting, L.G.: Postconflict (2003),
    http://postconflict.unep.ch/humanitarianaction/documents/
    02_08-04_05-11.pdf (accessed June 21, 2012)

Edwards, J., Cullinane, S., McKinnon, A.: GreenLogistics (2009),
    http://www.greenlogistics.org/SiteResources/7ffc66c2-4e53-
    4c3d-a29d-f62f49458dfa_J.Edwards%20-%20Carbon%20auditign%
    20conventional%20and%20online%20book%20supply%20chains.pdf
    (accessed September 2, 2012)

Fiksel, J.: Design for Environment, Second Edition: A Guide to Sustainable Product Development: Eco-Efficient Product Development, 2nd edn. McGraw-Hill Professional, London (2010)

Fortes, J.: Green Supply Chain Management: A Literature. Otago Management Graduate Review 7(1), 51–62 (2009)

Heying, A., Sanzero, W.: A Case Study of Wal-Mart ' s " Green " Supply Chain Management. Operations Management, 1–10 (May 4, 2009)

Hoek, R.: Using information technology to leverage transport and logistics service op-erations in the supply chain: an empirical assessment of the interrelation between technology and operations management. International Journal of Technology Management 23(1), 207–222 (2004)

James, M., Grosvenor, R., Prickett, P.: e-Distribution: Internet-based management of a merchandiser supply chain. Supply Chain Management: An International Journal 9(1), 7–15 (2004)

Klassen, R., McLaughlin, C.: The Impact Of Environmental Management On Firm Performance. Management Science 42(8), 1199–1213 (1996)

Lee, H., So, K., Tang, C.: The Value of Information Sharing in a Two-Level Supply Chain. Management Science 46(5), 626–643 (2000)

Lofland, J.: Analyzing social settings: a guide to qualitative observation and analysis, 1st edn. Thomson Wadsworth, London (1994)

McKinnon, A., Cullinane, S., Browne, M., Whiteing, A.: Green Logistics: Improving the environmental sustainability of logistics, 1st edn. KoganPage, London (2011)

Mortensen, O., Lemoine, W.: Information Technologies and Supply Chain Integration. A study among manufacturers and transport and logistics service providers. In: Netherlands, Workshop Supply Chain Management and Communication Technology. University of Groningen (2005)

Park, J., Roome, N.: The Ecology of the New Economy: Sustainable Transformation of Global Information, Communications and Electronic Industries, 1st edn. Greenleaf, Midsomer Norton (2002)

Parvenov, A.: SupplyChainDigest (2005),
    http://www.scdigest.com/assets/Reps/SCDigest_Best_Practices_W
    arehouse_Returns.pdf (accessed June 6, 2012)

Paulraj, A.: Environmental Motivations: a Classification Scheme and its Impact on Environmental Strategies and Practices. Business Strategy and the Environment 18, 453–468 (2008)

Philipp, B., Militaru, D.: Key Factors for Environmentally Friendly Logistics Services in the French Region of Picardy. International Journal of Logistics Research and Applications: A Leading Journal of Supply Chain Management 14(6), 413–426 (2011)

Preuss, L.: The Green Multiplier: A study of Environmentla Protection and the Supply Chain, 1st edn. Palgrave MacMillan, New York (2005)

Rao, P., Holt, D.: Do green supply chains lead to competitiveness and economic performance? International Journal of Operations & Production Management 25(9), 898–916 (2005)

Ribeiro, S.K., Kobayashi, S.: In Climate Change 2007: Mitigation. Contribution of Working Group III to the Fourth Assessment Report of the Intergovernmental Panel on Climate Change. In: Bose, R., Kheshgi, H. (eds.) Transport and its Infrastructure, pp. 325–380. Cambridge University Press, Cambridge (2007)

Rodrigue, J.-P., Slack, B., Comtois, C.: Green Logistics (The Paradoxes of). Business Administration Production, Operations and Manufacturing Management Papers, pp. 1–11 (2001)

Sarkis, J.: A strategic decision framework for green supplychain management. Journal of Cleaner Production 11(4), 397–409 (2003)

Sarkis, J., Meade, L.M., Talluri, S.: E-logistics and the natural environment. Supply Chain Management: An International Journal 9(4), 303–312 (2004)

Saunders, M., Lewis, P., Thornhill, A.: Research Methods for Business Students, 3rd edn. Prentice Hall, England (2003)

Scot, J., Fischer, K.: Introduction: The Greening of the Industrial Firm, 1st edn. Island Press, Washington (1993)

Silverman, D.: Interpreting Qualitative Data, 3rd edn. SAGE Publications Ltd., London (2006)

Srivastava, S.K.: Green supply-chain management: A state-of the-art literature review. International Journal of Management Reviews 9(1), 53–80 (2007)

Triantafyllou, M.K., Cherrett, T.J.: The logistics of managing hazardous waste: a case study analysis in the UK retail sector. International Journal of Logistics Research and Applications 13(5), 373–394 (2010)

Trunick, P.: A Green Role for Logistics. Logistics Today 47(6), 26–28 (2006)

Ubeda, S., Faulin, J., Arcelus, F.: Green logistics at Eroski: A case study. Int. J. Production Economics 131(1), 44–51 (2011)

Wang, C., J, V., Mercer, J., Zhao, Y.: A case-based model facilitating retailing op-erations going "green": A proposed research agenda with a consideration of recession. Dalian, Asia Pacific, s.n., pp. 1–4 (2011)

Bringing about Innovative Change: The Case of a Patient Flow Management System in an NHS Trust

Teresa Waring, Martin Alexander, and Rebecca Casey

Newcastle Business School
Northumbria University
Newcastle upon Tyne
NE1 8ST
teresa.waring@northumbria.ac.uk

Abstract. Bringing about innovative IT enabled change within organisations that have restricted funding and resources is a challenge currently facing hospitals in the UK National Health Service (NHS). This article explores an Action Research project which aimed to implement a Patient Flow Management System in an acute hospital in the North East of England. The project took place over a twelve month period and involved a number of stakeholders including nursing staff. The contribution of this paper is to recognise the importance of AR as an approach suitable for systems adoption and the need to 'know your stakeholder' and their culture especially when dealing with professional bodies.

1 Introduction

It can be argued that the UK National Health Service (NHS) does not have a glowing record of innovative change in their use of information technology to improve the effectiveness, efficiency and delivery of healthcare particularly in the hospital sector (NAO, 2011; HCCPA, 2011). The attempts at imposing large scale IT enabled change programmes on the hospital sector have been researched by a number of authors who have concluded for a variety of reasons both technical and social they are doomed to failure (Wainwright and Waring, 2000; Norris, 2002; Sauer and Willcocks, 2007; Brennan, 2007; Eason 2007; Currie, 2012). Nevertheless over the last twenty years successive governments have committed billions of UK tax payers' money to technology investment and infrastructure within the NHS with mixed results.

Today, like many across the world facing the current recession, NHS hospitals are tackling challenges that include reduction in funding, cutbacks, rising admissions, an ageing population and an increasing number of patients with complex, chronic and multiple illnesses. Attempting to address some of these challenges the 2012 NHS information strategy, *'The power of information'*, aims to *'provide the NHS with a framework to enable local innovation, driven by a stronger voice for service users and citizens, and clear ambitions for the next decade'* (DoH, 2012). Whether this can be achieved is still to be determined but given the unprecedented fiscal constraints imposed by government on the NHS there is an expectation that local hospital trusts and providers may find it difficult to finance IS development as opposed to investing in healthcare services (Raleigh, 2012).

Y.K. Dwivedi et al. (Eds.): TDIT 2013, IFIP AICT 402, pp. 164–183, 2013.

The aim of this paper is to explore how local hospital trusts can develop innovative solutions to their information needs in challenging times. Using Action Research (AR) a team at Town hospital in the NE of England implemented a patient flow management system (PFMS) during 2011-12. Utmost in their mind was stakeholder involvement and participation in the project. The main stakeholders who would be expected to work daily with the system and to ensure the currency of its data were the nursing staff who as a body are recognised to be slow to adopt IT in their workplace (Murphy, 2010). The paper focuses on the process of engagement and the issues which, in terms of stakeholder collaboration, challenge IS/IT staff. The outcome for Town hospital has been positive and the system has been rolled out across all wards. Yet there are still hurdles to be overcome including realising all the benefits promised by the system vendors. The paper begins with a review of the pertinent literature but is kept necessarily concise in order to devote sufficient effort to the AR project and its 'data generation' (Coghlan and Brannick, 2010). The contribution of this paper is to recognise the importance of AR as an approach suitable for systems adoption and the need to 'know your stakeholder' and their culture especially when dealing with professional bodies.

2 Literature Review

Innovation and innovative change are terms which have various meanings in different contexts. Amongst some of the more popular definitions are those shown in Table 1:

Table 1. Example definitions of innovation

Author	Definition
Moore (2005); Bessant (2005)	Explicitly reserve the term innovation for radical, permanent change and real breakthroughs. They prefer to use the term continuous improvement for smaller steps, while not judging one of the types to be superior to another
Hartley (2006)	Innovation represents a step change, or a disruptive change for the organization or service.
Rogers (1995); Mack et al. (2008)	Innovation "the adoption of an existing idea for the first time by a specific organization"
Buijs (2007)	Innovation is about coming up with and implementing something new.
Albury (2005)	Successful innovation is the creation and implementation of new processes, products, services and methods of delivery which result in significant improvements in outcome, efficiency, effectiveness or quality
Zhuang (1995)	The act of creation which is both new and unique. Moving outside of existing paradigms and finding new approaches lies at the innovation process including diffusion.

Within the UK public sector innovation has been occurring over the last twenty years but this mainly has been done in the context of 'purchase to innovate' where IT was seen as the main driver and big project change was the norm (Hartley, 2006; Kelman, 2005; Zouridis and Termeer (2005). This landscape has now radically changed to one faced with budgetary austerity and the increased drive for innovation focused on cost saving. In the UK NHS IT innovation has had mixed success and on the whole authors have seen much of the work over the last twenty years as ineffective and in some instances as out- right failure (Wainwright and Waring, 2000; Clegg and Shepherd, 2007; Currie, 2012). Yet other forms of technology are being used throughout the NHS to support patient care and in many instances to save and prolong life. The question is why is IT different and why do stakeholders such as nursing staff continually experience difficulty with it or appear to resist its use in the workplace?

2.1   The Nursing Profession and IT

There is international interest in the nursing profession and IT. Generally IT is seen as being beneficial, inevitable and desirable for nursing and related healthcare (Levett-Jones, 2009; Lupiáñez-Villanueva, 2011). Authors have argued that nurse training should be improved, that use of IT should be a core competency for nurses (Willmer, 2005; Fetter, 2008) and that nurses should engage more in IT systems design when implementing new systems in their workplace (Hayward-Rowse and Whittle, 2006). Nevertheless there are studies which see IT as a barrier between the nurse and the patient (Royal Society, 2006) and others which recognise the slow up take of IT within the nursing profession (Murphy, 2010).

The Royal College of Nursing is concerned that the profession's attitude to IT has been seen as negative and has conducted research into this issue (e.g. 2006, 2007). These studies acknowledge and support the view that poor consultation and involvement in IT projects in their direct workplace is a major barrier to success.

In response to evident failure to exploit new IT, despite their ever increasing encroachment into normal day to day life, academics and management within the NHS have sought new ways of addressing the problem. Urquhart and Currell (2005) and Oroviogoicoechea et al. (2006) stress the importance of looking at how information is used, involving nurses at the core of design, rather than simply seeking to automate administrative processes. Using theories of change emanating from academics such as Lewin (1951) and Rogers (2003), Huryk (2010) has sought answers to the problem of nurse engagement in IT projects and has suggested that this phenomenon can be examined from the perspective that there may be barriers to change which are not related to technology or resources and suggests that failure to implement IT in the NHS is due to a slow rate of adoption. Table 2 provides a brief summary of the literature relating to barriers to innovative change in the NHS with a focus on the nursing profession.

2.2   Diffusion of Innovation Theory and Its Relation to Healthcare

Within this healthcare research study, *diffusion of innovation* (DoI) is defined as programmes of change affecting the uptake of new technologies, working practices or behaviours within an organisation (Greenhalgh et. al, 2004). The study of innovative change and factors relating to its adoption are varied. The literature is consequently vast and has been the subject of a number of meta analyses and literature reviews (see, for example, Damampour 1991, Damanpour and Gopalarkrishnan, 2001; Granados et. al. 1997, Greenhalgh et.al., 2004, Mustonen-Ollila and Lyytinen, 2003, Schrijvers, Oudendijk and Vries, 2003). This research has been carried out within a large range of traditions, each of which has addressed the subject of innovative change within its own discipline, from different perspectives and with different objectives.

Table 2. Barriers to Innovative Change in the NHS

Barriers to innovative change	Source
The NHS does not have the capacity or structural readiness for change to happen.	Wainwright and Waring, 2000
The NHS is culturally and politically structured against change.	Redwood, 2000
Technology itself is opposed to the Cultural and Social norms associated with care giving.	Barnard, 2000
Nurses are not empowered to make the changes themselves, reducing the chances that innovative change will embed in individual organisations.	Hill and McNulty, 1998
Variation in outcomes for innovative change programmes derive from within individual organisations which are not receptive to new ideas.	Pettigrew, Ferlie and MkKee, 1992; Pettigrew, Woodman and Cameron, 2001
The NHS consists of micro-systems of culture and social structures which act against each other and act as a barrier to change.	Nelson et. al , 2002
Technology has not been adequately aligned to the work practices of nurses, preventing innovation in ICT.	Hughes, 2003; Oroviogoicoechea et. al. 2006
The NHS target driven culture, emerging over recent years, is altering behaviours and distracting staff away from improving service delivery.	Seddon, 2008

The study described here has utilised the work of three sources Rogers (2003), Greenhalgh et al.(2004) and Mustonen-Ollila and Lyytinen (2003) as shown in Table 3. Rogers (2003) is seminal work developed in the 1960s and updated over time in response to new data and critique; Greenhalgh et al. (2004) looks at DoI within service organisations and specifically the NHS; Mustonen-Ollila and Lyytinen (2003) examine DoI theory as it relates to information systems process innovations.

There have been several critiques of DoI theories. Some argue that innovation considered solely within the context of positive change is invalid (Greenhalgh et.al., 2004; Rogers, 2003; McMaster and Wastell , 2005; Berkun, 2010). It is seen as counter intuitive, as there are many examples of innovation, such as the wide scale use of DDT as an agricultural pesticide with its unexpected impact on the environment, which are profoundly negative (Berkun, 2010). This argument leads to the conclusion that observations of DoI on the basis of their inherent positive nature are, at best, incomplete and at worse misleading (McMaster and Wastell, 2005).

Table 3. Attributes of innovation affecting the rate of adoption from the perspective of the individual and organisation (adapted from Rogers, 2003, Greenhalgh et al., 2004 and Mustonen-Ollila and Lyytinen, 2003)

Attribute	Summary Description	Individual	Organisation
Relative Advantage	The degree to which an innovation is perceived better than the idea it supersedes	The user derives tangible personal benefit, such as reducing personal administration or making the job easier	The organisation derives tangible benefits such as increasing productivity or reducing administration costs
Compatibility	The degree to which an innovation is perceived consistent with the existing values, past experiences and the needs of potential adopters, similar to suitability	The innovation does not conflict with political, cultural, social or religious beliefs of the individual, for example use interferes with patterns of rest breaks.	The innovation supports organisational policies, strategies or corporate objectives.
Complexity / Ease of Use	The degree to which an innovation is perceived difficult to understand and use (inversely proportional)	Personal skills and capabilities support the innovation	Personnel development strategies are in place to develop a skilled workforce
Trialability	The degree to which an innovation may be experimented with a limited basis	The individual has access to the innovation and freedom to try it out	The organisation will tolerate experimentation and create opportunities for personal innovation
Observability	To what extend the innovation is visible to others	The individual can see the innovation in use	The organisation position the innovation in a visible location. There is a communication strategy

Early studies of change structured its process into distinct stages. Change models such as the "unfreeze, change, freeze" (Lewin, 1951), consider phases of development as distinct and manageable. Kotler's (1984) six stages of change, commonly referred to as the 'social marketing model' presents the pathway to change as controllable, manageable, linear and to some degree predictable. These models have been criticised as overly simplistic and not relevant to the modern world, as complex social interactions are considered to be more representative of reality (Morgan, 2006). Likewise Van de Ven et al. (1999) view change as often messy and organic, with much movement between initiation, development and implementation, punctuated by shocks, setbacks and surprises. A further criticism of DoI theory is the lack of empirical evidence supporting the efficacy of models and in particular there is insufficient research into how DoI theory relates to the degree to which an innovation is retained within a social or cultural system (Mustonen-Ollila & Lyytinen, 2003).

The context of healthcare has generated much interest in DoI theory. The tradition of 'evidence based medicine' has led some to call for 'evidence based management' within the NHS and this has become particularly popular with some clinicians (Sheaff et al., 2006; Hughes, 2003) who view DoI theory as a 'scientific' framework around which managerial reform can be based. Berwick (2003) has proposed some recommendations that are believed will support innovations within healthcare:

1. Find sound innovations and support innovators
2. Invest in early adopters of the innovation
3. Make early adopter activity observable
4. Trust and enable reinvention.
5. Create space for change
6. Lead by example.

Thus it is against this background that the patient flow project was developed by Town Hospital as an essential innovation to support its strategic aims, within a context of a shrinking budget and rising costs.

3   The Context of the Study – Town Hospital and the Patient Flow Management System (PFMS)

Town hospital is a relatively small district hospital offering a large range of diagnostic and treatment health services to a population of approximately 160,000 living in the neighbouring areas. The hospital has an accident and emergency department, offering walk-in and critical care services for around 50,000 patients per year; has 18 wards and 4 operating theatres, providing approximately 10,000 surgical procedures each year. As well as surgery, the hospital provides support for 23,000 medical admissions per year and over recent years Town has seen a sustained growth in emergency activity with an increasing number of emergency admissions to the hospital.

Prior to 2012 Town hospital managed its occupancy of beds through a manual system whereby every ward had a 'whiteboard' on which the name of the patient in each bed was written. The whiteboards were maintained by nurses and frequently updated using a board rubber and whiteboard pen. When patients admitted via the emergency department required a bed on a ward, bed managers would telephone around the hospital to find out if there were any vacancies. With increasing quality targets, set by government, relating to waiting times and infection control the manual system was ineffective at delivering the required information. Discussions at hospital board level led to a potential solution being identified: an electronic patient flow management system (PFMS). This system would replace whiteboards with electronic interactive displays, linked to Town's computerised patient administration system (PAS). These displays would have the 'look and feel' of a white board and would show, in real-time, the location of every patient in a hospital bed. It would also allow the capture of the various treatments and interventions that had taken place for each patient. This project would represent a major innovation within Town in the management of a patient journey throughout their stay in hospital and offered several perceived benefits both for the clinician and the organisation as shown in Table 4.

The difficulty for Town was that it had a mixed record in the adoption and use of IT in the past. For example in 2001 Town implemented an innovative electronic patient records system which combined all of the main hospital departmental computer systems into one integrated electronic patient records system. Although the core patient administration functionality has been adopted, with notable success in business management areas, the system as a whole has failed to take hold in clinical areas.

Table 4. Individual and Organisational benefits

Individual Stakeholder Benefits	Organisational Benefits
Reduction in time associated with updating the whiteboard	Improved planning for discharge and reduction in bed occupancy
Automation of the administration of a patient admission to a ward and between wards.	Ability to control and audit the patient journey through the hospital.
Ability to use the system to pass information between clinicians in a controlled and auditable manner.	Access to better management statistics reports concerning performance of in-patient departments.
Ability to locate individual and groups of patients by condition, making it easier to plan targeted care	Reduction of inappropriate delayed discharges, reducing the cost of admitted care.
The discharge process can be made more efficient across the hospital, reducing inappropriate delays in discharge from hospital – better patient experience.	Ability to plan for specialist intervention teams to target conditions and reduce emergency admission.
Access to up to date and accurate information about the treatment and care providers within the hospital during an in-patient episode.	Reduce administration associated with patient flow management and save money through efficiency in patient administration.
	Ability to see the hospital bed population in real time.

Some consultants and doctors were openly hostile to the computer system, refusing to use the new technology. The PFMS was seen as a strategic project within the hospital and senior management were keen to see it adopted. They, therefore, provided one of the authors with an opportunity to conduct an action research project around the implementation process.

4   Methodology

Action Research has its academic origins in sociology, social psychology, psychology, organisational studies, education and health studies. The term Action Research (AR) has been in the vocabulary of research for quite some time now (Lewin, 1946, 1947; Chein, et al, 1948; Blum, 1955) and has continued to gain credence in management research mainly through the work of Checkland (1981) and others such as Warmington (1980); Avison and Wood-Harper (1990); Jonsson (1991); Kemmis and McTaggart, (1988) Perry and Gummesson (2004); Zuber-Skerrit (2002), French (2009), Coghlan and Brannick (2010).

A wide range of approaches to AR have emerged over time on how it should be conducted (see overviews by Coghlin and Brannick(2010); French(2009); Greenwood and Levin(2007); Flood and Romm (1996); Moggridge and Reason(1996); Reason(1994); Dash(1999)). Denscombe (1998) and Kember (2000) consider it important that AR leads to practical outcomes as well as theoretical knowledge, contributing to social practice as well as theory development and bringing theory closer to practice. Achievement of change, not just knowledge acquisition, as well as a rigorous process of data generation and analysis, is essential in AR. O'Leary (2005:190) describes action researchers as working on 'real-world problems' at the 'intersection' of the production of knowledge and a 'systematic approach to continuous improvement' which she argues is part of management. AR is grounded in real problems and real-life situations.

4.1   The Methodological Process Adopted by This Study

In terms of a methodological approach the research team adopted the model utilised by Coghlan and Brannick (2010) which like other variants of AR is distinguished by a pre-step and four stages as shown in Figure 1. The pre-step is an important function in defining the context and purpose of the research. Avison et al. (1999) point to the need for determination of power over the structure of the project and process for renegotiation and/or cancellation. 'Diagnosing' is a collaborative act and seeks to identify provisional issues. 'Planning action' follows on from the diagnosis and is consistent with it. Taking action implements the planned interventions and 'evaluating action' examines outcomes intended or otherwise and links in to the next cycle of action research.

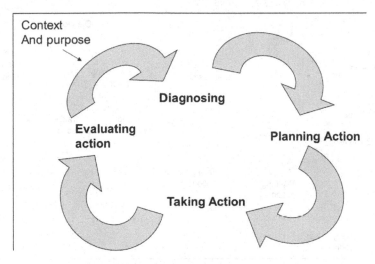

Fig. 1. The Action Research Framework used in this research

The study was designed around three action research cycles, two of which lasted approximately twelve months as shown in Figure 2. The first cycle was carried out prior to the system going live and it referenced theory based upon the diffusion of innovation (DoI) theory intended to maximise the rate of adoption of the system (e.g. Mustonen-Ollila and Lyytinen, 2003) as well as considering some of the research on the nursing profession and IT. The second cycle of AR was carried out post 'go live' and its purpose was to assess the effects of applying DoI theory and what lessons could be learned. Finally Cycle 3 explores how the benefits of the new system can in practice be completely realised bearing in mind the political, cultural and social difficulties associated with adopting IT which could be seen as an instrument of management control.

4.2   Involving the Clinical Staff and Generating the Data

Stringer (1993:35) suggests that an authentic socially responsive AR methodology must enable participation, acknowledge people's equality of worth and is most effective when it facilitates significant levels of active involvement, provides support for all stakeholders to learn and deals personally with people rather than with their representatives or agents.

In adopting a participative approach to AR the project team actively and ethically encouraged the hospital staff to be participants in the research. Consistent members of the AR team were the allocated IS staff and the Director of Information Services and during the research period a number of other clinical staff participated in the research at appropriate times. The project team were also keen to engage other stakeholders and this was reflected in the data generating methods used in the various cycles of the AR as shown in Table 5.

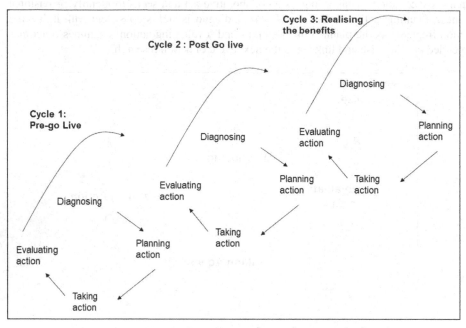

Fig. 2. Cycles of Action Research at Town Hospital

Table 5. Data Generation Methods

Cycle	Data Generation Methods
Pre- going live	Document analysis e.g. hospital strategy, minutes of meetings, emails, project journals Interviews with hospital staff Observation in the workplace (wards) Project meetings Workshops Project meetings
Post going live	Document analysis e.g. hospital strategy, minutes of meetings, emails, project journals, performance data. Interviews with hospital staff Ward visits Questionnaire, statistical analysis Workshops
Realising the benefits	Meetings with senior team Observation on wards Training plans Interviews with staff

Coghlan and Brannock (2010) argue that it is more appropriate to discuss data generation rather than data collection because AR data exists through engagement with others and attempts to collect data are themselves interventions.

4.3   Quality and Rigour in Action Research

Reason and Bradbury (2001) argue that AR should not be judged by the criteria of positivist science and requires its own criteria. Good quality AR should be explicit in developing a praxis of relational participation, should have practical outcomes, should engage in significant work and should result in significant change. Rigour in AR refers to how data are generated, gathered, explored and evaluated, how events are questioned and interpreted through multiple AR cycles (Reason, 2006)

The next section outlines the action research project undertaken at Town hospital and answers the three questions posed by Coghlan and Brannick (2010): *What happened?*; *How do you make sense of what happened?*; *So what?*

5   Data Generation – What Happened?

Before the AR cycles were enacted a participant AR team was assembled and this consisted of a project manager (PM), two application development officers one of whom was a nurse (ADO1 and ADO2), and one of the authors of this paper (AU).

5.1   Cycle 1 – Pre- 'Go Live'

Diagnosis: Recognising the past record of IT implementation in the hospital the first step in the cycle of AR was to consider pertinent issues around clinical engagement and possible theoretical approaches offered by DoI. The priority for the AR team was identifying the stakeholders in the PFMS and establishing how stakeholder engagement could be achieved across the hospital. (AU) brought to the discussion the DoI theory and it was clear that some of what was written did not translate easily into practice for the hospital. Members of the AR team believed much of what was presented was too complex and insufficiently IT focused. The team decided that the range of attributes offered by Mustonen-Ollila and Lyytinen (2003) around factors affecting the rate of adoption that related to the individual could be subject to immediate action. Thus the factors of relative advantage, compatibility, complexity, trialability, observability, reinvention, own testing, technological infrastructure, opinion leaders and change agents were considered strong candidates for developing tactical interventions to improve adoption of the system.

Following this analysis the team also constructed an 'issues log' which was intended to identify major issues that might arise from adopting this process. One issue that caused the most concern and discussion was the concept of 're-invention'- where users of the innovation adapt it to meet their individual perceived needs (Rogers, 2003; Greenhalgh et al., 2004). If the system was set up to meet individual stakeholder perceptions of their needs there would be a long 'wish list' not linked to corporate objectives resulting in chaos. On the other hand if there was no consultation and the system was imposed then stakeholders may be dissatisfied leading to lack of system use.

Planning: Recognising that the hospital was bound by NHS requirements to use a mandatory project management methodology (PMM) when implementing any form of IT the AR group had to think creatively within these parameters. Stakeholder consultation was planned and desired adaptations would be considered during the 'go live' period. There was agreement that as far as possible stakeholders should have the freedom to adapt the technology within the bounds of the system design. The hospital decided that a pilot implementation on a limited number of wards would allow for evaluation.

A workshop was organised by the AR team and the development team where the various aspects of the DoI theory was considered and planned action developed for each of the proposed relevant attributes (Mustonen-Ollila and Lyytinen,2003). These included:

- Creation of a 'sand pit' system
- Delivery of 'open' training sessions in wards
- A programme of ward visits
- Structured walk through of process flows with the key stakeholder groups
- Development of a communication strategy for the project.

Taking Action: The idea of creating a *'sand pit'* system was new to the hospital and generated some concerns. The purpose of a 'sand pit' environment was to 'play' with the system and allow users to try out new ways of working thus making the system more visible (Rogers, 2003). However, the system was largely un-configured, offering the possibility that the users would see any bugs or system set-up problems. The project development team, more familiar with a formal project management approach, were concerned that users would develop a negative impression of the software. Nevertheless the 'sand pit' environment was made available in March, 2012, two months prior to going live with the patient flow system.

Availability for training is always an issue for clinical staff because of shift working, the transient nature of the staff, and the need to call on 'bank' nursing staff (qualified nurses who can be called in at short notice to meet work demand). In the past Town hospital trained its staff in controlled classroom environments with planned lessons and defined objectives. However, it was not possible to provide this type of training within the available timeframe. Therefore the plan was for trainers to go to the wards at set times and wait for nursing staff to attend in situ with an 'open' agenda of training. In practice the trainers did have a planned structure for system training but had to be flexible to users' needs.

The project development team visited wards, usually in quiet periods, to assess the physical layout of the wards and the possible location of the proposed technology. They also took time to discuss the forthcoming system implementation and this was commented on by nursing staff who previously '*had never seen as many IT people on the wards*'.

Specific workshops were held with stakeholders to discuss the process flow models developed by the project analysts. These workshops challenged staff understanding of the 'as is' system and the 'to be' system. The hospital uses a formal documentation called UML process diagrams (Kratochvil and McGibbon, 2003) and this was shared in the workshops with the stakeholders.

The stakeholder analysis identified all of the potential groups who might have a vested interest in the PFMS. These included nurses, ward managers and clerks, junior doctors, consultants, the hospital board of directors, the IT team, the clinical intervention teams, clinical business managers, HR staff, modern matrons, infection control team, the vendors, A&E staff, the PAS supplier, system administrators and the information governance team. A detailed communications strategy was developed which contained the information required by each group, who would provide the information, how frequently it would be provided and the best method of communication to each group.

Evaluating the Action: The final stage of Cycle 1 involved reflecting on the outcomes of each action taken. The data generated was achieved through a series of meetings involving structured focus groups and opportunity sampling of staff feedback on the process. Formal meetings were recorded and focus group workshops were recorded in a structured manner. During this cycle data from ten focus groups and eighteen workshops were obtained and analysed. There was clear evidence of extensive stakeholder engagement. However this had led to many requests for changes to the system to suit individual needs, reflecting the concerns outlined by Greenhalgh et al. (2004). Stakeholders also identified issues around potential abuse of the system:

- Individuals looking at data they would not otherwise have access to.

- Management using the data to performance manage the nursing staff

- Individuals falsifying data entry for their own benefit

Politically, a ward being able to see the bed occupancy levels of another ward was challenging for staff and appeared to be an issue primarily about ownership and control of information.

The use of DoI theory had been seen to be useful and although not much different from the traditional approach the hospital might have taken it allowed more focus on the stakeholders. However, for some of the development team this had a negative effect as stimulating stakeholder expectation put pressure of the scope of the project. Thus going into Cycle 2 the AR team decided the following:

1. They would promote the concept of controlled and progressive change in dealing with user requests for change.
2. Issues relating to confidentiality and misuse of the system would be openly discussed with the senior management of the hospital.
3. The use of contentious performance related data, such as 'expected discharge date' would not be strongly promoted and the use of these functions would be accessed at a later date.
4. Senior management would not use the system to 'spy' on wards in early months of implementation and management reporting functions would be used in consultation with other stakeholders.

5.2   Cycle 2 – Post 'Going Live'

Diagnosing: The issues raised in the previous cycles were fed into Cycle 2 which was intended to ensure that the system went live with as little difficulty as possible.

The AR team wanted to explore what the key success factors (KSFs) might be and to what extent applying DoI had affected the rate of adoption. The team determined tests that would provide evidence that implementation of the system had been positively affected compared with expected outcomes. Table 6 outlines the KSFs:

Table 6. Key Success Factors

Key Success Factors as determined by the AR team
The system was used by all target areas, with no significant areas or populations refusing to use the system.
The system was used in excess of 90% for the management of patient flows in target areas.
Stakeholders/users were aware of the trial system and had actively used the system prior to going live and response to the system was positive.
There was demand to install the system in other areas of the hospital
Use of the system was not reduced due to concerns over confidentiality.

Planning Action: The roll out onto the pilot wards was planned and alongside this the measurement of the KSFs. The AR team decided to obtain evidence in two ways; first the take up of the system would be explored by carrying out a reconciliation of ward activity recorded in the core patient administration system (PAS) and the activity recorded in the new patient flow management system. In theory if the system was used as intended in real time, data from the PAS system would reconcile exactly with the data in the PFMS. The AR team considered the issues of performing a qualitative study of user responses to the PFMS in a busy hospital environment where ethically they could not compel individual stakeholders to participate in interviews. It was decided that the 'response to the system' study would be carried out by researchers attending the pilot wards and inviting willing participants to participate in an interview, an approach described by Arksey and Knight (1999) as 'opportunity sampling'.

Taking Action: The PFMS went live on all medical wards on the 15th May 2012. A month after live operation the analysis of system usage was started. The analysis showed rapid uptake of the system from going live to the 15th July, 2012 with excess of 99% of all activity tracked in the system within the first week of operation. This was considerably greater than expected from previous experience of similar projects conducted in Town Hospital. Having established that there was a rapid uptake of system use, a further analysis was conducted to identify the number of live user accounts in the system. This revealed that 43% of issued user accounts were in active use over the analysis period. This was worrying as there was a suspicion that PIN access codes were being shared among staff.

During the analysis period 20 interviews were conducted with stakeholders. These included nurses (13), ward clerks (2), ward manager and deputy ward manager (2), occupational therapist (1), ward housekeeper (1) and nurse practitioner (1). This covered all of the main roles present in a ward care setting. The development team then met to identify key themes that had emerged from their interviews.

Evaluating the Action: Themes identified in the work of Rogers (2003),Greenhalgh et al. (2004) and Mustonen-Ollila and Lyytinen (2003) were used to explore whether the PFMS had been successful   and are presented below:

'*Relative advantage*' was a theme to which 45 extracts of data were attributed and this was further sub-divided into 'personal advantage' and 'wider advantage'. Interviewees perceived that the system provided benefits for them individually in that it reduced their workload on the wards (e.g. by not having to regularly update and re-construct white boards with patient information) and it provided them with up to date information. Few interviewees identified benefits to patient care and five out of the twenty interviewees stated that the manual system using the whiteboards had not stopped and was running in parallel with the PFMS.

The extent to which the system was *'compatible with the culture'* of the stakehold-ers was a theme which was drawn out and 48 extract of data were grouped under this theme. Confidentiality of patient data is very important on wards and interviewees expressed concern about access to data beyond that which was possible using the manual whiteboards. Interviewees were anxious that managers might use data to con-trol ward staff in ways that currently does not happen.

In terms of the emergent theme *'simplicity of use'* most interviewees found that the system was on the whole easy to use and this had been a factor that the AR team per-ceived had contributed to the rapid rate of adoption of the PFMS.

The interviewees were asked about the use of the 'sand pit environment' set up to address the *'trialability'* of the system. It was indicated they enjoyed 'playing' with the system and that this opportunity developed user confidence. The AR team consi-dered this a positive response given the technical difficulties encountered in installing the temporary system and the limited time it was available. The conclusion was that this factor could have influenced the rate of adoption but it was not possible to gauge to what extent.

Entering the 'going live' phase the AR team were keen for the system to be *'visi-ble'* to all stakeholders. Most interviewees were using the PFMS and knew others around them who were using the new system. Yet seven interviewees stated that there were significant areas where the system was not being used. This required further investigation.

When asked about how the PFMS could be amended or improved the theme *'adaptation'* drew a number of suggestions and it was clear that stakeholders had been actively using the system and adapting it to their daily work. It was perceived that interviewees were engaged and thoughtful about how some small changes might im-prove it.

6   Discussion

AR is well recognised as an IS research method and is seen as highly relevant in the context of IS development (Avison et al., 1999). Nevertheless, conducting AR projects which involve substantial change or innovation within organisations can be challenging (Van de Ven et al., 1999). This section considers the meta-learning that has emerged from the project that has not only contributed to the local knowledge within Town hospital but also contributes to the IS methodological and IS develop-ment knowledge within the academic area. Coghlan and Brannick (2010) suggest that this meta- learning comprises 'premises', content and process. 'Premises' consist of *'...unstated and often non-conscious assumptions which govern attitude and beha-viour '*(p26). 'Content' relates to *'.. the issues, what is happening'* (p25) and 'process' relates to *'..strategies, procedures, how things are being done'* (p 25).

In terms of premises it is important to recognise that all the Town IT development staff have worked in the NHS for some time and have been inculcated into a public sector mind set: the proprietary project management methodology (PMM) used in systems development or adoption; the belief that clinicians resist change and will not take part in new systems development; the NHS and Town have a poor track record in systems acquisition and innovation in general. The AR project had to work with these premises and to develop new belief systems. This was done through inviting the AR team to access knowledge outside their normal area of expertise by exploring academic literature from nursing theory as well as DoI theory relevant to their situation. Understanding the nurse stakeholder became very important in this project. The AR team and the development team spent time on wards understanding nurse culture and then exploring what might work in terms of getting their engagement in the PFMS project. It became very clear that nurses do not resist change as long as the change benefits patient care and their role within the hospital. Thus within a healthcare environment taking an interdisciplinary approach to stakeholder knowledge is important in projects which have had a poor track record in implementing systems involving clinicians.

Many of the development team linked the PMM to poor implementation of systems in the hospital and believed that an AR approach could not work within these constraints. This assumption was challenged through finding ways of aligning DoI theory with some of the stages of the PMM. Once again the team were asked to think creatively about how the system could be introduced into the hospital in a way that satisfied nurse stakeholder needs first and then addressed management needs. This was very important to the success of the system as only by nurses engaging daily with the PFMS and ensuring the data was accurate would management be able to get the information they needed to make more strategic decisions.

The 'content' or issues of the meta-learning from the AR project relate to what happened. AR is often messy and non-linear. It can be highly stressful at times especially when researchers are closely involved. Berwick (2003) in a US study suggested ways of supporting DoI in healthcare. This AR project adopted some of the suggestions by identifying a pilot area for the PFMS, investing in training and development of the staff on the wards, communicating the progress of the pilot to the rest of the hospital and providing space and resource for the change. One of the AR team led the pilot. Nevertheless adjustments had to be made and the pilot lead faced challenges to the project from within his team and from a number of sceptical nurses. AR acknowledges this need for flexibility and applauds recognition of problems. The issues are important and need to be dealt with, not ignored and using this approach stands in stark contrast to the PMM used in Town.

The 'process' of carrying out the AR was done in a systematic manner by identifying the AR cycles early on in the project. The most difficult part of the research and the project in general was identifying the academic literature that would be of interest and relevant to a group of multi-disciplinary staff all of whom had their own epistemological and educational traditions. This was not an approach they had used before in systems acquisition though a number of nurses had used AR and evidence-based medicine in their professional work. The AR needed a champion within the hospital who was convinced that this was beneficial for the organisation and who was committed to seeing the project to an end. This individual, (AU), led the project throughout and ensured that the senior management of Town were kept informed of the work, issues and outcomes. AU also instigated a post-implementation review of the pilot project to inform the full roll out of the PFMS. This was unusual in Town but has helped to embed knowledge within the organisation.

In terms of quality and rigour in this AR project the research conducted here has ensured that the approach taken has developed praxis of relational participation, has been guided by a reflexive concern for the practical outcome of implementing the PFMS, has involved a plurality of knowing and has resulted in sustainable change (Reason and Bradbury, 2001). The AR team have demonstrated how there was engagement in the AR cycles, how the project was exposed to critique and how different views of what was happening were accessed. The team used scholarly theory, rigorously applied it and have reflected on the appropriateness of that work (Reason, 2006).

7   Conclusion

The' benefits realisation' cycle of this project is still underway and the intention is to provide information to support senior management decision making as well as support for other clinical stakeholders such as doctors. It is clear that the doctors could gain benefits from the system with discharge plans, discharge letters and with hand overs at the end of working shifts. Yet doctors are a difficult group of stakeholders to work with. As was discussed above a better understanding of the doctor stakeholder is needed in order to enable engagement on this project. Patients would also benefit from some of the facilities in the PFMS as their individual care plans can be tracked and treatment targeted. It is clear that patients are rarely consulted on how IT can improve their care and there are often assumptions made about this. Town are keen to involve patients and are researching ways of doing this. It is our intention to report on this work at a later date.

References

Albury, D.: Fostering Innovation in Public Services. Public Money & Management 25(1), 51–56 (2005)

Arksey, H., Knight, P.: Interviewing for Social Scientists. Sage, London (1999)

Avison, D.E., Wood-Harper, A.T.: Multiview - An exploration in information systems development. Blackwell Scientific, Oxford (1990)

Avison, D.E., Lau, F., Myers, M., Nielsen, P.A.: Action Research. Communications of the ACM 42(1), 94–97 (1999)

Barnard, A.: Alteration To Will As An Experience Of Technology And Nursing. Journal of Advanced Nursing 31(5), 1136–1144 (2000)

Berkun, S.: The Myths of Innovation, 2nd edn. O'Reilly, Farnham (2010)

Berwick, D.M.: Disseminating Innovations in Health Care. Journal of the American Medical Association 289(15), 1969–1975 (2003)

Bessant, J.: Enabling Continuous and Discontinuous Innovation: Learning From the Private Sector. Public Money & Management 25(1), 35–42 (2005)

Blum, F.H.: Action Research - A Scientific Approach? Philosophy of Science 22(1), 1–7 (1955)

Brennan, S.: The biggest computer programme in the world ever! How is it going? Journal of Information Technology 22, 202–211 (2007)

Buijs, J.: Innovation Leaders Should be Controlled Schizophrenics. Creativity and Innovation Management 16(2), 203–210 (2007)

Checkland, P.: Systems Thinking, Systems Practice. Wiley, Chichester (1981)

Chein, I., Cook, S.W., Harding, J.: The Field of Action Research. The American Psychologist 3, 43–50 (1948)

Clegg, C., Shepherd, C.: The biggest computer programme in the world...ever!': time for a change in mindset? Journal of Information Technology 22, 212–221 (2007)

Coghlan, D., Brannick, T.: Doing Action Research in your own organization, 3rd edn. Sage publications, London (2010)

Currie, W.: Institutional isomorphism and change: the national programme for IT – 10 years on. Journal of Information Technology 27, 236–248 (2012)

Damanpour, F.: Organizational innovation: a meta-analysis of effects of determinants and moderators. Academy of Management Journal 34, 555–590 (1991)

Damanpour, F., Gopalarkrishnan, S.: The Dynamics of the Adoption of Product and Process Innovations in Organizations. Journal of Management Studies 38(1), 45–65 (2001)

Dash, D.P.: Current Debates in Action Research. Systemic Practice and Action Research 12(5), 457–492 (1999)

Denscombe, M.: The Good Research Guide for Small Scale Research Projects. Open University Press, Buckingham (1998)

Department of Health. The power of information: Putting all of us in control of the health and care information we need (2012),   http://informationstrategy.dh.gov.uk/about/the-strategy/ (accessed September 27, 2012)

Eason, K.: Local sociotechnical system development in the NHS National Programme for Information Technology. Journal of Information Technology 22, 257–264 (2007)

Fetter, M.S.: Curriculum Strategies to Improve Baccalaureate Nursing Information Technology Outcomes. Journal of Nursing Education 48(2), 78–85 (2008)

Flood, R.L., Romm, N.R.A.: Emancipatory Practice: Some contributions from Social Theory and Practice. Systems Practice 9(2), 113–128 (1996)

French, S.: Action research for practicing managers. Journal of Management Development 28(3), 187–204 (2009)

Granados, A., Jonsson, E., Banta, H.D., Bero, L., Bonair, A., Cochet, C., Freemantle, N., Grilli, R., Grimshaw, J., Harvey, E., Levi, R., Marshall, D., Oxman, A., Passart, L., Raisenan, V., Reus, E., Espinas, J.A.: EUR-ASSESS project subgroup report on dissemination and impact. International Journal of Technology Assessment in Health Care 13(2), 220–286 (1997)

Greenhalgh, T., Robert, G., Macfarlane, F., Bate, P., Kyriakidou, O.: Diffusion of Innovations in Service Organizations: Systematic Review and Recommendations. The Milbank Quarterly 82(4), 581–629 (2004)

Greenwood, D., Levin, M.: Introduction to action research: Social research for social change, 2nd edn. Sage, Thousand Oaks (2007)

Hartley, J.: Innovation and its Contribution to Improvement: A Review for Policy-makers, Pol-icy Advisers, Managers and researchers (2006), http://www.communities.gov.uk/documents/localgovernment/pdf/151336.pdf (accessed October 24, 2012)

Hayward-Rowse, L., Whittle, T.: A pilot project to design, implement and evaluate an electronic integrated care pathway. Journal of Nursing Management 14, 564–571 (2006)

Hill, S., McNulty, D.: Overcoming Cultural Barriers To Change. Health Manpower Management 24(1), 6–12 (1998)

House of Commons Committee of Public Accounts The National Programme for IT in the NHS: an update on the delivery of detailed care records systems (2011), http://www.publications.parliament.uk/pa/cm201012/cmselect/cmpubacc/1070/107002.htm (accessed: October 20, 2011)

Hughes, R.: Clinical practice in a computer world: considering the issues. Journal of Advanced Nursing 42(4), 340–346 (2003)

Huryk, L.A.: Factors influencing nurses' attitudes towards healthcare information technology. Journal of Nursing Management (18), 606–612 (2010)

Jonsson, S.: Action Research. In: Nissen, H.E., Klein, H.K., Hirschheim, R. (eds.) Information Systems Research: Contemporary Approaches and Emergent Traditions, pp. 371–396. Elsevier Science Publishers, North Holland (1991)

Kelman, S.: Unleashing Change: A Study Of Organizational Renewal In Government. The Brookings Institution, Washington (2005)

Kember, D.: Action learning and action research: Improving the quality of teaching and learning. Kogan Page, London (2000)

Kemmis, S., McTaggart, R. (eds.): The action research planner, 3rd edn. Deakin University Press, Victoria (1988)

Kotler, P.: Social Marketing of Health Behaviour. In: Fredericksen, L.W., Solomon, I.J., Brehoney, K.A. (eds.) Marketing Health Behaviour: Principles, Techniques and Applications. Plenum Press, New York (1984)

Kratochvil, M., McGibbon, B.: UML Light: How to specify your software requirements. Cambridge University Press, Cambridge (2003)

Levett-Jones, T., Kenny, R., Van der Riet, P., Hazelton, M., Kable, A., Bourgeois, S., Lux-ford, Y.: Exploring the information and communication technology competence and confidence of nursing students and their perception of its relevance to clinical practice. Nurse Education Today 29(6), 612–616 (2009)

Lewin, K.: Action Research and Minority Problems. Journal of Social Issues 2, 34–46 (1946)

Lewin, K.: Frontiers in Group Dynamics: II. Channels of Group Life; Social Planning and Action Research. Human Relations 1, 143–153 (1947)

Lewin, K.: Field Theory in the Social Sciences. Harper, New York (1951)

Lupiáñez-Villanueva, F., Hardey, M., Torrent, J., Ficapal, P.: The integration of Information and Communication Technology into nursing. International Journal of Medical Informatics 80(2), 133–140 (2011)

Mack, W.R., Green, D., Vedlitz, A.: Innovation and Implementation in the Public Sector: An Examination of Public Entrepreneurship. Review of Policy Research 25(3), 233–252 (2008)

McMaster, T., Wastell, D.: Diffusion – or Delusion?:Challenging an IS research tradition. Information Technology & People 18(4), 383–404 (2005)

Moggridge, A., Reason, P.: Human Inquiry: Steps Towards Emancipatory Practice. Systems Practice 9(2), 159–175 (1996)

Moore, G.: Dealing with Darwin: How Great Companies innovate at every phase of their evolution (2005), http://www.dealingwithdarwin.com (accessed November 5, 2012)

Morgan, G.: Images of Organization. Sage Publications Ltd., London (2006)

Murphy, J.: Nursing and Technology: A Love/Hate Relationship. Nursing Economic 28(6), 405–408 (2010)

Mustonen-Ollila, E., Lyytinen, K.: Why organizations adopt information system process innovations: a longitudinal study using Diffusion of Innovation theory. Information Systems Journal 13, 275–297 (2003)

National Audit Office. The National Programme for IT in the NHS: an update on the delivery of detailed care records systems (2011),
http://www.nao.org.uk/publications/1012/npfit.aspx
(accessed October 20, 2011)

Nelson, E., Batalden, P., Huber, T., Mohr, J., Godfrey, M., Headrick, L., Wasson: Microsystems in Health Care, Part 1: Learning from High-Performance Front-line Clinical Units. Journal on Quality Improvement 28(9), 472–493 (2002)

Norris, A.C.: Current trends and challenges in health informatics. Health Informatics Journal 8, 205–213 (2002)

O'Leary, Z.: Researching Real-World Problems: A Guide to Methods of Inquiry. Sage Publications, London (2005)

Oroviogoicoechea, C., Elliott, B., Watson, R.: Review: evaluating information systems in nursing. Journal of Clinical Nursing 17, 567–575 (2006)

Perry, C., Gummesson, E.: Action research in marketing. European Journal of Marketing 38(3/4), 310–320 (2004)

Pettigrew, A., Ferlie, E., McKee, L.: Shaping Strategic Change. Making Change in Large Organizations: The Case of The National Health Service. Sage, London (1992)

Pettigrew, A., Woodman, R.W., Cameron, K.S.: Studying Organisational Change and Development: Challenges for Future Research. Academy of Management Journal 44(4), 697–713 (2001)

Raleigh, V.: The information strategy: a transformation in health and social care information on the way? The Kings Fund (2012), http://www.kingsfund.org.uk/blog/
informationstrate_1.html (accessed September 24, 2012)

Reason, P.: Three Approaches to Participative Inquiry. In: Denzin, N.K., Lincoln, Y.S. (eds.) Handbook of Qualitative Research. Sage, Thousand Oaks (1994)

Reason, P.: Choice and Quality in Action Research Practice. Journal of Management Inquiry 15(2), 187–203 (2006)

Reason, P., Bradbury, H.: Handbook of Action Research: Participative Inquiry and Practice. Sage Publications, London (2001)

Redwood. H.: Why Ration Health Care? : An international study of the United Kingdom, France, Germany and public sector health care in the USA, CIVITAS: Institute for the Study of Civil Society, London (2000), http://www.civitas.org.uk/pdf/cs08.pdf
(accessed March 20, 2012)

Rogers, E.M.: Diffusion of Innovations, 4th edn. Simon and Schuster, New York (1995)

Rogers, E.M.: Diffusion of Innovations, 5th edn. Simon & Schuster, New York (2003)

Royal College of Nursing. Nurses and NHS IT developments : Results of an online survey by Nursix.com on behalf of the Royal College of Nursing (2006),
http://www.rcn.org.uk/__data/assets/pdf_file/0009/78714/00307
9.pdf (accessed: March 12, 2011)

Royal College of Nursing. Market Research Report : RCN EHealth Study (2007),
http://www.rcn.org.uk/__data/assets/pdf_file/0015/111552/003166
.pdf (accessed: March 12, 2011)

Royal Society. Digital Healthcare: The impact of information and communication technologies on health and healthcare. London: Royal Society (2006),
http://royalsociety.org/Digital-healthcare-the-impact-of-
information-and-communication-technologies-on-healthcare/
(accessed: March 12, 2011)

Sauer, C., Willcocks, L.: Unreasonable expectations – NHS IT, Greek choruses and the games institutions play around mega-programmes. Journal of Information Technology 2, 195–201 (2007)

Seddon, J.: Systems Thinking in the Public Sector: The failure of the reform regime and a manifesto for a better way. Triarchy Press, Axminster (2008)

Sheaff, R., Pickard, S., Dowling, B.: Is Evidence Based Organizational Innovation a Delusion? In: Casebeer, A.L., Harrison, A., Mark, A.L. (eds.) Innovations in Health Care: A Reality Check. Palgrave Macmillan, New York (2006)

Stringer, E.T.: Action Research, 2nd edn. Sage Publications (1999)

Urquhart, C., Currell, R.: Reviewing the evidence on nursing record systems. Health Informatics Journal 11(3), 33–42 (2005)

Van de Ven, A.H., Polley, D.E., Garud, R., Venkataraman, S.: The Innovation Journey. Oxford University Press, Oxford (1999)

Wainwright, D.W., Waring, T.S.: The information management and technology strategy of the UK National Health Service: Determining progress in the NHS acute hospital sector. The International Journal of Public Sector Management 13(3), 241–259 (2000)

Warmington, A.: Action Research: Its Methods and Its Implications. Journal of Applied Systems Analysis 7, 23–39 (1980)

Willmer, M.: Promoting practical clinical management learning: the current situation about Information and Communications Technology capability development in student nurses. Journal of Nursing Management 13, 467–476 (2005)

Zhuang, L.: Bridging the gap between technology and business strategy: a pilot study on the innovation process. Management Decision 33(8), 13–21 (1995)

Zouridis, S., Termeer, C.J.A.M.: Never the twain shall meet. An oxymoron: innovation in government. Public Administration 7(8), 13–23 (2005)

Zuber-Skerrit, O.: The concept of action learning. The Learning Organization 9(3), 114–124 (2002)

Does Mandatory Pressure Increase RFID Adoption?
A Case Study of Western Australian Livestock Industry

Mohammad Alamgir Hossain[1,*] and Mohammed Quaddus[2]

[1] School of Business, North South University, Dhaka, Bangladesh
mahripon@yahoo.com
[2] Graduate School of Business, Curtin University of Technology, Western Australia
Mohammed.quaddus@gsb.curtin.edu.au

Abstract. Radio Frequency Identification (RFID) technology has been increasingly used in innovative applications around the world. It has caught attention of different industries and been mandated by resource dominant organizations and different countries in various applications. In Australia RFID is mandatory for cattle identification. The objective of this research is to investigate whether the mandatory pressure really makes the livestock farms to adopt RFID. This study took the broader aspect of external environment considering external pressure, external support, and external uncertainty. Applying a mixed method approach this is a prime initiative exploring and detailing the external environmental factors on RFID context. Following extensive literature on innovation and RFID adoption this paper, first, explores the relevant factors on miscellaneous innovations. The literature review was followed by a qualitative field study. The field study confirms and contextualizes the factors from the literature review. Finally, an empirical study investigates the adoption behavior of livestock farms in relation to RFID adoption in the context of Western Australia. Data were analyzed using Partial Least Square (PLS)-based Structured Equation Modeling (SEM) tool. The analysis finds that market pressure, cognitive pressure, government support, and external uncertainty are the main driving factors in RFID adoption. Implications of the results are highlighted.

Keywords: RFID, adoption, external environment, mixed method, PLS.

1 Introduction

Radio frequency identification (RFID) is one of the most effective technologies which identifies an object automatically and uniquely, and can store enormous amount of data for many years which can later be retrieved as information as required (Hossain and Quaddus 2011). Because of its enormous capabilities RFID enjoys a quick growth in recent decades in many innovative applications around the world and has drawn the attention of the innovation architects and researchers. Now-a-days, RFID technology

---

* Corresponding author.

Y.K. Dwivedi et al. (Eds.): TDIT 2013, IFIP AICT 402, pp. 184–202, 2013.

is used extensively from item-level tracking through the supply chain to fault monitoring in train tracks to electronic passports.

The revolution of RFID has not started before it was mandated by several key players of the external environment. In 2003 Wal-Mart and Department of Defense (DoD) of United States Stores mandated their suppliers to attach RFID tags at case/palette level (Bansal 2003; Jones et al. 2005; Roberti 2003; Whitaker et al. 2007). Around the same time Tesco, Metro AG, Target, and Albertsons issued guidelines for their suppliers to be RFID enabled (Poirier and McCollum 2006; Garry 2004). In livestock industry, the first significant external pressure was introduced by European Union (EU), in late 1990 (Semple 2007), which was followed by Japan, South Korea, and United States. A considerable amount of consumer awareness is also observed which increases with time and eventually is converted to a demand for a precise method of meat traceability. As not every farmer has "*the same enthusiasm and urgency for incorporating RFID technology*" (Nolz 2008), to entertain the consumers' demand, livestock agencies and organizations put pressure on the producers for the traceability information.

Hence, it is observed that the *external environment* plays a significant role on RFID adoption. Though a number of studies have been found which dealt with the effect of environmental, technological, and organizational (TOE) characteristics on RFID adoption but surprisingly, to the best of authors' knowledge, no study has been conducted detailing the external environment in RFID context; though external environment is regarded as the most influential factor for RFID adoption. Generally, there are only a handful of researches on the overall uptake of RFID in livestock sector though there is a significant body of research in logistics area. This paper thus takes the opportunity to study RFID adoption, in addressing the current literature gap, by exploring and examining the external environmental factors on RFID, taking Western Australian (WA) livestock industry as the context. Equipped with a background of environmental factors for RFID adoption, this paper performs an exploratory field study on eight livestock farms in WA, develops an initial research-model which is validated further with quantitative data to examine and identify the environmental factors affecting RFID adoption.

This paper is organized as follows. The next section presents the literature review and the theoretical grounds of external environmental issues on RFID adoption which is followed by presenting the research methodology, and then discusses the findings of the qualitative field study while developing the propositions. The following sections present and discuss the results from a quantitative survey. This paper ends with conclusion and further work sections.

2 Background

Scott (2001) indicates that, in order to survive, organizations must conform to the rules and demands prevailing in the environment. In other words, organizations' adoption decisions aim primarily at organizational achievements; however, the decisions sometimes are directly influenced by the external business-environments. Similarly, Social Cognitive Theory (SCT) argues that organizational factors regarding innovation are necessary but not sufficient (Bandura 2001); the process includes environmental effects including the pressure of social influence and incentives. SCT also recognizes that gaining social recognition and status are the main motivations for adopting an innovation which is termed as 'normative pressure' in the institutional theory. Institutional theory assumes that organizations cannot operate in isolation rather they need to respect and follow the trends and demands of the external environment where they operate. Institutional theories define the environment as an integrated set of political, economic, social, and legal conventions that establish the foundational of a productive business environment (Oxley 1999). It is agreed that institutional environment is a very important external factor to firms. Institutional theory, thus, emphasizes on institutional environments in organizational strategy, policy, and operations (Scott 2001). Moreover, firms usually do observe each other over time to gain competitive advantage and also to respond to the competitive pressure and market pressure (Gibbs and Kraemer 2004). In recent time Teo et al. (2003) applied the institutional theory to examine intention to adopt inter-organizational linkages; especially financial electronic data interchange (FEDI). Moreover, proactively, Gibbs and Kraemer (2004) applied institutional theory in conjecture with the Technology-Organization-Environment (TOE) framework, proposed by Tornatzky and Fleischer (1990).

Moberg et al. (2002) classified the adoption factors into environmental, organizational, and informational factors. To explore the adoption factors at organization-level and to study the adoption of technological innovations, Tornatzky and Fleischer (1990) proposed the Technology-Organization-Environment (TOE) model. TOE argues that the decision to adopt a technological innovation is based on factors in the organizational and environmental contexts, as well as the characteristics of the technology itself. However, the detail nature of external environment is somewhat missing in TOE studies. In investigating the external factors on RFID adoption, this study used the "environment" construct from TOE model. A similar type of study was performed by Teo et al. (2003).

2.1   External Environment

The external environment consists of those relevant factors outside the boundaries of the organization (or a specific decision unit) that are taken direct into consideration. External environment, therefore, consists the 'global' external factors which are beyond organization's control but are important in functioning and decision-making behavior (Quaddus and Hofmeyer 2007).

Numerous innovation studies have examined a variety of external environmental factors, including economic conditions, global competitiveness, transaction climate, industry concentration, and environmental uncertainty on decision to adopt new technologies (Gatignon and Robertson 1989; Quaddus and Hofmeyer 2007). In general, external environment has been recognized to play a very significant role in adoption diffusion research and so as for RFID adoption (Sharma and Citurs 2005; Wen et al. 2009). Based on literature external pressure, external support, and external environmental uncertainty are viewed as important environmental factors for RFID adoption (Hossain and Quaddus 2011).

2.1.1   External Pressure
External pressure has been considered as a significant factor in adoption research (Gatignon and Robertson 1989); not surprisingly is also treated similarly for RFID

adoption (Matta and Moberg 2007; Schmitt and Michahelles 2009). External pressure can be exercised by different authorities as follows:

Government Pressure: Government pressure or "regulative process" (Lawrence et al. 2001) is a kind of coercive pressure as government exercises its power to force the targeted people or industry in order to gain compliance to a desired system or practice. Government regulation can either encourage or discourage the adoption of innovation (Scupola 2003). Shih et al. (2008) considered government policy/legislation as one of the leading challenges for RFID adoption. More specifically, Luo et al. (2007) argued that government mandate can speed up the rate of RFID adoption.

Market Pressure: An ultimate reason to adopt RFID by livestock industry is the increasing market pressure and mandates by supply chain partners for RFID-based animal tracking systems (Li and Visich 2006; Schmitt and Michahelles 2009). Meat exporting agents follow the pressure of the market and impose it to the meat producers. Therefore, imposition from trading partners makes the livestock producers to adopt RFID because they are the most susceptible to such imposition. Such impositions are prevalent in case of RFID because of its network nature, like EDI (Iacovou et al. 1995).

Competitive Pressure: Larger retailers and also small farms keenly aware of what competitors are doing, with respect to new IT tools or technology that may provide competitive advantage (Brown and Russell 2007). One of the main sources of external pressure to adopt RFID is the pressure due to fierce competition (Iacovou et al. 1995). As more countries and competitors are becoming RFID-enabled, livestock farms in Australia are more inclined to adopt RFID in order to maintain their own competitive pressure, though Brown and Russell (2007) did not find so in retail sector.

Mimetic Pressure: "Mimetic pressure involves the perception of some value of mimicking a behavior from other referent actors" (Lawrence et al. 2001, p. 628). Mimetic pressure is exerted on an organization by itself when the organization perceives that another organization on the same business environment are getting benefit of an innovation or practice and thus feels the pressure to act on a same manner (Teo et al. 2003). This is a "cognitive process" (Lawrence et al. 2001). Sharma et al. (2007) suggests that mimetic pressure is positively and significantly related to RFID adoption.

Normative Pressure: Organizations may experience the normative pressure sharing the similar norms in a given environment; to be treated differently or to receive respect from the other members of the society such as the other farmers and supply chain partners. An organization with a direct or indirect relation to other organizations that have adopted an innovation may get interest to the innovation and finally adopt the innovation to gain the similar social recognition and benefits (Teo et al. 2003; Lawrence et al. 2001).

2.1.2   External Support
External support for relevant technology is considered as an important factor that matters to potential adopters (Huyskens and Loebbecke 2007). External support can have different sources varying from country to country and from region to region within a same country. External supports can be provided by the government, technology vendors and change agents.

Government Support: Government is an important environmental actor for RFID adoption (Lin and Ho 2009). Government can play an important role for an RFID adoption-diffusion through restructuring the infrastructure, information provision, research and development policies, providing incentives, building and enhancing the infrastructure, conducting pilot projects, provision of tax-breaks, and providing consultancy and counseling service (Lin 2009; Lin and Ho 2009; Luo et al. 2007). In fact, without government action and intervention it is treated by the individual adopters as a "risky" investment that demands a 'risk-share' by the government.

Vendor Support: Supports from technology providers (Huyskens and Loebbecke 2007) is also very important as many organizations may not have the internal expertise to trial and implement RFID projects, and would therefore rely on external providers (Lee and Shim 2007). Vendors may support the potential and already-adopters by providing training, incentives, discounted products, trial use, customized solutions, troubleshooting services, and conducting pilot projects. The availability of vendor supports may vary from place to places and have a significant influence on RFID adoption (Brown and Russell 2007).

2.1.3   Environmental Uncertainty

Uncertainty originates from lack of information, know-how, or the ability to predict developments and situations (Rogers 1995). Environmental uncertainty would influence the innovation adoption. Zhu et al. (2003) and Lee and Shim (2007) argued that market uncertainty is important to help understanding RFID adoption because organizations usually pay more attention on innovations when they face an environment with higher instability and chaos (Gatignon and Robertson 1989; Kimberly and Evanisko 1981; Patterson et al. 2003). Alternatively, uncertainty about the innovation itself may hinder the adoption process because organizations do not adopt an innovation if there is not a significant level of assurance of the utility of the innovation. On other words, uncertainty about RFID itself, and the future market and return negatively influence the adoption of RFID (Hossain and Quaddus 2011).

3   Methodology

To understand the research topic, to validate and understand the conceptual model, and to obtain and analyze data a combination of both qualitative and quantitative methods, which is referred to as the 'mixed method' (Tashakkori and Teddlie 1998), was applied in this study. A significant reason for adopting this approach is: as "The mixed method approach is appropriate as RFID research is still in its infancy" stage therefore, "a combination of methodological techniques assists in exploring the RFID adoption phenomenon more fully" (Brown and Russell 2007, p. 252).

Therefore, to study RFID adoption, theoretical factors and variables are needed to borrow from other established adoption studies namely innovation adoption, technology adoption, IS/IT adoption researches. However, it will be quite optimistic assumption that those factors can effectively be utilized to deal with RFID adoption in a very dissimilar environment; in the livestock field. Therefore, the widely acceptable factors need to be verified/ contextualized by a group of representatives of livestock farms. Moreover, the exploration of new factors is also not unlikely. The qualitative study meant to perform this role.

Similarly, the rational for a survey is also very strong for this study. The adoption diffusion behavior of a livestock-farm is a very subjective issue because each farm has its own perceptions, perspective, expectation, and experience. The rationales, motivations, and incentives to adopt and use RFID of one farm might be different from others. Further, there are a multitude parallel factors that contribute to such decision. Thus, conducting field study interviewing a number of farms that can represent the whole industry is time consuming, effort-driven, and not much an effective way. Furthermore, qualitative approaches can generate a social desirability bias. Instead, a nation-wide survey could perform this job in an efficient manner.

Since this research provides evidence of hypotheses, quantifiable measures of variables, hypotheses testing, and the drawing of inferences about a phenomenon from the sample to a stated population, the positivist paradigm has been considered to be appropriate for this research.

4 Qualitative Field Study

4.1 Sampling

The number of cases suggested by researchers varies. Some researchers suggest an open-ended number of cases while others recommend a restricted range. The most appropriate range falls between four and eight (Eisenhardt 1989). This study approached eight livestock-farms for investigations. As with many qualitative studies, we employed purposive sampling rather than random sampling (Corbin and Strauss 2008). The farms were chosen from the short-listed farms, prepared by discussion with several officials of Department of Agriculture and Food, Western Australia (DAFWA). The shortlisted farms were chosen, by considering their diversity, interest, and contribution to the livestock community. More family-owned small-farms have been considered because small farms are recognized as the major sector in the Australian livestock industry (Green 2009). Table 1 summarizes the profiles of each organization. In this study, farmer is defined as the decision-making unit of a livestock farm: for a corporate farm it is the 'manager' whereas in a family-owned-and-operated farm it is the "Owner-Manager". In both cases, s/he is usually responsible for the day-to-day operation of the farming business and may own or have a share in the business (Hooper 2010).

Table 1. Profile of the organizations

Farm ID	Farm type	Area (hectare)	No. of livestock
A	F	352	560 cattle
B	F	44	200 cattle, 40 sheep
C	C	20,000	12,000 cattle and 7,000 sheep
D	F	300	400 cattle
E	F	2,800	1,000 cattle, 130 sheep
F	C	10,000	8,000 cattle
G	F	1,000	800 cattle
H	F	1,114	7,000 sheep

F: Family-owned-operated, C: Corporate

4.2 Data Collection

This study involved face-to-face, one-to-one, infield, and in-person interviews and therefore all farms were within a 300 km radius of Perth, the capital city of WA. At the beginning of each interview the participant was given a brief outline of the research purpose, together with the ethical issues. The average interview time was around one hour. Reliability was achieved by using the same interview-protocol for each case. The interviewer inserted the questions into the conversation and prompted when needed. With the permission of the participants, the interviews were recorded.

4.3 Data Analysis

A *modus operandi* approach (Scriven 1976), which consists of triangulating independent indices, has been adopted for this study, which is achieved by analyzing the same factor from multiple instances. The analysis also involved browsing the information repositories to find the participants' views on similar issues. Interestingly, some of the comments (during the interview) of two respondents came up as contradicting to their previous comments on the same issues, published in public media. In those cases, the participant was called again to make his/her position clear. During developing the variables from the interviews, this study followed both the theoretical replication as well as the literal replication (Chan and Ngai 2007). Theoretical replication was made by contrasting cases between respondents; while literal replication occurred where the cases were obtained from their similarities. Using NVivo8, coding the interviews word-by-word, a number of free nodes were developed by naming each segment of data with a label. Each free node summarized and accounted for each concept about the data. Later, tree nodes were developed. Each tree node became a prospective construct, which consisted of a set of relevant free nodes with a similar concept.

5 Findings and Hypotheses Development

5.1 External Pressure

External pressure is the combination of a few types of pressures which are discussed in the following sections. From the analysis it is found that every farmer in Australia experienced at least one kind of pressure which drove them to adopt RFID. Without having such pressure, most of the farmers would not have implemented RFID in their farming.

5.1.1 Government Pressure

It is evident that the regulative pressure from the government made many farmers to adopt RFID, as four (A, B, E, and G) out of eight farms are directly influenced by government legislation and adopted RFID. They all are unanimous to say "*I just had to do it*" or "*...would not go for this system if it were not mandatory*". Farm C, however, felt "genuine push" by Department of Food, Western Australia (DAFWA) "for everyone to move in this way" and "a heavily saturated awareness program", and does not consider the "push" as a 'pressure'. On the contrary, RFID adoption in farm D and F was not influenced by government pressure as they found it as a "voluntary activity" and "commercial advantage", respectively; but agree that the legislation worked as a catalyst.

Based on the analysis, we assume that government pressure is one of the most important driving factors for RFID adoption in WA livestock industry. Therefore, the proposition is:

H1: Greater government pressure will lead to greater RFID adoption.

5.1.2   Market Pressure

The analysis found that the terms competitive pressure, competition, market demand, consumer demand and so on are generally considered, by the farms, as *market pressure*. They emphasize that food safety and product integrity are becoming non-negotiable requirements for food commodities in all Australian domestic and export markets. Half of the interviewed farms in this study, however, do not find much pressure from the market while other half do. Farms those are supplying their livestock and meat products to only the local markets do not feel any market pressure for RFID-based animal identification system whatsoever. However, lately there is an emerging market preference, though not the pressure, for lifetime traceable beef; *"Buyers are beginning to show a preference for cattle that can be quickly and accurately traced back to all properties on which they have resided"* or *"Many of our larger domestic customers are beginning to demand lifetime traceability, particularly the larger supermarket-chains"*.

Farms like D, F, and H find the RFID-based animal traceability system as a prerequisite to do business with the EU, Korean, and Japanese market, and those markets are *absolutely rigid about the identification and other requirements*. Farm C, therefore, does care RFID system because of the customer demand.

> *..... there is always competitive pressure. You have the competing organizations pushing their products with better than the other one. Therefore, if you have got this sort of traceability in place, it would give your product a push in the competitive market for a better position* (Farm C).

Sheep farmers perceive that, by the means of individual sheep-data, competitors can entertain the customers with accurate data and customized product which insists them to adopt RFID in their sheep management operations. However, as because the market pressure has come up as an important factor; this study assumes a contribution from market pressure per se towards RFID adoption.

H2: Greater market pressure will lead to greater RFID adoption.

5.1.3   Cognitive Pressure

A clear difference between mimetic and normative pressures is missing by the respondents, rather it is mingled; this pressure is termed as 'cognitive pressure' (Lawrence et al. 2001). Cognitive pressure comes from the farms' cognition, which is mediated by the external factors, which influences their adoption decision. Sheep farmers, particularly, perceive that the other farmers who adopted RFID for their sheep management system are getting operational efficiency as they can manage sheep individually, not as a flock, which enables improved decision-taking. It is also found that a farm may consider RFID as a means of 'image' or 'prestige'. Farm C stated that one of the reasons to adopt RFID was to "take a leadership role" in their community as "small farms around us expect that they would learn from our experience as some of the new things are too expensive" to be tried by the small farms. Farm H also did "try to be different". As the farm-owner of Farm H holds one of the top positions in livestock association, he realized the cognitive pressure "to prove the RFID efficiencies and make them [other farmers] convinced". The proposition is therefore:

H3: Greater cognitive pressure will lead to greater RFID adoption.

5.2   External Support

External support to adopt RFID comes from different sources.

> [At the beginning] *there was fairly a strong awareness program that was going on. The awareness was made by the agriculture department, government staffs, industry staff...*

As mentioned by the respondents, external support comes from various channels including government staffs, suppliers' staffs, and organizations staffs that inspires and make farmers confident to adopt RFID technology.

5.2.1   Government Support

Farmers are very satisfied with the supports from the government department. They all agreed that if they get any problems, DAFWA would be the first place to seek assistance from. "The agriculture department is pretty responsive. I am pretty happy with them" (Farm C). Except farm C, all asked for incentives, unanimously. "Without the subsidy, it's a bit of struggle" (Farm B). "The farmers should get subsidized tags and readers" (Farm A). They unanimously supported that government support, on RFID costs in particular, will increase RFID adoption. However, farm C does not agree: "I do not support if the total cost is reimbursed to the farmers because it would send the farmers wrong message. It was the lesson to blow for a management change; that's really came down to". However, Australian government is supporting the livestock industry by taking the expenses of building, maintaining, and developing infrastructure. The basic infrastructure includes identifying the farms uniquely, managing the NLIS database, and providing ICT infrastructure. Interestingly it is found that the then infrastructure did not have any influence in RFID adoption rather the RFID adoption has a positive influence in upgrading the infrastructure because government needed to provide internet facility, for example, to upload the data from the farm-site to the MLA-site. In fact, because of the growing pressure, the infrastructure is getting better. "Now, many of them (the farms) have satellite broadband which was actually done by the government in the remote area". However, the continuous existing support from the agriculture department is believed to be satisfactory towards RFID adoption. The proposition, thus, becomes:

H4: Greater government support will lead to greater RFID adoption.

5.2.2   Vendor Support

RFID is introduced, governed, and disseminated mainly by the government agencies. The respondents argued that the vendors have least involvement and influence in

Australian livestock, particularly in RFID context. However, three of the interviewees received troubleshooting support from the vendors at the initial stage which is now discontinued. It is apparent from the interviews that the providers were much proactive and supportive at the initial stage of RFID introduction and now, *may be,* have concentrated to other applications. Farmers stated that except for large-scale integration of RFID systems they do not need vendor support, *anyway.*

5.2.3 Associative Support

This study finds a distinctive source of support which can be called as 'union support' or 'association's support' or the 'support from the industry bodies'. It is found that the farmers have different formal associations (through which they bargain with externals and market their products) and informal networks (to share and seek knowledge). The level and frequency of involvement with those networks affects the speed and level of RFID adoption. Six participants do have a regular participation in their associations. However, one interviewee felt that the association is more concentric on general farming issues rather business issues like enhancing the brand image and exploring new international markets. The proposition, thus, becomes:

H5: More support from farming association will lead to greater RFID adoption.

5.3 Environmental Uncertainty

In contrast to the literature, this study finds that external uncertainty decreases the rate and level of RFID adoption as farmers do not know how long the demand will be for a RFID-based animal information system. Similarly some farmers are not interested to invest in keeping more information to entertain Japanese and Korean market as they are not certain about the other markets' future intention and timing of such extension of requirements. Instead, they would concentrate on finding new markets with less RFID requirements such as in the Middle East, Lebanon, Dubai, Philippines, and Russia. Moreover, Farm D worries that a better technology may replace the RFID technology which, they think, deters other farms to adopt RFID technology. Thus, the proposition supported is:

H6: Higher environmental uncertainty will decrease the speed and level of RFID adoption.

6   Proposed Framework for RFID Adoption

Based on the above analysis and literature review the research model is developed which is presented in Fig. 1. This model proposes that external pressure (consists of government pressure, market pressure, and cognitive pressure), external support (government support, and associative support) positively influence RFID adoption while external uncertainty negatively influences RFID adoption in Australian livestock industry.

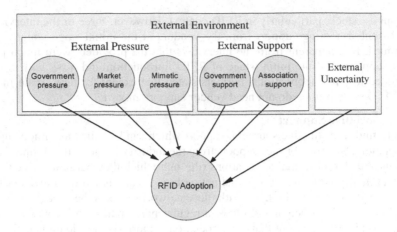

Fig. 1. The proposed framework for environmental effects on RFID adoption

7   Quantitative Study

7.1   Sample

This research struggled badly conducting the survey especially to collect the contacts of the sample. Because of the strong 'privacy' provision with every agencies and farmers' association the researchers found it very hard to collect the information. However, a technique was provided by the DAFWA which retrieves the contact of each farm from an online database. In this data-retrieval process 568 contacts were generated. Later, a contact list of 2,600 WA cattle farms were supplied by the DAFWA. In total, 1,200 farms were invited to participate the survey. The samples were chosen using a random sampling technique. Each paper-based questionnaire provided a temporary URL (web link) so that respondents could alternatively use the online version in *Survey Monkey*. Moreover, a national agency agreed to attach the e-questionnaire with electronic newsletters to its members/subscribers.

To secure the confidence of the respondents they were ensured that their identity could never be detected thus ensuring the privacy and anonymity. For the convenience of the respondents, a stamped and addressed reply-envelope was provided. Unlike other surveys, this survey did not include a 'follow-up' procedure. This was actually not possible; because, the questionnaire did not include any reference-code to check whether a particular respondent replied or not. This was intentionally done to increase the reliability and thus the response rate. Overall, 220 returned surveys were useable. The response rate could not be established; however, the rate is low which is not uncommon for small businesses in Australia (Dawson et al. 2002).

7.2   Data Examination

As mentioned earlier, this research was conducted through an online survey as well as through the traditional mail survey. The responses from the mail survey were split into early and late respondents. Also, the online survey-respondents were considered as the early respondents. Therefore, the responses were grouped into Wave 1 and Wave 2 sample. 139 responses were in Wave 1 and the rest 81 were in Wave 2. Independent sample *Mann-Whitney U Test* was performed to test the significant differences between two different waves. The test was performed in terms of *gender*, highest level of *education*, and *age* of the person completing the survey, *income* of the farm, and one indicator from the research model. The result established that in each instance z-values are not significant at 0.05 level. In other words, the distribution of gender, for example, is same across two different waves of the survey sample, and there was negligible non-response bias between Wave 1 and Wave 2 sample. Therefore, the response for Wave 1 and Wave 2 samples could be combined for data analysis (Quaddus and Hofmeyer 2007). The number of usable responses met the requirement level: 10 times the number of items in the most complex formative construct or the largest number of antecedent constructs leading to an endogenous construct in the research model, as argued by Barclay et al. (1995).

7.3   Measures

The six factors described earlier (see Fig. 1) have been measured with great care. The factors were operationalised first from the literature which was further enhanced through the field study. Six-point Likert scale ranging from 'strongly disagree' to 'strongly agree' has been used to measure 22 items while two items (of RFID adoption) were measure with "<1>, <2>, <3>, <4>, <5>, <more than 5> years/applications" scale.

7.4   Quantitative Results

The data gathered from the survey phase were analyzed by partial least squares (PLS)-based structural equation modeling (Barclay et al. 1995). This study used the standard PLS analysis of the individual item reliability, composite reliability, and discriminant validity to assess the adequacy of the measurement model (Barclay et al. 1995; Hulland 1999).

7.4.1   Assessment of Measurement Properties
The initial research model consisted of 24 observed variables. As par the PLS procedure (Barclay et al. 1995; Hulland 1999), this model was tested for item reliability, internal consistency, and discriminant validity to assess the measurement adequacy of the model. Referring to Igbaria et al.'s (1995) argument this research adopted the minimum cut-off level of 0.5 for item loading; following this rule, one item was discarded (GS3: 0.1679). The item loadings are detailed in Table 2 with the low loading item marked as 'a'. The revised model with 20 observed variables were again tested using PLS and all item reliabilities exceeded the 0.5 reliability criteria. This result confirms that all items are sufficient to represent their respective construct. The item loadings have not considered for the only formative construct external uncertainty. However, the items were checked with acceptable VIF values and the weight scores.

Table 2. The item loadings

	Construct	Item	PLS loading
Govt. Pressure	Legislation	GP1	0.5092
	Government intervention	GP2	0.9999
Market Pressure	Market demand	MP1	0.7922
	Trading requirement	MP2	0.6697
	Business pressure	MP3	0.8647
	Competitive pressure	MP4	0.5049
	Competition	MP5	0.8193
Cognitive Pressure	Mimetic pressure	CP1	0.6091
	Favorability	CP2	0.7052
	Normative pressure	CP3	0.7829
	Subjective norm	CP4	0.5915
Govt. Support	Information service	GS1	0.8137
	Infrastructure	GS2	0.8160
	Taxation	GS3	0.1679[a]
	Training	GS4	0.7450
Ass. Support	Demonstration	AS1	0.7732
	Publication	AS2	0.7152
	Discussion	AS3	0.6144
Adoption	Significance	ADP1	0.8788
	Duration	ADP2	0.5777
	Extent	ADP3	0.5161

'a' denotes for discarded item

The Fornell and Larcker's (1981) method was used to evaluate the model for internal consistency (see Table 3). Referring to Table 3, all constructs met the acceptable criterion for composite reliability (CR) (0.7 or more) and AVE (0.5) (Jiang et al. 2002). The highest CR was observed for *associative support* (0.857) followed by *cognitive pressure* (0.849) and *market pressure* (0.848), and the lowest being *adoption* (0.705). Similarly, the AVE values for every constructs exceeded the recommended value 0.5, which means that convergent analysis for these constructs is satisfied. The highest value for AVE was experienced by *associative support* (0.668) and the lowest was by *adoption* (0.507).

Table 3. Internal Consistency and AVE for the constructs

Construct	Composite Reliability	AVE
Government pressure	0.715	0.592
Market pressure	0.848	0.539
Cognitive pressure	0.849	0.584
Government support	0.795	0.531
Associative support	0.857	0.668
Adoption	0.705	0.507

Table 4 presents the detailed results of discriminant validity test. The square root of AVEs are shown as the diagonal elements and the off-diagonal elements represent the correlations among the latent variables. Table 4 indicates that the square root of AVE is greater than the off-diagonal elements across the row and down the column. The result indicates that all items demonstrate higher loadings in their respective constructs in comparison to their cross loadings in other constructs. Therefore, it confirms that the measurement model has strong discriminant validity at construct level - all the latent variables are different from each other.

Table 4. Correlation of Latent Variables and the Square Root of AVE

	GP	MP	CP	GS	AS	ADP
Government pressure (GP)	**0.769**					
Market pressure (MP)	0.127	**0.734**				
Cognitive pressure (CP)	0.097	0.656	**0.764**			
Government support (GS)	0.199	0.363	0.465	**0.729**		
Associative support (AS)	0.155	0.310	0.422	0.654	**0.817**	
Adoption (ADP)	0.118	0.580	0.519	0.432	0.299	**0.676**

Bold diagonal elements are the square root of AVE

Based on the outcomes as shown in Table 2, 3, and 4, overall result of the measurement model has provided satisfactory empirical support for the reliability, convergent, and discriminant validity. Having established that the measurement model is adequate and sufficient, the next phase of PLS analysis was to analyze the assessment of the structural model. This analysis is presented in the next section.

7.5   Assessment of the Structural Model

The score of R^2 is 0.425. R^2 value can be interpreted in the following way: the model explained 42.5% of the variance in *RFID adoption*. Overall findings show that all scores of R^2 value satisfy the requirement for the 0.10 cut off value (Quaddus and Hofmeyer 2007).

To provide a clearer picture, Table 5 is presented along with the result of the research hypotheses. As shown in the Table 5, the influence of *market pressure* (H2), *cognitive pressure* (H3), *government support* (H4), and *external uncertainty* (H6) are found to be significant on RFID adoption. However, the influence of *government pressure*, and *associative support* on RFID adoption are not supported.

Table 5. Evaluation of the research hypotheses for the antecedents factors

Hypothesis	Link	Path Coeff.	*t*-value	Result
H1	Govt. Pressure to Adoption	-0.002	0.0270	Not Supported
H2	Market Pressure to Adoption	0.416	6.0263***	Supported
H3	Cognitive Pressure to Adoption	0.125	1.6853*	Supported
H4	Govt. Support to Adoption	0.232	2.8306***	Supported
H5	Associative Support to Adoption	-0.080	1.0826	Not Supported
H6	Uncertainty to Adoption	0.142	2.5323**	Supported

Significance at $*p<0.05$, $**p<0.01$, $***p<0.005$

8   Discussion and Implications

This study provides a clearer understanding of the influence of external environmental factors on the adoption of RFID. The contributing environmental factors of RFID adoption are *market pressure, cognitive pressure, government support*, and *external uncertainty*.

In general, cattle farmers in Western Australia adopt RFID because of *market pressure* with the hope that it would give them a competitive-edge in the marketplace. Moreover, the *cognitive pressure* (particularly in sheep identification) is one of the contributing factors adopting RFID. It is found that *government pressure* does not have an influence on *RFID adoption* which is bit surprising in Australian-livestock context. Actually, to comply with the legislation, many of the farms attach RFID tags just immediately before the cattle are moved to another farm ('slap and ship' technique). Technically, this process is not treated as adoption. Hence, the lack of influence of *government pressure* on *RFID adoption* is not exceptional.

However, RFID adoption is dependent on *government support*. For example, for an effective system that ensures lifetime traceability of animals farms need to upload animal information in a central national database which requires unique (farm) identification number, Internet facilities and so on. Without a strong infrastructure of data management the whole initiative might go wrong/ useless. Moreover, a more proactive and aggressive approach from the vendors, by demonstrating RFID projects and providing technical support, would inspire farmers embracing more RFID applications and services. Finally, a positive approach from the farming associations toward RFID technology and thus educating the farmers is invaluable.

This study finds that *external uncertainty* decreases RFID adoption. Farms informed that there is a lack of consistency on data requirement; markets request for more and different data. To provide a new set of data farms may require making a major change in the RFID system. Therefore, farms that are not certain about the market-requirements are less interested adopting RFID. Some farmers are not interested to invest on keeping more information to entertain Japanese and Korean market, for example, as they are not certain about the other markets' future intention and timing of such extension of requirements. Consequently, this type of uncertainty hinders the RFID adoption as farmers do not know how long the demand for record keeping and how viable it will be. Instead, farms would concentrate on finding new markets with less RFID requirements such as in the Middle East, Lebanon, Dubai, Philippines, and Russia (Rees 2008).

The findings from this study are of considerable significance for RFID adoption, particularly for those countries which have a plan or are under pressure to apply RFID technology to identify objects. They may consider that supporting farms is more useful than exercising pressure. Government pressure sometimes develops a negative image, and negative perceptions about the technology. Moreover, in lieu of relying on other supports (e.g., vendors, associations, networks) government should take the leadership role and offer every-possible supports to the prospective adopters, and adopters; even after the adoption takes place. Furthermore, the government as well as technology providers must realize that (hence make the farms to realize) though the 'slap and ship' technique conforms the law but does not guarantee the optimum return. To get the best of the technology and cost effective, farms need to use RFID on every possible farm operations; mere adoption at the last minute is just underutilizing the technology and its associated costs. Hence, the government agencies can prepare their task-list realizing the outcomes of this study. For example, they may use 'incentive' as the main support for a quick adoption of RFID.

As a theoretical contribution, this paper is the first initiative investigating solely the environmental factors responsible for RFID adoption. This study presents a systematic presentation of those factors. The concept of 'cognitive pressure' is studied by the researches in individual-adoption but not in organizational perspective. This study proposes to use this term in organizational adoption research which could be viewed as the integration of two concepts from institutional theory: mimetic pressure and normative pressure. The survey result supports this presumption. Moreover, the field study in this research finds that, the associative support (farmers' associations and the relationship among other farmers) is very important for RFID adoption; which is not discussed in the literature with due importance. Finally, relevant organizations and bodies could pay attention reducing external uncertainty which would increase RFID adoption. One of the solutions of reducing many uncertainties, in RFID context, is setting and practicing a global standardization.

9   Future Research and Conclusion

This study presents the significance of external environmental factors on RFID adoption. The factors have been explored from an extensive literature review which were confirmed and contextualized from a field study. The contextualized factors, then, have been examined by a quantitative survey data. Following the 'mixed method' research approach this study is the first of its kind detailing the factors from external environment. The results and implications support that this research has the potential to be applied in other similar studies. However, future studies could integrate this current model with technological and organizational factors, and be tested to find the effects of those factors on RFID adoption.   Also, testing this model separately with adopters and yet-to-be adopters would be worthwhile and interesting.

References

Bandura, A.: Social Cognitive Theory of mass communication. Media Psychology 3(3), 265–299 (2001)

Bansal, R.: Coming soon to a Wal-Mart near you. IEEE Antenna and Propagation Magazine 45(6), 105–106 (2003)

Barclay, D., Higgins, C., Thomson, R.: The partial least squares (PLS) approach to causal modeling: Personal computer adoption and use as an illustration. Technology Studies 2(2), 285–309 (1995)

Brown, I., Russell, J.: Radio frequency identification technology: An exploratory study on adoption in the South African retail sector. International Journal of Information Management 27(4), 250–265 (2007)

Chan, S.C.H., Ngai, E.W.T.: A qualitative study of information technology adoption: how ten organizations adopted Web-based training. Information Systems Journal 17(3), 289–315 (2007)

Corbin, J.M., Strauss, A.L.: Basics of qualitative research: Techniques and procedures for developing grounded theory, 3rd edn. Sage, California (2008)

Dawson, S., Breen, J., Satyen, L.: The ethical outlook of Micro business operators. Journal of Small Business Management 40(4), 302–313 (2002)

Eisenhardt, K.M.: Building Theories from Case Study Research. The Academy of Management Review 14(4), 532–550 (1989)

Fornell, C., Larcker, D.F.: Evaluating Structural Equation Models with unobservable variables and measurement error. Journal of Marketing Research 18(1), 39–50 (1981)

Garry, M.: Albertsons launches RFID program. Supermarket News (2004)

Gatignon, H., Robertson, T.: Technology diffusion: an empirical test of competitive effects. Journal of Marketing 53, 35–49 (1989)

Gibbs, J.L., Kraemer, K.L.: A cross-country investigation of the determinants of scope of E-commerce use: An institutional approach. Electronic Markets 14(2), 124–137 (2004)

Green, B.: Implementation of the National Livestock Identification System (Cattle) Business Plan in Western Australia (2005-2008), Department of Agriculture and Food, WA (2009)

Hooper, S.: Australian Beef, Australian Bureau of Agricultural and Resource Economics (ABARE) (2010), http://www.abare.gov.au/publications_html/livestock/livestock_10/beef_10_1.pdf

Hossain, M.A., Quaddus, M.: The Adoption and Continued Usage Intention of RFID: An Integrated Framework. Information Technology & People 24(3), 236–256 (2011)

Huyskens, C., Loebbecke, C.: RFID Adoption: Theoretical Concepts and their Practical Application in Fashion. In: Organizational Dynamics of Technology-Based Innovation: Diversifying the Research Agenda, pp. 345–361. Springer, Boston (2007)

Hulland, J.: Use of partial least squares (PLS) in strategic management research: a review of four recent studies. Strategic Management Journal 20, 195–204 (1999)

Iacovou, C.L., Benbasat, I., Dexter, A.S.: Electronic Data Interchange and Small Organizations: Adoption and Impact of Technology. MIS Quarterly 19(4), 465–485 (1995)

Igbaria, M., Guimaraes, T., Davis, G.B.: Testing the Determinants of Microcomputer Usage via a Structural Equation Model. Journal of Management Information Systems 11(4), 87–114 (1995)

Jiang, J.J., Klein, G., Carr, C.L.: Measuring information system service quality: SERVQUAL from the other side. MIS Quarterly 26(2), 145–166 (2002)

Jones, M.A., Wyld, D.C., Totten, J.W.: The adoption of RFID technology in the retail supply chain. The Coastal Business Journal 4(1), 29–42 (2005)

Kimberly, J.R., Evanisko, M.J.: An integrated model of information systems adoption in small businesses. Academy of Management Journal 24(4), 689–713 (1981)

Lawrence, T.B., Winn, M.I., Jennings, P.D.: The temporal dynamics of institutionalization. The Academy of Management Review 26(4), 624–644 (2001)

Lee, C., Shim, J.: An exploratory study of radio frequency identification (RFID) adoption in the healthcare industry. European Journal of Information Systems 16(6), 712–724 (2007)

Li, S., Visich, J.K.: Radio frequency identification: supply chain impact and implementation challenges. International Journal of Integrated Supply Management 2(4), 407–424 (2006)

Lin, C.-Y.: An Empirical Study on Organizational Determinants of RFID Adoption in the Logistics Industry. Journal of Technology Management & Innovation 4(1), 1–7 (2009)

Lin, C.-Y., Ho, Y.-H.: An Empirical Study on the Adoption of RFID Technology for Logistics Service Providers in China. International Business Research 2(1), 23–36 (2009)

Luo, Z., Tan, Z., Ni, Z., Yen, B.: Analysis of RFID in China. In: Proceedings of IEEE International Conference on e-Business Engineering, pp. 315–318 (2007)

Matta, V., Moberg, C.: Defining the Antecedents for Adoption of RFID in the Supply Chain. Issues in Information Systems 8(2), 449–454 (2007)

Moberg, C.R., Cutler, B.D., Gross, A., Speh, T.W.: Identifying antecedents of information exchange within supply chains. International Journal of Physical Distribution & Logistics Management 32(9), 755–770 (2002)

Nolz, A.: Setting the RFID standard. In: Beef Magazine. Penton Media Inc. (2008)

Oxley, J.E.: Institutional environment and the mechanisms of governance: the impact of intellectual property protection on the structure of inter-firm alliances. Journal of Economic Behavior & Organization 38(3), 283–309 (1999)

Patterson, K., Grimm, C., Corsi, T.: Adopting New Technologies for Supply Chain Management. Transportation Research (Part E): Logistics and Transportation Review 39(2), 95–121 (2003)

Poirier, C.C., McCollum, D.: RFID Strategic Implementation and ROI: a practical roadmap to success,.J. ROSS Publishing (2006)

Quaddus, M., Hofmeyer, G.: An investigation into the factors influencing the adoption of B2B trading exchanges in small business. European Journal of Information Systems 16, 202–215 (2007)

Rees, T.: Globalisation impacts the Australian meat industry. In: Meat International, Meat International (2008)

Roberti, M.: Wal-Mart Spells Out RFID Vision. RFID Journal (2003),
http://www.rfidjournal.com/article/purchase/463

Rogers, E.M.: Diffusion of Innovation. Free Press, New York (1995)

Schmitt, P., Michahelles, F.: Status of RFID/EPC Adoption. In: Auto-ID Labs White Paper, Auto-ID Labs, 1-41 (2009)

Scott, W.R.: Institutions and Organizations. Sage Publications, CA (2001)

Scriven, M.: Maximizing the power of causal investigations: The modus operandi method. In: Evaluation Studies Review Annual, pp. 101–118. Sage Publications, CA (1976)

Scupola, A.: The adoption of Internet commerce by SMEs in the South of Italy: An environmental, technological and organizational perspective. Journal of Global Information Technology Management 6(1), 51–71 (2003)

Semple, K.: NLIS: On-farm Benefits. Agriculture Notes, Department of Primary Industries, Victoria, Australia (2007)

Sharma, A., Citurs, A.: Radio Frequency Identification (RFID) adoption drivers: a radical innovation adoption process. In: Proceedings of Americas Conference on Information Systems (AMCIS), NE, USA (2005)

Sharma, A., Citurs, A., Konsynski, B.: Strategic and institutional perspectives in the adoption and early integration of Radio Frequency Identification (RFID). In: Proceedings of the 40th Hawaii International Conference on System Sciences (2007)

Shih, D., Chiu, Y., Chang, S., Yen, D.: An empirical study of factors affecting RFID's adoption in Taiwan. Journal of Global Information Management 16(2), 58–80 (2008)

Tashakkori, A., Teddlie, C.: Mixed methodology: Combining qualitative and quantitative approaches. Sage Publications, Inc., California (1998)

Teo, H., Wei, K., Benbasat, I.: Predicting intention to adopt interorganizational linkages: An institutional perspective. MIS Quarterly 27(1), 19–49 (2003)

Tornatzky, L.G., Fleischer, M.: The process of technological innovation. Lexington Books, Lexington (1990)

Wen, L., Zailani, S., Fernando, Y.: Determinants of RFID Adoption in Supply Chain among Manufacturing Companies in China: A Discriminant Analysis. Journal of Technology Management & Innovation 4(1), 22–32 (2009)

Whitaker, J., Mithas, S., Krishnan, M.: A field study of RFID deployment and return expectations. Production and Operations Management 16(5), 599–612 (2007)

Zhu, K., Kraemer, K., Xu, S.: Electronic Business Adoption by European Firms: A Cross-Country Assessment of the Facilitators and Inhibitors. European Journal of Information Systems 12(4), 251–268 (2003)

Role of Innovation Attributes in Explaining the Adoption Intention for the Interbank Mobile Payment Service in an Indian Context

Kawaljeet Kapoor, Yogesh K. Dwivedi, and Michael D. Williams

School of Business, Swansea University, Swansea, United Kingdom
{kawalkap,ykdwivedi}@gmail.com,
m.d.williams@swansea.ac.uk

Abstract. This study presents an investigation on the role of innovation attributes that significantly influence the behavioural intention and actual adoption of potential consumers towards the *interbank mobile payment service*. Using attributes from Rogers' diffusion of innovations theory, along with one other attribute, cost, the diffusion of this IMPS application has been studied. The proposed model was empirically tested against the data gathered from both, the adopters and non-adopters of this technology. The SPSS analysis tool was used to perform the reliability tests, and linear and logistic regressions. While relative advantage, compatibility, complexity and trialability displayed significant relationships, observability exhibited a poor impact on behavioural intention. On the other hand, behavioural intention and cost showed significant impacts on the adoption of the IMPS application. The theoretical background, discussions, key conclusions, and limitations, alongside research implications of this study have been presented.

Keywords: Innovation, Adoption, Mobile Payment, IMPS, Diffusion of Innovations.

1 Introduction

The Interbank Mobile Payment Service (IMPS) is a 24/7 interbank electronic fund transfer service available as a mobile application, enabling customers to access their bank accounts via mobile phones to make the required fund transfers in a secured manner (NPCI, 2012). There are two types of this service – (a) *Person to Person* - where fund transfers between two individuals are allowed. (b) *Person to Merchant* - where fund transfers between a customer and a merchant are allowed (South Indian Bank, 2012). Liang et al. (2007) emphasize on one of the major advantages of using services on mobile phones as the ability to access services ubiquitously, through various devices. The positives of the IMPS application are clearly its round-the-clock availability, savings in terms of time and cost, transactions on a safe/secure mode, and the instant fund transfer ability. As of October, 2012, the national payments corporation of India [npci.org.in] claims that fifty banks have become the IMPS member banks. An article available on *Business Standard*'s (2012) website points out that the adoption rate of this technology has been low; the industry analysts pick on this mobile application's availability to only the smart phone users as a possible

Y.K. Dwivedi et al. (Eds.): TDIT 2013, IFIP AICT 402, pp. 203–220, 2013.

reason for the low adoption rate. *PayMate*, has now addressed this concern and provided the basic phone users with a hybrid SMS-IVR solution. However, PayMate has only partnered with three banks until date, which does not effectively provide a large scale solution to this problem.

Shyamala Gopinath, DG, RBI, at the inauguration of IMPS of the NPCI in Mumbai stated (22/11/2010) – "the twin challenge for India is to succeed in reducing the use of cash, while encouraging the spread and use of mobile wallet to reap the full benefits of this ubiquitous product". She identified three stakeholders of this IMPS application– the telecom partners, the member banks, and the participating merchants, who will have to invest combined efforts to deliver the true value to their consumers, whilst sharing the costs and generated revenues amongst themselves. While 50 banks have partnered with IMPS, more banks are yet to adopt this technology. Higher the success rate of this application with the member banks, more number of other banks would want to join the IMPS league. The potential members would be interested in obtaining an insight into the factors that influence the customers to use such a mobile payment facility. What do we know about the factors that encourage consumers to use IMPS? How can we reason the low adoption rate of this technology? Is it simply the lack of cognition? Unfortunately, there are no empirical studies or official adept reports available to address these questions.

Although, there have been numerous studies examining mobile payment in the m-commerce context (Barnes, 2002; Siau and Shen, 2003; Wu and Wang, 2005), IMPS is a very recent technology in the Indian context. The features of this particular application differ from the other mobile technologies. Since the technology is very new in India, there have been no studies/publications made yet on this application. Therefore, an empirical investigation is necessary to learn about the factors that entice the consumers to use IMPS. Hence, the research aim of this study is to empirically examine the role of innovation attributes on the adoption of the IMPS technology in an Indian context. Comprehending these influential attributes could serve in assisting the stakeholders to develop competitive strategies that could promote a wider acceptance of this technology. The next section provides theoretical basis for this study and proposes a conceptual model with hypotheses; after which, the research method is explained followed by a findings section presenting the SPSS statistics, which are then discussed against the proposed hypotheses; at closure, the key conclusions, limitations and future research directions have been presented.

2   Theoretical Basis and Development of the Conceptual Model

IMPS is clearly an integration of internet banking and mobile payment service. This application allows customers to access their bank accounts on mobile phones, using the internet from their mobile's network providers to make a successful payment to another person or merchant. There have been numerous publications on internet banking (IB) and mobile payment services in the past - two studies on IB adoption in Hong Kong use TAM (Yiu et al., 2007) and extended TAM models (Cheng et al. 2003) and find that perceived usefulness and perceived web security have a direct effect on the use intention, the former study extends implications for retail banks in Hong Kong. Brown et al. (2004) study the impact of national environment on the IB adoption in South Africa confirming attitudinal and behavioural control factors influence the IB adoption decision.

Chen (2008) expanded the TAM model and IDT to examine the consumer acceptance of mobile payments. They found that perceived use, perceived ease of use, perceived risk, and compatibility were the determinants of adoption. Mallat (2007) conducted an exploratory study on mobile payments which showed that relative advantage and compatibility influenced adoption decisions. Schierz et al. (2010) in their empirical study found that compatibility, individual mobility and subjective norm significantly influence consumer acceptance of m-payment services. These studies show that there has been no study on IMPS in the Indian context. More obviously, this can be reasoned for the IMPS application to be very new in the Indian context. Our study, therefore aims at focussing at this application to gain an understanding of the significant determinants of the IMPS acceptance. One of the most common problems faced by many individuals and organizations in an *innovation adoption and diffusion process*, despite the obvious advantages that their innovation already has to readily offer, is of how to speed up the rate of diffusion of their innovation(s) (Rogers, 2003). To address this concern with respect to the IMPS application, our study uses Rogers' *innovation attributes* alongside one another added attribute, *cost*, the justification of which has been provided in the later part of this section. There are many models available for predicting the user behaviour towards a given innovation like – TAM, UTUT, theory of reasoned action, and theory of planned behaviour, but all of these models tend to use similar attributes. The innovation of diffusion theory is more established and uses a set of attributes different from those used by the above mentioned models. Thus, our study borrows attributes from the Rogers' innovation diffusion theory for exploration purposes in the IMPS context.

To explain the process of diffusion, Rogers recognized five attributes – *Relative Advantage, Compatibility, Complexity, Trialability, and Observability* as the innovation attributes. Over the years, majority of the studies have chosen to use and study these five innovation attributes (Tornatzky and Klein, 1982; Greenhalgh et al., 2004; Legare et al., 2008; Hester and Scott, 2008). TRA (Ajzen and Fishbein, 1980) studied only intention on adoption. TPB (Ajzen, 2006) studied intention and actual behavioural control on adoption. The decomposed theory of planned behaviour (Taylor and Todd, 1995) studied intention and perceived behavioural control on adoption. TAM (Davis et al., 1989) also studied only behavioural intention on adoption. Based on the aforementioned theories, our study decided that Rogers' five attributes will be studied against behavioural intention, and behavioural intention in turn will be studied against adoption. Since IMPS is an innovation involving cost, this attribute was looked upon with interest. Previous studies on mobile payments consider cost as an important influencing factor in making the adoption decision – Dahlberg et al. (2007) point out that researchers find costs in the form of transaction fee to be a barrier of adoption. Another qualitative study on adoption of mobile payments found the premium pricing of payments to be a barrier of adoption (Mallat, 2007). Additional to the apparent costs of adopting an m-commerce innovation, a consumer is often subjected to relatively hidden transaction charges which could considerably influence the adoption decision of that particular innovation (Hung et al., 2003; Wu and Wang, 2005).

Interestingly, all of the above mentioned studies discuss the influence on cost on adoption and not on intention. This could be because a consumer can form favourable intentions towards such innovations (internet banking/mobile payments) without having to actually use (spend money on) that innovation, but when it comes to making an actual transaction, the different aspects of charges associated with that transaction

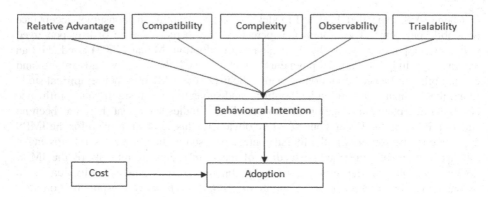

Fig. 1. Proposed conceptual model for examining intention and adoption of IMPS

come into picture. This is when the consumer makes the critical decision of adoption or rejection based on how appealing or unappealing is the charge associated to that transaction. Therefore, it was decided for cost to be regressed only against adoption. It was thereby concluded that - *relative advantage, compatibility, complexity, trialability, observability* and *cost* will be studied to examine the adoption intention and the actual adoption of the IMPS application in an Indian context (fig.1).

2.1 Relative Advantage

By definition, relative advantage is the degree to which an innovation is better than the idea that it is superseding (Rogers, 2003). This attribute has been studied across many different technologies – mobile internet (Hsu et al., 2007) and online portal (Shih, 2008) studies revealed in their findings that a higher degree of offered advantage is related to increased levels of adoption intentions. An organizational study on intention to adopt distributed work arrangements found relative advantage was positively related to use intention (Sia et al., 2004). Since the IMPS application supersedes the idea of performing financial transactions on laptops/personal computers, and allows the same transactions on-the-go, this attribute was deemed appropriate.

H1: *Relative Advantage will significantly influence the users' behavioural intentions.*

2.2 Compatibility

Compatibility is the degree to which an innovation is consistent with the existing values, past experiences and needs of potential adopters (Rogers, 2003). This attribute has been studied across different mobile technologies. Examples include the mobile network and mobile internet studies which reveal that compatibility has a significant and positive influence on the consumer intentions (Hsu et al., 2007; Shin, 2010). An empirical study on mobile ticketing service adoption found that compatibility was a strong predictor of use intention (Mallat et al., 2008). In the IMPS context, in order to learn how similar or different, the consumers find transferring money to the desired client/merchant accounts on a mobile phone, this attribute was studied in further detail.

H2: *Compatibility will positively influence the users' behavioural intentions.*

2.3   Complexity

It is degree to which an innovation is perceived as difficult to understand and use (Rogers, 2003). Greater complexity implies increased degree of difficulty in understanding the use of a given innovation. Therefore complexity is assumed to be negatively associated to use intentions. A mobile marketing adoption study shows that complexity has a direct influence on user's adoption intentions (Tanakinjal, 2010). Studies on online portal use (Shih, 2008) and automatic cash payment system (Yang et al., 2006) found, complexity had a significant negative impact on use intention. Using the IMPS application on a mobile phone may be perceived differently by different users on the complexity scale, based on their skill and adaptability levels.

H3: *Lower complexity will positively influence the users' behavioural intentions.*

2.4   Trialability

Rogers (2003) defines trialability as the degree to which an innovation is available to be experimented for a limited period prior to its actual adoption/rejection. Many internet banking and mobile internet studies are available – a mobile internet study found that trialability was not a significant predictor of adoption intention (Hsu et al., 2007). Arts et al. (2011) in generalizing consumer innovation adoption argue that trialability enhances consumer readiness and has a stronger effect at the behaviour stage, negatively affecting adoption behaviour. It is important to understand, how trialability of IMPS can affect its adoption intention.

H4: *Trialability will significantly influence the users' behavioural intentions.*

2.5   Observability

Observability is defined as the degree to which the results of an innovation become clearly visible to others (Rogers, 2003). A technology products study (Vishwanath and Goldhaber, 2003) found observability significantly impacted intention. Arts et al (2011) in their meta-analysis on drivers of intention and behaviour, showed a partial support to the notion that observability will have a stronger effect at the intention stage. In order to receive more clarity on the effect of this attribute, it has been posited as,

H5: *Observability will significantly influence the users' behavioural intentions.*

2.6   Cost

Tornatzky and Klein (1982) posited cost to be negatively associated with the adoption of an innovation. According to them lesser the cost of adopting an innovation, higher will be the probability of it being adopted immediately. A study on mobile virtual network hypothesizes for cost to negatively influence usage behaviour (Shin, 2010). More conclusions on the effect of cost on the adoption of an innovation (from the previous studies) have already been discussed in section 2. In using the IMPS application, the consumers incur a certain charge per transaction, plus this application is not compatible with all mobile phones. It more specifically runs best on smart phones. In order to account for these potential costs, this attribute was taken into consideration.

H6: *Lower Costs will positively influence the adoption of IMPS.*

2.7   Behavioural Intention

Apart from the aforementioned six attributes, the effect of behavioural intention on adoption was also included to be measured. Gumussoy and Calisir (2009) cite Ajzen and Fishbein (1980) to define behavioural intention as a measure of the likelihood of a person getting involved in a given behaviour. They point at behavioural intention to be an immediate determinant of actual use. Stronger the intention, greater will be the probability of use. Most studies supported for this attribute to have a positive influence on the actual use (Chen et al., 2002; Ajjan and Hartshorne, 2008; Gumussoy and Calisir, 2009); Ajjan and Hartshorne (2008) also cite Ajzen (1991) suggesting that behavioural intention acts as the most important determinant of the adoption decision.

H7: *Behavioural Intention positively influences the adoption of IMPS.*

3   Research Method

3.1   Survey Instrument

The instrument used for data collection was a questionnaire comprising of 36 questions, out of which, eight were demographic by nature – four out of these were multiple choice, respondent specific questions - focussed on *age, gender, education* and *occupation* of the respondent; the remaining four were multiple choice, technology specific questions - focussed on the *adoption factor, innovation type, duration of adoption,* and *frequency of usage.* A seven point likert scale was used to measure the attitude of the respondents to the remaining 28 questions. These 28 questions were designed to cover the seven shortlisted constructs. The seven attributes were made up of four items each (table 1).

Table 1. Constructs-Questions Mapping

Constructs	Questions	Source(s)
Behavioural Intention	BI1: I plan to continue using/use IMPS. BI2: My willingness of using/continuing to use IMPS is high. BI3: I intend to use/continue using IMPS. BI4: The likelihood that I will use/continue using IMPS is high.	Karahanna et al. (1999); Teo and Pok (2003); Shih and Fang (2004)
Trialability	T1: I know the bank which provides/offers IMPS. T2: IMPS mobile application is easily available to get familiar with. T3: I do/did not have to expend much effort in trying the IMPS. T4: I do/did not have adequate opportunities to try the IMPS application.	Moore and Benbasat (1991)
Relative Advantage	RA1: IMPS provides quicker access to the transactions that I need to make. RA2: IMPS provides greater flexibility. RA3: IMPS will help/helps me gain greater control over my finances. RA4: IMPS will help/helps complete all my financial transactions on time.	Moore and Benbasat (1991)
Compatibility	CT1: IMPS is/will be compatible with all of my financial transfer needs. CT2: IMPS will fit/fits well with the type of transactions that I perform. CT3: Using IMPS fits/will fit well with my lifestyle. CT4: My mobile phone is compatible with the IMPS application.	Moore and Benbasat (1991)
Complexity	CP1: Using IMPS will be/is challenging and frustrating. CP2: Learning to use IMPS will be/is easy for me. CP3: Easy to operate interbank service is important to me. CP4: I find it easy for me to be skilful at using the IMPS mobile application.	Moore and Benbasat (1991); Shih and Fang (2004); Yang et al. (2006); Richardson (2009)
Cost	C1: IMPS is inexpensive. C2: The cost of making a financial transfer with IMPS is reasonable. C3: Buying a phone compatible with this IMPS application is expensive. C4: IMPS Transactions are the most affordable single transfer type for me.	Mallat et al. (2008); Koenig-Lewis et al. (2010)
Observability	O1: Being seen as a user of IMPS is good for my image. O2: People who use IMPS are not very visible in my social circle. O3: I have seen others using IMPS. O4: I do not know anyone who uses IMPS.	Meuter et al. (2005); Richardson (2009)

3.2   Pilot Study

The questionnaire was tested against a small sample size to improve upon the instrument design prior to the full scale roll-out of this study. The pilot study was done on a sample of 30 respondents. It was ensured that the population for this study included respondents from all age groups to ensure their understandability of the questionnaire. The respondents' feedback revealed that although the questionnaire was clear and simple by understanding, it appeared to be repetitive. Minor suggestions that were made were addressed and the questionnaire was amended suitably.

3.3   Data Collection

All-India data was to be accumulated and therefore it was decided to collect equal number of responses from all of the four – *northern (Delhi City), eastern (Kolkata City), western (Mumbai City)* and *southern (Bangalore City)* regions of India. A total of 330 respondents participated in this survey. Upon the receipt of the questionnaires, it was found that seven questionnaires were incomplete. In the interest of data accuracy and reliability, these seven questionnaires were discarded, and a total of 323 questionnaires were subjected to further analyses. The SPSS data analysis software was used to produce results on the gathered data, the findings of which are made available in section 4. The findings section will provide for results from the (a) frequency tests on the demographic characteristics (b) *reliability test* showing the internal consistencies of the construct items (c) *descriptive test* generating the means and standard deviations for all of the seven constructs (d) *regression analyses*, both *linear* and *logistic*, in order to test the stated hypotheses, and (e) *multicollinearity test* to check for the correlation amongst the predictor variables.

4   Findings

4.1   Demographics

Table 2 is descriptive of the demographic characteristics for this study's respondent-profile. Clearly, the 18-24 age group, the male respondents (53.6%), and the graduates (38.1%) formed the largest proportion groups for our dataset.

Table 3 discloses the demographics specific to use of IMPS, and shows that out of the 323 respondents, there were 249 non-adopters and only 74 adopters (22.9%) of IMPS.

Table 2. Demographic Characteristics

Variable	Group	Frequency	Percentage
Age	18-24	104	32.2
	25-34	101	31.3
	35-44	51	15.8
	45-54	46	14.2
	55-64	21	6.5
	65-74	0	0
	Above 75	0	0
	Total	323	100.0
Gender	Male	173	53.6
	Female	150	46.4
	Total	323	100.0
Education	Secondary School	3	0.9
	Higher Secondary	62	19.2
	Diploma	31	9.6
	Graduate	123	38.1
	Postgraduate – Taught	71	22.0
	Postgraduate – Research	12	3.7
	Other	21	6.5
	Total	323	100.0

Table 3. Use-Specific Demographic Characteristics

Variable	Group	Frequency	Percentage
Application Type	Person to Person	32	9.9
	Person to Merchant	42	13
	Non Adopters	249	77.1
	Total	323	100
Usage Duration	<=12 Months	30	9.3
	12-24 Months	37	11.5
	25-36 Months	4	1.2
	>36 Months	1	0.3
	Other	2	0.6
	Non Adopters	249	77.1
	Total	323	100
Usage Frequency	Several times a day	1	0.3
	Once a day	7	2.2
	1-2 days a week	20	6.2
	3-5 days a week	19	5.9
	Once every few weeks	16	5
	Less often	11	3.4
	Non Adopters	249	77.1
	Total	323	100

4.2   Reliability Test

A reliability test was carried out to learn the internal consistencies of the individual items forming each of the utilized constructs (Table4). There were four constructs for which one item each was deleted in order to arrive at better α values. Hinton et al. (2004) illustrated that as a representative of reliability, the Cronbach's alpha could be read across four different reliability types: ≥ 0.90 - excellent; 0.70-0.90 - high; 0.50-0.70 - moderate; and ≤ 0.50 - low. Out of the seven constructs, there were four constructs with high, and three with moderate reliabilities. Higher the Cronbach's alpha values, greater is the consistency amongst the individual items making up a given construct.

Table 4. Reliability Test

Constructs	Sample Size	Number of Items	Cronbach's Alpha (α)	Number of Items	Improvised Alpha (α)	Reliability Type
Behaviuoral Intention	323	4	0.87	4	0.87	High
Trialability	323	4	0.569	3	0.649 (T4)	Moderate
Relative Advantage	323	4	0.788	4	0.788	High
Compatibility	323	4	0.713	4	0.713	High
Complexity	323	4	0.497	3	0.629 (CP1)	Moderate
Cost	323	4	0.659	3	0.752 (C3)	High
Observability	323	4	0.523	3	0.585 (O3)	Moderate

4.3   Descriptive Statistics

Table 5 provides for the results from the descriptive test. The statistics were extracted in the ascending order of the mean values.

Table 5. Descriptive Statistics: Importance of various innovation-attributes

Constructs	N	n	Mean	Std. Deviation
Observability	323	4	4.28	1.114
Trialability	323	4	4.61	1.063
Behaviuoral Intention	323	4	4.63	1.242
Cost	323	4	4.69	1.021
Complexity	323	4	4.74	0.961
Compatibility	322	4	4.77	1.224
Relative Advantage	323	4	4.89	1.113

4.4   Regression Analysis

Regression analysis is a statistical technique that predicts the values of one dependent variable using the values of one or more other independent variables (Allen, 2004). This study underwent two types of regression analysis – (a) Linear regression (b) Logistic Regression, which were performed on a total of 323 cases.

Linear Regression

Worster et al. (2007) stated that linear regression assumes a linear relationship between the dependent and independent variable(s). A linear regression was performed taking *Behavioral Intention* as the dependent variable, and the Rogers' five attributes as the independent variables (Table6). The resultant model significantly predicted the behavioral intention of the target population towards IMPS (F (5, 323) = 40.919, p=0.000). The model explains 39.3% of the variance. While four variables were found to have a significant effect, observability did not have any effect on the behavioral intention.

Table 6. Linear Regression

Independent Variables	Standardized Coefficients (Beta)	t	Sig.	Collinearity Statistics (VIF)	Hypotheses Support
(Constant)		.032	.974		
Relative Advantage	.386	6.655	.000	1.749	H1: Supported
Compatibility	.164	2.707	.007	1.904	H2: Supported
Complexity	.156	2.824	.005	1.589	H3: Supported
Trialability	.111	2.057	.040	1.502	H4: Supported
Observability	-.080	-1.51	.132	1.456	H5: Not Supported
MODEL DETAILS					
Adjusted R square = 0.393; *F* = 40.919; *Significance* = 0.000					

Multicollinearity Test

According to Brace et al. (2003) multicollinearity is a situation where a high correlation is detected between two or more predictor variables, which cause problems in drawing inferences about the relative contribution of each predictor variable to the success of the model. The VIF values for this regression analysis vary between 1.456 and 1.904 (Table6). Clearly, these values are significantly lower than the maximum value of 10 (Irani et al., 2009). Thus, the independent variables for this study are free from the multicollinearity problem. The likelihood of the reported variance explained by these independent variables to be close to the real situation is therefore very high.

Logistic Regression

According to Worster et al. (2007), in logistic regression, the outcome variable must be categorical with two possible outcomes, i.e. it should be dichotomous. A logistic regression was performed with adoption as the dependent variable, and behavioural intention and cost as the predictor variables, the results of which are available in table7. The full model significantly predicted the adoption decision of the IMPS users. The model accounted for between 11.1% and 16.8% of the variance (Table8) in the adoption decision. As available in table9, 95.2% of the non-adopters were successfully predicted. However, only 6.8% of predictions for the adopter group were accurate. Overall, 74.9% of the predictions were accurate. Table 10 gives coefficients, Wald statistics, associated degrees of freedom, and probability values for the two predictor variables.

Table 7. Omnibus Tests of Model Coefficients

		Chi-square	df	Sig.
	Step	38.000	2	.000
Step 1	Block	38.000	2	.000
	Model	38.000	2	.000

Table 8. Model Summary

Step	-2 Log likelihood	Cox & Snell R Square	Nagelkerke R Square
1	309.670	.111	.168

Table 9. Classification Table

				Predicted	
	Observed		Installed or Not		Percentage
			Yes	No	Correct
Step 1	Adoption	Yes	24	50	6.8
		No	14	233	95.2
	Overall Percentage				74.9

Table 10. Variables in the equation

Variables	B	S.E.	Wald	df	Sig.	Exp(B)	95% C.I.for EXP(B)		Hypotheses Support
							Lower	Upper	
Behavioural Intention	-.531	.145	13.385	1	.000	.588	.443	.782	H6: Supported
Cost	-.423	.165	6.545	1	.011	.655	.474	.906	H7: Supported
Constant	5.871	.907	41.944	1	.000	354.6			

5   Discussion

5.1   Hypotheses Testing

A total of seven hypotheses were formulated and tested to examine the influence of the independent variables on the dependent variables (Adoption and Behavioural Intention). Only six of these seven hypotheses were supported by data (H1, H2, H3, H4, H6, and H7). As posited, the data confirms that relative advantage, compatibility, complexity and trialability have significant impacts on the *behavioural intentions* of the targeted consumers in the IMPS context. Internet banking and telebanking can be seen as the predecessors of IMPS in the Indian context. In terms of compatibility, IMPS is much faster than telebanking. IMPS provides consumers with quicker access to their bank accounts, and offers greater flexibility in terms of the type of payment they need to make. Along with its 24/7 availability, the mobility feature of the IMPS application surpasses internet banking, in that, IMPS allows access to the consumers from anywhere, anytime, via their mobile networks, without having the need to connect through routers/modems to gain internet/Wi-Fi access. From the data results, clearly, the users perceive IMPS to be an easy to use mobile application. Studies from the past are a supportive proof of these facts - Slyke et al. (2002) used IDT in studying groupware applications and found that *relative advantage, complexity* and *compatibility* significantly influenced intention. Chen et al. (2002) applied IDT to study the consumer attitudes towards virtual stores and found *compatibility* to be strong determinant of consumer intentions. Hsu et al. (2007) studied the adoption of MMS using IDT, and concluded for *relative advantage* and *compatibility* to significantly influence the user intentions. Lee and Kozar (2008) combined IDT, TPB, IT ethics, and morality in an empirical investigation on the anti-spyware software adoption, and found that relative advantage and compatibility showed significant effect on adoption intention. Trialability also succeeded in successfully explaining the consumer's adoption intention (hypothesis 4). Meuter et al. (2005) concluded that trialability serves in clarifying the role of potential adopters by helping evaluating their ability to use that innovation, and thus enhancing the consumer readiness towards the given innovation. IMPS is an application which comes with no installation charge or usage clause, i.e. it is a service available for the consumers to use if and when required. In other words, IMPS comes with an unlimited trial period. The consumers can opt to use this application once, or any number of times without any trial obligations, and return to using it again if the service is appealing to them, or simply quit using it, otherwise.

Hypothesis 5 for this study was not supported by the data, in which *observability* failed to make a significant impact on the consumer intention to adopt IMPS. A recent study on consumer innovations adoption also found that observability was not significantly related to intention (Arts et al, 2011). According to Meuter et al. (2005), observability may assist in showing positive outputs, which in turn may motivate the adopters to receive that innovation's rewards. IMPS is purely a mobile application. The visibility of this innovation is not that apparent. To illustrate in more detail – a study on e-book reader (Jung et al., 2011) found that observability had a significant relationship with consumers' intention to use. This is because an e-reader is a whole instrument in itself which is visible when carried around, and whose outcomes can be observed at visibility, thereby significantly affecting the potential consumers' intentions. The case of IMPS, here, is a complete opposite. The use of IMPS application by an active user will not be evidently visible to the eyes of the others, unless the use and the outcomes of using the IMPS application are explicitly discussed with its active users. This effectively makes IMPS less observable in comparison to other innovative products like tablets, e-readers, smart phones etc. This in turn can be reasoned to justify the insignificance displayed by our study's data for observability towards the use intentions.

The data for this study also confirms the hypotheses with respect to the *adoption* of the IMPS application. It was confirmed that both, cost and behavioural intention significantly affected the adoption of IMPS. Tornatzky and Klein (1982) identified increased costs as inhibitors of the adoption of any innovation. As previously explained in section 2, the former studies are in conformance with the fact that high costs act as retarding agents in the acceptance of a diffusing innovation. In terms of cost, clearly an application like IMPS can incur three kinds of charges – (a) charge per transaction (b) cost of the compatible mobile phone (c) charges on the data being used from the mobile network providers. Our study's results however show that the existing and potential consumers find these charges to be affordable. Thus, it can be concluded that although IMPS comes with a cost, this application is viewed as inexpensive which in turn encourages adoption.

Similarly, with behavioural intention, the past studies have been in accordance with our findings – Taylor and Todd (1997), while studying the determinants of consumer compositing behaviour found that behaviour was significantly influenced by behavioural intention. Shin (2010), in studying the policy implications of mobile virtual network adopter diffusion also found for behavioural intention to have a significant effect on the actual behaviour. Hartshorne and Ajjan (2009) cite Sheppard et al., (1998) and Ajzen (1991) to support that the previous literature also finds a strong association between actual behaviour and the behavioural intention, which has also been confirmed in the IMPS context, in our study.

5.2   Validated Conceptual Model

Figure 2 is representative of the validated model for the factors influencing the behavioural intention and adoption of the IMPS application, as proposed in section 2. The dotted line running from observability to behavioural intention represents that path as insignificant, and the remaining paths from the remaining attributes to behavioural intention are shown to be the significant. Similarly, the paths from cost and behavioural intention to adoption have been shown as significant.

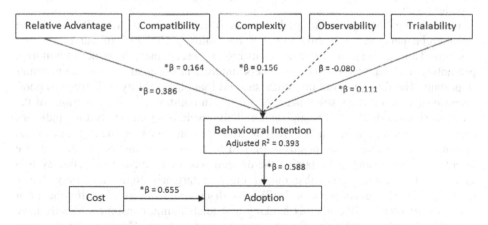

Fig. 2. Validated model illustrating attributes influencing the intention and adoption of IMPS

In terms of performance, the R^2 values for adoption were measured across the Cox and Snell R^2 (0.111) and Nagelkerke R^2 (0.168). These two values were found to be comparatively lower than the values from the earlier studies measuring influences of different independent variables on the adoption of a given innovation (Ungan, 2004;

Gounaris and Koritos, 2008; Li. 2008). To exemplify a few, Ramamurthy et al (2008) reported values of Cox and Snell R^2 – 0.412 and Nagelkerke R^2 – 0.550; Wang et al (2010) reported Cox and Snell R^2 value of 0.51 and Nagelkerke R^2 value of 0.69, which are again higher than the values reported by our study (the variance is not very well explained). The adjusted R^2 value for behavioural intention was 0.393. These R^2 values are comparative to the values from former studies (Taylor and Todd, 1997; Ajjan and Hartshorne, 2008; Hartshorne and Ajjan, 2009). For instance, Gumussoy and Calisir (2009) reported an adjusted R^2 value of 0.14, which is much lower than the R^2 value of 0.393 (which is higher in value and better) reported by our study. Similarly, another study by Lin (2008) reported an R^2 value of 0.30 for a TAM model and an R^2 value of 0.35 for a decomposed TBP model, both of which are clearly lower than the reported R^2 value of this study. The above comparisons evidently suggest that the performance of the validated model (figure 2) is satisfactory (the variance is well explained).

5.3   Research Contributions and Practical Implications

This piece of work is a contribution to the existing literature on the diffusion of innovation attributes, as Rogers' five attributes were studied and tested in a new context with this study: *IMPS application in the Indian context*. According to the authors' best knowledge, the IMPS technology is very new in the Indian context, and there have been no research publications made on this technology yet. Hence, the findings from this study should succeed in providing the first insights into how Rogers' attributes, alongside cost, behave with behavioural intention and adoption aspects of the IMPS application. Both, adoption and intention have been studied in parallel to augment the existing research paradigm with more constructive and broader results.

Considering the statement made by the director general of RBI, from the commercial perspective, mobile wallet is becoming a vital part of our transaction systems. Thus, in order to work towards its broader acceptance, the issues of building, promoting, and maintaining the consumers' interest in using such a service becomes important. The findings from this study showed that observability of IMPS was poor, because of which this construct made no impact in building positive intentions of the consumers towards the IMPS application. This result from our study thus indicates that it is important for the banks to rethink strategies on educating the target mass and making them aware of the positives of IMPS, to promote this application in the interest of improvising and attaining the desired type of financial transaction system in India. The results reveal that out of the 323 targeted population, only 22.9% (table3) formed the adopters of IMPS. As discussed in section5, with the prior existence of systems like internet banking and telebanking, consumers already have established banking styles and finance management systems. The low adoption rates indicate that, for mobile banking to overpower these already existing systems, the real challenge for the banks promoting the IMPS application will be to offer consumers with not just the equivalent services (from its predecessors), but with more attractive, easy to use features to draw more consumers towards its adoption.

6   Conclusions

This study affirms the many established innovation adoption and diffusion notions established by former studies by extending them in the IMPS context. Using Rogers' innovation attributes, alongside cost and behavioural intention, we develop an integrative model to study the influence of these attributes on the adoption of the IMPS application in the Indian context. The results from this study yielded key insights concerning the determinants of IMPS adoption from the proposed conceptual model. The model confirmed that a consumers' usage of IMPS can be predicted from their intentions. It also revealed that IMPS was perceived as inexpensive, and that the low costs associated to this mobile application facilitated its adoption. On the other hand, relative advantage, compatibility, lower complexity and trialability were found to be the significant determinants of the consumers' intention to use the IMPS application. The model also rendered observability as an insignificant determinant of the consumer's intention to use IMPS.

6.1   Limitations and Future Research Directions

Although, the current research aims to study the diffusion of IMPS in an Indian context, the data collected was limited to only four states representing each of the north, east, west, and south regions of India. The other cities of the country may bear certain cultural differences that may facilitate or impinge the adoption of IMPS. The future researchers may focus on the cultural factors, and more importantly focus on gathering the data from more number of cities in the country to bring to light the differences in state-wise adoption of this application, if any. Also, future researchers may want to investigate issues such as social influences using qualitative data, which may also fairly impact the adoption of such mobile payment innovations.

This study restricted its focus to only five of Rogers' innovation attributes, alongside cost as an added attribute of study. However, there are other innovation attributes apart from Rogers' five attributes that have been used and reviewed in the past, but not as much as Rogers' attributes. One study that has remarkably reviewed and listed more of such innovation attributes is the meta-analysis presented by Tornatzky and Klein from 1982. They recognized 25 other attributes as innovation attributes, in addition to Rogers' five attributes. Another significant contribution in this field has been a study by Moore and Benbasat from 1991, wherein they developed an instrument to measure individual perceptions taking a total of eight attributes into consideration. It would be interesting to get an insight into how the adoption of IMPS is affected by these other innovation attributes. Therefore, the future research may shift focus towards studying these other innovation attributes in the IMPS context to attain a deeper understanding of its diffusion process.

Our study focussed on studying the relationship between Rogers' innovation attributes and behavioural intention only, the future researchers may consider studying the direct influence of Rogers' attributes on the adoption aspect on IMPS. The findings from the logistic regression (Table8) showed low R^2 values for Cox and Snell and Nagelkerke, indicating that the total variance explained for adoption of IMPS is slightly lesser for our model. The future researchers may consider incorporating more number of adoption attributes for attaining a better explanation of the variance. Finally, as Rogers' (2003) states, diffusion is a process by which an innovation is communicated through certain channels over time. Given how new the IMPS application is, to have a more collective and constructive understanding, its adoption and diffusion process will have to be empirically investigated at different points in time.

References

Ajjan, H., Hartshorne, R.: Investigating faculty decisions to adopt Web 2.0 technologies: Theory and empirical tests. Internet and Higher Education 11, 71–80 (2008)

Ajzen, I.: The theory of planned behaviour. Organizational Behaviour and Human Decision Processes 50, 179–211 (1991)

Ajzen, I., Fishbein, M.: Understanding attitudes and predicting behaviour. Prentice Hall, Englewood Cliffs (1980)

Ajzen, I.: Behavioural interventions based on the theory of planned behavior. Journal of Applied Social Psychology 32, 665–683 (2006)

Allen, M.P.: Understanding Regression Analysis. Springer (2004)

Arts, J.W.C., Frambach, R.T., Bijmolt, T.H.A.: Generalizations on consumer innovation adoption: A meta-analysis on drivers of intention and behaviour. International Journal of Research in Marketing 28, 134–144 (2011)

Barnes, S.J.: The mobile commerce value chain: analysis and future developments. International Journal of Information Management 22, 91–108 (2002)

Brace, N., Kemp, R., Snelgar, R.: SPSS for psychologists: a guide to data analysis using SPSS for windows. Palgrave Macmillan, New York (2003)

Brown, I., Hoppe, R., Mugera, P., Newman, P., Stander, A.: Environment on the Adoption of Internet Banking: Comparing Singapore and South Africa. Journal of Global Information Management 12, 1–26 (2004)

Business Standard (2012), http://www.business-standard.com/india/news/paymate-powers-inter-bank-mobile-payment-services-in-india/438160/ (accessed on: October 20, 2012)

Chen, L.-D., Gillenson, M.L., Sherrell, D.L.: Enticing Online Consumers: an extended technology acceptance perspective. Information and Management 39, 705–719 (2002)

Chen, L.-D.: A model of consumer acceptance of mobile payment. International Journal of Mobile Communications 6, 32–52 (2008)

Chen, L., Gillenson, M.L., Sherrell, D.L.: Enticing online consumers: an extended technology acceptance perspective. Information and Management 39, 705–719 (2002)

Davis, F.D., Bagozzi, R.P., Warshaw, P.R.: User acceptance of computer technology: A comparison of two theoretical models. Management Science 35, 982–1003 (1989)

Dahlberg, T., Mallat, N., Ondrus, J., Zmijewska, A.: Past, present and future of mobile payments research: A literature review. Electronic Commerce Research and Applications 7, 165–181 (2007)

Gumussoy, C.A., Calisir, F.: Understanding factors affecting e-reverse auction use: An integrative approach. Computers in human behaviour 25, 975–988 (2009)

Greenhalgh, T., Robert, G., Macfarlane, F., Bate, P., Kyriakidou, O.: Diffusion of Innovations in Service Organizations: Systematic Review and Recommendations. The Milbank Quarterly 82, 581–629 (2004)

Gounaris, S., Koritos, C.: Investigating the drivers of internet banking adoption decision: A comparison of three alternative frameworks. International Journal of Bank Marketing 26, 282–304 (2008)

Greenhalgh, T., Robert, G., Macfarlane, F., Bate, P., Kyriakidou, O.: Diffusion of Innovations in Service Organizations: Systematic Review and Recommendations. The Milbank Quarterly 82, 581–629 (2004)

Grepott, T.J.: Attribute perceptions as factors explaining Mobile Internet acceptance of cellular customers in Germany – An empirical study comparing actual and potential adopters with distinct categories of access appliances. Expert Systems with Applications 38, 2148–2162 (2011)

Hartshorne, R., Ajjan, H.: Examining student decisions to adopt Web 2.0 technologies: theory and empirical tests. Journal of Computer Higher Education 21, 183–198 (2009)

Hernandez, J.M.C., Mazzon, J.A.: Adoption of internet banking: proposition and implementation of an integrated methodology approach. International Journal of Bank Marketing 25, 72–88 (2007)

Hester, A.J., Scott, J.E.: A conceptual model of wiki technology diffusion. In: Proceedings of the 41st Hawaii International Conference on System Sciences (2008)

Hsu, C.-L., Lu, H.-P., Hsu, H.-H.: Adoption of the mobile Internet: An empirical study of multimedia message service (MMS). Omega 35, 715–726 (2007)

Irani, Z., Dwivedi, Y.K., Williams, M.D.: Understanding Consumer Adoption of Broadband: An Extension of Technology Acceptance Model. Journal of Operational Research Society 60, 1322–1334 (2009)

Jung, J., Chan-Olmsted, S., Park, B., Kim, Y.: Factors affecting e-book reader awareness, interest, and intention to use. New Media and Society 14, 204–224 (2011)

Karahanna, E., Straub, D.W., Chervany, N.L.: Information technology Adoption Across Time: A Cross-Sectional Comparison of Pre-Adoption and Post-Adoption Beliefs. MIS Quarterly 23, 183–213 (1999)

Lee, Y., Kozar, K.: An empirical investigation of anti-spyware software adoption: A multitheoretical perspective. Information & Management 45, 109–119 (2008)

Le´gare´, F., Ratte´, S., Gravel, K., Graham, I.D.: Barriers and facilitators to implementing shared decision-making in clinical practice: Update of a systematic review of health professionals' perceptions. Patient Education and Counselling 73, 526–535 (2008)

Li, Y.-H.: An empirical investigation on the determinants of E-procurement adoption in Chinese manufacturing enterprises. In: 15th International Conference on Management Science and Engineering, pp. 32–37 (2008)

Liang, T.-P., Huang, C.-W., Yeh, Y.-H., Lin, B.: Adoption of mobile technology in business: a fit-viability model. Industrial Management and Data Systems 107, 1154–1169 (2007)

Lin, H.-F.: Predicting consumer intentions to shop online: An empirical test of competing theories. Electronic Commerce Research and Applications 6, 433–442 (2008)

Mallat, N.: Exploring consumer adoption of mobile payments–A qualitative study. The Journal of Strategic Information Systems 16, 413–432 (2007)

Mallat, N., Rossi, M., Tuunainen, V.K., Oorni, A.: An empirical investigation of mobile ticketing service adoption in public transportation. Pers Ubiquit. Comput. 12, 57–65 (2008)

Meuter, M.L., Bitner, M.J., Ostrom, A.L., Brown, S.W.: Choosing among alternative service delivery modes: An investigation of customer trial of self-service technologies. Journal of Marketing 69, 61–83 (2005)

Moore, G.C., Benbasat, I.: Development of an Instrument to Measure the Perceptions of Adopting an Information Technology Innovation. Information Systems Research 2, 192–222 (1991)

NPCI (2012), http://www.npci.org.in/aboutimps.aspx (accessed on: October 20, 2012)

Ramamurthy, K., Sen, A., Sinha, A.P.: An empirical investigation of the key determinants of data warehouse adoption. Decision Support Systems 44, 817–841 (2008)

Richardson, J.W.: Technology adoption in Cambodia: Measuring factors impacting adoption rates. Journal of International Development 23, 697–710 (2009)

Rogers, E.M.: Diffusion of Innovations, 5th edn. The Free Press, New York (2003)

Schierz, P.G., Oliver Schilke, O., Wirtz, B.W.: Understanding consumer acceptance of mobile payment services: An empirical analysis. Electronic Commerce Research and Applications 9, 209–216 (2010)

Shih, H.-P.: Continued use of a Chinese online portal: an empirical study. Behaviour and Information Technology 27, 201–209 (2008)

Shih, Y.-Y., Fang, K.: The use of a decomposed theory of planned behavior to study Internet banking in Taiwan. Internet Research 14, 213–223 (2004)

Shin, D.-H.: MVNO services: Policy implications for promoting MVNO diffusion. Telecommunications Policy 34, 616–632 (2010)

Siau, K., Shen, Z.: Building customer trust in mobile commerce. Communications of the ACM 46, 91–94 (2003)

Sia, C.-H., Teo, H.-H., Tan, B.C.Y., Wei, K.-K.: Effects of environmental uncertainty on organizational intention to adopt distributed work arrangements. IEEE Transactions on Engineering Management 51, 253–267 (2004)

Slyke, C.V., Lou, H., Day, J.: The impact of perceived innovation characteristics on intention to use groupware. Information Resource Management Journal 15, 5–12 (2002)

South Indian Bank (2012), http://www.southindianbank.com/UserFiles/FAQ-IMPS.pdf (accessed on: October 20, 2012)

Tanakinjal, G.H., Deans, K.R., Gray, B.J.: Third Screen Communication and the Adoption of Mobile Marketing: A Malaysia Perspective. International Journal of Marketing Studies 2, 36–47 (2010)

Tornatzky, L.G., Klein, K.J.: Innovation Characteristics and Innovation Adoption-Implementation: A Meta-Analysis of Findings. IEEE Transactions on Engineering Management 29, 28–43 (1982)

Taylor, S., Todd, P.: Understanding information technology usage: a test of competing models. Information Systems Research 6, 144–176 (1995)

Teo, T.S.H., Pok, S.H.: Adoption of WAP-enabled mobile phones among Internet users. Omega 31, 483–498 (2003)

Vishwanath, A., Goldhaber, G.M.: An examination of the factors contributing to adoption decisions among late-diffused technology products. New Media and Society 5, 547–572 (2003)

Ungan, M.: Factors affecting the adoption of manufacturing best practices. Benchmarking: An International Journal 11, 504–520 (2004)

Wang, Y.-M., Wang, Y.-S., Yang, Y.-F.: Understanding the determinants of RFID adoption in the manufacturing industry. Technological Forecasting and Social Change 77, 803–815 (2010)

Worster, A., Fan, J., Ismaila, A.: Understanding linear and logistic regression analyses, pedagogical tools and methods. CJEM 9, 111–113 (2007)

Wu, J.-H., Wang, S.-C.: What drives mobile commerce?: An empirical evaluation of the revised technology acceptance model. Information and Management 42, 719–725 (2005)

Yang, H.-J., Lay, Y.-L., Tsai, C.-H.: An implementation and usability evaluation of automatic cash-payment system for hospital. Journal of Scientific and Industrial Research 65, 485–494 (2006)

Yiu, C.S., Grant, K., Edgar, D.: Factors affecting the adoption of internet banking in Hong Kong – implications for the banking sector. International Journal of Information Management 27, 336–351 (2007)

The Success of Google Search, the Failure of Google Health and the Future of Google Plus

Marcel Landeweerd[1], Ton Spil[1,*], and Richard Klein[2]

[1] Dept. of Industrial Engineering and Business IT, University of Twente
Marcel@landeweerd.nl,
a.a.m.spil@utwente.nl
[2] Florida International University Miami, Florida, U.S.A.
kleinrich@yahoo.com

Abstract. What makes an e-commerce company successful? In 2011 24% of venture capital in the US went into Internet companies adding up to a total of $6.9 billion (PwC & NVCA, 2011). With such high stakes the question of e-commerce success is more topical than ever. Google, one of the biggest e-commerce companies in the world, despite huge successful products like Google Search, has also seen failures. In this paper, we explore factors associated with successful and unsuccessful adoption of Google products using a literature study in conjunction with qualitative analysis of the Google Search, Google Health, and Google Plus products. Our research identifies key success factors for user adoption of Google products and predicts that Google Plus in its present form will lead to failure. The study shows that perceived compatibility, perceived usefulness, information quality, balancing risks with trust, and finally social pressure are important success factors for Google. Despite limiting the examination to Google products, results can serve as a guideline for other e-commerce ventures.

Index Terms: User adoption, User acceptance, E-commerce, Google, TAM.

1   Introduction

With the Internet integrated in all aspects of our society, fast growing Internet companies like Google and Facebook have become part of our daily lives as they have grown from small startup firms to multinational corporations in a matter of years. Despite economic difficulties in many countries, e-commerce continues to provide opportunity. Nevertheless, for every Internet success story, failures abound. Consider that Peapod and WebVan pursued similar online grocery initiatives. The former having started in the United Kingdom facing larger profit margins succeeded, while the latter fell victim to extremely narrow margins in the United States attracting few adopters. Similarly, WebMD rose to tremendous success drawing revenue from advertising and healthcare provider subscriptions; yet, DrKoop.com, attempting to capitalize on the reputation of its namesake, could not attract even a fraction of the user base of its competitor.

---

[*] Corresponding author.

Y.K. Dwivedi et al. (Eds.): TDIT 2013, IFIP AICT 402, pp. 221–239, 2013.
© IFIP International Federation for Information Processing 2013

Even within the same firm some projects realize tremendous success while others fail. Explanations for success versus failure can be derived from user adoption of e-commerce. Looking at two projects from Google, we see both success and failure, with Google Search engine realizing widespread adoption (comScore, 2012), while Google's electronic personal health record (ePHR) under the name Google Health failed to reach a critical mass in audience (Google, 2011). Accordingly, user adoption constitutes a key concern, which leads to the question, "what yields user adoption of one e-commerce initiative and failure for another?"

The leading model in the area of user adoption is the Technology Acceptance Model (TAM) (Davis, 1989), which proposes usefulness, ease of use and attitude as leading success factors. A good runner up is the UTAUT model (Venkatesh et al, 2003); however, recent studies show that there is a lot of criticism specific to this model (Dwivedi et al, 2011). Both user adoption models do not fully cover all factors associated with user adoption of e-commerce as important domain specific factors including trust (Chervany, 2001–2002) (Corritore, Kracher, & Wiedenbeck, 2003), service quality (Lee & Lin, 2005), and risk (Lee M.-C. , 2009) remain unaddressed, many attempts have tried to extend the TAM model (Han & Jin, 2009; Gefen, Karahanna, & Straub, 2003; Chen, Gillenson, & Sherrell, 2002) to cover e-commerce specific success factors. The Delone & McLean Model of IS success (DeLone, 2003) constitutes another leading model and includes e-commerce specific measures. In contrast to the user focus of the TAM model, the D&M IS Success Model views success more from the technology perspective looking at service quality, information quality and system quality as key determinants of user satisfaction. Despite sharing constructs and like propositions, no single model fully addresses all success factors of user adoption of e-commerce.

Employing a grounded literature search approach, we explore factors associated with user adoption of e-commerce explaining these in greater detail through interviews of potential Google product users. The next section provides background on evolution of Google's product offerings, followed by an in-depth review of our literature study of user adoption factors related to e-commerce. We then provide an overview of the research design and methodology; followed by a review of our results. Last, we discuss the findings and use our results to make a prediction for the future of Google's social network; Google Plus.

2   Background

E-commerce is a popular term associated with almost every business activity conducted on the Internet. The academic literature defines e-commerce very narrowly as "the buying and selling of information, products and services via computer networks" (Kalakota, 1997) to very broadly as "the sharing of business information, maintaining business relationships, and conducting business transactions by means of telecommunications networks." (Zwass, 1996). In order to keep focused on the transactional part of e-commerce, we adopt the narrow definition put forth by Kalakota and Whinston (1997). Noteworthy, buying and selling, not per definition, takes place via direct monetary transactions, but also by different means like showing adds, building user profiles, and other mechanisms of monetizing electronic services.

Google is one of the biggest companies operating on the Internet. Using our definition, Google is considered an ecommerce company as the firm sells information and electronic services. Google does not draw direct money for these services, but monetizes services primarily through advertisements. Products of Google include both hugely successful products as well as ones that resulted in failure. This makes Google the ideal case to compare successful with unsuccessful ventures.

The first product studied is Google Search. Google Search started in March of 1996 as a research project of Larry Page and Sergey Brin, students at Stanford University. The project, name BackRub, sought to develop enabling technologies for a universal digital library (Google Inc., 2012). The new algorithm used links placed on the Internet (similar to academic citations), a technique known by the name Page-Rank. The new search engine adopted the name Google in 1997 and started a rapid growth trajectory that resulted in its first billion URL indexes by June of 2000, making it the largest search engine. Research identified Google as the most widely used search engine among students (Griffiths, 2005). By May of 2011 Google grew to the most visited website within the European Union with a reach of 94% of Internet users (comScore, 2012). By June of 2012 Google gained almost 67% of the United States market share (comScore, 2012), making Google the most successful search engine in the world.

The second product studied is Google Health. Google Health offers the user the opportunity to manage their own health information. Introduced in 2008 and retired on January 1st of 2012, Google Health failed to capture widespread adoption achieving only limited use (Google, 2011). Google Health can be classified as an electronic personal health record (ePHR). ePHRs offer users a variety of advantages aimed at patient empowerment. Personal health records allow users to control their own information, creating a more balanced and complete view than current provider maintained health records (Ball, Smith, & Bakalar, 2007). Further, ePHRs afford extra features such as making online appointments, supplemental information about illnesses, information about health care providers, self-care possibilities, and more (Pagliari, 2007). Sunyaev (2010) presents a framework for the evaluation of ePHRs based on functionality and adopts this to evaluate both Google Health as Microsoft Health Vault. Subsequently, finding it difficult to evaluate a service based only on end-user functionality.

The third product studied is Google Plus. Google Plus launched in June of 2011 as a rival to Facebook. Google Plus introduced the concept of circles as an easy way of dividing relations into groups and deciding what information to share with specific groups of people. This feature allows for better privacy settings, but has also seen debate given equivalent options available on Facebook (Desmedt, 2011). Further, Google Plus introduced hangouts, or a video chat function for groups of up to 10 people. This does not constitute Google's first attempt at launching a social network. Google Buzz started in 2010 ending a year later, Google Friend Connect launched in 2008 to retired in March of 2012. Orkut hit the market in 2004 with Google Brazil the only remaining operational unit in 2013. An important reason for Google to enter the social network market lies in harvesting user information, allowing Google to personalize both search results as advertisements (Poelhekke, 2011).

3   Literature Study

An extensive literature search provides for an overview of the current academic insights in the area of e-commerce adoption. Academics have widely debated the topic of user adoption of e-commerce. Despite many valuable works in the area of user adoption of information system, we limited our search to literature applicable to user adoption of e-commerce, because of the different nature of IS adoption and the availability of sufficient literature on user adoption of e-commerce.

3.1   Service Quality

Service quality is of great importance for every company. Reducing defections by customers by only 5% has the potential to boost profits by as much as 85% to 100% (Reichheld & Sasser, 1990). Good service quality increases good behavioral intentions and decreases bad behavioral intensions (Zeuthaml, Berry, & Parasuraman, 1996), such as stimulating customer retention and improved loyalty versus preventing bad word-of-mouth communications. Given the impersonal nature of e-commerce, service quality is especially important to such transactions (Kim, Galliers, Shin, Ryoo, & Kim, 2012) (Zeithaml, Parasuraman, & Malhotra, 2002). Service Quality measurements for e-commerce tend vary broadly and include information quality, usability, and trust (Collier & Bienstock, 2006) (Santos, 2012). In the context of our research, the inclusion of a broad service quality measure results in an "overall" quality measurement of the business enterprise. Hence, we chose a more limited measure focusing on support and customer service. Factors associated with service quality include quick responsiveness, assurance, empathy, reliability, follow-up service, and personalization (Liu & Arnett, 2000) (Lee & Lin, 2005).

3.2   Information Quality

Information quality influences both perceived usefulness (Green & Pearson, 2011) (Chen & Tan, 2004) and perceived usability mediated by trust (Zhou & Zhang, 2009). Information quality can be measured in terms of accuracy, timeliness, completeness, relevance, and consistency (DeLone, 2003). Egger (2001) gives some guidelines for informational content, and these encompass product and service information, information about the company, and information limiting user risks. First product information should create value as well as instill credibility and transparency. Company information should present the firm, describe organizational achievements, and communicate company values; hereby increasing consumer trustworthiness and making it possible for the user to identify with the organization. Information that limits risks should include security and privacy policies in addition to contractual terms.

3.3   System Quality

System quality measures system design aspects and the way in which the system was built, through measures like usability, availability, reliability, adaptability, and response time (DeLone, 2003). Individual measures of system quality have overlap with other success factors in our study including perceived usability (Green & Pearson,

2011) and perceived usefulness, which encompass measures like system features (Kim, Galliers, Shin, Ryoo, & Kim, 2012) (Urbach & Müller, 2012). For the Web some specific measures exist such as security, valid links, page load times, search facilities, and anonymity (Aladwani & Palvia, 2002).

3.4   Perceived Usefulness

Venkatesh et al. (2000) define perceived usefulness as *"the extent to which a person believes that using the system will enhance his or her job performance"*, in other words, the system must deliver some value. Distinct from perceived usefulness (Wang, 2008), usefulness is often not objectively measurable, but rather a subjective perception of an individual user. Perceived usefulness consistently predicts purchase intention across a large variety of research contexts (Bhattacherjee, 2000) (Pavlou, 2003) (Venkatesh V. A., 2000) (Dubinsky, 2003) and is thereby an important CSF in e-commerce. Value derives in different ways including task-based timesavings, task ease enablement, as well as user entertainment and innovativeness. To deliver value, system use should incorporate efficiency, resulting in a close connection with perceived usability (Al-Gahtani, 2011).

3.5   Perceived Usability

Usability or ease of use defines how effortlessly a user can interact with a system. The International Standard Organization (ISO) defines usability as "the extent to which a product can be used by specified users to achieve specified goals with effectiveness, efficiency, and satisfaction in a specified context of use". Hence, usability is both user and goal specific, making it difficult to create universal guidelines; however, despite this, some practices likely prove more beneficial for many purposes. Consider, minimal clicks to reach a desired result (Hicks, 2002), placing important information before the page fold, clear navigation (Bhatia, 2002), use of breadcrumbs, good search possibilities (Freeman & Hyland, 2003), read fonts, and cross browser compatibility. Research posits higher usability increases both perceived usefulness (Crespo, 2008) and intention to use (Bhattacherjee, 2000), but studies show weak, or no support, for a direct effect on intention to use (Chen & Tan, 2004) (Klopping & McKinney, 2004) (Crespo, 2008) (Shih, 2004).

3.6   Trust

The relative novelty of e-commerce and online shopping gives rise to greater (feelings of) uncertainty and risks. Hence, perceived risks and feelings of safety potentially drive the adoption of e-commerce, trust, or trustworthiness, an important and related underlying factor (Turban, 2011). Previous research shows trust as an important indicator of willingness to buy (Andrea Basso, 2001), particularly with respect to the initial purchase (Gefen, Karahanna, & Straub, 2003) (Koufaris & Hampton-Sosa, 2004) with a stronger influence than even perceived price (Kim, Xu, & Gupta, 2012). Furthermore, trust is known to reduce perceived risks (Corritore, Kracher, & Wiedenbeck, 2003).

McKnight and Chervany (2001, 2002) define trust to encompass attitude, belief, intention, and behavior. Within the context of the current work, trust constitutes "an attitude of confidence formed by a combination of faith and knowledge that a second actor can and will perform as expected." The "will perform" implicitly encompasses the intention to do so, hereby capturing all four characteristics of trust as described by McKnight and Chervany (2001, 2002).

User privacy constitutes an additional issue for e-commerce firms. In a survey of 158 online users, privacy concerns ranked as the most important concern when transacting via the Internet at 55% of all respondents (Udo, 2001), highlighting the importance of privacy online. The right to privacy has existed for decades (Brandeis, 1890), but recent research shows users believe privacy a growing concern (Ackerman, 1999). That said, when using websites these same users take little to no precautions to protect their privacy online (Berendt, 2005) (Spiekermann, 2001) (Ackerman, 1999). Accordingly, users' willingness to disclose privacy-sensitive information to trusted organizations constitutes an important factor shaping e-commerce adoption.

3.7   Perceived Risks

By using an e-commerce service, users incur different risks. Lee (2009) identifies different perceived risks from the user perspective. Specifically, she identifies *performance risk, social risk, time risk, financial risk*, and *security risks* as facets of perceived risks (Lee M.-C. , 2009). Perceived risks has a negative influence on perceived usefulness, user attitude, and intention to use (Lee M.-C. , 2009) Lee, Park, & and Ahn, 2001). In situations of higher risks, higher trust is also necessary as trust can reduce perceived risk (Corritore, Kracher, & Wiedenbeck, 2003).

3.8   Social and Personal Influence

"Much of human behavior is not best characterized by an individual acting in isolation" (Bagozzi, 2007)

People are both influenced by their environment and their own attitude towards a specific e-commerce service and e-commerce in general. Attitude encompasses the sum of beliefs weighted by its evaluations (Miller, 2005). Hence, attitude implicitly derives from past experiences. Social pressure, a subjective norm (Venkatesh V. A., 2000) (Crespo, 2008), influences one's attitudes specific to intention to use (Venkatesh V. A., 2000) (Crespo, 2008). In an online context, social pressure can result from interactions with friends and acquaintances, but also from informational social influences (Lee, Shi, Cheung, Lim, & Sia, 2011) like online reviews. The theory of planned behavior (Ajzen, 1991) adds perceived behavioral control as an influential factor explaining the difference between intention and actual behavior. Perceived behavioral control captures one's perception of internal and external controls that constrain a certain behavior.

3.9   Perceived Compatibility

Rogers (1983) defines compatibility as "the degree to which an innovation is perceived as consistent with the existing values, past experiences, and needs of potential adopters'', and the degree to which an innovation is compatible can "either speed up or retard its rate of adoption" (Rogers, 1983) (Eastin, 2002). Karahanna et al. (2006) validates three distinct aspects of compatibility, namely, compatibility with prior experience, compatibility with existing work practices, and compatibility with values. These compatibility beliefs can be instrumental in shaping beliefs about usefulness and ease of use, and they also influence usage directly (Karahanna, Agarwal, & Angst, 2006). In addition to the effect of compatibility on perceived usefulness and ease of use, compatibility also influences attitude (Hernández-García, Iglesias-Pradas, Chaparro-Peláez, & Pascual-Miguel, 2010).

4   Research Method

The main question answered in this study is "What factors result into user adoption of one e-commerce product, or service, and not another?" We subsequently chose to examine Google because the firm is one of the biggest companies in e-commerce with both hugely successful products as well as ones that resulted in failure. The products selected for our research include Google Search, Google Health, and Google Plus. These products were selected because of sufficient availability of interview data and variation in success. Substantial market share (comScore, 2012) makes Google Search the pre-eminent success; Google Health retired in January of 2012 as a result of lagging interest (Google, 2011), classifying it as an unsuccessful venture. The success of Google Plus, one of the newest Google offerings, is still up in the air. Comparing characteristics of Google Search and Google Health derived from the interviews we can make a prediction regarding the potential user adoption of Google Plus.

4.1   Interview Method

We employ an interview model-based research method called PRIMA (Spil & Michel-Verkerke, 2012) (also known as USE IT) (Spil, Schuring, & Michel-Verkerke, 2004), the model is based on a large body of knowledge including TAM (Venkatesh V. A., 2000), the Information System Success Model of Delone and McLean (2003) and the innovation diffusion model of Rogers (1983). The model has two dimensions; the innovation-dimension and the domain dimension. The innovation dimension is separated into the process and the product. Both process and product determine the success of an innovation (Saarinen & Sääksjärv, 1992). The domain-dimension is separated into the user domain and the information technology domain. The user domain primary covers factors associated with end-user adoption measurements. The information technology domain primary covers factors associated with quality of implemented system measures. This makes the method very suitable for studying adoption of e-commerce services. The qualitative research method is chosen to afford a more detailed understanding of the success measures, while complementing literature study with the interview method to allow the unraveling of the underlying end-user motivations. Further, few qualitative research initiatives in the area of e-commerce user adoption appear within the existing literature.

Data is collected by multiple interviewers that were trained to commence interviews using the PRIMA model (Spil & Michel-Verkerke, 2012). This allows us to triangulate data using different interviewers and vary interviewees across different socio demographic criteria to improve validity (Miles & Huberman, 1994). The interviewers where given the same instructions and question lists.

4.2   Interview Contents

The PRIMA model (Spil & Michel-Verkerke, 2012) consists of five areas of analysis, namely, (1) Process, (2) Relevance, (3) Information needs, (4) Means and people, and finally (5) Attitude. For our research primary the micro definitions of the constructs are used. In the following sections we explain which success factors we expect to measure by each construct. The validation of these expectations follow in the discussion.

Looking at the PRIMA method (Spil & Michel-Verkerke, 2012), all success factors from our literature study are expected to appear either directly or indirectly as shown in table 1.

Table 1. Expected success factors to be measured by PRIMA construct

PRIMA construct	Success factors expected to be measured	Examples of questions asked
Process	Perceived compatibility	Which search engines you regularly use? Are you using a fixed sequence of actions when searching online? Which alternatives you have to find information?
Relevance	Perceived usefulness Perceived usability	Which functions of a search engine are most important for you? Which parts of the system you experience as a bottleneck? Do you have suggestions for improvements?
Information needs	Information quality	Which information you need to get from the service? Do you get sufficient information from the system? Is the information quality sufficient?
Means and people	Service quality System quality Perceived risks	Do you get sufficient support? Is the system reliable? Does the system offer enough privacy?
Attitude	Trust Social and personal influence	Do you think IT is necessary to improve health information? Do you feel social pressure of using the service? How much time do you want to spend for learning to use the service?

4.3   Interviewees

Interviewees were given an introduction of the Google product and had the possibility to test the product before starting the interview, this to get familiarity with the Google product. As prescribed, our interviews should represent all homogenous groups (Yin, 1994). Drawing on the UTAUT (Venkatesh, Morris, Davis, & Davis, 2003) model we include gender, age, and experience as moderators influencing the determinants of behavioral intention and actual use behavior. Previous research shows that experience positively influences adoption, while users that adopt one service express a greater likelihood to adopt another (Eastin, 2002) (Rogers, 1983) with perceptions evolving over time (Hernández, Jiménez, & Martín, 2010).

4.4   Processing Interviews

We obtained a total of 127 interviews among potential users of Google Search (46), Google Health (27) and Google Plus (54). These interviews represented different homogenous groups (Yin, 1994). First individual outcomes are extracted while scanning the interviews by using the success factors found in literature. Several studies have tried to extend existing models like TAM (Han & Jin, 2009) (Gefen, Karahanna, & Straub, 2003) (Chen, Gillenson, & Sherrell, 2002) and the Delone and McLean model (Wang, 2008), while other work has integrated different models (Lee M.C., 2009) (Klopping & McKinney, 2004). Despite sharing constructs and like propositions, no single model fully addresses all success factors of user adoption of e-commerce. Therefore, rather than draw upon a single model, we extract success factors identified across the literature and independently evaluate these factors using interview data. Success factors found by the extensive literature study are used as input for our research.

5   Results

First, we individually examine the interview outcomes for Google Search and Google Health. We then use these outcomes to draw an overall conclusion related to user adoption of Google products. We subsequently use this conclusion to predict potential user adoption of Google Plus.

5.1   Google Search

Different interviewers conducted a total of 45 interviews across the period 2008 till 2012. Experience with IT in general and search engines specifically fluctuated from very experienced to reasonable and moderate experience. Most were in the 15-25 age group (32), and the gender split was roughly equal (24 males, 22 females). All participants indicated a reasonable familiarity with Google Search with only two not using Google as their primary search engine, confirming the success in user adoption of Google Search.

In general older users need more time to find the right results, consistent with previous research findings (Freudenthal, 2001). Users expressed satisfaction with Google Search, noting ease of use in addition to fast, good, and well-organized results. Despite 7 users mentioning privacy concerns, it did not stop them from using Google.

All users see the value of Google, as the alternative would involve time consuming and potentially unsuccessful library searches. The perceived compatibility is high, while most users spent significant time behind the computer and using Google, as searching with Google fits into their work patterns. Sparse negatives mentioned specific to Google include sometimes not getting satisfactory results, too many results, the presence of commercial advertisements, and limited specialized information. These negatives did not, however, dissuade using Google Search.

Table 2. Interview results Google Search

Google Search	✔ Positive		✘ Negative
Process	Compatible with current (work) practices and experiences		
	Frequent usage	**Little usage**	
	Small usage sessions	Long usage sessions	
	Usage pattern	No fixed pattern	
	Study & Work	Hedonic & Work	
Relevance	Getting the right results		Wrong results
	Fast results, Well-organized		Commercial adds
	Advanced search options		To much results
	Objective, Complete, Simple		Privacy concerns
Information needs	Trusting the information		Limited specialized and technical information, Too much information
	Fast results, Simple, Trustworthy, Freely accessible		Not relevant enough
Means and people	Free , Easy accessible		
Attitude	Environment positive, Innovative Positive experiences in past		

5.2   Google Health

In 2012, different interviewers conducted a total of 27 interviews. The experience among interviewees with ePHR was very limited. Most were in the 15-25 age group (15), and the gender split was roughly equal (11 males, 16 females). Most users didn't know of Google Health prior to the interview and only one actually used Google Health. Privacy concerns emerged as the biggest threshold for users with 23 out of 27 noting the issue as a big concern. Out of all the interviews emerges a view that users consider health information as very personal with a commercial company like Google not trusted with this information.

The second threshold is usefulness of the e-commerce service. Despite some positive reactions, most of the interviewees failed to see the direct value of Google Health for themselves. Currently, they do not hold their own health information, so why would they need to in the future? This indicates a low compatibility with current practices. Additionally, they noted relative good health as a reason not to use such eHealth systems. When asked if they saw barriers to using Google Health, one participant noted:

> "…in addition to the fact that I don't have any information to put onto Google Health, I really would want privacy guarantees before putting my information into the system to prevent my information getting public on the internet"

This sentiment illustrates the general opinion emerging from the interviews.

The main problems, or objection points, are highlighted within the table below. Users do not see the relevance of Google Health with primarily negative attitude towards the product

Table 3. Interview results Google Health

Google Health	✅ Positive	❌ Negative
Process		Time consuming Currently calling doctor to get medical information, almost no time in current efforts.
Relevance	*Maybe useful for other people*	No need Security concerns
Information needs	Simple looking Clear results	Only available in English Usage of medical terms Concerns about quality when filling in data yourself Current information enough
Means and people	Easy accessible Free	Support needed Privacy risks
Attitude	Trust Google More than Facebook	No trust, Privacy concerns No social pressure to use, No added value

5.3   Google Plus

Different interviewers conducted a total of 53 interviews during 2012. Again the majority were in the 15-25 age group (41) with an even gender split (20 males, 23 females). Every user had some experience with social media, varying between sometimes using YouTube to classifying themselves as being an expert. The most popular platform mentioned was Facebook, which was used by almost all interviewees. Users employed social media primary to stay in touch with friends both nearby and far away. Other goals include sharing study and work information and using it for fun or killing time.

Most interviewees (45 out of 53) had heard of Google Plus with only 4 using it. The main reason for this is that none of their friends are using Google Plus. Users adopting Google Plus primary use it for work in the Internet industry like online marketing and programming. So it seems Google Plus has not realized widespread adoption, but a niche of users employ the product. When asked about the advantages of Google Plus, 24 users saw advantages compared to 29 perceiving disadvantages. The advantages found are primary the use of circles and the possibilities for video chat, but as many users noted, this is also possible with Facebook. The concept of circles has been received positively, while users like to separate, for example, work and friends. This indicates that their view of social relations is in line with the concept of circles. Users only see small differences with current social media available, which is an indicator of good compatibility. All users mention privacy concerns when using social media, this is not a reason to stop use, but a reason to be careful with what to share. Many users neither trust Google nor Facebook with their information, but 21 have a preference for Google compared to 8 having a preference for Facebook. Through all interviews there emerges a view of minor advantages against a big disadvantage due to lack of friends on Google Plus, i.e., a requisite critical mass. Looking at our success factors from literature, usefulness, information fit, social pressure, and trust, we see that Google Plus has a low usefulness due to a lack of critical mass, there is a bad fit with information needs while no friends are using Google Plus resulting in a lack of information about friends and no social pressure to use Google Plus. Only trust of Google emerges higher, which may result in a higher willingness to use. To reach a widespread user adoption Google needs user information, while user adoption seems necessary to get this user information. To become a success Google needs to find an answer to this causality dilemma, otherwise Google Plus will follow Google Health in its early retirement.

Table 4. Interview results Google Plus

Google Plus	✅ Positive	❌ Negative
Process	Keeping in touch with friends Just for fun Sharing study and work information Ability to separate work and friends Google plus almost the same as currently used Facebook	Social media in general distracting from normal activities
Relevance	Option for group video Ordering relations in groups Good usability Integration with other Google products	Copy of Facebook Options also available on Facebook Not enough advantages to switch
Information needs	Same possible information as Facebook Tech information available	No information because of lack of friends
Means and people	Easy accessible Free	Risks of bad privacy
Attitude	Trust Google More than Facebook	No social pressure to use Only using when friends use it Don't see really big advantages

6   Discussion

The value of **compatibility** as a success factor was supported. Google Search fits well with current work practices that often included working many hours behind a computer. Further users were already familiar with the way the search engine works and presents results. In the case of Google Health, low compatibility prevailed as users currently didn't administer their own Health information and didn't see the value of doing so. Current practices included calling the doctor, which was less time consuming. Keeping an ePHR is seen as a task for medical specialist, and accordingly, Google Health seems incompatible with existing practices (Rogers, 1983). In the case of Google Plus, compatibility seemed positive. While there were not big differences with existing social media, the concept of circles was in line with their view of social relationships. A higher compatibility increases the perceived usefulness of a service (Karahanna, Agarwal, & Angst, 2006) (Hernández-García, Iglesias-Pradas, Chaparro-Peláez, & Pascual-Miguel, 2010), this is both supported by the literature and our study.

The **usefulness** of the service is in line with literature and demonstrated an important success factor. The usefulness of the services differs with all seeing Google Search as useful, or even essential, and viewing Google Health as of limited usefulness. Participants do not currently retain their personal health information and fail to see added value in doing so. The alternative to Google Health, calling the doctor seems easy and fast. By comparison, the difficult and time-consuming alternative to Google Search necessitates visiting a library. Hence, users considered the functionality of Google Plus similarly useful and easy to use, but the overall usefulness of Google Plus as a service emerged as low because of a lack of friends who use Google Plus, an essential part of social media. . In that context the relative advantage construct of Rogers (1983) seems more appropriate than the perceived usefulness construct of TAM (Venkatesh V. A., 2000). The usability of all three services was viewed favorably by interviewees.

Information needs align closely with usefulness of the e-commerce service as usefulness of services rests in providing the right information. Users expressed positive sentiments about the information provided by Google Search classifying it as reliable, simple, and fast. Users of Google Health, however, saw providing their own information as unreliable with usage of medicinal terms complicated. Not all interviewees deemed the information provided by and use of Google Health negatively, failing to see relevance to their own situation, which resulted in a bad fit to their specific situation. This result supports the theory saying that the better the fit between information needs and information provided by the e-commerce service, the higher the user adoption of the service. Our analysis of Google Plus revealed the service lacked information. While users like to receive updates from friends, many were not Google Plus users.

Consistent with the theory of planned behavior (TPB) (Ajzen, 1991), sufficient means implies external controls influence both intention to use and actual use. All services saw no restrictions to use the service with the Internet and computers readily available and requisite knowledge sufficient, resulting in users making little to no use of customer support. Widespread acceptance of the Internet, mitigates restrictions on searches to use Google products. Also, **system quality** was considered good with all services fast and no availability problems mentioned. Only Internet problems at home or at work were mentioned, but these problems were not related to Google. Furthermore users didn't see the need of contacting Google's customer service, while all necessary information was readily available online.

Our literature search found that the **social pressure** of using a service will increase the likelihood the user consistently uses the service. Our interviews showed that there was an absence of social pressure to use Google Health, while Google Search saw significant pressures. In the case of Google Plus, there is a lack of social pressure in the absence of a critical mass of friends using the service.

A balance between **trust** and **risk** is necessary. The results of our interviews support this proposition. Despite users trusting Google with their search queries, they are very reticent to share personal health information, as users considered this information far more personal and privacy-sensitive. In other words, the perceived risks of Google Health are higher than the perceived risks associated with Google Search. The most plausible explanation lies in a negative correlation between trust and risks, in other words trust should be in balance with risk. Google Health carries higher risks necessitating greater trust. Conversely Google Plus users expressed privacy concerns, but trusted Google more than Facebook, which they already used. So in the case of Google Plus, trust seems sufficient. Many studies used trust as a success factor, but few studies recognize the relationship to risk. Our study showed evidence that trust can't be seen as an isolated factor, but should be viewed as inseparably couple. In situations of high risk, high trust is necessary as trust can reduce specific risks perceptions.

Table 5. Success factors in literature with findings at Google

	Google Search	Google Health	Google Plus		Google Search	Google Health	Google Plus
Service quality	✓	✓	✓	Perceived risks	Low	High	Medium
Information quality	✓	✗	✗	Perceived usefulness	✓	✗	✗
System quality	✓	✓	✓	Social and personal influence	✓	✗	✗
Trust	✓	✗	✓	Perceived compatibility	✓	✗	✓
Perceived usability	✓	✓	✓				

Strengths and Weaknesses of Study

The number of qualitative studies in the area of e-commerce user adoption is limited. The combination of an extensive literature search with a qualitative analysis using interviews of potential Google users constitutes a unique contribution. The qualitative method allows us to see relationships between success factors, which would be unknown using a quantitative approach. The study explains the user adoption of Google Search and the failure of Google Health. Last, but not least, the study shows the causes plaguing Google Plus adoption.

Our research has several limitations. Different interviewers conducted the interviews, the risks of biasing the results by the interviewers is limited by giving these interviews the same protocols and instructions and above all an extensive training. The subject of our interviews, Google products, restricts our findings to a single firm but since the products are three totally different e-commerce services we strongly belief the result can be generalized to all e-commerce services. The products researched were free to use with information the primary value, potentially resulting in a close relation between information quality and usefulness. This doesn't neglect the value of the method used. The widespread adoption of Google Search resulted in sample of users familiar with the product, with this knowledge possibly influencing interview results.

7   Conclusion and Implications

This study combined an extensive literature search with a total of 127 interviews among potential users of Google Search (46), Google Health (27) and Google Plus (54) to come to an overview of success factors associated with successful e-commerce user adoption at Google. Factors found in the literature include service quality, information quality, system quality, perceived usefulness, perceived usability, perceived enjoyment, trust, perceived risks, in addition to social and personal influences.

Although these factors come from different theories with different backgrounds and assumptions we think that by handling them all in a qualitative interview model explains more than evaluating the new innovation with one of the underlying methods in a quantitative way. A combination would be very time consuming but would be best.

Analyzing these success factors in our interview the following findings arise. First perceived compatibility proved a good indicator of user adoption at Google and can be used to explain while certain innovations are considered useful while others are not. Second there should be a fit between information supplied and the information needs of the user. The better the fit between information needs and information provided by the e-commerce service, the higher user adoption of the service. In this case it is important to know which information users expect to get from a service and meet these expectations. Third our study showed that perceived usefulness is not only a subjective perception, but also a relative perception as in relative advantage. E-commerce ventures should not be studied as a closed system, but in the context of its competitive environment. Fourth findings suggest that risks should be in balance with trust for successful adoption of e-commerce projects. Further findings show that social pressure of using a service increases the likeliness of using the service. Google search saw some pressure, Google health no pressure and Google plus still lacks social pressure. In the case of Google Plus this social pressure is closely related to the usefulness of the service, which makes it hard to isolate the effect from social pressure from the effect of usefulness on user adoption.

With current results Google Plus is deemed to fail. A solution has to be found to overcome a lacking information quality and usefulness resulting from a lacking user adoption. Possible solutions include more radical innovations or inclusion of friends data from external sources. Looking at the interviews no single success factor on its own can explain the success or failure of a service. A service which scores high on all success factors, but is not compatible with current values and work practices will probably not be successful. The right balance of success factors is necessary for a service to be successful. Results show no significant differences in age, experience or gender supporting the generalizability of the results.

Rather than drawing on a single model or adapting a selection of success criteria, services should be evaluated based on all success criteria. The used PRIMA method is proven valuable, but could be adjusted to more explicitly measure our e-commerce success factors in a voluntary user environment. Our list of success factors could be translated in a PRIMA interview for e-commerce services by selecting different success measures for each of the individual factors. Such a list could be used to evaluate a service from the user perspective and would increase success rates of new e-commerce startups. The user adoption of e-commerce is a widely debated topic, and our study showed a wide variety of success factors all partially explaining the adoption of e-commerce. That said, the complete answer remains hidden. Till that time rather than to draw on a single model our collection of success factors can serve as a valuable guideline both for research as practice.

8   Future Research

In general current research fails to incorporate a sense of time, while user perceptions like usefulness and intention to use may change over time. Despite theories like

Rogers Innovation Diffussion Theory (1983) incorporating a staged innovation-decision process, this theory didn't got much attention in studies addressing the user adoption of e-commerce. More attention should be for this changing user perception. Furthermore, existing models explore adoption of innovations as an isolated event, while the Internet constitutes a social happening with different influences including competitors, new technologies, and users among other external factors. The models use a single user as unit of analysis, in some cases using a group of users as unit of analysis may be more appropriate. Models like TAM may be over simplified for adoption of complex technologies like the Internet, but are used in most research addressing the user adoption of e-commerce. services. Finally, no single article within our literature study included all factors associated with successful user adoption of e-commerce in a single model. Future research might study if and how factors relate to each other. Finally our study illustrated the value of qualitative efforts in the area of e-commerce adoption. The Prima model should be adjusted for e-commerce specific applications and could be used in more studies. This would allow for a more detailed understanding of user motivations behind e-commerce user adoption.

References

Ackerman, M.S.L.F.: Privacy in E-Commerce: Examining User Scenarios and Privacy Preferences. In: ACM Conference on Electronic Commerce, pp. 1–8. ACM, Denver (1999)

Ahn, T., Ryu, S., Han, I.: The impact of the online and offline features on the user acceptance of Internet shopping malls. Electronic Commerce Research and Applications 3, 405–420 (2004)

Ajzen, I.: The theory of planned behavior. Organizational Behavior and Human Decision Processes 50(2), 179–211 (1991)

Aladwani, A.M., Palvia, P.C.: Developing and validating an instrument for measuring user-perceived web quality. Information & Management 39, 467–476 (2002)

Al-Gahtani, S.S.: Modeling the electronic transactions acceptance using an extended technology acceptance model. Applied Computing and Informatics 9, 47–77 (2011)

Andrea Basso, D.G.: First impressions: emotional and cognitive factors underlying judgments of trust e-commerce. In: 3rd ACM Conference on Electronic Commerce, pp. 137–143. ACM, New York (2001)

Bagozzi, R.: The legacy of the technology acceptance model and a proposal for a paradigm shift. Journal of the Association for Information Systems 8(4), 244–254 (2007)

Ball, E.F., Carla Smith, N.F., Richard, S., Bakalar, M.: Personal Health Records: Empowering Consumers. Journal of Healthcare Information Management 21(1), 76–86 (2007)

Bettina Berendt, O.G.: Privavy in e-commerce: Stated Preferences vs. Actual Behavior. Comms. ACM 48(4), 101–106 (2005)

Bhatia, B.S.: A Framework for Determining Success Factors of an E-Commerce Initiative. Journal of Internet Commerce 1(2), 63–75 (2002)

Bhattacherjee, A.: Acceptance of E-Commerce Services: The Case of Electronic Brokerages. IEEE Transactions on Systemens, Man, And Cybernetics - Part A: Systems and Humans 30(4), 411–420 (2000)

Brandeis, S.D.: The Right to Privacy. Harvard Law Review 4(5), 193–220 (1890)

Chen, L.-D., Tan, J.: Technology Adaptation in E-commerce: Key Determinants of Virtual Stores Acceptance. European Management Journal 22(1), 74–86 (2004)

Chen, L.-D., Gillenson, M.L., Sherrell, D.L.: Enticing online customers: an extended technology acceptance perspective. Information & Management 39, 705–719 (2002)

Chervany, D.H.: What Trust Means in E-Commerce Customer Relationships: An Interdisciplinary Conceptual Typology. International Journal of Electronic Commerce / Winter 6(2), 35–59 (2001-2002)

Collier, J.E., Bienstock, C.C.: Measuring Service Quality in E-Retailing. Journal of Service Research 8, 260 (2006)

ComScore. comScore Releases June 2012 U.S. Search Engine Rankings (July 11, 2012,) retrieved from comScore, http://www.comscore.com/Press_Events/Press_ Releases/2012/6/comScore_Releases_June_2012_U.S._ Search_Engine_Rankings

Corritore, C.L., Kracher, B., Wiedenbeck, S.: On-line trust: concepts, evolving themes, a model. Int. J. Human-Computer Studies 58, 737–758 (2003)

Crespo, A.H.: Explaining B2C e-commerce acceptance: An integrative model based on the framework by Gatignon and Robertson. Interacting with Computer 20, 212–224 (2008)

Davis, F.D.: Perceived usefulness, perceived ease of use, and user acceptance of information technology. MIS Quarterly 13(3), 319–340 (1989)

DeLone, W.: The DeLone and McLean model of information systems success: a ten-year update. Journal of Management Information Systems 19, 9–30 (2003)

Desmedt, S.M.: Preliminary Analysis of Google+'s Privacy. In: 18th ACM Conference on Computer and Communications Security, pp. 17–21 (October 2011)

Dubinsky, Z.C.: A Conceptual Model of Perceived Customer Value in E-Commerce: A Preliminary Investigation. Psychology & Marketing 20(4), 323–347 (2003)

Dwivedi, Y., Rana, N., Chen, H., Williams, M.: A Meta-analysis of the Unified Theory of Acceptance and Use of Technology (UTAUT). In: Governance and Sustainability in Information Systems. Managing the Transfer and Diffusion of IT, pp. 155–170 (2011)

Eastin, M.S.: Diffusion of e-commerce: an analysis of the adoption of four e-commerce activities. Telematics and Informatics 197, 251–267 (2002)

Egger, F.N.: Affective Design of E-commerce User Interfaces: How to Maximise Perceived Trustworthiness. In: International Conference on Affective Human Factors Design. Asean Academic Press, London (2001)

Freeman, M., Hyland, P.: The current state of Australian Online Supermarket Usability. In: ACIS 2003 Proceedings. Paper 102, vol. 1 (2003)

Freudenthal, D.: Age differences in the performance of. Behaviour & Information Technology 20(1), 9–22 (2001)

Gefen, D., Karahanna, E., Straub, D.W.: Trust and TAM in Online Shopping: An Integrated Model. MIS Quarterly 27(1), 51–90 (2003)

Google. An update on Google Health and Google PowerMeter (June 24, 2011) Retrieved from Google Official Blog, http://googleblog.blogspot.nl/2011/06/update- on-google-health-and-google.html

Google Inc. Our History in depth (August 14, 2012) retrieved from Google, http://www.google.com/intl/en/about/company/history/

Green, D.T., Pearson, J.M.: Integrating website usability with the electronic commerce acceptance model. Behaviour & Information Technology 30(2), 181–199 (2011)

Griffiths, J.R.: The Commercialized Web: Challenges for Libraries and Democracy. library trends, 539–554 (2005)

Han, L., Jin, Y.: A Review of Technology Acceptance Model in the E-commerce Environment. In: International Conference on Management of e-Commerce and e-Government, pp. 28–31. IEEE, Nanchang (2009)

Hernández, B., Jiménez, J., Martín, M.J.: Customer behavior in electronic commerce: The moderating effect of e-purchasing experience. Journal of Business Research 63, 964–971 (2010)

Hernández-García, A., Iglesias-Pradas, S., Chaparro-Peláez, J., Pascual-Miguel, F.: Perceived Compatibility and the Adoption of B2C E-Commerce by Non-buyers,Organizational, Business, and Technological Aspects of the Knowledge Society. Communications in Computer and Information Science 112, 186–192 (2010)

Hicks, M.: Plug in to customers – Usability testing, tools help prevent site flaws, reveal secrets to Web success. eWeek 19(4) (2002)

Kalakota, R.A.: Electronic Commerce: A Manager's Guide. Addison-Wesley (1997)

Karahanna, E., Agarwal, R., Angst, C.: Reconceptualizing Compatibility Beliefs. MIS Quarterly 30(4) (2006)

Kim, C., Galliers, R.D., Shin, N., Ryoo, J.-H., Kim, J.: Factors influencing Internet shopping value and customer repurchase intention. Electronic Commerce Research and Applications 11, 374–387 (2012)

Kim, H.-W., Xu, Y., Gupta, S.: Which is more important in Internet shopping, perceived price or trust? Electronic Commerce Research and Applications 11, 241–252 (2012)

Klopping, I.M., McKinney, E.: Extending the Technology Acceptance Model and the Task-Technology Tit model to consumer e-commerce. Information Technology, Learning, and Performance Journal 22(1), 35–48 (2004)

Koufaris, M., Hampton-Sosa, W.: The development of initial trust in an online company by new customers. Information & Management 41, 377–397 (2004)

Lee, D., Park, J., Ahn, J.-H.: On the Explanation of Factors Affecting E-Commerce Adoption. In: ICIS 2001 Proceedings. Paper 14 (2001)

Lee, G.-G., Lin, H.-F.: Customer perceptions of e-service quality in online shopping. International Journal of Retail & Distribution Management 33(2), 161–176 (2005)

Lee, M.K., Shi, N., Cheung, C.M., Lim, K.H., Sia, C.L.: Consumer's decision to shop online: The moderating role of positive informational social influence. Information & Management 48, 185–191 (2011)

Lee, M.-C.: Factors influencing the adoption of internet banking: An integration of TAM and TPB with perceived risk and perceived benefit. Electronic Commerce Research and Applications 8, 130–141 (2009)

Liu, C., Arnett, K.P.: Exploring the factors associated with Web site success in the context of electronic commerce. Information & Management 38, 23–33 (2000)

McKnight, D.H., Chervany, N.L..; (2001-2002),What Trust Means in E-Commerce Customer Relationships: An Interdisciplinary Conceptual Typology,International Journal of Electronic Commerce,Volume 6, Number 2, p35-59

Miles, M.B., Huberman, A.M.: Qualitative data analysis: An expanded sourcebook. Sage (1994)

Miller, K.: Communications theories: perspectives, processes, and contexts. McGraw-Hill, New York (2005)

Pagliari, D.D.: Potential of electronic personal health records. BMJ 335, 330–333 (2007)

Pavlou, P.A.: Consumer Acceptance of Electronic Commerce: Integrating Trust and Risk with the Technology Acceptance Model. International Journal of Electronic Commerce 7(3), 69–103 (2003)

Poelhekke, K.: Over Google's personaliseringsmechanismen, de gevaren ervan en de rol van Google+ (2011)

PwC & NVCA, MoneyTree report. PricewaterhouseCoopers (PwC) and the National Venture Capital Association, NVCA (2011)

Reichheld, F.F., Sasser, W.J.: Zero Defections: Quality Comes to Services. Harvard Business Review, 105–111 (1990)

Rogers, E.M.: Diffusion of Innovations. Free Press, New York (1983)

Saarinen, T., Sääksjärvi, M.: Process and product success in information systems development. Journal of Strategic Information Systems 1, 266–277 (1992)

Santos, J.: E-service quality: a model of virtual service quality dimensions. Managing Service Quality 13(3), 233–246 (2012)

Shih, H.-P.: An empirical study on predicting user acceptance of e-shopping on the Web. Information Management 41, 351–368 (2004)

Spiekermann, J.G.: E-privacy in 2nd Generation E-Commerce: Privacy Preferences versus actual Behavior. In: EC 2001, October 14-17. ACM, Tampa (2001)

Spil, T.A., Schuring, R.W., Michel-Verkerke, M.B.: Electronic prescription system: do the professionals USE IT? Int. J. Healthcare Technology Management 6(1), 32–55 (2004)

Spil, T.A., Michel-Verkerke, M.B.: De waarde van informatie in de gezondheidswereld, Eburon, Delft (2012)

Sunyacv, D.C.: Evaluation Framework for Personal Health Records: Microsoft HealthVault vs. Google Health. In: 43rd Hawaii International Conference on System Sciences, pp. 1–10 (2010)

Turban, M.K.: A Trust Model for Consumer Internet Shopping. International Journal of Electronic Commerce 6, 75–91 (2011)

Udo, G.J.: Privacy and security as mojor barriers for c-commerce: a survey study. Information Management & Computer Security, 165–174 (2001)

Urbach, N., Muller, B.: The Updated DeLone and McLean Model of Information Systems Success. Information Systems Theory Integrated Series in Information Systems 28, 1–18 (2012)

Venkatesh, V.A.: A theoretical extension of the Technoly Acceptance Model: Four longitudal field studies. Management Science 46(2), 186–204 (2000)

Venkatcsh, V., Morris, M.G., Davis, G.B., Davis, F.D.: User Acceptance of Information Technology: Toward a Unified View. MIS Quarterly 27(3), 425–478 (2003)

Wang, Y.-S.: Assessing e-commerce systems success: a respecification and vali on of the De-Lone and McLean model of IS success. Info Systems 18, 529–557 (2008)

Yin, R.K.: Case study research: Design and methods, 2nd edn. Sage, Thousand Oaks (1994)

Zeithaml, V.A., Parasuraman, A., Malhotra, A.: Service Quality Delivery Through Web Sites: A Critical Review of Extant Knowledge. Journal of the Academy of Marketing Science 30(4), 362–375 (2002)

Zeuthaml, V., Berry, L., Parasuraman, A.: The behavior consequences of service quality. Journal of Marketing 60, 31–46 (1996)

Zhou, T., Zhang, S.: Examining the Effect of E-commerce Website Quality on User Satisfaction. In: Second International Symposium on Electronic Commerce and Security, pp. 418–421. IEEE, Nanchang (2009)

Zwass, V.: Electronic commerce: structures and issues. International Journal of Electronic Commerce 1(1), 3 (1996)

Examining the Factors Affecting Intention to Use of, and User Satisfaction with Online Public Grievance Redressal System (OPGRS) in India

Nripendra P. Rana, Yogesh K. Dwivedi, and Michael D. Williams

School of Business, Swansea University, Swansea, SA2 8PP, United Kingdom
{nrananp,ykdwivedi}@gmail.com, M.D.Williams@swansea.ac.uk

Abstract. The purpose of this paper is to examine the success (by measuring intention to use and user satisfaction) of the online public grievance redressal system (OPGRS) from the perspective of the citizens of India. This is the first time that the success of this e-government system is examined using an IS success model. The model developed includes the constructs such as *system quality, information quality, perceived usefulness, user satisfaction,* and *intention to use.* The empirical outcomes provided the positive significant connections between all eight hypothesized relationships between five constructs. The empirical evidence and discussion presented in the study can help the Indian government to improve upon and fully utilize the potential of OPGRS as a useful tool for transparent and corruption free country.

Keywords: Online public grievance redressal system, OPGRS, e-government, DeLone and McLean, Seddon, India.

1   Introduction

Starting from the early 1990s, the revolution of information and communication and technologies (ICTs) has made major and brisk changes in the day-to-day life of people and governments (Floropoulos et al., 2010). Realizing this, many governments across the world are transforming into new forms of government called electronic government (hereafter, e-government) (Akman et al., 2005) to reinforce and maintain their positions in the global competition (Sharifi and Zarei, 2004). Though e-government provides obvious benefits to governments, professionals, and organizations, it is citizens who actually predicted to receive a number of benefits (Jaeger, 2003). Looking at this aspect, one of the most significant requirements of citizen's day-to-day life such as their grievances against the government systems, officials, organizations, and bureaucratic structures in a country like India is quite evident. As governments develop e-government systems to deliver services to the people, there is a need for evaluation efforts that could examine their effectiveness (Wang and Liao, 2008) and success. OPGRS is one such e-government system which is primarily meant for addressing the grievances, issues, and problems of citizen's everyday life and gets them resolved online by the high-level government officials

Y.K. Dwivedi et al. (Eds.): TDIT 2013, IFIP AICT 402, pp. 240–260, 2013.

designated for it. It provides a huge benefit to the people by resolving their problems without much hassle.

Grievance redress mechanism is a part and parcel of the machinery of any administration. No administration can claim to be answerable, responsive, and user-friendly unless it has established a proficient and effectual grievance redress mechanism. In fact, the grievance redress mechanism of a firm is an estimate to examine its efficiency and effectiveness as it provides significant feedback on the working of the administration. The grievances from public are accepted at various points in the Government of India. There are mainly two designated agencies in the central government handling these grievances namely Department of Administrative Reforms and Public Grievances (under Ministry of Personnel, Public Grievances and Pensions) and Directorate of Public Grievances (under Cabinet Secretariat). The public grievance redress mechanism in India functions on a decentralized basis. An officer of the level of Joint Secretary is designated as the Director of Grievances of the Ministry/Department/Organization.

The major reasons of grievances primarily include the socio-economic reasons such as prevalent corruption in the ministries, government organizations, and bureaucratic systems, which are ubiquitous in the current society. The people feel themselves helpless against it and are bound to tolerate it in their day-to-day lives. But, the factors such as lack of awareness and lack of relevant information about whom to complain make this process even more tedious. Looking at this aspect, OPGRS has been designed and developed to take care of such problems of the people without stepping in the offices of ministries and government organizations or even without knowing sometimes where to go to lodge their complaints. In majority of the cases, they don't even know who is accountable to listen to their problems. Therefore, the significance of such e-government systems is felt even more for smooth, transparent and impartial running of the governments. The success of this system can be measured only when a large section of the society adopts this system and the government responds properly to their problems leading to the citizens' satisfaction.

Although, OPGRS offers several advantages (as outlined above), its adoption is currently low. Despite low adoption rate, existing literature has not yet attempted to examine citizens' adoption behaviour and their satisfaction with the use of such an important public administration system. It is evident from the discussion presented above that it would be useful to study intention to adopt or adoption of and satisfaction with this system. Hence, the aim of this study is to undertake an exploratory study to examine the success of OPGRS by exploring citizens' adoptive intention.

The remaining paper is organised as follows to fulfill the desired aim: next section undertake a review of e-government literature based on IS success model, this would be followed by a brief discussion on the utilised theoretical background of DeLone and McLean's (1992, 2003) and Seddon's (1997) IS success models. Section 4 then provides an overview of the proposed research model and justification for the proposed hypotheses followed by a brief discussion on utilised research method. Findings are presented and discussed in Section 6 and 7 subsequently. Finally, conclusion including limitations and future research directions and implications for theory and practice are presented in Section 8.

2   Literature Review

As far as e-government adoption research is concerned, some studies (Chai et al., 2006; Chen, 2010; Floropoulos et al., 2010; Gotoh, 2009; Hsu and Chen, 2007; Hu et al., 2009; Sambasivan et al., 2010; Scott et al., 2009; Teo et al., 2008) have used IS Success Models to analyse the use, intention to use, and satisfaction toward adopting an e-government system. In recent years, many citizens centric Internet based enhanced services implemented by governments of various countries including India. As government develops e-government systems to offer such enhanced services to the citizens, further assessment efforts are required to measure the effectiveness of the e-government systems. Such evaluation efforts would allow government agencies to determine whether they are capable to deliver what citizens require and provide expected services accordingly (Gupta and Jana, 2003; Wang and Liao, 2008).

From the analysis of the research findings of the various literature studies, Chai et al. (2006) implied that success of e-government depends on how governments offer high quality and user-oriented e-government services to the citizens. One of the major factors of the success of the e-government was government websites. The relationship between the quality of a website and its success has been analysed in some research papers (Chai et al., 2006). Palmer (2002) discussed that quality of a website can be measured by its connection speed, navigability, interactivity, responsiveness, and quality substance. On the other hand, it was found that website quality is supposed to have positively linked toward developing trusting intention on e-commerce website (McKnight et al., 2000). Therefore, website service quality can be considered as one of the strong interpreters of e-government success and user's intention to constantly use an e-government website (Chai et al., 2006).

Hsu and Chen (2007) provided an alternative conceptualization of the IS success model for examining the IS use behaviour of e-government in Taiwanese context. Their analysis indicated that user intention to use IS in e-government is governed by social (i.e. normative pressure) and functional value (i.e. information and system quality) rather than conditional value (i.e. system quality) and satisfaction. Teo et al. (2008) have analysed the influence of trust on the specific e-government systems on the quality constructs (i.e. information, system, and service quality) of the IS success model. They argued that higher level of citizen's trust would be positively associated with information, system, and service quality of the systems (Teo et al., 2008). Similarly, backed by the IS success model, Wang et al. (2010) devised a model for citizen's sustainable trust in e-government.

Gotoh (2009) undertook a similar analysis of the online tax declaration services for the Japanese government and examined it quantitatively to elucidate the factors that enhance user's satisfaction with such services. The paper used IS success models with two amendments where preparation quality and result quality were the constructs used apart from system quality, which was directly driven from the IS success model. Hu et al. (2009) examined the determinants of service quality and continuance intention on the eTax system in context of Hong Kong. The data analysis supported both service traits (i.e. security and convenience) and one technology trait (i.e. perceived ease of use) as the key determinants of the service quality. They also observed that perceived usefulness was not found as the strongest predictor of continuance intention but service quality was.

Scott et al. (2009) provided a multi-faceted framework for understanding the success of e-government websites from the citizen's perspectives. They established the role of net benefits in the evaluation of e-government success and extended the knowledge of e-government success by determining the influence IT quality constructs. Chen (2010) discussed taxpayer's satisfaction with the online system for filing the individual income tax returns in context of Taiwan. The system under discussion covered its information, system, and service qualities, which are the precursors of the user's satisfaction with any system. By the use of DeLone and McLean's IS success model, the author intended to demonstrate how the use of the system could be enhanced by the increasing software satisfaction with it. The research also found that information and system quality are significant factors toward achieving this goal (Chen, 2010).

Floropoulos et al. (2010) measured the success of the Greek taxation information system (TAXIS) from the perspective of expert employees using the constructs including information, system, and service quality, perceived usefulness, and user satisfaction and found the strong links between five success constructs. However, they found the effect of system quality on perceived usefulness quite low and on user satisfaction as non-significant. Sambasivan et al. (2010) used an extended IS success model of DeLone and McLean (2003) to examine the factors that influence the intention to use and actual use of the electronic procurement system by various ministries in the Malaysian government. They used DeLone and McLean IS success model by extending it with the factors such as trust, facilitating conditions, and web-design quality and found them strongly linked with intention to use.

3   Research Model Development and Hypotheses

3.1   Theoretical Background - IS Success Models

There are primarily three theories given in the area of IS success. The first IS success model was given by DeLone and McLean (1992) with six factors namely system quality, information quality, use, user's satisfaction, individual impact, and organizational impact (DeLone and McLean, 1992). In order to address criticism by several studies (such as Seddon and Kiew, 1996) relating to some of its constructs such as individual and organizational impact and use, Seddon (1997) introduced a re-specified model of DeLone and McLean where use of the system was considered to have results of various types, perceived usefulness was introduced in the model as an IS measure. Latter in the year 2003, DeLone and McLean discussed many of the significant IS research efforts that have applied, validated, challenged, and offered enrichments to their original model. The updated IS success model (DeLone and McLean, 2003) incorporated a new construct 'service quality' and substituted the variables, individual and organizational impact, with net benefits with accounting for benefits at different levels of analysis.

3.2   Overview of Proposed Research Model for Examining Success Factors of OPGRS

The theoretical development is based on the above described IS success models (DeLone and McLean, 1992; 2003; Seddon, 1997). The decision for not considering certain constructs of these models for proposing research model for this study is based on certain logical facts. For example, service quality is concerned with measuring the quality of service obtained by the IT departments as opposed to the specific IT applications. It mainly examines user's beliefs and their insight of IT department (Petter et al., 2008). Since this study is concerned with a specific application (i.e. OPGRS), it was deemed inappropriate to include service quality in the proposed research model. The construct 'use' was also excluded from the proposed model as respondents of this study were potential adopters ('not actual users') of the systems. Although, they were shown the working of the system and its benefits and are expected to use this system in the future, they had not have yet experience with the system. For the purpose of this study the perceived usefulness construct from the Seddon's (1997) model was added to replace use. Seddon and Kiew (1996) and Seddon (1997) argued that non-use of a system does not necessarily indicate that it is not useful; it may simply indicate that the potential users have other tasks to perform (Seddon, 1997; Seddon and Kiew, 1996). Such logical arguments further justifies basis for the inclusion of perceived usefulness as an appropriate construct in the proposed model.

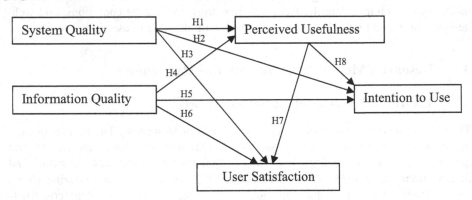

Fig. 1. The proposed research model

Considering above discussion, proposed research model (see Fig. 1) postulate that system quality, information quality will have significant influence on perceived usefulness and these three constructs together will be significantly related to intention to use, and user satisfaction. Testing the postulated relationships (See Table 2 for the list of hypotheses) can help to extrapolate the success of online public grievance redressal systems.

3.3   Hypotheses Development

As illustrated in Fig. 1, a total of eight hypotheses are proposed based on the relationships between five constructs. The core (independent) constructs are listed and defined in Table 1.

Table 1. Definitions of core constructs used in proposed model (Adopted from Seddon, 1997)

Variable/Construct	Definition
System Quality	System quality is concerned with whether or not there are 'bugs' in the system, the consistency of the user interface, ease of use, quality of documentation, and sometimes, quality and maintainability of the program code.
Information Quality	Information quality is concerned with the issues such as the relevance, timeliness, and accuracy of information generated by an information system. Not all applications of IT involve the production of information for decision-making (e.g., a word processor does not produce any information) so information quality is not a measure that can be applied to all systems.
Perceived Usefulness	Perceived usefulness is a perceptual indicator of the degree to which the stakeholder believes that using a particular system has enhanced his or her job performance, or his or her group's or organization's performance.

Table 2. A list of proposed hypotheses

H#	Hypothesis
H1	System quality has a positive and significant relationship with perceived usefulness
H2	System quality has a positive and significant relationship with intention to use
H3	System quality has a positive and significant relationship with user satisfaction
H4	Information quality has a positive and significant relationship with perceived usefulness
H5	Information quality has a positive and significant relationship with intention to use
H6	Information quality has a positive and significant relationship with user satisfaction
H7	Perceived usefulness has a positive and significant relationship with user satisfaction
H8	Perceived usefulness has a positive and significant relationship with intention to use

System Quality → Perceived Usefulness

Seddon and Kiew (1994) examined a part of DeLone and McLean (1992) IS success model and replaced 'use' with 'usefulness' and their outcomes partially supported DeLone and McLean (1992) IS success model. After replacing use by usefulness, the influence of system quality on perceived usefulness was found very significant. Latter, Fraser and Salter (1995) also obtained a very similar result after replicating Seddon and Kiew's (1994) study. Ease of use has been devised as one of the characteristics of system quality, and the meta-analytic results of this very frequently occurring relationship (in other words, impact of ease of use on usefulness) have been supported and found positive and significant for various categories (King and He, 2006). Examining the success of a Greek taxation information system (TAXIS), Floropoulos et al. (2010) found a strong connection of system quality on perceived usefulness. However, the effect of system quality on perceived usefulness was found to be very low. It was argued that sample considered was largely based on computer and Internet literates and hence might not be a crucial factor for determining perceived usefulness. Therefore, we hypothesize:

H1: System quality has a positive and significant effect on perceived usefulness of the online public grievance redressal systems.

System Quality → Intention to Use

The individual meta-analyses results of DeLone and McLean (2003) IS success model supported and indicated a positive and a highly significant relationship of system analysis on intention to use (Petter and McLean, 2009). The impact of ease of use, which is considered as one of the measures of system quality is already established as positive and significant on intention to use in majority of cases (58 out of 101 relationships found significant as per Lee et al., (2003)) and through the meta-analysis under various categories (King and He, 2006) as well. Therefore, we hypothesize:

H2: System quality has a positive and significant effect on intention to use of the online public grievance redressal systems.

System Quality → User Satisfaction

The prior empirical findings (Iavari, 2005; Rai et al., 2002; Seddon, 1997; Seddon and Kiew, 1996; Wang and Liao, 2008) have supported the positive and significant impact of system quality on user satisfaction as discussed in DeLone and McLean's model. That indicates that the higher levels of system quality are positively associated to higher levels of user satisfaction. However, analysing TAXIS in context of Greece, Floropoulos et al. (2010) found it non-significant. The authors argued that the system quality may not be the prominent factor in measuring satisfaction given the nature of sample being sufficiently computer and Internet literate. However, measuring the e-government system success using the validation of DeLone and McLean model, Wang and Liao (2008) found a significant impact of system quality on user's satisfaction. Therefore, we hypothesize:

H3: System quality has a positive and significant effect on user satisfaction of the online public grievance redressal systems.

Information Quality → Perceived Usefulness

This relationship has been supported by Seddon (1997) IS success model, where they substituted 'IS use' of DeLone and McLean (1992) success model by perceived usefulness. Seddon (1997) pointed out that perceived usefulness is impacted directly by beliefs about information quality. Latter, Rai et al. (2002) analysed and validated Seddon's (1997) and its amended models and found the effect of information quality on perceived usefulness as positive and significant. Similarly, Franz and Robey (1986), Kraemer et al. (1993) and Seddon and Kiew (1996) have also argued that augmented information quality leads to enhanced usefulness. Moreover, Floropoulos et al. (2010) explored the effect of information quality on perceived usefulness in context of Greek TAXIS systems and confirms the Seddon's (1997) argument. Therefore, we hypothesize:

H4: Information quality has a positive and significant effect on perceived usefulness of the online public grievance redressal systems.

Information Quality → Intention to Use

DeLone and McLean (2003) IS updated model has hypothesized and supported the link of information quality on intention to use. Moreover, the effects of information quality on intention to use is also strongly supported by the meta-analytic outcomes of DeLone and McLean IS success model, which showed the strong relationship strength of these variables even for the least overall sample size obtained to perform the meta-analysis (Petter and McLean, 2009). As far as e-government based studies are concerned, they yet need to validate this relationship. Hence, the following hypothesis can be formulated:

H5: Information quality has a positive and significant effect on intention to use of the online public grievance redressal systems.

Information Quality → User Satisfaction

Several prior studies on IS success have demonstrated support for the argument that higher degree of information quality leads to enhanced user satisfaction (Chae and Kim, 2001; Floropoulos et al., 2010; Iavari, 2005; McGill and Hobbs, 2003; Rai et al., 2002; Seddon, 1997; Seddon and Kiew, 1996; Wang and Liao, 2008; Zhang et al., 2005). Petter and McLean's (2009) meta-analytic assessment of DeLone and McLean model has also strongly supported in effect of information quality on user's satisfaction. In context of e-government adoption research, Wang and Liao (2008) presented and validated a model of e-government system success (based on DeLone and McLean (2003) IS success model) and found the influence of information quality on user satisfaction being significantly supported. Similar, results were obtained for TAXIS systems analysed by Floropoulos et al. (2010), where the findings indicated system quality as an important and stronger determinant of employee's satisfaction. Hence, we hypothesize:

H6: Information quality has a positive and significant effect on user satisfaction of the online public grievance redressal systems.

Perceived Usefulness → User Satisfaction

Seddon (1997) has validated and supported the positive effect of perceived usefulness on user's satisfaction. Rai et al. (2002) specified and empirically measured Seddon (1997) and its amended IS success model and found the significant correlation between perceived usefulness and user's satisfaction. Moreover, findings of Floropoulos et al. (2010) confirmed that perceived usefulness is a strong determinant of user satisfaction in context of TAXIS systems of Greece. They also argued that this relationship has not been explored much by the researchers in the extant literature (Floropoulos et al., 2010). Moreover, the studies like Franz and Robey (1986) and Seddon and Kiew (1996) have also supported a positive correlation between these constructs. Therefore, we hypothesize:

H7: Perceived usefulness has a positive and significant effect on intention to use the online public grievance redressal systems.

Perceived Usefulness → Intention to Use

Building on the prior IS research, the technology acceptance model (TAM) conceptualized usefulness as one of the significant insights leading to intention to adopt new systems (Lee et al., 2003). Research has shown that perceived usefulness influences intended adoption of IT (Gefen and Straub, 2000). As far as e-government adoption research is concerned, this relationship has been examined through the models such as the TAM and extended TAM (TAM2). Subsequently, out of being examined for a total of 24 times, it was found significant in 21 cases across different studies. The meta-analysis also found the collective effect of perceived usefulness on intention to use as significant. However, as per our knowledge, this relationship has not been explored in context of IS success model in e-government research. Considering the overall performance of this relationship across IS research in general and e-government adoption research in particular, the following hypothesis can be formulated:

H8: Perceived Usefulness has a positive and significant influence on intention to use the online public grievance redressal systems.

4   Research Methodology

For the purpose of examining e-government system success of OPGRS, the researchers considered survey as an appropriate research method (Cornford and Smithson, 1996; Choudrie and Dwivedi, 2005). There are various ways to capture the data, however, a self-administered questionnaire was found to be a suitable as a primary survey instrument of data collection in this research. This is due to the fact that this tackles the issue of reliability of information by reducing and eliminating the way the questions are asked and presented (Conford and Smithson, 1996). Moreover, collecting data from the majority of respondents within a short and specific period of time was a critical issue of this research (Fowler, 2002). Therefore, only closed and multiple-choice questions were included in the questionnaire. The final questionnaire consisted of total 30 questions including 10 questions from respondent's demographic characteristics and 20 questions on the five different constructs of the proposed research model. All these questions were multiple-type, closed-ended and seven-point Likert scale type questions. Likert scales (1-7) with anchors ranging from "strongly disagree" to "strongly agree" (Wang and Liao, 2008) were used for all non-demographic based questions. Appendix A lists all the items for the constructs used in this study.

The sample of the study consists of wide spectrum of respondents from different cities of India including New Delhi, Pune, Mumbai, Bangalore, Patna, Siliguri, and Gangtok. From the literature on IS success models, five factors were identified and a questionnaire for examining intention to use and satisfaction was then created and pilot tested with 34 respondents. While the results of the pilot test were found to be valid and reliable measuring instrument, the researchers agreed that further analysis could reduce the set of factors and that further validation efforts were required (Griffiths et al., 2007). Deriving from the success of the pilot test, a total of 1500 questionnaires distributed to respondents through one-to-one and group interaction. The respondents were briefed and demonstrated about the functioning of the online public grievance redressal system and in some cases they were given maximum two days of time to complete the questionnaire. This was done considering the long list of questions in the questionnaire. However, some of the questionnaires were made to respond on spot. A total of 485 completed survey questionnaires were received back. The further scrutiny of questionnaires revealed that 66 of them were partially completed and so rejected from the subsequent analysis. Hence, we were left with 419 usable responses, which made our basis for the empirical analysis for measuring the IS success of OPGRS. The overall response rate was found to be 32.3% with 27.9% valid questionnaires.

5   Research Findings

5.1   Respondents' Demographic Profile

This section analyses demographic data (in Table 3) obtained from the respondents. As per the questionnaire results, the average respondent's age ranges from 20 to 34, with males accounting for 67.8% of the sample and 32.2% were female. The majority of the population (i.e., 56.1%) belongs to student community with a fair representation from public- and private-sector employees (i.e., 29.3%). As far as the educational qualifications are concerned, 82% of the total population are having a minimum degree of graduation. The computer and Internet literacy and awareness of the respondents can be judged from their very high computer and Internet experience percentage ($\approx$ 96%). This higher frequency is also supported by their computer and Internet access at various places and Internet use frequency, which is very high. Therefore, it is argued that the sample of respondents could be the best-fit potential users and adopters of the systems such as online public grievance redressal system.

Table 3. Demographic characteristics of respondents

Characteristics	Frequency	%
Age		
20-24 Years	228	54.4
25-29 Years	70	16.7
30-34 Years	52	12.4
35-39 Years	27	6.4
40-44 Years	11	2.6
45-49 Years	13	3.1
50-54 Years	7	1.7
55-59 Years	1	0.2
>= 60 Years	10	2.4
Gender		
Male	284	67.8
Female	135	32.2
Education		
Non-Matriculation	7	1.7
Matriculation	13	3.1
10+2/Intermediate	55	13.1
Graduate	161	38.4
Post-Graduate	169	40.3
Post-Graduate Research	14	3.3
Occupation		
Student	235	56.1
Unemployed	18	4.3
Pensioner	7	1.7
Employee-Public Sector	29	6.9
Employee-Private Sector	94	22.4
Self-Employed	36	8.6
Computer Access		
Home	273	46.4
Office	107	18.2
Internet Cafe	83	14.1
College/University	100	17.0
Common Service Centre	12	2.0
No Access	13	2.2
Computer Experience (in Years)		
No Experience	17	4.1
1-3 Years	99	23.6
4-6 Years	98	23.4
7-9 Years	91	21.7
>= 10 Years	114	27.2

Internet Access		
Home	246	42.6
Office	104	18.0
Internet Cafe	109	18.9
College/University	103	17.8
Common Service Centre	10	1.7
No Access	6	1.0
Internet Experience (in Years)		
No Experience	16	3.8
1-3 Years	132	31.5
4-6 Years	122	29.1
7-9 Years	80	19.1
>= 10 Years	69	16.5
Internet Use Frequency		
Never	12	2.9
Very Rarely	21	5.0
Rarely	39	9.3
Occasionally	77	18.4
Very Frequently	137	32.7
Always	133	31.7

5.2   Reliability Analysis - Cronbach's Alpha (α)

Reliability analysis was performed using Cronbach's alpha. It was used for determining the reliability of the scale, which provides an indication about the internal consistency of the items measuring the same construct (Hair et al., 1992; Zikmund, 1994). Cronbach's alpha reliability for all the constructs except system quality is in the range 0.796-0.881, which is quite good. A Chronbach (α) of greater than 0.7 is considered to be good (Nunnaly, 1978; Hair et al., 1992). Therefore, alphas imply strong reliability for all constructs, but system quality which is at satisfactory level.

Table 4. Cronbach's alpha (α) of constructs

Construct	Cronbach's Alpha (α)
System Quality	0.548
Information Quality	0.810
Perceived Usefulness	0.800
Intention to Use	0.796
User Satisfaction	0.881

5.3   Descriptive Statistics

Table 5 presents the mean and standard deviation (S.D.) for all the five constructs and their individual items. The high overall as well as individual items' means for most of the constructs, except user satisfaction, indicate that respondents react favourably to the IS success measures examined.

Table 5. Descriptive statistics of the constructs and their items

Measure	Item	Mean	S.D.
System Quality (SQ)		5.19	0.97
	SQ1	5.17	1.31
	SQ2	5.33	1.35
	SQ3	5.06	1.37
Information Quality (IQ)		5.02	1.08
	IQ1	5.11	1.28
	IQ2	4.92	1.38
	IQ3	5.05	1.40
	IQ4	4.98	1.35
Perceived Usefulness (PU)		5.29	0.96
	PU1	5.51	1.35
	PU2	5.06	1.41
	PU3	4.97	1.51
	PU4	5.05	1.36
	PU5	5.58	1.23
	PU6	5.55	1.23
Intention to Use (IU)		5.26	1.23
	IU1	5.31	1.50
	IU2	5.20	1.46
	IU3	5.27	1.40
User Satisfaction (US)		4.15	0.95
	US1	5.08	1.45
	US2	5.12	1.45
	US3	5.21	1.33
	US4	5.35	1.30

5.4   Hypotheses Testing

Table 6, 7, and 8 present output of linear regression model analysed using SPSS 19.0. The analysis presented in Table 6 supported all the hypotheses (i.e. H2, H5, and H8) on intention to use as positive and significant. The constructs SQ, PU, and IQ explain 25.1% (adjusted R^2) of the variance in respondents' intention to use the online public grievance redressal system. Since, the overall model is significant (F=47.811, p=0.000), the significance of the independent variable was further examined. All independent variables were found significant with 1% significance level except IQ, which was found significant with 5% significance level. Therefore, all the three hypotheses H2, H5, and H8 are supported.

Table 6. Effect of system quality, perceived usefulness, and information quality on intention to use

Model	Unstandardized Coefficients		Standardized Coefficients	t	Sig.	Result
	B	S.E.	Beta			
(Constant)	1.409	0.326		4.319	0.000	
SQ	0.245	0.071	0.194**	3.469	0.001	Supported
PU	0.369	0.072	0.288***	5.147	0.000	Supported
IQ	0.126	0.060	0.111*	2.098	0.036	Supported
Model R^2	0.257					
Adjusted R^2	0.251					
F	47.811					
Significance	0.000					

[Note: *: $p<0.05$, **: $p<0.01$; ***: $p<0.001$][Legend: S.E. = Standard Error, Sig. = Significance]

Table 7 presents the β-value of independent variables such as SQ, PU, and IQ on US. The analysis exhibits a stronger effect of SQ ($\beta=0.310$) and IQ ($\beta=0.355$) on US than IU. However, PU seems to have better influencing BI ($\beta=0.288$) than US ($\beta=0.109$). That means, higher the usefulness, higher the intention to use the system rather than being more satisfied. Higher the system and information quality, respondents tend to be more satisfied with the system. That means, OPGRS enhances the overall satisfaction of the respondents by providing accurate, reliable, updated information to name a few in the bureaucratic government system in a country like India.

Table 7. Effect of system quality, perceived usefulness, and information quality on user satisfaction

Model	Unstandardized Coefficients		Standardized Coefficients	t	Sig.	Result
	B	S.E.	Beta			
(Constant)	0.437	0.221		1.982	0.048	
SQ	0.303	0.048	0.310***	6.343	0.000	Supported
PU	0.109	0.049	0.109*	2.246	0.025	Supported
IQ	0.312	0.040	0.355***	7.723	0.000	Supported
Model R^2	0.434					
Adjusted R^2	0.430					
F	106.098					
Significance	0.000					

[Note: *: $p<0.05$, **: $p<0.01$; ***: $p<0.001$][Legend: S.E. = Standard Error, Sig. = Significance]

All the three hypotheses H3, H6, and H7 have been found positive and significant on user satisfaction. The same set of independent constructs (i.e. SQ, PU, and IQ)

explains 43% (adjusted R^2) of the variance in the respondents' user satisfaction on the system. The overall model was found significant (F=106.098, p=0.000), and the significance of the individual independent variables was further verified. It was found that both SQ and IQ were found significant on US with 0.001 significant level whereas PU at 0.05 significant level.

Table 8 summarizes the results of the hypotheses testing the dependent variable perceived usefulness. This model explains 42.6% of variance of the system OPGRS on respondent's perceived usefulness. Again, the overall model was found significant (F=154.538, p=0.000) with the individual independent variables IQ and SQ are significant determinants of respondent's perceived usefulness with a significance level of 0.001. More precisely, the hypotheses H1 and H4 are supported. This time, SQ exhibits stronger effect (β=0.447) on perceived usefulness than IQ (β=0.293). That indicates, higher the system quality higher will be its usefulness as perceived by its users.

Table 8. Effect of information quality and system quality on intention to use

Model	Unstandardized Coefficients		Standardized Coefficients	t	Sig.	Result
	B	Std. Error	Beta			
(Constant)	1.706	0.207		8.249	0.000	
IQ	0.259	0.039	0.293***	6.672	0.000	Supported
SQ	0.440	0.043	0.447***	10.178	0.000	Supported
Model R^2	0.426					
Adjusted R^2	0.424					
F	154.538					
Significance	0.000					

[Note: *: p<0.05, **: p<0.01; ***: p<0.001]

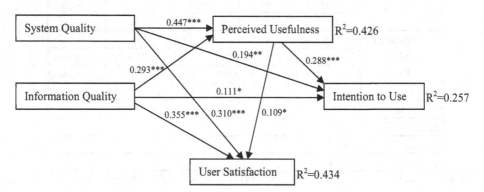

Fig. 2. Validated research model to measure intention to use and user

The hypothesis testing results of linear regression analysis with the coefficient values (i.e. β-value), p-value, and R^2-value are presented along the research model in Fig. 2.

6   Discussion

The hypothesis testing results indicated that there are strong links between the five constructs supporting the hypotheses. The regression coefficient outcomes indicated that system and information quality are significant positive determinants of perceived usefulness. Moreover, their effect on user satisfaction was even stronger. However, unlike the system and information quality, the effect of perceived usefulness on user satisfaction was significant but its influence on intention to use exhibited even stronger affect as far as OPGRS is concerned. Finally, the findings also revealed that system and information quality are the stronger predictors of perceived usefulness

It is evident from the above analysis that perceived usefulness of the system leads the respondents more toward their intention to use it rather being satisfied. This is due to the fact that although perceived usefulness is found as an effective determinant to measure both intention to use as well as user satisfaction, it is more significant toward intention to use than satisfaction. This may be due to the fact that users would tend to use the system more than being satisfied to the level based on the usefulness of the system. The argument of intention to use a system based on its perceived usefulness has already been well established by Davis (1989) through TAM model and supported by a number of studies using this model. Moreover, a significant impact of perceived usefulness on user's satisfaction (established by Seddon, 1997) has also been supported by Colesca and Dobrica (2008) in their study of e-government adoption in Romanian context.

As OPGRS is relatively a new system and not being used by the sample population for lodging their complaints and grievances, the stronger significant relationship between perceived usefulness and satisfaction can be expected only when the system is used to a certain extent. On the other hand, the predictors such as system and information quality make the respondents more satisfied than intending to use the system though all the relationships were found significant. This may be due to the fact that the respondents believed about how the system is going to benefit them without much hassle. The other significant reason for the respondents being more satisfied to this system is it does not involve any transactions and would take away their fear to lose anything monetarily. However, all these relationships were found significant as described in DeLone and McLean IS success Model (2003). Finally, the constructs system and information quality strongly determines the perceived usefulness of the system. This is due to the simple reason that this is the flexibility, conciseness, ease of use, faster response time, user-friendly interface, accuracy, completeness, and significance of the system which can make it more useful for its use. This strong empirical evidence also supports Seddon (1997) view of IS success model.

7   Conclusion

This research is a response to a call for the continuous challenge and validation of IS success models in different contexts (DeLone and McLean, 2003, Rai et al., 2002). The purpose of this study is to examine the success of OPGRS through an e-government based IS success model, which is developed using DeLone and McLean's and Seddon's IS success models. Therefore, we integrated the constructs of these two models to form a model that could explain the success of OPGRS as perceived by the sample of respondents in context of India. All the eight hypotheses performed significantly as per the expectations of the IS success models. Therefore, it is quite evident from the empirical findings that the implementation of OPGRS seems to be quite successful even though it is not a very old system. However, it was sensed that the government should take more initiatives to enhance the information quality of the system to attract more positive responses from the citizens toward their inclination to use the system. Moreover, there should be an emphasis to highlight the usefulness of the system as a whole to make the citizens aware, prompted, and satisfied.

7.1   Limitations and Future Research Directions

Even though the thorough process has allowed us to develop and validate the e-government based system success model, this study has a number of limitations that can be taken care of in the future research. Firstly, the exploration of IS system success model in context of e-government system is relatively new to the e-government researchers. Therefore, the caution needs to be taken while generalizing its findings to the other categories of users (i.e. in G2B and G2G contexts) as well as applying this model in other developing country even in G2C context. Secondly, this model does not measure the concerns of net benefits as defined in the IS success model (DeLone and McLean, 2003; Seddon, 1997). Hence, measuring net benefits from the citizen's points of view can reveal some more facts about the system. However, future researchers need clearly and carefully define the stakeholders and situations under which the net benefits are to be examined (DeLone and McLean, 2003). Thirdly, the study has not validated this system for specific cultural and geographical contexts. Future research can dig out more on these aspects. Finally, this study has performed empirical investigation of e-government systems success based on the snapshot view of the sample. The longitudinal view of sample data would allow the researchers to better explore the facts about the actual use of the system and it's after effect.

7.2   Implications for Theory and Practice

The first theoretical implication of this research is that this system is tested for the first time for its success measure. Secondly, we have integrated DeLone and McLean's (2003) and Seddon's (1997) IS success models to provide a better understanding of OPGRS's success. The model presented here can be tested further based on longitudinal nature of data gathered from the same set of sample after they use the system for some time or data collected from those respondents who are already using the system. The empirical testing outcomes of the hypotheses linked to the model can help researchers toward a better understanding of citizen's intention to use and satisfaction with the system. The results will allow the e-government practitioners to realize about the factors to give more attention for increasing the citizen's satisfaction and intention to use the system. The current link of information quality with intention to use the system is although significant, it is not strong. The system designer should pay more attention toward enhancing the standard of information quality of the system to strengthen people's intention to use it. The practitioners should be asked to reinforce perceived usefulness of the system in such a way that they can ensure user's satisfaction to a larger extent.

References

Adams, D.A., Nelson, R.R., Todd, P.A.: Perceived usefulness, ease of use, and usage of information technology: A replication. MIS Quarterly 16(2), 227–247 (1992)

Akman, I., Yazici, A., Mishra, A., Arifoglu, A.: E-Government: A global view and an empirical evaluation of some attributes of citizens. Government Information Quarterly 22, 239–257 (2005)

Chae, M., Kim, J.: Information quality for mobile internet services: A theoretical model with empirical validation. In: Proceedings of the Twenty-second International Conference on Information Systems New Orleans, LA, USA, pp. 43–54 (2001)

Chai, S., Herath, T.C., Park, I., Rao, H.R.: Repeated Use of E-Gov Web Sites: A Satisfaction and Confidentiality Perspective. International Journal of Electronic Government Research 2(3), 1–22 (2006)

Chen, C.-W.: Impact of quality antecedents on taxpayer satisfaction with online tax-filing systems - An empirical study. Information & Management 47, 308–315 (2010)

Choudrie, J., Dwivedi, Y.K.: Investigating the research approaches for examining technology adoption issues. Journal of Research Practice 1(1), Article D1 (2005)

Colesca, S.E., Dobrica, L.: Adoption and use of e-government services: The case of Romania. Journal of Applied Research and Technology 6(3), 204–217 (2008)

Cornford, T., Smithson, S.: Project Research in Information Systems: A Student's Guide. Macmillan Press Ltd., London (1996)

Davis, F.D.: Perceived usefulness, perceived ease of use, and user acceptance of information technology. MIS Quarterly 13(3), 318–346 (1989)

DeLone, W.H., McLean, E.R.: Information systems success: The quest for the dependent variable. Information Systems Research 3(1), 60–95 (1992)

Delone, W.H., McLean, E.R.: The DeLone and McLean model of information systems success: A ten-year update. Journal of Management Information Systems 19(4), 9–30 (2003)

Floropoulos, J., Spathis, C., Halvatzis, D., Tsipouridou, M.: Measuring the success of the Greek Taxation Information System. International Journal of Information Management 30, 47–56 (2010)

Fowler, F.J.: Survey Research Methods. SAGE Publications Inc., London (2002)

Franz, C.R., Robey, D.: Organisational context, user involvement and the usefulness of information systems. Decision Sciences 17, 329–356 (1986)

Gefen, D., Straub, D.: The Relative Importance of Perceived Ease of Use in IS Adoption: A Study of E-Commerce Adoption. Journal of the Association for Information Systems 1(8), 1–28 (2000)

Gotoh, R.: Critical factors increasing user satisfaction with e-government services. Electronic Government, an International Journal 6(3), 252–264 (2009)

Griffiths, J.R., Jhonson, F., Hartley, R.J.: User satisfaction as a measure of system performance. Journal of Librarianship and Information Science 39(3), 142–152 (2007)

Gupta, M.P., Jana, D.: EGovernment evaluation: A framework and case study. Government Information Quarterly 20(4), 365–387 (2003)

Hair, J.F., Anderson, R.E., Tatham, R.L., Black, W.C.: Multivariate data analysis, with readings, 3rd edn. Macmillan Publishing Company, New York (1992)

Hsu, F.-M., Chen, T.-Y.: Understanding Information Systems Usage Behavior in E-Government: The Role of Context and Perceived Value. In: Pacific Asia Conference on Information Systems, pp. 477–490 (2007)

Hu, P.J.-H., Brown, S.A., Thong, J.Y.L., Chan, F.K.Y., Tam, K.Y.: Determinants of Service Quality and Continuance Intention of Online Services: The Case of eTax. Journal of the American Society for Information Science and Technology 60(2), 292–306 (2009)

Iavari, J.: An empirical test of the DeLone-McLean model of information system success. The Data Base for Advances in Information Systems 36(2), 8–27 (2005)

Jaeger, P.T.: The endless wire: E-Government as global phenomenon. Government Information Quarterly 20(4), 323–331 (2003)

King, W.R., He, J.: A meta-analysis of the technology acceptance model. Information & Management 43(6), 740–755 (2006)

Kraemer, K.L., Danzinger, J.N., Dunkle, D.E., King, J.L.: The usefulness of computer-based information to public managers. MIS Quarterly 17(2), 129–148 (1993)

Lee, Y., Kozar, K.A., Larsen, K.R.T.: The Technology Acceptance Model: Past, Present, and Future. Communications of the Association for Information System 12, 752–780 (2003)

McGill, T., Hobbs, V.: User-developed applications and information systems success: A test of DeLone and McLean's model. Information Resources Management Journal 16, 24–45 (2003)

McKnight, D.H., Choudhury, V., Kacmar, C.: Trust in e-commerce vendors: A two-stage model. In: Proceedings of the 21st International Conference on Information Systems, Brisbane, Queensland, Australia (2000)

Nunnaly, J.: Psychometric theory. McGraw-Hill, New York (1978)

Palmer, J.W.: Web site usability, design, and performance metrics. Information Systems Research 13(2), 151–167 (2002)

Petter, S., McLean, E.R.: A meta-analytic assessment of the DeLone and McLean IS success model: An examination of IS success at the individual level. Information & Management 46(3), 159–166 (2009)

Petter, S., DeLone, W., McLean, E.: Measuring information systems success: models, dimensions, measures, and interrelationships. European Journal of Information Systems 17, 236–263 (2008)

Rai, A., Lang, S.S., Welker, R.B.: Assessing the validity of IS success models: An empirical test and theoretical analysis. Information Systems Research 13(1), 50–69 (2002)

Sambasivan, M., Wemyss, G.P., Rose, R.C.: User acceptance of a G2B system: A case of electronic procurement system in Malaysia. Internet Research 20(2), 169–187 (2010)

Scott, M., DeLone, W.H.: Understanding Net Benefits: A Citizen-Based Perspective on E-government Success. In: International Conference on Information Systems, pp. 1–11 (2009)

Seddon, P.B.: A respecification and extension of the DeLone and McLean model of IS success. Information Systems Research 8(3), 240–253 (1997)

Seddon, P.B., Kiew, M.-Y.: A partial test and development of the DeLone and McLean model of IS success. In: DeGross, J.I., Huff, S.L., Munro, M.C. (eds.) Proceedings of the International Conference on Information Systems, pp. 99–110. Association for Information Systems, Atlanta (1994)

Seddon, P.B., Kiew, M.Y.: A partial test and development of DeLone and McLean's model of IS success. Australian Journal of Information Systems 4(1), 90–109 (1996)

Sharifi, H., Zarei, B.: An adaptive approach for implementing e-government in I.R. Iran. Journal of Government Information 30, 600–619 (2004)

Teo, T.S.H., Srivastava, S.C., Jiang, L.: Trust and Electronic Government Success: An Empirical Study. Journal of Management Information Systems 9(3), 99–131 (2008)

Wang, T., Cao, Y., Yang, S.: Building the Model of Sustainable Trust in E-government. In: 2nd IEEE International Conference on Information and Financial Engineering, pp. 698–701 (2010)

Wang, Y.-S., Liao, Y.-W.: Assessing eGovernment systems success: A validation of the DeLone and McLean model of information systems success. Government Information Quarterly 25, 717–733 (2008)

Zhang, Z., Leeb, M.K.O., Huanga, P., Zhang, L., Huang, X.: A framework of ERP systems implementation success in China: An empirical study. International Journal of Production Economics 98, 56–80 (2005)

Zikmund, G.W.: Business research methods, 4th edn. The Dryden Press, New York (1994)

Appendix A. Survey items used in this study

Information Quality

IQ1 The public grievance redressal system would provide sufficient information

IQ2 Through public grievance redressal system, I would get the information I need in time

IQ3 Information provided by public grievance redressal system would be up-to-date

IQ4 Information provided by public grievance redressal system would be reliable

System Quality

SQ1 The public grievance redressal system would be user friendly

SQ2 I would find the public grievance redressal system easy to use

SQ3 I would find it easy to get the public grievance redressal system to do what I would like it to do

Perceived Usefulness

PU1 Using the public grievance redressal system would enable me to accomplish lodging complaint more quickly

PU2 Using the public grievance redressal system would improve my overall performance

PU3 Using the public grievance redressal system would increase my productivity

PU4 Using the public grievance redressal system would enhance my effectiveness

PU5 Using the public grievance redressal system would make it easier to lodge my complaint

PU6 I would find the public grievance redressal system useful in lodging and monitoring complaint

User Satisfaction

US1 I feel that public grievance redressal system would adequately meet my needs of interacting with government agency

US2 Public grievance redressal system would efficiently fulfill my needs of interacting with government agency

US3 Overall, I would be satisfied with the public grievance redressal system

Intention to Use

IU1 I intend to use the public grievance redressal system

IU2 I predict that I would use the public grievance redressal system

IU3 I plan to use the public grievance redressal system in the near future

Tensions between Individual
Use and Network Adoption of Social Media Platforms

Nikhil Srinivasan and Jan Damsgaard

Department of IT Management, Copenhagen Business School, Frederiksberg, Denmark
{ns.itm,jd.itm}@cbs.dk

Abstract. Social media have diffused into the everyday lives of many but still pose challenges to individuals regarding use of these platforms. This paper explores the multiple manners in which social media platforms gets employed by individuals based on an examination of 4 vignettes generated by interviewing individuals within a university context. An analysis of the vignettes and individual use behaviors highlights the tension between network-based adoption of social media platforms and the constraints that the network places on individual use of the platform.

Keywords: social media, adoption, use, social network, tensions.

1 Introduction

Social media platforms have in a very short time integrated well into people´s lives, both socially and professionally. Long-lost school mates reconnect with one another, friends and family share news, and professional bonds are easily continued after a work relation has ended; all as a result of social media platforms. A social media platform is built around social relations that individuals establish or confirm with each other through information and communication technologies for the purpose of communication, collaboration and coordination of information, knowledge and activities. A social media platform is inherently a participative environment where the consumers of information and knowledge are simultaneously the co-creators and consumers of new information and knowledge, while at the same time interacting with and engaging with individuals (Parameswaran et al. 2007).

Academic studies have examined the diffusion and adoption of specific social media technologies (Hester 2008; Hester et al. 2008) and employed popular and widely acknowledged models such as Diffusion of Innovation (DOI) (Rogers 1995), Technology Acceptance (TAM) or Unified Theory of Acceptance and Use of Technology (UTAUT) (Davis et al. 1989; Venkatesh et al. 2003) that have proven themselves in the past as useful vehicles in explaining the diffusion and adoption of IT in general. However extensions of DOI and TAM to cover social media platforms do so without revisiting the basic assumptions of the models and their validity domain (Sledgianowski et al. 2009; Tufekci 2008). This results in a conflation of individual use behaviors on the part of the individual with social network adoption contexts.

Y.K. Dwivedi et al. (Eds.): TDIT 2013, IFIP AICT 402, pp. 261–278, 2013.

This conflation of individual use and network adoption is significant because the one profound difference between general IT and social media platforms is that social media platforms are communal and have inherent network effects. Social media platforms only have value when many are using them, which is not paramount for many previous IT applications that were perfectly useful for the individual alone: e.g. word-processing. Consequently, examining social media platforms from the perspective of TAM and DOI tend to emphasize their individual use behaviors and the antecedents to those behaviors, rather than a broader examination of those individual use behaviors within a situated network (Granovetter 1973).

We contend that while DOI and TAM do shed light on examining adoption and diffusion of IT in general, social media represents a new paradigm in IT and as such traditional models of adoption and diffusion may not readily apply. The goal of this paper is to explore the adoption and diffusion of social media platforms. The central point of departure is the following research question.

How does the networked nature of social media platforms influence their use by individuals?

The remainder of this paper is organized the following way. In the next section we revisit classical adoption and diffusion theories in light of social media platforms. We then examine the nature of social media platforms and the characteristics that describe them. We then describe a field study designed to examine the tension between individual use and network adoption of social media platforms. We subsequently discuss our field study results and make some conclusions and note some limitations in our study.

2 Revisiting Classical Adoption and Diffusion Theory

This section discusses how the diffusion and adoption of technologies have been previously examined.

2.1 Technology Adoption

The individual adoption of a technology is based on two broad theories from social psychology i.e. the theory of reasoned action (Fishbein et al. 1975) and the theory of planned behavior (Ajzen 1985). The theories were immediately absorbed by information systems researchers and formed the basis for some of the most interesting, vibrant and comprehensive research programs of the discipline. The first work by Davis, Bagozzi and others (1989; 1989) was referred to as the technology acceptance model (TAM) and was subsequently built on by others to extend the model. The theory has been applied to compare across cultures (Straub et al. 1997) and genders (Gefen et al. 1997), extended with social influence (Malhotra et al. 2002), accounted for task-technology fit (Dishaw et al. 1999), and other similar extensions. A comprehensive examination of the theory of technology acceptance was performed by Venkatesh et al. (2003) who compared 8 different user acceptance models and synthesized them into a comprehensive model referred to as the Unified Theory of Acceptance and Use of Technology (UTAUT). Work still continues in this program of research with an examination of IS continuance (Bhattacherjee 2001) that examines the nature of continued use past the point of initial adoption and the role of habit (Limayem et al.). Since a complete review of the theory is beyond the scope of the paper please refer to Venkatesh (Venkatesh et al. 2007; Venkatesh et al. 2003) and the special issue of JAIS[1] for a more extensive review of the literature in this domain.

Broadly speaking within the individual technology acceptance literature, characteristics such as habit, self-efficacy, experience, task relevance, and others are primary and important determinants of behavior regarding individual technology adoption and use (Davis et al. 1989; Venkatesh et al. 2003). This perspective specifically privileges endogenous characteristics of the individual and individual motivations in ultimately determining behavior. Characteristics such as social norms and self-image are employed as mediating or moderating roles in influencing individual perceptions of the usefulness of a specific technology or service.

2.2   Technology Diffusion

The second perspective on the spread of technology exists at a broader level and examines the factors that contribute to the manner in which technologies diffuse across a population of potential adopters. This second perspective is often referred to as the diffusion of innovation (DOI) theory. While developed in the late 19th century, it is only recently that IS researchers have started examining and applying the theory. The seminal work of Rogers (1995) examines a large body of work in this domain and synthesizes it. Since the work of Rogers, DOI theory has been extensively applied in the context of IT (Attewell 1991; McFarlan et al. ; Moore et al. 1991; Mustonen-Ollila et al. 2003) to examine the diffusion of technological innovations and information technologies. Much of the information systems research literature has examined the adopter populations within organizations with a focus on the factors that influence adoption (Bala et al. 2007; Lin 2006; Melville et al. 2008). However despite its extensive application and popularity, DOI has also received some criticism (Lyytinen et al. 2001b; Lyytinen et al. 2011) noting that information technologies are often quite complex and that diffusion theories may not be sophisticated enough to address such complex technological innovations. DOI theory is especially effective at examining singular, monolithic technologies or well-defined systems with an apparent function such as TV sets or coffee makers (Lyytinen et al. 2001b). Such technologies typically rely on economies of scale on the supply side. The use of the system on the demand side is fairly independent of others' use of the same technology.

2.3   Other Related Theories

Social influence theories have also been applied to examine technology adoption among individuals with the basic premise that individual decisions and attitudes are not developed in isolation (Salancik et al. 1978). Individuals refer to a social context and environmental cues in order to aid in the decision making process. Social and

---

[1] http://aisel.aisnet.org/jais/vol8/iss4/

structural cues are conveyed through the social relations that individuals share and behavioral grammars reflect the influencers' autonomy, consistency or rigidity (Kraut et al. 1998). Social influence and social information processing theories do lend insight into examining use and adoption behaviors of individuals; but while it explains certain types of use, it does not explain non-use by individuals that exist in similar social contexts.

Critical mass theories of information technology postulate that mass adoption and diffusion of technologies take place based on momentum built up by a social system. The momentum builds up based on social factors within a system such as size, interrelatedness of individuals and levels of communication. Critical mass theories also suggest that there is a point at which enough users have adopted an innovation or technology that the acceleration of adoption process is self-sustaining (Sledgianowski et al. 2009) which is also referred to as the "bandwagon effect" (Peng 2010). Critical mass theories have also been examined in the context of adoption of new telecommunication services (Mahler et al. 1999), online gaming (Hsu et al. 2004), contribution to public knowledge databases (Peddibhotla et al. 2007), adoption of EDI systems (Iacovou et al. 1995) and more. These studies highlight the self-sustaining effects that adoption behavior of certain technologies may have. Markus (1987) proposed a critical mass theory for interactive media where she suggests that examining individuals' technology adoption and use decisions may not be sufficient to predict behavior at the community level due to the interdependence in the use of certain technologies. This suggests that certain information and communication technologies need to have a unique lens applied to examine their adoption and diffusion processes.

2.4   Revisiting the Assumptions of TAM and DOI

In the TAM approach to the adoption of innovations and technologies, individual characteristics are the primary determinant of individual adoption and use behavior. The limitation of such a theory is that the individual is the primary unit of analysis without an examination of the embeddedness (Granovetter 1973) of the individual in the context of their social networks. The role of social networks and embeddedness in such theories takes the form of subjective norms through which influence operates (Vannoy et al. 2010). DOI theory has been found as ineffective when examining diffusion of complex, networked information technologies (Lyytinen et al. 2001b). In examining the adopter population, individuals are treated as relatively isolated from the group, thereby separating them from the social setting in which they are embedded. By treating individuals as independent in their adoption behavior, the TAM and DOI perspectives do not focus on the interplay between users and between user behaviors (Benbasat et al. 2007) that involve more than one system and might involve an infrastructure of systems. This is a specific neglect of group, social and cultural aspects of decision-making behavior and a lack of examination of self-regulation processes (Bagozzi 2007). Traditional TAM and DOI models are less suitable in situations where adoption decisions are joint processes of decision-making or "we-intention" (Bagozzi 2007), that are rooted in a collective intention to adopt. Attention paid to the collective or "we-intention" examines the role of valence or feelings that individuals in a group have to each other and to choices of the group on the intention to adopt a technology (Sarker et al. 2005). "We-intention" or "we-ness" refers to the interdependence of individuals in making technology adoption decisions where relational linkages play a key role (Sarker et al. 2010).

Furthermore, TAM and associated theories of adoption do not adequately explain why parts of the population are more likely to adopt the technology or service and the other parts of the population less so, despite sharing similar individual characteristics (Lyytinen et al. 2001a). While they do a good job of explaining why specific individuals adopt technologies and service, they do a relatively poor job of understanding and explaining why others do not adopt a technology or service despite being similar and belonging to the same pool of potential adopters (Lyytinen et al. 2001a).

3   The Nature of Social Media Platforms

Social media platforms refer to technological and social infrastructures that are used to support specific and generalized modes of communication and collaboration between distributed individuals that share a common interest. They are also avenues for content generation where persons individually and collaboratively create, contribute and build on others' information contribution. Social media has been described as having the unique feature of "active creation of content by their users or members" (Scott et al. 2009) where the creation of content takes place through the building and maintaining of social networks and relations. Social media or social media platforms are collective, distributed and fluid, and as such are both complex and highly topical. While social media and social media technologies are easier to distinguish from traditional computer mediated communication environments, they are harder to distinguish from one another (Hanna et al. 2011). Social media technologies enhance communication effectiveness with customers and make them part of the organization's environment. The technologies extend the organization's antenna and moves it closer to the customer (Jones et al. 2009). The social media technologies described, and the organizations and social networks adopting them, are presented with several opportunities and challenges. Several strategies (Dutta 2010) have actively been developed for managing the social media technology environment ranging from personal to professional and private to public.

A honey comb structure (Figure 1) can be used to represent the various capabilities of social media and social media platforms (Kietzmann et al. 2011). The structure encapsulates seven functional capabilities that social media may have. These capabilities are presence, sharing, relationships, identity, conversations, groups and reputation. The *identity* component represents the extent to which users reveal their identities in the social media setting such as disclosing their name, age and other personal information. *Conversations* represent the extent and abilities of the system to enable users to communicate with other users in the social media and social media environment. *Sharing* represents the extent to which users exchange, distribute and receive content. Social media is based around the social interconnectedness between individuals and consequently sharing forms an important part of social media and social media environments. *Presence* represents the capability in the system to inform the users as to whether other users are accessible within the system. Identifying co-presence in virtual environments   such as social media and social media platforms the *relationships* components represents the extent to which individuals can relate to or establish relationships with other users. This represents the sociality component of social media. *Reputation* is the extent to which users can identify the standing of others in a social media and social media setting. *Groups* represent the extent to which users can form communities and subgroups within the social media and social media setting.

These 7 elements of the honeycomb structure represent characteristics and functionalities that are present within applications of the social media ecosystem. Various tools provide combinations of these functionalities to achieve their intended purpose. For instance, Facebook is based around the characteristic of relationships but goes on to provide functionality in the domains of identity, reputation, conversations and presence. Foursquare, another social media and social media tool is based around the notion of presence but also provides functionality around the notions of identity and relationships.

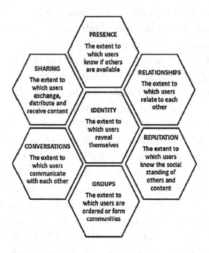

Fig. 1. Social Media Functionality

These 7 characteristics also highlight the Janus-faced nature (Arnold 2003) of social media platforms. Social media platforms provide individual use affordances through identity, reputation and presence functionality but enable network behaviors through sharing, relationship, conversation and grouping functionality.

The value to the users of social platforms is based on their appropriation of the functionalities based on individual use behavior or network appropriations based on number of their friends, family and colleagues they can communicate and collaborate with, within the specific social media platform. Thus while a single individual may be mobile across social media platforms, the social network and an individual's interactions with that network are locked into the specific platform used by the social network. Subsequently an individual's use of social media platforms is poised between individual use of functionalities and network use based on their communication and information needs with the relevant social networks.

Differentiating Social Media Platforms from other Technologies

Social media platforms are complex and are composed of disparate and fragmented networked systems that are the infrastructure on which social networks create content, communicate and collaborate. Individuals are not isolated on social media platforms. Architectures of participation and networks of users are fundamental to the notion of "collective intelligence" that form the basis of social media platforms (O'Reilly 2005). Social media platforms as infrastructures bind social networks together through which existing and new social relations are established and maintained. Network externalities result from the use of systems by friends, neighbors and families of individuals and consequently make social media platforms more valuable.

In addition to the network effects that are inherent in social media platforms; social networks add their own unique twist to technology adoption. Social networks are important in social media services since they are likely the first and major sources of influence in adoption decisions. The local configuration of relationships and the social network's adoption of technology represents a "we-intention" (Bagozzi 2007) on part of the social network. The migration of traditional social networks of friends, colleagues, family and acquaintances to digital networks has often resulted in the clash of these various networks. In addition to making the various social networks available on common technological platforms, these networks now are visible to each other. The availability and visibility of social networks however come at a price; the flattening or collapsing of the relationships into single homogeneous relationships, resulting in uncomfortable experiences with them (Boyd 2007). Furthermore, Boyd (2007) found that in the case of Friendster, the social network of individuals played a significant role in both the initial and second phases of adoption. This adoption was prior to the discussion in popular media, and invitation to use the service was based on whether your friends considered you a fit within the specific community that you were invited to. The observation that individuals belong to several social networks; e.g., professional, sports, relatives etc., suggests that social networks may adopt different social media platforms for supporting their social relations. This may mean that an individual may adopt several such platforms, essentially one for each network that they participate in or belong to. Thus the social network must form the key factor in the adoption of social media platforms, given the network effects associated with them.

The honeycomb framework that was described in figure 1 identifies several functional characteristics of social media platforms. These characteristics are centered on the affordances provided to the individual by social media platforms. While the affordances and functional capabilities of social media are individual centered, they are also relationship and network oriented. For instance, the functional capability of *sharing* which is the ability to exchange and distribute content is provided by the social media platform to the individual, but the exchanging and distribution of the content can either be one-to-one, one-to-many or one-to-all. Similarly, *presence,* a functional capability provided to the *individual* to communicate with and share presence information with *others* highlights the individual use nature of social media platforms while *conversations* highlights the social network oriented nature of social media platforms.

4   Research Method

Through a field study, we examine the central thesis in this paper, which is that social media platforms exist within a duality of individual use and social network adoption. The field study allows us to examine the context of adoption, and the adoption and use process of the social network's use of social media platforms (Lee 1989; Yin 1989).

4.1   Field Study Design

We employed semi-structured interviews as a data collection technique. The semi-structured interview started by focusing on the broad concept of the study and then narrowed down into specific instantiations of the adoption of social media by the interviewees. We started by probing into the use of social media and other communication technologies by the individual. We then asked the individual to describe the specific technologies in detail with emphasis on the social media technologies that specific groups and cliques employ in the interviewee's network. As such we asked for an individual interviewee to speak on the various social networks he or she may be participating in and his or her adoption and use of the social media platform for these networks.

4.2   Data Collection

This field study was conducted in a university setting. This setting is appropriate for data collection purposes as such populations are likely to use the social media services and are more amenable to having their behavior and use. The informants employ a variety of communication technologies and of course belong to a number of social networks. We probed the informant about the communication technologies their social networks employed, and for each social network that the person named we asked:

1.   The genesis, name, size and history of the social network
2.   The social network´s general use of social media platforms and other communication technologies
3.   The date of initiation and the adoption among the members of the social network
4.   The number of close friends, followers and relationships the social network has.

5. If there is a core of strong ties that forms the network, and what weak ties are common
6. How the members of the social network previously communicated.

The interviews lasted between 30 to 45 minutes. The interviewees were recruited from a marketing class. Students were invited to participate in the study by one of the authors.

4.3   Data Analysis

We employ vignettes (Avital et al. 2009; Jarvenpaa et al. 2000) to describe the adoption and use of social media platforms by social networks and individuals. We start by discussing the data analysis process and the manner by which various vignettes were constructed. We then proceed to discuss the vignettes that were elicited.

Method

Vignettes are used to illustrate the complex use of social media platforms. Our analysis of the observed social networks has been summarized in four vignettes. The interview subjects themselves did not provide the vignettes that are described. These vignettes were constructed by the authors from the narratives described by the interviewees and are used to illustrate the Janus-faced nature of social media platforms.

The vignettes were identified based on questions discussed previously. The interviewees were asked to respond to the questions and upon identification of a specific network, were asked to detail specific characteristics of the network and the communication tool used therein. When the interviewee provided a social network that employed the social media platform as a tool, they were asked about the unique characteristic or feature of the tool they employed for that social network and the reason why such a feature was employed. This enquiry process across all the interviews provided opportunities for the interviewees to reflect on their unique experience as it relates to social media. It also allowed researchers to focus on both the overlapping and unique characteristics of social media platform use. Interviewees identified several overlapping vignettes and a few unique ones. The vignettes subsequently represent the various manners of use of the social media platform by the interviewees. We use the vignettes as short illustrations of these use scenarios. These vignettes are summarized in Table 1.

Prior to the actual discussion of communication and social media technology use, the interviewees were asked to describe their daily use of the Internet and other IT. All interviewees were very accomplished with respect to communication and social media technologies. Most if not all of them spent several hours a day on the Internet. The time they spent on the Internet was a combination of school activities, job activities and hedonic activities. They attempted to articulate the amount of time spent on each of these activities but were cognizant of the fact that the manner in which they allocate time to each of these specific activities was fluid. They switched

Table 1. Characteristics of the four vignettes

Vignette	Social network	Representative	Social media platform	Frequency
As a Communication and Coordination Medium	Jewish Summer Camp, High school cohort and Soccer Team	Udi Jannik	Facebook	A few times a week
As a Relational Continuance Device	University Cohort	Shu	Facebook	A few times a week
As an Observational Platform	Squash Team, College Network Professional Network	Casper Udi Khaled	Facebook LinkedIn	A few times a month Once a week
As Emerging Social Infrastructure	Family and friends	Casper Khaled Shu	Facebook, LinkedIn	A few times a month

seamlessly between the activities. The interviewees were highly fluent in the use of computer and communication technologies such as phone calls, e-mail, SMS, internet chat, Voice over IP calls and social media environments such as Facebook, Twitter, LinkedIn and others. They often employed more than one form of communication technology and were able to articulate the communication and social media technologies effectively. Most of them spent about 25-50% of their daily time on the Internet on communicative activities.

Vignette 1: Social media is a **Communication and Coordination Medium**

This vignette focuses on one specific social network that was formed during participation in a Jewish summer camp and it illuminates how a social network uses a social media platform as a communication and coordination medium. The social network is made up of people that were present at the camp during the same summer. After the camp, communication in the social network was through e-mail threads used to sustain conversation or initiate new communication. Any new communication would employ previous threads to start the communicative or coordinative activity. This e-mail thread switched over to a Facebook group in 2006. When the core of the camp network moved to Facebook, the remainder of the cohort were de facto forced to drop the use of e-mail chains to communicate and started employing the Facebook Social media platforms to communicate in the social network. Furthermore new camp networks form their own social networks within the Facebook platform and employ the platform to communicate and coordinate their activities. These activities may include future summer camp participation, visits to Israel, parties and events, travels abroad, etc. In addition to the network of the summer camp, high school cohort and soccer club networks also communicate through the Facebook Social media platform.

While the familial and friend networks of the informants may employ the more traditional modes of communication, other networks employ social media based platforms. For instance, squash-based social networks rely on weak ties to organize games that rely on Facebook-based social media platform to schedule court times.

The visibility that the social media platform provides exposes the various social networks to each other. Despite the exposure of these networks to each other, observation and communication across the social network is based on participation in the social media platform. The Facebook platform is primarily used for monitoring purposes.

Vignette 2: Social media is a **Relational Continuance Device**

Illustrative of social networks employing social media platforms as a relational continuance device we find that high school and secondary school social networks that use the platform. On these platforms the social networks communicate on a one-to-one or a one-to-many basis.

A university cohort social network that we identified through the interviews interacts through Facebook. Facebook use by the network is simultaneously private to the individual, while also being public. Parts of the social network like to flaunt behavior across the remainder of the social network while parts of the social network remain very subdued. Flaunting behavior is performed through sharing photos, videos and other types of provocative posts. Parts of the social network that flaunt, and the related commenting and posting behavior inform the remainder of the social network as to who is doing what and where. Facebook is used to observe the social network and occasionally touch them through the use of the commenting and the liking feature. The maintenance of relational linkages is dispersed, and social networks take place through the social media platform. Although the platform is not used for communication and coordination activities, it serves as a way to observe individuals in the network and as a way to maintain conversational and relational continuance through other modes of communication. In this vignette we saw the social media platform employed to maintain relational linkages across a specific network. These relational linkages are the weak ties that allow individuals to pick up lost threads of conversation.

Vignette 3: Social media as an **Observational Platform**

Some social networks use Facebook and LinkedIn as an observational platform rather than for direct and frequent interaction. Social networks employ these platforms to passively share information about their recent activities, and acts of direct communication or close coordination in the social network get transferred from the social media platforms to the more traditional modes of communication. For instance, informants have professional circles on LinkedIn and these professional circles include social networks of software developers, engineers and IT specialists. These social networks are referred to as a job opportunity networks. These social networks employ the social media platform to monitor the job opportunities and career opportunities that may be accessed through the network and platform.

In the case of our informants, various social networks are accessed through social media platforms. The social media platform affords them the *observational capability* to peek into their social networks. Facebook is a platform through which interviewees observe the network at a distance and subsequently take direct communicative action. On the other hand, colleague-based social networks are within the LinkedIn social media platform. The informants for this vignette belong to social networks that employ social media technologies such as Facebook and LinkedIn.

Vignette 4: Social media is an Emerging Social Infrastructure

Social networks are diverse, fluid, geographically dispersed and are continually added to with new individuals. Fluid social networks are only one type of social network; social networks may also be highly stable and static. Static and stable social networks are typically family, extended family and high and secondary school networks.

The social networks described by our informants employ social media platforms to observe their networks but rely on traditional modes of communication for in-depth communication and coordination. However, specific networks encourage peripheral members of the network to communicate on social media platforms. While some networks treat Facebook as an observational platform they are aware of the need to engage further with their social network through the use of these platforms. They are aware of the increasing number of "friends" on these platforms and the need to interact with them. The social media platforms are an emergent social infrastructure for social networks in which they need to participate to potentially leverage their connections. For instance, the colleague social circle on LinkedIn is one that recognizes that such platforms provide access to a broad range of social networks that may be leveraged.

Social networks also use the social media platform to maintain relational continuance. Relational continuance in the network is important for participation in projects. For example, maintaining weak ties and awareness of the social network allows the network to function after the study abroad programs come to a close. In addition to maintaining relational continuance through these platforms, image projection on these platforms is also vital in maintaining certain social networks. The social network's continued engagement with the medium suggests that it recognizes the resources that are available through the social infrastructure embedded in these social media platforms.

5   Analysis and Discussion

The vignettes presented by the interviewees may be analyzed from two separate but complementary perspectives i.e. that of individual use and that of network-based adoption.

Our informants were quite capable of differentiating between the social media platforms they used and the social networks that they belonged to. They were also able to clearly articulate the adoption rationale, general use, benefits and barriers on behalf of the social network in their search for a suitable social media platform. We find in our research that the information and communication technologies adopted and used by individuals in the network in some instances were subsumed by the greater wishes of the social network. This is an interesting phenomenon where a higher level entity (the social network) is created by lower level entities (individuals and their relations), yet the higher level entity cannot be reduced to its parts (Andersen et al. 2000). Furthermore the higher-level entity has a direct causal effect on the lower level parts´ behavior that created the higher-level entity in the first place, which is called *downward causation*. Here is means that the social network which is itself the result of many individuals and their mutual relations, exercises behavioral constraints on the very same individuals that constitute it.

The vignettes for social media as a communication and coordination medium and as a relational continuance device illustrate that the social network of the individual dictates adoption. This social network may be real or imagined on the part of the individual. Thus individuals that employ social media for these purposes employ the functional characteristics (Kietzmann, Hermkens, McCarthy, & Silvestre, 2011) of conversation, groups, sharing and relationships to maintain and establish connections to their social networks. Vignette 1 illustrates this point as the grouping and conversation functionality of the Facebook social media technology was employed to participate in the social network of a high school camp. However vignette 1 also illustrates the individual use of the social media platform to establish and maintain presence on social media platforms. This presence can take many forms including the formation and maintenance of identities through the use of profiles or the monitoring of other identities and profiles. Consequently, the individual use of the social media platform takes place within the process of coordination within the social media platform.

Individual interviewees stated at several instances their conflicting use of social media vis-à-vis their adoption behavior. The quotes illustrate the manner in which individual use of the platform may not correspond with characteristics that the platform has despite these very characteristics driving adoption behavior.

> *"You have friends you want to talk to and you have friends you don't want to talk to"....Udi*

> *"I'm using Facebook to be social and show my life, there are some people I don't care for looking at my photos, so, I have been deleting a lot of friends"....Jannik*

Vignette 2 describes the unique role that social media platforms play in maintaining social networks. These social networks are a result of dynamic and static ties between individuals but become a phenomenon of its own right. Naturally individuals belong to many such networks, some of which are very stable and established, and some of which are dynamic and much more fluid. Living in a digitalized age, digital natives employ information and communication technologies to establish, maintain and develop these social networks with social media being the most recent and principal of these technologies. As a relational continuance device the interviewees employed the relationship functional characteristic of the technology to create and maintain ties to other individuals within their social network. However their adoption and use of the social media platform was conditioned based on the existence of the social network on the platform.

However, the relationship continuance based on participation within social networks is moderated by the types of participants with whom individuals wish to interact. Individual use of the social media platform is moderated by the ease within which relationships are formed within the platforms. As the quotes illustrate, individuals condition their use based on the adoption by large parts of the network.

> " I don't use Facebook for my buddies, I use Facebook for my friends...."...Shu

> "Kammarat..its like a pal rather than a friend, a casual acquaintance. That's the word I use for people I just ignore and on Facebook I have a 300 (air quotes) "friends" but I don't want them to see what I am sharing with friends"...Shu

Vignette 3 illustrates the role of social media as observational platforms for dynamic social networks. Social media platforms serve as an observational platform where the individual can observe the changing nature of relationships and the formation of new ones through the use of the social media platform. As a communication and coordination medium, social media platforms offer the individual transparency. Communication in the social network on social media platforms is transparent to the entire global network. The boundaries of the network are porous and the addition of new members to the network may also be actively encouraged.

While individuals may adopt social media as an observation platform, the use of the media as such a platform does not necessarily imply they employ other communicative characteristics of the platform. Interviewees describe the use of the platform as observational and then the use of other media modes as a way to communicate and coordinate.

> "I use Facebook for pictures mainly, vacation pictures, party pictures, videos, YouTube videos. I don't post on Facebook. I generally post once or twice a month." "I don't talk to them on Facebook. I use it to see what is going on and then send them an e-mail."....Casper

> "I prefer the use of closed forums."....Khaled

Vignette 4 describes the social media platform as an emerging social infrastructure for the informal social networks. Relations are significantly altered when moved into the social media platform. On this platform, social networks participate by exposing some of the private into the public and as such expose the social networks to each other. One manner in which to manage this would be to maintain several social media platforms as infrastructure in which to manage networks. As we find, our informants' social networks do so by maintaining several networks in the social media platform, or by having more than one social media platforms as a basis for their social networks.

However individual use of the platform is constrained by the exposure the networks have to one another. Several interviewees exhibited concern that their relatives, family and other networks may get to see their behavior and participation with friends in other settings. Specifically individuals who employed the platform to communicate and interact with several social networks reflected this concern. Despite the adoption of the platform to maintain a social infrastructure by individuals, this participation constrained their individual use of the platform by constraining their use of characteristics and features.

6   Conclusions

In this paper we specifically examine the tension between individual use and network-based adoption of social media platforms. The social network is an emergent entity of many individuals and their relations, yet it cannot be reduced to its constituent parts. Adoption perspectives on social media discuss the role that network effects and network behavior have on the adoption of the technology by the individual. The network lens drives us towards examining relations and relational structures that comprise groups and social networks. Consequently adoption behavior of individuals within social media platforms follows related network structures and relationships. However the adoption of a social media platform by an individual due to network behaviors constrains the use of the platform by the same individuals. These tensions have been referred to as socially mediated publicness (Baym et al. 2012) where collapsing contexts requires differing strategies on parts of individuals. We attempt to explore these strategies on the part of individuals and to explore how individuals manage or attempt to manage identities, relationships, and information in such social media platforms. While some individuals display behaviors of closing down communication and coordination on these platforms due to concerns of visibility (Marwick et al. 2012) others may choose strategies that are more suited to their concerns. Such strategies may take many forms that use affordances and characteristics of the technology to engage in posturing, power aggrandizement and reputation management (Lim et al. 2012). As the vignettes illustrate, the adoption of social media platforms have several facets, but each vignette illustrates the Janus-faced nature of the platform.

Vignette 1 illustrates the adoption of the technology as a communication and coordination medium but its affordances simultaneously constrain its use. Vignette 2 illustrates the adoption of the platform to maintain relationships but the use of the technology by individuals creates numerous relationships that are hard to distinguish and necessitate corrective behaviors in the part of individuals. Vignette 3 illustrates use of social media as an observational platform; however, the very act of observation is an act of communication that individuals are not comfortable with. And finally Vignette 4 illustrates the use of the platform as emerging social infrastructure; however, their use in such a form implies exposure of networks to one another.

The challenges of examining social media platforms with such an approach is that it requires researchers to focus on two fundamentally related processes, i.e. adoption and use. The primary question that emerges from the examination of this tension is; *how do individuals make sense of conflicting goals within the adoption and use of social media platforms?* While previous research may have examined social media adoption through individualistic lenses, they have included certain social network components in their analysis. Our focus has been to examine the individual use of the platform within the context of network-based adoption. We find that the tension between network-based adoption by individuals and individual use, points to interesting dynamics within the adoption and use of social media and the understanding of such dynamics may aid in understanding the success and failures of such technologies.

References

Ajzen, I.: From intentions to actions: A theory of planned behavior. Action-control: From Cognition to Behavior (11), 39 (1985)

Andersen, P.B., Emmeche, C., Finnemann, N.O.: Downward Causation: Minds, bodies and matter. Aarhus University Press (2000)

Arnold, M.: On the phenomenology of technology: the "Janus-faces" of mobile phones. Information and Organization 13(4), 231–256 (2003)

Attewell, P.: Technology diffusion and organizational learning: The case of business computing. Organization Science 3(1), 1–19 (1991)

Avital, M., Te'eni, D.: From generative fit to generative capacity: exploring an emerging dimension of information systems design and task performance. Information Systems Journal 19(4), 345–367 (2009)

Bagozzi, R.P.: The legacy of the technology acceptance model and a proposal for a paradigm shift. Journal of the Association for Information Systems 8(4), 244–254 (2007)

Bala, H., Venkatesh, V.: Assimilation of interorganizational business process standards. Information Systems Research 18(3), 340 (2007)

Baym, N.K., Boyd, D.: Socially Mediated Publicness: An Introduction. Journal of Broadcasting & Electronic Media 56(3), 320–329 (2012)

Benbasat, I., Barki, H.: Quo vadis, TAM. Journal of the Association for Information Systems 8(4), 211–218 (2007)

Bhattacherjee, A.: Understanding information systems continuance: An expectation-confirmation model. MIS Quarterly 25(3), 351–370 (2001)

Boyd, D.M.: None of this is Real: Identity and Participation in Friendster. In: Karaganis, J. (ed.) Structures of Participation in Digital Culture, Social Science Research Council, United States of America (2007)

Davis, F.D.: Perceived usefulness, perceived ease of use, and user acceptance of information technology. MIS Quarterly 13(3), 319–340 (1989)

Davis, F.D., Bagozzi, R.P., Warshaw, P.R.: User acceptance of computer technology: A comparison of two theoretical models. Management Science 35(8), 982–1003 (1989)

Dishaw, M.T., Strong, D.M.: Extending the technology acceptance model with task-technology fit constructs. Information & Management 36(1), 9–21 (1999)

Dutta, S.: What's Your Personal Social Media Strategy? Harvard Business Review 88(11), 127–130 (2010)

Fishbein, M., Ajzen, I.: Belief, attitude, intention, and behavior: An introduction to theory and research. Addison-Wesley, Reading (1975)

Gefen, D., Straub, D.W.: Gender differences in the perception and use of e-mail: An extension to the technology acceptance model. MIS Quarterly 21(4), 389–400 (1997)

Granovetter, M.S.: The Strength of Weak Ties. The American Journal of Sociology 78(6), 1360–1380 (1973)

Hanna, R., Rohm, A., Cittenden, V.L.: We're all connected: The power of the social media ecosystem. Business Horizons (54), 265–273 (2011)

Hester, A.: Innovating with organizational wikis: factors facilitating adoption and diffusion of an effective collaborative knowledge management system, pp. 161–163. ACM (2008)

Hester, A.J., Scott, J.E.: A conceptual model of wiki technology diffusion, p. 32. IEEE Computer Society (2008)

Hsu, C.L., Lu, H.P.: Why do people play on-line games? An extended TAM with social influences and flow experience. Information & Management 41(7), 853–868 (2004)

Iacovou, C.L., Benbasat, I., Dexter, A.S.: Electronic data interchange and small organizations: Adoption and impact of technology. MIS Quarterly, 465–485 (1995)

Jarvenpaa, S.L., Staples, D.S.: The use of collaborative electronic media for information sharing: an exploratory study of determinants. The Journal of Strategic Information Systems 9(2), 129–154 (2000)

Jones, B., Temperley, J., Lima, A.: Corporate reputation in the era of Web 2.0: the case of Primark. Journal of Marketing Management 25(9), 927–939 (2009)

Kietzmann, J.H., Hermkens, K., McCarthy, I.P., Silvestre, B.S.: Social media? Get serious! Understanding the functional building blocks of social media. Business Horizons (2011)

Kraut, R., Rice, R., Cool, C., Fish, R.: Varieties of Social Influence: The Role of Utility and Norms in the Success of a New Communication Medium. Organization Science 9(4), 437–453 (1998)

Lee, A.S.: A scientific methodology for MIS case studies. MIS Quarterly 13(1), 33–50 (1989)

Lim, S.S., Vadrevu, S., Chan, Y.H., Basnyat, I.: Facework on Facebook: The Online Publicness of Juvenile Delinquents and Youths-at-Risk. Journal of Broadcasting & Electronic Media 56(3), 346–361 (2012)

Limayem, M., Hirt, S.G.: Force of habit and information systems usage: Theory and initial validation. Journal of the Association for Information Systems 4, 65–97 (2003)

Lin, H.F.: Interorganizational and organizational determinants of planning effectiveness for Internet-based interorganizational systems. Information & Management 43(4), 423–433 (2006)

Lyytinen, K., Damsgaard, J.: What's wrong with the diffusion of innovation theory. In: Proceedings of the IFIP TC8 WG8 (1), pp. 173–190 (2001a)

Lyytinen, K., Damsgaard, J.: What's wrong with the diffusion of innovation theory? Diffusing Software Products and Process Innovations, 173–190 (2001b)

Lyytinen, K., Damsgaard, J.: Inter-organizational information systems adoption - a configuration analysis approach. European Journal of Information Systems 18(1) (2011)

Mahler, A., Rogers, E.M.: The diffusion of interactive communication innovations and the critical mass: the adoption of telecommunications services by German banks. Telecommunications Policy 23(10-11), 719–740 (1999)

Malhotra, Y., Galletta, D.F.: Extending the technology acceptance model to account for social influence: theoretical bases and empirical validation, p. 14. IEEE (2002)

Markus, M.L.: Toward a "critical mass" theory of interactive media. Communication Research 14(5), 491 (1987)

Marwick, A., Ellison, N.B.: There Isn't Wifi in Heaven!" Negotiating Visibility on Facebook Memorial Pages. Journal of Broadcasting & Electronic Media 56(3), 378–400 (2012)

McFarlan, F.W., McKenney, J.L., Pyburn, P.: The information archipelago–plotting a course. Harvard Business Review 61(1), 145

Melville, N., Ramirez, R.: Information technology innovation diffusion: an information requirements paradigm. Information Systems Journal 18(3), 247–273 (2008)

Moore, G.C., Benhasat, I.: Development of an instrument to measure the perceptions of adopting an information technology innovation. Information Systems Research 2(3), 192–221 (1991)

Mustonen-Ollila, E., Lyytinen, K.: Why organizations adopt information system process innovations: a longitudinal study using Diffusion of Innovation theory. Information Systems Journal 13(3), 275–297 (2003)

O'Reilly, T.: What is web 2.0. Design patterns and business models for the next generation of software (30), 2005 (2005)

Parameswaran, M., Whinston, A.B.: Research issues in social computing. Journal of the Association for Information Systems 8(6), 336–350 (2007)

Peddibhotla, N.B., Subramani, M.R.: Contributing to public document repositories: A critical mass theory perspective. Organization Studies 28(3), 327 (2007)

Peng, G.: Critical Mass, Diffusion Channels, and Digital Divide. Journal of Computer Information Systems, 63–71 (2010)

Rogers, E.M.: Diffusion of innovations. Free Press (1995)

Salancik, G., Pfeffer, J.: A Social Information Processing Approach to Job Attitudes and Task Design. Administrative Science Quarterly 23(2), 224–253 (1978)

Sarker, S., Valacich, J.S.: Technology adoption by groups: A valence perspective. Journal of the Association for Information Systems 6(2), 37–71 (2005)

Sarker, S., Valacich, J.S.: An Alternative to Methodological Individualism: A Non-Reductionist Approach to Studying Technoogy Adoption by Groups. MIS Quarterly 34(4), 779–808 (2010)

Scott, S.V., Orlikowski, W.J.: 'Getting the truth': exploring the material grounds of institutional dynamics in social media (2009)

Sledgianowski, D., Kulviwat, S.: Using social network sites: the effects of playfulness, critical mass and trust in a hedonic context. Journal of Computer Information Systems 49(4), 74–83 (2009)

Straub, D., Keil, M., Brenner, W.: Testing the technology acceptance model across cultures: A three country study. Information & Management 33(1), 1–11 (1997)

Tufekci, Z.: Grooming, Gossip, Facebook and MySpace. Information, Communication & Society 11(4), 544–564 (2008)

Vannoy, S.A., Palvia, P.: The social influence model of technology adoption. Communications of the ACM 53(6), 149–153 (2010)

Venkatesh, V., Davis, F.D., Morris, M.G.: Dead or alive? The development, trajectory and future of technology adoption research. Journal of the Association for Information Systems 8(4), 267–286 (2007)

Venkatesh, V., Morris, M.G., Davis, G.B., Davis, F.D., DeLone, W.H., McLean, E.R., Jarvis, C.B., MacKenzie, S.B., Podsakoff, P.M., Chin, W.W.: User acceptance of information technology: Toward a unified view. Information & Management 27(3), 425–478 (2003)

Yin, R.: Case Study Research: Design and Methods. Sage Publications, London (1989)

Discursive Co-development
of Agile Systems and Agile Methods

Richard Baskerville[1] and Jan Pries-Heje[2]

[1] Georgia State University, USA
Baskerville@acm.org
[2] Roskilde University, Denmark
janph@ruc.dk

Abstract. Agile methods continue their growth in popularity. This spreading usage increases the need for adapting agile approaches to specific organizations. Hence, we investigate how system developers engage in the evolution of both agile systems and agile methods in practice. We study adaptation of the agile method *Scrum* in six organizations. Based on this study we design a framework explaining how agile methods, and in particular Scrum, are constantly articulated and re-articulated when diffused in practice. This framework includes a two-by-two dimensional grouping that includes three classes of fragments: Objects, Organization, and Process. The fourth class involves a discursive articulation that occurs on the same logical plane as the fragments. Unlike method engineering, the discourse is an inseparable part of the methodology itself, not a separate "meta" method.

Keywords: Agile Methods; Discourse; Adaptation of Methods; Technological Rules; Scrum.

1   Introduction

Agile development approaches assume continuous method evolution, but sometimes offer little guidance how to go about managing this evolution. There is considerable work on the construction of information systems development methods, but this work largely has an engineering orientation of most value to plan-based development. There is a need for more work specifically on the alternatives to such engineering approaches for developing and redeveloping agile methods on the fly. Agile methods involve frequent, fast, and continuous change. On-the-fly redevelopment of agile methods also involves frequent, fast, and continuous change. The research reported here indicates that such evolution of agile methods involves the engagement of a discursive mode of method development.

Our research question regards "How do system developers over time engage in the evolution of both agile systems and agile methods in practice?" The research reported below indicates the presence of a co-development discourse within which both the methodologies and the systems that the methodologies create are evolving.

Y.K. Dwivedi et al. (Eds.): TDIT 2013, IFIP AICT 402, pp. 279–294, 2013.

This methodological evolution progresses through a process of fragmentation, articulation, and re-articulation continuously throughout a software development project.

2   Agile Development Methods

Agile information systems development has been adopted successfully by practitioners partly or completely replacing more linear or plan-driven approaches. Agile is a success in systems development, and acknowledged as such by both the practitioner and researcher community [1]. Agile IS development can be defined either as an approach focusing on delivering something useful at high speed [2] or as an approach that can adapt to a continuously changing target or requirements [3]. Agile development is organized as iterations, repeating the same activities in short cycles [4]. In 2001 the agile manifesto provided a statement of values and principles (agilemanifesto.org) that has spawned many agile methods. Conboy [3] defined agility as the intersection of speed, change, learning, and customer value. He used these characteristics to propose a taxonomy and an instrument for assessing the agility of a particular practice. This assessment operated across agile, plan-driven, or in-house methods. The agility of a methodology is: "the continual readiness of an ISD method to rapidly or inherently create change, proactively or reactively embrace change, and learn from change while contributing to perceived customer value (economy, quality, and simplicity), through its collective components and relationships with its environment" [3, p. 340].

2.1   Scrum

Our cases below use Scrum, a frequent example of agile methodology. Scrum originated as The Rugby Approach [5]. This approach used small cross-functional teams produce better results. The Rugby theme arose from concepts like "Scrum" and "Sprint" that referred to the game to describe how work was carried out by a team in this approach. We have read and categorized literature on Scrum [6]. As a result we identified four objects (abbreviated "OB"), three types of organization (abbreviated "OR"), and five types of process (abbreviated "PR").

Scrum is iterative as with other agile approaches to IS development. The iteration in Scrum is called a Sprint. Work is organized in short iterations no more than 2-4 weeks long (PR-1). The team is a self-organizing team of equals (OR-1) The user or customer is deeply integrated in the development and has representation through the Product Owner role (OR-2). This role is defined as a user or customer with power and ability to make decisions. The Product Owner defines the desired functionality in a new IT system and originates it as a User Story (OB-1). The Product Owner then prioritizes User Stories in a Product Backlog (OB-2). The functionality from a User Story with the highest priority is broken down into tasks in a Sprint Planning Meeting (PR-2) on the first day of a Sprint. This breakdown of User Stories into tasks is a collaborative effort involving the participation of the project team as well as the Product Owner. Planning Poker (PR2.1) is a mechanism for ensuring the right level of breakdown. All participants estimate the tasks using a number of pre-defined esti-mates. The allowable estimates are "Less than one day for one developer", "One day", "Two days", "Three days", and "Too big". If the group agrees a task is "Too big" then the task needs to be broken down further. If the group agrees on "Less than one day for one developer" then the task needs to be merged with another task.

The Sprint continues after the planning meeting. Each day the project team meets in a Daily Stand-up Meeting (PR-3) that takes place in front of a Scrum Board (OB-3). A Scrum Master (OR-3) is responsible for the meeting, which should take no more than 15 minutes. In the meeting, each team member chooses one or more of the tasks. During the meeting every team member answers three standardised questions. (1) What did you do yesterday? (2) What are you doing today? (3) What problems did you encounter?

The Scrum Board (OB-3) is usually a whiteboard with four columns. The columns are titled "Ready", "In-progress", "Done", and "Done-Done". *Ready* details the task breakdown and Planning Poker estimates. *In-Progress* indicates tasks that a team member has chosen the task and work is underway. Upon task completion, this team member moves moved the task to *Done*. After this, a different team member may quality-assure the task, and afterwards the task moves to *Done-Done*. After this, the task is registered on a Burn-Down Chart (OB-4) that depicts "expected" versus "real-ized" production.

During the Daily Stand-up meeting (PR-3) team members record their answers to the first two of the three standardised questions by moving tasks from column to col-umn on the Scrum Board. For example the answer to, "What did you do yesterday?" could move a task from *In-Progress* to *Done*. The answer to, "What are you doing today?" can move a task from *Ready* to *In-Progress*. Team members usually write their names on the card associated with the task card as a self-commitment made ap-parent through the Scrum Board.

After the Sprint iteration completes, the product is demonstrated to the Product Owner in a Sprint Review Meeting (PR-4). First, the Product Owner reflects on the value of the deliverable. Second, the team conducts a learning Retrospective (PR-5). In this retrospective, the team considers what succeeded and failed in the Sprint. Fi-nally, the team determines one or two changes to implement or at least pursue in the next Sprint.

3 Research Method

The research reported in this paper operated from a staged research design (two stages). The first stage involved a multiple case study with six cases. Originally the cases were chosen to study the diffusion and adoption of Scrum. But an early finding of the studies was that all the case companies had evolved agile methods. Hence the focus in this paper is to develop a framework that helps explain how developers evolve agile methods during projects. We chose six cases in order to build a *replication logic* for contrasting results across the cases [7]. The specific agile methodology was held constant (Scrum) to reduce the ontological noise that would arise from differing perspectives of alternative agile methods. The different cases were selected to provide diversity in organizations using a common agile approach. Thereby the replication logic captures shifts in a more cohesive agility viewpoint across diverse settings. Table 1 provides details of the six organizations represented in our cases. The second stage created an evaluation engagement in which 25 practicing software developers received an orientation to the framework and were given the opportunity to evaluate its use in appraising the agile method adaptation processes in their own organizations.

Table 1. The six companies studied. Pseudonym names used to preserve anonymity.

Name (Pseudonym)	Characteristics	Roles and Number of Subjects
GlobeRiver	Develops engineering products. 500 employees in R&D function world-wide when interviewed	3 people interviewed: Danish and Indian Scrum master, and Danish Facilitator
SuperSystem	Develops software for the military, the banking industry, hospitals, etc. Approx. 400 employees when interviewed.	4 people interviewed: a Lead developer, a Scrum master, manager, and person in charge of implementing Scrum
DareYou	An off- and online gaming company; works with several suppliers located in different places	2 people interviewed: The Project manager and the Product owner.
ShipSoft	A software house producing software for international production. 150 employees	20 people interviewed. Observation over three periods of time including full week
PubliContract	Public organization that contracted a private software house.	All people in Scrum team interviewed. Three product owners interviewed.
InterFin	International financial organization with IT development in Europe and India.	Scrum team followed for a full project (one year in length). Scrum in Europe and India.

In the six stage-one-cases we collected data using techniques appropriate for each setting. For example, the Interfin case involved interviews and observation, both in India and Europe, over the course of the project. In general, analytic induction (inductive reasoning about a social phenomenon) was used for data analysis [8]. This approach involved inducing concepts, so-called "social laws", from a deep analysis of empirically isolated instances [9]. The research question drove this analytic inductive reasoning. It was an analytical process whereby data was coded when found in the six cases and when it was related to the diffusion and evolution of agile methods [10]. The analysis revealed that the phenomena in the case could be classified as either objects or organization. An alternative classification also surfaced in which the phenomena could be classified as either static concepts/processes, or as elements that were dynamic and ever changing. There were 12 concepts in this classification scheme that were labeled method fragments (a term adopted from the method engineering literature). In concert with the analytic induction, we followed an interrogatory data analysis process described by Pascale [11]. In our implementation, the interrogatives included, "Under what contexts does this adaptation of Scrum arise?" "Under what circumstances may we find exceptions to this general adaptation rule?" The results were coded as technological rules [12].

4   Fragmentation and Articulation

Agile development meets the need for systems development where a setting is subjected to continual change. Planned methodologies (which invoke mechanistic organization) are less suitable in such settings. But agile approaches (which involve organic organization) fit such settings well [13]. Agile methodologies, like other kinds of methodologies share certain general characteristics. Methodologies are organized collections of concepts, beliefs, values, and normative principles that are supported by material resources [14]. Methodologies often adopt a particular perspective intended for a particular application domain involving particular prerequisites and activities. Because methodologies are rarely used in the exact way described [15, 16], method fragments become cobbled together with novel elements that comprise a situated methodology unique to its setting. For example, in agile development often embodies an ad-hoc mix of fragments intuitively assembled from Scrum, XP, etc, [17].

A method fragment is a concept, notation, tool, technique, etc. that has been coherently separated from the overall methodology. It is lifted from its original methodological framework and used in a different one. The use of "method fragments" or "method chunks" is a central principle in method engineering [18]. These method fragments can have varying levels of abstraction and granularity [19]. Method fragments are a concept best known within the frameworks and processes of method engineering. Such frameworks engineer IS development methods by assembling them from an inventory of components: methodologies, method fragments, and innovations [20]. Computer-based method engineering uses formal models to enable the rapid development of computer-aided systems analysis and software engineering (CASA/CASE) tools that provide a unique methodology for each unique development settings [21].

This discourse involving organizations, settings, developers, and their method fragments should not be mistaken for the several variations of agile engineering and agile method engineering. Such variations include obtaining feedback from users of the subject methods, or method engineering of agile methods [22], or meta-meta-method engineering or the representation of agile ways to semantically capture the domain knowledge [23]. A key discovery found in our data is the participation of the fragments themselves (along with developers, settings, etc.) in the process. Because of its discursive character, *articulation* engenders an emergent form of methodology evolution that subsumes its complexity into a holistic and reflective social discourse. It does not deal with complexity through reduction, as an engineering approach might, but rather approaches it as a conversation between people, their problems, and their tools.

Method engineering provides a strategy for method adaptation. Situated method engineering is a strategy for continual integration of fragments such that methods can adapt as developers learn about their changing environment [24]. This work has also been used as an approach to software process improvement for agile methods and for object-oriented methods [25]. One objective has been the rational transformation of unique methodologies using fragment assemblies [26]. The approach provides a form of meta-method for configuring off-the-shelf methods componentization [27].

Our agile cases seemed to choose a mode of fragmentation and articulation that differed from the method engineering mode. They used a discursive perspective instead of an analytical design perspective. These were evolving agile methodologies as a discourse shared between organizations, settings, developers, and their method fragments. Fragmentation is retained because it is common beyond engineering. Method fragmentation is found in business process management [28], security method adaptation [29], self-organizing systems [30], requirements traceability [31], and for requirements elicitation [32]. Articulation has a discursive character that subsumes complexity into a holistic and reflective social discourse. Unlike an engineering approach that uses reduction to eliminate complexity, it approaches adaptation as a conversation between people, their problems, and their tools.

5   Co-developing Systems and Methods

The process of co-development in the cases above can be expressed in terms of method fragments, technological rules, and articulation. We analyzed the major method fragments in the Scrum cases seeking an understanding of how these fragments were adopted or adapted in the cases. This analysis revealed two central dimensions that characterized the fragments.

5.1   Dimensions of Agile Method Fragmentation

As discussed above, the analysis provided two central dimensions in the fragmentation and articulation of evolving agile methodology. One dimension distinguishes static fragmentation versus dynamic fragmentation as distinguishing characteristics of the fragments. This was more of a criteria for articulation or re-articulation of the method   than it was a factor of the criteria for fragment use [33]. Static fragments are often used or reused without changing the fragment internally. Dynamic fragments are often used or reused only after internal modifications or adaptations. These dynamic fragments were often themselves re-articulated in innovative ways. Dynamic fragments required internal changes before the next re-use in the method.

The second dimension distinguished actor fragments versus artifact fragments. In actor fragments, human autonomy was somehow featured in the fragment. Actor fragments tended to be loosely articulated; imbued with a permissive spirit giving people the latitude to re-arrange their behaviors during the development project. In contrast, artifact fragments suppressed human autonomy; imbued with a restrictive spirit that limited changes in individual behavior during the project.   Together, these two dimensions define four classes of fragments: Process, Objects, Organization, and Articulation.   See Figure 1. Each of these classes is described below.

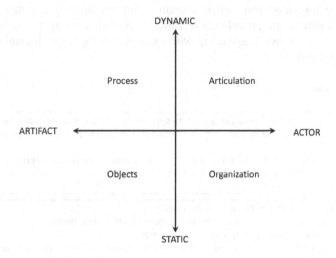

Fig. 1. Dimensions of agile fragmentation and reassembly

6   Scrum Fragment Technological Rules

For the purpose of expressing the method fragments in Scrum, we adopt the notion of technological rules.   Van Aken's design rules operate in the following manner. In a management vision of design science, there are two possible outputs: artefacts or interventions, and there may be three kinds of design in a professional episode: The object-design defines the artefact or intervention. The realization-design is the plan for implementing the artefact or intervention. The process-design is the plan for the design process itself. In this sense designing is similar to developing prescriptive knowledge. Van Aken suggests expressing a design in the form of technological rules: 'A technological rule follows the logic of "if you want to achieve Y in situation Z, then perform action X". The core of the rule is this X, a general solution concept for a type of field problem' [12, p. 23]. Van Aken emphasises that technological rules need grounding [12, p. 25]: 'Without grounding, the use of technological rules degenerates to mere "instrumentalism", that is, to a working with theoretically ungrounded rules of thumb'. The rules need to be grounded in a way acceptable from a social science perspective.

Based on our analysis of the six cases we were able to formulate the following technological rules for the specific parts of Scrum.   In each rule, we note the way in which each rule is empirically grounded in the data collected and the analysis and coding of data from the six cases.   Note that the version presented below is the refined version that resulted from an evaluation described later in this paper.

6.1   Objects

Object fragments are Static Artifacts. This means they are frequently used for (re)assembly in new variants of situated Scrum without changing (re-articulating) the fragment. These fragments marginalize human autonomy in the sense that these involve structures that do not provide much variance according to the individual actors in the setting. These are listed here along with examples of the technological rules that inhabit each fragment.

Object: User Stories

> OB-1: If you want to express requirements for new systems in a simple user-oriented form that is easier to communicate to and with end users than "classic" rigorous requirements (e.g. following the IEEE standard)
> - In a situation where you are considering the use of agile methods; specifically Scrum
> - - then write User Stories on index cards in your projects
> *Grounding: Used at SuperSystem*

> OB1.1: If you want to involve users more in projects
> - In a situation where you have decided to express requirements as user stories
> - - then let users write or participate in writing user stories
> *Grounding: In DareYou the customer had written the User Stories on how to play a specific game.*

Object: Product Backlog documentation

> OB-2: If you want to have a dynamic list of functionality where it is easy to add new or subtract "old" functions
> - In a situation where you are considering the use of agile methods; specifically Scrum
> - - then maintain a list called Product Backlog and let user update list dynamically and prioritize list regularly; i.e. before each sprint
> *Grounding: All companies maintained a product backlog list of wished-for functionality*

> OB2.1: If you need to have more documentation, e.g because it is required by law or regulation or because you need to maintain the resulting systems for years after
> - In a situation where you are considering the use of agile methods; specifically Scrum
> - - then you need to decide specifically what additional documentation is required
> *Grounding: Avoiding unnecessary documentation is a general principle of agile methods. (Cf. the agile Manifesto)*

Object: Scrum Board

> OB-3: If you need a visible coordination mechanism for project teams where it is easy to progress and whether anyone in the team needs help or have problems finishing tasks assigned
> - In a situation where you are considering the use of agile methods; specifically Scrum
> - - then use a Scrum Board in your projects
> *Grounding: All cases except DareYou used a Scrum Board as a visible coordination mechanism*

> OB3.1: If Scrum-team is located in different locations
> - In a situation where you have decided to use the Scrum Board object
> - - then use an electronic Scrum Board that can be seen in all locations simultaneously. Possibly coupled with a video-link so people at all locations can see Scrum Board and each other at the same time
> *Grounding: GlobeRiver and ShipSoft did this with good results*

OB3.2: If Scrum-team needs to focus more on increased quality
- In a situation where you have decided to use the Scrum Board object
- - then consider assigning quality or tester role to person in the team and/or add a *Done Done* column to Scrum Board
Grounding: PubliContract and some projects in ShipSoft did this

Object: Burn-Down Chart

OB-4: If you want to have simple visible mechanism for follow-up in projects where it is possible in one glance (on the chart) to see how close or far you are from having achieved the work planned
- In a situation where you are considering the use of agile methods; specifically Scrum
- - then implement a Burn Down Chart in your projects
- Alternatively use more traditional follow-up techniques such as Earned Value
Grounding: ShipSoft had Burn-Down charts for every project. SuperSystem also maintained Burn-Down charts in every project

6.2   Organization

These fragments are Static Actors.   This means they are frequently used for (re)assembly without necessarily rearticulating the fragment itself. Roles such as Scrum Master and Product owner are common, and seldom changes.   Beyond this role, however, these fragments do privilege human autonomy in the sense that the actors have much latitude in how they enact this role. These organization fragments are listed along with the technological rules that inhabit each fragment.

Organization: Self-organizing team of equals

OR-1: If you have a team of experienced professionals, with more or less the same level of competence, in a culture where hierarchy is not desired
- In a situation where you are considering the use of agile methods; specifically Scrum
- - then consider organizing the team as a self-organizing teams of equals without a project manager to assign tasks
Grounding: InterFin showed that this may be hard in a culture with high power-distance (in the Hofstede sense)

OR1.1: If you want to want to use Scrum in a team where the team members have different (or very uneven) competences
- In a situation where you have decided to use self-organizing teams of equals
- - then you may need to assign specialist roles to different team members. You need to adapt the *process*-elements (PR-1 to PR-5) to allow for non-equals.; and you may consider having a traditional project manager
Grounding: InterFin had a test specialist in a Scrum team. SuperSystems also used specialist roles as part of their Scrum adaptation

Organization: Product Owner role

OR1.2: If you have a larger team than 8-10 people
- In a situation where you have decided to use self-organizing teams of equals
- - then you may organize a number of Scrum-teams each with a Scrum Master, and then the Scrum Masters can meet (daily) in a Scrum-of-Scrum
Grounding: We saw this done in both DareYou and InterFin with good results

OR-2: If you need a decision making ability in relation to all user- or functionality-oriented issues (e.g. to make firm decisions on what functionality is included and excluded)
- In a situation where you are considering the use of agile methods; specifically Scrum
- - then you should have a highly decisive customer take on the role as Product Owner
Grounding: DareYou for example had a manager from the customer site in the Product Owner role.

OR2.1: If you cannot assign the role of product owner to one person but have many stakeholders that want to be heard and to be part of the decision making
- In a situation where you need the decision making ability of the product owner
- - then organize a product owner forum and name a chief product owner who can make the final decision when disputing views arise among stakeholders
Grounding: Exactly the solution chosen in PubliContract where they see it as very beneficial and a way to preserve the effectiveness of the product owner role

OR2.2: If you want to have a product owner
- In a situation where you do not have access to customers (e.g. because you are doing product development)
- - then find a person with a good market understanding to fill the role as product owner
Grounding:SuperSystem, Globeriver, Interfin and ShipSoft were all doing this

Organization: Scrum Master role

OR-3: If you want to have a person specifically responsible for ensuring that agile process is followed
- In a situation where you are considering the use of agile methods; specifically Scrum, and you have decided to have a self-organizing team of equals (OR-1)
- - then have one person in each team take on the role as Scrum Master
- Alternatively just use existing Project Manager role
Grounding: Found as described in SuperSystem,

OR3.1: If you want to maintain *both* a Project Manager and a Scrum Master role *and* not enacted by same person
- In a situation where you have decided to have Scrum Master role enacted
- - then you need to negotiate responsibilities for the two roles and the interface between them
Grounding: PubliContract did exactly this. In DareYou the customer was also the project Manager. In InterFin the Project Manager was placed above two Scrum masters that each had a team of their own

6.3 Process

These fragments are Dynamic Artifacts. This means they are more often modified, adapted, and rearticulated as the method evolves. Nevertheless, these fragments do not afford much latitude to the individual actor in changing their behavior within the process. They are listed here along with examples of the technological rules that inhabit each fragment.

Process: Organize work in short iterations

PR-1: If you want to organize work in small iterations to deliver something of value *fast*
- In a situation where you are considering the use of agile methods; specifically Scrum
- - then use *Sprints*
Grounding: All six companies did this. The shortest iterations we saw were one week (ShipSoft). The longest was eight weeks

Process: Sprint Planning Meeting

PR-2: If you want to start the iteration with a planning meeting where work breakdown and estimation takes place
- In a situation where you are considering the use of agile methods; specifically Scrum
- - then have a one day Sprint Planning meeting on the first day of the iteration with the development team and the product owner present
Grounding: All six companies did this. In a few instances the product owner was not present which caused delays and indecisiveness due to the lack of needed information on what the user actually wanted

PR2.1: If you need estimates for tasks fast
- In a situation where you have decided to use agile method and Sprint Planning meetings
- - then use Planning Poker to come up with estimates
- Alternatively you can use any other estimation techniques
Grounding: Several companies used Planning Poker i.e. DareYou and ShipSoft

Process: Daily Stand-up Meeting

PR-3: If you have meetings in teams that take up too much time and you want to have shorter and more effective meetings without long discussions of the agenda and/or specific problems
- In a situation where you are considering the use of agile methods; specifically Scrum
- - then use daily stand-up meeting lasting no longer that 15 minutes and with a standard agenda: (1) What have you been doing? (2) What are you doing now? (3) Problems encountered?
Grounding: Five out of six companies did this. In one ShipSoft project they were even standing in front of PC screen when doing daily meeting between Denmark and India. In one project in InterFin they were not standing up for their daily meeting because they were in an open office environment where it bothered other projects when they were standing. And in DareYou the daily meeting was conducted on phone with same standardised agenda but sitting down

PR3.1: If you want to use short stand-up meetings
- In a situation where you do not have full-time resources (people)
- - then organise the stand-up meeting weekly, bi-weekly, every 2nd day or the like
Grounding: In GroundRiver they did not have meetings every day due to part-time resources. Instead they had a weekly meeting between the people working in India and the people from Europe (a project manager and a facilitator)

Process: Demo of value at the end

PR-4: If the functionality that is developed in a sprint can be put into production immediately and you want customers or end users to see what they are getting out of each sprint (e.g. because you know that is likely to increase their satisfaction with the development)
- In a situation where you are considering the use of agile methods; specifically Scrum
- - then demonstrate that you have developed something of value at the end of a sprint
Grounding: PubliContract and DareYou did this

PR4.1: If you want to adapt to an existing release schedule
- In a situation where you uses agile methods in combination with more traditional schedule
- - then demonstrate value but do not release
Grounding: InterFin did this to fit Scrum with traditional mainframe-oriented release plan every 3-4 months

Process: Retrospective at the end

PR-5: If you want to capture learning and put lessons learned into use quickly - In a situation where you are considering the use of agile methods; specifically Scrum - - then carry out a retrospective at the end of a sprint (iteration) *Grounding: All six companies had adopted adapted this practice*

7   Articulation

The articulation group is too poorly structured for expression using technological rules. The articulation of fragments is itself a fragment because it is the on-the-fly, discursive process where developers assemble the fragments into a working methodology. While similar to the method engineering notions of design rationale or design model, it was not a "meta" process or a "meta" design. In agile development, the discourse about the adaptation and evolution of the methodology is part of the normal development conversation. Articulation fragments were distinctly dynamic actors. Fragments in this group often specified criteria for articulation or re-articulation of the method. It was dynamic because the articulation fragments changed internally on each use in the method. Articulation fragments are actor fragments that privilege human autonomy. They allow people to adjust their future behaviors as the development project evolved.

A more complete framing of this method articulation is the theory nexus [34, 35]. A theory nexus encompasses the interaction between theories and designed artifacts. It helps frame the process that results when multiple theories overdetermine the design for an object that, in fact, represents a setting where the design outcome is at least partly the result of the use of the object. In our cases, the theories are embodied in the technological rules. Agile methodologies are designed and re-designed on-the-fly, in concert with the use of the methodology, creating a theory nexus as technological rules and fragments-in-use are combined, separated, and recombined. Within the theory nexus, a discourse is present. This discourse articulates and rearticulates the dynamic objects in the presence of the static objects. In the six cases, such discourse episodes were embodied by each Sprint. Only experience with the methodology can determine the exact effects of an evolving methodology in relation to underlying technological rules.

The nexus is a discourse, a complex conversation that extends across (1) a deductive view of the relationship between fragmentation and methodology, (2) a reciprocal relationship between the articulation and re-articulation of technological rules; and (3) the evolutionary iterations of methodological framing (Carroll and Kellogg 1989). A nexus binds method fragments with realities and shapes a momentary version of a methodology. This moment immediately initiates a new episode in the discourse (a Sprint in the cases). The fragments, the participants, the methodology, the setting, and the problem are engaged in this discourse. Each re-articulation of the methodology results in a new momentary version that necessarily precipitates a new episode (the next Sprint). These re-articulation episodes within the nexus persist throughout the life of an agile development project. There is not a methodology, but a succession of different methodologies that momentarily provide structure through regularities that are present only for unique episodes.

8   Evaluating the Co-development Framework

To evaluate the framework, we engaged with 25 software practitioners from mainly engineering-oriented companies, each of whom represented different software development companies and each with extensive experience from companies that had adapted Scrum or were considering doing so. After having been introduced to the framework and the technological rules they were asked to fill out a questionnaire with the purpose of improving the framework. Thirteen of the 25 participants decided voluntarily to participate. Six of the 13 could immediately use the framework to evaluate the Method-System Co-Development activities in their own organizations whereas the seven others reflected on past situations in which they adapted Scrum or imagine such a future situation. The results indicate that the framework was easy to learn and very helpful in their own practice. It was clear from the responses that there was substantial interest in further development of the framework for future use. Further the evaluation pointed to four things that have been changed in the version of the framework presented in this paper.

First, many of the technological rules were formulated too briefly (e.g., using a phrase such as "if you want to …"). For version 2 (presented above) we considerably elaborated the technological rules with a focus on the benefits to be achieved from adapting the object, organization or process.

Second, it was stated in the evaluation that the framework was "…not detailed enough for implementation. An example was the relationship between Scrum Master and Project Manager". For version 2 (above), we have added more details and we have made it clear that there are relationships between some of the fragments by adding a numbering system for easy reference and by adding references from fragments to other fragments. See for example "OR1.1" where the technological rule now includes a reference to "PR-1 to PR-5".

Third, it was pointed out that the technological rules on the product owner role were too rudimentary. It didn't include the "hard things" such as "product owner availability" and "what to do if the product owner was only interested in final results and not in partial results after each sprint?". To cope with this comment we added several statements to the technological rule on product owner (see OR-2 above).

Fourth, one evaluator pointed out that he did not believe in the "supermarket approach" that we were using and that he believed there was a minimum level of Scrum elements necessary to regard the approach as Scrum. Nevertheless, the six cases we originally analyzed clearly show that companies in practice do use a supermarket approach, taking some Scrum fragments into use and eschewing others. But our study of the six cases also showed that at least six-seven fragments of the 12 identified were taken into use in all six cases. This effect suggests that there is indeed a minimum of at least 50% of the fragments that are intuitively taken into use.

Finally, the evaluation confirmed that for none of the six companies had adapted Scrum as a one-shot event. They were all continuously adapting Scrum in a discursive process as we have presented in this paper.

9   Conclusion

Among the limitations in the work above, the approach used cases representing one instance of agile methodology (Scrum). While observationally consistent, it limits the confidence that the study findings will generalize across all agile methodologies. We also studied instances of Scrum projects, which limited observations of any longitudinal evolution from project-to-project.

The adaptation of agile methods is a special case of an adoption process where users purposefully adopt parts of the methodology and discard other parts. In this sense our study has implications for future studies of adoption in which a technology (such as a tool, method, or process) grows more adoptable by promoting its re-articulation through discursive usage.

The main contribution of this paper is the framework explaining how Agile methods, and in particular Scrum, are constantly articulated and re-articulated when diffused in practice. This framework includes a two dimensional groupings that include three classes of fragments: Objects, Organization, and Process. The fourth class involves a discursive articulation that occurs on the same logical plane as the fragments. Unlike method engineering, the discourse is an inseparable part of the methodology itself, not a separate "meta" method. Agile method adaptation is a functional part of routine development practice.

There is practical value in the nexus and the technological rules. They have a demonstrated prescriptive design value useful for many development managers employing agile methods.

References

Dybå, T., Dingsøyr, T.: Empirical studies of agile software development: A systematic review. Information & Software Technology 50(9-10), 833–859 (2008)

Ågerfalk, P.J., Fitzgerald, B., Slaughter, S.: State of the Art and Research Challenges. Information Systems Research 20(3), 317–318 (2009)

Conboy, K.: Agility from First Principles: Reconstructing the Concept of Agility in Information Systems Development. Information Systems Research 20(3), 329–354 (2009)

Austin, R.D., Devin, L.: Research Commentary–Weighing the Benefits and Costs of Flexibility in Making Software: Toward a Contingency Theory of the Determinants of Development Process Design. Information Systems Research 20(3), 462–477 (2009)

Takeuchi, H., Nonaka, I.: The New New Product Development Game. Harvard Business Review (January-February 1986)

Sutherland, J., Schwaber, K.: The Scrum Papers: Nut, Bolts, and Origins of an Agile Framework. SCRUM Training Institute (2010)

Yin, R.K.: Case Study Research: Design and Methods, 4th edn. Sage, Thousand Oaks (2008)

Ragin, C.C.: Constructing Social Research: The Unity and Diversity of Method. Pine Forge Press (1994)

Znaniecki, F.: The method of sociology. Farrar & Rinehart, New York (1934)

Miles, M.B., Huberman, A.M.: Qualitative Data Analysis: A Sourcebook of New Methods, 2nd edn. Sage, Newbury Park (1994)

Pascale, C.-M.: Cartographies of Knowledge: Exploring Qualitative Epistemologies. Sage (2010)

van Aken, J.E.: Management Research as a Design Science: Articulating the Research Products of Mode 2 Knowledge Production in Management. British Journal of Management 16(1), 19–36 (2005)

Burns, T., Stalker, G.M.: The Management of Innovation. Tavistock, London (1961)

Lyytinen, K.: A Taxanomic Perspective of Information Systems Development. Theoretical Constructs and Recommendations. In: Boland, R., Hirschheim, R. (eds.) Critical Issues in Information Systems Research. Wiley, New York (1987)

Bansler, J., Bødker, K.: A reappraisal of structured analysis: Design in an organizational context. ACM Transactions on Information Systems 11(2), 165–193 (1993)

Truex, D.P., Baskerville, R., Travis, J.: Amethodical Systems Development: The Deferred Meaning of Systems Development Methods. Accounting, Management and Information Technology 10(1), 53–79 (2000)

Chiniforooshan Esfahani, H., Yu, E., Cabot, J.: Situational Evaluation of Method Fragments: An Evidence-Based Goal-Oriented Approach. In: Pernici, B. (ed.) CAiSE 2010. LNCS, vol. 6051, pp. 424–438. Springer, Heidelberg (2010)

Rolland, C., Prakash, N.: A proposal for context-specific method engineering. In: Brinkkemper, S., Lyytinen, K., Welke, R. (eds.) Method Engineering: Principles of Method Construction and Support, pp. 191–208. Chapman & Hall, London (1996)

Tan, W.-K., Tan, C.-H.: Teaching Information Systems Development via Process Variants. Journal of Information Systems Education 21(2), 159–172 (2010)

Brinkkemper, S., Lyttinen, K., Welke, R. (eds.): Method Engineering. Chapman & Hall, London (1996)

Odell, J.J.: A primer to method engineering. In: Brinkkkemper, S., Lyytinen, K., Welke, R. (eds.) Method Engineering: Principles of Method Construction and Tool Support, pp. 1–7. Chapman & Hall, London (1996)

Schapiro, S.B., Henry, M.H.: Engineering agile systems through architectural modularity. In: IEEE International Systems Conference, SysCon (2012)

Berki, E.: Formal metamodelling and agile method engineering in metaCASE and CAME tool environments. In: Tigka, K., Kefalas, P. (eds.) Proceedings of The 1st South-East European Workshop on Formal Methods, pp. 170–188. SEERC, Thessaloniki (2004)

Van Slooten, K.: Situated method engineering. Information Resources Management Journal 9(3), 24–31 (1996)

Henderson-Sellers, B., Serour, M.K.: Creating a Dual-Agility Method: The Value of Method Engineering. Journal of Database Management 16(4), 1–23 (2005)

Karlsson, F., Wistrand, K.: Combining method engineering with activity theory: theoretical grounding of the method component concept. European Journal of Information Systems 15(1), 82–90 (2006)

Karlsson, F., Agerfalk, P.J.: Method configuration: adapting to situational characteristics while creating reusable assets. Information and Software Technology 46(9), 619–633 (2004)

Ravesteyn, P.: A Context Dependent Implementation Method for Business Process Management Systems. Communications of the IIMA 9(1), 31–45 (2009)

Low, G., Mouratidisb, H., Henderson-Sellers, B.: Using a Situational Method Engineering Approach to Identify Reusable Method Fragments from the Secure TROPOS Methodology. Journal of Object Technology 9(4), 91–125 (2010)

Puviani, M., et al.: A Method Fragments Approach to Methodologies for Engineering Self-Organizing Systems. ACM Transactions on Autonomous and Adaptive Systems 7(3), Article 33 (2012)

Domges, R., Pohl, K.: Adapting traceability environments to project-specific needs. Association for Computing Machinery. Communications of the ACM 41(12), 54–62 (1998)

Haumer, P., Pohl, K., Weidenhaupt, K.: Requirements elicitation and validation with real world scenes. IEEE Transactions on Software Engineering 24(12), 1036–1054 (1998)

Aydin, M.N., et al.: On the Adaptation of an Agile Information Systems Development Method. Journal of Database Management 16(4), 24–40 (2005)

Pries-Heje, J., Baskerville, R.: The design theory nexus. MIS Quarterly 32(4), 731–755 (2008)

Carroll, J.M., Kellogg, W.A.: Artifact as theory-nexus: hermeneutics meets theory-based design. In: CM SIGCHI Bulletin–Proceedings of the SIGCHI Conference on Human Factors in Computing Systems: Wings for the Mind, vol. 20(SI), pp. 7–14 (1989)

Is Agile the Answer? The Case of UK Universal Credit

Rosa Michaelson

School of Business, University of Dundee, Dundee, Scotland, UK
r.michaelson@dundee.ac.uk

Abstract. In 2010 the UK government responded to a catalogue of failing large-scale IT projects by cancelling most of them. In 2011 they announced the Universal Credit (UC) project, described as "the biggest single change to the system of benefits and tax credits since 1945, affecting some 6 million households and 19 million people". UC will integrate a number of legacy databases with the Real Time Information (RTI) system, administered by Her Majesty's Revenue and Customs (HMRC) and due to complete by October 2013. The coupling of these two large-scale IT projects will affect millions of UK citizens; it is crucial that both complete successfully and on time. Government has responded to criticisms by stating that the use of Agile methods will solve the failures of the past. This paper critically assesses the adoption of Agile methods for software development, project management and procurement in the case of Universal Credit.

Keywords: failure analysis, sociotechnical framework, Agile methods, large-scale systems.

1   Introduction

Whilst investigating wide-reaching UK Taxation problems which came to light in 2010 and 2011, research into the limitations of the UK Pay-As-You-Earn system were overtaken by events. Firstly, despite the problems of under and over payment of tax associated with the delays in this large-scale public sector project, an announcement was made that instead of continuing with year-end reconciliations of employee data, HMRC (Her Majesty's Revenue and Customs) was adopting a new system which would receive real-time information from employers throughout the year, on a monthly basis, so that tax collection was more frequent and employee tax status was kept up-to-date. What is more, this new system, known as RTI, was to be delivered in 18 months, a relatively short time-scale compared with the time for procurement and implementation associated with previous large-scale public sector IT projects. Within 6 months of this announcement, the basis and rationale for RTI was further expanded; the RTI system was now the enabling technology for a complete overhaul of the UK welfare system. The delivery of the simplified payment system of benefits called Universal Credit (UC) requires the integration of 6 separate legacy systems administered by the Department of Work and Pensions, and features data sharing with tax systems (administered by the separate government division of HMRC) via RTI.

Y.K. Dwivedi et al. (Eds.): TDIT 2013, IFIP AICT 402, pp. 295–309, 2013.
© IFIP International Federation for Information Processing 2013

The deadline for this ambitious change was originally planned within the timescale for RTI completion, with the stated aim of both RTI and UC being live in October 2013.

The Universal Credit project is a messy one, as are many of the large-scale public sector projects of the last 20 years - messy in the sense that Law applies to social science case studies (Law, 2007). Law uses a number of sociotechnical case studies which deploy ethnographic methods to illustrate a range of ways to deal with "what happens when social science tries to describe things that are complex, diffuse and messy" (Law, 2007). Here, I use a socio-technical framework in order to make sense of the many factors and viewpoints that influence a real world problem, that of the histories of inter-linked large-scale public sector IT projects. In this paper, I present what Geertz called "a thick description" of policy and practise with respect to the Universal Credit project, where the process of amassing data and writing the case study forms part of the analysis (Geertz, 1975). This is similar to Beynon-Davies' 'web-based analysis' of failure which focuses on the social and political contexts of software adoption as a way of improving our understanding of such examples (Beynon-Davies, 1999).

In 2010, the UK Coalition government responded to the legacy of disastrous public IT projects by cancelling most of them (DoH, 2010; NAOa, 2011; Tarr, 2012). Given this response, what makes government sure that the ambitious Universal Credit project will succeed? Their answer is a fundamental change in ICT development by the public sector, abandoning the overly bureaucratic processes of the past by adopting Agile methods for software development, project management and procurement (CO, 2011; 2012). This paper assesses to what extent Agile is the solution to the historical problems of large-scale public sector IT failure by examining the case of Universal Credit. The structure is as follows: firstly, Agile methods are briefly discussed, and recent changes in government attitudes to software project design, development and acquisition are noted; secondly, the story of the HMRC RTI project is presented, with a description of PAYE, the organisational context, the technologies and history; thirdly, I describe the case of Universal Credit with responses from several different interested parties. Finally, I discuss to what extent Agile methods can or will ensure the successful outcome the government expects.

2   Agile Methods and UK Government ICT Development

2.1   Agile Methods

Agile methods were originally defined by programmers and software developers in the Agile Manifesto of 2001. The focus of Agile development is on (i) individuals and interactions rather than processes and tools; (ii) the production of working software rather than extensive documentation; (iii) collaboration with the customer not contract negotiation; and (iv) responding to change rather than following a plan (Agile Manifesto, 2001). Further, the methods requires developers and clients to work together on a daily basis and insists that face-to-face interactions are vital. Thus Agile development applies to projects which are: modular, iterative, responsive to change, and in which the users' needs are central to the delivery. Such projects are characterised by not having a fixed or detailed knowledge of the final solution at initiation, but must have clear business objectives. Agile has been of recent interest to many in Computer Science and Information Systems fields, with caveats concerning what type of organisation and scale of IT project are suitable for such methods (Nerur, 2005; Denning, 2008). In fact, the roots of Agile can be found in earlier software engineering methods of the 60s which deploy iteration and incremental processes, and eschew overly-bureaucratic documentation and project management techniques (Larman, 2003). Similar development techniques of more recent times include Prototyping, Rapid Application Development and Extreme Programming, amongst others (Larman, 2003).

In a footnote in the Cabinet Office report entitled *One Year On: Implementing the Government ICT Strategy,* we find this definition for agile:

> Agile is an iterative development process where deliverables are submitted in stages allowing projects to respond to changing business requirements and releasing benefits earlier. (CO, 2012)

However, the way Agile is discussed in the government documents detailed below shows a difference between the Agile Manifesto objectives and how Agile is understood by managers and civil servants. For example, Agile is frequently presented as the opposite of the 'waterfall' method, but the definition above is not the opposite of a classic waterfall approach, rather it echoes some of the waterfall methodology – that is the iterative nature of development.

2.2   Changes in UK Government ICT Development

Failure in software development and adoption has been analysed in several different ways over the last 30/40 years. There are those who differentiate between development failure and system failure, and classify project abandonment in terms of total, substantial and partial, as noted in (Beynon-Davies, 1999). In 2002 Wilson and Howcroft revisited and reconceptualised ideas of failure classification by noting that even after successful adoption software could be regarded as having failed at a later date, given the contextual changes and inherent uncertainties of system use over time (Wilson, 2002). Fincham goes so far as to suggest that we cannot use the labels of failure or success as those concerned modify their views as the project unfolds (Fincham, 2002). Goldfinch takes the pessimistic view that large-scale projects of this nature are so inherently driven by politics that they should not be attempted in the first place (Goldfinch, 2007). However, though it is difficult to distinguish between software projects that have a strong possibility of success and those that may succeed, but deliver incomplete solutions, it is self-evident that some software does actually fail to work, and much is not fit for purpose when implemented.

The UK has a history of large-scale public-sector IT failures which include (i) the e-Borders project; (ii) the UK ID central database project; (iii) the NHS for IT project in England and Wales; (iv) 5 shared services projects for central government departments; (v) the integrated Fire Services Management project; and (vi) the Rural

Payments project (Anderson et al., 2009; NAO, 2011a). Several factors are regarded as contributing to each of these failures, namely size, spiralling costs and over-runs, the software acquisition process, political contexts, and so on (PAC, 2011). Major reviews of these failures have resulted in a change in government views about development and procurement of ICT. These are documented in several reports, namely (i) UK Government changes in ICT strategy (CO, 2011; 2012); and (ii) in responses from the National Audit Office to this change of strategy (NAO, 2011b; NAO, 2011c).

In particular, the idea that Agile methods might be preferable to previous overly-bureaucratic processes emerged in an important Public Administration Committee report in 2011 (PAC, 2011). Here, having recommended that departments look at alternative development methods, the report summary notes the tension between the need for in-house expertise in Agile methods, and the major outsourcing of such expertise because there is little or no in-house civil service knowledge of such matters. Others also suggested that Agile methods might solve the problems of failure (Magee, 2012); this idea was then taken up and expanded in the new government ICT strategy that emerged after the 2010 election: "Applying lean and agile methodologies that will reduce waste, be more responsive to changing requirements and reduce the risk of project failure and moving away from large projects that are slow to implement" (NAO, 2011c). This strategy included the aim that Agile would be used in 50% of all government IT projects by April 2013 (NAO, 2011b). In these and subsequent statements, Agile is presented as not only the answer to project failure and cost over-runs, but also a means to challenge the oligopoly of large software companies in large-scale IT procurement, allowing more SME (Small to Medium-sized Enterprise) involvement in public sector projects: "Government is consulting on new frameworks that will enable more agile procurement, and open the market to more SMEs" (NAO, 2011c).

3   The Real Time Information Project

3.1   PAYE

Pay-as-you-earn (PAYE) was introduced in 1944 as a means of maximising revenue during the inter-war and post-war period (HMRC, 2011). PAYE is a method of collecting tax at source via employee payments, so that taxpayers pay their tax as they work. The employee pays in advance each month (or payment period) towards an estimated amount of tax which is then checked against actual employment and allowances at each year end. An employee is given a tax code by HMRC which consists of items which show the allowances for an individual. The employer is responsible for sending on the total tax owed by the employees of the organisation to HMRC in an annual payment. However, given the need for annual reconciliations of employee status, often the employer is in arrears for the overall tax burden to the state.

In September 2010, HMRC announced that due to errors in PAYE coding a total of 6M people in the UK had paid the wrong amount of tax in previous periods. It was estimated that 4.3M had paid too much and were due a refund, and 1.4M had underpaid (on average each had underpaid by £1,428.) A Treasury report into the administration and effectiveness of HMRC noted that "these over-and underpayments had arisen because the amounts of tax collected from individual taxpayer under the PAYE system in 2008-09 and 2009-10 had not been checked" (Treasury, 2011). Soon after, in October, more errors in payments of tax (of up to £24,000 in some cases) were announced by HMRC. Further details emerged at this point; in particular, it was said that the 2009 introduction of a computer system had produced the large number of anomalies in tax payment. Prior to the roll-out of 2009, the previous PAYE system was based on manual as well as computer-based processes. There were 12 different regional databases across the UK, and taxpayers' details were often cross-checked manually. HMRC stated that the old system led to mistakes which were then flushed out by the new system. With the previous system, HMRC manually reconciled between 16-17M cases at the year-end; once the 2009 system was fully embedded it was hoped that this would fall to around 3M cases, but this proved to be over optimistic (CIT, 2011).

The problems appeared to date from 2008, but were, in fact, an accumulated set of PAYE coding errors which had a far longer history. In 2010, it was estimated that 15 million taxpayers had not had their tax affairs settled since 2004. Previously in December 2009, it was suggested that 7M people had mispaid in 2008/09 as a result of coding anomalies. The problems of tackling these mispayments was further compounded by additional disruption in January 2010, when HMRC issued nearly 26M new tax codes to taxpayers, almost twice as many as expected on an annual basis. It appeared that the annual reconciliation of PAYE codes based on the returns of data from employers compared with those held by HMRC had not happened for several years. In 2011 the Treasury noted that HMRC had committed to clearing the backlog of open cases, which stood at 17.9M in late 2010, by 2012 (Treasury, 2011).

3.2   Organisational Context

The organisational context for RTI involves changes to the structure and role of HMRC over the last decade (Treasury, 2011). In 2005/6 the UK Tax and Inland Revenue departments were merged. In 2007, the department had to reduce its annual operational costs by five per cent each year over the period 2007/08 to 2010/11 (Kablenet, 2007). Between 2006 and 2011, it is estimated that 25,000 jobs were lost, many as a result of the merger in 2005/6, leaving HMRC with 74,000 posts in 2011. By 2009, it was claimed that staff morale at HMRC was at an all-time low. In 2010, the closure of 130 local offices was announced, and planned reductions in staffing levels with the loss of what managers at HMRC claimed was 3000 jobs over 5 years. However, it is estimated that the Comprehensive Spending Review of 2010 in reality threatens a further 10,000 jobs over the next 4 years (ICAEW, 2010).

A recent external report on employment issues at HMRC stated: "At the heart of the engagement challenge in HMRC is a disconnect between employees and the overall organisation. Many employees feel that the organisation as a whole neither values, listens to, nor respects them" (Clarke, 2012). Low levels of morale in HMRC have been reported over the last 10 years (Brookes, 2009). This is due to constant re-structuring, changes to conditions of services, job reductions and lack of resources (Clarke, 2012). Several internal surveys have shown that employees do not feel trusted by management and that there is a "strong blame culture". This low morale is reflected in the number of strikes that have occurred in recent years. Carter et al. argue that the impact of Lean management processes within HMRC has had "a detrimental effect on employees, their working lives, and the service that is provided to the public" (Carter et al., 2011).

2010 saw a major government review of HMRC in light of complaints from clients, and with regard to the loss of crucial tax income due to mistakes and errors in data handling, as noted above in 3.1. Perhaps it is no coincidence that over this period there have been issues with the suppliers of computing systems, and problems with the resulting processes and tax collections.

3.3   Technologies

The main commercial supplier for the Inland Revenue's Tax and National Insurance system from 1994 to 2004 was EDS, then the second largest software company in the world (BBC, 2003). In 2003, the launch of a new tax credit system led to over-payments of £2B to over two million people and the contract with EDS was scrapped. After eight years, EDS paid £71.25M in compensation for this debacle (Oates, 2009). In 2004, the computing systems contract was awarded to Capgemini with Fujitsu and BT as minor partners (Oates, 2009). This contract, which was originally to run until 2014, was one of the biggest ever IT outsourcing contracts, with a value of £2.6B, and a lifetime value of £8.5B (Computer Weekly, 2009). Aspire (Acquiring Strategic Partners for the Inland Revenue) was set up to replace the contracts Inland Revenue had with EDS and Accenture for IT services respectively (Kablenet, 2007).

In 2009, HMRC revised the contract for the Aspire system with Capgemini and extended it until 2017 (Computer Weekly, 2009). This locking in of IT services for such a long period has been heavily criticised, and illustrates the issues associated with assessing the claims made for cost-savings as a result of Aspire:

> The Aspire contract between HMRC and Capgemini covers a 13 year period and was originally valued at £2.8 billion. This contract is a case study of what is wrong with the present procurement culture. Such a large contract is too complex to manage. The assessment of costs and benefits is opaque and it commits too much power and money to a single supplier. (PAC, 2011)

Unfortunately the new computer systems implementation overran, and software problems, which were estimated to cost £395M, delayed the processing of the 2008-2009 PAYE details for at least a year.

3.4   RTI

In 2010, further changes were proposed to the HMRC PAYE computing system in order to avoid the annual reconciliation process, which was producing large numbers of anomalies in tax codes, and to obtain real-time data from organisations with regard to employee status. The argument was that in comparison to the early period of PAYE when an individual had the same job for many years, nowadays there are rapidly changing patterns of employment, which lead to increases in the under or overpayment of tax each year. To allow for these rapid changes in employment, an individual's details will be held in a large database known as the Real-Time Information (RTI) system (a data warehouse). The new system requires high levels of data quality (presumably because there is no plan for recovery from the errors that are present in the un-reconciled tax payments based on estimates), and all organisations have been briefed on the need for the provision of clean data. However, the current status of the quality of data held by HMRC is in doubt. As noted by the 2011 Treasury report: "Data quality has been a key weakness in the PAYE system to date. The success of both the National Insurance and PAYE Service and Real-time Information will depend to a large extent on how effectively HMRC can 'cleanse' the data it receives and holds" (Treasury, 2011).

In 2010, a one-off payment of £100M was given to HMRC to help fund RTI which was to be rolled out over a period of 18 months, starting with a pilot in spring 2011. The timetable slipped somewhat, and the pilot started in April 2012 using a selected number of partners, and then proceeding to a full engagement from all employers by October 2013, despite opposition from several interested parties (such as major employers, and professional tax bodies). By July 2012 the pilot involved 500 employers, with approximately 1.7m employees (Fuller, 2012). The pilot was widened further in November 2012.

RTI requires all employers to change their reporting systems to be compliant with HMRC software. Few of the software suppliers who support businesses in PAYE returns had developed appropriate packages in the early part of the project. The original specification also required employers to make payments to HMRC using BACS (Bankers' Automated Clearing Services) instead of EDI (Electronic Data Interchange), competing standards for electronic cash transfers. Since the majority of SME were using EDI there were objections from interested parties, and other problems arose with moving from EDI to BACS as a means of communicating employee records, by September 2011, HMRC had agreed to continue to use several channels for payment, including both EDI and BACS (Say, 2012).

This is but one of several changes made to specifications for RTI during the development phase. Other objectives that were changed due to stakeholder responses include the following examples. Firstly, 'end of work period' P45 forms were to be abolished. A P45 is the document which allows for continuity in the tax process as an individual changes job. However, this decision was reversed after extensive complaints from employers and accountants (Woods, 2012). Secondly, the pilot was originally planned to take under 12 months. The idea that employers should then use a system that had not been fully tested for a complete tax year in pilot form caused some concern:

> We welcome the move to introduce Real-time Information (RTI). We agree with the professional bodies that the system must be tested thoroughly before full implementation, with full consultation with users and close co-operation with the Department for Work and Pensions at all stages. We note that large employers will be required to use the new system in January 2013, which is before the system has been tested through one complete tax year. (Treasury, 2011)

As a result of growing external pressure, in October 2012 it was announced that the pilot would continue until April 2013, at which point all employers would use RTI, though larger firms were given between April and October to join the new system.

This responsiveness might be seen as a positive way of developing a new system, if it were not for the impression that the scoping of requirements had been rushed and did not take account of stakeholder views. If anything, these reverses added to the mistrust of HMRC technologies.

The HMRC web-site is predicting that the complete RTI system will be in place for October 2013, or rather that this final date for completion cannot be changed due to the pressure from Ministers who are driving welfare reform. Given the history of overrun on previous HMRC projects, as noted above, and UK public sector IT projects in general, this is a worrying stance. The Treasury has warned of the dangers of such inflexibility in the roll-out of RTI:

> HMRC has committed to an ambitious timescale to deliver Real-time Information, driven in part by the importance of the project in delivering the Universal Credit. The history of large IT projects subject to policy-driven timescales has been littered with failure. The timetable is made more ambitious by the fact HMRC will still be resolving the legacy of open cases and stabilising the National Insurance and PAYE Service during the project's early stages. Introducing Real-time Information before HMRC and the Government can be sure it will work correctly would run unacceptable risks for the reputation of the Department and the tax system. (Treasury, 2011)

As of March 2013, though the pilot has been described as a success, the numbers of small businesses ready for the April change is as low as 32% (PAC, 2012). Not only does HMRC have no contingency plans in place if RTI fails, all remaining 281 tax advice centres will close during 2013-2014 during the period of the roll-out of Universal Credit (Wade, 2013; BBC, 2013).

4   Universal Credit

> Universal Credit is a new benefit for people of working age which will be introduced over a four year period from 2013 to 2017. It will replace existing means-tested benefits and tax credits (including income-based Jobseekers; Allowance and Employment and Support Allowance; Income Support; Child Tax Credits; Working Tax Credits; and Housing Benefit). It is the Government's key reform to simplify the benefits systems and to promote work and personal responsibility. (CSC, 2012)

Mark Hoban, who became a minister at the Department for Work and Pensions (DWP) in September 2012, produced figures for the estimated cost of the UC project of £638M, which included IT development, associated integration with other systems and infrastructure requirements. The cost of design, development and software was estimated at £492M, with the remainder for changes to dependant systems and infrastructure (Work & Pensions, 2012). Accenture was awarded the £500M 7-year contract to manage the IT systems that support UC; IBM was awarded a £525M contract which runs until 2018, to provide computing systems across 60 services and will also be involved in the integrating UC project. They are providing a customer information system, resource management, and fraud referral and intervention management, some of which will be used in the delivery of Universal Credit. The DWP also signed a £100 million deal with HP for delivery of software covering the core benefits system and department application support (King, 2011). In addition DWP signed a contract with Capgemini for 7 years, of between £5M and £10M per year, for the provision and maintenance of business applications (Hall, 2011).

The effects of the roll-out of the Universal Credit project can be gauged by reading the transcripts of Select Committee reviews, the reports of various government bodies such as the National Audit Office and the Cabinet Office. In addition there are the reports and briefings which each public department makes about the management of IT and special projects, including the metrics and key performance indicators. All of these are in the public domain. There are over 70 organisations directly affected by changes to benefits and which have responded to consultation exercises. The Local Government Association (LGA) is one these and it has made several representations to the DWP and other committees asking that the Agile methodology for UC be revised as it is 'not grounded in reality' (Hitchcock, 2012).

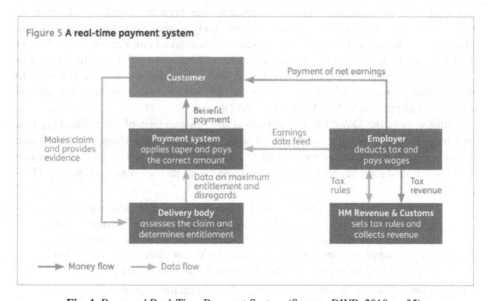

Fig. 1. Proposed Real-Time Payment System (Source: DWP, 2010, p. 35)

In addition, UK Local Authorities have an interest in the change to Universal Credit, since there are various benefits which affect the holder's status with regard to local taxes, such as council tax, and the subsequent need to reconcile monies between central and local government. Local authorities also provide the face-to-face contact for those who receive many benefits. The locally managed Council Tax is not part of the overhaul of Universal Credit, but is part of the total benefit assessment. There are differences as to how benefit payments are made across the UK which directly affect the integration process (Tarr, 2012). Benefit payments have weekly cycles; RTI operates on a monthly cycle. As a result UC has also been planned as a monthly cycle of payment, thereby creating problems for the disadvantaged who are used to budgeting on a weekly basis. Benefits are to be calculated per household not for an individual which may lessen income for women.

Other sources of information concerning policy and practise are the publications of interested bodies including (i) public sector unions, such as Unison; (ii) Charities, such as the Joseph Rowntree Foundation; and (iii) representatives of professions, including accountants and tax professionals, such as the Institute of Chartered Accountants and the Chartered Institute of Taxation, amongst others. For example, the Chartered Institute of Taxation has a group called the Low Income Tax Reform Group (LITR) which is very worried by the possible effects of Universal Credit. They have warned of problems with the accumulation and transition of tax credit debt which may occur as a result of linking benefits payments with taxation in this way, stating "HMRC and DWP need a clear and well thought-out strategy to ensure that the start of UC is not blighted by inheriting the £6.5 billion debt that may have accumulated in tax credits by 2014/15" (LITR, 2012).

Under the new system all claimants will be 'digital by default'. The plan is to have all communications from an individual about benefits online, and for payments to be made into an online account. 'Digital by Default' has been criticised for affecting the most vulnerable, who are those who are most likely to receive many of the benefits (Tarr, 2012). Many of those claiming benefits do not have bank accounts, and budget with cash set aside for specific items such as rent, debts and food. Community charity Citizens Advice warns that the Universal Credit system "risks causing difficulties to the 8.5 million people who have never used the internet and a further 14.5 million who have virtually no ICT skills" (WPC, 2012).

Unfortunately the DWP has not published the fuller details of the technology that will integrate the existing systems (See Figure 1 for a dataflow diagram of real-time payments for Universal Credit proposed in 2010 by DWP). The October 2012 Joseph Rowntree Foundation report discussed the problem of lack of details about the IT as follows:

> However, there is still very limited publically available information on how the IT will operate and what will happen if things go wrong; DWP should address this and provide reassurance on how the system will operate, what training staff will undergo to understand it, and what processes will be in place in case IT systems fail. (Tarr, 2012)

Other information that is not in the public domain includes how Agile methods are actually being deployed in UC development (Slater, 2012). Is Agile regarded as a software development method, a project management process, at odds with the 'waterfall' method, or scalable? This is the main focus of the next section in which the efficacy of the adoption of Agile methods is discussed.

5   Is Agile the Answer?

In September 2012, in response to criticisms of timescale, the DWP claimed that "'The IT is already mostly built. It is not a single IT system, but is being built part-by-part on an agile basis as well as bringing in existing systems. It is built and tested, on-time and on-budget" (Hall, 2011). Iain Duncan Smith, the government Work and Pensions Secretary, told the Commons Select Committee when it took evidence on Universal Credit in September 2012:

> The thing about the agile process which I find frustrating at times, because we cannot quite get across to people, is that agile is about change. It is about allowing you to get to a certain point in the process, check it out, make sure it works, come up with something you can rectify, and make it more efficient. So you are constantly rolling forward, proving, and making more efficient. (CSC, 2012)

The Cabinet Office Major Projects Authority (MPA) issued the *Starting Gate Review of Universal Credit* in September 2011. This report notes some concerns about the take-up of agile methods as follows: "Overall, the use of an agile methodology remains unproven at this scale and within UK Government however, the challenging timescale does present DWP with few choices for delivery of such a radical programme." Thus Agile was chosen not because it was a tried and tested methodology, but because of the short timescale (Collins, 2011). This report also shows that there are doubts about the scalability of the Agile process stating further that the programme is using conventional, multi-million pound contracts with large suppliers to deliver the system, with RTI being developed simultaneously using a conventional waterfall methodology (Ballard, 2011; Collins, 2011).

There is a lack of understanding in the government and civil service that adopting agile processes will require changes to organisational structures (Nerur, 2005). Commenting that government IT is not just a cost to be managed, Sir Ian Magee, who co-edited the 'System Upgrade?' report, questioned the ability of senior civil servants as follows:

> Agile requires real changes in departmental procurement, policy development and operational management processes, and it is not clear that government IT leaders feel sufficiently confident or supported to challenge departmental board leaders and ministers to do things differently. Meanwhile, in my experience, many top level civil servants express discomfort about challenging IT leaders to deliver better, more responsive services, in part due to a shortage of knowledge but also due to a distinct shortage of information on chief information officer (CIO) performance. (Magee, 2012)

In the case of Universal Credit, Agile has become an answer to critics of the scale and speed of the process, a means by which SME can become part of the software solution, and is also regarded as a project management and procurement process, rather than a software development method.

Many questions are as yet unanswered with respect to this example of interlinked large-scale public sector IT projects. Will the use of Agile design in government departments mean that the 'IT rip-offs' of the past are no longer going to happen? How can Agile be used successfully if civil servants and managers appear to have little or no technical understanding in the first place? To what extent can such grandiose schemes be decoupled from the political contexts in which they are conceived and driven? There is growing evidence that the use of Agile methods is not compatible with large-scale projects or organisations that are bureaucratic (Nerur, 2005). In 2011 the US Department of Defence had to impose an emergency reform of IT projects using Agile methods, after 11 major computer systems went $6bn over budget and were estimated to be 31 years behind schedule (Ballard, 2012). As noted in section 2.1 above, Agile requires a daily commitment from clients to meet with developers. In large-sale projects it can be hard to identify appropriate clients for sub-projects, and for those clients to be available for daily meetings with small development teams. It is also difficult to imagine how the needs of public accountability can be met without some level of administrative control and documentation.

The DWP states in the *21ˢᵗ Century Welfare paper*: "In planning the transition to the new system, we would be guided by our principles of simplicity, fairness and affordability" (DWP, 2010). What is evident in the analysis presented above is that the addition of major IT change adds complexity to the process of simplification. Whether this grand project is affordable will only be determined at some point in the future. Howver, it seems likely that there will be losers in this roll-out – those with the most dependency on benefits and welfare, which is hardly fair.

It is unlikely that we can identify one factor in particular that is the main cause of systems failure, but given the complex nature of large-scale public sector projects it is also unlikey that relying on one factor alone, such as a change in software methodology, will guarantee success. The rationale of government entering on new large-scale complex IT projects after the experiences of the previous disasters discussed above was the use of Agile methods. In the cases of RTI and UC outlined above, I would argue that Agile has become a rhetorical device rather than the answer to large-scale public sector IT failure. Ian Watmore, who was Permanent Secretary of the Cabinet office in 2011, at the time of the major review, identified three main reasons for large-scale IT failure: "policy problems, business change problems or big-bang implementation" (PAC, 2011). The Universal Credit project has all of these features. It is unlikely that the adoption of a new method of software design and procurement will affect such major structural processes.

6   Glossary

ASPIRE   Acquiring Strategic Partners for the Inland Revenue
BACS   Bankers' Automated Clearing Services
DWP Department of Work and Pensions
EDI   Electronic Data Interchange
HMRC   Her Majesties Revenue and Customs

IT   Information Technology
IS   Information Systems
LITR Low Income Tax Reform Group
LGA   Local Government Association
MPA   Major Projects Authority
NPS   National Insurance and PAYE Service
PAYE   Pay As You Earn
RTI   Real Time Information
SME   Small to Medium-sized Enterprise
UC   Universal Credit

References

Anderson, R., Brown, I., Dowty, T., Inglesant, P., Heath, W., Sasse, A.: Database State: A Report Commissioned by the Joseph Rowntree Reform Trust Ltd. Joseph Rowntree Reform Trust Ltd., York (2009)

Ballard, M.: Universal Credit deadline forced DWP to use "unproven" agile development. Computer Weekly (October 4, 2011)

Ballard, M.: Soldiers nail data for agile offensive on $6bn cock-up. Public Sector IT, Computer Weekly (June 2012)

BBC: Inland Revenue dumps IT provider, BBC News (December 11, 2003)

BBC: HMRC to close all of its 281 Enquiry Centres, BBC News (March 14, 2013), http://www.bbc.co.uk/news/business-21789759

Beynon-Davies, P.: Human error and information systems failure: the case of the London ambulance service computer-aided despatch system project. Interacting with Computers 11, 699–720 (1999)

Brookes, R.: Morale among HMRC workers falls to new low. Accountancy Age (July 9, 2009)

Carter, R., Danford, A., Howcroft, D., Richardson, H., Smith, A., Taylor, P.: Lean and mean in the civil service: the case of processing in HMRC. Public Money & Management 31(2), 115–122 (2011)

CIT: PAYE Reconciliation - questions and answers, Chartered Institute of Taxation (2011), http://www.tax.org.uk/media_centre/blog/Technical/PAYE%20QAs

Clarke, N.: People Engagement in HMRC: A report to ExCom and the HMRC trade unions (May 2012)

CO: Government ICT Strategy - Strategic Implementation Plan: Moving from the 'what' to the 'how' (March 2011)

CO: One Year On: Implementing the Government ICT Strategy (May 2012)

Collins: Universal Credit review now published, Campaign4Change (October 10, 2011)

CSC: Universal Credit, Commons Select Committee (September 20, 2012)

Computer Weekly: HMRC revises Aspire contract with Capgemini. Computer Weekly (October 29, 2009)

Denning, P.J., Gunderson, C., Hayes-Roth, R.: Evolutionary system development. Communications of the ACM 51(12), 28–31 (2008)

DoH: The future of the National Programme for IT Department of Health press release (September 9, 2010)

DWP: 21st Century Welfare, Presented to Parliament by the Secretary of State for Work and Pensions by Command of Her Majesty. The Stationery Office Limited (July 2010)

Fincham, R.: Narratives of Success and Failure in Systems. British Journal of Management 13(1), 1–14 (2002)

Fuller, C.: Gauke rejects postponement of RTI. Accountancy Age (July 2012)

Geertz, C.: The interpretation of cultures. Hutchinson, London (1975)

Hall, K.: IBM signs £525m DWP contract to provide Universal Credit systems. Computer Weekly (September 29, 2011)

Goldfinch, S.: Pessimism, Computer Failure, and Information Systems Development. Public Administration Review (September/October 2007)

Hall, K.: DWP hits back at criticism over Universal Credit IT systems. Computer Weekly (September 17, 2012)

Hitchcock, G.: LGA: revise 'agile' approach to universal credit. Government Computing, Kable (2012), http://central-government.governmentcomputing.com/news/lga-revise-agile-approach-to-universal-credit

HMRC (2012), http://www.hmrc.gov.uk/history/taxhis6.htm

ICAEW: Comprehensive Spending Review (2010), http://www.ion.icaew.com/TaxFaculty/20858

Kablenet: HMRC extends Aspire deal to 2017: Cost cutting drive, The Register (2007), http://www.theregister.co.uk/2007/11/08/hmrc_extends_aspire

King, L.: DWP signs fifth large deal with HP. Computer World (October 7, 2011)

Law, J.: After Method: Mess in Social Science Research. Routledge, London (2007)

LITR (2012), http://www.litrg.org.uk/News/2012/work-and-pensions-committee-of-mps-scrutinises-universal-credit

Magee, I., Gash, T., Stephen, J.: System upgrade? The first year of the Government's ICT strategy. Institute for Government (June 25, 2012)

NAO: The failure of the FiReControl project, National Audit Office (2011a)

NAO: ICT in government: landscape review, National Audit Office (February 17, 2011b)

NAO: Implementing the Government ICT Strategy: six-month review of progress, National Audit Office (December 21, 2011c)

Nerur, S., Radhakanta, M., Mangalaraj, G.: Challenges of migrating to agile methodologies. Communications of the ACM 48(5), 73–78 (2005)

Oates, J.: EDS pays for tax failure: Final divorce settlement. The Register (2009), http://www.theregister.co.uk/2009/01/07/eds_hmrc_tax_credit_fail/

PAC: Government and IT- "A Recipe For Rip-Offs": Time For A New Approach, Public Administration Committee Report (July 28, 2011), http://www.publications.parliament.uk/pa/cm201012/cmselect/cmpubadm/715/71502.htm

PAC: Minutes of Evidence (HC 716), Public Accounts Committee (November 5, 2012), http://www.publications.parliament.uk/pa/cm201213/cmselect/cmpubacc/716/121105.htm

Say, M.: RTI: Inside the massive IT project at the heart of universal credit, Guardian professional. The Guardian (March 5, 2012)

Sherman, J., Savage, M.: Whitehall's Wasted Billions. The Times, pp. 6–7 (January 9, 2102)

Slater, J.: Universal Credit Programme: Freedom of Information request (2012), http://www.whatdotheyknow.com/request/universal_credit_programme

Tarr, A., Finn, D.: Implementing Universal Credit: will the reforms improve the service for users? Joseph Rowntree Foundation, Centre for Economic and Social Inclusion, London (2012)

The Agile Manifesto (2001), http://agilemanifesto.org/

Treasury: Sixteenth Report: Administration and effectiveness of HM Revenue and Customs (HMRC). Findings of the select Committee (January 19, 2011)

Wade, N.: A Taxing Time as PAYE Regulations Change. Accountancy and Tax, No 1, The Guardian (March 2013)

Wilson, M., Howcroft, D.: Reconceptualising Failure: Social Shaping Meets IS Research. European Journal of Information Systems 11(4), 236–250 (2002)

Work & Pensions, Universal Credit Work & Pensions, response to Frank Field (September 18, 2012), http://www.theyworkforyou.com/wrans

Woods, D.: HMRC performs u-turn on plans to axe P45. HR Excellence Magazine (February 8, 2012)

WPC: Work and pensions Committee – Written Evidence, Contents: HC576 - Progress towards the implementation of Universal Credit, House of Commons, Select Committees (2012)

The Cross-Cultural Knowledge Sharing Challenge: An Investigation of the Co-location Strategy in Software Development Offshoring

John Stouby Persson

Department of Computer Science, Aalborg University, Aalborg, Denmark
john@cs.aau.dk

Abstract. Cross-cultural offshoring in software development challenges effective knowledge sharing. While research has suggested temporarily co-locating participants to address this challenge, few studies are available on what knowledge sharing practices emerge over time when co-locating cross-cultural software developers. This paper presents a longitudinal case study of an offshoring project with co-location of Indian and Danish software developers for 10½ months. A community-of-practice (CoP) analysis is offered of what knowledge sharing practices emerge over time and how these where facilitated. The study supports previous studies' suggestion of co-location in offshoring for helping cross-cultural knowledge sharing. However, the short initial period of co-location suggested in these studies, was insufficient for achieving knowledge sharing practices indicating a CoP. In conjunction with a longer period of co-location four facilitators of cross-cultural knowledge sharing were shared office, shared responsibility for tasks and problems, shared prioritization of team spirit, and a champion of social integration.

Keywords: cross-cultural software projects, offshore outsourcing, knowledge sharing, communities-of-practice, longitudinal case study.

1 Introduction

The substantial research knowledge base on information technology and systems accumulated over decades does not prevent the persistent failures in both public and private enterprises. One explanation is the challenge of sharing knowledge such that it becomes embedded in the working practices of the involved practitioners. The knowledge sharing challenge is present throughout most aspects of information technology and systems development in and across organizations. The challenge can even be further exacerbated by cultural diversity when crossing not only organizational but also national boundaries. Offshoring in software development is a setting where the cross-cultural knowledge sharing challenge has a very persistent presence. With a history of numerous failures, many research efforts have investigated risks particular to offshoring and distribution (Iacovou & Nakatsu, 2008; Lamersdorf et al., 2012; Persson & Mathiassen, 2010; Singh & Nigam, 2012). Knowledge sharing is one of the key challenges in software development with offshoring that is further

Y.K. Dwivedi et al. (Eds.): TDIT 2013, IFIP AICT 402, pp. 310–325, 2013.

exacerbated by different national cultures (Boden et al., 2012; Dibbern et al., 2008; Nakatsu & Iacovou, 2009; Persson et al., 2009). A general suggestion to alleviate risks related to offshoring in software development is co-location of developers. Previous research suggest that liaisons between sites address the risks related to knowledge management and cultural diversity in distributed software development projects (Persson et al., 2009). A recent study of knowledge sharing practices and the impact of cultural factors found that spending time at the other site in software development offshoring, is very good (Boden et al., 2012). In global software development, face-to-face meetings, temporal co-location, and exchange visits are best practices with benefits such as trust, cohesiveness, and effective teamwork but also constrained by extra costs (Šmite et al., 2010). While these suggestions has also been argued for virtual work in general, other research has found that teams composed of distributed members can perform effectively without ever meeting face-to-face (Watson-Manheim et al., 2012). However, co-location of project participants is still an often-reoccurring suggestion for addressing the knowledge sharing challenge in the offshore software development with cross-cultural relations. The extent, to which this suggestion of co-location should be taken, has been given little attention in the above literature. Thus, a longitudinal case study has been conducted to investigate the following research question: *When co-locating cross-cultural software developers, what knowledge sharing practices may emerge over time and how can such practices be facilitated?*

The research question was investigated through a case where a financial company engaged a large amount of software developers from an Indian outsourcing provider and collocated them with their own developers in Denmark. Based on a Communities-of-Practice (CoP) perspective on knowledge sharing, an analysis is conducted of what practices emerged over time and how they were facilitated. The following sections present the literature on cultural diversity and offshoring (2) and CoP (3). Followed by the case study research approach (4) and findings (5) of knowledge sharing practices in a collocated cross-cultural software project. The contribution and implications of these findings are discussed (6) followed by the conclusion (7).

2   Cultural Diversity and Offshoring in Software Development

Culturally and geographically distributed collaborators in software development projects or organizations have different conceptualizations. Three common conceptualizations are 1) virtual teams (Bergiel et al., 2008; Gibson & Gibbs, 2006), 2) global software development (Damian & Moitra, 2006; Mishra & Mishra, 2011), and 3) offshore outsourcing (Doh, 2005; Nakatsu & Iacovou, 2009). Indicated by several literature studies in different research fields, virtual teams is a widespread and frequently used conceptualization (Persson, 2010). The majority of studies see virtual teams as functioning teams that rely on technology-mediated communication while crossing several different boundaries (Martins et al., 2004). Commonly-noted boundaries are geographic, time, and organizational dispersion, while additional characteristics are electronic dependence, structural dynamism, and national diversity(Gibson & Gibbs, 2006; Martins et al., 2004; Powell et al., 2004). The term "team" suggests groups displaying high levels of interdependency and integration (Powell et al., 2004). However, virtual teams are often assembled from different organizations via outsourcing, or through joint ventures crossing organizational boundaries (Martins et al., 2004; Zigurs, 2003). A virtual team perspective on collaboration has also been adopted for software development with offshore outsourcing (Persson, 2010; Siakas & Siakas, 2008). Offshore outsourcing involves cross-organizational transactions by the use of external agents to perform one or more organizational activities (Dibbern et al., 2004) crossing national borders. This can apply to everything from the use of contract programmers to third-party facilities management. Offshore outsourcing arrangements can include a virtual team setting, pursuing high levels of interdependency and integration, while other arrangements go in opposite directions pursuing high levels of independence (Dibbern et al., 2004; Kaiser & Hawk, 2004; Siakas & Siakas, 2008).

The participants in offshore software development may not share language, traditions, or organizational culture, which makes knowledge sharing very difficult. Language barriers are typically present in cross-national projects when sites and participants do not share a common native language or norms of communication resulting in misinterpretations and un-conveyed information (Krishna et al., 2004; Sarker & Sahay, 2004). Overall, it takes more time and effort to communicate effectively in offshore projects (Iacovou & Nakatsu, 2008). However, studies have also shown successful knowledge sharing and collaboration among geographically and culturally distributed software developers through information and communication technologies (Persson et al., 2012; Yalaho & Nahar, 2010). Differences in work culture, team behavior, or organizational culture may also lead to difficulties (Connaughton & Shuffler, 2007; Nakatsu & Iacovou, 2009; Persson, 2010), that can be caused by divergence between sites, in balancing collectivism and individualism, perception of authority and hierarchy, and planning and punctuality (Herbsleb & Moitra, 2001; Krishna et al., 2004). This may lead to decreased conflict-handling, lower efficiency, or even paralyze the software project. In general, when projects are distributed across time, space, and culture, it is difficult to obtain the same level of group cohesion and knowledge sharing expected in collocated teams (Sakthivel, 2005). One suggestion for addressing the risks in offshore software development is working face-to-face (Sakthivel, 2007). Working face-to-face for limited periods of time in global or offshore software development has been suggested by numerous studies (Boden et al., 2012; Kotlarsky & Oshri, 2005; Krishna et al., 2004; Šmite et al., 2010). This may include the use 'cultural bridging' staff with people rooted in both cultures or locals as on-site workers at the supplier (Krishna et al., 2004), exchange visits (Šmite et al., 2010), or the use of liaisons between sites to address the risks related to knowledge management and cultural diversity (Persson et al., 2009; Persson & Mathiassen, 2010). Boden et al. (2012) found in their study of knowledge sharing practices and the impact of cultural factors in offshore software development, that spending time at the other site is very good. While, the suggested best practices in face-to-face meetings, temporal co-location, and exchange visits can give rise to benefits in trust, cohesiveness, and effective teamwork it is constrained by the extra costs (Šmite et al., 2010). In general, it has been argued that in order to avoid project failures that the onshore and offshore teams from the vendor and client sides should work as an integrated project team (Philip et al., 2012).

While numerous studies have suggested co-location for alleviating knowledge sharing difficulties in cross-cultural and offshored software development, there is an apparent need for in-depth studies of how knowledge sharing practices can emerge with co-location. This may help managers make more informed decisions on how and to what extend co-location can be used for alleviating the risks associated with cross-cultural knowledge sharing in offshore software development. The following section presents the CoP framework for understanding knowledge sharing in practice.

3   Communities of Practice

Software development in and across organizations requires extensive knowledge sharing, that can be conceptualized as collective learning.

> ... collective learning results in practices that reflect both the pursuit of our enterprises and the attendant social relations. These practices are thus the property of a kind of community created over time by the sustained pursuit of a shared enterprise. It makes sense, therefore, to call these kinds of communities communities of practice. (Wenger, 1998 p.45)

The CoP conceptualization has been used extensively for explaining or cultivating knowledge sharing in distributed settings (Hildreth et al., 2000; Kimble & Hildreth, 2005; Wenger et al., 2002) also called virtual communities of practice (Ardichvili, 2008; Dubé et al., 2006). However, the influential works introducing CoP (Brown & Duguid, 1991; Lave & Wenger, 1991; Wenger, 1998; Wenger et al., 2002) conceptualize it differently (Cox, 2005). These works differs markedly in their conceptualizations of community, learning, power and change, diversity, and informality, for instance is the concept of community presented in the following ways (Cox, 2005):

- A group of people involved in a coherent craft or practice, e.g. butchers OR Not a neatly group at all (Lave & Wenger, 1991).
- An informal group of workers doing the same or similar jobs (Brown & Duguid, 1991).
- A set of social relations and meanings that grow up around a work process when it is appropriated by participants (Wenger, 1998).
- An informal club or Special Interest Group inside an organization, set up explicitly to allow collective learning and cultivated by management action (Wenger et al., 2002).

This study investigates what knowledge sharing practices emerge over time when co-locating a project's cross-cultural software developers. Thus, Wenger's (1998) focus in the third bullet above on social relations and meanings (knowledge sharing) that grow up around a work process (software development project) when it is appropriated by participants (Indian and Danish Software developers), is adopted instead of his more recent work in the fourth bullet above (Wenger et al., 2002). Cox summarize Wengers (1998) definition of CoP as "*a group that coheres through 'mutual engagement' on an 'indigenous' (or appropriated) enterprise, and creating a common repertoire*" (Cox, 2005). Wenger (1998) associates community with practice that is the source of coherence for a community. He proposes three dimensions of the relation including, mutual engagement, joint enterprise, and shared repertoire (Fig. 1).

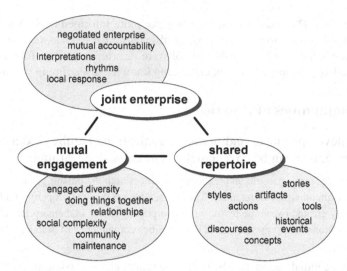

Fig. 1. Dimensions of practice as the property of a community (Wenger, 1998 p.73)

Wenger (1998) presents 14 indicators of CoP (Table 1), that show an emphasis of close relations created by sustained mutual engagement opposed to the less tight knit community relations in his following work (Wenger et al., 2002). While these indicators can be a strong aid in clarifying the nature of CoP, they have not been widely referenced by subsequent researchers (Cox, 2005). These indictors serve as the analytical framework for identifying knowledge sharing practices emerging over time in the investigated cross-cultural software project.

Table 1. Indicators of CoP (Wenger, 1998 p.125-126)

1) Sustained mutual relationships – harmonious or conflictual
2) Shared ways of engaging in doing things together
3) The rapid flow of information and propagation of innovation
4) Absence of introductory preambles, as if conversations and interactions were merely the continuation of an ongoing process
5) Very quick setup of a problem to be discussed
6) Substantial overlap in participants' descriptions of who belongs
7) Knowing what others know, what they can do, and how they can contribute to an enterprise
8) Mutually defining identities
9) The ability to assess the appropriateness of actions and products
10) Specific tools, representations, and other artifacts
11) Local lore, shared stories, inside jokes, knowing laughter
12) Jargon and shortcuts to communication as well as the ease of producing new ones
13) Certain styles recognized as displaying membership
14) A shared discourse reflecting a certain perspective on the world

The following section presents the investigated case, the date collection, and how the content of these data was analyzed for any supportive or opposing findings in relation each of the 14 indicators of CoP.

4   Research Approach

The research question was investigated through a longitudinal case study, exploiting that *"knowledge sharing practices need to be studied in context and longitudinally"* when dealing with knowledge sharing and cultural diversity in software development with offshoring (Boden et al., 2012). The adopted case study approach was in the terms of Cavaye (1996) single case with use of qualitative data for discovery based on an interpretive epistemology. Interpretive research allow investigation of knowledge sharing and CoP in its organizational and cross-cultural context as socially constructed and thus open to several interpretations by organizational actors but also to the researcher (Klein & Myers, 1999; Walsham, 2006).

4.1   The Case

The case was a software development project in a large financial company in northern Europe with a history of national mergers and acquiring companies in neighboring countries. Each acquisition requires a significant effort from the company's IT division, implementing the standard IT platform as quickly as possible in all new branches to achieve economies of scale. The responsibility for the IT platform resides at the company's headquarters. However, some acquired companies have their own IT departments that became engaged in making the shared IT platform adhere to specific financial software system requirements in their respective countries. The company's most recent acquisition is different from previous acquisitions. It's significantly larger, has a sophisticated IT platform, and is located in a country with a different language tradition from the dominant language within the company. Previous acquisitions were smaller, had an inferior IT platform, and involved a language tradition similar to or easily understandable to the employees of the company. This implementation project of the company's standard IT platform had more than 500 participants and a strict one-year deadline. The project required a large number of software developers and the company engaged an Indian software outsourcing provider. The company had limited experience with offshore outsourcing but had engaged an Indian outsourcing provider experienced in outsourcing relations with financial companies. The large integration project consisted of numerous subprojects associated with different departments of the company's IT division. This case study was initiated through contact with a department manager who would supply the project managers and developers for the subprojects related to his department. Participants from the company's internal consultancy organization, responsible for both locally recruited employees and the consultants from the Indian outsourcing provider, would also populate these subprojects. The Indian consultants available for the department's subprojects were placed in a single subproject and collocated with the Danish participants at the department offices in Denmark. This subproject with the Indian participants was the focus of this case study. The sub-project manager had two rather different tasks, one related to the company's telephone system and the other to the system managing payment agreements. Thus in practice, the subproject had two subprojects working on these tasks. Eleven people were involved in this subproject, including a project manager, a business developer, a test coordinator who left the company and was replaced by one of the developers, and eight developers. Three of the developers were Indian consultants, while the developer who replaced the test coordinator was a newly hired employee from the consultancy organization within the company.

The sub-project delivered on the two tasks on time without a high level of last minute pressure and with only one reported error that was easily amendable. Following delivery, the subproject participants spent most of their time on documentation and helping other subprojects. Other sub-projects of the integration project also had extended co-location of Indian developers, but some of these projects experienced limited success in making them valuable contributing members. The overall integration project was implemented at the acquired company on the initially set date. However, the implementation was followed by numerous errors and a large amount of negative attention from the news media in the country of the acquired company. Within the company, the integration project was initially perceived as successful. However, the negative press eventually influenced this view. Over time, the news media attention is now more positive to the company and the integration project. However, the integration project cannot easily be labeled as one of the grand successes or failures in IT, even though different stakeholders have attempted to label the project as either a big success or failure.

4.2   Data Collection and Analysis

The data collection spanned 1 year and 6 months (Fig. 2) and included various documents and audio-recorded meetings, observations, and interviews for understanding the context of the subproject with collocated Indian developers. The subproject was investigated through six rounds of semi-structured interviews with all available participants (Fig. 2) resulting in 56 audio-recorded interviews.

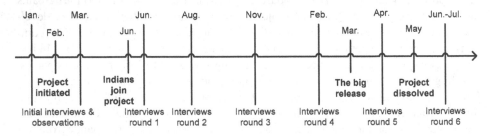

Fig. 2. Timeline of project

The author conducted the six rounds of interviews with an interview guide based on Wenger's (1998) conceptualization of CoP. The interview guide included questions to the activities on an ordinary day, use of tools, collaborators, collegial relations, professional inspiration, current challenges, and changes since last interview. The interviews were planned to take ½-hour pr. person but some were longer while others were shorter. The first round of interviews was conducted two weeks after the first Indian developer arrived while they went back to India few days after the fifth round of interviews 10 months later. The knowledge sharing practices revealed through analysis of the first (9 interviews lasting 4h7m) and fifth (9 interviews 4h4m) rounds (Fig. 2), is the primary focus of this paper.

The author conducted a content analysis of the audio-recordings of the first and fifth round of interviews using Nvivo 8. A content analysis involves observing repeating themes and categorizing them using a coding system elicited in a grounded way (built up from the data) or from some external source (in this case the indicators of CoP presented in the theory section, Table 1). The content analysis was qualitative as the indicators of CoP were studied in their location in the source audio-recording, where the addition of context can help to identify additional relevant factors. The analysis software NVivo 8 was used for the code-based analysis, distinguishing between theoretical constructs (Wengers (1998) indicators of CoP) and descriptive codes based on the language of the interviewees (Fielding & Lee, 1998).

5   Findings

The analysis of the interviews two weeks after the Indians arrival and two days before their departure resulted in 208 coded indications of CoP with 86 opposing and 112 supportive findings. The arrival interviews had 99 CoP indicators, while the departure interviews had 109 CoP indicators (Table 2).

Table 2 summarizes the supportive and opposing findings indicating CoP from interviews with the project manager, Indian developers, and Danish developers. An example of this coding, with the descriptive code "Indians are colleagues, but the language is difficult", is part of a Danish developer's response to the question of whether he considers the Indians his colleagues:

> " I share an office with one... I think we try to include him (the Indian developer) and he tries to be included. There are off course some language issues. Sometimes we want to discuss something with the person next to you in Danish because it is difficult to do in English. Then he is excluded because we talk Danish in some situations. But, when we have had a discussion, we sometimes follow up with a summary to him- saying we have just discussed this and this, what do you think of that?" (DD, arrival)

The interpretation of this quote was that the Danish developer described the Indian as belonging (CoP indicator 6) and that they have a sustained mutual relationship (CoP indicator 1). However, the quote also showed opposition to rapid flow of information (CoP indicator 3), a very quick setup of problems to be discussed (CoP indicator 5), and shortcuts to communication (CoP indicator 12). Thus, this quote was coded with

Table 2. Indications of CoP from the project manager (PM), Indian Developers (IDs) and, Danish Developers (DDs) (V: Supportive, X: Opposing, !: Mixed, "empty field": No findings)

Indicators of CoP	Two weeks after Indians arrival			10 months later, two days before Indians departure		
	PM	IDs	DDs	PM	IDs	DDs
1) Sustained mutual relationships – harmonious or conflictual	V_1	X_1	$!_{5/2}$	$!_{1/1}$	V_4	$!_{7/7}$
2) Shared ways of engaging in doing things together	X_3	X_5	X_6	V_2	V_5	V_7
3) The rapid flow of information and propagation of innovation	X_3		X_7	V_2		V_1
4) Absence of introductory preambles, as if conversations and interactions were merely the continuation of an ongoing process	X_1	X_1				V_1
5) Very quick setup of a problem to be discussed	X_2	X_5	X_2	V_2	V_1	V_3
6) Substantial overlap in participants' descriptions of who belongs	V_1	V_2	$!_{7/2}$		V_1	$!_{6/3}$
7) Knowing what others know, what they can do, and how they can contribute to an enterprise	X_1		X_1		V_2	V_6
8) Mutually defining identities	X_1	X_1	X_5	V_2	V_3	V_7
9) The ability to assess the appropriateness of actions and products	X_2	X_1		V_2		V_3
10) Specific tools, representations, and other artifacts		X_4	X_3		V_1	V_1
11) Local lore, shared stories, inside jokes, knowing laughter			X_2	V_1	V_4	V_7
12) Jargon and shortcuts to communication as well as the ease of producing new ones	X_3		X_4	V_1	V_1	
13) Certain styles recognized as displaying membership	X_1	X_2	X_3		V_1	V_4
14) A shared discourse reflecting a certain perspective on the world.	X_1	X_1	X_2	V_2	V_3	V_6

two supportive and three opposing indicators of CoP. Some of the 14 CoP indicators had neither supportive nor opposing findings, while two of the indicators had both supportive and opposing findings in the interview or interview grouping. Most of the statements reflecting CoP involved more than one of the 14 indicators presented in Table 2. In total, 73 statements reflecting CoP was coded with a description based on the language of the interviewees. Of the 73 statements, 25 had only opposing indicators, 36 had only supportive indicators, while 12 had both opposing and supportive indicators (as the example presented above).

5.1   Two Weeks After the Indians Arrival

The nine interviews after the Indians arrival included the project manager, two Indian developers, and six Danish developers and a test coordinator. The analysis revealed 99 indicators of CoP of which 75 were opposing and 24 were supportive (Table 2). The second CoP indicator, "shared ways of engaging in doing things together" was with 14 opposing findings from all but one Danish developer the most frequently identified. The project manager shows an example of differences in ways of engagement between the Danish and Indian developers in this quote:

> "... I have introduced project meetings every two weeks; I call them "buzz meetings"... I have not invited the Indians because people sometimes need to talk to me in Danish..." (PM, arrival)

In this way, the project manager established distinct engagement practices for the Indian and Danish developers. One Indian also mentioned that he usually eats lunch with the 10-15 other Indians participating in different projects at different departments and rarely with the other project participants. In addition, does his description of a regular workday differ from that of the Danes'; by being more individualized work on tasks from a schedule defined by the Danish project participants. These distinctive practices between the Indians and Danes also appeared in the use of software development tools (CoP indicator 10):

> " ... at present in the specification phase I am using RSM [IBM Rational Software Modeler]... it's a customized version for *the company*... *name of the other Indian project participant* is also making use of it, the others are also supposed to use it, but since it is a new tool they need some training... they do the work they are comfortable with, and I do the work I am comfortable with..." (ID, arrival)

The quote shows the Indian developers bring knowledge to the project not held by the other participants. The Indians are not sharing this knowledge through mutual engagement with the Danish developers; instead, it is used for a division of labor. However, the Danes valued the Indians held this knowledge and they used it later to present the Indian developers as valuable project participants. The Danes did also reveal resistance to the inclusion of the Indian developers:

> " ... I think that we all would prefer to avoid having the Indians because it takes time and nobody has time... " (DD, arrival)

Not all the project participants shared this resistance towards the Indian developers. At the time of their arrival most of the participants described the Indians as belonging and the Indians also described themselves as belonging (CoP indicator 6). The project manager and some of the Danish developers also emphasized the current and future mutual relationship between them and the Indians (CoP indicator 1).

5.2   Two days before the Indians departure

The nine interviews two days before the Indians departure after 10½ months of co-location included the project manager, three Indian developers, and five Danish developers and a test coordinator. The analysis revealed 109 indicators of CoP of which 98 were supportive and 11 were opposing (Table 2). In the interviews close to the Indians departure, the second CoP indicator "shared ways of engaging in doing things together" was also one of the most frequently identified but now with 14 supportive findings. This time, the project manager shows an example of a shared way of engaging both the Danish and Indian developers in the project planning with small responsive meetings:

> " ... we did not make a plan, saying this is the plan for the next three months, you continuously relate to it and if it is drifting, then we have a small meeting in payment agreement [subproject] to deal with it..." (PM, departure)

In the above quote, the project manager is inclusive of the Indians in the term *we* while mainly distinguishing between project participants based on what subproject they belong. Thus, they have a joint enterprise but also high mutual engagement between the two nationalities, as stated by an Indian developer:

> "... They feel we are one among them, not separated by you being from India. Their treatment brought us close. Our thoughts are similar, that is the thing, that made us more close. We used to make fun in our rooms when we are working and we used to laugh together and that gives a better relation..." (ID, departure)

The quote show their mutual engagement have a shared repertoire in laughing together (CoP indicator 11) and an inclusive treatment of the Indian developers as members (CoP indicator 13) with similar ways of thinking (CoP indicator 14). The Danish developers mentioned elements of a mutual engagement with a shared repertoire in their joint enterprise, such as a good team spirit, also mentioned by the Indian developers:

> "... There is a good team spirit... Off course, we know the Indians are going home now, so we need to get something out of them before they disappear. We have been involved in most of the things they have been doing, but some of the details are unknown to us..." (DD, departure)

While the good team spirit show the Indians was seen as belonging to the project (CoP indicator 6), this Danish developer also know what they have contributed to their joint enterprise (CoP indicator 7). Knowing this, there was a concern related to the end of the collocated sustained mutual relationship with the Indian developers (CoP indicator 1).

5.3   Change in Knowledge Sharing Practices

The 10 months of collocated software development in addition to the two initial weeks, resulted in considerable changed knowledge sharing practices when comparing CoP indicators (Table 2). All of the 14 knowledge sharing practices indicating CoP had emerged over the 10 months of co-location in the cross-cultural software project. The following four knowledge sharing facilitators, was synthesized from the descriptive codes attached to the indicators of CoP in the interviews two days before the Indians departure. The Danish project participants viewed these facilitators as distinguishing their successful integration of Indians compared to the other subprojects. These other subproject had limited success in making the Indians valuable contributing members, despite of similar extended co-location. The four knowledge sharing facilitators are exemplified with a quote from the interviews:

Shared office	"… they have been sitting close together, that is what everybody says, it would not have been the same, if they have been sitting in an entirely different office…" (PM, departure)
Shared responsibility for tasks and problems	"… once *name of Danish developer* felt stressed and asked for help, the others working on lower priority tasks immediately offered their help…it helps a lot that I am not alone with a task, it is a group assignment we are doing…" (DD, departure)
Shared prioritization of team spirit	"I think we all wanted to create a good working relationship and we all know the importance of team spirit." (DD, departure)
A champion of social integration	"… One of the reasons for the high integration of our Indians in our project is *name of ID* who arrived first… it is rare to see Indians eating lunch with Danes, but he often did that from day one, and influenced the other Indian project participants in that way… he tries to learn Danish and he is good at being extrovert… he did not come just to sit with the other Indians …" (DD, departure)

6   Discussion

The cross-cultural knowledge sharing challenge and the co-location strategy was investigated in software development offshoring with the research question *"When co-locating cross-cultural software developers, what knowledge sharing practices may emerge over time and how can such practices be facilitated?"*. This study show that with co-location of a project's cross-cultural software developers, knowledge sharing practices covering all of Wenger's (1998) 14 indicators of CoP can emerge, but not after only two weeks of co-location. These knowledge sharing practices was according to the project participants facilitated differently to projects with less successful use of co-location by: 1) shared office, 2) shared responsibility for tasks and problems, 3) shared prioritization of team spirit, and 4) a champion of social integration.

The study contributes to our understanding of the cross-cultural knowledge sharing challenge in the context of software development offshoring (Dibbern et al., 2008; Nakatsu & Iacovou, 2009; Persson et al., 2009). Investigating the suggestion of working face-to-face proposed by numerous studies of global and offshore software development (Boden et al., 2012; Kotlarsky & Oshri, 2005; Krishna et al., 2004; Šmite et al., 2010). The study supports the potential value of co-location for risk alleviation (Persson & Mathiassen, 2010; Sakthivel, 2007), but also extend these studies by showing how longer periods of co-location can support alleviation of the knowledge sharing challenge in cross-cultural offshoring. This investigation supports the Boden et al. (2012) study of knowledge sharing practices and the impact of cultural factors in offshore software development, in their finding that spending time at the other site is very good. However, this study adds, that an extended period of co-location may benefit cross-cultural knowledge sharing more substantially. This is based on the finding that knowledge sharing practices reflected in Wenger's (1998) indicators of CoP was not achieved in the first two weeks of co-location. Thus, this study extends the research suggesting face-to-face work for supporting cross-cultural knowledge sharing

(Boden et al., 2012; Kotlarsky & Oshri, 2005; Krishna et al., 2004; Šmite et al., 2010) by showing that shorter periods of co-location may only have limited effect on achieving knowledge sharing practices that indicate a CoP. Yet the achievement of a CoP may be critical to the success of software development offshoring. This is supported by Philip et al. (2012) claiming that in order to avoid project failures, the onshore and offshore teams from the vendor and client sides should work as an integrated project team. The CoP framework (1998) provide a sophisticated theoretical explanation of working as such an integrated project team, without being a team in the traditional sense (Powell et al., 2004). However, this study found that co-location without facilitation, even for extended periods, might not result in successful cross-cultural knowledge sharing. Thus, four ways to facilitate cross-cultural knowledge sharing was proposed, when adopting the extended period of co-location strategy in software development offshoring. These suggestions may contribute to frameworks for guiding the co-location strategy in software development offshoring or supplement other studies' suggestions (Krishna et al., 2004; Persson et al., 2009) in managing cross-cultural knowledge sharing in distributed settings without co-location.

The study has implications for managers in software development with offshoring, who may consider extended co-location as a potentially costly but effective mitigation strategy for projects with high risk-exposure related to cross-cultural knowledge sharing. But also taking a critical stance towards the effect of initial short co-location on cross-cultural knowledge sharing practices at the level of ambition reflected in Wenger's (1998) indicators of CoP. Choosing an extended co-location period strategy, managers should carefully monitor and facilitate the emergence of knowledge sharing practices over time. Future research is however needed of what knowledge sharing practices can emerge over shorter periods of time when co-locating a project's cross-cultural software developers, exploring the possibility of reducing the cost constraints of this strategy (Šmite et al., 2010). More research is also needed of why the four facilitators of cross-cultural knowledge sharing in collocated settings may be successful and how they should be implemented. Furthermore, future research is needed of the possibility for bringing CoP knowledge sharing practices from a collocated to a distributed setting. However, such research should consider the limitation of this study in the adopted conceptualization of CoP based on Wenger's (1998) indicators, emphasizing close relations created by sustained mutual engagement. The findings based on this conceptualization of CoP, may not be directly transferable to other conceptualizations of CoP (Cox, 2005) more suitable for exploring less tight knit community relations, as in Wenger's later work (Wenger et al., 2002).

7   Conclusion

This paper presents an investigation of the cross-cultural knowledge sharing challenge addressed by the co-location strategy in software development offshoring. A longitudinal case study of collocated Indian and Danish software developers revealed a positive change on 14 indicators of CoP over 10 months. While almost none of the 14 indicators of CoP had emerged after 2 weeks of co-location. The participants' contrasting with less successful use of collocated Indian developers in other projects, was synthesized into four distinctive facilitators of cross-cultural knowledge sharing: 1) shared office, 2) shared responsibility for tasks and problems, 3) shared prioritization of team spirit, and 4) a champion of social integration. This study helps understand the potential of the co-location strategy for mitigating the cross-cultural knowledge sharing challenge in software development offshoring, but also presents a critical stance towards the effect of shorter periods of co-location on cross-cultural knowledge sharing at project initiation.

References

Ardichvili, A.: Learning and Knowledge Sharing in Virtual Communities of Practice: Motivators, Barriers, and Enablers. Adv. Develop. Hum. Resour. 10, 541–554 (2008)

Bergiel, B.J., Bergiel, E.B., Balsmeier, P.W.: Nature of Virtual Teams: A Summary of their Advantages and Disadvantages. Management Research News 31, 99–110 (2008)

Boden, A., Avram, G., Bannon, L., et al.: Knowledge Sharing Practices and the Impact of Cultural Factors: Reflections on Two Case Studies of Offshoring in SME. Journal of Software: Evolution and Process 24, 139–152 (2012)

Brown, J.S., Duguid, P.: Organizational Learning and Communities-of-Practice: Toward a Unified View of Working, Learning, and Innovation. Organ. Sci. 2, 40–57 (1991)

Cavaye, A.L.M.: Case Study Research: A multi - faceted Research Approach for IS. Information Systems Journal 6, 227–242 (1996)

Connaughton, S.L., Shuffler, M.: Multinational and Multicultural Distributed Teams A Review and Future Agenda. Small Group Research 38, 387–412 (2007)

Cox, A.: What are Communities of Practice? A Comparative Review of Four Seminal Works. J. Inf. Sci. 31, 527–540 (2005)

Damian, D., Moitra, D.: Guest Editors' Introduction: Global Software Development: How Far have we Come? IEEE Software 23, 17–19 (2006)

Dibbern, J., Goles, T., Hirschheim, R., et al.: Information Systems Outsourcing: A Survey and Analysis of the Literature. ACM SIGMIS Database 35, 6–102 (2004)

Dibbern, J., Winkler, J., Heinzl, A.: Explaining Variations in Client Extra Costs between Software Projects Offshored to India. MIS Quarterly 32, 333–366 (2008)

Doh, J.P.: Offshore Outsourcing: Implications for International Business and Strategic Management Theory and Practice. Journal of Management Studies 42, 695–704 (2005)

Dubé, L., Bourhis, A., Jacob, R.: Towards a Typology of Virtual Communities of Practice. Interdisciplinary Journal of Information, Knowledge, and Management 1, 69–93 (2006)

Fielding, N.G., Lee, R.M.: Computer analysis and qualitative research. Sage Publications Limited, London (1998)

Gibson, C.B., Gibbs, J.L.: Unpacking the Concept of Virtuality: The Effects of Geographic Dispersion, Electronic Dependence, Dynamic Structure, and National Diversity on Team Innovation. Adm. Sci. Q. 51, 451–495 (2006)

Herbsleb, J.D., Moitra, D.: Global Software Development. IEEE Software 18, 16–20 (2001)

Hildreth, P., Kimble, C., Wright, P.: Communities of Practice in the Distributed International Environment. Journal of Knowledge Management 4, 27–38 (2000)

Iacovou, C.L., Nakatsu, R.: A Risk Profile of Offshore-Outsourced Development Projects. Commun ACM 51, 89–94 (2008)

Kaiser, K.M., Hawk, S.: Evolution of Offshore Software Development: From Outsourcing to Cosourcing. MIS Quarterly Executive 3, 69–81 (2004)

Kimble, C., Hildreth, P.: Dualities, Distributed Communities of Practice and Knowledge Management. Journal of Knowledge Management 9, 102–113 (2005)

Klein, H.K., Myers, M.D.: A Set of Principles for Conducting and Evaluating Interpretive Field Studies in Information Systems. MIS Quarterly 23, 67–93 (1999)

Kotlarsky, J., Oshri, I.: Social Ties, Knowledge Sharing and Successful Collaboration in Globally Distributed System Development Projects. Eur. J. Inform. Syst. 14, 37–48 (2005)

Krishna, S., Sahay, S., Walsham, G.: Managing Cross-Cultural Issues in Global Software Outsourcing. Commun. ACM 47, 62–66 (2004)

Lamersdorf, A., Münch, J., Viso Torre, A.F., et al.: A rule‐based Model for Customized Risk Identification and Evaluation of Task Assignment Alternatives in Distributed Software Development Projects. Journal of Software Maintenance and Evolution: Research and Practice 24, 661–675 (2012)

Lave, J., Wenger, E.: Situated learning: Legitimate peripheral participation. Cambridge university press, Cambridge (1991)

Martins, L.L., Gilson, L.L., Maynard, M.T.: Virtual Teams: What do we Know and Where do we Go from here? Journal of Management 30, 805–835 (2004)

Mishra, D., Mishra, A.: A Review of Non-Technical Issues in Global Software Development. Int. J. Comput. Appl. Technol. 40, 216–224 (2011)

Nakatsu, R.T., Iacovou, C.L.: A Comparative Study of Important Risk Factors Involved in Offshore and Domestic Outsourcing of Software Development Projects: A Two-Panel Delphi Study. Information & Management 46, 57–68 (2009)

Persson, J.S.: Managing distributed software projects. PhD Thesis, Department of Computer Science, Aalborg University, Denmark (2010)

Persson, J.S., Mathiassen, L.: A Process for Managing Risks in Distributed Teams. IEEE Software 27, 20–29 (2010)

Persson, J.S., Mathiassen, L., Aaen, I.: Agile Distributed Software Development: Enacting Control through Media and Context. Inform. Syst. J. 22, 411–433 (2012)

Persson, J.S., Mathiassen, L., Boeg, J., et al.: Managing Risks in Distributed Software Projects: An Integrative Framework. IEEE T. Eng. Manage. 56, 508–532 (2009)

Philip, T., Wende, E., Schwabe, G.: Exploring Failures at the Team Level in Offshore-Outsourced Software Development Projects. In: Kotlarsky, J., Oshri, I., Willcocks, L.P. (eds.) Global Sourcing 2012. LNBIP, vol. 130, pp. 194–211. Springer, Heidelberg (2012)

Powell, A., Piccoli, G., Ives, B.: Virtual Teams: A Review of Current Literature and Directions for Future Research. ACM SIGMIS Database 35, 6–36 (2004)

Sakthivel, S.: Managing Risk in Offshore Systems Development. Commun ACM 50, 69–75 (2007)

Sakthivel, S.: Virtual Workgroups in Offshore Systems Development. Information and Software Technology 47, 305–318 (2005)

Sarker, S., Sahay, S.: Implications of Space and Time for Distributed Work: An Interpretive Study of US–Norwegian Systems Development Teams. Eur. J. Inform. Syst. 13, 3–20 (2004)

Siakas, K.V., Siakas, E.: The Need for Trust Relationships to Enable Successful Virtual Team Collaboration in Software Outsourcing. Int. J. Technol. Pol. Manage. 8, 59–75 (2008)

Singh, A., Nigam, A.R.K.: Risks Identification in an Offshore-Onshore Model Based IT Engagement. International Journal of Computer Applications 48, 31–41 (2012)

Šmite, D., Wohlin, C., Gorschek, T., et al.: Empirical Evidence in Global Software Engineering: A Systematic Review. Empirical Software Engineering 15, 91–118 (2010)

Walsham, G.: Doing Interpretive Research. Eur. J. Inform. Syst. 15, 320–330 (2006)

Watson-Manheim, M.B., Chudoba, K.M., Crowston, K.: Perceived Discontinuities and Constructed Continuities in Virtual Work. Inform. Syst. J. 22, 29–52 (2012)

Wenger, E.: Communities of practice: Learning, meanings, and identity. Cambridge university press, New York (1998)

Wenger, E., McDermott, R.A., Snyder, W.: Cultivating communities of practice: A guide to managing knowledge. Harvard Business Press, Boston (2002)

Yalaho, A., Nahar, N.: Key Success Factors for Managing Offshore Outsourcing of Software Production using the ICT-Supported Unified Process Model: A Case Experience from Finland, India, Nepal and Russia. In: Proceedings of Technology Management for Global Economic Growth (PICMET), pp. 1–14 (2010)

Zigurs, I.: Leadership in Virtual Teams:-Oxymoron Or Opportunity? Organ. Dyn. 31, 339–351 (2003)

An Integrative Model Linking Risk, Risk Management and Project Performance: Support from Indian Software Projects

Sam Thomas[1] and Bhasi Marath[2]

[1] School of Management Studies, Cochin University of Science and Technology, Cochin, India
[2] School of Management Studies, Cochin University of Science and Technology, Cochin, India
Sam8570@gmail.com, mbhasi@cusat.ac.in

Abstract. Software development organizations across the globe are concerned about the high rate of project failures. Two constructs which are hypothesized to have significant impact on project outcome are risk and risk management. Risk points to an aspect of a development task, process or environment which, if ignored, tends to adversely affect the project performance. Risk management is defined as the mechanism for identifying, addressing and eliminating software risk items before they become threats to project success. Based on the data collected from 527 software development projects in India, this research develops an integrated model linking these three constructs. Structural Equation Modeling was used to develop and validate the models. The models show how the impact of risk management on project outcome may be mediated by risk.

Keywords: Risk, Risk management, Project Outcome, Software project in India, Structural Equation Modeling.

1   Introduction

Research on software project risk and project outcome has attracted attention among academicians and practitioners all over the world. One of the reasons why this topic remains relevant across time is that the failure rate continues to be very high among software projects. The latest "chaos" report (2011) from Standish Group research shows that 66% of projects are either "challenged" or downright failures, leaving 34% of projects to be considered successful. Jørgensen and Moløkken-Østvold (2006) suggest that failure rates for software development projects could be up to 85%. As software companies continue to invest time and resources into the development of software, how software development problems and failures can be minimized continues to be a focus area.

Most of the researchers on software project risk broadly agree on a two- step approach to managing risk: risk assessment and risk control. Risk assessment involves identifying, analyzing and prioritizing the risk factors that are likely to compromise a project's success, and risk control involves acting on each risk factor in order to eliminate or control it ((Boehm, 1991; Charette, 1996; Lyytinen et.al, 1998; Wallace et al., 2004, Keil et al., 2008, Wen-Ming Han, 2007). Literature review shows that the past research on software project risk has mainly focused on:

Y.K. Dwivedi et al. (Eds.): TDIT 2013, IFIP AICT 402, pp. 326–342, 2013.
© IFIP International Federation for Information Processing 2013

(a) *Risk identification and assessment* (McFarlan, 1981; Barki et al., 1993; Neumann, 1995; Keil et al., 1998; Lyytinen et al., 1998; Ropponen & Lyytinen, 2000; Schmidt et al., 2001; Wallace et al., 2004; Tiwana &Keil, 2004; Cuellar & Gallivan, 2006; Costa et al., 2007)

(b) *Risk management strategies for project performance improvement* (Alter & Ginzberg, 1978;Boehm, 1991; Fairley, 1994; Powell & Klein, 1996; Keil et al., 1998; Barki et al., 2001; Barki & Rivard, 2003; Jiang & Klein, 2004; Iversen et al., 2004; Taylor, 2006; Camprieu et al., 2007; Keil et al., 2008)

(c) *Relationship between risk and risk management* (Kirsch,1996; Ropponen and Lyytinen, 2000; Jiang et al,2000; Barki et al,2001; Addision and Vallabh,2002)

(d) *Link between risk and project performance* (Nidumolu, 1995; Jiang & Klein, 1999; Na et al., 2004; Wallace et al.,2004; Han & Huang, 2007; Na et al., 2007)

Most of the previous research takes an isolated view of software project risk and risk management strategies. Empirical evidence on the relationship between risk, risk management and project outcome is rare. Arguments are largely based on theory or case studies. Yet, this is an important step for advancing our knowledge on software project risk. Most of the projects will have risk management strategies adopted from the beginning of the project. But risk factors continue to exist in the project. What defines the project success will be the combined impact of the risk factors present and the effectiveness of the risk control strategies adopted. This can be analyzed only through an integrated study on the linkages among risk, risk management and project outcome. This can help project managers to select the needed implementation strategies to achieve their desired project outcomes.

The past research on software project risk is predominantly reported from the western world. This has been acknowledged as a major limitation of the research in this domain (Ropponen and Lyytinen, 1997; Schmidt et al., 2001;Shan Liu et al., 2009). Whenever research was conducted in emerging economies, particularly where cross-cultural research indicates likely differences in behavior or practices, differences were observed in software development risk factors -Schmidt et al. (1996) in USA, Finland and Hong Kong, Na et.al (2006) in Korea, Mursu (2000) in Nigeria, Mann et.al (2002) in Thailand, Shan Liu et al (2009) in China and Thomas et.al (2011) in India. Cultural differences can impact work related values and play a significant role in the success or failure of projects (Hofstede, 1980). There is a need for more risk related studies across varying socio-economic contexts to validate the models. Also, previous studies have looked at software projects in all types of companies without focusing on software development with only IT companies.

This research is undertaken with an objective of developing insights into the linkages among risk, risk management and project outcome. Based on the data collected from 527 projects executed within the leading software development companies in India, this paper validates an integrated model linking these constructs using Structural Equation Modeling (SEM). Reliable and validated instruments were used for measuring risk, risk management and project outcome. We begin this article with a brief review of the relevant literature. Next the methodology for collecting and analyzing the data is discussed. Finally, the results of the model testing are reported and the implications of the study are discussed.

2   Background

The research focus on three constructs namely risk, risk management and project out come with respect to software development projects. Previous work related to these studies is briefly reviewed here.

2.1   Software Project Risk

A software project risk points to an aspect of a development task, process or environment, which if ignored tends to increase the likelihood of software project failure (Lyyttinen et al., 1993). Such incidents pose danger to the development of a successful project leading to inadequate software operations, software re-work, implementation difficulty, delay or uncertainty (Boehm, 1991). Barki et al. (1993) define software development project risk as the product of the uncertainty surrounding a software development project and the magnitude of potential loss associated with project failure.

The most common method for identifying the presence of risk factors has been the use of checklists. These checklists present a list of all potential risks that might be applicable in a software development project. One of the pioneering studies in this regard is the top 10 risk list of Boehm (1991). Barki et al (1993) tried to produce a more comprehensive list of risk factors based on the data collected from 120 ongoing projects in 75 organizations. Jiang and Klein (2002) supplemented this study through a survey among project managers asking them to rank these risk categories in order of importance. One of the most quoted international studies on software project risk factors was conducted by Schmidt et al. in 1996. Their research developed an extensive list of risk factors through three simultaneous Delphi surveys in three different settings: Hong Kong, Finland and the United States. Keil et al (1998) improved upon their international Delphi study exploring the issue of IT project risk from the user perspective and compared it with risk perceptions of project managers. The study was repeated in China (Shan Liu et al., 2009) and Nigeria (Anja Mursu ,1999) .The Software Engineering Institute (SEI)'s Taxonomy-Based Risk Identification Instrument, which contains 194 questions, is probably one of the largest checklists of software development risk factors. Moynihan (1997) through his survey on project managers produced a huge collection (113) of risk related constructs and showed that many of the real world issues are not captured in the Barki list and the SEI list. The work by Ropponen and Lyytinen (1997) contributes to the empirical studies on software development risks. Wallace (1999) developed a valid and reliable measure of software project risk to study risk from a common perspective and to compare findings across studies in a more meaningful manner. Addison (2003) through a Delphi study among expert practitioners identified the most important risks in the development of e-commerce projects. IT implementation risk and its impact on the organization have been stressed by many researchers (Alter, 1979; Chatzoglou et.al, 2009, Malhotra et.al, 2009).

2.2   Software Project Risk Management

Once the risk factors are successfully identified and assessed, the next logical step is to manage the risk (Boehm, 1991). Software project risk management is one mechanism for minimizing project failure (McFarlan, 1981; Boehm, 1991; Barki et. al., 1993). Risk management is concerned with a phased and systematic approach to analyse and control the risks occurring in a specific context (Charette, 1996). Project risk management encompasses both hard skills such as estimating and scheduling tasks, and soft skills, which include motivating and managing team members (Kirsch 1996).

Research on software risk management has primarily focused on crafting guidelines for specific tasks. Risk management strategies use observations from the past; they learn from analogical situations, and they use deductive reasoning to detect risky incidents. Alter and Ginzberg's (1978) focused on problems associated with the organizational acceptance and implementation of the information system. Davis' model (1982) is concerned with selecting procedures that lead to complete and correct information requirements. McFarlan (1982) classified risk resolution techniques into four types, namely External integration, Internal integration, Formal planning and Formal control mechanisms. Boehm's model (1991) suggests a comprehensive set of steps and guidelines to manage software development risks. Drawing from contingency research in Organizational theory and IS literature, Barki et al (2001) developed an integrative contingency model of software project risk management. Ropponen and Lyytinen (2000) researched on how risk management practices and environmental contingencies help in addressing the risk components in software projects. Kirsch (1996) proposed to build an integrated contingency model of software project management linking project management practices to the characteristics of the project and attributes of the individuals involved. Jiang et al (2000) studied the relationship between the major risk factors and the risk mitigation strategies. A similar analysis was performed by Addision and Vallabh (2002) to determine whether there were significant relationships between risks and risk controls in software projects.

2.3   Project Outcome and its Linkages with Risk and Risk Management

A project is usually deemed as successful if it meets the desired requirements, is completed on time and is delivered within budget (Powell and Klein, 1996). A number of success criteria have been developed and empirically tested for IS projects. The triple criteria of project success – meeting cost, schedule and performance targets - have been widely used by researchers to analyze project success (Barki et. al 2001; Nidumolu 1995; Deephouse, 2005; Wallace, 2000; Ravichandran, 1996). Performance measures like meeting the original specifications, reliability, easy to use, portability etc. are subjective measure whereas time and cost overruns are objective measures. Studies are reported based on both subjective and objective measures (Nidumolu, 1996; Wallace et al., 2004b; Rai and Al-Hindi, 2000).

Linda Wallace (1999) validated the second order factor model of risk through the establishment of co-alignment, a structural model of the relationship between risk and project outcome. Jiang et. al. (2000) has independently done a study similar to the one described above and arrived at similar conclusions. But both these studies failed to include the risk management in the model which is stated as a major limitation by the authors. Barki et al (2001) showed how the outcome of the software project is influenced by the fit between the project risk and the project management. Deephouse et al (2005), through an exploratory study, developed a conceptual model linking effectiveness of software processes such as project planning, training, user contact, design reviews, prototyping and cross functional teams on project outcome. But there is no reference to the risk items. Nidumolu's (1995) model introduced residual performance risk as an intervening variable clarifying the relationship between risk, coordination mechanisms and performance. Na et al (2006) replicated this study in Korea revealing that both functional and system development risks are important predictors of software project performance. Jiang and Klein (2000) related software development risks to project effectiveness and Deephouse et al (2005 linked effectiveness of software processes to the project outcome.

Building on the limitations of the past research to include comprehensive measures of risk, risk management and project outcome into a single framework, we have undertaken this study. We are attempting to empirically validate the linkages among risk, risk management and project outcome in a single integrated model.

3   Research Methodology

The current research was designed as a survey. Operationally, risk is defined as the presence of the factors that will adversely affect the software development project. Risk management is defined as the presence of practices which are crafted to reduce the impact of risk in software projects. Project outcome is defined in terms of time overrun, cost overrun and quality of the software developed. The level of risk, risk management and project outcome were measured by collecting data from software projects through validated instruments.

3.1   Instrument Development

An exhaustive survey of literature was performed to identify the major risk and risk management items from the previous studies. This list was edited by five senior software professionals working with leading companies in the IT industry as well as five senior professors in software engineering. The project outcome was measured with the validated tool used by Wallace (1999) with nine questions on the product quality and one question each on time and cost overrun. The draft questionnaire was pretested to a convenient sample of 100 software professionals with at least one year of software development project experience. The final instrument was developed incorporating the modifications based on the pretest data. It had 68 items representing the risk construct and 42 items representing the risk management construct. The Wallace (1999) instrument on project outcome was retained without any change.

The population for the study was defined as completed software development projects undertaken by software development organizations based in India. The data had to be provided by a project representative who had been part of the project from the beginning to the completion. The respondent was asked to read each statement and indicate the extent to which the risk / risk management item was present his/her project. The response format for each item was a five-point Likert-type scale ranging from "strongly disagree" to "strongly agree". Product quality was measured through a five point rating scale where the respondent rated the software developed on nine dimensions of software quality. The time and cost overrun (or underrun) had to be indicated as a percentage of variation from the original estimate.

3.2   Data Collection

The survey was conducted in Chennai, Bangalore (tier I cities) Cochin and Trivandrum (tier II cities) in India. National Association of Software Companies (NASSCOM) is the most respected and recognized body of Indian software industry. NASSCOM listed companies account for over 90% of the revenue of the software industry in India. NASSCOM list of software companies in the selected cities was accepted as the sample frame for data collection. Letters were sent via email to the centre heads/HR managers of all the companies requesting them to allow their IT professionals to participate in the study. Reminder letters were sent after three weeks. 105 companies agreed to participate in the study. Data was collected from different types of projects and members in different roles but keeping the condition that only one response should be solicited from one project. The researchers distributed 1350 questionnaires via email to the 105 companies who agreed to participate. After two rounds of reminders, 574 filled questionnaires were collected back from 95 companies. Detailed examination of the data based on grossly missing or inappropriate values resulted in the deletion of 47 records. Thus the final data set had 527 usable records representing 527 projects from 95 companies. Table 1 shows how the sample projects are distributed across various categories.

Table 1. Type of the project in the sample

Sl. No.	Domain	Percent (%)
1	Business Applications	48.3
2	Engineering Applications	20.2
3	System Software	10.5
4	Web Application	17.5
5	Others	3.5
Total		100

4   Developing the Risk and Risk Management Measurement Models

The data was randomly divided into two groups: An estimation sample of 250 responses and validation (hold out) sample of 277 responses. Exploratory Factor Analysis (EFA) was performed on the estimation sample to identify the underlying dimension structure for the risk and risk management constructs. The identified factor structures were confirmed (validated) through a Confirmatory Factor Analysis (CFA) on the validation sample. This approach is recommended by many researchers (Moore and Benbasat, 1991; Hair et. al., 2006, Thomson S.H. Teo et.al, 2006). Finally, the proposed model was tested on the validation sample using structural equation modeling.

4.1   Exploratory Factor Analysis (EFA)

The estimation sample data was subjected to an exploratory factor analysis using principal component analysis with varimax rotation. This has been the most popular and accepted procedure for similar data analysis (Moore and Benbasat, 1991, King and Teo, 1996, Thomson S.H. Teo et.al, 2006). The number of factors was to be decided looking into (a) percentage of variance explained (b) eigen values (c) interpretability of the factor structure (Hair et.al, 2006).

The analyses led to the representation of risk construct as a five factor structure and risk management as a four factor structure. Kaiser–Meyer–Oaklin measure of sampling adequacy and Bartlett Test of Sphericity values were seen to be acceptable. Items that did not load on a factor or cross load on multiple factors were identified. They were deleted if they didn't affect the face validity of the instrument in which case they were retained under the factor where the loading was highest. The final instrument had 55 risk items under risk construct loading onto five risk dimensions (Thomas et al, 2012) and 36 items under the risk management construct loading onto 4 risk management dimensions (Thomas et.al, 2011(2)).

4.2   Confirmatory Factor Analysis (CFA)

Confirmatory Factor Analysis (CFA) which is part of the structural equation modelling (SEM) is used to confirm a factor structure known beforehand or developed through EFA. The validation sample data was used to confirm the factor structures developed with EFA on the estimation sample. Software package AMOS 4.0 was used to do the analysis. The overall fit of a model was assessed using a number of fit indices like Goodness of Fit Index (GFI) (Joreskog and Sorbom, 1989), Comparative Fit Index (CFI) (Bentler, 1990), Non-normed Fit Index (NFI) (Bentler and Bonet`t, 1980) and Root Mean Squared Residual (RMSR). The reliability of each dimension as well as the total construct was tested by computing Cronbach alpha (α) value. The risk and risk management dimensions with the fit indices are presented in tables 2 and 3. Thomas et.al (2012) describes in details the procedure followed.

Table 2. Fit indices for the measurement models of risk

Dimensions of risk	No. of items	GFI	CFI	NFI	RMSR	Cron bach α
Team Risk	26	0.894	0.953	0.913	0.048	0.9667
Proj. Plan & Exec Risk	14	0.804	0.807	0.790	0.09	0.9196
External Risk	5	0.914	0.837	0.831	0.08	0.8466
User Risk	6	0.962	0.967	0.958	0.07	0.8309
Proj. Complex Risk	4	0.990	0.986	0.982	0.03	0.7663
Full Risk Model	55	0.908	0.895	0.896	0.04	0.813

Table 3. Fit indices for the measurement models of risk management

Dimensions of Risk Management	No. of items	GFI	CFI	NFI	RMSR	Cron bachα
Execution Management Strategies	13	0.937	0.953	0.937	0.038	0.9204
Human Resource Management Strategies	11	0.930	0.913	0.895	0.050	0.8630
User Coordination Strategies	6	0.983	0.975	0.965	0.030	0.7001
Project Planning Strategies	6	0.994	0.999	0.989	0.034	0.8059
Full Risk Management Model	36	0.921	0.914	0.907	0.037	0.8340

5   Risk Management-Risk-Project Outcome Model

The objective of this research to empirically develop and validate an integrated model linking risk, risk management and project outcome. Risk management is designed to reduce risk in the project and reduction in risk is expected to improve the project outcome (Nidumolu,1995; Na et al, 2006). Thus the impact of the risk management on project outcome may be mediated by risk in the project. The proposed research model shown in figure 1 model postulates that risk management will be related to project outcome, both directly and indirectly, being mediated by risk. The hypothesized direct and indirect relationship between the predictor variables (risk, risk management) and the dependent variable (project outcome) is explored. Separate models were tested for each of the project outcome measures. Figure 2 shows the proposed model for the project outcome "quality".

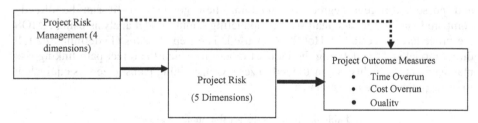

Fig. 1. Integrated model

Structural equation modeling (SEM) is often used for testing theory associated with latent variable models because it enables the inference of complex relationships among variables which cannot be directly observed. SEM is a multivariate statistical methodology, which takes a confirmatory approach to the analysis of a structural theory. SEM provides researchers with the ability to accommodate multiple interrelated dependence relationships in a single model. (Hair et al., 1998). As mentioned earlier, the overall fit of a model was assessed using a number of fit indices as well as the values of the loading coefficients.

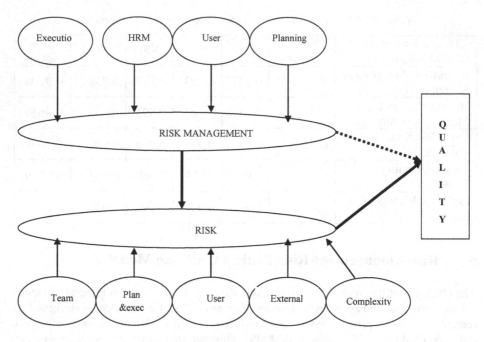

Fig. 2. Hypothesized model of quality

5.1   Modeling the Outcome Variable - Quality

The posited model presented in figure 2 contains two models — (1) the full direct model, which incorporates all identified paths and (2) the indirect model, in which the direct path (dotted) linking risk management to Quality will not be estimated. As both these models are nested (i.e., they are hierarchical models based on the same data set) and possess different degrees of freedom, their goodness-of-fit can be directly compared via multimodel analysis. In conducting a multimodel analysis using AMOS the procedure suggested by Ho(2006) is used. The step involves (1) defining the full direct model and (2) defining the indirect model in which the direct path linking risk management to Quality is constrained to zero. Constraining paths to zero is equivalent to those paths not being estimated.

Table 4. Fit measures for the quality models

Fit measures	Values for the direct model for quality	Values for the indirect model for quality
Chi square (χ2)	72	134
GFI	0.974	0.953
CFI	0.988	0971
RMSR	0.029	0.038
Akaike Criterion Information	132	192

As seen in table 4, both the models are fitting the data very well. But the direct model has better fit indices values. The reduction in chi square (from 134 to 72) is statistically significant for a corresponding reduction of 1 in the degree of freedom as we move from indirect model to direct model. Therefore, although both models fitted the data relatively well, the direct model represents a significantly better fit than the indirect model, and is to be preferred. This conclusion is further supported by the Akaike Criterion Information (AIC) comparison statistics which shows a lower value for direct model which indicates that the direct model is both better fitting and more parsimonious than the indirect model. Table 5 presents the standardized regression coefficients of the paths in the hypothesized direct model.

Table 5. Standardized path coefficients for the quality model

Paths			Standardized Path coefficients	Significance (P)
risk management	->	risk	-0.498	0.000
risk management	->	Quality	0.351	0.000
risk	->	Quality	-0.318	0.000
risk	->	complexity risk	0.892	0.000
risk	->	user risk	0.826	0.000
risk	->	external risk	0.685	0.000
risk	->	team risk	0.870	0.000
risk	->	plan & exec	0.658	0.000
risk management	->	exec mgmt	0.930	0.000
risk management	->	HR mgmt	0.865	0.000
risk management	->	user mgmt	0.752	0.000
risk management	->	planning mgmt	0.834	0.000

The results indicated that all the paths highly significant at p = 0.01 level. The risk had a significant negative link with risk management. Quality had a significant negative link with risk and positive link with risk management. Risk management is related indirectly to quality being mediated by risk. Thus better risk management result in reduced risk (β = -0.498) and reduction in risk results in increased quality (β = -0.318). Also, the better risk management results in a direct improvement in quality ((β = -0.351) and indirect improvement through risk (-0.498*-0.318= 0.158) . The loadings of the first order factors onto risk and risk management constructs were strong and positive, thereby providing further support for the model (Segars and Grover., 1993).

5.2 Modeling the Outcome Variable -Time Overrun

A similar analysis was performed on the second project outcome variable "time overrun". Both the direct and indirect models were tested. The values of the fit measures are reported in table 6:

Table 6. Fit measures for the time overrun models

Fit measures	Values for the direct model for time	Values for the indirect model for time overrun
Chi square (χ2)	68	73
GFI	0.957	0.953
AGFI	0.906	0.900
CFI	0.982	0.980
RMSR	0.154	0.155
Akaike Criterion Information	128	131

Table 7. Standardized path coefficients for the time overrun model

Paths		Standardized Path coefficients	Significance (P)
Risk management ->	risk	-0.467	0.000
Risk	-> Time overrun	0.754	0.000
Risk management ->	Time overrun	-0.110	0.030
Risk	-> complexity risk	0.901	0.000
Risk	-> user risk	0.841	0.000
Risk	-> external risk	0.736	0.000
Risk	-> team risk	0.900	0.000
risk	-> plan & exec risk	0.595	0.000
risk management ->	execution mgmt	0.915	0.000
risk management ->	HR mgmt	0.862	0.000
risk management ->	user mgmt	0.809	0.000
risk management ->	planning mgmt	0.831	0.000

As seen both models are fitting well. The direct model shows slightly better fit. The standardized path coefficients for the direct mode are shown in table 7. The path linking risk management to time overrun is not significant at p = 0.01 level but significant at 5% level. The magnitude of the coefficient is very weak (β = -0.11). Thus it can be concluded that the impact of risk on time overrun is strong and significant(β =0.754). But the direct effect of risk management on the outcome variable is very weak (-0.11) and the effect is mainly indirect(-0.467*0.754 =-0.352) mediated through risk.

5.3   Modeling the Outcome Variable -Cost Overrun

The final outcome variable cost overrun was also modeled and analyzed similar to the other two variables. The values of the fit measures for the two models are reported in table 8.

Table 8. Fit measures for the cost overrun models

Fit measures	Values for the direct model for cost overrun	Values for the indirect model for cost overrun
Chi square	70.7	70.9
GFI	0.957	0.956
AGFI	0.904	0.908
CFI	0.980	0.981
RMSR	0.152	0.162
Akaike Criterion Information (AIC)	132	131

Table 9. Standardized path coefficients for the cost overrun model

Paths		Standardized Path coefficients	Significance (P)
Risk management ->	risk	-0.472	0.000
Risk ->	Cost overrun	0.559	0.000
Risk management ->	Cost overrun	-0.019	0.730
Risk ->	complexity risk	0.901	0.000
Risk ->	user risk	0.854	0.000
Risk ->	external risk	0.727	0.000
Risk ->	team risk	0.890	0.000
risk ->	plan & exec	0.603	0.000
risk management ->	execution	0.914	0.000
risk management ->	HR mgmt	0.862	0.000
risk management ->	user mgmt	0.813	0.000
risk management ->	planning mgmt	0.827	0.000

The two models show equal fit and statistically there is no difference between the two. The reduction in chi square value is not significant for a one degree difference in the degrees of freedom. This supports the indirect model. The path coefficients (Table 9) shows that the path linking risk management to cost overrun is insignificant even at p=.05 level. Thus we conclude that the risk has direct impact on cost overrun where as the effect of risk management is indirect through the mediating variable risk.

6   Limitations of the Study

Risk and risk management are complex constructs which many researchers constantly work on. Hence it is quite possible that this research may not have captured every aspect of these construct even though an extensive literature review was conducted and experts in the area were consulted for inputs.

The study was designed as a single-respondent survey. Although it is common to use a single respondent in academic research, it would be more desirable to have multiple respondents from each project and independently assess risk in order to validate the results. Future researchers can address this issue by administering the instrument in this study to different stakeholders involved with the same project and comparing their perceptions of risk. The data is confined to projects executed with IT companies in India. It doesn't account for software development happening with non IT companies.

This research looks at software projects at a generic level. This lays the foundation for future research for studying the possible variation in the models depending on the organizational and project characteristics. Future researchers can follow the procedures laid out in this study to develop models on projects which are at different stages in project life cycle rather than studying them at the completion of the project.

7   Discussion and Conclusion

This study showed the integrated relationship among risk, risk management and project outcome. The implications of this research for researchers and practitioners are highlighted.

The study showed that the impact of the risk management on project outcome is mediated by the levels of risk present. This indirect impact is more visible in the case of time and cost outcome measures. The quality of the software developed had a positive relationship with risk management and negative relationship with risk. The direct impact of risk management was seen to be stronger than the indirect impact through risk. The other outcome variables namely time overrun and cost overrun had strong negative relationship with risk. Risk management did not have much direct effect on overrun variables. Risk was seen to be acting as an intervening variable between risk management and overrun variables.

The direct link between risk and project outcome measures is consistent with literature. Wallace (1999) proved that the second order model of risk directly influenced all the three outcome measures. Jiang and Klein (2000) also demonstrated the negative impact of risk items on a range of project effectiveness measures.

The findings on the direct as well as indirect impact of risk management on project outcome also find support from literature. Deephouse et.al (2005) found that effectiveness of the software processes had a stronger and direct linkage with project quality than with overrun measures. Nidumolu (1995) showed that the risk control measures such as coordination strategies may have a direct and/or indirect impact on project outcome measures.

The impact and the importance of different risk and risk management dimensions can be understood looking at their loading coefficients in the models. The complexity risk and team risk are seen to be the most important risk dimensions in all the three models. Similarly execution management and HR management are seen to be the most effective risk management components.

It is important for project managers to understand this relationship among these constructs in the integrated environment. A clear assessment of risk helps project managers to perform risk control better. They can develop appropriate strategies for mitigating the risk in order to reduce the chance of project failure. Thus it can be concluded that only an integrated model accounting for the direct and indirect impact of risk and risk management can explain the variation in project outcome measures satisfactorily.

References

Addison, T.: E-commerce project development risks: Evidence from a Delphi survey. International Journal of Information Management 23(1), 25–40 (2003)

Alter, S.: Implementation risk analysis. TIMS Studies in Management Sciences 13(2), 103–119 (1979)

Alter, S., Ginzberg, M.: Managing Uncertainty in MIS Implementation. Sloan Management Review, 23–31 (fall 1978)

Barki, H., Rivard, S.: Toward an assessment of software development risk. Journal of Management Information Systems 10, 203 (1993)

Barki, H., Rivard, S., Talbot, J.: Toward an assessment of software development risk. Journal of Management Information Systems 10(2), 203–225 (1993)

Barki, H., Rivard, S., Talbot, J.: An integrative contingency model of software project risk management. Journal of Management Information Systems 17(4), 37–69 (2001)

Bayer, J., Muthig, D.: A view-based approach for improving software documentation practices. In: 13th Annual IEEE International Symposium and Workshop on Engineering of Computer Based Systems (2006)

Bentler, P.M.: Comparative fit indexes in structural models. Psychological Bulletin 107, 238–246 (1990)

Bentler, P.M., Bonett, D.G.: Significance tests and goodness of fit in the analysis of covariance structures. Psychological Bulletin 88, 588–606 (1980)

Boehm, B.: Theory-W software project management principles and examples. IEEE Transactions on Software Engineering 15(7), 902–916 (1989)

Boehm, B.W.: Software risk management: Principles and practices. IEEE Software 8(1), 32–41 (1991)

Charette, R.N.: Software engineering risk analysis and management. McGraw-Hill Software Engineering Series (1996)

Chatzoglou, P.D., Diamantidis, A.D.: IT / IS implementation risks and their impact on firm performance. International Journal of Information Management 29(2), 119–128 (2009)

Costa, H.R., Barros, M.O., Travassos, G.H.: Evaluating software project portfolio risks. Journal of Systems and Software 80, 16–31 (2007)

Cuellar, M.J., Gallivan, M.J.: A framework for ex ante project risk assessment based on absorptive capacity. European Journal of Operational Research 173, 1123–1138 (2006)

Davis, G.B.: Strategies for Information Requirements Determination. IBM Systems Journal 21(1), 4–30 (1982)

Deephouse, C., Mukhopadhyay, T., Goldenson, D.R., Kellner, M.I.: Software Processes and Project Performance. Journal of Management Information Systems (Winter 1995-1996) 12(3), 185–203 (2005)

Ewusi-Mensah, K., Przasnyski, Z.H.: On information systems project abandonment: An exploratory study of organizational practices. MIS Quarterly 15(1), 67–85 (1991)

Fairley, R.: Risk management for software projects. IEEE Software 11(3), 57–67 (1994)

Ginzberg, M.: Early diagnosis of MIS implementation failure: Promising results and unanswered questions. Management Science 27(4), 459–478 (1981)

Hair Jr., J.F., Black, W.C., Babin, B.J., Anderson, R.E., Tatham, R.L.: Multivariate data analysis. Pearson Prentice-Hall, Englewood Cliffs (2006)

Hair, J.F., Anderson, R.E., Tatham, R.L., Black, W.C.: Multivariate Data Analysis. Prentice-Hall International, New Jersey (2006)

Ho, R.A.: Handbook of Univariate and Multivariate Data Analysis and Interpretation with SPSS. Francis and Taylor Group, LLC (2006)

Hofstede, G.: Cultures and organizations: Software of the mind: Intercultural cooperation and its importance for survival. McGraw-Hill, London (1980)

Iversen, J.H., Mathiassen, L., Nielsen, P.A.: Managing risk in software process improvement: an action research approach. MIS Quarterly 28, 395–433 (2004)

Jiang, J., Klein, G.: Information system success as impacted by risks and development strategies. IEEE Transactions on Engineering Management 48, 46–55 (2004)

Jiang, J.J., Klein, G.: Software development risks to project effectiveness. Journal of Systems and Software 52(1), 3 (2000)

Jiang, J.J., Klein, G.: The importance of building a foundation for user- involvement in information system projects. Project Management Journal 33(1), 20–26 (2002)

Jiang, J., Klein, G.: Risk to different aspects of system success. Information & Management 36(5), 263–271

Jones, C.: Assessment and control of software risks. Yourdon Press, Englewood Cliffs (1999)

Jørgensen, M., Moløkken-Østvold: How large are software cost overruns? A review of the 1994 CHAOS report. Information and Software Technology 48, 297–301 (2006)

Keil, M., Cule, E.P.: Framework for identifying software project risks. Communications of the ACM 41(11), 765–783 (1998)

King, W.R., Teo, T.S.H.: Key dimensions of facilitators and inhibitors for the strategic use of information technology. Journal of Management Information Systems (12), 4 (1996)

Kirsch, L.J.: The management of complex tasks in organizations: controlling the systems development process. Organization Science 7, 1–21 (1996)

Lyytinen, K., Mathiassen, L., Ropponen, J.: Attention Shaping and Software Risk – A categorical Analysis of Four Classical Risk Management Approaches. Information Systems Approach 9(3), 233–255 (1988)

Lyytinen, K.: Expectation failure concept and systems analysts view of information system failures: Results of an exploratory study. Information and Management 14, 45–46 (1988)

Lyytinen, K., Mathiassen, L., Ropponen, J.: An organizational analysis of software risk management approaches. Working Paper, University of Jyvaskyla, Jyvaskyla, Finland (1993)

Lyytinen, K., Mathiassen, L., Ropponen, J.: Attention shaping and software risk – A categorical analysis of four classical risk management approaches. Information Systems Approach 9(3), 233–255 (1998)

Malhotra, R., Temponi, C.: Critical decisions for ERP integration: Small business issues. International Journal of Information Management 30(1), 23–37 (2010)

Mann, J.: Undergraduate global IT education: An experiential approach using the concept of fit. In: IRMA Conference 2000, pp. 917–918 (2002)

McFarlan, F.W.: Portfolio approach to information systems. Harvard Business Review 59(5), 142–150 (1981)

Moore, G.C., Benbasat, I.: Development of an instrument to measure the perceptions of adopting an information technology innovation. Information Systems Research 2(3), 173–191 (1991)

Moore, J.E.: One road to turnover: an examination of work exhaustion in technology professionals. MIS Quarterly 24(1), 141–168 (2000)

Moynihan, T.: How experienced Project Managers access risk. IEEE Software 14(3), 35–41 (1997)

Mursu, A.: From software risks to sustainable information systems: Setting the stage for a Delphi study in Nigeria. Journal of Global Information Technology Management 2, 57–71 (1997)

Mursu, A.: University of Jyväskylä, Dept. of Computer Science and Information Systems, PL 35, FIN 40351 Jyväskylä, Finland (2000)

Na, K., Li, X., Simpson, J.T., Kim, K.: Uncertainty profile and software project performance: A cross-national comparison. The Journal of Systems and Software 70, 155–163 (2004)

Na, K., Simpson, J.T., Li, X., Singh, T., Kim, K.: Software development risk and project performance measurement: Evidence in Korea. Journal of Systems and Software 80(4), 596–605 (2006)

Neumann, P.G.: Computer related Risks. Addison-Wesley, Reading (1995)

Nidumolu, S.: The Effect of Coordination and Uncertainty on Software Project Performance: Residual Performance Risk as an Intervening Variable. Information Systems Research, 191–219 (1995)

Powell, P.L., Klein, J.H.: Risk Management for Information Systems Development. Journal of Information Technology 11, 309–311 (1996)

Rai, A., Al-Hindi, H.: Effects of development process modeling and task uncertainty on development quality performance. Information and Management 37, 335–346 (2000)

Ravichandran, T.: Special issue on component-based software development. ACM SIGMIS Database 34(4), 45–46 (2003)

Ropponen, J., Lyytinen, K.: Can software risk management improve system development: An exploratory study? European Journal of Information Systems 6(1), 41–50 (1997)

Ropponen, J., Lyytinen, K.: Components of software development risk: how to address them? A project manager survey. IEEE Transactions on Software Development 26(2), 98–112 (2000)

Schmidt, J., Kozar, K.: Management's role in information system development failures: A Case Study. MIS Quarterly 2, 7–16 (1978)

Schmidt, R., Lyytinen, K., Keil, M., Cule, P.: Identifying software project risks: an international delphi study. In: Proceedings of the 17th International Conference on Information Systems, Cleveland, OH (1996)

Segars, A.H., Grover, V.: Re-Examining Perceived Ease of Use and Usefulness: A Confirmatory Factor Analysis. MIS Quarterly 17(4), 517–525 (1993)

Shan, L., Jinlong, Z., Keil, M., Chen, T.: Comparing senior executive and project manager perceptions of IT project risk: Chinese Delphi study. Information Systems Journal (2009)

Taylor, H.: Risk management and problem resolution strategies for IT projects: prescription and practice. Project Management Journal 37, 49–63 (2006)

Teo, T.H., Ranganathan, C., Dhaliwal, J.: Key dimensions of inhibitors for the deployment of web-based business-to-business electronic commerce. IEEE Transactions on Engineering Management 53(3) (2006)

Sam, T., Bhasi, M.: How does software project risk vary across projects? An exploratory study from India. International Journal of Intercultural Information Management 2(4) (2011)

Sam, T., Bhasi, M.: A Structural Model for Software Project Risk Management. Vilakshan XIMB Journal of Management VIII (February 2011)

Sam, T., Bhasi, M.: Software Development Project Risk: A Second Order Factor Model Validated in the Indian Context. International Journal of Information Technology Project Management 3(4), 41–55 (2012)

Tiwana, A., Keil, M.: The One-Minute Risk Assessment Tool. Communications of the ACM 47, 73–78 (2004)

Wallace, L.: The development of an instrument to measure software project risk. Thesis 1/1999, Georgia University (1999)

Wallace, L., Keil, M.: Software project risks and their effect on outcomes. Communications of the ACM 47(4), 68–73 (2000)

Wallace, L., Keil, M., Rai, A.: Understanding Software Project Risk: A Cluster Analysis. Information and Management 42(1), 115–125 (2004)

Wen-Ming, H., Sun-Jen, H.: An empirical analysis of risk components and performance on software projects. The Journal of Systems and Software 80, 42–50 (2007)

Legitimation of E-Government Initiatives:
A Study of India's Identity Project

Jyoti M. Bhat

Indian Institute of Management, Bangalore, India
jyoti.bhat@iimb.ernet.in

Abstract. Legitimation is an important aspect of e-government initiatives due to the complex and diverse issues related to policy and technology implementation which create huge demands for resources. Legitimation is one of the core concepts of Institutional theory. Though institutional theory is gaining importance in IS and e-government research, there are very few studies on the strategies and process of legitimation in e-government implementations. In this paper we use institutional theory and examine the institutionalization of India's Unique Identification (UID) project. Given the novelty and uniqueness of the UID initiative, we find that the predominant strategy used is that of conformance and proactive manipulation of the environment. The main contribution of the paper is in identifying that different strategies are used for supply side and demand side stakeholders of e-government projects.

Keywords: E-government, legitimation, Institutional theory.

1   Introduction

E-government projects cover a variety of applications depending on the content, the stakeholders involved and the specific context of use. While typical e-government projects cater to specific categories of stakeholders (Rowley 2011), National identity (NI) projects are relevant to a wider range of contexts and stakeholders. NI projects leverage the latest technologies like smart cards and biometrics to enable identity management and impact large numbers of people in various economic, social and political activities. While the primary driving forces behind identity projects in developing countries are efficient delivery of government welfare services and developmental goals, in some of the developed countries, especially in Europe (Kubicek and Noack, 2010), the current focus is national security, travel document management, e-commerce and e-services. The evolving expectations, diverse stakeholders, large scale of implementation, untested technologies and the huge demands for financial and human resources make NI projects complex and risk prone. Countries like the UK and Australia had to abandon their identity projects as the public debate and opposition raised issues which turned these projects into technical, financial and even political liabilities.

NI projects are similar to other infrastructure projects taken up by the state, as they provide a basic service (i.e. identity management) to citizens, which can then be used by other government, private, social and economic actors. NI project creates a *new*

Y.K. Dwivedi et al. (Eds.): TDIT 2013, IFIP AICT 402, pp. 343–358, 2013.

institutional field with its own set of norms, processes and practices through which government, commercial and other parties interact. The benefits of identity projects take a longer time to become visible as they depend on large scale usage across diverse applications and on network effects. Hence the success of NI project depends on it gaining legitimacy and achieving a taken-for-grantedness among the various stakeholders.

Legitimizing a novel idea is very critical, especially if it involves both technology and practice novelty (Boxenbaum 2008). The institutionalization of NI involves the acceptance of the new identity management processes in addition to the adoption and diffusion of the identity management technologies. The planned interventions and tactics adopted by the NI project managers to gain legitimacy are critical to creating the new institutional field. While gaining legitimacy is critical for e-government success, there exists a gap in literature related to the legitimation processes and strategies adopted by e-government projects. In this paper we examine the legitimation strategies adopted by NI projects and address a critical gap in e-government literature. We study the institutionalization of India's Unique Identification (UID) project and examine the strategies being adopted to gain legitimacy.

The Indian government has taken up Aadhaar[1], an ambitious biometric based identity for its billion plus residents in order to provide a clear identity to its citizens that would be primarily used as the basis for efficient delivery of welfare services (UIDAI, 2009). UID has many firsts to its credit as an e-government project with respect to technology, scale and application, even when compared to other public and private ICT implementations across the globe. The current discourse is slowing moving away from UID enrolments and technological debates related to data security, reliability of biometric technology and authentication to the UID based delivery of welfare services. Given the novelty of the UID initiative with its dependence on IT as a paradigm changer, we found the strategies for legitimation of the IT/IS process to be different from the legitimation of the identify management process in government departments (Avgerou, 2000). Though a repertoire of tactics is employed, UID is focusing on gaining cognitive legitimacy. It uses acquiescence or conformance strategies for the IT/IS dimension and proactive environment manipulation strategies for institutionalization of the identity management process. The main contribution of the paper is in identifying that the legitimation strategies adopted for supply side stakeholders differ from those adopted for demand side stakeholders. While context is critical in studying IS innovation diffusion, our findings can be applied to other large e-government projects which involve the creation of institutions where IT can be seen as an active change agent.

In the next section we discuss the theoretical background for legitimation of e-government projects. We then describe the research question and method used. We provide an overview of Aadhaar and its institutional field to help understand the context. The analysis section details out our findings related to the legitimation strategies being adopted by Aadhaar. We discuss our study with respect to existing studies on legitimation strategies and conclude by identifying the contributions made by this study and the future work.

---

[1] Aadhaar means "foundation" in many Indian languages. UID and Aadhaar have been used interchangeably in this document.

2   Theoretical Background

Institutional theory "considers the processes by which structures, including schemas, rules, norms, and routines, become established as authoritative guidelines for social behavior" (Scott, 2005). Institutional theory recognizes that the environment places a variety of technical, economic, social and cultural demands on organizations. Institutionalization is the process by which social practices conform to environmental pressures and eventually become taken for granted (Scott, 2008). Institutional theorists describe three kinds of institutional pressures the environment exerts on organizations and organizational actors: coercive – formal and informal pressures due to the legal environment, standards and norms; normative – due to professionalism resulting from education and professional networks; and mimetic – as a response to uncertainty when organizations mimic or model themselves on other organizations that are perceived to be more legitimate or successful (DiMaggio and Powell, 1983).

The concept of agency is also gaining importance in institutional theory where interested actors work to influence their institutional contexts. Jepperson (1991) considers agentic action and defines institutions as the product of specific purposive actions taken to reproduce, alter and destroy mechanisms of control. Lawrence and Suddaby (2006) through a review of empirical work in institutional entrepreneurship, identify ten distinct sets of practices through which actors engaged in actions that resulted in the creation of new institutions. These include advocacy, defining, vesting, constructing identities, changing normative associations, constructing normative networks, mimicry etc. Advocacy, defining and vesting are actions which have political tones and define access to material resources. Constructing identities and changing normative associations focus on how actors' belief systems are reconfigured. Mimicry and educating are actions which focus on altering abstract categorizations. Oliver (1991) suggests an active approach of organizational actors in managing legitimacy. She suggests that organizational actors and managers do not always conform or comply with institutional pressures, but adopt other strategic responses which vary in active resistance. The five types of strategic responses which are each exerted through tactics are: acquiescence, compromise, avoidance, defiance, and manipulation. Boxenbaum (2008) suggests that there are varying degrees between the two extremes of institutional pressures and managerial response in gaining legitimacy. Rao (1994) classifies legitimacy into sociopolitical and cognitive. Cognitive legitimacy is the acceptance of new ideas as desirable and appropriate within a widely shared system of norms and values, while endorsements by legal authorities, governmental bodies, and other powerful organizations provides sociopolitical legitimacy.

Suchmann (1995) synthesizes the strategic and institutional groups of legitimation studies and proposes an inclusive, broad-based definition of legitimacy:

"Legitimacy is a generalized perception or assumption that the actions of an entity are desirable, proper, or appropriate within some socially constructed system of norms, values, beliefs, and definitions."

He proposes three primary forms of legitimacy: pragmatic, based on audience self-interest; moral, based on normative approval: and cognitive, based on comprehensibility and taken-for-grantedness. While the three forms co-exist, there are some underlying distinctions: pragmatic legitimacy rests on audience self-interest, whereas moral and cognitive legitimation involves larger cultural rules; pragmatic and moral legitimacy rest on discursive evaluation and organizations can gain legitimation by participating in public discussions and dialogues. Suchmann proposes 30 legitimation strategies and classifies them under gaining, maintaining and repairing legitimation within the 'institutional field' which is the environment within which legitimacy must be gained. Further the mechanism for gaining legitimacy can be classified as conforming, selecting or manipulating the institutional field.

A cross-disciplinary literature review by Weerakkody et al. (2009) finds that the use of institutional theory is in its infancy within the IS discipline. King et al. (1994) recognizing the institutional factors in the diffusion of IT innovations propose six types of interventions which can be employed by the government to facilitate IT innovations. The six types of institutional interventions are mobilization, knowledge building, knowledge deployment, innovation directive, subsidy, and standard setting. While these interventions were proposed for guiding government's support for IT innovation, Henriksen and Damsgaard (2007) adapt the interventions proposed by King et al. to study and classify the initiatives used to stimulate e-government diffusion in Denmark. They find that the demand-pull based approach has not been successful and the Danish government is changing its strategy to imperatives and regulations. An examination of IS research publications by Mignerat and Rivard (2009) found that though the Institutional theory is being used by IS researchers; there are very few papers which adopted institutional theory to study e-government. Another finding was that 'acquiescence' or conformance was the only legitimation strategy studied by most of the IS papers reviewed. IS innovations may be initially adopted and diffused for its technical merits (Zucker 1983), and partly under the influence of powerful actors (Granovetter and McGuire 1998). Avgerou (2000) finds that IS development and organizational transformation are two different institutionalization processes, and ongoing sustenance of IS adoption is based on its legitimacy, irrespective of its contribution to the processes of organizational change.

According to Whitley and Hoisen (2010) most governments approach their NI projects as a technology implementation without considering the eventual social impact and economic opportunities possible through innovative applications of NI. Crosby (2008), by studying various NI usages across countries and private sector players, highlights the opportunities for new services and markets based on the NI infrastructure. He also brings out the need to involve various stakeholders and sectors in designing and implementing the NI project. The role of stakeholders and the importance of their participation in the e-government initiative for its long-term success are well-recognized in the literature (Flak and Rose, 2005). De' (2005) provides an appropriate framework for stakeholder groups in e-government considering their role as demand-side or supply-side and the impact felt by them as first order, second order or higher-order effects. These stakeholder groups exert institutional pressures on the e-government project.

Studies on technology acceptance and user satisfaction focus on individual's adoptions of ICT based on their perceptions of the technology (Venkatesh et al, 2003). E-government projects differ as the acceptance involves a social and political process with different adoption motivations across stakeholders. Current e-government approaches take a project management approach and do not address the facilitation process required across various stakeholders such as policymakers, public officials, and business persons (Sarantis et al., 2010). Hence an institutional perspective considering the various institutional pressures, developmental goals, existing social norms and beliefs which forces e-government projects to seek legitimacy more than efficiency (DiMaggio and Powell, 1983) is more appropriate to study the diffusion of NI initiatives.

The literature review identifies the need for the legitimation process in e-government projects, especially NI projects, given the novelty, complexity and scale of the initiatives. There is a need to gain a positive cognitive personal response from salient stakeholders to gain support and access to resources. Existing studies of legitimation of IT-enabled changes focus on organizations (private or public). There exists a gap in literature related to studies on legitimation strategies adopted in e-government projects. We attempt to address this gap by examining the legitimation strategies adopted by India's UID project.

3   Research Question and Method

The research objective is to identify and analyze the interventions and legitimation strategics adopted by Aadhaar for success of the NI initiative. As NI initiatives involve creating a new institutional field with new actors, norms and procedures, the legitimation strategies are used to institutionalize NI. Legitimation of NI initiatives would involve two separate sets of strategies (Avgerou, 2000); one for the legitimation of the identity technologies and infrastructure and the other for the identity management processes used in e-government projects (enrolments, authentication and related applications). Hence

RQ1: *Are there different sets of strategies for gaining IS/IT infrastructure legitimation and e-government process legitimation in NI initiatives?*

The success of NI depends on large scale usage across diverse contexts and e-government applications. While pragmatic and moral legitimation strategies will be adopted, gaining cognitive legitimacy is important for long term success of NI initiatives. But government departments and agencies using NI to reengineer their process would evaluate the NI processes against their pragmatic expectations and benefits. The large numbers of people impacted and the novelty of technology and processes may force NI project managers to adopt manipulation strategies like co-opt, influence, or control the institutional pressures.

RQ2: *Are there specific clusters and legitimation strategies which are more suitable for gaining specific types of legitimacy in NI projects?*

The above research questions have been framed specific to NI projects, but can be generalized to other large e-government or IS implementation projects which involve the creation of a new institutional field.

The research methodology adopted in this paper is a case study approach using document analysis. Before beginning our study, we had an informal discussion with one of the senior members of the UIDAI technical team, who provided us with details on the events, choices and decisions made which lead to the current design and process for UID enrolments. The discussion also helped us identify relevant documents on the UIDAI website. We studied all the documents and articles related to Aadhaar available at the website of UIDAI (http://uidai.gov.in/). These indicate the explicit legitimation strategies adopted. Several news articles related to UID which highlight the activities of UIDAI were accessed through popular search engines using the keywords "UID", "UIDAI" and "Aadhaar". Documents and reports related to UID available in the public domain like websites of various government departments and agencies (like Parliament debates, GoI circulars, welfare benefit department websites) and discussions on social media sites dedicated to UID discussions were also studied (like http://thinkuid.org/ and http://aadhararticles.blogspot.in/). The documents and news articles for the period of two years (2011 and 2012) were examined. Each document and source was examined by the author and the legitimation strategy identified. Each strategy was then coded using the categorization proposed by Suchmann (1995) for gaining legitimation along two dimensions - pragmatic, moral and cognitive legitimacy; and conforming, selecting and manipulating the institutional field.   The legitimation strategies were further classified as IT/IS oriented strategies and NI process strategies.

4   Aadhaar – India's UID

Aadhaar, India's Unique Identity project (UID), which aims to provide a unique identity to 1.2 billion is the largest ICT roll-out using IT, biometrics and mobile technologies. In the last decade various national identity options have been evaluated by the Indian government. The current national identity project, initially proposed in 2003, was called the Multipurpose National Identity card and was initiated to address the national security issues. The current government which came to power in 2004 carried the project forward but renamed it as UID in January 2009 indicating a shift to a development goal for the project. The context in which Aadhaar project has been taken up is for efficient delivery of the socio-economic benefit services of the government. According to the strategy overview document developed by UIDAI, the statutory body set up to handle the Aadhaar project (UIDAI, 2010) –

"The purpose of UIDAI is to issue a unique identification number (UID) to all Indian residents that is (a) robust enough to eliminate duplicate and fake identities, and (b) can be verified and authenticated in an easy, cost effective way"

The current focus of UID is the poor and underprivileged communities who lack any form of identity documentation. Therefore, UID enrolments are not being mandated though it is envisaged as the de facto identity for most applications in the future (GoI, 2008). UIDAI issues a 12-digit randomly generated number as the Aadhaar number after collecting the demographic (Name, address, gender, date of birth) and biometric (Iris scans, fingerprints and photographs) details of individuals. These details are subsequently verified against a central repository to check for duplicates before the UID is issued. Unlike most other countries UIDAI issues only a number and not a card. The residents' enrolment is done by partnering with central and state departments (Registrars) who process the UID applications and connect to a central repository for the de-duplication check and issue of Aadhaar. The Registrars that the UIDAI has partnered with are the government departments involved in providing welfare services like employment guarantee, health insurance, food distribution; who will use the UID in providing subsidies and other benefits.

The usage of UID by the various government and private agencies has been planned as a federated set of databases with the central repository containing a minimal set of fields. Registrars can provide their own account number for each resident which is the derived ID, while the UID/Aadhaar number forms the base ID. The registrars' database will access individual resident's details using the UID or the derived ID. UIDAI offers online authentication services by checking the resident's data against that stored in the central repository, but provides only "Yes"/"No" responses in order to protect residents' privacy. The authentication services are implemented using service agencies that have the connectivity to the Aadhaar authentication module. User agencies that require Aadhaar authentication have to sign up with the authentication service agency.

While the technological and implementation challenge of enrolling and providing IDs to 1.2 billion is broadly acknowledged, the common opinion is that UID is otherwise a very simplistic problem of a unique 12-digit number. But the achievement of the development objective is dependent on a base infrastructure consisting of connectivity, financial inclusion and identity on which various government and private agencies would build their own applications and platforms. This requires Aadhaar to have a taken-for-grantedness for identity management. As the extensions of the Aadhaar infrastructure are context dependant, various stakeholders like government agencies (registrars), regulators, residents, etc. are involved. We provide two examples below to highlight the possible variations. The Madhya Pradesh state government has reengineered its food distribution processes based on Aadhaar and has built the MPePDS platform for its food distribution system (MPePDS, n.d.). Figure 1 shows the proposed MPePDS process where the identity verification is done offline.

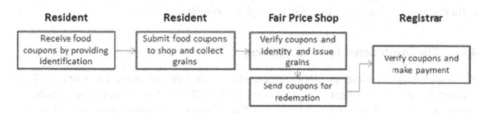

Fig. 1. A sample usage of Aadhaar in food distribution process

To ensure financial inclusion and electronic payments, the Indian Central Bank and the banking association are building a payment platform consisting of Aadhaar Payments Bridge System, Aadhaar enabled payment systems and microATMs. This platform forms the base on which benefits are transferred to residents and basic financial transactions can be carried out using microATMs. UIDAI has signed up several banks to open the "no-frills" account after the central bank made policy changes to allow such accounts. Banking correspondents (BC) (can be the local small retailers) using the microATMs are planned as providing this last mile banking services in remote villages. Figure 2 provides an illustration of cash withdrawal using online authentication and electronic payments.

While the above examples illustrates only the first order effects of Aadhaar, the higher-order effects such as the residents' ability to participate in economic activity due to access to banking services, reduction of transaction costs due to the last mile banking is not directly visible. The ability to provide identity and access to financial services may further increase the trustworthiness of the individual and increase his abilities to participate in market transactions by providing services and products.

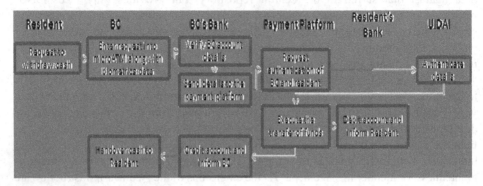

Fig. 2. Aadhaar enabled Payments Platform

The UIDAI has identified the various welfare schemes and relevant stakeholders who would be involved in adopting Aadhaar enabled services. Various regulatory bodies are also involved in establishing standards for different aspects of Aadhaar and its usage for e.g. UIDAI for biometrics, the Central Bank for microATM devices, etc. These standards are used by the suppliers involved in the UID enrolments, authentication and usage, who form the higher order stakeholders.

4.1   The Institutional Field of Aadhaar

With upcoming elections in 2014, the current ruling political party has reinforced its support for the UID project and announced new welfare schemes which are Aadhaar-based for e.g., direct cash transfers. The Planning Commission provides the administrative support for UIDAI and is actively pushing for Aadhaar as a basic requirement for inclusive development. But Aadhaar faces opposition from many other institutional actors and organizations at other levels in the government. The UIDAI bill has not yet been presented in the parliament as it has openly met resistance from various political parties and Parliamentary Standing Committee on Finance. Resistance has been seen from other government departments like the National Population Registry (NPR) which is collecting details of citizens with the objective of national security and views Aadhaar as intruding on its territory. While Aadhaar has been initiated by the central government, the welfare programs are state level responsibilities and hence Aadhaar-based applications have to be developed and supported by state governments in most cases. The implementation of the Aadhaar based welfare initiatives also depends on the executive officers in the Indian Administrative system who are posted at various levels of district and local governments.

One of the initial objections raised against UID was that if such projects have failed in other developed countries, its success in India is highly improbable. There are many public debates by social activists speaking on behalf of the poor and marginalized raising questions on the importance and applications of Aadhaar based on the feasibility of technology and policy implementation. Differing perspectives of Aadhaar are available on social media sites where opinions and news items are posted related to Aadhaar. Some of the common discussions revolve around data privacy, data aggregation, reliability of the technology, legality of UID, errors and delays in UID allocation.

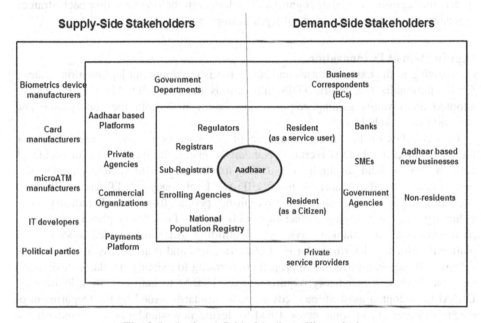

Fig. 3. Institutional field of Aadhaar (illustrative)

We provide an illustrative institutional field using the stakeholder diagram in Figure 3 which highlights the numerous and diverse stakeholders of the Aadhaar project. Each consecutive square represents higher-order stakeholders on the supply and demand side of Aadhaar (De' 2005).

5   Analysis of the Legitimation Strategies Adopted by Aadhaar

Organizations taking up activities or initiatives which have few precedents in the social order face the overwhelming task of acquiring acceptance either for the propriety of the activity or their own validity as practitioners (Suchmann 1995). In the case of Aadhaar overcoming this "liability of newness" is extremely formidable as the technologies used are untested and the initiative still lacks legal support. The acceptance of Aadhaar as the national identity, when currently many other forms of identity documents exist, involves convincing existing entities to support Aadhaar and get involved in a risky and lengthy relationship for offering Aadhaar enabled services.

We analyze the legitimacy gaining activities adopted by Aadhaar using two dimensions. The first dimension is based on whether the tactics are used for legitimizing the IT/IS innovation or the NI processes and the second dimension is the stakeholders being addressed with these tactics – supply side or demand side. The 2x2 matrix in Table 1 summarizes the predominant legitimation strategies adopted by UID. For each legitimation tactic we also identify the mechanisms used (C-conform, S- select and M-manipulate environment) and the type of legitimation being sought (p-pragmatic, m-moral and c- cognitive).The letters in the brackets after each strategy indicates the mechanism and type of legitimation sought.

Legitimation of IS Innovation:
Conforming to the existing norms and standards is the dominant legitimation strategy for institutionalization of the IT/IS innovations used in UID. Most of the tactics adopted are towards gaining *cognitive legitimacy* with both the supply side and demand side stakeholders.

UIDAI relies on the strong reputation of the key people and partners from the Indian IT industry. UIDAI recruited Nandan Nilekeni, the ex-CEO of an Indian IT firm which is held in high regard for its business ethics, transparency and performance, as the Chairperson of UIDAI. Legitimacy of IT knowledge and execution capabilities is sought by recruiting people from the IT industry on a voluntary basis and forging partnerships with various IT industry players. UIDAI is partnering with the Banking system for building Aadhaar enabled systems and platforms which will form the basis of cash transfers and transactions for the welfare schemes. Being an e-government project conforming to existing standards or defining new standards is a mandatory requirement for UIDAI to gain cognitive legitimacy. UIDAI has adopted most of the e-government standards issued by the Department of electronics and IT. In some cases it had to define new standards like standards for biometrics and microATM. In response to the doubts and concerns raised by various institutional actors over the biometrics technology UID has invested in the creation of the Biometrics Centre of Competence. In some aspects of the technical architecture and choice of technologies, UIDAI has adopted externally accepted competencies like open source and a server farm architecture to avoid lock-in and be cost-efficient. Given the failure of several e-government initiatives which adopted a kiosk-based model (De' 2005); UIDAI is riding on the mobile penetration in India as a means to access the rural and remote regions.

Demonstration of success has been actively pursued by UIDAI as a means to gain moral legitimacy. Success is operationalized as the number of Aadhaar enrolments. Announcing the number of Aadhaar numbers issued and handing over of specific milestone numbers by prominent people like the Prime Minster or ruling party chairperson are some of the strategies adopted.

Table 1. Legitimation Strategies adopted by UID

	Supply-side stakeholders	Demand-side stakeholders
IS Innovation Institutionalization	• Rely on reputation of key personnel (C,p) • Co-optation with the Banking System (C,p) • Adopt existing e-government standards (C,c) • Define new hardware/device standards (C,c) • Adopt open source (C,c) • Mimic hardware architecture of large cloud infrastructure providers (C,c) • Undertake research and competency development in biometrics (C, c)	• Rely on reputation of IT industry, outsourcing partners (C,p) • Co-optation with the Banking System (C,p) • Adopt existing e-government standards (C,c) • Define new hardware/device standards (C,c) • Leverage the mobile penetration (C,c) • Demonstrate success through announcements of number of Aadhaar enrolment and specific milestones (M,m)
NI Processes Institutionalization	• Seek legislation of UID (M, c) • Co-opt salient and influential stakeholders (M, c) • Use task forces (C, p) • Engage with government departments and public agencies (C, p) • Identify receptive state governments and district level officers for pilots (S, p) • Communicate the 'efficiency' goal to registrars (M, p)	• Seek legislation of UID (M, c) • Co-opt salient and influential stakeholders (M, c) • Communicate the benefits of Identity (M, p) • Advertise an image of transparency and openness through actions like sharing data (M, p) • Form coalition of initial adopters and highlight success (M, m) • Persist with UID enrolments in spite of lack of regulatory support (M, c) • Popularize usage of UID authentication by through advocates of UID in the state government and administrative department (M, c) • Established Aadhaar as a de facto standard by mandating it for welfare schemes, retirement benefits and payroll of government employees (M,c).

Legitimation of NI Processes:

The dominant strategy adopted for legitimization of the NI processes is to *manipulate the environment*. This is more applicable to ensure participation from demand side stakeholders during the UID enrolments as they are the salient stakeholders for this stage of UID. Once the UID gains legal status, the manipulation mechanism may be visible even on the supply-side stakeholders as government departments and agencies would have to adopt UID-based services.

Communicating the benefits of identity to the residents, and highlighting the goal of efficiency in distribution and monitoring of welfare schemes to government departments is a clear manipulation strategy. UIDAI is seeking cognitive legitimacy through the UIDAI bill which has yet to be enacted. In the meantime, it is using the support of salient and influential stakeholders like the Prime Minister and Finance minister to enable it to continue operating in its current set of welfare departments and locations and enter new application areas like direct cash transfers. The UIDAI uses task forces with members from relevant government departments as a means to offer them decision making access to the design on the technical solution and policy implications. UIDAI engages them as registrars allowing them to collect information in addition to the basic details required for Aadhaar. UIDAI has engaged with certain welfare departments like public distribution system and employment guarantee scheme in its search for friendly audiences for the initial Aadhaar based applications. Under these welfare schemes it has identified receptive state governments and district level administrative officers to partner for the initial pilots of these applications.

While UID enrolments are claimed to be voluntary, mandating it for availing welfare benefits and other services, send a very explicit message that without an Aadhaar number, welfare benefits cannot be availed. It has persisted in Aadhaar enrolments in spite of lack of legislative and regulatory support. In spite of many technical and process related setbacks which led to delays and temporary hold up of Aadhaar enrolments, UIDAI has continued to retain its enrolment partners like the state governments and other departments who are keen to resume the Aadhaar enrolments. Aadhaar is approaching a de facto standard for identity and people are enrolling for Aadhaar numbers to take advantage of the advertised welfare benefits or the fear of exclusion.

UIDAI communicates an image of transparency and openness in all its communications. In accordance with this image it has an Aadhaar portal with current status and a website where it makes available data of UID enrolments and authentication which can be used for various analyses and research by anyone.

Legitimation Strategies for Demand Side and Supply Side:
The strategies adopted for gaining acceptance from the supply side and the demand side for the NI process are different. UIDAI attempts to gain *pragmatic legitimacy* with the supply side stakeholders like the government departments and agencies for the NI processes. UIDAI uses *cognitive legitimation strategies* to popularize the UID technology and processes among the demand side stakeholders.

Linkages between strategies:
UIDAI has adopted a repertoire of the legitimation strategies for gaining legitimacy and has accumulated a group of supporters across various kinds of stakeholders. Many of the specific actions taken for a strategy may be due to the existing context or situation at the time of decision-making by the organizational actors. We found during our analysis that some of the legitimation strategies lead to a new situation (or failure) where another legitimation strategy may need to be applied

to gain or maintain legitimacy. For example, we found that UIDAI had initially planned to adopt the IT architecture as per the existing e-government project guidelines, but on obtaining a quote from the hardware vendors it was found that the cost effectiveness requirement of the initiative would be at risk. Hence it was decided to adopt a farm of servers similar to the cloud based architecture using low-end servers. This was a novelty in government projects, though it had been quite successfully adopted by commercial IT organizations. But this required gaining legitimacy for the new architecture by defining new standards, advertising the product and popularizing the new model. Another instance is related to the lack of confidence in the existing biometric standards due to which UIDAI had to invest in research and competence building biometrics. Hence many of the strategies have a linkage and an order which we have not described in our analysis.

6   Findings and Discussion

Our analysis of the strategies adopted by UIDAI for institutionalization of Aadhaar identified the following
- IS innovation legitimation involves gaining cognitive legitimacy and conforming to existing environmental norms.
- NI projects need to use manipulative mechanisms to gain legitimacy of the NI processes. This strategy is more dominant with the demand side stakeholders during the initial stages of the NI project.
- Pragmatic legitimacy strategies are adopted for gaining acceptance of the NI processes with the supply side stakeholders. These stakeholders evaluate the NI project based on the benefits and norms of interactions to deliver NI based services, hence gaining pragmatic legitimacy is important.
- Cognitive legitimation strategies are used to popularize both NI processes and technologies with the demand side stakeholders.

With respect to our research questions we found that the legitimation of the IS innovation requires different sets of strategies as compared to the strategies adopted for NI processes (RQ1). The legitimation strategies for gaining acceptance with demand side and supply side stakeholders differ. The mechanisms for gaining legitimation are either conforming to the environment or manipulating the environment using cognitive and pragmatic legitimation strategies (RQ2). The strategies related to environment selection have only limited usage for e-government projects as the initiatives are constrained by their objectives and goals.

Our findings support the argument by Avgerou (2000) that IT and organizational change undergo two different institutionalization processes and the legitimation of IT does not automatically lead to organizational change. Mignerat and Rivard (2009) found that acquiesce or conformance to environment was the most dominant response studied in IS literature. IS initiatives within an organization usually conform to the institutional field of the organization as the sponsors of the project are usually the senior management. We found this to be true even in the case of e-government projects as IS legitimation strategies use mechanisms whereby the IS innovation conforms to standards and norms in the professional discipline, even if the technology is untested and new. Our study finds empirical support for Henriksen and Damsgaard (2007) conclusion that manipulative or regulations are needed to embed IS innovations in organizational processes. While the technology may be accepted, usage of the technology in processes needs manipulative strategies. We also found that the legitimation strategies needed to gain the support of the supply side stakeholders differs from that required to popularize the concept among the larger demand side stakeholders. Pragmatic legitimacy is sought by supply side partners while cognitive legitimacy is required to gain the demand side acceptance. Cousins and Robey (2005) found that the B2B metal exchanges which survived had established pragmatic legitimacy in their business relationship among their trading partners. As the UID initiative is still in the initial adoption phase, it is too early to decide whether these strategies would result in sustained success and legitimacy of UID. While there are not many studies which has studied the legitimation strategies adopted by e-government projects, some of the existing IS innovation literature supports these findings.

Though we used Suchmann (1995) classification for analyzing the legitimation tactics, we could map them to the strategic responses and tactics in response to institutional pressures identified by Oliver (1991). But we did not find examples for some of the tactics proposed by Oliver. For example, the strategic response and tactics related to "Defy" like 'Assaulting the sources of institutional pressure' is not addressed as part of the legitimation strategies. Is it because such a tactic does not help in gaining legitimacy? We approached this study of legitimation of NI projects assuming planned actions by organizational actors to institutionalize the new idea. But if we assume legitimation as a socially constructed concept Structuration theory by Giddens can be used as another lens to study legitimation of e-government projects.

We have identified the legitimation strategies adopted by UIDAI for gaining legitimacy using document analysis. Boxenbaum (2008) argues that this approach does not help identify the process of legitimation which involves the choices available to organizational actors and the context and trade-offs made while taking decisions. While we recognize the limitation of our method, we argue that the process of legitimation can be inferred from document analysis in the case of e-government initiatives. Being an e-government initiative UIDAI publishes all information through their website. Some of the details can be reconstructed using news articles, blogposts and other social media postings. But we realize that the sequence and linkages among strategies may not always be identifiable through methods like document analysis.

7   Conclusions

Aadhaar - the national identity project of India is unique and novel in many aspects and gaining legitimacy in its institutional field is critical for its long term survival. We used the lens of institutional theory to study the legitimation strategies adopted by this e-government initiative in India. One of the contributions of the paper is in identifying that NI projects adopt different strategies for institutionalizing the IS innovation and the NI processes. While conformance to environment is the dominant strategic mechanism for legitimizing IS innovation, manipulation of the environment is the mechanism adopted for institutionalizing the NI processes. The main contribution of the paper is that IT-enabled changes seek cognitive legitimacy with demand side stakeholders and pragmatic legitimacy with their supply side stakeholders.

This paper contributes to the e-government research by filling the gap in studying legitimation strategies in e-government. It also contributes to the institutional theory literature by bringing in the e-government context to legitimation strategies. Some of the future research areas are identifying the linkages between legitimation strategies, and associating the strategies to specific stages of the innovation diffusion cycle.

Acknowledgements. The author would like to thank Prof. Abhoy Ojha, Prof. Rahul De' and Pramod Varma for their guidance and comments on previous versions of this paper. The author is also grateful to the two anonymous reviews of the IFIP WG 8.6 conference for their constructive comments which helped improve this paper.

References

Avgerou, C.: IT and organizational change: an institutionalist perspective. Information Technology & People 13(4), 234–262 (2000)

Boxenbaum, E.: The Process of Legitimation. In: Scheuer, S., Scheur, J.D. (eds.) The Anatomy of Change, pp. 237–262. CBS Press (2008)

Crosby, S.J.: 'Challenges and Opportunities in Identity Assurance' (2008), http://webarchive.nationalarchives.gov.uk/+/http://www.hm-treasury.gov.uk/d/identity_assurance060308.pdf

Cousins, K.C., Robey, D.: The social shaping of electronic metals exchanges: an institutional theory perspective. Information Technology & People 18(3), 212–229 (2005)

De', R.: E-government systems in developing countries: Stakeholders and conflict. In: Wimmer, M.A., Traunmüller, R., Grönlund, Å., Andersen, K.V. (eds.) EGOV 2005. LNCS, vol. 3591, pp. 26–37. Springer, Heidelberg (2005)

DiMaggio, P.J., Powell, W.W.: The Iron Cage Revisited: Institutional isomorphism and collective rationality. American Sociological Review 48(2), 147–160 (1983)

Flak, L.S., Rose, J.: Stakeholder governance: Adapting stakeholder theory to the e-government field. Communication of the Association for Information Systems 16(31), 1–46 (2005)

Granovetter, M., McGuire, P.: The making of an industry: electricity in the United States. The Law of Markets. M. Callon (1998)

GoI: Press Release of the Press Information Bureau, Government of India (2008), http://pib.nic.in/release/release.asp?relid=44711 (retrieved on April 10, 2012)

Henriksen, H.Z., Damsgaard, J.: Dawn of E-Government – An institutional analysis of seven initiatives and their impact. Journal of Information Technology 22(1), 13–23 (2007)

Jepperson, R.L.: Institutions, institutional effects, and institutionalism. In: Powell, W.W., DiMaggio, P.J. (eds.) The New Institutionalism in Organizational Analysis, pp. 143–163. The University of Chicago Press, Chicago (1991)

King, J.L., Gurbaxani, V., Kraemer, K.L., McFarlan, F.W., Raman, K.S., Yap, C.S.: Institutional Factors in Information Technology Innovation. Information Systems Research 5(2), 139–169 (1994)

Kubicek, H., Noack, T.: Different countries-different paths extended comparison of the introduction of eIDs in eight European countries. Identity in the Information Society 3, 235–245 (2010)

Lawrence, T., Suddaby, R.: Institutions and Institutional Work. In: Clegg, S., Hardy, C., Lawrence, T., Nord, W. (eds.) Handbook of Organization Studies. Sage, London (2006)

MPePDs (n.d.) Madhya Pradesh ePDS, http://mpepds.in/ (retrieved on April 10, 2012)

Mignerat, M., Rivard, S.: Positioning the institutional perspective in information systems research. Journal of Information Technology 24, 369–391 (2009)

Oliver, C.: Strategic responses to institutional processes. Academy of Management Review 16, 145–179 (1991)

Rao, H.: The social construction of reputation: Certification contests, legitimation, and the survival of organizations in the American automobile industry. Strategic Management Journal 15, 29–44 (1994)

Rowley, J.: e-Government stakeholders—Who are they and what do they want? International Journal of Information Management 31, 53–62 (2011)

Sarantis, D., Smithson, S., Charalabidis, Y., Askounis, D.: A critical assessment of project management methods with respect to electronic government implementation challenges. Systemic Practice and Action Research 23(4), 301–321 (2010)

Scott, W.R.: Institutional theory: contributing to a theoretical research program. In: Smith, K., Hitt, M. (eds.) Great Minds in Management: the Process of Theory Development. Oxford University Press, New York (2005)

Scott, W.R.: Institutions and organizations: ideas and interests, 3rd edn. Sage, Thousand Oaks (2008)

Suchman, M.C.: Managing Legitimacy: Strategic and institutional approaches. Academy of Management Review 20(3), 571–611 (1995)

UIDAI, Creating a Unique Identity Number for Every Resident in India'. UIDAI (2009), http://uidai.gov.in/ (retrieved on March 10, 2012)

UIDAI, UIDAI Strategy Overview: Creating a Unique Identity Number for Every Resident in India. UIDAI (2010), http://uidai.gov.in/ (retrieved on March 10, 2012)

Venkatesh, V., Morris, M.G., Davis, G.B., Davis, F.D.: User acceptance of Information technology: Toward a unified view. MIS Quarterly 27, 425–478 (2003)

Weerakkody, V., Dwivedi, Y.K., Irani, Z.: The Diffusion and Use of Institutional Theory: A Cross Disciplinary Longitudinal Literature Survey. Journal of Information Technology 24(4), 354–368 (2009)

Whitley, E.A., Hoisen, G.: Global Identity Policies and Technology: Do we Understand the Question? Global Policy 1(2), 209–215 (2010)

Zucker, L.G.: Organizations as Institutions. In: Bacharach, S.B. (ed.) Research in the Sociology of Organizations, vol. 2, pp. 1–47. JAI Press, Greenwich (1983)

Designing an Information System
for Updating Land Records in Bangladesh:
Action Design Ethnographic Research (ADER)

Laurence Brooks and M. Shahanoor Alam

Department of Information Systems and Computing, Brunel University, UK
{Laurence.Brooks, Muhammad.Alam}@brunel.ac.uk

Abstract. Information Systems (IS) has become a research discipline accommo-
dating and adapting diverse methodologies, methods, and techniques from reference disciplines as well as generating them. Action Design Research (ADR) has
been developed as a broad research method, based on empirical study within developed countries. However, there remains a lack of methodologies for studying IS
in the complex context of developing counties. This pioneering application of ADR
in a developing country context identified that ADR requires additional lenses for
understanding this additional complexity. Further, combining ADR with an ethnographic methodological framework has potential complementarity within IS research. This helps the researchers cycle through the problem formulation, design,
evaluation, reflection and learning cycles. This paper therefore argues that Action
Design Ethnographic Research (ADER) is a potential methodological framework
for IS research. While developed from a specific case of land records service in
Bangladesh, ADER shows potential as a rigorous methodology for conducting IS
research in any complex context.

Keywords: Action Design Research, Action Design Ethnographic Research,
Land Records Management, Bangladesh.

1 Introduction

Information Systems (IS) research already draws methodological and theoretical contributions from many reference disciplines (Thompson, 2012). Anthropology is one of
these valuable reference disciplines and ethnography, as a subfield of anthropology
which has potential contributions in qualitative studies in IS (Nandhakumar and
Jones, 1997; Myers 1999). Ethnography refers to a paradigm, a methodology and a
basket of tools and techniques (Geertz, 1973; Westbrook, 2008). As a research methodology, it has been used in IS research for over the last 20 years and played a substantial role in theory building (Walsham, 1995; Orlikowski, 1992). The nature of
ethnographic research is empirical, longitudinal, inductive, long term, participant
observation oriented and interventional. Thus ethnographic research is helpful for
theory building (Orlikowski, 1992; Orlikowski and Gash, 1992; Walsham and Sahay,
1999). Ethnographic research provides a unique opportunity for insight into everyday

Y.K. Dwivedi et al. (Eds.): TDIT 2013, IFIP AICT 402, pp. 359–374, 2013.

practices through applying the dual perspective of the emic view (insider) and etic view (outsider) (Geertz, 1983). It provides insights into IS research (Walsham 1995) and shows complementarity with applied and interpretive research e.g., action research (Nilsson, 2000), design research (Barab et. al., 2004). This paper aims to explore how an ethnographic methodological perspective contributes to Action Design Research (ADR) (Sein et. al., 2011), a newly developed research method in IS.

The main objective of this paper is to seek a broader methodological framework for understanding complex organizational contexts, everyday organizing, practices, informal organizational behavior and networks and dichotomy in organizational processes. These features are commonly visible in IS research in developing countries. This paper shows that ADR is a potential research method for understanding IS in the complex context of developing countries, whereby an ethnographic methodological framework has potential complementarity for conducting ADR. The findings are derived from a longitudinal empirical study in a public sector organization in Bangladesh, in which an ethnographic methodological framework and ADR has been applied, as Action Design Ethnographic Research (ADER). A recent study has demonstrated how ethnographic perspectives, approaches and tools are potentially very useful for conducting ADR in these complex developing countries contexts (Alam et. al., 2012).

2   Action Design Ethnographic Research

Action Design Research (ADR) aims to build ensemble artifacts in organizational contexts to generate prescriptive design knowledge through building and evaluating ensemble IT artifacts in organizational settings (Sein et. al., 2011; Hevner et. al. 2004). ADR thus harnesses complementarity between Action Research (AR) and Design Research (DR) to build a rigorous methodology for studying these artifacts. Hence, ADR aims to build artifacts in organizational contexts through framing DR into AR cycles. Similarly, Gregor and Jones (2007) show that designing an ensemble artifact requires interactions between technological and organizational dimensions while organizational contexts, structures and networks play significant roles. Ensemble IT artifacts emerge from design, use, practice and on-going refinement in organizational contexts.

However understanding organizational context and building artifacts in organizational context are highly challenging because organizational context refers to the complex fabric of local culture, people, resources, purposes, earlier events and future expectations that are bounded by time-space-situation (Evered and Louis, 1981). Understanding the organizational context of IS research in developing countries is equally important and complicated. Therefore, in order to understand organizational context, IS research suggests applying different modes of enquiries, perspectives and roles of researcher – Barley's (1986) 'emic and etic' perspectives; Evered and Luis's (1981) 'outsider and insider mode of inquiry'; Nandhakumar and Jones' (1997) 'distance and engagement' perspectives. These perspectives, derived from an ethnographic methodological framework, are briefly discussed to understand the framing of ADR in such a framework.

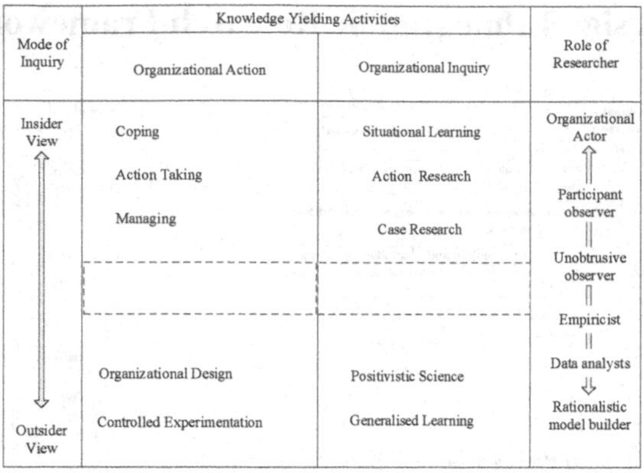

Mode of Inquiry	Knowledge Yielding Activities		Role of Researcher
	Organizational Action	Organizational Inquiry	
Insider View ↑	Coping	Situational Learning	Organizational Actor ↑
	Action Taking	Action Research	Participant observer
	Managing	Case Research	Unobtrusive observer
			Empiricist
	Organizational Design	Positivistic Science	Data analysts ⇓
Outsider View	Controlled Experimentation	Generalised Learning	Rationalistic model builder

Fig. 1. Insider and Outside Modes of Inquiry (Evered and Louis, 1981)

Evered and Louis (1981) suggested applying insider and outsider views to the ethnographic perspectives, to understand organizational contexts with different roles and involvement of researchers along with methods, learning and epistemological strands (see figure 1). Both views are complementary to elicit insights of the situation under study.

The outsider view generates research findings usually with quantitative data, questionnaires and passive observation. The insider view generates data by 'being there' and becoming immersed in the organizational activities through participant observation and playing the role of organizational actor. Further, there is the opportunity to examine one situation from different lenses and stances. So, it is possible to derive situational learning and generalized learning. Thus applying both perspectives enhances the validity of analyses and interpretations by bringing the world of interpretations and the world of scientific theory together (Schutz, 1973). Ethnographic perspectives, therefore, have the potential for understanding organizational contexts with various roles, modes of inquiry, actions from various dimensions and generating both situational and generalized learning.

Nandhakumar and Jones (1997) emphasize the ethnographic perspective along with participant observation and argue that though researchers enter into the actors' world, there are a number obstacles, including deceptive behavior, sensitivity, deliberately misleading, dominant perception, actors' inability of expression, to understand their interpretations (Nandhakumar and Jones, 1997). Researchers, therefore, need to observe actors' response, note their gesture and watch bodily responses to what's going around them with an engagement (Goffman, 1990).

Finally, Barley (1986) applied both insider view (emic) and outsider view (etic); the insider view elicits context, practices and way of life from the perspective of participants along with concepts of the native's worldview; the outsider view relies heavily on the perspective of the researcher, uses the concepts of social science and aims to analyse the context, practices and ways of life theoretically (Barley, 1986). Applying both perspectives gives rich insights but it is difficult to apply them. Barley (1986) suggests two ways: a) taking a collaborating role and b) a commitment to long term involvement.

3   Action Design Ethnographic Research Framework (ADER)

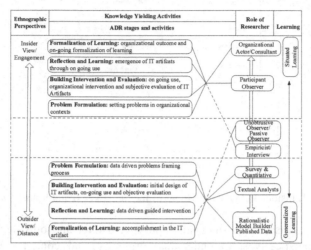

Fig. 2. Ethnographic Perspectives in ADR Process

ADR aims to build artifacts in organizational contexts and to refine them through on-going use, intervention and evaluation in organizational contexts whereby the ethno-graphic perspective(s) is a potential lens for understanding it. Thus it can be seen that an ethnographic methodological framework has complementarity with all the stages and activities of ADR (see figure 2). Formulating problems in organizational contexts entails a mutually influential and reciprocal role in shaping artifacts, objective evalua-tion, emergence of artifacts and learning as organizational actors are significantly relied on to provide understanding from an insider perspective. On the contrary, data driven problems formulation, initial design, on-going evaluation, guided intervention and learning as researcher all come from an outsider perspective. Therefore the eth-nographic perspective in ADER (see figure 3) allows for better integration of the in-side/outside perspective than traditional ADR alone and can be seen as an extended variant of ADR.

3.1   Problem Formulation

ADR formulates problems in organizational contexts drawing from empirical evidence and data driven by end-users and existing technologies (Sein et. al., 2011). Researchers' engagement, long term involvement, observation, participant observation and being an actor in the context bring a type of empirical evidence derived from applying the insider view which discovers underlying meanings of organizational contexts that are expressed through actions and artifacts (Prasad, 1997). The outsider view applies 'looking on' in the sense of witnessing and examining processes and contexts externally to produce logi-cal meaning and measurement (Evered and Louis, 1981). Consequently, this view allows the researcher to frame data driven problems. ADR also formulates data driven problems because it follows a cyclical process between problems formulation to evaluation stages ie. problem, fix, problem, fix, as if in a 'systems development life-cycle' (see figure 3) (Sein et. al., 2011; Mantei and Teorey, 1989).

3.2   Building Intervention and Evaluation (BIE)

This stage iteratively interweaves between three core activities i.e., building artifacts; intervening in organizational settings and evaluating concurrently and objectively (Sein et. al., 2011). BIE principles (reciprocal shaping between artifact and organizational contexts; mutual learning between researcher and practitioners; applying on-going and objective evaluation) require both insider and outsider views. These principles include observation, involvement, interpretation and intervention whereby the insider view elicits insights from them. In contrast, the outsider view is important for these BIE principles for applying the researcher's theory of knowledge according to existing technologies and resources and conducting context free objective evaluation.

Researchers' engagement as participant observation (insider view) is significant in information systems design, implementation and use because it sees nothing as surprising (Nandhakumar and Jones, 2002). It seeks meaning of every observation; what those observations mean and why (Kelly and Gibbons, 2008). Thus, applying the insider view develops meaningful interpretations from the iterative relation between organizational contexts and designed artifact.

Further, an ethnographic perspective brings forth 'live experience', including behavior, attitudes, practices, roles of actors and how they help to design change supported by local transformation (Barab et. al., 2004). Applying the insider view, therefore, enhances the mutually influential role between researcher's knowledge and the actors' practices. As Sim (1999) noted, the ethnographic perspective has the potential to design artifacts and redesign them through contextualizing organizational practices. Furthermore, the insider view provides insights from evaluation in organizational contexts (Nedevschi et. al., 2006) because it does not leave actions as: being absurd, peculiar, pointless, irrational, surprising or confusing, rather finds their existing meanings lying in the local context and culture (Lee, 1991). We refer to it as interpretive subjective evaluation; where subjective does not mean bias, rather it aims to seek contextual meanings and examine how the meanings interact with artifacts. This evaluation aims to reflect the actors view and situated learning from ADER.

On other hand, the outsider view gives an opportunity to conduct a context free and objective evaluation. Moreover, it allows researchers to filter the on-going activities as well as learning through their preset categories, codings that derive factual data and results as an objective evaluation (Evered and Louis, 1981). Although ADER is highly situated, objective evaluation seeks to generalise its outcome. Since the researchers' involvement in organizational context might hinder objective evaluation and give rise to a conflict of interests. Thus the outsider view gives objective and context free evaluation in ADR.

3.3   Reflection and Learning

Reflection and learning is derived from formulated problems, theoretical premises and emerged solutions that contribute towards research processes and knowledge

(Sein et. al., 2011). It applies 'guided emergence' a principle containing two contrasting views 'guided' and 'emergence' (Sein et. al., 2011). The former refers to guided intervention i.e. an outsider's view, and the latter displays a sense of organic evolution i.e. an insider's perspective. ADR, therefore, recognizes that understanding emerging artifacts through on-going use requires both insider and outsider views (Sein et. al., 2011). It can be seen that organizational contexts, practices and users' roles reshape the initial design of artifacts whereby alone the outsider view/distance relation cannot trace the emerging shape of artifacts because it requires close observation and engagement. However it requires guided intervention with logic, model and theory to redesign the emerged artifacts. Thus, both perspectives enhance the reflection and learning process of ADR.

3.4   Formalization of Learning

This stage aims to formalize learning through generalizing the 'situated learning' (van Aken, 2004). The situated nature of ADR outcomes includes organizational change and implementation of an artefact. Researchers, therefore, need to describe organizational outcomes and outline the accomplishments in artefact formalised learning.

The ethnographic perspective in IS bridges the gap between academics and practitioners through generating valuable learning and contributing to knowledge (Myers, 1999). It provides analyses that are communicable and predictable (Sanday, 1979). Organizational outcomes can be best expressed by organizational actors and in order to identify that the researchers' engagement as an actor (insider perspective) is important. Contrary, applying the outsider view transmits situated learning into generalised learning that could be applicable to other similar contexts (Evered and Louis, 1981). The outsider view helps to build a rationalistic model to transmit the situational learning into generalized design principles, and outline the accomplishment in the artifacts from the ADR.

Therefore, the ethnographic perspective fits throughout the stages and activities of ADR with a complementarity towards the end of advancing ADR in complex contexts (see figure 3). They allow the formulation of problems and design artifacts (BIE) in multiple cycles; evaluate the on-going use of artifact from different positions and identifying and transferring learning. More importantly, applying the ethnographic perspectives iteratively in problem formulation and BIE generates significant insights and detailed findings. Thus applying ADR with an ethnographic methodological framework means it is able to draw out an ethnographic description as an outcome that can be seen as Geertz's (1973) thick description. 'Thick description' unfolds multiple layers of meaning held by the members and practices of the organization (Nilsson, 2000). Notably thick description aims to contribute to knowledge through providing detailed analysis of ADR findings. Therefore ADER is a potential methodological framework for IS studies and it is illustrated with a case of the service for updating land records in Bangladesh.

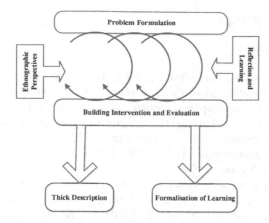

Fig. 3. Action Design Ethnographic Research (Adapted from Sein et. al., 2011)

4   Data Collection Methods

Both ADR and ethnography seek long term involvements and commitments of re-searchers. With these notions, this study gathered data from longitudinal, interventional and participant observation oriented approaches and processes. The study was conducted for about 2½ years in a public sector organization in a sub-district of Bangladesh, called Upzila, Land Office, Rooppur (not real name). The study focused on improvements to the service involved in updating land records locally and throughout the country.

The ADER was been initiated by the Office of the Divisional Commissioner, head of the land and revenue administration divisional level. The ADER team comprises of both professional and practitioners. The lead author worked as the Section Officer in the Divisional Commissioner Office and presented the problems updating land records in several meetings, workshops and training sessions with the officers involved. In addition, the lead author took the opportunity to use participant observation arising from his responsibilities i.e., coordinating with the decision makers of this service and the decision implementers of this service.

This ADER was been initiated in October 2009 and the findings tracked until June 2012. Therefore throughout the ADER process, the findings are derived from participant observation and interventions arising from field visits, inspections, official reports and documents analyses, workshops, meetings, consultations and training exercises, policy formulation and implementation, all relating to updating land records.

The initial design process was been launched in December, 2009 in just one district. Thereafter nine districts have implemented the initial design in January, 2010. The initial design was further redesigned and that has been implemented throughout the country since April 2010. This paper now focuses on how organizational context has further redesigned the implementation process (the redesign) of the land records updating service in Bangladesh.

5   ADER Findings

5.1   Background

Updating land records is a core service delivery for citizens in Bangladesh. It has been identified as problematic and outdated, a source of corruption and litigations by the government itself, the development partners, practitioners and civil society. Rampant corruption in this service delivery is a barrier to economic growth. In addition to fraud, forgery and physical assaults, some murders took place due to land record litigations, which are also responsible for 80% of all civil cases and 70% of all criminal cases (Barakat and Prasanta, 2004).

Bangladesh is a populous country with a total of 160 million people, while the average land per person is only 0.22 acre. However, it relies on an agro-economy because agriculture contributes 60% of total GDP. It is noteworthy that land is the only capital and source of livelihood for the majority of people. About 80% of people depend on agriculture and the rate of land ownership transfer is very high. Updating of land records is, thus, a significant service to the citizens.

Updating land records refers to updating the name of the owner of land in record registers after land registration (purchase) or inheritance (either loosing or gaining). This process is called 'mutation'; mutating records from one name to other. This service is delivered from a public sector organization namely the Upazila Land Office (ULO). Upazila refers to a sub-district, the bottom tier of public administration in the country. There are a total of 500 ULOs in the country. The ULO is headed by the Assistant Commissioner of Land (ACL). A ULO comprises of several local union Land Offices (LO) that is headed by a Union Assistant Land Officer (UALO).

There are two ways of updating land records: ULO's initiatives and citizens' application. Firstly, the ULO can update land records on the basis of two information networks: one, receiving a Land Transfer Notice after land registration is completed by the Sub-Registrar Office and the other is a report from a LO. According to the government rules, following land registration a Land Transfer Notice is issued to the ULO for updating the appropriate records. On the other side, where there is the death of a land owner or any change takes place in the type of land, the LO reports to the ULO for the purpose of updating land records. However, functionally, updating land records by ULO's initiative rarely takes place. The ULO, therefore, updates land records on the basis of citizens' applications which require fees and lists of documents; land registration deeds, certified copy of original records, sketch map of the land plots, inheritance certificate from local union council. Thereafter the ULO conduct an initial scrutiny on the fees and supporting documents and ask the concerned LO for its field inspection report. The ACL calls the applicant the first party (or new owner) and the second party, the seller and related individuals, and consults the LO's report and scrutinizes the registers of the ULO. Finally, the ACL either approves the application i.e., updates the land record, or rejects the application i.e., no change in the original details.

5.2   Problems Formulation

Citizens' access to this service is complicated because from application submission to service delivery requires a number of documents and processes. The ULO often neither has application forms nor the guidelines on supporting documents and the processes that need to be followed. Therefore, in order to mediate access to this service, several vested interest networks, known as 'bribery networks', have been developed within and beyond the organization which they mediate as informal intermediaries.

Data Driven Problems Formulation
Citizens are not well acquainted with filling out the application form, the exact amount of fees, required documents and to whom and where the application should be submitted and how the service is to be delivered. Even after submission, it's common for the application to go missing or be rejected without any notification. Since access to this service requires filing applications with appropriate documents and a follow up set of processes, it is difficult for citizens to submit an application and track the processes without any actor in the vested interest networks – the middleman, the stamp vendor, lawyers, deed writers and the subordinate staff of ULO or LO.

Context Driven Problems
From the inception of this service it has been kept as a complex set of processes and used as a source of vested interests by the actors within the organization and beyond. Citizens rarely understand the process because there is no information system explaining this service. Even educated citizens enter into this service through the vested interest networks either through buying the application form, using the service to accomplish tasks within the shortest period of time or making possible an impossible or legally challenging case. The actors in the vested interest networks maintain application format, requirements and supporting documents privately and only use them in the case of their vested interests. Further, they expedite this service delivery in the cases of their clients' applications. As a result, applications with vested interests receive the fastest service delivery and all others are kept pending, sometimes for several months.

Therefore, the data driven and problem context can be summed up as the ULO does not have any information systems for citizens; for example, the application form, point of application submission, exact amount of fees, specific list of supporting documents, receipt for application submission, tracking options after submission, duration of service delivery and decision on the application. Whereas the organization failed to develop and maintain the information systems for this service, the actors of the vested interest networks have developed and maintained them. It could be seen as mutually dependent because the vested interest networks maintain the information systems for this service, but the organization is both dependent on them and do not find ways to overcome the problems of vested interests.

5.3   Building Interventions and Evaluation

Fieldwork
ADER aims to support the design of an IS to address the problems with and enhance citizens' access to the land records management service, to eradicate the vested interest networks. To this end, two pieces of fieldwork took place (one for 2½ months and one for 2 months) as well as relevant documents and reports were reviewed.

In addition, three interactive workshops were arranged, for reciprocal consultations with the officers and staff of this service delivery. As a result, a number of components have been designed.

Initial Design

Initially, through the ADER a single application form was developed that aims to enhance citizens' access to this service through the organizational process, rather than through the vested interest networks. The newly designed application form has been kept as simple and informative as possible for citizens. Anyone with basic literacy and writing would be able to fill in the form. The application form contains the necessary information and instructions relating to this service delivery – with no fee for the application form; updating land records fee BDT 250.00; and 30 working days duration for service delivery. All this information is printed on the opposite side of the application form. The application form has been divided into two parts: the first part is filled in by the citizens and the second part is the acknowledgement of application receipt and for issuing an application ID. In addition, the date of the hearing is given on receipt of the application. Thus the initial design of the application form has tracking options. Nearly all the tracking information contains the acknowledgement receipt of the application form. This is issued to the applicant at submission by the ULO staff.

On-going Use and Evaluation

This initial design was implemented in 10 districts for about five months. During this period the ADER team closely observed and evaluated the on-going use and implementation. Since the newly designed application form is available and given freely by the ULO, it has attracted citizens to come to the ULO. Consequently, the practice of submitting and mediating citizens' applications by the actors of the vested interest networks has been significantly reduced compared to the previous system. Furthermore, observation and empirical findings showed that $1/3$ of the applicants' submitted applications directly to the ULO while previously it was less than $1/10$.

However, it has not become possible to uproot the vested interest networks totally. While implementing the newly designed application form, the actors of the vested interest networks found that their application forms, the previous one, are no longer required for this service. The actors beyond the organizational process are involved in assisting in filling in the form for illiterate people, processing the supporting papers and submitting applications on behalf of their clients in the newly designed system.

Equally, the actors both within the organization and beyond reprint/copy the newly designed form for their clients. Consequently, they shift from their old version of the application form to the newly designed one. As a result, the benefits of the new system do not fully reach the citizens because it has been also partially utilized by the vested interest networks. While a significant number of citizens submit their application by themselves, applications from vested interest networks receive better and quicker service delivery than the rest.

Reflection and Learning: Emergence of Artifacts

The on-going use of the new system reflects two aspects: one, the actors in the vested interest networks remain visible through filling in and submitting the application forms for illiterate people. Secondly they are involved in processing papers and expediting the service delivery for their clients. Since the application submission process did not exclude them from submission of applications, they continue their alternative route. Further, the long list of supporting documents means the application remains a complicated process, especially for illiterate and inexperienced citizens. Thus a section of citizens need to rely on the vested interest networks to appropriately arrange the list of supporting documents. Therefore, the initial design has been reshaped through on-going use.

Redesign: Guided Intervention

From the initial design and its on-going use, three things have emerged as artifacts that reshaped the initial design – a) submitting applications for their clients; b) assisting in filling and arranging complex set of supporting documents and c) expediting applications with the vested interests. In order to address them, guided interventions were made.

Firstly, receiving applications only from the applicant or his/her representative is one way to exclude the vested interest networks. Therefore, the application form has been redesigned so that the applicant needs to put his/her or his/her representative's photo on the application. If an applicant fails to submit his/her application, s/he could nominate a competent representative related to his family to the ULO for application submission.

Secondly, the list of supporting documents has been reduced and simplified so that citizens' do not need to rely on actors of the vested interest networks for arranging them. To this end, the supporting documents have been documents redesigned in such a way that if updating of the land record (mutation) has been done previously, then only that updated record is needed for the supporting document, nothing else. It makes it easier for citizens to process their application by themselves. Further, if there is any lack of supporting documents with applications, the applicant could submit them during the hearing. This reduces rejection of applications submitted by citizens.

Thirdly, the first come first served rule has been introduced in order to prevent the process of expediting applications by vested interests. Since every application is to be given an ID number during its submission by the ULO, this also provides the basis for a chronological order. In addition, it has been taken as policy to complete the application within 30 working days. Together, these interventions have given citizens' easy access and greater reliability.

Subjective Evaluation

However, within a year of implementation the redesigned system has also been further reshaped by the vested interest networks. Firstly although it is mandatory to submit the application with the applicant/representative photograph on the application form, it could be faked or be one of the actors from the vested interest networks. Mainly the actors from the vested interest networks from outside of the organization are involved in the process of fake photograph pasting on the applications that they submit. While an applicant comes into contact with actors of the vested interest networks, either it is the requirement of the applicant or it is the offer of the actor of vested interest networks to manage every process on their behalf. It provides greater profit to the actors and less hassle to the applicant for the vested interest network actors to process everything on behalf of the applicants.

In addition, the vested interest networks reshaped the chronological order of the process in order to deliver this service. Since, the application receipt register is maintained manually it is possible to tamper with application IDs and receiving dates. The application ID and date of receipt become significant because of the 'first come first served' system.

5.4   Reflection and Learning: Emergence and Intervention

Adding a photograph to the application aims to ensure that only the applicant could submit an application. With the help of a photograph, it should be easy to identify whether s/he is an applicant or not. However, the issue of the photograph has been kept outside the service delivery process because it does not have any other role and reflection in the record updating process.

Equally, a paper-based and manual receipt register has allowed the opportunity for tampering with the date of receipt and the chronology of application ID number. The staff have several means and techniques to do this. From observation, it appeared that while issuing an application receipt, the staff allocates the application ID number to the application but they put all the applications' ID number into the register once a week or fortnightly. This allows them to manipulate the chronological order of the service delivery.

5.5   Formalization of Learning

The initial design was implemented for 5 months in 10 administrative districts in Khulna division. Following the Ministry of Land engagement with this ADER project a divisional level workshop was conducted with ACLs by the researcher; this enabled the decision making officers and the Secretary of the Ministry of Land to share their ideas and learning derived from the initial design. On the basis of the initial design and reciprocal learning from the 10 districts, the redesigned process has been issued as an official circular for the whole county by the Ministry of Land. The redesigned process has been in operation since May 2010.

Learning by organizational actors

The actors in the vested interest networks belong within the organizational process and those beyond the organizational process are mutually dependent on each other in intra and inter dimensions (ULO staff with citizens; ULO-LO staff; ULO staff). So, the initial design and the redesign process have been reshaped through the intra-action within the organizational staff and mutual interaction between the organizational staff and the other actors in the vested interest networks. Incorporating the applicants photograph has played a small role in excluding the actors of the vested interest networks from the application submission process because the identifier, the staff of ULO and user of the fake photograph in the application and the actors of the vested interest networks have mutual vested interests. Similarly, expediting service delivery for applications having vested interests is taking place through their mutual interaction. Therefore, the actors of vested interest networks in this service shift their position according to shifting of the design and redesign of the service process.

6   Empirical Outcomes

The initial design and redesign process has significantly increased citizens' direct access to this service delivery. The empirical findings show that about ½ of the total applications are now submitted by citizens to the ULO, compared with before the initial ADER redesign process. On the other hand, the redesigned process has ensured service delivery for all applications within 30 working days compared with previously where there was no time frame and consequently at least $1/3$ of the applications took more than 90 working days. Further the delays often took place in the cases of weaker sections of society. The redesigned process has simplified the application submission and tracking process, empowered the citizens through putting guidelines and necessary information with the application form and achieved chronological order in service delivery, to some extent.

However, the limitation of the redesigned process is that there is no scope for prioritizing service delivery. It has both advantages i.e., visibly no scope of discrimination; and disadvantages i.e., no scope to prioritize service delivery. Consequently, prioritizing service delivery has become a hidden process through vested interest networks and the citizens need to pay a significant extra amount ('bribe') for the prioritized service. Further, the centralized application submission process in the ULO and the manual receipt register still do not stop tampering with the chronological order.

7   Future Design

There are many socio-economic reasons behind the existence of the vested interest networks. The paper has addressed only a few, others include: low paid organizational staff; low literacy rates; complicated records; the presence of the actors in the vested interest networks outside the organization rooted in socio-political contexts and connected with organizational staff. Removing the vested interests overnight throughout the system is difficult. It requires long term strategic interventions through iterative design and redesign of this service delivery process.

The ADER generalized a list of learning points: the distance of the relationship between the service provider and the service recipients; installing technology to prevent and reduce intervention from vested interests networks in reshaping of the design process and reducing tampering in application ID as well as chronology of the service; and decentralization of the application submission process.

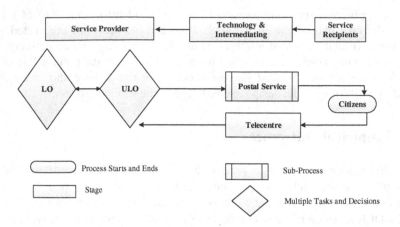

Fig. 4. Model for Further Design of Land Records Update in Bangladesh

On the basis of the generalized learning, a model (see figure 4) can be framed for further design of this service. Since the literacy rate is low, most of the citizens would require a mediator to access this service. Therefore technology mediated actors as intermediaries could help to remove the actors of the vested interest networks. They would be able to reduce citizens' interaction with service providers. Further, the country already has a network of 4501 telecentres across the rural areas. The telecentres could be technology mediated intermediaries in this service. In this way it is possible to decentralize the submission process, stop tampering and break chronological disorder. Updates could be received through SMS service or online tracking from the telecentres. Furthermore, the processed service is possible to deliver through the post, since there is countrywide public postal coverage.

The telecentres have already been mediating the service delivery of certified copies of land records to the citizens from the Deputy Commissioners office. Thus, to decentralize the application submission through the telecentres is compatible. To this end, there needs to be interfaces between the telecentres, the ULOs and the postal service developed.

Further, the Ministry of Land should revise the concept of chronological order service delivery because there should be a provision for urgent service delivery in emergency situations. In the case of urgent service, citizens are ready to pay 10-20 times higher than the usual fee to the government, which they currently pay as a bribe. Therefore, the government income would increase, the citizens would receive better service delivery and whereby incentives for the low paid service delivery staff might be possible.

8   Conclusion

This paper applied ADR together with an ethnographic methodological framework in order to gain a deeper understanding of the organizational contexts around updating land records in Bangladesh. It has applied an iterative process of problem formulation and design (BIE). ADR originally shared many of its activities and principles latently with an ethnographic perspective. Applying ADR in a developing country, it is clear that while understanding organizational contexts and building artifacts in organizational contexts remains unattainable and challenging due to the complex contexts, informal practices dominate over the organizational rules and the design processes. Thus applying ADR together with an ethnographic methodological framework helps to elicit insights into the organizational context. More importantly, an ethnographic methodological framework allows researchers to iterate throughout the ADR process. For instance, it gives an opportunity to formulate problems and interact with BIE through multiple cycles such that the context problems can be formulated from the data i.e. rather than relying on the researchers' knowledge and perceptions, the problem can be formulated through empirical evidence arising from engagement and observation. Further, understanding on-going use and redesign of artifacts is challenging in developing countries where practices are diverse, hidden and deliberately deceptive and where the researchers' engagement with the insider view is potentially very powerful. An objective evaluation is often helpful in the case of interventional research, thus applying an outsider viewpoint helps to conduct context free evaluation. However, the insider view also brings forth the researchers' reflection that could be seen as subjective evaluation. Finally, ADER has the potential to identify learning and transfer it to the practitioners through model building. Although conducting ADER is challenging because it requires long term involvement, commitment and skills, it has the potential to provide valuable ethnographic analysis i.e. 'thick description', for both IS practitioners and IS professionals.

References

Alam, M.S., Brooks, L., Khan, N.I.: Action design ethnographic research (ADER): Vested interest networks and ICT networks in service delivery of land records in Bangladesh. In: Bhattacherjee, A., Fitzgerald, B. (eds.) Shaping the Future of ICT Research. IFIP AICT, vol. 389, pp. 51–67. Springer, Heidelberg (2012)

Barab, S.A., Thomas, M.K., Dodge, T., Squire, K., Newell, M.: Critical design ethnography: Designing for change. Anthropology & Education Quarterly 35(2), 254–268 (2004)

Barakat, A., Prasanta, K.R.: Political Economy of Land Litigation in Bangladesh: A Case of Colossal National Wastage. Nijera Kori, Dhaka (2004)

Barley, S.: Technology as an occasion for structuring: evidence from observation of CT Scanners and the social order of radiology departments. Administrative Science Quarterly 31, 78–108 (1986)

Evered, R., Louis, M.R.: Alternative Perspectives in The Organizational Sciences: Inquiry from the Inside and Inquiry from the Outside. The Academy of Management Review 6(3), 385–395 (1981)

Geertz, C.: From the Native's Point of View: On the Nature of Anthropological Understanding. In: Geertz, C. (ed.) Local Knowledge, pp. 55–70 (1983)

Geertz, C.: Thick Description: Toward an Interpretive Theory of Culture. Basic Book Inc., New York (1973)

Goffman, E.: The Presentation of Self in Everyday Life. Penguin, London (1990)

Gregor, S., Jones, D.: The Anatomy of a Design Theory. Journal of the Association for Information Systems 8, 312–335 (2007)

Hevner, A.R., March, S.T., Park, J., Ram, S.: Design Science in Information Systems Research. MIS Quarterly 28(1), 75–105 (2004)

Kelly, D., Gibbons, M.: Ethnography: The good, the bad and the ugly. Journal of Medical Marketing 8, 279–285 (2008)

Lee, A.S.: Integrating positivist and interpretive approaches to organizational research. Organization Science 2(4), 342–365 (1991)

Mantei, M.M., Teorey, T.J.: Incorporating behavioral techniques into the systems development life cycle. MIS Quarterly 13(3), 257–274 (1989)

Myers, M.D.: Investigating Information Systems with Ethnographic Research. Communications of the Association for Information Systems 2, 1–20 (1999)

Nandhakumar, J., Jones, M.: Development Gain? Participant observation in interpretive management information systems research. Qualitative Research 2, 323–341 (2002)

Nandhakumar, J., Jones, M.: Too Close for Comfort? Distance and Engagement in Interpretive Information Systems Research. Information Systems Journal 7, 109–131 (1997)

Nedevschi, S., Jaspal, S.S., Joyojeet, P., Rodrigo, F., Kentaro, T.: Bayesian networks: An exploratory tool for understanding ICT adoption. In: Information and Communication Technologies and Development, ICTD 2006, pp. 277–284 (2006)

Nilsson, M.: Organizational Development as Action Research, Ethnography, and Beyond. Paper Presented at the Annual Meeting of the American Educational Research Association (2000)

Orlikowski, W.J., Gash, D.: Changing Frames: Understanding Technological Change in Organizations. Working Paper No. 236. MIT, Sloan School of Management (1992)

Orlikowski, W.J.: The Duality of Technology: Rethinking the Concept of Technology in Organizations. Organization Science 3, 398–427 (1992)

Orlikowski, W.J.: The Sociomateriality of Organisational Life: Considering Technology in Management Research. Camb. J. Econ. 34, 125–141 (2010)

Prasad, P.: Systems of Meaning: Ethnography as a methodology for the study of information technologies. In: Lee, A., Liebenau, J., DeGross, J.I. (eds.) Information Systems and Qualitative Research: Proceedings of the IFIP TC8 WG 8.2 International Conference, pp. 101–118. Chapman & Hall, London (1997)

Sanday, P.R.: The Ethnographic Paradigm(s). Adm. Sci. Q. 24, 527–538 (1979)

Schutz, A.: Concept and theory formation in the social sciences. In: Natanson, M. (ed.) Collected Papers, pp. 48–66. Martinus Nijhoff, The Hague (1973)

Sein, M.K., Henfridsson, O., Purao, S., Rossi, M., Lindgren, R.: Action Design Research. MIS Quarterly 35, 37–56 (2011)

Sim, S.E.: Evaluating the evidence: Lessons from ethnography. In: Proceedings of the Workshop Empirical Studies of Software Maintenance, p. 66 (1999)

Thompson, M.: People, Practice, and Technology: Restoring Giddens' Broader Philosophy to the Study of Information Systems. Information and Organization 22(3), 188–207 (2012)

van Aken, J.E.: Management research based on the paradigm of the design sciences: The quest for field-tested and grounded technological rules. Journal of Management Studies 41(2), 219–246 (2004)

Walsham, G., Sahay, S.: GIS For District-Level Administration in India: Problems and Opportunities. MIS Quarterly 23, 39–65 (1999)

Walsham, G.: Interpretive Case Studies in IS Research: Nature and Method. European Journal of Information Systems 4, 74–81 (1995)

Westbrook, D.A.: Navigators of the Contemporary: Why Ethnography Matters. University of Chicago Press, Chicago (2008)

Governance in the Technology Era: Implications of Actor Network Theory for Social Empowerment in South Asia

Akhlaque Haque[1] and Kamna L. Mantode[2]

[1] University of Alabama at Birmingham
ahaque@uab.edu
[2] ACR Analytics
Lal.kamna@gmail.com

Abstract. Information and communication technologies (ICT) have proven their value in delivering time-sensitive and relevant information to targeted communities. Information has been the key resource to social development. Social entrepreneurs have leveraged ICT to reach out to people who are marginalized from public discourse. Despite successes however, some ICT initiatives have failed due to underestimating the social requirements of technology and to relying more on information systems than on the information the system transports. How information is produced and applied to a social context to create meaning is more important than the means by which it is represented through portable monitors and mobile devices. The paper argues in order to take advantage of today's ICT, it is critical that we understand how technology and society mediate within a socio-technical framework. Using the Actor Network Theory, the paper explains the process of mediation to highlight that the journey to technology-based solutions is not smooth. The Village Knowledge Center (VKC) project in India and the Access to Information (A2I) project in Bangladesh provide sound evidence of how ICT-led social development can be effective in the short run but meaningful long term changes will depend on the collaboration of social entrepreneurs and public administrators.

Keywords: Social entrepreneurship, governance, information utilization, actor network theory, public administration.

1   Introduction

The success of social entrepreneurship has regenerated interest in partnerships between government and civil society organizations (CSO) to solve the world's most pressing problems including, among others, dealing with demands for democratic rights, coping with climate change, and giving access to healthy living and social justice for marginalized communities. With the hopes of mobilizing citizens to become productive partners in economic revival, the international development agencies including The World Bank, United Nations Development Program (UNDP),

Y.K. Dwivedi et al. (Eds.): TDIT 2013, IFIP AICT 402, pp. 375–390, 2013.

the DFID (Britain), and GIZ (Germany) have invested in sustainable social development projects through collaborating with social entrepreneurs.[1] Social entrepreneurship is arguably a mobilization tool used by catalytic entrepreneurs who leverage the social capital in helpless communities to develop sustainable partnership as they empower and transform the human condition (Waddock and Post, 1991; Waddock, 1991).

Information plays a critical role in motivating citizens by identifying and contextualizing information towards a purposeful goal. Indeed, democracy is strengthened by an informed citizenry as citizens take ownership of their situation to become empowered and take charge of their destiny. In this regard, information and communication technologies (ICT) have proven advantage in delivering time-sensitive and relevant information to targeted communities. However, evidence suggests there are more failures than successes using ICT for social empowerment because of over reliance on the information systems rather than on the information it transports within a given social context. A systematic surveillance of the social context is a precondition to applying technology for social benefit. The paper uses actor network theory to show how linkages between human actors and the new technology can be established to form the *social basis* of technology deployment. Social entrepreneurs have been important catalyst in introducing new ideas through technology for social transformation. Social entrepreneurs' use of ICT for social development provides sound evidence of social mobilization using ICT.

The purpose of the proposed research agenda is to evaluate the process by which social entrepreneurs as leaders, in conjunction with public administrators, utilize information technology to activate and mobilize citizens to reach a sustainable and socially desirable outcome. For empowerment initiated through technology, the outcome depends on a complex social process independent of the technological supremacy. The growing literature on Actor Network and ethnomethodology will support discussion of the implications of action oriented information for empowerment in two independent civil society led projects in Bangladesh and India. The case studies highlight how new information that becomes available through ICT can mediate within society to build social relationships. Despite similarities in the mediation process, the approach taken by social entrepreneurs will ultimately determine the sustainability of ICT-based developments.

The paper comprises three broad sections. The first section delves into the discussions of the sociology of association as it affects our understanding of the role of technology in the larger scheme of human and non-human interaction. This section introduces Actor Network Theory (ANT). The second section connects the

---

[1] Investment in social entrepreneurship in the developed world is also noteworthy. For example, the Obama administration, through its newly created Office of Social Innovation and Civic Participation (OSICP) has allocated 1.1 billion dollars. The newly created Social Investment Fund (SIF) has given to some of America's most successful non-profit organizations to expand their work and encourage investment in health care, vocational training and direct assistance to bring people out of poverty.

theoretical discussion of ANT to the case study on the Village Knowledge Center project in Pondicherry, India, and the Access to Information (A2I) project in Bangladesh. In conclusion, we discuss the implication of social entrepreneurship in public administration.

2   Social Entrepreneurship and ICT

The roots of social entrepreneurship can be traced in the works by scholars engaged in civic and community empowerment, social responsibility and social justice (Harmon, 2006; Frederickson, 1997; King, 1998); however, the role of information and information systems in the process of achieving the same goals needs further investigation. As opposed to business entrepreneurs who take risk for making new opportunities to profits, the social entrepreneurs are interested in making mission-related social impact (Martin and Osberg, 2007; Yunus and Weber, 2010). Although a growing literature on social entrepreneurship is emerging, the creative process of leveraging resources towards social mobilization is not well understood (Dacin et. al, 2010). This becomes particularly of interest in developing countries where public agencies play a critical role in realizing the social entrepreneurial goals.

The role of ICT for social empowerment is unclear, due in part to the fact that far more ICT dependent projects fail than succeed (Goldfinch, 2007; Heeks and Bhatnagar, 1999; Korac-Boisvert and Kouzmin, 1995). Institutional impediments and failures to mobilize government support for action have often confounded ICT's role in the process (Heeks, 2005; De Rahul and Ratan, 2009). Understanding the impact of technology on social empowerment requires a deeper understanding of ICT, beyond institutional receptivity (Fountain, 2001) and into comprehension of social institutions including cultural norms and standardization of routine work (Northrop et al., 1990). These can have direct impact on the livelihood of the population in question.

Social entrepreneurs are unelected bodies who need to be competent in what they do. Competency provides one of the bases by which policy decisions are deemed legitimate (Dahl, 1970). Therefore, how to mobilize information and knowledge authoritatively in the society is a fundamental task of the social entrepreneurs. Whereas elected politicians can make value judgments about policy decisions, they have a disadvantage when it comes to gathering empirically sound, unbiased information to validate their judgments and make them acceptable to the public. The public may question the neutrality of elected officials. In addition, the qualities that helped someone win election may not always include competency in data gathering and validation (Vibert, 2007, p. 49). When it comes to policy issues, respectable social entrepreneurs and independent international development organizations can offer the skills to gather empirical evidence about what works and what does not. They can apply the technical knowledge and leverage resources specific to the mission of the development projects. However, the normative judgments about what is best for the society are reserved by the politicians; they ultimately decide what ought to be the public interest. Whereas the technocratic function (i.e. information gathering and resource mobilization) can be performed by independent social entrepreneurs, political value judgments are made by the politicians, be they liberal or conservative, pro-business vs. pro-liberation, or otherwise. Therefore, the social development formula in a democracy has a technocratic component for developing techniques and a political component to justify implementing projects seen as critical in maintaining a stable democracy. Social entrepreneurs can bring innovative ideas and technical knowledge to reach specific social goals. In places where development challenges have been an uphill battle due to political and/or socioeconomic situations, ICT has become an expedient tool for social connectivity and access to information hastening social mobilization and empowerment. But the process is not always clear as to how ICT can be effective in social mobilization. Actor network theory provides a framework that can be helpful to link ICT to society in general.

3   Actor Network Theory (ANT)

Social problems are complex and require comprehensive understanding of the relationships of the social networks and each actor's relationship to technology and the artifacts that define the *socio-technical* network. In other words, the society is technologically shaped as we tie ourselves to routines that are built around a network of relations to humans as well as non-human actors. Actor-Network Theory (ANT) describes how society is an assemblage of actors, each linked to create meaningful relationships. The seminal works of Bruno Latour (1987, 2005), John Law and Michael Callon (1986, 1992) are recognized as foundations of ANT. The subsequent work and related research within Science and Technology Studies (STS) provides further basis for understanding the evolution of ANT as a multidisciplinary study (See for example, Bijker, Hughes and Pinch, 1987; MacKenzie and Wajcman, 1999; Feenberg, 1991.) The theory asserts that the role of technology in society depends on the interpretation of the actors who use their social lenses to arrive at a *mutually recognizable usage* of the technology towards a given routine, while at the same time balancing their social network relationships. Technology therefore is a social construct whereby technical artifacts in society become meaningful as reliance on them becomes part of the society's routine. By way of becoming part of a societal routine, the technology is stabilized to affect social roles and relations, political arrangements, organizational structures and even cultural beliefs. Figure 1 is an attempt to describe the ANT process. The ANT defines the non-linear negotiation

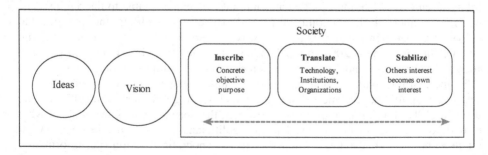

Fig. 1. Actor Network

among differing actors as they interpret the role of other actors' (including non-human actants) which culminates to a shared *mode of thinking* about the normative role of technology within existing social and organizational relationship.

The figure describes, in general, the process of change within a socio-technical framework where an individual initiator of change (the actor) creates his or her own vision of the future based on understanding of the societal motives, socio-cultural and political biases, and assuming that morality, technology, science and economy will evolve in particular ways. A large part of the work of the actors involved in the initial phase of deploying an artifact is that of *"inscribing"* the vision or prediction about the world in the technical context of the new idea. In other words, the individual vision is combined with the technical world to meet the purpose. Until the individual idea crystalizes as an organized action, the negotiation of "idea" and "reality" continues in *translation*. Translation is the phase in which existing social settings including agents and institutions are aligned to meet the demands of the new idea. The evolutionary process is fraught with failures and improvisations at each stage of translation by differing actors in the process. The formal world of institutions and technology is used to translate the message (of the change) and to standardize the process so the desired change can emerge specific to the people and their context. The negotiation is said to have been resolved or standardized when one form of the initial idea appears to be acceptable by others given the human and non-human contingencies. Once the idea reaches a standard interpretation, it provides the stability and continuity required to replicate and translate it to the masses. What has been eventually "created" is the result of collective interpretation of the actors, what Heideggar (1977) calls "revealing" through *"enframing"* of the human mind. The essence of technology therefore, according to Heideggar, is nothing technological; it is the collective realization of transforming (revealing) idea into an art (or *technè* as defined by Plato; see Heidegger, 1977, p. 34) as if it is pleasing to see it from different perspectives. Therefore, technology reveals itself by meshing with the given societal norms.

The ANT's emphasis on giving equal weight to non-human actors (technology) and human actors in social development is to differentiate between *situated* information and *objective* information. Whereas, objective information is imposed on the existing social setting, situated information is applied and improvised to match the existing social norms. Translation varies with people, time and context, yet once it is stabilized it becomes part of the routine. For example, social entrepreneurs can utilize technology as a supporting element in an effort to shape the environment to favor a desired effect on a community; yet the social entrepreneurs do not have full control of the outcome given the inherent limitations within the translation phase. The outcome could be affected by, for example, differing understandings of the technology's role within existing routine. The flexibility of the translation process is directly associated with how technology may be used.

Regardless of the technological sophistication, moral reasoning as to "why do it?" must take precedence above technical rationality in the translation process. The greater the reliance on technology, not the human and cultural beliefs, to standardize the desired result, the more difficult it becomes to translate idea into action. The question of "why do it?" is answered when others' interests becomes one's own.

Social entrepreneurs and civil society organizations provide that moral basis for initiating change. For successful implementation, however, the moral basis must also be congruent with the social values and the political judgments of the elected officials. In the translation process, the instrumental knowledge required to make the change is critical but secondary to social and political knowledge. In other words, the global knowledge must be in line with the local knowledge. This is also described as the micro-macro problem or the local-global problem in the translation process discussed in the next section (Misa, 2003). Local and global perception must be synchronized in order to sustain a stable network.

4   Accountability of Information Technology

The concept of ANT allows us to focus specifically on the accountability of technology to society. Just as individuals are accountable for their role in society as responsible citizens, technology must also account for its role in shaping society. That accountability can be measured by the *value* ICT generates through to its users. If the shared information that is gathered and disseminated among members using a particular ICT raise conflicts with the cherished values of the society, the given ICT will have a harder time *situating* itself in the social group. Thus, "information has an inalienable ethical dimension," noted information scientist Joseph Goguen (1997, p. 47). If technologies, such as surveillance tools, are used to compromise citizens' rights, such technologies will be incompatible with democratic values. Whether it is the right kind of information for social advancement will depend how well the ICT is able to integrate itself into the normal and acceptable routine of the social group. If the technology demands a significant shift from normal routine, adaptation will be slower and the failure rate will increase to the point where the user critical mass will not be sufficient to have significant impact in social behavior. It becomes incumbent that the local actors embrace ICT for their social advantage, and for that, global actors should pay adequate attention to the social-self of the local actors. Otherwise, the local-global conflict will destabilize a negotiated network.

How fast the local actors embrace a particular technology has to do with the type of technology introduced in the early phases of technology deployment. Elected representatives often fail to address the social value of ICT, particularly if they are deployed in large scale. In the absence of actions from elected representatives, social entrepreneurs can easily fill the void by bringing pertinent ideas of social mobilization using technological means. As Waddock (1991) carefully noted: "Social entrepreneurs generate followers' commitment to the project by framing it in terms of important social values, rather than purely economic terms, which results in a sense of collective purpose [Burns, 1978] among the social entrepreneur and those who join the effort" (p. 394).

Social entrepreneurs capitalize on a local network to earn trust as they focus on a target population to address pertinent social concerns. They leverage social capital to articulate larger, complex social problems within the *task environment* (concept coined by Thompson [1967]). Aiding the process of translation are intermediaries, technical resources employed to mobilize the actors. Examples of intermediaries can be maps, policy documents, mobile apps and even financial resources which symbolize a social order and power in the network. The intermediaries aid in the translation by standardizing the message across time and place. Inscriptions like "reports, texts and documents refer to the way technical artifacts embody pattern of use" (Rhodes, 2009). Government can play a key role in facilitating development of intermediaries. Modern day internet and ICT in general are powerful intermediaries, providing standardized platforms to expedite e-government services (paying taxes, getting licenses, online procurement, etc.) and other useful functions. Intermediaries are passive when it comes to transforming the social order to address larger socioeconomic concerns such as poverty, social equity and social justice issues.

Unlike intermediaries, *mediators* transform the message as opposed to just transport it without distortion or addition.[2] With respect to mediators, when a message is being transported, it customizes it based on local context. Therefore mediators impede standardization of the message as it finds ways to channel the message through improvisation to address the needs of the day.

While clearly the internet and ICT in general are effective intermediaries; they can also be powerful mediators when used to disseminate situated information for social transformation. Intermediaries are the primary vehicles for creating "black-boxes" or closed systems where the input leads to a given output and the interlocking of the coordination between input and output is not clearly identified (Kaghan and Bowker, 2001). When a network or part of the network is successfully black-boxed, it can be treated as a simple input/output device that is expected to perform a routine operation with precision and without creating any disturbances within the larger system. Since black boxes work with near certainty, they can be transferred from one black box to another set or subset of black boxes. They can be effectively used to mobilize an individual or group to mediate in addressing larger socioeconomic concerns such as poverty, social equity and social justice issues. For example, social media tools (targeted apps, twitter, Facebook, etc.) can be powerful intermediaries to mobilize a large mass for a certain cause. The masses can then become mediators to make changes on the ground or even utilize the same social media tools to start-off another series, effectively mobilizing another group of masses for some other cause. Look for example at "the Arab Spring" of 2012 and subsequent movements in Libya, Syria and other parts of the world. What intermediary is to technique is what mediator is to act on that technique for specific solutions. The two case studies refer in this paper highlight how information technology can become an active "social tool" to change the human condition as local actors utilize the tools of their daily social routine for expanded purpose. With the help of global actors such as social entrepreneurs and governmental agencies who provide technical or political or moral support, technology can be an effective tool to mobilize social empowerment.

---

[2] A good discussion about intermediaries and mediator can be found in Latour (2005), pp. 37-42.

5   Information Technology and Society: Case Studies

5.1   Village Knowledge Center Project (VKC), India

The Village Knowledge Center project started as a pilot initiative in 1998 in Pondicherry, India, a rural region that was once a French colony in the southern state of Tamil Nadu. The project was initiated by the M. S. Swaminathan Research Foundation (MSSRF), a rural development nonprofit organization founded by Professor M. S. Swaminathan in 1988. Among many different projects undertaken by MSSRF, the village center project is of particular interest to this study because it systematically blends technology with social context for social development. The materials for the case study are gathered from the work of Swindell (2006, 2007), Bhatnagar et.al., (2006), published reports by the MSSRF (Senthikumaran S. and Arunachalam, 2002; Nanda and Arunachalam, 2009) and the archived reports from the official website of MSSRF http://www.mssrf.org.

The vision of the MSSRF projects is to increase the capacity of the marginalized communities in the rural areas through community-demand driven technology. At the initial phase of the VKC project, a need assessment survey was conducted in the target area of Pondicherry to find what the local people already knew about the resources available to them and what they needed to know to improve their livelihood. Rather than creating a new technology-driven system, technology was brought in to improve upon the existing socio-technical design. There was clear methodology about how to create Village Knowledge Centers, methodology which was refined over more than 10 years. A large group of volunteers have been trained to maintain and operate the VKCs. A detailed handbook titled *Toolkit for setting up Rural Knowledge Centers (RKC)* is widely circulated to standardize the process. Once established, VKCs worked as the information hub for a several communities. For example, the farmers had incomplete or, in some cases, no information about market prices for their crops. Fishermen had no scientific way to forecast the weather or their prospects for good fishing the next day. Technology helped deliver such information through very high frequency radio wave broadcast within a 12 kilometer radius. Technology also enabled voice data transfer to be converted to text and then to fax out which then was uploaded and displayed on a computer screen.

The village centers were initially housed in private residences with limited access to all farmers, particularly those belonging to the lower caste, poor communities. Inability to ensure equitable access to all the farmers was seen a major obstacle for mobilizing the local network. Once MSSRF recognized the drawback, they had to revisit the strategy. They closed the village information centers after a few months. When they reintroduced the project with a revised action plan, they also established VKCs for an additional 12 villages.

Participation in VKCs was contingent on an expressed request of the village community. Also the village community was required to provide premises in a public building and to ensure the center was accessible to everyone in the village. In most cases these centers were located in public places like temples, government offices, noon meal program centers and *panchayat* (village assembly) office. The village community was responsible for the upkeep of the rooms and utility bills. Finally, every village was also required to provide local volunteers who were trained by the foundation staff and placed in the centers to function as information facilitators, computer maintenance experts and local information gatherers. In order to establish and *stabilize* the new information gathering method, a great number of volunteers, especially women, were trained in basic PC operations, use of data cum voice networks, maintenance of user log register, management of queries and handling data requests. Involving the village community from the beginning and encouraging local people to take ownership of the VKC was critical to the longevity of the project. Involvement was essential to drive the amount of social impact necessary to empower people in the communities through information and knowledge sharing. In terms of power, the global network represented by MSSRF was scaling back its control when it allowed the villages to control the location and provide the volunteers. By providing autonomy to the local network, MSSRF was able to mobilize and strengthen stakeholders in the implementation of the project. Transferring ownership was critical for building trust among global and local networks. VKCs clearly focused on situational information as opposed to objective information, and this helped the citizens to incorporate technology into their daily routine. The new technology was able to earn trust which in turn speeded deployment to larger groups. The special value of this project is the manner in which local knowledge was given importance. In particular, for example, all information including databases was translated into the local Tamil language. A variety of visual multimedia resources were also used to standardize the message.

The VKCs vision and commitment to learning and engaging the poor attracted the support of the Indian government in the form of a monetary grant of 100 core rupees and technical support from Indian Space Research Organization (ISRO) for launching a separate satellite for the program. Under the National Virtual Academy (NVA) program women empowerment groups are being trained in organic farming, herbal healing. Self-help groups also hold regular video conferences with rural communities and experts, manufacturers, government officials and experts. Fishermen are being offered training in the use of GPS and fish finding equipment. NVA launched a program called "Knowledge on Wheels" in 2007, in partnership with the Sankara Nethralaya Medical Research Foundation. The purpose of the project is to provide eye care information and eye care facilities to the rural poor. In collaboration with Hindustan Petroleum and ISRO, NVA has plans to use a mobile soil testing van that will help to detect the chemical composition of soil, including its pH and availability of various nutrients. This mobile equipment can propagate knowledge about crop cultivation, livestock management and harvesting technologies to locations not yet connected to permanent centers. NVA also plans to help educate villagers on methods of agro packaging. In collaboration with Bosch, a machine is made available to NVA for them to use for demonstrations across the villages to spread knowledge about hygienic packaging.

In 2004, MSSRF created a multiple stakeholder ICT partnership labeled as "Mission 2007: Every Village a Knowledge Centre". The target for this partnership was to connect 600 thousand villages via internet and radio communication by the year 2007. In 2007, global partners of MSSRF Microsoft and Telecenter.org (a joint effort of Microsoft, IDRC, Canadian and Swiss development agencies constituted a rural innovation fund (RIF). The sole purpose of this fund is to provide resources for development of technologies customized to fit the needs of rural population and their development. In particular, the mission of the fund is to encourage technology entrepreneurs. The response to RIF was encouraging; of the 1400 applications received, 9 software programs have been developed by the project. The software applications range from an e-commerce web portal, to animal husbandry, to account maintenance for self-help groups. As of 2009, MSSRF had Village Knowledge Centers in 5 states of India: Tamil Nadu, Kerala, Orissa, Maharashtra and Pondicherry, in total about 101 village knowledge centers and 15 village resource hubs.

5.2   Access to Information (A2I) Project – Bangladesh

A2I is the one of the largest technology-driven initiatives undertaken by the United Nations Development Program to expand e-Services capacity for the Government of Bangladesh (GoB). The A2I initiative used a grassroots approach to training and educating a critical mass of government officials, individual entrepreneurs and volunteers in ICT to create ICT-driven services (e-Services) at the door steps of citizens. Initially launched in 2009, the overall goal of the project is to create an e-Service environment to provide access to information and services that can reach the most vulnerable population in society. Unlike the Village Knowledge Centers discussed earlier, the A2I partnered with the government from the beginning of the project. This approach not only mobilized resources quickly but also placed the large governmental apparatus at the disposal of the A2I initiative. The primary information discussed in this paper about A2I is gathered from reports published by UNDP (2012) and reports published on the official A2I website by the Government of Bangladesh (http://a2i.pmo.gov.bd/index.php).

The A2I project aimed to utilize situated information to build capacity for local actors and give them ownership for sustainable e-Services throughout the country. The GoB took the A2I as one of their own projects as it was synonymously identified with the "Digital Bangladesh" goal within the national development agenda declared by the current government. The project attracted a large critical mass through its Quick Wins (QW) e-Services projects. Quick Wins is referred to e-Services that could be quickly developed to facilitate citizen government interaction at the grass root level to work at the district, Upazila (regional jurisdiction) and village levels to create accessibility infrastructure. In the first two years of the project, 53 QW e-service projects encompassing 9,000 independent entrepreneurs trained to run and manage over 4,500 Union Information and Service Centers (UISC), were begun, covering the whole country. Currently, there are 700 QW projects in the pipeline.

A notable outcome of the project has been the development of multimedia classrooms in some 500 schools. This is expected to be scaled up to 15,000 secondary schools within two years. The following table highlights some of the signature QW projects that are significant due to their social impact on ordinary citizens of the country.

Table 1. Impact of Popular A2I-Quick Win Initiatives

Initiative	Impact
UISC (Union Information Service Center)	Three million users have access to growing e-service portfolio; saves citizens time & money through reduction in travel 3M grassroots people/month generating $150K/month
DESC (District E-service center)	Significant reductions in delay (time for certified document reduced by half); 50% more requests processed per day; more transparent 5,000 applicants/month
Multimedia Classroom	Students interest in lessons increased 50%
E-Purjee (Digital Cane Procurement System)	Over 200,000 sugar cane farmers benefitting from more transparent system where they are informed of when to deliver sugar (in the past they sometimes never received the paper "chalan", or had to pay rent seekers a fee or travelled to the mill in vain) and when they will be paid; mills are benefitting from more efficient delivery

Source: UNDP, 2011

Over 200,000 sugar cane farmers benefit from a more transparent system through which they are informed of the best time to deliver sugar and when they will be paid. In the past the farmers sometimes failed to receive the paper (*chalan*) or they were obliged to pay a fee for information to unscrupulous petty officials. Sometimes the farmers traveled to the mill in vain. The new system to disseminate accurate information in a timely manner minimizes such problems. Mills too receive benefits from more efficient delivery

One of the unique features of the project was to enroll top level bureaucrats, senior government officials at the ministerial/federal level, public representatives and local entrepreneurs in ways that made them aware and informed about the developing services. Therefore they felt less threatened by the new means of *governing-from-a-distance* (e-Services). Awareness was followed by ownership which was fundamental in the translation phase to mobilize citizens towards using any particular e-Service activity. For example, all Ministries had to come up with their own Quick Win projects that were tied to the existing infrastructure of ongoing A2I projects. Although ministries varied in terms of their competency and commitment for such projects, there was a sense of pride among peers when a particular e-Service was launched and citizens embraced those services. The A2I project has interested many businesses and international donor organizations including the World Bank, Intel, International Rice Research Institute, D.Net, Asian Development Bank, UNESCO and UNICEF.

5.3   Policy Implications of VKC and A2I

We can glean very important insights from these two projects. First, the application of technology must directly address the fundamental matter of improving the quality of life of the local actors even if the new activity appears to be trivial or mundane in the eyes of the global actors, i.e., social entrepreneurs or the government. The technology adaptation can be smoother when the normal routine within the social association remains undisturbed. This is critical because during the translation phase when the new technology is introduced the actors can easily negotiate common definitions and meanings of the new way of doing things. Second, rather than introducing a big change through a big project, a gradual and incremental approach can have a wider and more meaningful impact in the society. This is because by keeping things simple, the standard definition can be easily and quickly replicated to serve greater numbers of people in a greater variety of small ways. For example, thorough the Quick Win projects for A2I in Bangladesh, the farmers were not learning anything new about farming, but they were getting valuable information quickly at insignificant cost. This enabled the farmers to focus on increasing production and diversifying their greater earnings to invest in other productive uses, perhaps for their children's education or for beginning a small handicraft business.

The VKC project in India started as a small scale, pilot investment in private homes. Within the first few months of operation the problems were revealed within the existing infrastructure regarding lack of access by potential beneficiaries within the lower caste population. We note that technology must be adjusted and in some case improvised in order to meet the demands of the existing socio-cultural circumstances. Whereas technical adjustment can be easier, especially when undertaken in smaller scale, value adjustments take time and may be difficult without political support. When technocratic functions are imposed without regard to both political and sociocultural context, a high failure rate is inevitable, at least when measured in terms of usage and mobilization. Whether the global actors are NGOs or governments, the values of the local actors involved must take precedence to the values or demands of the global actors. As argued earlier, the greater the supremacy of technology in the design of a project over the values that justify the project, the more difficult it becomes to translate the idea into action. Technology cannot address questions of values. Therefore, the ideals of democracy, freedom and justice must be addressed through avenues that deal with empowerment and awareness of the citizens' limitations. Information technology has proven that it can mobilize and empower the citizenry.

The deep rooted caste system that pervades rural India provided the impetus for the global actors (social entrepreneurs) to intervene to override the societal bias via information technology tools. Values drove the strategy and design of the Village Knowledge Centers to introduce technological tools for the benefit of all citizens. VKCs placed technology in the role of a mediator, less as an intermediary, and that effective policy enabled the VKCs to address social bias and help to empower masses that had been marginalized.

Similarly, in Bangladesh where political turmoil and corruption impede social development, social entrepreneurs intervened and played a dominant role in transforming the way the central government and its local counterparts ran their business. By partnering with international NGOs, the social entrepreneurs were able to break through political barriers to reach out to citizens via Quick WIN projects. The applications (apps) are more often intermediaries than mediators. Whereas in India technology was able to mediate deep into the social prejudices and the culture; Bangladesh was able to solve a problem quickly and to replicate the simple model exponentially to deliver accessible benefits widely throughout the country. The extent of the cultural shift which was very apparent in Pondicherry may not be as apparent in Bangladesh, at least in the short run, but both case studies reveal Actor Network Theory succeeding to improve the quality of life through applications of technology. In both cases the values and realities of the citizen beneficiaries informed the design and implementation of the technological tools.

The balance of societal values with functional abilities of technology is a promising formula for success, yet all projects are vulnerable. Many of the gains brought about by the social entrepreneurs, NGOs, or any global actors can easily be undermined unless vigilant and engaged public administrators act on behalf of the local citizens. For example, in India the elite class may find it to their advantage to reinforce historical norms of social discrimination and devise means to incapacitate the VKCs. The sustainability of the VKCs will depend on how effectively local citizens take ownership of the centers' mission and services. Should they be blinded to the advantages or doubtful of their need to be involved, they may withdraw their support and see the demise of the project. In Bangladesh, diligent oversight by village citizens and the public managers who represent their interests may well be necessary to protect the large scale, widely uniform ICT projects from abuse by ruling political parties who can misuse the projects for their own political gain. To compound the risks, successful projects can and do attract the attention of national or even international interests with no regard to the quality of life of the participating local actors. Projects are vulnerable to sophisticated hi-jacking orchestrated by distant powers who can exploit the local citizens. Anecdotal evidence suggests that both VKCs and A21 projects are becoming vulnerable to some or all of these intrinsic risk factors. Public administrators have the responsibility to monitor and maintain the innovative projects that have direct social and economic implications for their societies.

6   Conclusion

Information technology plays a critical role in balancing our life and work in society today. Applications of technology are instrumental in shaping our values as we develop a deeper understanding of the roles they can take in all aspects of our lives. The modern era has seen a sudden shift towards ICT-based policy developments, a shift with wide ranging implications in our social and economic life. Being in the midst of the transition, the millennia generation may take for granted the changes without questioning how the social and economic values have shifted in response to ICTs role in society.

Information technology enthusiasts have long argued that ICT is an empowerment tool and liberator for the marginalized. They argue, by introducing ICT into the governing process (i.e., automation of service delivery through E-Government) government can be accessible and convenient for citizens. Indeed today government is much closer to citizens through electronic means and is probably more transparent as far as service delivery is concerned. Even so, whether the citizens are empowered in the sense of taking control of their own livelihood is debatable. Societal empowerment demands sustainable social and economic development for all people including the most vulnerable populations. Technology can be the mediator for connecting citizens, but it cannot be the translator for action. Action requires the support of global network visionaries who help to mobilize the local citizenry network.

In the information age, implications of this study for public managers must not be underestimated. Public administrators, as non-elected representatives, occupy the desks where citizens come to ask for what they need their government to do; yet public administrators are bounded by procedures that are often antithetical to empowerment of the citizens who stand before them. Restricted by limitations of their ability to reach out to citizens, public managers can use ICT as the mediator to deliver an essential resource, information, to the doorsteps of citizens who will use it. Unlike food that will almost certainly be consumed when provided to the hungry, information may not be readily consumed. Potential beneficiaries require strategic direction about where and how to use the information. They need to comprehend the benefits of using the new information. In other words they ask, "What's in it for me?" When the "fundamental purpose of social entrepreneurship is creating social value for the public good," (Christie and Honig, 2006, p.3) it is only fitting for public administrators to answer that question and align with such a cause that brings social value to the public.

As our study alludes, social entrepreneurs provide the vision for information resources to be utilized for individual advantage. In the absence of visionaries within the local elected representatives, public administrators can partner with social entrepreneurs and civil society organizations. In the U.S., organizations such as Imagine Chicago (http://www.imaginechicago.org) and Everyday Democracy (http://www.everyday-democracy.org) have provided exemplary social entrepreneurial leadership within their communities.

Zukin et al. (2006) points out, "citizens need to be able to engage in the institutions and process of government and of civil society, since both are authoritative determiners of how goods, services, and values are allocated in a society" (p. 207). Today civic participation is an integral part of democracy, but it is open to question whether awareness of government and of political issues and participation in government services are constructive within the society. Leadership from public administrators dedicated to represent the citizens is crucial. Public administrators and public managers will best succeed in their efforts to deliver service when they accurately assess the local situation – the abilities, impediments, cultural mores and values -- and devise strategies to serve the citizens through technologies designed with the local situation in mind. Indeed, what is needed is an intention and desire to change the nature of the relationships amongst and between citizens and government. Some initial relationships may have to come from active citizens who will mobilize the resources towards a sustainable, beneficial impact in our communities.

References

Bhatnagar, D., Dewan, A., Torres, M., Kanungo, P.: M.S. Swaminathan Research Foundation's Information Village Research Project (IVRP). Union Territory of Pondicherry, World Bank (2003)

Bijker, W.E., Hughes, T.P., Pinch, T.J. (eds.): The Social Construction of Technological Systems, New Directions in the Sociology and History of Technology. MIT Press, Cambridge (1987)

Callon, M.: Some Elements of a Sociology of Translation: Domestication of the scallops and the fishermen of St Brieuc Bay. In: Law, J. (ed.) Power, Action and Belief: A New Sociology of Knowledge, pp. 196–233. Routledge & Kegan Paul, London (1986)

Dacin, P.A., Dacin, M.T., Matear, M.: Social Entrepreneurship: Why We Don't Need a New Theory and How We Move Forward From Here. Academy of Management Perspectives 24(3), 37–57 (2010), doi:10.5465/amp.2010.52842950

Dahl, R.A.: After the revolution; authority in a good society. Yale University Press, New Haven (1970)

De, R., Ratan, A.L.: Whose gain is it anyway? Structurational perspectives on deploying ICTs for development in India's microfinance sector. Information Technology for Development 15(4), 259–282 (2009), doi:10.1002/itdj.20129

Feenberg, A.: Critical Theory of Technology. Oxford University Press, New York (1991)

Fountain, J.E.: Building the virtual state: Information technology and institutional change. The Brookings Institution, Washington (2001)

Frederickson, H.G.: The spirit of public administration. Jossey-Bass Publishers, San Francisco (1997)

Goguen, J.: Social Theory of Information. In: Bowker, G.C. (ed.) Social Science, Technical Systems, and Cooperative Work: Beyond the Great Divide, pp. 27–56. Lawrence Erlbaum Associates, Mahwah (1997)

Goldfinch, S.: Pessimism, Computer Failure, and Information Systems Development in the Public Sector. Public Administration Review 67(5), 917–929 (2007)

Harmon, M.M.: Public Administration's Final Exam: A Pragmatist Restructuring of the Profession and the Discipline. University of Alabama Press (2006)

Heeks, R.: ICTs and the MDGs: On the Wrong Track? Information for Development, III(3). Retrieved from ICTs and MDGs in Wrong Track website (2005), http://www.sed.man.ac.uk/idpm/research/publications/wp/di/short/di_sp07.pdf

Heeks, R., Bhatnagar, S.: Understanding success and failure in information age reform. In: Heeks, R. (ed.) Reinventing Government in the Information Age: International Perspectives in IT-Enabled Public Sector Reform, pp. 49–74. Routledge, London (1999)

Heeks, R., Seo-zindy, R.: ICTs and Social Movements under Authoritarian Regimes: An Actor-Network Perspective. Centre for Development Informatics, Institute for Development Policy and Management, SED, Manchester, UK (2013)

Heidegger, M.: The question concerning technology, and other essays. Harper & Row, New York (1977)

Kaghan, W.N., Bowker, G.C.: Out of machine age?: complexity, sociotechnical systems and actor network theory. Journal of Engineering and Technology Management 18(3-4), 253–269 (2001), http://dx.doi.org/10.1016/S0923-4748

King, C.S., Stivers, C., Box, R.C.: Government is us: public administration in an anti-government era. Sage Publications, Thousand Oaks (1998)

Korac-Boisvert, N., Kouzmin, A.: Transcending soft-core IT disasters in public sector organizations. Information Infrastructure and Policy 4(2), 131–161 (1995)

Latour, B.: Science in action: How to follow scientists and engineers through society. Harvard University Press, Cambridge (1987)

Latour, B.: Reassembling the social: an introduction to actor-network-theory. Oxford University Press, Oxford (2005)

Law, J.: Notes on the Theory of the Actor-Network: Ordering, Strategy and Heterogeneity. Systems Practice 5, 379–393 (1992)

Law, J., Callon, M.: The Life and Death of an Aircraft: A Network Analysis of Technical Change. In: Bijker, W.E., Law, J. (eds.) Shaping Technology/Building Society: Studies in Sociotechnical Change, pp. 21–52. MIT Press, Cambridge (1992)

MacKenzie, D.A., Wajcman, J.: The social shaping of technology. Philadelphia: Open University Press, Buckingham (1999)

Martin, R.L., Osberg, S.: Social entrepreneurship: the case for definition. Stanford Social Innovation Review 5(2), 28 (2007)

Misa, T.J., Brey, P., Feenberg, A.: Modernity and Technology. MIT Press (2003)

Nanda, S., Arunachalam, S.: Reaching the Unreached. M S Swaminathan Research Foundation, Chennai (2009)

Northrop, A., Kraemer, K.L., Dunkle, D., King, J.L.: Payoffs from Computerization: Lessons over Time. Public Administration Review 50(5), 505–514 (1990)

Rhodes, J.: Using Actor-Network Theory to Trace an ICT (Telecenter) Implementation Trajectory in an African Women's Micro-Enterprise Development Organization. Information Technology and International Development 5(3), 1–20 (2009)

Swindell, J.: The Information Villages of Pondicherry: a case study in capacity building for sustainable development. In: Leal, W. (ed.) Innovation, Education and Communication for Sustainable Development, pp. 515–534. Peter Lang., Frankfurt (2006)

Swindell, J.: Rural empowerment through access to knowledge: a comparison of two projects on two continents. Paper Presented at the European Federation for Information Technology in Agriculture (EFITA), Glasgow, England (2007)

Thompson, J.D.: Organizations in Action: Social science bases of administrative theory. Transaction Publishers, New Brunswick (2003)

UNDP, Bangladesh: Access to Information (A2I) Evaluation (5398). Dhaka, Bangladesh: United Nations Development Programme, UNDP (2011), http://erc.undp.org/evaluationadmin/downloaddocument.html?doc id=5398 (retrieved)

Vibert, F.: The rise of the unelected: democracy and the new separation of powers. Cambridge University Press, Cambridge (2007)

Yunus, M., Weber, K.: Building social business: the new kind of capitalism that serves humanity's most pressing needs. Public Affairs, New York (2010)

Zukin, C., Keeter, S., Andolina, M.W., Jenkins, K., DelliCarpini, M.X.: A new engagement? Political participation, civic life, and the changing American citizen. Oxford University Press, New York (2006)

Persuasive Pressures in the Adoption of E-Government

Vincent Homburg[1] and Andres Dijkshoorn[2]

[1] Erasmus University Rotterdam, Faculty of Social Sciences, Rotterdam, The Netherlands
homburg@fsw.eur.nl
[2] Novay, Enschede, The Netherlands
andres.dijkshoorn@novay.nl

Abstract. In this paper, we describe the diffusion of personalized services among municipalities in the Netherlands over the period 2006-2010 and investigate how and why various municipalities adopted personalized electronic services. Using qualitative data gathered in fifty interviews in ten selected Dutch municipalities, we synthesize the findings in an explanatory model of personalized electronic service delivery diffusion. The model shows how persuasive pressure (as perceived by adopters) is followed-up by organizational search activities, and how, in various circumstances, the idea of personalized services is 'framed' by innovation champions, knowledge brokers and new members of staff as to appeal to specific organizational priorities and ambitions. In doing so, this article contributes to an institutional view on adoption and diffusion of innovations, in which (1) horizontal and vertical channels of persuasion and (2) human agency, rather than technological opportunity and rational cost-benefit considerations, account for actual diffusion of innovations.

Keywords: e-government, adoption, diffusion, public sector, public management, institutions, channels of persuasion.

1   Introduction

In many western countries, it is especially local governments that are developing one-stop shops that serve as a point-of-entry to the whole range of government (Ling, 2002; Ho, 2002). Some contributions in the literature present high hopes of 'transformation' of the public sector (Weerakkoddy & Reddick, 2013). The actual implementation and take-up of the e-government phenomenon by public sector organizations, however, has lagged behind policy ambitions and rhetoric of transformation, reform and re-engineering (Moon, 2002; Homburg & Dijkshoorn, 2011). In trying to explain the actual diffusion of e-government, various empirical studies have identified city size, citizen demand, organizational structure, geographic location and capacity (see Table 1 for details of the literature reviewed) as the most important determinants of e-government adoption by public sector organizations. Implicit in the explanations that are featured by these authors seems to be the idea that public sector organizations – as organizations in general – are rational, utility-maximizing entities. In order for these organizations to survive, they may adopt innovative ideas and technologies, but the

Y.K. Dwivedi et al. (Eds.): TDIT 2013, IFIP AICT 402, pp. 391–406, 2013.

empirical evidence suggests they are sometimes hampered by the identified determinants. Such a rational explanation suffers from two weaknesses.

First, researchers working in the burgeoning institutional perspective have asserted that organizations in general are not entities that necessarily maximize efficiency and effectiveness, but rather accept and follow social norms, and seek long-term survival through legitimacy rather than efficiency and effectiveness (Orlikowksi & Barley, 2001; Mignerat & Rivard, 2009). Zorn et al. (2011) have argued that, especially for non- and not-for-profit organizations, technological innovations are a means for establishing legitimacy in the eyes of key stakeholders as much as they are means for enhancing operational efficiency. Frumkin and Galaskiewicz (2004) indicate that institutional pressures to adopt specific innovations are very relevant for public sector organizations.

Table 1. Literature review of explanatory e-government studies

Determinants of e-government adoption	Author(s)
City size	Moon (2002); Reddick (2004); Moon and Norris (2005); Norris and Moon (2005); Homburg and Dijkshoorn (2011)
Citizen demand (perceived usefulness)	Holden et al. (2003); Reddick (2004); Gilbert et al. (2004); Horst et al. (2007)
Organizational structure	Moon (2002); Reddick (2004); Holden et al. (2003);
Geographic location	Holden et al. (2003); Reddick (2004); Norris and Moon (2005)
Managerial, financial and technological capacity	Reddick (2004, 2009); Moon and Norris (2005)

Second, there seems to be an underemphasis in the literature on how the process of innovation looks like. In rational models of adoption and diffusion (e.g. Rogers, 1995), potential adopters figure as rather passive entities, adapting to prevailing norms of efficiency, without paying attention to ways in which human actors reflect on external pressure to behave in a particular way, nor to the types of responses human actors display in decision-making processes regarding the decision to adopt or not adopt a specific technology. In short, with the exception of studies by theorists like Orlikowksi (2000), Cziarniawska and Sevon (2005), Bekkers and Homburg (2005) and Homburg and Georgiadou (2009), 'agency' seems to be lacking in existing explanations (see also Orlikowksi & Barley, 2001). Therefore, questions like *why* public sector organizations actually adopt (or fail to adopt) e-government innovations, and *how* organizations actually learn to innovate, are scarcely given attention.

In this paper, the research question is how the actual adoption of e-government can be explained. Our intention is that, by focusing on 'agency' alongside 'structure' (Orlikowksi and Barley, 2001), and by emphasizing norms, values and taken for granted assumptions other than efficiency and utility-maximization alone, more light will be shed on the *process* of technological and organizational change. The analysis reported in this paper extends the existing literature on e-government to include institutional, 'agency' and 'process' aspects of e-government innovation.

2   Personalization and Personal Public Service Delivery

In this paper, focus on a specific empirical phenomenon: the delivery of personalized public services (OECD, 2009; Peterson et al., 2007; Homburg and Dijkshoorn, 2011) as a 'case' of the diffusion of a specific innovation. A characteristic of personalized services is that they generally make use of authorization, profiling and customization in such a way that, eventually, one-to-one relationships between public service providers and citizens are established. One-to-one relationships may provide citizens with, for example, pre-filled forms, suggestions for permits or benefits that maybe relevant given past requests, automatically generated reminders, and news updates based on customer preferences. The eventual aim is to provide services that are geared towards the needs of citizens, and less towards the existing supply-oriented organizational routines of service providers. Personalized services are presented as fairly 'mature' e-government levels (Andersen & Henriksen, 2006).

Examples of personalized services at national or federal levels are the Belgian MyMinFin e-tax initiative, the Danish borger.dk portal, the Estonian eesti.ee initiative, the French mon.service-public.fr website, the Norwegian Norway.no portal, the British direct.gov.uk site and the Dutch mijnoverheid.nl site. In the Netherlands, various municipalities offer personalized sections on their websites including http://www.eindhoven.nl/mijn-eindhoven.htm for the city of Eindhoven, and http://www.rotterdam.nl/mijn_loket _digid for Rotterdam.

3   Related Research: The Theoretical Antecedents of Diffusion

Diffusion of a new idea, product or service is defined as the spread of its use in a population of potential adopters (Rogers, 1995; King et al., 1994). The process of diffusion has been linked to characteristics of the innovation itself, the social system (community of potential adopters), channels of communication, and time (Rogers, 1995). Given the lack of a rigorous theory that acknowledges the embeddedness of e-government diffusion processes by municipalities in the larger context of governance (including central-local relationships and the activities of outreach programs), we scanned and searched related concepts in the organizational sociology and institutional theory disciplines - two related literature streams that explicitly address how organizations absorb prevailing ideas from their environments into their operations and structures. However, this literature tends to be relatively abstract, and does not address the diffusion of personalized e-government in the specific context of municipalities.

Advancements in the discipline of organizational sociology in recent decades (DiMaggio and Powell, 1983; Tolbert and Zucker, 1996) have highlighted the significance of the professional and/or legal rules, cognitive structures, norms and the prevailing values in which innovation takes place. Institutionalism emphasizes the persuasive control over the practices, beliefs and belief systems of individuals or organizations through an institution's sway (Kimberley, 1979, in King et al., 1994). Persuasion can be achieved not only through directives, but also through more gentle but nevertheless potentially convincing means such as deploying specific knowledge, subsidizing activities deemed 'appropriate' by national government, standard-setting, raising awareness and generally promoting specific technologies (King et al., 1994). Moreover, Venkatraman et al. (1994) have stated that persuasion can occur both through vertical channels of communication (initiated by actors outside the set of potential adopters, such as central government; see also Moon and Bretschneider, 1997; Bobrowski and Bretschneider, 1994) as well as through processes of mimicking and 'word-of-mouth' diffusion (Wang and Doong, 2010) involving communication, interaction and persuasion among potential adopters (DiMaggio and Powell, 1983).

The organizational sociology and institutional theory literatures are helpful in identifying an organization's environment as a source of 'pressure' for organizations to behave in a particular way (Suchman, 1995). Nevertheless, these literature streams do not explicitly address how, through 'pressure', innovations are diffused among organizations. Additional theoretical guidance related to this issue is provided by the so-called Scandinavian Institutionalism (Czarniawska and Sevon, 2005). This school of thought sees innovations as 'ideas' insofar as they can be viewed as artifacts. In order for ideas (such as 'personalization') to spread (using either horizontal or vertical channels of communication) they must be translated into, or associated with, a success story, image or even a myth. During its travel, the idea itself is likely to change (Czarniawska and Sevon, 2005). As such, the idea of translation is a much more complex concept than the notions of 'diffusion, 'adoption, 'mimicry' and 'direction' suggest, and involves various phases in which so-called change agents (Caldwell, 1996) are actively engaged in the process of adoption. Agency in the process of translation takes place in horizontal as well as vertical modes of persuasion, and change agents (experts, boundary-spanning agents, consultants, knowledge brokers etc.) may operate on both the supply and the demand sides of the translation (King et al., 1994).

To sum up, we draw on concepts selected from organizational sociology and institutional theories, such as horizontal and vertical 'persuasive' pressures in the form of beliefs, cognitive structures, norms and values. Scandinavian Institutionalism adds the aspect of 'agency' to this: diffusion is not a deterministic process but an intricate social process that involves translation activities by experts, boundary-spanning agents and knowledge brokers. At this moment, however, there is no complete theory available that fully explains the diffusion process.

4   Methods and Data

In order to explain the diffusion of personalized e-government services, we first define our population of interest, that is, the set of potential adopters of the innovation being scrutinized: personalized e-government. We chose to analyze diffusion within one national jurisdiction (in our case, the Netherlands), and our first step was to describe the diffusion pattern of personalized e-government services over a four-year period (2006-2010) delineated by two consecutive municipal elections. For this purpose, we used an existing dataset that is assembled annually by the Dutch 'Government has an answer' project. This project monitors directly observable characteristics of e-government initiatives by Dutch ministries, provinces, municipalities and water regulatory authorities, and annually reports its findings.

In line with our objective to further extend the e-government body of knowledge (that is, to actually build theory), we first described general trends in a population of 441 municipalities[1] and then, as a second step, we selected ten municipalities for an in-depth analysis of adoption processes. As the e-government literature consistently reports city size as being a major determinant of e-government adoption (see Table 1; see also Reddick, 2004), from the 2008 data we selected both adopters ('early adopters') as well as non-adopters ('laggards') from substrata, based on city size, of the population (see table 2 for a list of the selected municipalities). In each of the selected municipalities, qualitative interviews were held with key stakeholders such as council members, city managers, senior ICT managers and managers of public service provision. The starting point for the interviews was a topic list through which it was attempted to identify the antecedents, critical events, ongoing activities and interactions with internal and external stakeholders in relation to e-government and public service delivery.

Table 2. Selected municipalities

Number of inhabitants	Personalisation adopted	Personalisation not adopted
200,000+	Eindhoven	Tilburg
150,000-200,000	Enschede	Nijmegen
100,000-150,000	Haarlem	Amersfoort
50,000-100,000	Capelle aan den IJssel	Lelystad
0-50,000	Moerdijk	Lemsterland

All the interviews were recorded, transcribed and analyzed[2] using back-and-forth coding techniques[3]. Following recommended practices for qualitative research (Miles and Huberman, 1994; Patton, 2002), data analysis was conducted in parallel with data gathering, starting with the constructs that emerged from the theoretical antecedents of diffusion. In an iterative process, construct categories were refined, added or combined, and new categories sometimes led to new constructs being identified in the empirical data. In the analysis, both the prevalence of categories of empirical constructs are presented (which are identified as being values of categorical variables), as well as illustrative quotes that serve to furthermore illustrate processes of adoption and diffusion. Furthermore, the five 'non-adopter' cases were compared to the 'adopter'-cases based on the occurrence of specific, coded constructs or themes. As a final step, using both theoretical plausibility and induction, relationships between

---

[1] In the interval 2006-2010, the population of municipalities shrunk from 458 to 418 due to planned mergers.

[2] Note that the interviews were held in Dutch; the authors have translated the quotations given in the analysis section into English.

[3] Using the MaxQDA qualitative analysis tool.

constructs were made explicit: first through 'conjectures' (statements that, through induction, follow from empirical observations, patterns and theoretical analogy), and second through including concepts and relationships in a conceptual framework for understanding the adoption of personalized e-government. In doing so, it is attempted to actually contribute to *induction* (defined as distilling variables and explanatory relations from observed empirical patterns) in a transparent way, consistent with sound principles of qualitative research methodology (Patton, 2002; Bringer, Johnston, & Brackenridge, 2006).

5   Analysis: Explaining the Diffusion of Personalized E-Government

5.1   Description of Personalized E-Government Services in Dutch Municipalities

Table 3 lists the prevalence of certain attributes of personalized electronic service delivery by Dutch municipalities in the years 2006, 2007, 2008 and 2009. Overall, in the period covered, there is an increase in the offered possibility of using DigiD[4] authentication (from 20.7% in 2006 to 88.2% in 2009) and on-line payments (from 15.9% in 2006 to 80% in 2009). The growth of possibilities for receiving personalized newsletters, using pre-completed forms, assessing personalized policy consequences and using personalized counters lagged somewhat.

Table 3. Prevalence of personalization attributes in Dutch municipal e-government services

	2006 (n=458)	2007 (n=443)	2008 (n=443)	2009 (n=441)	2010 (n=418)
DigiD authentication	20.7%	56.7%	76.3%	88.2%	94.6%
Personalized newsletter	16.4%	21.2%	21.2%	N/A	27.9%
Tracking and tracing	10.0%	16.0%	28.2%	26.5%	41.3%
Payment	15.9%	42.4%	61.4%	80.0%	91.6%
Pre-completed forms	N/A	N/A	17.8%	19.1%	33.9%
Personalized counters (MyMunicipality.nl)	5.2%	14.2%	23.7%	28.8%	40.9%
Personalized policy consequences	N/A	N/A	19.4%	18.7%	22.2%

5.2   Pressure: Persuasive Influence on Adoption Decisions

We identified various categories of pressure (see Table 4) as sources of 'pressure' on decisions to adopt personalized e-government services. Most prominent was the perceived expectations of citizens. As one councillor phrased it:

---

[4] DigiD stands for Digital Identity. With a DigiD users can access a large number of online services offered by Dutch (central and municipal) government agencies.

> *"... a clamor for service provision, less bureaucracy, transparency: that is external pressure, as I perceive it. (...) Simply because society does not tolerate other kinds of organizational behavior ..."* (Councillor)

Another form of influence that was mentioned quite frequently was the existence of benchmarks against which municipalities can be judged. The fact that municipalities keep a sharp eye on benchmarks and rankings sometimes results in somewhat perverse incentives to adopt personalized services, such as one respondent noted:

> *"Our decision to implement personalized service delivery was due to our low ranking ... Our councillor wanted to improve our ranking, and we found out that we could improve our ranking quite easily by implementing a Personalized Internet Page ... and so we did"* (Project manager).

To summarize, what can be witnessed is that, in line with institutional theory (DiMaggio and Powell, 1983; Ashworth et al., 2009; Lai et al., 2006), all the municipalities reported perceiving persuasive pressure to adopt personalization measures, both from outside the set of potential adopters (referring to norms to conform to citizens' needs, or to be receptive towards national initiatives) as well as from within the set of potential adopters (referring to the norm to excel in relation to one's peers). Adopters are associated with a higher perceived persuasive pressure than non-adopters.

Table 4. Prevalence of 'pressure' on adoption decisions

Perceived pressures	Adopters	Non-adopters
Citizen expectations	56	36
Legislation	40	50
Benchmarks	57	26
National initiatives	52	24
Reputation	54	17
Other municipalities	16	7

The abovementioned observations lead us to formulate the conjectures 1A and 1B.

Conjecture 1A: Municipalities experience environmental pressures that persuade them to adopt personalized electronic service delivery.

Conjecture 1B: Perceptions of persuasive pressure are reported more frequently by adopters than by non-adopters.

5.3   Organizational Search: Scanning for Knowledge, Experiences and Courses of Action

Respondents from the municipalities reported that perceptions of persuasive pressure were followed by organizational searching and scanning activities, through which municipalities attempted to seek, identify and choose relevant knowledge, experiences and courses of action (see also Levinthal and March, 1982; Tidd et al., 2009). One respondent clearly illustrated how municipalities react to pressure:

> *"One member of our support staff made an inventory of associations that staff members are participating in, and she managed to compile a list of three or four pages..."* (Manager of service provision)

Typical targets for search and scan operations are forums and national outreach programs, companies and financial institutions, other municipalities generally, municipalities with which the municipality has an alliance, and within the organization itself (see Table 5).

Table 5. Organizational search

Organizational search	Adopters	Non-adopters
Forums and outreach programs	59	48
Companies	49	51
Other municipalities	60	27
Municipal alliances	29	7
Own organization	22	9

Respondents reported that pressure did not directly result in new connections with other organizations, but rather that it resulted in more intensive contact with forums and associations (for instance, the Public Service Provision Managers' Association, the Association of Dutch Municipalities, and also outreach programs such as GovUnited and DIMPACT) with which one was already involved. As one public manager reported:

> *"We meet each other at meetings of municipalities with 100 000+ residents. One talks to others, exchanges experiences, we report our practices, and listen to other ideas ... in this way, we converge on similar solutions as we all offer similar services"* (Manager Population Affairs and Taxes)

One respondent explained how one's own organization could serve as a source of relevant knowledge (see also Isabella, 1990):

> *"It happened partly due to one of our developers (...) She said she had knowledge of how personalized counters could be implemented but, until then, she had no time to work on them. She said it could be realized given that we already owned the necessary software packages - and she could develop it further. So we felt we were quite lucky to have such a developer who was able to build these facilities..."* (Program manager)

To summarize, in all the selected municipalities we witnessed how pressure was followed by organizational search activities, both in the external environment, as well as in existing alliances and within one's own organization for solutions and inspiration that might already be available. It can also be concluded that both adopters and non-adopters seek and scan for relevant knowledge in national forums, outreach initiatives and companies, but that adopters more frequently report seeking out ideas, inspiration and solutions in alliances, other (often similar) municipalities and their own organization than non-adopters do. These observations lead us to formulate a second pair of conjectures (2A and 2B).

Conjecture 2A: Municipalities respond to persuasive external pressure by searching and scanning for knowledge, inspiration and suggested courses of action related to personalized electronic service delivery.

Conjecture 2B: Searching and scanning activities are more prevalent in adopters than in non-adopters.

5.4   Framing: Translating Pressure into Local Priorities and Opportunities

According to Sahlin and Wedlin (2008; see also Silva and Hirscheim, 2007), and in line with the Scandinavian Institutionalism mentioned in the discussion on theoretical antecedents of diffusion, knowledge and ideas cannot simply be transfused from one organization to the other: rather, ideas, concepts and knowledge has to be repackaged and re-embedded (Isabella, 1990; Sahlin and Wedlin, 2008). In our field study, respondents explained that comparable ideas and 'chunks' of knowledge on personalization were framed completely differently in various adopting organizations (see Table 6 for a summary). Personalization was sometimes framed in terms of:

- A precursor to an organization becoming a service champion (enabling genuine citizen-centric service delivery);
- A means for achieving efficiency (*"If the processes are well-organized, I am convinced that in the long run we can do without large numbers of staff"*, Councillor);
- Boosting reputation (*"We think that we, being part of a high technology region, are obliged to modernize our service delivery"*, Head of Customer Relations Department); and
- Exerting control (*"Now the focus is on the front office ... but in the near future we intend to reengineer processes in the back office as well, so as to simplify and speed up processes..."*, Project Manager Service Delivery).

Table 6. Framing of personalized e-government services

Framing in terms of:	Adopters	Non-adopters
Service delivery, being a 'service champion'	84	40
Efficiency	46	21
Reputation	24	16
Management and control	13	18

Overall, we conclude that persuasive pressures are actively framed by stakeholders so as to appeal to local priorities and ambitions, which are found to be enhancing citizen orientation, organizational efficiency and reputation (see also Deephouse & Suchman, 2008). These findings result in conjectures 3A and 3B.

Conjecture 3A: In municipalities, persuasive pressure and sought knowledge are actively framed in order to legitimize the adoption of personalized e-government.

Conjecture 3B: Framing occurs more frequently in adopters than in non-adopters.

5.5   Activation Triggers: Enabling Episodic Changes

From the transcripts of the various interviews, we distilled concepts that did not directly affect adoption but that, nevertheless, can be interpreted as being important in explaining adoption. Activation triggers of various kinds (coined discrepant events by Tyre and Orlikowksi (1994); see also Kim (1998); Zahra and George (2002); Tidd et al. (2009)) were reported by respondents as moderating the impact of persuasive pressures. Van Waarden and Oosterwijk (2006) see activation triggers as precursors of episodic as opposed to more linear forms of diffusion. In our study, we came across general shocks, staff changes and organizational mergers as activation triggers (see Table 7).

Table 7. Activation triggers

Activation triggers	Adopters	Non-adopters
External shocks (accidents, rehousing)	17	4
Staff changes	8	5
Organizational merger	5	2

One clear example of an activation trigger was a firework factory exploding in the municipality of Enschede. This triggered a political crisis and, in the subsequent reorganization, personalized service delivery was seen as an opportunity to help shape the new organization. Respondents also mentioned new members of staff. As one respondent explained:

> "With new members of staff, new ideas and new energy entered our organization (...). A new city manager, ICT developers, new departmental managers: they all managed to get up to speed with evolving developments" (Head of Service Delivery)

The merging of municipalities was also reported as a trigger event that helped boost ongoing developments. The idea of service delivery in general, and the more advanced forms of personalized e-government in particular, were embraced by some stakeholders as helping to shape the identity of a new municipal organization and to get away from the pre-existing local identities of the former smaller municipalities.

The above activation triggers were reported more often by respondents from adopting councils than by respondents from non-adopters (see Table 7; see also conjectures 4A and 4B).

Conjecture 4A: External trigger events moderate the impact of perceived persuasive pressure on organizational searching and scanning activities.

Conjecture 4B: External trigger events are reported more frequently by adopters than by non-adopters.

5.6   Social Integration Mechanisms: Translating and Framing by Actors

From fieldwork observations, and informed by our theoretical discussion of Scandinavian Institutionalism, we could see that translation, transfusion and repackaging of knowledge and ideas does not take place in a vacuum, but is a social integration process in which specific actors play a role (Czarniawska and Sevon, 2005; see also Pawlowski and Robey, 2004). Szulanski (1996, p. 29) states that "as time passes, a shared history of jointly utilizing the transferred knowledge is built up in the recipient, actions and actors become typified, and types of actions are associated with types of actors".

The actual framing, transformation and transfusion of ideas and knowledge, that occurs between the processes of organizational searching and scanning and the framing of ideas, involves various social integration processes. An example was given by one respondent who commented:

> "... *John Doe, of Consulting Inc[5], he is a remarkable character. He has access to senior management levels, where normally no-one understands the potential of modern ICTs. However, he is able to come up with brilliant applications, stories and examples...*" (Program manager)

In our study, we identified three types of social integration: activities by in-house innovation champions, activities involving knowledge brokers and staff exchanges (see Table 8).

Table 8. Social integration

Social integration mechanisms	Adopters	Non-adopters
Activities of innovation champions (internal)	43	11
Activities of knowledge brokers (external experts)	26	14
Staff exchange	13	6

---

[5] The names of the respondent and the consultancy firm have been changed to maintain anonymity.

The importance of innovation champions can be illustrated by means of a quote which identifies a specific innovation champion:

> "...the idea of personalization, that was more or less Erik's business. Our councillor was never a digital enthusiast, and despite limited resources we managed to make things happen. And that was due to the persistence of Erik, who kept on fighting, although the councillor said that he'd never succeed..." (ICT policy advisor).

Staff exchange was also mentioned as a moderator of adoption (in line with Mignerat & Rivard, 2009). One respondent explained:

> "... We moved on when a member of Enschede's staff temporarily joined our organization. Due to personal circumstances, he was able to stay for a while in the Province of Noord-Brabant and we were able to make use of his experience. That helped quite a lot" (Departmental Manager Service Operations).

It is especially through these kinds of integration mechanisms that ideas and knowledge are actually transfused, translated and framed rather than merely being imitated (Howell and Shea, 2001; see also Bressant and Rush, 1995; Rice and Rogers, 1980; Sahlin and Wedlin, 2008; Silva and Hirscheim, 2007). These observations lead us to identify conjectures 5A and 5B.

Conjecture 5A: Knowledge gathered on personalized e-government services is spread and organizationally embedded through the activities of innovation champions, knowledge brokers and temporarily assigned staff members.

Conjecture 5B: Activities aimed at integrating the knowledge gathered within municipalities are more prevalent in adopters than in non-adopters.

6   Synthesis: Conjectures and Explanatory Model

The findings from this study provide a detailed account of how persuasive pressure is channeled within organizations, and of how various processes (searching and seeking, framing) and moderators (external shocks, social integration) are related to the adoption of personalized electronic service delivery. The conjectures can, through a process of induction, be included in graphic model that displays the processes of persuasion at work. We identify activation triggers and social integration mechanisms not as direct influences but as moderating influences on conjectures 1A and 1B, and 2A and 2B, respectively (see Figure 1).

The format of the framework is similar to Zahra and George's (2002) absorptive capacity (ACAP) model that generally explains organizational innovativeness. However, much more than in Zahra and George's ACAP model, the model displayed in Figure 1 acknowledges the 'push'-influence of institutions through channels of persuasion, rather than 'pull'-absorptive capacities (initiated by adopting organizations) emphasized by Zahra and George.

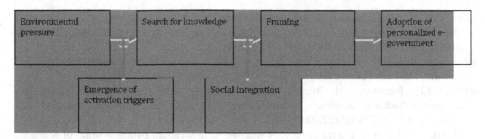

Fig. 1. Model of institutional influence on adoption of personalized e-government

7   Discussion and Conclusions

This paper has explored the process through which public organizations – or rather Dutch municipalities – adopt personalized e-government services and has resulted in a conceptual model of institutional influence on the adoption of personalized e-government services. This model contributes to the literature on diffusion and adoption of new technologies in a number of ways.

First, this study acknowledges and gives a distinct conceptualization of the concept of 'institutional pressure'. We have coined the term 'persuasive pressure' to exemplify that organizations are confronted with various types of pressure: both vertical (stemming from beyond the set of potential adopters) and horizontal (related to reputation and rivalry considerations that stem from within the set of potential adopters). Furthermore, various sources of pressure were identified: citizens' expectations, benchmarks, national programs, as well as considerations of reputation and rivalry.

Second, in line with the Scandinavian school of Institutionalism, human 'agency' was concluded to be an important part of the explanation. Persuasive pressure was not found to determine eventual outcomes, but was mitigated by active knowledge gathering by organizational actors, 'framing' of solutions and social integration processes initiated by innovation champions, knowledge brokers and through staff exchange (see also Mignerat & Rivard, 2009).

Third, and, related to the second conclusion, we conclude that institutionalization is not a deterministic process, but a rather political process that includes activities by key stakeholders, power and politicking. As a whole, it can be seen as a dynamic 'legitimization game' (see also Zilber, 2008).

References

Andersen, K.V., Henriksen, H.Z.: E-Government Maturity Models: Extension of the Layne and Lee Model. Government Information Quarterly 23(2), 236–248 (2006)

Ashworth, R., Boyne, G., Delbridge, R.: Escape from the iron cage? organizational change and isomorphic pressures in the public sector. Journal of Public Administration Research and Theory 19(1), 165–187 (2009), doi:10.1093/jopart/mum038

Bekkers, V.J.J.M., Homburg, V.M.F. (eds.): The information ecology of E-government (E-government as institutional and technological innovation in public administration), 2nd edn. IOS Press, Amsterdam (2005)

Bobrowski, P., Bretschneider, S.: Internal and external interorganizational relationships and their impact on the adoption of new technology: An exploratory study. Technological Forecasting and Social Change 46(3), 197–211 (1994)

Bessant, J., Rush, H.: Building bridges for innovation - the role of consultants in technology-transfer. Research Policy 24(1), 97–114 (1995), doi:10.1016/0048-7333(93)00751-E

Bringer, J.D., Johnston, L.H., Brackenridge, C.H.: Using computer-assisted qualitative data analysis software to develop a grounded theory project. Field Methods 18(3), 245–266 (2006), doi:10.1177/1525822X06287602

Caldwell, R.: Models of change agency: A fourfold classification. British Journal of Management 14(2), 131–142 (2003)

Czarniawska, B., Sevon, B.: Global ideas: How ideas, objects and practices travel in the global economy. Copenhagen Business School Press, Copenhagen (2005)

Deephouse, D.L., Suchman, M.: Legitimacy in Organizational Institutionalisation. In: Greenwood, R., Oliver, C., Sahlin, K., Suddaby, R. (eds.) Sage Handbook of Organizational Institutionalism, pp. 49–77. SAGE, Thousand Oaks (2008)

Dos Santos, B., Peffers, K.: Competitor and vendor influence on the adoption of innovative applications in electronic commerce. Information & Management 34(3), 175–184 (1998)

DiMaggio, P.J., Powell, W.W.: The iron cage revisited: Institutional isomorphism and collective rationality in organizational fields. American Sociological Review 48(2), 147–160 (1983)

Esping-Andersen, G.: The Three Worlds of Welfare Capitalism. Polity Press, Princeton University Press, Cambridge, Princeton (1990)

Frumkin, P., Galaskiewicz, J.: Institutional isomorphism and public sector organizations. Journal of Public Administration Research and Theory 14(3), 283–307 (2004)

Gilbert, D., Balestrini, P., Littleboy, D.: Barriers and benefits in the adoption of e-government. International Journal of Public Sector Management 17(4), 286–301 (2004)

Ho, A.T.: Reinventing local governments and the E-government initiative. Public Administration Review 62(4), 434–444 (2002)

Holden, S.H., Norris, D.F., Fletcher, P.D.: Electronic government at the local level. Public Performance & Management Review 26(4), 325–344 (2003)

Homburg, V.M.F.: Understanding E-government: Information systems in public administration. Routledge, London (2008)

Homburg, V.M.F., Dijkshoorn, A.J.D.: Diffusion of Personalized E-Government Services among Dutch Municipalities (An Empirical Investigation and Explanation). International Journal of E-Government Research 7(3), 21–37 (2011)

Homburg, V.M.F., Georgiadou, Y.: A tale of two trajectories: How spatial data infrastructures travel in time and space. Information Society 25(5), 303–314 (2009)

Howell, J., Shea, C.: Individual differences, environmental scanning, innovation framing, and champion behavior: Key predictors of project performance. Journal of Product Innovation Management 18(1), 15–27 (2001), doi:10.1016/S0737-6782(00)00067-9

Horst, M., Kuttschreuter, M., Gutteling, J.M.: Perceived usefulness, personal experiences, risk perception and trust as determinants of adoption of e-government services in the Netherlands. Computers in Human Behavior 23(4), 1838–1852 (2007)

Isabella, L.: Evolving interpretations as a change unfolds - how managers construe key organizational events. Academy of Management Journal 33(1), 7–41 (1990), doi:10.2307/256350

Kim, L.: Crisis construction and organizational learning: Capability building in catching-up at hyundai motor. Organization Science 9(4), 506–521 (1998)

Kimberley, J.R.: Issues in the Creation of Organizations: Initiation, Innocation and Institutionalization. Academy of Management Journal 22, 437–457 (1979)

King, J., Gurbaxani, V., Kraemer, K., McFarlan, F., Raman, K., Yap, C.: Institutional factors in information technology innovation. Information Systems Research 5(2), 139–169 (1994)

Lai, K., Wong, C.W.Y., Cheng, T.C.E.: Institutional isomorphism and the adoption of information technology for supply chain management. Computers in Industry 57(1), 93–98 (2006), doi:10.1016/j.compind.2005.05.002

Levinthal, D.A., March, J.G.: A Model of Adaptive Organizational Search. Journal of Economic Behavior and Organization 2, 307–333 (1981)

Ling, T.: Delivering joined-up government in the UK: dimensions, issues and problems. Public Administration 80(4), 615–642 (2002)

Loh, L., Venkatraman, N.: Diffusion of information technology outsourcing influence sources and the Kodak effect. Information Systems Research, 334–358 (1992)

Mignerat, M., Rivard, S.: Positioning the institutional perspective in information systems research. Journal of Information Technology 24(4), 369–391 (2009)

Moon, M.J.: The evolution of E-government among municipalities: Rhetoric or reality? Public Administration Review 62(4), 424–433 (2002)

Moon, M.J., Bretschneider, S.: Can state government actions affect innovation and its diffusion?: An extended communication model and empirical test. Technological Forecasting and Social Change 54(1), 57–77 (1997)

Moon, M.J., Norris, D.F.: Does managerial orientation matter? The adoption of reinventing government and e-government at the municipal level. Information Systems Journal 15(1), 43–60 (2005)

Miles, M.B., Huberman, A.M.: Qualitative data analysis, 2nd edn. Sage, Thousand Oaks (1994)

Norris, D.F., Moon, M.J.: Advancing E-government at the grassroots: Tortoise or hare? Public Administration Review 65(1), 64–75 (2005)

Orlikowski, W.J.: Using Technology and Constituting Structures: A Practice Lens for Studying Technology in Organizations. Organization Science 11(4), 404–428 (2000)

Orlikowski, W.J., Barley, S.: Technology and Institutions: What Can Research on Information Technology and Research on Organizations Learn from Each Other? MIS Quarterly 25(2), 145–165 (2001)

OECD. Rethinking e-government services (user-centred approaches). OECD, Paris (2009)

van Os, G.S.: The challenge of coordination: Coordinating integrated electronic service delivery in Denmark and the Netherlands. Information Polity 16(1), 51–61 (2011)

Patton, M.Q.: Qualitative Research and Evaluation Methods. Sage Publications, Thousand Oaks (2002)

Pawlowski, S.D., Robey, D.: Bridging User Organizations: Knowledge Brokering and the Work of Information Technology Professionals. MIS Quarterly 28(4), 645–672 (2004)

Pieterson, W., Ebbers, W., van Dijk, J.: Personalisation in the public sector: An inventory of organizational and user obstacles towards personalisation of electronic services in the public sector. Government Information Quarterly 24(1), 148–164 (2007)

Pollitt, C., Bouckaert, G.: Public management reform: A comparative analysis. Oxford University Press, Oxford (2004)

Reddick, C.G.: Empirical models of E-government growth in local governments. E - Service Journal 3(2), 59–84 (2004)

Reddick, C.G.: Factors that explain the perceived effectiveness of E-government: A survey of united states city government information technology directors. International Journal of E-Government Research 5(2), 1–15 (2009)

Rice, R.E., Rogers, E.M.: Reinvention in the innovation process. Knowledge-Creation Diffusion Utilization 1(4), 499–514 (1980)

Rogers, E.: Diffusion of innovations, 4th edn. Free Press, New York (1995)

Sahlin, K., Wedlin, L.: Circulating ideas: Imitation, translation and editing. In: Greenwood, R., Oliver, C., Sahlin, K., Suddaby, R. (eds.) Organizational Institutionalism, pp. 218–242. Sage, London (2008)

Silva, L., Hirschheim, R.: Fighting against windmills: Strategic information systems and organizational deep structures. MIS Quarterly 31(2), 327–354 (2007)

Suchman, M.C.: Managing Legitimacy: Strategic and Institutional Approaches. Academy of Management Review 20(3), 571–611 (1995)

Svensson, J.: Legal expert systems in social administration: From fearing computers to fearing accountants. Information Polity 7(2,3), 143–154 (2002)

Szulanski, G.: Exploring internal stickiness: Impediments to the transfer of best practice within the firm. Strategic Management Journal 17, 27–43 (1996)

Tidd, J., Bessant, J., Pavitt, K.: Managing innovation. John Wiley & Sons Ltd., Chichester (2009)

Tolbert, P.S., Zucker, L.G.: The Institutionalization of Institutional Theory. In: Clegg, S.R., Hardy, C., Nord, W.R. (eds.) Handbook of Organization Studies, pp. 175–190. Sage, Thousand Oaks (1996)

Tyre, M.J., Orlikowski, W.J.: Windows of opportunity - temporal patterns of technological adaptation in organizations. Organization Science 5(1), 98–118 (1994)

Venkatraman, N., Loh, L., Koh, J.: The Adoption of Corporate Governance Mechanisms: A Test of Competing Diffusion Models. Management Science, 496–507 (1994)

Van Waarden, F., Oosterwijk, H.: Turning tracks? Path dependency, technological paradigm shifts, and organizational and institutional change. In: Hage, J.T., Meeus, M. (eds.) Innovation, Science, and Institutional Change. Oxford University Press, Oxford (2006)

Wang, H., Doong, H.: Does government effort or citizen word-of-mouth determine e-government service diffusion? Behaviour & Information Technology 29(4), 1–15 (2010)

Zahra, S.A., George, G.: Absorptive capacity: A review, reconceptualization, and extension. The Academy of Management Review 27(2), 185–203 (2002)

Zilber, T.B.: The Work of Meanings in Institutional Processes and Thinking. In: Greenwood, R., Oliver, C., Sahlin, K., Suddaby, R. (eds.) The Sage Handbook of Organizational Institutionalism, pp. 151–169. SAGE, Thousand Oaks (2008)

Zorn, T.E., Flanagin, A.J., Shoham, M.D.: Institutional and Noninstitutional Influences on Information and Communication Technology Adoption and Use Among Nonprofit Organizations. Human Communication Research 37(1), 1–3 (2011)

Information as "Commons":
Applying Design Principles to ICTD Projects

V.L.V. Kameswari

G.B. Pant University of Agriculture and Technology
Pantnagar, Uttarakhand, India
vlvkameswari@yahoo.co.in

Abstract. Information is considered as a prerequisite for development in to-day's world. This belief has led to several measures to make information freely available to the citizens. Use of ICTs for development is a step in that direction, as they are expected to make communication more democratic and easy, leading to developmental outcomes. It is estimated that 60% of all ICT projects in Asia are located in India. Many players - national and state governments, private business organizations and civil society groups are engaged in their implementation. Despite huge investments, studies indicate that the developmental use of such projects is very low. ICTs for development projects have been studied using diverse tools and theories. Failure has been attributed to several factors including various types of barriers, faulty institutions, and technology related issues. This paper places analysis on ICTD projects within the context of CPR (Common Pool Resources) studies. In recent years, the definition of CPR has been expanded to include information as "new commons" and robust institutions are deemed essential for survival of all CPRs. In this paper, ICT based development projects have been interpreted as CPR institutions and CPR design principles have been used to explain the functioning of two ICTD projects. Both these studies were carried out in the state of Uttarakahnd, India and analysis is confined to use of agricultural information by the farming community.

Keywords: Information commons, Design principles, ICT projects.

1 Introduction

Information is posited as the prime mover of development in today's world. Hence, terms like knowledge society, knowledge economy, information movement, etc are in wide currency. There is a growing conviction that the future growth of nations will be limited less by financial/ capital resources in the years to come. It is oft repeated statement that countries will fail in their quest for development due to their inability to produce, process and use information. This belief is underlined by the growing number of ICT (Information and Communication Technology) projects, especially in the developing world. According to Yunus (2006), ICT is transforming the world into a distanceless, borderless world of instantaneous communication and access to ICTs can change the lives of poor people. The mushrooming number of ICT based development projects in India can be seen as a testimony to this view.

Y.K. Dwivedi et al. (Eds.): TDIT 2013, IFIP AICT 402, pp. 407–419, 2013.
© IFIP International Federation for Information Processing 2013

According to the World Resources Institute, India accounts for 60% of the ICT projects in Asia. The idea behind most of these initiatives is to democratise information and make it more easily available to the citizens with a hope that access to information will have developmental outcomes. However, studies on the impact of such projects indicate low usage for development purpose (Kiri and Menon, 2006; Veeraraghavan et al, 2006; Toyoma, 2010).

ICTs for development projects are institutions developed for governing the use of information, which is a Common Pool Resource (CPR). This paper analyzes two ICTD projects (*Janadhar* and IFFCO Airtel Green Card) using CPR design principles put forth by Ostrom (1990). Low usage by the intended users (farmers in these cases) has been traced to absence of most of the design principles deemed essential for the survival of long enduring CPR institutions. The scope of both the studies was limited to use of agricultural information by the farming community through these projects.

The study on *Janadhar* project was taken up to develop a profile of users of "Rural Knowledge Centres" and their perception about these Centres vis-à-vis traditional extension system (Barala, 2006). On the other hand, the study on IFFCO Airtel Green Card was designed to understand the factors affecting use of mobile phones by farmers for seeking agricultural information and their relationship with the socioeconomic status of the respondents. In both cases, in-depth interview schedules were used for data collection. Sample size comprised of 152 farmers in the first study and 277 (out of which only 70 were primarily engaged in agriculture) in the second instance. In the case of IFFCO Airtel Green Card study, respondents were scattered over a large geographical area. Hence, interview schedule was administered through telephonic as well as face to face interviews. Socio-economic status of the farmers and subsequent classification into low, medium and high categories in this study was done using standardised scale developed for rural population in India ($r = 0.93$). The scale comprises of nine items. After an in depth review of literature and consultation with experts, five factors; viz; ease of use, message comprehension, usefulness of information, trustworthiness and cost were selected for the study. The effect of these factors on the use of mobile phone by the farmers and their relationship with the socio-economic status of the users was analyzed using $\chi 2$-test at 5% level of significance (Sahota, 2009).

Rest of this paper is divided into six sections. Section two elaborates the concept of Common Pool Resources and evolution of the term to include information as "commons". Third section discusses the characteristics of institutions that govern long enduring CPRs. Section four briefly describes the ICTD projects analysed in this paper and section five applies CPR design principles to these projects. Sixth section briefly discusses ways of incorporating CPR design principles in ICTD projects and concluding remarks constitute the last section of the paper.

2   Common Property Resources and the "New Commons"

The term Common Pool Resource (CPR) has been used with diverse connotations to represent a wide variety of resources by scholars from various disciplines. While most of the work on common pool resources has been attributed to economists, CPR literature is replete with contributions from historians, political scientists, anthropologists, sociologists, ecologist and others. At an elementary level, Common Pool Resources (CPR) or simply "commons" are resources that are shared by a group of people and are subject to social dilemmas. However, much of traditional CPR studies use two biophysical attributes: non excludability and non rivalrous consumption to delineate CPRs from other types of goods. As per this classification, in case of CPRs, it is difficult to develop institutional or physical means to exclude beneficiaries or users and consumption of the resource by one person limits or subtracts from the quantity available to others. Hence, the term is commonly defined as "a natural or man-made resource from which it is difficult to exclude or limit users once the resource is provided by nature or produced by humans" (Ostrom, 1990). The "commons", however, are different from public and private goods while sharing some of their characteristics. Like public goods, they can be used by a number of people. But, their use by an individual who appropriates a portion of the resource makes it unavailable to others (Oakerson, 1990). De Moore (2011), however, argues that two more characteristics which were inherent to historical "commons"; viz; institutionalisation and self governance, need to be included while defining a Common Pool Resource. Though the term itself is often confused with a type of property right, Ostrom (1994) succinctly points out that CPRs can be owned by national, regional or local governments, communities, individuals or may even be used as an open access resource. In other words, a common pool resource may not always be governed through a common property regime.

According to Hess (2000) most of the initial literature on CPRs was concerned with the use and governance of natural resources and included such broad categories as agriculture, fisheries, grazing and forest land, water bodies, wild life, etc. In an in-depth analysis of CPR literature, the author notes that the scope was widened towards early 1990s to include technology driven human made resources. Non traditional CPR studies included analysis of apartments, streets, highways, parking places, etc. which were grouped as "new commons". The term was soon expanded to include "global commons" such as radio spectrum, atmosphere, high seas, polar regions, etc. which have "remained unclaimed due to lack of technology for extracting their value and for establishing and sustaining property rights".

Information is a fuzzy term and has been used in several ways. One way of reducing this confusion is by using the distinction between data-information-knowledge. Data is viewed as information in raw form, information is defined as organized data in a context, and knowledge as the assimilation of the information and understanding of how to use it (Machlup, 1983). While there is a definite distinction between information and knowledge, for the purpose of this paper the terms have been used interchangeably.

A resource is a good that can be transformed to produce a benefit which fulfils a need or want. It has utility, limited availability and faces depletion. People use information as a resource. They covet it, collect it and try to deny access to other using rules or technology. Massive amount of shared information made possible due to digital technologies (especially internet) coupled with infusion of scholarly works from other disciplines has given rise to studies that place information in the realm of "new commons". Broadly speaking, these studies examine both physical facilities (eg; digital libraries) and digital information (eg. open access journals) as "commons". The notion that information in the present age can be treated as "commons" and analysed as such is a contested issue. Hofmolk (2010) argues that "internet goods do not fall within the common pool category of goods". Such reservation in categorising information as "commons" is understandable in light of the key characteristics used to identity CPRs.

Prior to the digital age and advent of Information and Communication Technologies (ICTs), information was either a private good (due to limited individual ownership of scholarly works) or a club good (available in libraries, etc. whose membership was limited to some extent). Some may argue that opening of public libraries and other venues of storing scholarly works democratised information and turned it into a public good. However, conditions for access to such facilities and their limited number did not entail unlimited access and sharing of information, a key feature of public good. While it is difficult to exclude other users in case of information available through digital technologies (anyone with a computer and internet connection can access a wide range of information free of cost), information as "commons" does not meet the other key characteristic of CPRs i.e subtractability. As pointed out earlier, in case of traditional CPRs, use of a resource unit by one person limits or makes it unavailable to others. But, information as such is not divisible into subtractable resource units. In other words, access or use of information by one person does not make it unavailable to others. In fact, it may just be the opposite in some cases, where greater use leads to more value (eg; number of citations of a scholarly article). Information, therefore, has the attribute of non excludability but not subtractability. However, in rare cases, issues related to network congestion, limited number of terminals, band width restrictions, etc. may make information "commons" both excludable and subtractable.

With CPR literature gaining maturity and depth, it was realised that the distinction between various goods based on excludability and non rivalrous consumption is not as clear cut as it may seem in the first instance. Goods which were previously thought of or placed under one category may shift due to change in environment (e.g. air), technology (e.g radio spectrum) or legal measures (high seas). Hence, it is more useful to see both the key attributes of CPRs as a continuum rather than as dichotomous categories and some goods may fall and/ or shift in between the two extremes (De Moore, 2011).

Nevertheless, the general consensus is that information in the digital age is a Common Pool Resource, for which exclusion of beneficiaries is difficult, costly, or technically infeasible, and in which exploitation by one user may limit availability of the resource or reduces its value to others to some extent. Information is also vulnerable to classic CPR dilemmas like free-riding: either through overuse (dumping of irrelevant and redundant information, mingling of unreliable and high quality information making it difficult for the users to put it to use) or as a result of inadequate investment and maintenance necessary to sustain and enhance the physical facility (Bernbom, 2000).

In CPR literature, the term "information" commons is used synonymously with or confused with "knowledge" and "internet" commons. This confusion has been addressed in several ways. Bernbom (2000) labels internet as a global collection of multiple, interrelated resource facilities and contends that each one may be analyzed as a Common Pool Resource (CPR). Internet is viewed as an amalgam of three types of commons; viz; network commons (physical network infrastructure), information commons (vast and distributed collection of information resources that is available through use of physical infrastructure), and social commons (global communications forum). Internet commons has also been analysed as a composite good with three distinct layers; viz; physical (mainly comprising of equipment), logical (underlying code), and content (the message) (Benkler, 2002).

Common Pool Resource studies (especially those concerned with composite/multiple CPRs) differentiate between resource system and resource units. A resource system holds the resource unit and is usually not owned by an individual. On the other hand, resource units are individual transferable goods that can be put to use/exploited by each user. Hess and Ostrom (2001) note that while trying to extend the evolving theory of common-pool resources to "new commons", especially information and the intellectual public domain, this distinction can be modified into a three-way division between the *artifact*, the *facility*, and the *content*. An *artifact* is "a discreet, observable, nameable representation of an idea or set of ideas". Articles, books, database, etc are typical examples of *artifacts*. While physical *artifacts* are used in a sequential manner by multiple readers, digital *artifacts* can be used simultaneously by several users. On the other hand, a *facility* is a storehouse of *artifacts*. They can be compared to the resource system in conventional CPR theory and are subject to deterioration. They are usually governed by rules and norms and have a physical limitation on the number and type of *artifacts* that can be stored. Internet is a digital *facility*. Finally, "the *content* of an *artifact* in a *facility* is information........and is the nonphysical flow unit". For the purpose of this paper, only *content* is being interpreted as a Common Pool Resource.

3   ICTD Initiatives as Institutions for Information "Commons"

"Most works written to date studying the Internet as a common-pool resource centre on the technology infrastructure and the social network issues rather than the institutions developed about the distributed information per se" (Hess and Ostrom, 2001). Governance arrangements are extremely important for provision, production, appropriation, and use of long enduring CPRs as they are subject to free riding, resource degradation and competing users. Oakerson (1990) put forth a conceptual framework that can be used to analyse "commons" across a wide variety of resources and facilities. The framework has four sets of variables; viz, physical attributes, decision making arrangements, patterns of interaction and outcomes. These four variables can be used to describe any "commons" and each one of these is further subdivided into precise and measurable items.

The Institutional Analysis and Development (IAD) Framework (Oakerson, 1990) analyzes the physical attributes of the "commons" to decide on the scope, nature and boundaries of the resource. The physical attributes of the resource effect and are in turn influenced by the decision making arrangements, which are primarily concerned with governance issues (rules, etc.). Patterns of interaction refer to peoples' behaviour under established rules and physical constraints. People not only interact among themselves, but patterns of interaction may lead to compliance, donation or free riding of the resource. According to this framework, both physical attributes and patterns of interaction influence the final outcome or result. The framework can, however, be modified to gain a better understanding of institutional change. Outcomes can have a learning affect and thereby influence patterns of interaction, which in turn may lead to modified strategies. In the long run, decision making arrangements and technology can also be changed (thereby changing the physical attribute of the resource) to prevent destruction of the resourced or to get better outcomes.

Some of the attributes and their sub-components in the IAD framework are overlapping with CPR design principles developed by Ostrom (1990). Following an analysis of case studies involving a variety of CPRs, she developed eight design principles that characterise institutions governing long-enduring CPRs. She defines a design principle as "...a conception used either consciously or unconsciously by those constituting and reconstituting a continuing association of individuals about a general organising principle" and goes on to add that specific rules-in-use show a wide variation. These design principles include: (1) clearly defined boundaries which authorise individual users with rights to withdraw the resource units and clear cut boundaries for the CPR, (2) congruence between appropriation and provision rules and local conditions that ensure preservation of the resource, (3) collective choice arrangements that enable most resource users to participate in crafting rules, (4) monitoring resource condition and user behaviour, (5) graduated sanctions which are applicable to all violators of rules, (6) conflict resolution mechanism that is low cost and local, (7) minimal recognition of rights to organize that give some authority to users without undue interference, and (8) nested enterprises through which appropriation, provision, monitoring, enforcement, conflict resolution and governance activities are organised at multiple layers. These design principles have stood the test of time, have been widely used for analysing CPRs across the globe (especially natural CPRs) and have since acquired a prescriptive status. Only the initial seven design principles have been used for present discussion as the eighth principle (nested enterprises) applies mostly to larger and more complex CPRs.

4   Brief Description of Projects

Use of ICTs for development including agricultural growth started in India in late 1990s. Many players - national and state governments, private business organizations and civil society groups are engaged in their implementation and provide a wide variety of information ranging from government schemes, market information, technical advice and capacity building. Both the projects described below provide a variety of information that can be used by farmers.

Janadhar: Janadhar is an internet based e-governance initiative of the Government of Uttarakhand (a state in Northern India). It was started mainly to deliver information of public interest and services related to various government departments at the doorsteps of the citizens and also provide agriculture information to the farmers of the state. The project was started in March 2005 with funding from the United Nations Development Programme (UNDP) and technical guidance was provided by Indian Institute of Technology (IIT), Roorkee. The project was implemented through Rural Information Centres (popularly known as *Soochna Kutir*). These Rural Information Centres were managed by local youth who were trained in both organizational and technical aspect. At these Centres, information was provided to the citizens through a portal - *UTTARA* - especially developed for the project by IIT, Roorkee. *UTTARA* contains a wide variety of information on the state and is a centralized "databank". The portal is hosted on a group of servers located in the data centre at IIT, Roorkee. Information is predominantly in Hindi (local language), while a few pages are in English and the homepage and information of more general interest is in both Hindi and English.

Janadhar highlights a case where more than one type of property regime is in place. The project itself (hence the portal) was owned by the Government of Uttarakahnd, through IIT, Roorkee. But, the Rural Information Centres were essentially a private property as the service delivery was handed over/ contracted to individuals who were responsible for establishing and running the *Soochna Kutir* as a self employment venture. Hardware and internet connectivity was provided by IIT, Roorkee and the owner (who also acted as an infomediary) provided physical space for the Centre. It was found that only 10% of the sampled population had used the services offered under the project since its inception (Barala, 2006).

There are several reasons for low usage by the farmers. Firstly, the infomediaries (*Sanchalak*), who were also owners of the Rural Information Centres, did not find these centres economically viable and attempted to augment their income by providing market driven services like public telephony, DTP work, coaching classes, internet browsing, etc. This resulted in dilution of services offered by the project. Secondly, in most cases, the Centres were contracted to small time businessmen who were already engaged in a similar enterprise (like computer center/ internet cafe). This decision resulted in the infomediaries using the project equipment for personal business purpose. Lastly, much of the information posted on the site was "routine" and hence, not of much use to the farmers. The portal also has a facility for sending farmers' queries to experts to address specific farm problems. This can be done via an exclusive email account that could be accessed only by the *Sanchalak*. The farmer can request the *sanchalak* to send his/ her query to an expert after paying a fixed price. He/ she can view the reply by approaching the *Sanchalak* a second time and payment of the requisite fee. It was found that the response rate was very slow and reply was usually received after 7-10 days. In the intermittent period, the farmer would visit the *Soochna Kutir* two/ three times hoping for a reply. Every time he approached the *Sanchalak* to check for the reply (which can be done only by logging into the system), he had to pay the required fee, thereby losing money. On an average, farmer incurred an expenditure of Rs 5o/- (approximately 1US $) per query.

IFFCO Airtel Green Card: IFFCO is primarily a fertilizer producing unit, but also provides other agricultural services like crop insurance, agricultural extension, soil testing facilities, etc., to the farmers. IFFCO Kisan Sanchar Limited (IKSL) was incorporated in April, 2007 as a joint venture (JV) company between Indian Farmers Fertilizer Cooperative Limited (IFFCO) and Bharti Airtel in which IFFCO has 50% stake and Bharti Airtel and Star Global have 25% equity each. Bharti Airtel Limited is a part of Bharti enterprises and is one of India's leading integrated telecom service provider. The joint venture company offers "IFFCO Airtel Green Card". Under this scheme, affordable mobile handsets are bundled with Airtel mobile connection. The cost of the hand set, Airtel connection with one year validity and IKSL services was Rupees One Thousand (Rs 1000/- or approximately 20 US$). In addition, farmers could call others farmers subscribing to the service at cheaper call rates (@ fifty paisa per minute). All the farmers having IFFCO Airtel Green Card have access to a unique VAS platform that sends five free voice messages related to agriculture (market prices, farming techniques, weather forecasts, dairy farming, animal husbandry, rural health initiatives and fertilizer availability, etc.) every day. But, if the farmer wants to listen to the information a second time, (s)he had to pay the call charge (@ one rupee per minute). In addition, the farmer can also call a dedicated helpline (Helpline number- 534351), manned by experts to seek answers to specific queries. These calls were also charged at the rate of one rupee per minute.

Majority of the farmers felt that the information delivered by IKSL was useful. However, usefulness was interpreted in different ways by farmers belonging to different socio-economic categories. Farmers with high socio-economic status said that the service acted as a reminder for timely agricultural operations. Further, messages about likely pest/insect infestation helped them to take precautionary measures and save their crop from potential loss. On the other hand, farmers belonging to medium and low socio economic status found the service useful as they received relevant agricultural information at their doorsteps. This saved their time and cost (required for travelling to extension agency). However, none of the farmers made proactive use of the service, i.e. they have never used the helpline service.

5   Applying Design Principles and ICTD Initiatives

How far do these projects incorporate design principles characteristic of enduring CPRs?

Clearly Defined Boundaries: Ostrom (1990) argues that well defined boundaries apply both to the resource system and authorised users. In case of both these initiatives, boundaries of the resource system are well defined. Quantum, nature, types and form of information (though not the actual content) was predetermined. The technology through which information was made available to users has also remained unchanged during the period. On the other hand, users were amorphous due to operational and financial reasons. In case of *Janadhar*, due to economic factors, informediaries encouraged the youth (50% users were students) to use Rural Information Centres (RIC) for internet browsing, playing games, academic work, etc. At the same time, primary or authorised users were pushed into the background due to apathy of the infomediary, lack of relevant content, cost related issues, etc. On the other hand, IFFCO Airtel Green Card offered handset, connection and information services at a subsidized rate. In order to take advantage of the subsidy, many non-farmers subscribed to the scheme and used reduced call rates to maintain social networks (for making calls to friends, relatives, etc.) and their developmental use was only incidental and limited. This point is borne out by the fact that only 31.43% respondents were primarily engaged in agriculture. Authorised users were also few due to logistical issues (non-availability of inputs suggested by the experts in local market) and use of highly technical terms in voice messages.

Congruence between Appropriation and Provision Rules and Local Conditions: This implies a restriction on the number of authorized users and making rules regarding harvesting pattern, how much, when and how a resource can be harvested. This is essential for resource conservation. "How much" is not relevant in this case, as "extraction" of information through digital technologies does not deplete/ limit its availability to others. Similarly, "how" information can be accessed is also clear cut in these two cases (through a databank and expert system that can be accessed only with the permission of the infomediary in first case and using mobile telephony in the second case). "When" in case of Janadhar was problematic as information could be accessed only at the convenience of the infomediary (timings of the Centre were dependent upon the *Sanchalak* convenience), expert (when he/she is able to respond to the farmers' query), infrastructure (electricity connection, seating capacity, etc.). Further, in both the cases, there were no rules concerning who would be the primary users (which appears to be a more appropriate term when compared to authorized users). While the initiatives themselves were aimed at rural people/farmers for developmental purpose, there was no mechanism to ensure use by them. Hence, users were predominantly students in first case and non-farmers in the second case. In a way, both initiatives highlight "underprovision" of the resource to primary users instead of utilizing the excess capacity for providing the resource to subsidiary users.

Collective Choice Arrangements and Monitoring: Peoples' participation in framing rules that govern the day-to-day operation of the resource is essential as they can be tailored to local and resource conditions in a dynamic environment. Peoples' participation was the leitmotif in development theory and practice during the 1980s. This concept extended to communication projects as can be made out from terms like participatory communication, participatory message design, participatory evaluation, etc. It seems ironic that ICT based development projects that aim to democratize communication process and seek to use information as the prime mover of development have little to contribute in terms of peoples' involvement. Most of them are top down and view citizens as consumers of expert information. External enforcement has largely failed in case of conventional development projects and similar outcomes have been observed in case of several ICT initiatives. In the cases cited above, all decisions regarding technology, content, mode of delivery, operational procedures, etc were taken by "experts" leading to a mismatch between peoples' needs and project outputs at several levels. Peoples' involvement in monitoring and evaluation is considered most mature and highest level of participation. In the absence of sense of ownership, there was no involvement of the people to take/ enforce corrective measures when resource (information) was not provided/ underprovided and the resource system itself was not working efficiently or was highjacked by others.

Graduated Sanctions: Ideally, sanctions against those who break the rules should be developed by the users themselves through consensus. This requires monitoring of resource use by authorized users in the first place and the sanctions themselves should vary with the nature and extent of violation of rules. In case of traditional CPRs, graduated sanctions often take the form of payment in cash or kind coupled with loss of prestige or social disgrace. Is there a violator in these cases? If so, who are they? The studies present an interesting situation as the violators are not the authorized users themselves. Use of RIC by youth and neglect of farming community was a consequence of the infomediary's actions (need to make a success of the enterprise) and provisions within the project (which do not stipulate use by farmers, decision to use a business model which incentivizes use of the Centres by others, etc.). In case of IFFCO Airtel Green Card, violators include authorized users (who subscribed to the subsidized connection and passed it on to others due to low cost) and disbursement agency (which allowed ownership by subsidiary users). Sanctions can also be developed by officials, which may be necessary if the user group is not powerful or is unable to come to a consensus regarding sanctions. In these cases, that was clearly absent due to discrepancies at the implementation stage.

Conflict Resolution Mechanisms: All joint use arrangements face disputes at some point in time or the other. Hence, it is vital that the users and officials have access to low cost conflict resolution venues and mechanisms. In its absence, some users may be tempted to free ride or outsiders may appropriate the resource. In many CPR studies it was found that the conflict resolution mechanism is localized and informal with elders/ leaders acting as the arbitrator. However, "the presence of conflict resolution mechanisms does not guarantee that appropriators are able to maintain enduring institutions" (Ostrom, 1994). Conflict is expressed struggle between competing positions held by individuals or groups. It is pertinent to note that, absence of conflict does not always indicate harmony. Often the underrepresented or less powerful individual or group may withdraw. While the farmers in these cases cannot be labelled a less powerful, they were underrepresented/ unrepresented at planning, implementation and evaluation stages. This partially explains underuse of the facility by them rather than expressing discontent.

Minimal Recognition of Rights to Organize: For effective functioning of CPR institutions, it is essential that the authorised users have a right to devise their own institution and that such rights are not challenged by external authorities. When external authorities presume that only they have the authority to make rules, then it is difficult for local users to sustain the "commons" over long run. In the context of natural CPRs, Ostrom (1994) notes that once "the economic and social base has been weakened enough, then simply assigning a local authority to make rules related to the use of common-pool resources would probably not be a sufficient way out of a major dilemma." Decision making, including the best way of disseminating information to farmers through ICT, was centralized in both the cases. Even informediaries (in case of *Janadhar*) had no say in the payments charged for the services. If they were free to decide on charges on a case to case basis, the infomediaries may not have charged the farmer (when no reply was received from the expert) or the farmer may have negotiated the price. IFFCO Airtel Green Card is operational in most states in India. Pricing, content, mode of implementation is the same across the country. This centralized structure gives rise to problems surrounding cost and content. What may be considered a reasonable cost in an agricultural advanced state like Punjab may not be viewed as such by farmers in Uttarakahnd. Even within the state, farmers from low economic strata felt that the service was expensive. But the scheme has no provision for differential pricing. Also, most of the information delivered to the farmers centred on crops grown in the plains (cereals, pulses, etc.). Hence, farmers from the hilly region of the state did not find the information useful as they were mainly engaged in cultivation of horticultural crops.

6   Discussion

To date, myriad guidelines and criteria have been used for analysis and evaluation of ICTD projects. They mostly include supply side parameters like access, ICT infrastructure, presence of supportive environment, etc. Demand side issues have received less attention but include assessing the actual benefits accrued to the community. This approach has been extended to study the long term impact of ICT projects by Madon (2004) using Sen's capabilities approach. It has been argued that "there is a need to measure what people in practice can or cannot do with a range of ICT applications that are available and benefits they do or do not derive."

Applying CPR design principles to ICT projects is one way of explaining why people may not be able to use ICT based applications or derive benefits from them. In the present analysis, it was found that the intended users were marginalised due to financial considerations and unrestricted access to other users. This dilemma was compounded by restrictions on use by farmers due to logistical and infrastructure bottlenecks and absence of corrective mechanism. Lack of user participation led to dumping of content that did not address farmers' needs and apathy towards the project.

Users' or community participation in development efforts including ICTD projects have been strongly advocated as it instils a sense of ownership, reflects peoples' needs and incorporates their knowledge. Participation, however, is a tricky concept. In conventional development literature, the concept has been challenged on grounds of lack of resources and skills on part of the people, ideological fuzziness, and problems during actualization. These considerations are equally valid for ICTD projects. One possible way out can be to use existing farmers' groups/ organizations as intermediaries/ representatives in a partnership approach. The conventional Public-Private Partnership model can be modified to involve a technology provider and farmers' organizations or a tri partite arrangement between technology provider, public extension system and farmers' groups. At present, these groups are engaged in input supply, training, networking, marketing, etc. and are attuned to the real needs of the farming community. Involvement of farmers' groups in itself will not ensure total community "participation", but will only lead to greater acceptance of the project resulting in active contribution towards content and operations. At the policy level, the Eleventh Five Year Plan, Government of India stipulates that at least 10% of the funds allocated for extension activities should be channelized through private agencies, making it feasible to involve farmers' groups.

7   Concluding Remarks

Institutions are dynamic structures whose survival and longevity depends upon their ability to adapt to a changing environment. Strong institutions are essential for long term sustainability and scalability of ICT projects. All long enduring Common Pool Resources (CPRs) are governed by robust institutions that change with time and need. Application of design principles vary widely across CPRs and as Ostrom points out, sustainability of the resource and governing institutions cannot be explained by the presence or absence of a particular design principle. The fact that they "….do differ partly explains the sustainability of these systems. By differing, the rules take into account specific attributes of the physical systems, cultural views of the world, and the economic and political relationships that exist in the setting".

It would be erroneous to imply that the less than optimal performance of the ICT based projects discussed in this paper is due to the absence of a particular design principle. But, as pointed out during the analysis, the projects seem to be falling short on many design principles deemed essential for strong CPR institutions. It would be fair to admit that the application of CPR design principles to ICT base projects is neither easy nor clear cut. It is complicated by several stakeholders, absence of clear cut "authorised owners", technology related issues and multiple property regimes.

Lastly, the whole discussion hinges on the assumption that information is considered as a resource by the farmers. This supposition may not be true for all farmers. Information is a resource only if it can be converted into a benefit or fulfils a particular need. Agriculture in India (especially Uttarakhand) is limited by several factors like pricing policy, infrastructure, inputs, etc. In such a scenario, farmers are rarely motivated to contest for more and better information. Information is just one component of the system that can make agriculture profitable and farmers seem to realize this better than development agencies with "good intentions".

References

Barala, P.: A Study of Rural Knowledge Centers in Nainital District of Uttaranchal. Unpublished M.Sc. Thesis, Department of Agricultural Communication, GBPUAT, Pantnagar (2006)

Benkler, Y.: Coase's Penguin, or Linux and the nature of the firm. Yale Law Journal 112, 369–446 (2002)

Bernbom, G.: Analyzing the Internet as a Common Pool Resource: The Problem of Network Congestion. In: Eighth Biennial Conference of the International Association for the Study of Common Property, Bloomington, Indiana (2000)

De Moor, T.: From common pastures to global commons. An historical perspective on interdisciplinary approaches to commons. In: Thirteenth Biennial Conference of the International Association for the Study of Common Property, Hyderabad, India (2011)

Hess, C.: Is There Anything New Under the Sun? A Discussion and Survey of Studies on New Commons and the Internet. In: Eighth Biennial Conference of the Interna-tional Association for the Study of Common Property, Bloomington, Indiana (2000)

Hess, C., Ostrom, E.: Ideas, Artifacts, and Facilities: Information as a Common-Pool-Resource. Law and Contemporary Problems 66 (2003)

Hess, C., Ostrom, E.: Ideas, artifacts and facilities: Information as a Common Pool Resource, http://www.law.duke.edu/journals/66LCPHess

Hofmokl, J.: The Internet commons: towards an eclectic theoretical framework. International Journal of the Commons 4, 1 (2010)

Kiri, K., Menon, D.: For Profit Rural Kiosks in India: Achievements and Chal-lenges, http://www.i4donline.net/articles/current-rticle.asp?articleid=700&typ=Features

Machlup, F.: The Economics of Information: A New Classification. InterMedia 11, 2 (1983)

Madon, S.: Evaluating the developmental impact of e-governance initiatives: An ex-ploratory framework". The Electronic Journal of Information Systems in Developing Countries 5, 1–13 (2004)

Oakerson, R.J.: Analyzing the Commons: A Framework. In: Bromley, D. (ed.) Making the Commons Work: Theory, Practice and Policy. ICS Press, San Francisco (1992)

Ostrom, E.: Governing the Commons: The Evolution of Institutions for Collective Action. Cambridge University Press, Cambridge (1990)

Ostrom, E.: Neither market nor state: Governance of Common Property Resources in Twenty First Century. IFPRI Lecture Series (2) (1994)

Sahota, C.: Use of Mobile Phones in Agricultural Extension: A Study in Uttarakhand. Unpublished M.Sc. Thesis, Department of Agricultural Communication, GBPUAT, Pantnagar (2009)

Toyama, K.: Can Technology End Poverty?, http://www.bostonreview.net/BR35.6/toyama.php

Veeraraghavan, R., Singh, G., Toyama, K., Menon, D.: Kiosk Usage Measure-ment Using a Software Logging Tool, http://research.microsoft.com/en-us/um/india/projects/kiosktool/rajesh_vibelog_berkeley.pdf

Yunus, M.: Foreword. In: Digital Review of Asia Pacific 2007-2008. Sage, New Delhi (2006)

E-Participation and E-Government Maturity: A Global Perspective

Satish Krishnan[1], Thompson S.H. Teo[1,2], and John Lim[1]

[1] Department of Information Systems, School of Computing
[2] Department of Decision Sciences, School of Business
National University of Singapore, Singapore
{satishk,tteo,jlim}@comp.nus.edu.sg

Abstract. Utilizing the Technology-Organization-Environment (TOE) theory and the literature on citizen engagement (or participation), we formulated a multiple-mediation model, examining (1) the contextual antecedents of e-participation and e-government maturity; and (2) the mediating role of e-participation (in form of e-information sharing, e-consultation, and e-decision-making) on the relationships between the TOE contextual factors and e-government maturity. Based on archival data from 187 countries, our results showed that ICT infrastructure, human capital and e-participation had a direct relationship with e-government maturity. Of the three dimensions of e-participation, e-information sharing and e-decision-making were positively associated with e-government maturity, and e-consultation was negatively related. Further, all three dimensions of e-participation partially mediated the influence of ICT infrastructure and human capital on e-government maturity. Results also indicated that governance in a country did not significantly contribute to its e-government maturity, and their relationship was not mediated by e-participation. Our findings contribute to the theoretical discourse on e-government by identifying the contextual factors affecting e-government maturity, and provide indications to practice on enhancing government's willingness in implementing relevant e-participation initiatives.

Keywords: ICT infrastructure, human capital, governance, e-participation, e-government maturity.

1   Introduction

E-government can be defined as the delivery of government information and services using the Internet or other digital means (Krishnan and Teo 2012). Research on e-government can be classified into three broad streams, namely, evolution and development, adoption and implementation, and impact on stakeholders (Srivastava 2011). While there is a vast amount of research carried out in these three areas, most studies were concerned with specific aspects of e-government in reference to specific region or country (Srivastava and Teo 2008). Although the need for considering a macro-level (i.e., cross-country level) perspective is largely stressed in past literature (Srivastava and Teo 2010), researchers with few exceptions (e.g., Krishnan and Teo

Y.K. Dwivedi et al. (Eds.): TDIT 2013, IFIP AICT 402, pp. 420–435, 2013.
© IFIP International Federation for Information Processing 2013

2012), ignored or overlooked them due to the lack of cumulative theoretical development in e-government research (Heeks and Bailur 2007) to devise an empirical study addressing macro-level issues. Predicated by this concern, the present study addresses the need for conducting cross-country quantitative empirical study.

E-government maturity in a country represents the extent to which a government has established an online presence (West 2007). Implicitly, it constitutes a continuum of developmental stages, from publishing information to supporting transactions, with some countries having progressed further than others (West 2007). Despite numerous motivations and service targets underlying public institutions, furthering e-government, and reaching the stage of maturity is a challenging task faced by government agencies in most countries. Motivated by this challenge faced by majority of governments, a major purpose of this study is to identify the country-level factors influencing e-government maturity.

It is widely acknowledged that "citizen engagement" is key to growth and maturity of e-government (Chan and Pan 2008; Olphert and Damodaran 2007). The concept of citizen engagement is exercised through e-participation, which involves the extension and transformation of participation in societal democratic and consultative process mediated by ICTs and the Internet (Saebo et al. 2008). Emerging research on e-participation is limited in two ways. First, most studies remain – except a few recent studies – at best anecdotal, conjectural, and descriptive. While such studies offer benchmarks for practitioners to assess and evaluate their practices pertaining to e-participation, they provide little value to theory. Second, among few recent studies, most (e.g., Hartwick and Barki 2001) focus on the demand side of e-participation (i.e., citizens' perspective) rather than the supply side (i.e., governments' perspective). Motivated by the fact that there is a dearth of macro-level studies examining e-participation from supply side, in this study, we focus on the G2C aspect of participation, and adopt the definition as defined by the UN; e-participation is defined as the willingness of a government (and its agencies) to use online tools (e.g., email and discussion forums) for the specific purpose of empowering people for able participation in consultations and decision-making, both in their capacity as consumers of public services and as citizens (UN-Report 2005).

E-participation consists of three dimensions, namely, e-information sharing, e-consultation, and e-decision-making (UN-Report 2005). E-information sharing is concerned with the willingness of governments to offer tools (e.g., web forums, e-mail lists, newsgroups and chat rooms) for dissemination of information (e.g., list of elected officials, policies and programs, and point of contact) on their websites for timely access and use by citizens. E-consultation is concerned with the willingness of governments to encourage their citizens to participate in discussions by offering a choice of public policy topics online with real time and archived access to audios and videos of public meetings. Finally, e-decision-making is related to governments' willingness in indicating that it will take its citizens' e-inputs into account in decision-making, and provide actual feedback on the outcome of specific issues. A recent study conducted by the UN highlighted that e-participation is still in a "nascent state" indicating disconnectedness between government and its citizens (UN-Report 2010). Given that e-participation plays a pivotal role in growth and maturity of e-government (Chan and Pan 2008) by serving as a mechanism to manage the development of e-government services (Olphert and Damodaran 2007); it is necessary to identify the determinants that facilitate countries to attain varying levels of e-participation.

With these motivations, using the Technology-Organization-Environment (TOE) theory (Tornatzky and Fleischer 1990) as a guiding theoretical lens, we identify the contextual factors facilitating e-participation (in form of e-information sharing, e-consultation, and e-decision-making) and e-government maturity in a nation. Further, by drawing from the citizen engagement literature, we investigate the effects of e-information sharing, e-consultation, and e-decision-making on e-government maturity, and the mediating effects of e-information sharing, e-consultation, and e-decision-making on the relationships between the TOE factors and e-government maturity. In sum, the research questions are: *(1) What TOE contextual factors facilitate e-participation and e-government maturity? (2) What is the relationship between e-participation and e-government maturity? (3) How does e-participation mediate the effects of TOE contextual factors on e-government maturity?*

The rest of the paper is organized as follows. In the ensuing section, we present our theoretical background and hypotheses. This is followed by a section on research design. Thereafter, using archival data from 187 countries, we test the hypothesized model. We then discuss the results and the implications for future research. The final section provides concluding remarks with a restatement of the value of the work.

2   Theory and Hypotheses

We use the theoretical framework proposed by Tornatzky and Fleischer (1990) as our foundation. According to them, innovation adoption or technology deployment in a firm is influenced by three contexts, namely, technological context, organizational context, and environmental context. Based on our review of academic (e.g., Krishnan and Teo 2012; Siau and Long 2009) and practitioner literature (e.g., UN-Report 2003; 2010) on e-government, we identify three factors that might be influential in facilitating e-participation and e-government maturity in a country (see Fig. 1): (1) ICT infrastructure; (2) human capital; and (3) governance. These three factors correspond to the three contexts defined in the TOE theory. ICT infrastructure is the gradual convergence of broadcasting content, telecommunications, and computing (Tapscott 1996). Human capital, on the other hand, refers to the knowledge, skills, and abilities embodied in people (here, citizens) (Coff 2002). Governance is defined as the traditions and institutions by which authority in a country is exercised (Kaufmann et al. 1999). We next derive and explain each hypothesis.

2.1   ICT Infrastructure, E-Government Maturity, and E-Participation

According to neoclassical and new growth theories, technological progress and creativity is a critical determinant of growth and development (Lucas 1988; Romer 1990). Extending this argument in the context of e-government, we argue that ICT infrastructure can contribute towards the growth and maturity of e-government systems as e-government needs to utilize the information infrastructure to deliver online public services (Siau and Long 2009). In a similar vein, Srivastava and Teo

(2010) stressed that government and its agencies can fulfill their duties related to the daily activities of citizens and businesses only when they are connected with the citizens and businesses, which indeed is possible only with a sound ICT infrastructure. Warkentin et al. (2002) emphasized that e-government is characterized by extensive use of ICTs that stimulates the growth and maturity of e-government. Koh et al. (2005) and Singh et al. (2007) highlighted that reaching the stage of e-government maturity will remain an "unrealized dream" in the absence of sound and reliable ICT infrastructure. Hence, we posit: *'H1: ICT infrastructure in a country is positively associated with its e-government maturity.'*

For governments to be more willing to implement e-participation initiatives, robust ICT infrastructure that allows citizens access to decision makers is required (UN-Report 2005). Meso et al. (2009) indicated that the availability of ICTs (1) allows greater access by the population to government services; (2) facilitates public participation in policy-making process by rapidly disseminating news and information to the citizens; and (3) eliminates or minimizes barriers to participation in the country's economic markets. Further, information infrastructure (e.g., Web 2.0) plays a critical role in empowering citizens to become more active in expressing their views on issues concerning environment, health, education and other areas of government policy (UN-Report 2010). In sum, a government's willingness to (1) request, receive and incorporate feedback from its constituents; and (2) tailor the policy measures to meet the needs and priorities of citizens can be enhanced only when a sound, robust and reliable ICT infrastructure is in place. Therefore, we propose: *'H2: ICT infrastructure in a country is positively associated with its (H2a) e-information sharing; (H2b) e-consultation; and (H2c) e-decision-making.'*

2.2   Human Capital, E-Government Maturity, and E-Participation

Human capital indicates how well educated are the citizens in a nation. Schultz (1961) and Lewis (1955) in their human capital theory have stressed the critical role of "human capital" in growth and development of individuals and nations. Specifically, Schultz argued that human capital is one of the critical reasons that explain the differences in growth (e.g., income and productivity) between human beings as well as nations. Like human capital theory, the new growth theory also supported knowledge-based economy by recognizing the importance of human capital and indicates that the investment in human capital generates returns in the future (Lucas 1988; Romer 1986). Flak and Rose (2005) indicated that citizens is one of the important stakeholder groups for successfully implementing e-government initiatives, and their knowledge is a valuable resource for e-governments to attain the stage of maturity. Further, Singh et al. (2007) found that human capital is a significant determinant of e-government maturity, and Srivastava and Teo (2010) established that human capital (in terms of education and training) in a country is positively associated with the level of its e-government. Therefore, we propose: *'H3: Human capital in a country is positively associated with its e-government maturity.'*

UN established the expectations of citizens to be directly involved in designing government programs and services (UN-Report 2005). That is, at various stages of policy process, from elections to policy planning and implementation, citizens are becoming increasingly involved (Phang and Kankanhalli 2008). Such participation is possible only when the citizens have sufficient learning skills and knowledge capabilities embodied within them. This will indeed facilitate governments' willingness to (1) increase e-information sharing; (2) enhance e-consultation; and (3) support e-decision-making. Hence, when citizens are empowered, they are not only able to participate, but also create a different relationship with their respective governments, characterized by enhanced effectiveness (UN-Report 2010). Hence, we posit: 'H4: Human capital in a country is positively associated with its (H4a) e-information sharing; (H4b) e-consultation; and (H4c) e-decision-making.'

2.3   Governance, E-Government Maturity, and E-Participation

Governance refers to the collection of processes and institutions that creates the conditions for ordered rule and collective action (Kazancigil 1998). Madon et al. (2007) established that effective implementation of government-based information systems (IS) for the provision of services is impacted by the macro-level policy-making organs; thereby shaping the type of system that eventually gets implemented. Moon (2002) found that institutional factors significantly contributed to the adoption of e-government among municipalities. Norris and Moon (2005) showed that the level of adoption and sophistication of e-government systems are correlated with the presence of well-developed institutional factors. A study conducted by West (2004) and Srivastava and Teo (2010) highlighted the importance of governance mechanisms in ensuring e-government growth and maturity. As effective governance assures an environment conducive to investment (Meso et al. 2006), we posit: 'H5: Governance in a country is positively associated with its e-government maturity.'

Governance entails public debate and open, participatory decision-making. According to the participatory model of governance in e-government implementation (Chadwick and May 2003), governance is seen as open communications, where the opinions are not directed only to government but to all players within the governance communications space. Hence, governance fosters the collaboration and information sharing among disparate stakeholders. In addition, effective governance ensures an enhanced supply of the desired services, eliminates or minimizes the barriers to participation, and promotes rule of law (Meso et al. 2006). Also, governance provides direction to creation of environment in which citizens can be more active and supportive of their governments, and increase the willingness of governments to use ICTs to provide high quality information and effective communication tools for able participation in consultations and decision-making. Therefore, we propose: 'H6. Governance in a country is positively associated with its (H6a) e-information sharing; (H6b) e-consultation; and (H6c) e-decision-making.'

2.4   Relating E-Participation to E-Government Maturity

According to e-government stage models, e-government maturity cannot be thought as a one-step project or implemented as a single project (Siau and Long 2006). The implication from the stage models is that the growth and maturity of e-government is evolutionary in nature and the stages (of growth) are theoretically ascending in the level of maturity or sophistication of e-government (UN-Report 2003). Given that citizen engagement via e-participation is pivotal in the evolutionary process of e-government maturity (Chan and Pan 2008; Olphert and Damodaran 2007), it is logical to presume that as government's willingness to engage its citizens in e-government processes increases, so does the level of e-government maturity in a country. That is, when the government is willing to implement e-participation initiatives, citizens become "active creators" or "feedback providers," thereby contributing information to the success of e-government (Ekelin 2003). This fact is also emphasized in a study by Tan and Pan (2003). According to them, a bureaucratic government organization can move towards anticipative and responsive practices only when it treats its citizens as "strategic value networks" in the process of e-transformation. Further, they stress that such a relationship will not only lead to "total customer satisfaction" but also create "multi-directional strategic value." Consequently, we posit: *'H7. E-participation (H7a. e-information sharing; H7b. e-consultation; and H7c. e-decision-making) in a country is positively associated with its e-government maturity.'*

2.5   Mediated Effects of E-Participation

Having assembled each of the piecewise elements and relations in our research model (see Fig. 1), we logically deduce one more set of hypotheses. We posit that e-participation (in form of e-information sharing, e-consultation, and e-decision-making) serves as an intervening mechanism or, at the least, partial conveyors of the effects of TOE contexts onto e-government maturity. That is, TOE contexts indirectly influence e-government maturity by raising the levels of e-information sharing, e-consultation, and e-decision-making. More formally, we therefore offer the following: *'H8: TOE contexts' (H8a. ICT infrastructure; H8b. human capital; and H8c. governance) effects on e-government maturity are mediated by e-information sharing, e-consultation and e-decision-making.'*

3   Research Design

To test the formulated hypotheses, we gathered archival data (for each of the main constructs) as it offers several advantages such as easy reproducibility, ability to generalize the results arising from larger datasets, and robust to the threat of common method bias (Jarvenpaa 1991). Hypotheses were tested via a cross-sectional analysis of 187 countries (after omitting the missing values).

The dependent construct, *e-government maturity*, reflecting the demonstrated behavior of e-government in a country, is measured as the extent to which a government has established an online presence (West 2007). The scores for this construct were obtained from the Global E-Government Report 2007 (West 2007), and has been used in past academic studies such as Singh et al. (2007). The mediating construct, *e-participation* was measured on three dimensions: (1) e-information sharing; (1) e-consultation; and (3) e-decision-making. The UN assessed e-participation (qualitatively with values running between 0 and 1, with the higher values corresponding to the better results) by measuring the willingness of governments to engage citizens in public policy-making through the use of relevant programs (UN-Report 2005). The scores for these three dimensions were obtained from the UN Global E-Government Survey Report 2005 (UN-Report 2005).

The technology construct, *ICT infrastructure* is indicated by the Telecommunication Infrastructure Index, the values for which were taken from the UN global e-government survey report 2003 (UN-Report 2003). This index is a composite weighted average of six primary indices (PCs/1000 persons, Internet users/1000 persons, telephone lines/1000 persons, online population, mobile phones/1000 persons, and TVs/1000 persons), which define a country's ICT infrastructure capacity. This index has been used in past academic studies like Krishnan and Teo (2012), and Srivastava and Teo (2010). The organizational construct, *human capital* is indicated by the Education Index, the values (running between 0 and 1, with the higher values corresponding to the higher levels of human capital) for which were obtained from the UN global e-government survey report 2003 (UN-Report 2003). This index is a composite of the adult literacy rate and the combined primary, secondary and tertiary gross enrolment ratio, with two-thirds of the weight given to adult literacy and one-third to the gross enrolment ratio. This index has been used in past academic studies like Srivastava and Teo (2008). The environmental construct, *governance* was operationalized using six aggregated measures of governance (with values running between -2.5 and 2.5, with the higher values corresponding to the better governance) originally presented in Kaufmann et al. (1999). The measures are: (1) voice and accountability; (2) political stability and absence of violence; (3) government effectiveness; (4) regulatory quality; (5) rule of law; and (6) control of corruption. Data for these measures were taken from the Worldwide Governance Indicators Database, and is for year 2003 (Kaufmann et al. 2010). These measures have been used in past academic studies like Krishnan and Teo (2012), and Meso et al. (2006).

Additional control variables consisted of *economic conditions* (measured in terms of GDP per capita, adjusted for purchasing power parity) and *regional difference*, operationalized as the country-level difference across various regions of the world.

4   Analysis and Results

4.1   Descriptive Statistics and Correlations

Table 1 present the descriptive statistics and correlations for all variables. As shown, most correlations were significant at $p < 0.001$. In addition, as correlations were below the threshold value of 0.8, the concern for multicollinearity would be minimal (Gujarati and Porter 2009). Nevertheless, we followed up with the collinearity tests that measure variance inflation factor (VIF). The results revealed that our VIFs ranged from 1.31 to 3.43 (all tolerance levels above 0.29). As per Fox (1991), a VIF > 4.0, or a tolerance level < 0.25, may indicate the potential for multicollinearity; thus, the concern in our model appeared to be minimal.

Table 1. Descriptive statistics and correlations

Variable	Mean	SD	1	2	3	4	5	6	7	8
1. EC[a]	7.75	1.63	-							
2. RD	2.72	1.16	-29	-						
3. ICT	0.18	0.21	72	-20	-					
4. HC	0.72	0.25	54	-25	50	-				
5. GOV	-0.08	0.91	71	-27	73	45	-			
6. EIS	0.22	0.23	56	-25	69	45	60	-		
7. ECN	0.13	0.22	46	-20	61	39	49	71	-	
8. EDM	0.13	0.19	50	-21	65	38	54	69	70	-
9. EGM	28.01	4.61	66	-22	68	57	53	70	71	68

Note: [a]Log transformed variable; N = 187; EC: Economic Condition; RD: Regional Difference; ICT: ICT Infrastructure; HC: Human Capital; GOV: Governance; EIS: E-Information Sharing; ECN: E-Consultation; EDM: E-Decision-Making; EGM: E-Government Maturity; Decimal points are omitted for correlations; All correlations (except underlined) are significant at $p < 0.001$ and underlined correlations are significant at $p < 0.01$.

4.2 Hypotheses Testing

Given the importance of the mediating effects in our research model, it is necessary to conduct a systematic analysis exploring these effects. Since the research model has more than one mediator, this study refers to the method that Preacher and Hayes (2008) recommended for testing multiple-mediator models. A Preacher and Hayes analysis includes an examination of the total and direct effects of the independent variable on the dependent variable, the difference between which is the indirect effect of the independent variable on the dependent variable through mediators. The analysis also yields an estimation of the indirect effect of each mediator. In addition, the bias-corrected (BC) bootstrap will generate a 95% confidence interval (CI) for each mediator. If the interval for a mediator does not contain zero, it means the indirect effect of this mediator is significantly different from zero. In addition, a contrast between two mediators shows how their indirect effects can be distinguished in terms of magnitude. Fig. 1 shows the regression results.

As shown in Fig. 1, the results revealed that the paths from ICT infrastructure to e-government maturity ($\beta = 0.78$, $p < 0.001$) and from human capital to e-government maturity ($\beta = 0.23$, $p < 0.001$) were significant. Hence, H1 and H3 were supported. As the path from governance to e-government maturity ($\beta = 0.03$, n.s.) was not significant, H5 was not supported. Results also revealed that the paths from ICT infrastructure to e-information sharing ($\beta = 0.81$, $p < 0.001$), e-consulting ($\beta = 0.76$, $p < 0.001$) and e-decision-making ($\beta = 0.65$, $p < 0.001$) were all significant. This confirmed H2a, H2b, and H2c. Similarly, while the paths from human capital to e-information sharing ($\beta = 0.15$, $p < 0.01$) and e-consulting ($\beta = 0.12$, $p < 0.05$) were significant, the path concerning e-decision-making was not significant ($\beta = 0.08$, n.s.). Hence, H4a and H4b were supported and H4c was not supported. Further, the paths from governance to e-information sharing ($\beta = 0.03$, n.s.), e-consulting ($\beta = 0.01$, n.s.) and e-decision-making ($\beta = 0.02$, n.s.) were not significant. Hence, H6a, H6b, and H6c were not supported. Lastly, the paths from e-information sharing ($\beta = 0.60$, p < 0.001), e-consultation (β = -0.23, p < 0.05), and e-decision-making (β = 0.27, p < 0.01) to e-government maturity were all significant. However, while the direction of the relationships of e-information sharing and e-decision-making with e-government maturity was consistent with our initial prediction, the direction of the relationship between e-consultation and e-government maturity was contrary to our initial prediction. Hence, H7a and H7c were supported, and H7b was not supported. While unexpected, this finding is interesting and will be discussed in greater detail in the next section. Finally, the control variables, economic conditions (β = -0.004, n.s.) and regional differences (β = 0.003, n.s.) were not significantly associated with e-government maturity.

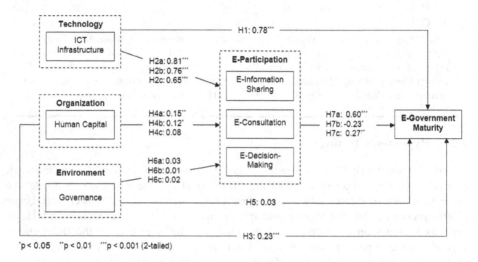

Fig. 1. Regression results

Table 2 presents the mediation results. First, model 1 was examined, in which ICT infrastructure was the independent variable with human capital and governance treated as covariates. Next, model 2 was examined, in which human capital was the independent variable with ICT infrastructure and governance treated as covariates. As shown in Table 2, ICT infrastructure [human capital] had a significant total effect on e-government maturity. When the mediators were introduced, the direct effect of ICT infrastructure [human capital] on e-government maturity remained significant. This meant that e-information sharing, e-consultation, and e-decision-making partially mediated the impact of ICT infrastructure [human capital] on e-government maturity. Furthermore, the difference between the total and direct effects was the total indirect effect as mediated through e-information sharing, e-consultation, and e-decision-making, with a point estimate of 0.4974 [0.0861] and a 95% BC bootstrap CI of 0.3435 to 0.6783 [0.0287 to 0.1543]. Since the CI did not contained zero, the total indirect effect was different from zero. An examination of the specific indirect effects indicated that e-information sharing, e-consultation, and e-decision-making were mediators as their 95% CIs did not contain zero. The point estimate of the indirect impact through e-information sharing and e-consultation were 0.4965 [0.0932] and -0.1800 [-0.0298] respectively, and of that through e-decision-making was 0.1809

[0.0226]. Examination of the pairwise contrasts of the indirect effects (i.e., C1, C2, and C3 in model 1 [2] of Table 2) showed that (1) the specific indirect effect through e-information sharing was larger than the specific indirect effect through e-consultation, with a BC 95% CI of 0.3281 to 1.1492 [0.0477 to 0.2437]; (2) the specific indirect effect through e-information sharing was larger than the specific indirect effect through e-decision-making, with a BC 95% CI of 0.0220 to 0.6512 [0.0130 to 0.1513]; and (3) the specific indirect effect through e-consultation was larger than the specific indirect effect through e-decision-making, with a BC 95% CI of -0.7436 to -0.0348 [-0.1325 to -0.0048]. In sum, H8a [H8b] was supported.

Table 2. Mediation results

Total Effect of IV on DV		Direct Effect of IV on DV		Indirect Effects				
COEF	TV	COEF	TV			PE	BC 95% CI	
							Lower	Upper
Model 1: ICT Infrastructure as IV								
0.7801^{***}	6.9609	0.2912^{**}	2.8892	Total		0.4974	0.3435	0.6783
				MED	EIS	0.4965	0.2705	0.7601
					ECN	-0.1800	-0.4219	-0.0066
					EDM	0.1809	0.0096	0.3756
				CON	C1	0.6765	0.3281	1.1492
					C2	0.3156	0.0220	0.6512
					C3	-0.3609	-0.7436	-0.0348
Model 2: Human Capital as IV								
0.2374^{***}	4.2752	0.1513^{**}	3.4035	Total		0.0861	0.0287	0.1543
				MED	EIS	0.0932	0.0351	0.1769
					ECN	-0.0298	-0.0774	-0.0008
					EDM	0.0226	0.0005	0.0664
				CON	C1	0.1230	0.0477	0.2437
					C2	0.0706	0.0130	0.1513
					C3	-0.0524	-0.1325	-0.0048
Model 3: Governance as IV								
0.0318	1.2747	0.0068	0.3436	Total		0.0251	-0.0017	0.0562
				MED	EIS	0.0230	-0.0009	0.0538
					ECN	-0.0031	-0.0213	0.0060
					EDM	0.0051	-0.0042	0.0295
				CON	C1	0.0260	-0.0044	0.0711
					C2	0.0178	-0.0003	0.0454
					C3	-0.0082	-0.0459	0.0102

Note: N = 187; 5000 bootstrap samples; R^2 = 78% (Adjusted R^2 = 77%); IV: Independent Variable; DV: Dependent Variable; MED: Mediators; COEF: Coefficient; TV: T-Value; PE: Point Estimate; BC: Bias-Corrected Bootstrap; CI: Confidence Interval; 'Total' is the total relation between independent variable and dependent variable without the consideration of other variables; 'CON (Contrast)' indicates if the indirect effects could be distinguished in terms of magnitude; EIS: E-Information Sharing; ECN: E-Consultation; EDM: E-Decision-Making; C1: E-Information Sharing vs. E-Consultation; C2: E-Information Sharing vs. E-Decision-Making; C3: E-Consultation vs. E-Decision-Making; $^{**}p < 0.01$ $^{***}p < 0.001$.

Next, model 3 was examined, in which governance was the independent variable with ICT infrastructure and human capital treated as covariates. As shown in Table 2, governance did not have a significant total effect on e-government maturity. While some researchers (e.g., Baron and Kenny 1986) suggested that a significant total effect of the independent variable on the dependent variable is a prerequisite for testing the mediating effects, others (e.g., Shrout and Bolger 2002) argued that this is not necessary. Thus, we continued to examine the mediating effects. However, as shown in Table 2 (model 3), the total indirect effects were not significant, with a point estimate of 0.0251 and a 95% BC CI of -0.0017 to 0.0562. Examination of the specific indirect effects showed that neither of the e-participation variables were mediators, since their 95% CIs contained zero. Hence, H8c was not supported.

5   Discussion

Our findings raise several issues that deserve mention. First, the level of ICT infrastructure in a country significantly contributed to its e-participation and e-government maturity. Within e-participation, the effect of ICT infrastructure was positively associated with all the three dimensions of e-participation. Further, the relationship between the levels of ICT infrastructure and e-government maturity was partially mediated by all the three dimensions of e-participation. Thus, the availability of robust, reliable and sound ICT infrastructure will not only facilitate the growth and maturity of online public services (Siau and Long 2009; Srivastava and Teo 2010) but also enhance the willingness of governments to engage its citizenry in e-government process. Hence, this result suggests that when a country's investment in ICT infrastructure increases (1) its e-government should be able to attain maturity; and (2) it should be more willing to encourage the public to be active in promoting participatory decision-making in public policy matters.

Second, human capital in a country was positively associated with its e-participation and e-government maturity. Within e-participation, while the effect of human capital facilitated e-information sharing and e-consultation, there was no relationship between human capital and e-decision-making. Further, the effect of human capital was stronger in e-information sharing than in e-consultation. While our study did not come to the expected conclusions with respect to the influence of human capital in a country on the dimensions of e-participation, given its positive associations, we suggest that stimulating the evolution of human consciousness and emergence of mentally self-conscious individuals in a country via education and training will facilitate the maturity of e-government systems and enhancement of e-participation for promoting citizen engagement. Mediation results also indicated that the relationship between the levels of human capital and e-government maturity was partially mediated by all the three dimensions of e-participation.

Third, our results indicated that governance in a country had little impact on e-government maturity and on all the dimensions of e-participation. While strong positive correlations (see Table 1) of governance with e-government maturity and e-participation variables suggested strong positive relationships between them, the results indicated that the technological and organizational contexts in the form of ICT infrastructure and human capital respectively were pivotal for e-government maturity and e-participation, compared to the environmental context, governance. Further, mediation results indicated that the relationship between the levels of governance and e-government maturity was not mediated by e-participation. Though several past studies (e.g., Moon 2002; Norris and Moon 2005; Srivastava and Teo 2010) had suggested governance as a significant determinant and contributor to e-government, our study did not elicit a similar result. However, it is gratifying that our findings (though not statistically significant) are in the same direction as past studies.

Finally, turning to the relationship between e-participation and e-government maturity, our results indicated that of the three e-participation dimensions, e-information sharing and e-decision-making were positively associated with e-government maturity, and e-consultation was negatively associated. Further, between e-information-sharing and e-decision-making, the former had a stronger positive association with e-government maturity than the latter. One possible reason for variations in results may be due to the relative differences in perceived threats (e.g., implementation delays) associated with deployment of various e-participation initiatives. In sum, our results suggest that not all dimensions of e-participation will positively contribute to the growth and maturity of e-government in a country.

Our study makes several key contributions. To theory, we extend and enrich the TOE theory in three ways. First, via theoretical synthesis, we combine the attributes of the TOE theory with the citizen engagement perspective to study the phenomenon of e-government maturity. Second, while the TOE theory has served as a useful theoretical lens for understanding innovation adoption in firms, our study is one among the few studies to extend its theoretical arguments in the global context and to explore its usefulness at the macro-level. Third, while most studies applying the TOE theory have used primary survey data for analyses, our study is among the few studies to demonstrate its applicability by making an innovative use of publicly available archival data. In sum, this study heeds the call of researchers (e.g., Baker 2011) to extend and enrich TOE theory via approaches such as theoretical synthesis.

Our study also contributes to research on e-government and e-participation in three ways. First, while much research has been carried out in all three streams of e-government research (i.e., evolution and development, adoption and implementation, and impact on stakeholders), most of them addressed research questions that are "micro" in orientation. That is, there is a paucity of research investigating the determinants of e-government maturity from a global perspective (Siau and Long 2009). Realizing the need for conducting cross-country quantitative empirical research, our study identified the contextual factors facilitating the maturity of e-government in a country. Second, while most extant studies on e-participation looked into the demand side of participation, our study offered a supply side view of participation. Specifically, by drawing from citizen engagement perspective, our study (1) has strived to further our understanding as to why differing levels of e-government maturity among countries continues to prevail; and (2) emphasize that the willingness of government (and its agencies) in a country to deploy e-participation initiatives will serve as a "mechanism" through which the growth and maturity of e-government projects could be managed. Third, by a deeper analysis of the mechanism of e-participation based on its dimensions (i.e., e-information sharing, e-consultation, and e-decision-making), our study indicate that the willingness of a government to deploy e-participation initiatives varies based on the nature and purpose of the e-participation activity, which in turn affects the maturity of e-government.

From a practical standpoint, our study offers several important insights. First, by identifying the determinants of e-government maturity in a country, our study not only facilitates to understanding of why differing levels of growth and maturity of e-government continues to prevail but also shows directions for attaining the stage of maturity. Specifically, our findings suggest that through investments in technological and human capabilities, it might be possible for a country to move up the ladder of e-government maturity. Second, by identifying the facilitators of e-participation in a country, our study helps practitioners showing directions to increase governments' willingness towards deployment of e-participation initiatives. Specifically, ICT infrastructure and human capital in a country over its governance are critical determinants of e-participation. Third, our findings indicate that all dimensions of e-participation play significant roles in affecting e-government maturity. Specifically, while e-information sharing and e-decision making contributes positively to e-government maturity, e-consultation negatively affects the growth and maturity of e-government in a country. These findings suggest to practitioners that while e-consultation might provide feedback on e-government process, it is vital for practitioners to realize that it might delay e-government from reaching the stage of maturity. Thus, our findings suggest that e-consultation is a double-edged mechanism.

This study has three major limitations. First, we used archival data obtained from different sources. While primary data might have given us a better control over the definition of variables, it is less feasible for a small group of researchers to undertake a large scale cross-country data collection given the limited amount of resources and time. However, considering the fact that the data have been collected by reputable and authorized organizations, and the indices have been formulated using suitable statistical procedures to ensure the reliability and validity; relying on these secondary sources provides a cost-effective way for conducting our study. Second, we analyzed data only from the countries commonly available in all the primary sources. For instance, we could not include countries like Hong Kong and Taiwan as these countries were not commonly available in all the data sources. However, given that we have only seven main variables and sample size as 187, discarding few countries may not make a significant difference in the results. Further, bootstrapping approach to mediation with a sample size of 100 and above will detect fairly small R-square values (10%-15%) with up to 10 independent variables and a significance level of 0.05 (Hair et al. 2006). Third, while e-participation scores for later years (e.g., 2010) are available, we used the scores from the UN Global E-Government Survey Report published in 2005 as the reports published in later years offered only an aggregate score for e-participation rather than scores for individual dimension within e-participation. However, considering the fact that e-participation is still in a "nascent state" (UN-Report 2010), we believe that the concern for direction and strength of the relationship among variables (due to the usage of e-participation data from earlier report) would be minimal. Despite these potential limitations, our study is one among the few studies with macro-level orientation striving to address the knowledge gaps described in the earlier sections of this paper.

Future research may focus on several directions. First, while our study has mainly focused on the antecedents of e-government maturity, future studies may consider examining its consequences (i.e., payoffs). Further, researchers may also consider studying both antecedents and consequences jointly by integrating them cohesively in a unified theoretical framework (e.g., Srivatsava and Teo 2010). Second, given the differences in relationships between the dimensions of e-participation and e-government maturity, future researchers may also test how the relationships are affected by introducing several contingency variables such as public institutions and macro-economy (e.g., Krishnan and Teo 2012; Srivatsava and Teo 2008).

6   Concluding Remarks

In conclusion, despite an extensive recognition on the importance of e-participation and e-government maturity in a nation as a predictor of its growth and performance, both research and practitioner communities knows relatively little with regards to managing e-government maturity. As an initial step to be taken towards raising awareness for the pivotal role of e-participation in managing e-government maturity, we have constructed and validated a theoretical model (specifically, a multiple mediation model) that examined the effects of the TOE contextual factors on e-participation and e-government maturity. In addition, we reasoned and demonstrated empirically the relationships of different dimensions of e-participation on e-government maturity, and the mediating role of e-participation variables on the relationships between TOE contextual factors and e-government maturity.

References

Barker, J.: The Technology–Organization–Environment Framework. In: Dwivedi, Y., Wade, M., Schneberger, S. (eds.) Information Systems Theory: Explaining and Predicting our Digital Society, vol. 1, pp. 231–246. Springer, New York (2011)

Baron, R.M., Kenny, D.A.: The Moderator–Mediator Variable Distinction in Social Psychological Research: Conceptual, Strategic, and Statistical Considerations. Journal of Personality and Social Psychology 51, 1173–1182 (1986)

Chadwick, A., May, C.: Interactions between States and Citizens in the Age of the Internet: 'E-government' in the United States, Britain and the European Union. Governance 16, 271–300 (2003)

Chan, M.L., Pan, S.L.: User Engagement in E-Government Systems Implementation: A Comparative Case Study of Two Singaporean E-Government Initiatives. Journal of Strategic Information Systems 17, 124–139 (2008)

Coff, R.W.: Human Capital, Shared Expertise, and the Likelihood of Impasse in Corporate Acquisitions. Journal of Management 28, 107–128 (2002)

Ekelin, A.: Working with the Fogbow: Design and Reconfiguration of Services and Participation in E-government. Licentiate Dissertation. Blekinge Institute of Technology, Sweden (2003)

Flak, L.S., Rose, J.: Stakeholder Governance: Adapting Stakeholder Theory to E-Governance. Communications of the Association for Information Systems 16, 662–664 (2005)

Fox, J.: Regression Diagnostics, Newbury Park. Sage, CA (1991)

Gujarati, D.N., Porter, D.C.: Basic Econometrics. McGraw-Hill, New York (2009)

Hair, J.F., Anderson Jr., R.E., Tatham, R.L., Black, W.C.: Multivariate Data Analysis with Readings. Prentice Hall, Englewood Cliffs (2006)

Hartwick, J., Barki, H.: Communication as a Dimension of User Participation. IEEE Transactions on Professional Communication 44, 21–36 (2001)

Heeks, R., Bailur, S.: Analyzing E-government Research: Perspectives, Philosophies, Theories, Methods, and Practice. Government Information Quarterly 24, 243–265 (2007)

Jarvenpaa, S.: Panning for Gold in Information Systems Research: 'Second-Hand' Data. In: Nissen, H.E., Klein, H., Hirschheim, R. (eds.) Information Systems Research: Contemporary Approaches and Emergent Traditions, IFIP TC/WG 8.2, pp. 63–80. Alfred Waller Ltd., North Holland (1991)

Kaufmann, D., Kraay, A., Mastruzz, M.: The Worldwide Governance Indicators: Methodology and Analytical Issues. Draft Policy Research Working Paper, The World Bank Development Research Group, Washington, DC (2010)

Kaufmann, D., Kraay, A., Zoido-Lobotan, P.: Governance Matters. Policy Research Working Paper 2196, The World Bank Development Research Group, Washington, DC (1999)

Kazancigil, A.: Governance and Science: Market-like Modes of Managing Society and Producing Knowledge. International Social Science Journal 50, 69–79 (1998)

Koh, C.E., Ryan, S., Prybutok, V.R.: Creating Value through Managing Knowledge in an E-Government to Constituency (G2C) Environment. Journal of Computer Information Systems 45, 32–41 (2005)

Krishnan, S., Teo, T.S.H.: Moderating Effects of Governance on Information Infrastructure and E-government Development. Journal of the American Society for Information Science and Technology 63, 1929–1946 (2012)

Lewis, W.A.: The Theory of Economic Growth, Irwin, Homewood, Ill (1995)

Lucas, R.E.: On the Mechanics of Economic Development. Journal of Monetary Economics 22, 3–42 (1988)

Madon, S., Sahay, S., Sudan, R.: E-Government Policy and Health Information Systems Implementation in Andhra Pradesh, India: Need for Articulation of Linkages between the Macro and the Micro. Information Systems 23, 327–344 (2007)

Meso, P., Datta, P., Mbarika, V.: Moderating Information and Communication Technologies' Influences on Socioeconomic Development with Good Governance: A Study of the Developing Countries. Journal of the American Society for Information Science and Technology 57, 186–197 (2006)

Meso, P., Musa, P., Straub, D., Mbarika, V.: Information Infrastructure, Governance, and Socio-Economic Development in Developing Countries. European Journal of Information Systems 18, 52–65 (2009)

Moon, M.J.: The Evolution of E-Government among Municipalities: Rhetoric or Reality? Public Administration Review 62, 424–433 (2002)

Norris, D.F., Moon, M.J.: Advancing E-Government at the Grassroots: Tortoise or Hare? Public Administration Review 65, 64–75 (2005)

Olphert, W., Damodaran, L.: Citizen Participation and Engagement in the Design of E-Government Services: The Missing Link in Effective ICT Design and Delivery. Journal of the Association for Information Systems 8, 491–507 (2007)

Phang, C.W., Kankanhalli, A.: A Framework of ICT Exploitation for E-Participation Initiatives. Communications of the ACM 51, 128–132 (2008)

Preacher, K.J., Hayes, A.F.: Asymptotic and Resampling Strategies for Assessing and Comparing Indirect Effects in Multiple Mediator Models. Behavior Research Methods 40, 879–891 (2008)

Romer, P.M.: Endogenous Technological Change. Journal of Political Economy 98, S71–S102 (1990)

Saebo, O., Rose, J., Flak, L.S.: The Shape of E-Participation: Characterizing an Emerging Research Area. Government Information Quarterly 25, 400–428 (2008)

Schultz, T.W.: Investment in Human Capital. American Economic Review 51, 1–17 (1961)

Shrout, P.E., Bolger, N.: Mediation in Experimental and Nonexperimental Studies: New Procedures and Recommendations. Psychological Methods 7, 422–445 (2002)

Siau, K., Long, Y.: Using Social Development Lenses to Understand E-Government Development. Journal of Global Information Management 14, 47–62 (2006)

Siau, K., Long, Y.: Factors Impacting E-Government Development. Journal of Computer Information Systems 50, 98–107 (2009)

Singh, H., Das, A., Joseph, D.: Country-Level Determinants of E-Government Maturity. Communications of the Association for Information Systems 20, 632–648 (2007)

Srivastava, S.C.: Is E-Government Providing the Promised Returns? A Value Framework for Assessing E-Government Impact. Transforming Government: People, Process and Policy 5, 107–113 (2011)

Srivastava, S.C., Teo, T.S.H.: The Relationship between E-Government and National Competitiveness: The Moderating Influence of Environmental Factors. Communications of the Association for Information Systems 23, 73–94 (2008)

Srivastava, S.C., Teo, T.S.H.: E-Government, E-Business, and National Economic Performance. Communications of the Association for Information Systems 26, 267–286 (2010)

Tan, C.W., Pan, S.L.: Managing E-Transformation in the Public Sector: An E-Government Study of the Inland Revenue Authority of Singapore (IRAS). European Journal of Information Systems 12, 269–281 (2003)

Tapscott, D.: The Digital Economy: The Promise and Peril in the Age of Networked Intelligence. McGraw-Hill, New York (1996)

Tornatzky, L.G., Fleischer, M.: The Processes of Technological Innovation. Lexington Books, Lexington (1990)

UN-Report.: UN Global E-Government Survey 2003: E-Government at the Crossroads (2003), http://www.unpan.org/egovkb/global_reports/08report.htm

UN-Report.: UN Global E-Government Readiness Report 2005: From E-Government to E-Inclusion (2005), http://www.unpan.org/egovkb/global_reports/08report.htm

UN-Report. UN Global E-Government Survey 2010: Leveraging E-Government at a Time of Financial and Economic Crisis (2010), http://www.unpan.org/egovkb/global_reports/08report.htm

Warkentin, M., Gefen, D., Pavlou, P.A., Rose, G.M.: Encouraging Citizen Adoption of E-Government by Building Trust. Electronic Markets 12, 157–162 (2002)

West, D.M.: E-Government and the Transformation of Service Delivery and Citizen Attitudes. Public Administration Review 64, 15–27 (2004)

West, D.M.: Global E-Government (2007), http://www.insidepolitics.org/

A Framework of Reference for Evaluating User Experience When Using High Definition Video to Video to Facilitate Public Services

Andreea Molnar, Vishanth Weerakkody, Ramzi El-Haddadeh,
Habin Lee, and Zahir Irani

Brunel University, Kingston Lane, Uxbridge, UB8 3PH, Middlesex, United Kingdom
{Andreea.Molnar,Vishanth.Weerakkody,Ramzi.El-Haddadeh,
Habin.Lee,Zahir.Irani}@brunel.ac.uk

Abstract. This paper proposes the use of high definition video to video as a means to facilitate the adoption of public services. High definition video can be delivered over the public Internet infrastructure by using a Right of Way platform that guarantees no interference from unwanted traffic. In this paper, we discuss the benefits of using high definition video to video communication in the public sector to facilitate services such as health, education and city experience/administration. Drawing from the dominant theories on Information Communication Technology we then propose a framework of reference to evaluate user experience of such services based on the Unified Theory of Acceptance and Use of Technology 2 (Venkatesh et al., 2012), the Information Systems success model (DeLone & McLean, 1992) and inclusion of the perception on information privacy.

Keywords: public services, video to video, user experience, evaluation framework.

1   Introduction

Despite the fact that it was introduced over a decade ago as a mainstream mechanism for the delivery of public services, electronic government has failed to fulfil initial expectations (Chadwick, 2009; Ferro & Molinari, 2010). To alleviate this problem, several projects have used other channels of service delivery such as mobile applications (Abdelghaffar & Magdy, 2012) or digital TV (da Silva et al., 2012). Although successful, these initiatives are still in pilot stages and their impact has yet to be proven on a broad scale.

Furthermore, the problems encountered during the adoption and diffusion of public services are not uniform. Simple customer facing services such as payments for services, fines or renewals of applications through the use of e-government have been successfully adopted, while more complex services are struggling with being accepted. Indeed, the research literature suggests that average citizens often prefer to have face-to-face contact when dealing with complex public services. This is particularly true for complex services such as health, education, and social or domestic

Y.K. Dwivedi et al. (Eds.): TDIT 2013, IFIP AICT 402, pp. 436–450, 2013.

services such as social security, housing, or employment (Andreassen et al., 2007; Santana et al., 2010). Among the problems that online services face is that they are distant and impersonal (Pavlou, 2003). Furthermore, there is no assistance offered to the citizens when they have problems using them (Ahmad et al., 2012; Venkatesh et al., 2011).

In this article, we argue that enhancing government services with high definition (HD) video to video (V2V) has the potential to offer citizens better and more person-alised services, similar to those offered by face-to-face, but maintaining the advantages of electronic services, i.e. citizens being able to access them regardless of their location and delivery channel. V2V will be used to facilitate service delivery (such as teaching from a remote location, connecting a patient with a specialist), but also in assisting citizens with their queries, or with the usage of an online service. The potential benefits of facilitating public services through V2V range from an easier usage to saving someone's life by providing the relevant stakeholders with adequate information when it is needed. To be able to improve the delivery of HD V2V on public Internet infrastructure, a new technology has to be introduced to alleviate some of the shortcomings that current video communication faces. However, due to the novelty of such technology, an established method to evaluate it does not exist. In this paper, we draw from existing theories to evaluate technology adoption and diffusion in order to propose a framework of reference to evaluate the user experience for V2V facilitated services.

The rest of this paper is organised as follows. First, we briefly present how HD V2V can be used on public infrastructure and the potential of using high definition video on the Internet for providing public services and the associated benefits that they can offer society. Second, the existing literature on technology adoption and diffusion is presented. We draw conclusions from this literature in order to propose a framework of reference for evaluating user experience. The next section discusses the conceptual development in relation to the proposed V2V framework. Finally, we conclude by outlining future directions for the use of V2V services in the public sector.

2   High Definitions Video to Video and Its Applications on Public Infrastructure

Although V2V communication has been previously used in public infrastructure by using applications such as Skype, FaceTime etc., it is often limited by technological constraints that affect delivery and have as consequences low image definition, delays in delivery etc. that put strain on user experience. In this article, we propose a LiveCity environment, where citizens communicate with each other and their governments anytime, anywhere using HD V2V on public infrastructure. HD V2V delivery will be implemented by using Right of Way (RoW) to guarantee a lack of interference from non-desired traffic, hence alleviating some of the problems imposed by current video delivery over public infrastructure. The LiveCity environment will be community driven and aims at improving core public services such as education, health, and city experience, empowering the citizens of a city to interact with each other in a more productive, efficient and socially useful way by using HD V2V.

Several public services could benefit from being enhanced with HD V2V. Some such services are Health, City Experience/Administration, and Education. For example, in health, a V2V service will be used for communicating live video images from the scene of a fatal accident to the emergency room of a hospital where an expert consultant can guide (real time) the paramedics on the ground on the best course of life saving treatment. Likewise, HD V2V can be used in tele-medicine where a doctor based in his/her surgery room can be guiding a patient at home on self-treatment (such as using eye drops to treat glaucoma). V2V will also be used to improve city administration where a municipality worker can assist a citizen with their service needs by guiding the citizen over the video link. Similarly, V2V can be used in education scenarios where teachers can assist pupils to complete their homework using a video link; or groups of students can have interactive debates (between schools) using a high definition video link. Furthermore, HD video will be used to promote the cultural heritage and art in a museum environment where people can view and interact with museum artefacts while at the same time interacting with museum workers regardless of their location.

3   Framework of Reference for Evaluating the User Experience in LiveCity

Due to the innovative nature of V2V usage in the context of the LiveCity environment, the evaluation is considered complex due to the difficulty of quantifying the benefits and inefficiencies. There does not exist an established way of evaluation yet. Therefore, we draw from existing theories on evaluating technology adoption and diffusion in order to propose an evaluation framework for LiveCity. Drawing on the dominant theories applied in Information and Communication Technology (ICT), a proposal for an integrated model of evaluation of V2V services is developed, based on the Unified Theory of Acceptance and Use of Technology 2 (Venkatesh et al., 2012), the Information Systems success model (DeLone & McLean, 1992) and inclusion of the perception on information privacy. The information privacy concept is introduced due to the fact that in the event of wide adoption of V2V on the Internet, potential users may be exposed to information security and privacy concerns.

State of the art key performance indicators for LiveCity are developed from a behavioural perspective. Hence, the related performance indexes refer to the assessment of LiveCity services from an end-users' viewpoint, and specifically with regards to the acceptance of using the V2V service and satisfaction from the service. As a result, we draw from the state of the art for technology adoption and associated behavioural evaluation.

Several researchers have proposed indicators for evaluating user satisfaction with innovative and/or new technology based services. Johnston (1995) compiled 18 determinants of service quality that have been used for assessing electronic services' (e-services) quality including availability, reliability, friendliness, functionality, access, aesthetics, etc. Parasuraman et al. (1988) have developed a widely accepted model namely SERVQUAL for measuring service quality that includes five dimensions: tangibles, reliability, responsiveness, assurance, and empathy. Information system researchers have adopted and modified the SERVQUAL model for e-service quality, including dimensions of website design, reliability, fulfilment, security, responsiveness, personalization, information (accuracy, comprehensibility, etc.) and empathy (Li and Suomi, 2009). Similarly, Zeithaml et al. (2001) adopts the SERVQUAL model for e-service quality evaluation and proposes 11 dimensions: access, ease of navigation, efficiency, flexibility, reliability, personalization, security/privacy, responsiveness, assurance/trust, site aesthetics, and price knowledge. Moreover, several information system researchers have applied technology acceptance theories in order to evaluate e-services from a user's perspective. During the past three decades there have been numerous studies regarding ICT acceptance and numerous information system (IS) acceptance studies have focused on the reasons why potential users accept or do not accept technology. Many research models have been developed and empirically validated, mainly including: The theory of Reasoned Action (TRA) (Fishbein and Ajzen, 1975), Social Cognitive Theory (SCT) (Bandura, 1986), Technology Acceptance Model (TAM) (Davis, 1989) and extended TAM 2 (Venkatesh and Davis, 2000), TAM 3 (Venkatesh and Bala, 2008), Theory of Planned Behaviour (TPB) (Ajzen, 1991), Model of PC Utilisation (Thompson et al, 1991), Motivation Model (Davis et al, 1992), the model combining TAM and the TPB (Taylor and Todd, 1995), the Innovation Diffusion Theory (IDT) (Rogers, 1995).

Table 1. Prominent Models used to study User Behaviour in Technology Adoption

Model	Reference
Theory of Reasoned Action (TRA)	Fishbein and Ajzen (1975)
Technology Acceptance Model (TAM)	Davis (1989)
Motivational Model (MM)	Davis, Bagozzi and Warshaw (1992)
Theory of Planned Behaviour (TPB)	Ajzen (1991)
Combination of Technology Acceptance and Theory of Planned Behaviour models (combined TAM – TPB)	Taylor and Todd (1995b)
Model of PC Utilization (MPCU)	Thompson, Higgins and Howell (1991)
Innovation Diffusion Theory (IDT)	Moore and Benbasat (1991)
Social Cognitive Theory (SCT)	Compeau and Higgins (1995)

The line of research in technology acceptance models culminates with the Unified Theory of Acceptance and Use of Technology (UTAUT) that was developed by (Venkatesh et al., 2003). The UTAUT aims to explain user intentions for using an information system. The subsequent usage behaviour and the model have been empirically examined by numerous studies. The UTAUT model integrates eight previously developed models and theories that relate to technology acceptance and use. Venkatesh et al. (2003) observed that IT researchers had a choice among a multitude of models and were confronted to choose constructs across models or choose an ideal model, thus ignoring the contribution from alternative ones. Therefore researchers compared the eight dominant models in explaining technology acceptance behaviour that have been previously used by researchers and scholars. The eight prominent models included are outlined in Table 1.

Another dominant stream of research in information systems and technology evaluation focuses on information system (IS) success. This includes several conceptual and empirical studies. In 1979, an assessment of IS research factors was conducted by Zmud (1979) to review issues addressed by most academics and practitioners concerning the influence of individual differences upon management information system design, implementation, and usage. In 1983, Bailey and Pearson (1983) outlined that evaluating and analysing computer user satisfaction is performed as an aspiration to improve the productivity of information systems by organizational management. According to the authors, productivity in computer services means both efficiently supplied and effectively utilized data processing outputs (Bailey and Pearson, 1983). In 1984, a study was conducted by Ives and Olson (1984) that emphasizes the importance of user involvement. After a decade, a study followed by Davis (1989) developed TAM. This explained the relationship among information system beliefs (e.g. perceived usefulness and ease of use, attitudes, and behavioural intentions and systems usage). DeLone and McLean (1992) reviewed over 180 articles and came up with the information systems success model that consisted of information quality, system quality, use, user satisfaction, individual impact, and organizational impact. In 1995, Goodhue and Thompson (1995) developed the task-technology fit model. The authors argued that the model services as the basis for a strong indicative tool to assess whether an information system including systems, policies, IS staff, and services in a given organization are meeting user needs. Among the above mentioned studies, DeLone and McLean's IS success model (1992) has gained great attention from scholars and widespread attention in the information success literature.

Given the above discussed context for the study of information technology and systems adoption, we present the two most widely accepted evaluation models, UTAUT and IS success model, which will be used to investigate the Key Performance Indicators (KPIs) for LiveCity from a behavioural perspective.

3.1   The Unified Theory of Acceptance and Use of Technology

The Unified Theory of Acceptance and Use of Technology provides a useful tool for managers that aim at assessing the likelihood of success for new technology introduction and helps them understand the drivers of technology acceptance in order to proactively design interventions targeted at users that might be less inclined to adopt and use new systems respectively (such as, training, marketing, etc.). The UTAUT model consists of three indirect determinants of behavioural intention, and two direct determinants of use behaviour. The three core constructs in the UTAUT model that declare to impact behavioural intention (BI) directly are: (1) performance expectancy, (2) effort expectancy, and (3) social influence. Intention to use and facilitating conditions (FC) are declared to impact indirectly on use behaviour. UTAUT includes four moderators (i.e. age, gender, experience and voluntariness of use), which contribute to a better understanding of the complexity of technology acceptance by individuals. Figure 1 illustrates UTAUT's core constructs.

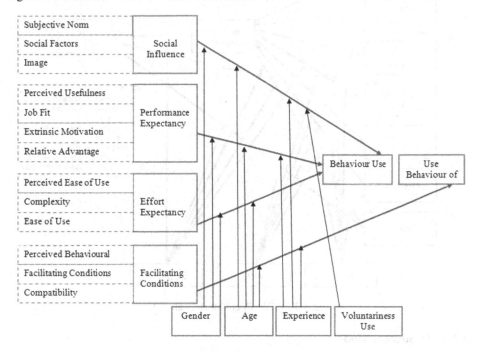

Fig. 1. UTAUT's Constructs and Root Core of Constructs

Additionally, the UTAUT model suggests the following: (1) gender and age moderate the relationship between performance expectancy and behavioural intention, (2) gender, age, and experience moderate the relationship between effort expectancy and behavioural intention, (3) gender, age, experience and voluntariness are suggested to moderate the relationship between social influence and behavioural intention, and (4) age and experience are declared to moderate the relationship between facilitating conditions and behaviour intention.

UTAUT2 (Figure 2) is an extension of UTAUT "to study acceptance and use of technology in the consumer context" (Venkatesh et al., 2012). UTAUT2 adds three more constructs that affect BI: (1) hedonic motivation, (2) price value, and (3) habit. Voluntariness use is no longer kept as one of the moderators, as in the consumer context most activities are voluntary; hence no variation will occur by including it (Venkatesh et al., 2012). A link is also added between facilitating conditions and behavioural intention.

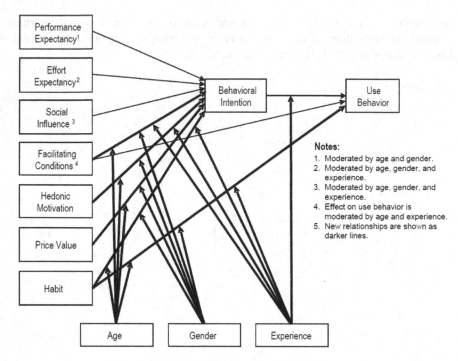

Fig. 2. UTAUT2   (Venkatesh et al., 2012)

3.2   IS Success Model

One of the most popular information systems success assessment models that resulted in highly significant contributions in the research literature is the DeLone and McLean IS success model conceptual model (IS Success model). The IS success model categorizes existing IS success measures under six dimensions (Gable, Sedera and Chan, 2003; Seddon, 1997). As Gable, Sedera and Chan (2003) note the development of IS success models, such as the DeLone and McLean model, has been an important contribution toward our improved understanding of IS management.

The IS success taxonomy and its six success categories are based on a process model of information systems (DeLone and McLean, 1992). Additionally, strong cause and effect relations exist among the six dependent variables. The six dimensions are interrelated, resulting in a success model that illustrates that causality flows in the same direction as the information process does (DeLone & McLean, 2002). The six major variables of the IS success model are:

1. system quality
2. information quality
3. use
4. user satisfaction
5. individual impact
6. organizational impact

In the IS Success model, system quality measures technical success, information quality measures semantic success and use, user satisfaction, individual impact, and organizational impact measure effectiveness success of the system measured. Figure 3 illustrates the IS Success model.

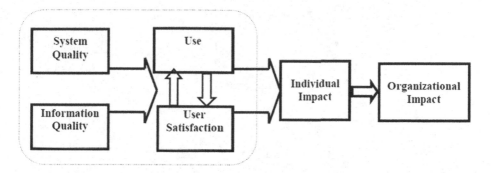

Fig. 3. DeLone and McLean IS Success Model (1992)

One of the strongest criticisms about the IS Success model is the lack of service quality among variables. According to Pitt, Watson and Kavan (1995), there is a danger that researchers will mis-measure IS effectiveness if they do not include in their assessment criteria a measure of IS service quality. Service is an important part of information systems departments; thus, service quality is a critical measure of information system effectiveness (Van Dyke, Kappelman and Prybutok, 1997). As a result, in order to measure information system effectiveness properly, many researchers believed that service quality should be included in the IS success model as a success measure (Kettinger and Lee, 1997; Myers, Kappelman and Prybutok, 1997; Pitt, Watson and Kavan, 1997). Pitt, Watson and Kavan (1997, p.210) posit that "the IS community needs to be aware of problems that might be experienced in using an instrument to measure so critical a construct as IS service quality".

Having realised the importance of e-services, DeLone and McLean (2003) outlined that in frequently used systems not only the benefits to the users, but also the quality of the system should be considered as well. In response to the calls of other researchers that criticized the original model, and due to the advent and growth of Internet based e-services, DeLone and McLean (2003) decided to add service quality to their new model as an important dimension of IS success noting the significance of customer service in the e-services environment. Therefore, in an attempt to contribute towards a universal model, DeLone and McLean (2003) introduced their updated model after ten years of its first induction in 1992. The model includes six success dimensions, and holds that the constructs of information quality, system quality, and service quality individually jointly affect the factors of use and user satisfaction, whereas user satisfaction and use jointly affect net benefit. Figure 4 illustrates the updated DeLone and McLean Success Model.

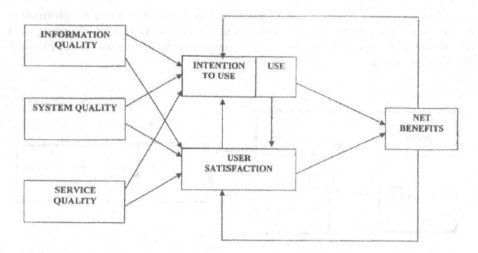

Fig. 4. Updated DeLone and McLean IS Success Model

The updated model of DeLone and McLean (2003) includes six success dimensions to measure the success of a system in the e-services domain. The six major variables of the 2003 IS success model are:

1. System quality, which measures the desired characteristics of an e-Commerce system. It refers to the quality of (usability, availability, reliability, adaptability, and response time (e.g., download time),
2. Information quality, which measures the e-Commerce content issues, the dimension of this variable are (personalization, currency, relevance, reliability, completeness, easy to understand and secured for (to gain user's trust when conducting a transaction via the internet),
3. Service quality, which is the "overall support delivered by the service provider, applies regardless of whether the support is delivered by the information systems' department or a new organizational unit or is outsourced to an internet service provider" (DeLone & McLean, 2004, p. 34),
4. Usage, which measures everything from a visit to a web site and navigation within the site to information retrieval and execution of a transaction,
5. User satisfaction, which measures customers' opinions of an e-Commerce system and should cover the entire experience cycle of customers from information retrieval to purchase, payment, receipt, and service, and
6. Net benefits that capture the balance of the positive and negative impacts of e-Commerce on customers, suppliers, employees, organizations, markets and even society as a whole.

Hu et al. (2005) attempted to establish a suitable and systematic appraisal framework of public sector e-services success based on the IS Success Model presented by DeLone and McLean in 1992, which is relevant to the LiveCity project. Table 2 summarizes the relevant KPIs for evaluating the LiveCity project.

Table 2. IS Success Model Factors

System Quality	Reliability	The dependability of system operations	(Wixom and Todd, 2005)
	Flexibility	The way the system adapts to changing demands of the user	
	Integration	The way the system allows data to be integrated from various sources	
	Accessibility	The ease with which information can be accessed or extracted from the system	
	Timeliness	The degree to which the system offers timely responses to requests for information or action	
Information Quality	Completeness	The degree to which the system provides all necessary information	(Wixom and Todd, 2005)
	Accuracy	The user's perception that the information is correct	
	Format	The user's perception of how well the information is presented	
	Currency	The user's perception of the degree to which the information is up to date	
Service Quality (SERVQUAL Scale)	Tangibles	Physical facilities, equipment, and appearance of personnel	(Parasuraman, Zeithaml and Berry, 1988)
	Reliability	Ability to perform the promised service dependably and accurately	
	Responsiveness	Willingness to help customers and provide prompt ability to inspire trust and confidence	
	Assurance	Knowledge and courtesy of employees and their ability to inspire trust and confidence	
	Empathy	Caring, individualized attention to firm provides its customers	
Information Use	Usefulness	The degree to which a person believes that a particular information system would enhance his or her job performance	(Davis, 1989)
	Ease of Use	The degree to which a person believes that using a particular system would be free of effort	
User Satisfaction	Information Satisfaction	The application of that information useful in enhancing work performance	(Wixom and Todd, 2005)
	System Satisfaction	A degree of favourableness with respect to the system and the mechanics of interaction	

3.3   Integrated Model for Evaluating User Experience of LiveCity

For the purpose of evaluating the user experience related to LiveCity technology and services, the two noteworthy models, UTAUT2 and DeLone and McLean IS Success model, are integrated based on theoretical evidence presented in the previous two sections as depicted in Figure 5 below.

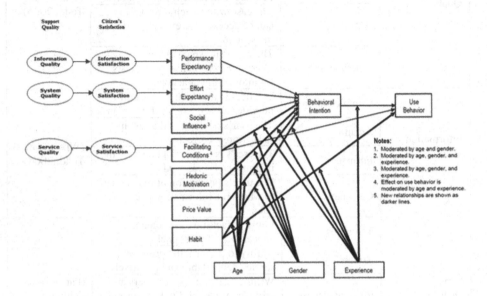

Fig. 5. Integrated Model of UTAUT and IS success model

The integrated research model presented in Figure 5 attempts to merge quality dimensions from the IS Success model together with the UTAUT2 model as antecedents for the intention to use with an attempt to reveal the role of perceived service quality towards intention to use the LiveCity application. The acceptance of the LiveCity application is defined through the behaviour intention to use the associated services. The proposed integrated research framework consists of thirteen constructs; one dependent variable and ten independent variables. The dependent variable is behaviour intention to use LiveCity services, while the independent variables are: (1) information quality, (2) information satisfaction, (3) system quality, (4) system satisfaction, (5) service quality, (6) service satisfaction, (7) social influence, (8) performance expectancy, (9) effort expectancy, (10) facilitating conditions, (11) hedonic motivation, (12) price value, and (13) habit.

Moreover, a key for adopting Internet based (V2V) services is the perceived customer or end-user perception on information security and privacy. Therefore, information privacy should be an assessment variable integrated in the model as an independent variable. For that purpose we adopt the research of Dinev and Hart (2006) who identify the factors representing elements of a privacy calculus in the e-commerce domain.

Therefore, under the user satisfaction variables, we add the parameter of willingness to provide personal information (Figure 6).

Table 3. Information privacy construct (adopted by Dinev and Hart, 2006)

Willingness to provide personal information to an e-service	Perceived Internet privacy risk	Perceived risk related to the disclosure of personal information submitted by the relent stakeholders in their specific context (use cases) in general
	Internet privacy concerns	Concerns related to the personal information submitted over the internet by the respondent in particular
	Internet trust	Trust beliefs that personal information submitted to V2V based services will be handled competently, reliably, and safely
	Personal Internet interest	Personal interest or cognitive attraction to V2V internet content overriding privacy concerns

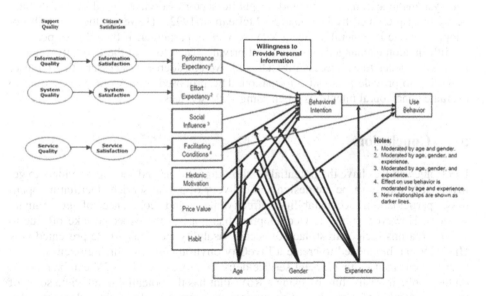

Fig. 6. Integrated model for V2V services on the Internet incorporating Trust

The model proposed in Figure 6 endeavour to merge UTAUT2 model, IS Success model and enhance them with the willingness to provide personal information. The framework consists of one dependent variable (the behaviour intention to use LiveCity services) and fourteen constructs; one dependent variable and ten independent variables.

The dependent variable is behaviour intention to use LiveCity services, while the independent variables are: (1) information quality, (2) information satisfaction, (3) system quality, (4) system satisfaction, (5) service quality, (6) service satisfaction, (7) social influence, (8) performance expectancy, (9) effort expectancy, (10) facilitating conditions, (11) hedonic motivation, (12) price value, (13) habit and, (14) willingness to provide personal information. This reference model will serve as an evaluation framework for LiveCity users' experience.

4   Discussion

Taking into consideration that the use of high definition, uninterrupted V2V oriented platforms is new and yet to evolve, and limited normative literature exists specifically for the evaluation of such services. For that reason we drew upon existing literature and added constructs that are particularly important for the diffusion and adoption of Internet Based e-services such as V2V as well as other socio economic and information privacy factors that may influence the V2V offered on the Internet.

As the V2V platform will offer mostly consumer services, we draw from UTAU2 that is an extension of UTAUT to reflect the acceptance and use of technology in the consumer context. As the services covered in the LiveCity project are public services we refer to Hu et al. (2005) that show results from their attempt to establish a suitable and systematic appraisal framework of public sector e-services based on the IS Success Model presented by DeLone and McLean in 1992. However, the user will not adopt a service in general, hence a V2V service in particular, if they do not perceive the information exchanged as secure and private. Therefore, in the LiveCity context, for V2V services to be successfully adopted, we considered it necessary that the user is willing to provide personal information. The proposed framework will be used to evaluate behavioural intentions when using V2V services.

5   Conclusion

Electronic services have the potential of allowing citizens and service providers to get involved to jointly shape the design and delivery of public services facilitating openness, participation, accountability, effectiveness, and coherence of government services. However, public service adoption has not had the expected take off due to various reasons such as trust, lack of access, usability etc. This article presented how HD V2V can be utilised to create a LiveCity environment, in which citizens can actively be engaged in government service delivery processes. HD V2V can be realised on the public infrastructure by using a RoW that has the potential to alleviate some of the consequences of the technical constraints that currently affect video delivery. This article offers an insight on how using HD V2V can enhance public services such as health, education, and city experience and what the potential benefits and impact added by the video communication. However, due to the novelty of the technology involved, there is no established method to quantify its benefits. Therefore, we draw from previous literature and we propose a framework of reference for evaluating user experience on LiveCity by drawing from previous literature on technology adoption.

Acknowledgements. The authors wish to acknowledge the contributions made to this article by the LiveCity consortium of partners and the European commission.

References

Abdelghaffar, H., Magdy, Y.: The Adoption of Mobile Government Services in Developing Countries: The Case of Egypt. International Journal of Information 2(4) (2012)

Ahmad, M.O., Markkula, J., Oivo, M.: Factors Influencing the Adoption of e-Government Services in Pakistan. In: Proceedings of the 9th European, Mediterranean & Middle Eastern Conference on Information Systems (2012)

Ajzen, I.: The Theory of Planned Behavior. Organizational Behavior and Human Decision Processes 50, 179–211 (1991)

Andreassen, H.K., Bujnowska-Fedak, M.M., Chronaki, C.E., Dumitru, R.C., Pudule, I., Santana, S., Wynn, R.: European citizens' use of E-health services: a study of seven countries. BMC Public Health 7(1), 53 (2007)

Bandura, A.: The Explanatory and Predictive Scope of Self-Efficacy Theory. Journal of Social and Clinical Psychology 4 (Special Issue: Self-Efficacy Theory in Contemporary Psychology), 359–373 (1986)

Bailey, J.E., Pearson, S.W.: Development of a tool for measuring and analyzing computer user satisfaction. Management Science 29(5), 530–545 (1983)

Chadwick, A.: Web 2.0: New Challenges for the Study of E-Democracy in an Era of Informational Exuberance. I/S: A Journal of Law and Policy for the Information Society 5(1), 9–41 (2009)

Compeau, D.R., Higgins, C.A.: Application of social cognitive theory to training for computer skills. Information Systems Research 6(2), 118–143 (1995)

Davis, F.D.: Perceived Usefulness, Perceived Ease of Use, and User Acceptance of Information Technology. MIS Quarterly 13(3), 319–340 (1989)

Davis, F.D., Bagozzi, R.P., Warshaw, P.R.: Extrinsic and intrinsic motivation to use computers in the workplace1. Journal of Applied Social Psychology 22(14), 1111–1132 (1992)

da Silva, J.C.F., Barbosa, H.P., Tavares, P.B.T.A.: The Importance of digital TV for countries in development: A case study of Brazil. Journal of Communication and Computer 9, 847–851 (2012)

DeLone, W.H., McLean, E.R.: Information systems success: The quest for the dependent variable. Information Systems Research 3(1), 60–95 (1992)

DeLone, W.H., McLean, E.R.: The DeLone and McLean model of information systems success: A ten-year update. Journal of Management Information Systems 19(4), 9–30 (2003)

Dinev, T., Hart, P.: An extended privacy calculus model for e-commerce transactions. Information Systems Research 17(1), 61–80 (2006)

Ferro, E., Molinari, F.: Making Sense of Gov 2.0 Strategies: No Citizens, No Party. Journal of eDemocracy and Open Government 2(1), 56–68 (2010)

Fishbein, M., Ajzen, I.: Belief, Attitude, Intention, and Behavour: An Introduction to Theory and Research. Addison-Wesley (1975)

Gable, G.G., Sedera, D., Chan, T.: Enterprise systems success: a measurement model. In: International Conference on Information Systems, pp. 576–591 (2003)

Goodhue, D.L., Thompson, R.L.: Task-Technology Fit and Individual Performance. MIS Quarterly 19(2), 213–236 (1995)

Hu, Y., JingHua, X., JiaFeng, P., Kang, X.: A research on the framework of e-government project success. In: International Conference on Electronic Commerce, ICEC, Xian, China (2005)

Ives, B., Olson, M.H.: User involvement and MIS success: a review of research. Management Science 30(5), 586–603 (1984)

Johnston, R.: The determinants of service quality: satisfiers and dissatisfies. International Journal of Service Industry Management 6(5), 53–71 (1995)

Kettinger, W.J., Lee, C.C.: Perspectives on the Measurement of Information Systems Service Quality. MIS Quarterly 223 (1997)

Li, H., Suomi, R.: A proposed scale for measuring e-service quality. International Journal of u- and e-Service, Science and Technology 2(1), 1–10 (2009)

Myers, B.L., Kappelman, L.A., Prybutok, V.R.: A comprehensive model for assessing the quality and productivity of the information systems function: Toward a theory for information systems assessment. Information Resources Management Journal 10(1), 6–25 (1997)

Moore, G.C., Benbasat, I.: Development of an instrument to measure the perceptions of adopting an information technology innovation. Information Systems Research 6(2), 144–176 (1991)

Parasuraman, A., Zeithaml, V.A., Berry, L.L.: SERVQUAL: A multiple-item scale for measuring customer perceptions of service quality. Journal of Retailing 64(1), 12–40 (1988)

Pavlou, P.A.: Consumer acceptance of electronic commerce: Integrating trust and risk with the technology acceptance model. International Journal of Electronic Commerce 7(3), 101–134 (2003)

Pitt, L.F., Watson, R.T., Kavan, C.B.: Service quality: a measure of information systems effectiveness. MIS Quarterly, 173–187 (1995)

Pitt, L.F., Watson, R.T., Kavan, C.B.: Measuring Information Systems Service Quality: Concerns for aComplete Canvas. MIS Quarterly 21(2), 209–221 (1997)

Rogers, E.M.: Diffusion of Innovations, 4th edn. The Free Press, New York (1995)

Santana, S., Lausen, B., Bujnowska-Fedak, M., Chronaki, C., Kummervold, P.E., Rasmussen, J., Sorensen, T.: Online communication between doctors and patients in Europe: status and perspectives. Journal of Medical Internet Research 12(2) (2010)

Seddon, P.B.: A Respecification and Extension of the DeLone and McLean Model of IS Success. Information Systems Research (8), 240–253 (1997)

Taylor, S., Todd, P.: Assessing IT Usage: The Role of Prior Experience. MIS Quarterly 19(4), 561–570 (1995)

Thompson, R.L., Higgins, C.A., Howell, J.M.: Influence of experience on personal computer utilization: testing a conceptual model. Journal of Management Information Systems, 167–187 (1994)

Van Dyke, T.P., Kappelman, L.A., Prybutok, V.: Measuring information systems service quality: Concerns on the use of the SERVQUAL questionnaire. MIS Quarterly 21(2), 195–208 (1997)

Venkatesh, V., Bala, H.: Technology Acceptance Model 3 and a Research Agenda on Interventions. Decision Sciences 39(2), 273–315 (2008)

Venkatesh, V., Chan, F., Thong, J.Y.: Designing e-Government Services: Key Service Attributes and Citizens' Preference Structures. Journal of Operations Management 30, 116–133 (2011)

Venkatesh, V., Davis, F.D.: A Theorieical Extension of the Technology Acceptance Model: Four Longitudinal Field Studies. Management Science 46(2), 186–204 (2000)

Venkatesh, V., Morris, M.G., Davis, F.D., Davis, G.B.: User Acceptance of Information Technology: Toward a Unified View. MIS Quarterly 27, 425–478 (2003)

Venkatesh, V., Thong, J., Xu, X.: Consumer acceptance and use of information technology: extending the unified theory of acceptance and use of technology. MIs Quarterly 36(1), 157–178 (2012)

Wixom, B.H., Todd, P.A.: A Theoretical Integration of User Satisfaction and Technology Acceptance. Information Systems Research 16(1), 85–102 (2005)

Zeithaml, V., Parasuraman, A., Malhorta, A.: A conceptual framework for understanding e-service quality: implications for future research and managerial practice. working paper, pp. 100–115. Marketing Science Institute, Cambridge (2001)

Designing Sustainable Open Source Systems: The Cuban National Health Care Network and Portal (INFOMED)

Ann Séror

eResearch Collaboratory, Quebec City, Canada
annseror@eresearchcollaboratory.com

Abstract. Integrating research, education and evidence-based medical practice requires complex network linkages among these critical activities. This study examines the Cuban National Health Care Network and Portal (INFOMED) in the context of the regional Virtual Health Library of the Latin American and Caribbean Health Sciences System (BIREME) led by Brazil. INFOMED is a virtual infrastructure for integration of scientific research with education and expert intervention in evidence-based medicine. Virtual infrastructures refer to an environment characterized by overlapping distribution networks accessible through Internet portals and websites designed to facilitate integrated use of available resources. The objective of this paper is to examine system design at the regional and national levels of analysis using theoretical perspectives from complexity theory, institutional economics and knowledge ecology. In conclusion model transferability to other national health care systems is considered.

Keywords: Cuba, national health care systems, INFOMED, qualitative research methods, virtual infrastructures, open source software.

1   Introduction

Recent literature in development, sustainability and health care has recognized the importance of comparative research on large systems for understanding of complexity and performance at the national and global levels of analysis (Reimers *et al.*, 2010). Despite recognition of the importance of systems science in medical informatics(Coiera, 2003), only fragmented progress has been made in theory development and research methods to address issues of critical importance in large scale health care system reform. The objective of this research is to contribute to an interdisciplinary perspective on theory and methods for this emerging scientific domain.

The diversity of such systems means that technology varies, in particular as a function of technological choices based on local and regional ideologies and traditions. The boundaries of the ecological field under study pose both conceptual and methodological dilemmas. (Thrift, 2006) The health care system is defined here as a complex set of interconnected individuals, institutions, organizations, and projects offering products and services in health care markets (Alliance for Health Policy and Systems Research, 2004). The functions of the health care system include

Y.K. Dwivedi et al. (Eds.): TDIT 2013, IFIP AICT 402, pp. 451–466, 2013.
© IFIP International Federation for Information Processing 2013

all categories of service delivery, resource generation and allocation, and governance. Service delivery encompasses information, research, and educational services as well as public health and delivery of patient care, both preventative and curative. Performance of complex health care systems depends on patterns of interdependence of these diverse system functions through extended interorganizational information systems and virtual infrastructures. Virtual infrastructures refer to an environment characterized by overlapping distribution networks, systems brokerage functions, and the adoption of a software perspective emphasizing the devices and channels through which information is processed and distributed (Séror, 2006a).

Integration of health information systems at the country and regional levels of analysis is particularly evident in the Latin American and Caribbean Health Sciences System (BIREME) led by Brazil, national systems share common ideologies (Committee for Economic Development (CED), 2006) associated with universal health care, public education in medicine and the health sciences, open access publishing of health information and research, and infrastructure creation through open source software development.[1] The principle of *open access*[2] is the responsibility to extend the unrestricted availability of scientific information and research publications to all who may be interested or have need of it (Albert, 2006;Cockerill, 2006;Willinsky, 2006). Similarly, *open source* software development is founded on the principles of freely shared source code with a license that permits redistribution as well as the creation of derived works (Benkler, 2001;Edwards, 2001). Some experience suggests that the open source model for software development may be extended to research in the health sciences, pointing to the ideological coherence between infrastructure development and productive activities conducted within such infrastructure(Maurer *et al.*, 2004;Mueller, 2008;Scacchi & et al., 2010).

A useful perspective on this system driven by the open source model is complexity theory. Characteristics of complex systems include emergent properties and qualitative rather than incremental change. (Byrne, 2009;Kannampallil *et al.*, 2011). INFOMED within the larger network of BIREME can be viewed as a complex adaptive system of nested entities(Dagnino, 2004). Open source systems possess the capability to grow and self-organize through sharing of tools and resources. The self-organizing system adapts to its environment with the capacity to replicate and renew itself from within. These systems may be considered closed by virtue of the rules of interaction, while at the same time they are open as they extend – for example – from one national entity to another. Coevolution of INFOMED and other national health information systems within BIREME also affects the distribution of roles at regional and nested national levels of analysis. As nested entities coevolve, emergent features transform the larger system. (Morrison, 2008)

---

[1] The ideology shared by these related communities of practice may also profoundly affect the broader functions of the knowledge ecology, including the conduct of research and delivery of care. (Anonymous, 2004;Benkler, 2002;Maurer *et al.*, 2004).

[2] See the Public Library of Science definition of *open access* at http://www.plos.org/oa/definition.html (accessed 28 April 2008).

Open access publication remodels information flows across virtual spaces with no exchange of physical materials or financial transactions in a process of shared content development and ever reduced restrictions on access to health information.(Packer, 2000) While online publication extends global access to both international and local scientific journals, the linkage between these resources may be configured to contextualize user knowledge and practice. (Ofori-Adjei *et al.*, 2006) The shared space linked through virtual infrastructures of the health information system is defined here as a knowledge ecology - including institutional and network portals, electronic journals and other resources, online courses, collaborative spaces, human resources, and search engines arranged according to language, knowledge domain, or geographical location.

Trist suggested as early as 1977 the importance of "clustering" in social ecologies and the need for inquiry into the cognitive mapping of large scale socio-ecological systems characterized by network structures expressing negotiated rather than bureaucratic order. (Trist, 1977) He identified conceptual and methodological difficulties posed by this new area of inquiry. First, the ecological domain is difficult to identify – requiring a "figure-ground reversal" to render its features observable or measurable. Second, the structure of middle-level fields - bridging the divide between local and global(Barrett *et al.*, 2005) - is particularly elusive, as singular institutions are generally more visible in networks than - for example - chambers of commerce or regulatory councils. Virtual infrastructures made visible on the Internet reflect the resources of the knowledge ecology. These institutional infrastructures may control access to associated resources through regulatory or certification processes, or they may be created and controlled by their constituencies through membership and democratic governance. Where no referent structures order the system, market dynamics and ideologies determine the configuration of the ecological domain(Séror, 2011).

Virtual infrastructures of INFOMED - accessible on the Internet - offer visible evidence of ecological domains for mapping and analysis of their configurations at micro-, meso- and meta-levels of structure. The research objectives here are to describe INFOMED in the context of BIREME as a complex knowledge ecology using qualitative case analysis – and to make some recommendations regarding national strategies for model transferability.

This case analysis contributes to a broad research program designed to develop a framework for comparative analysis of national health care system infrastructures using qualitative case research methods. (Séror, 2012, 2011, 2002, 2006a, 2006b). The next section of the paper describes the methodology for study of the Cuban National Health Care Network and Portal (INFOMED).

2   Research Methodology

The research methodology used for this study is embedded qualitative case analysis(Hannan, 2005;Yin, 1999;Yin, 2009). The regional and national infrastructures selected for study - the Latin American and Caribbean Health Sciences

System (BIREME) as a context for the Cuban National Health Care Network and Portal (INFOMED) – form a complex interorganizational information system (Byrne, 2009;Reimers *et al.*, 2010) (Dagnino, 2004). Such large, complex systems pose significant challenges to design of research methods for a number of reasons. First, the degree of interrelatedness and the evolutionary nature of system change make it very difficult to identify a nomological model (Kannampallil *et al.*, 2011). Second, the process definition of causality associated with the scientific method (Morrison, 2012) cannot be applied in development of theoretical frameworks, nor can it be the objective of research designs focused on complexity. Rather, the lens of complexity theory suggests an interconnected system with reciprocal relationships for mutual constitution of the observed characteristics of the system (Reimers *et al.*, 2010).

Specifically this is an embedded case according to the typology suggested by Yin (2009) where the regional BIREME forms the context in which INFOMED has grown and developed at the Cuban country level of analysis. This choice of case is revelatory of the reciprocal roles of regional and country level leadership in health information system development. The Cuban case is unique, in some ways offering a natural experiment in the values of social medicine. While this study may not yield generalizable conclusions, it sheds light on the critical coevolution of regional and national knowledge ecologies and the ideological role of the social medicine model shared among countries of the Latin American region (Collier & Mahoney, 1996). Historical description of the institutional context shows how virtual infrastructures have emerged over time and how this temporal evolution has affected the forms and functions expressed in the system ecology (Bennett & Elman, 2006).

Data include published accounts of system development and the websites of the constituent organizations, networks and services to describe the configuration of virtual infrastructures(Vidal Ledo *et al.*, 2007). The mapping methodology reveals complex infrastructural patterns of health care information system management and control(Rodriguez Pina & Guerra Avila, 2008). Qualitative interpretation facilitates identification of complex and sometimes paradoxical effects of information and communication technologies on knowledge ecologies (Robey & Boudreau, 1999). E-mapping software[3] is used to visualize maps of the linkages among resources identified in the knowledge ecology of the Cuban National Health Care Network and Portal (INFOMED) in the context of the regional Virtual Health Library of the Latin American and Caribbean Health Sciences System (Egbu & et. al, 2006;Ruffini, 2008). The maps generated using this methodology show how global, regional and national resources are shared and integrated in the virtual infrastructure (Ebener *et al.*, 2006;Lavis *et al.*, 2006). Figure 1 below shows a partial view of a map of INFOMED. Nodes in this map identify virtual organizations and resources. Edges represent Internet linkages among these virtual entities. The resulting configuration reveals the relational logic of the system as well as patterns of connectedness and self-organization both within INFOMED and among emergent entities of BIREME. Figure 1 below shows a partial view of a map of INFOMED. This database is available online for review.

---

[3] See The Brain - Visual Information Management at http://www.thebrain.com/

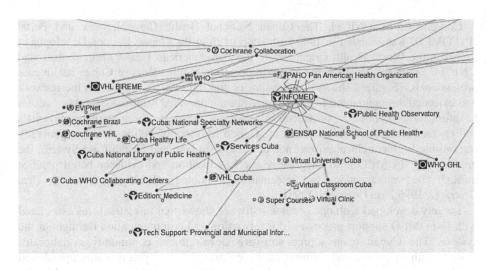

Fig. 1. The virtual infrastructure of INFOMED

3   Case Analysis

According to Article 4 of the Cuban Public Health Law No. 43, the ideological principles underpinning Cuban health care services include (Asamblea Nacional del Poder Popular de la República de Cuba, 1983): adequate health care defined as a human right, free and universal access to health care services offered by the state, emphasis on preventive care, and active participation of the population in public health promotion. The performance of this national system is reflected in statistics for population life expectancy of 78 years (2009) and infant mortality of 5 per thousand live births - indicating standards similar to those observed in the developed countries. Expenditure per capita of $495 contrasts sharply with the US expenditure of $7,164 in 2008, particularly in light of poor US performance among other OECD countries(Davis *et al.*, 2010). Also significant is the concentration of 64 physicians per 10,000 population (2000-2010) – the highest in the world (World Health Organization, 2011).

Since the Cuban revolution in 1959, the country's leadership have pursued strategies to integrate national research and innovation policies through development of traditional institutions and, since 1990, information and telecommunication infrastructures(Amaro, 2000;Capote, 1996;Séror & Fach Arteaga, 2000). In 1963, municipal polyclinics were first created to form the basic units of the Cuban health care system and to manage all health care activities within their jurisdictions, including workplaces, schools, and childcare centers. These activities were the first programs of the current community-based health care model(Campion & Morrissey, 2013;Keck & Reed, 2012;Séror, 2006a). In 1965 the National Center for Scientific Research (Centro Nacional de Investigaciones Cientificas, CNIC) and the National Information Center for the Medical Sciences (Centro Nacional de Información de Ciencias Médicas de la República de Cuba-CNICM) were founded to serve the institutional needs of science and research in health care.

Coordinated by CNICM, The Cuban National Health Care Network and Portal (INFOMED) was founded in 1992 with support from the United Nations Development Program, the World Health Organization, the Pan-American Health Organization, and UNICEF. INFOMED serves the health information requirements of Cuban health care professionals. (Figure 2 shows a screenshot of the INFOMED Portal.) As the network was extended throughout the 14 Cuban provinces, it provided health care workers' access to information - connecting provincial information centers, research institutes, hospitals and universities(Séror, 2006a). While the Cuban Ministry of Public Health is generally responsible for hierarchical governance of the Cuban National Health Care System, the mission of INFOMED is to integrate research, education and evidence-based practice through telecommunications and information technologies(Rodríguez Pérez & Urra González, 1996;Urra González, 1995).

Largely developed with open source software, the virtual infrastructures associated with INFOMED support processes of information and communication throughout the system. The Cuban open source software development community collaborates closely with scientific and administrative communities of practice through shared ideological values expressed in open access to health information and universal health care services (Schweik & Semenov, 2003).

Fig. 2. The INFOMED Portal at http://www.sld.cu/ (accessed 15-3-2013)

In particular, BIREME forms the context for development of national health information systems serving Latin America. It was founded in 1967 with the collaboration of the Brazilian Ministry of Education, Ministry of Health, Secretary of Health of the State of São Paulo, and the Federal University of São Paulo as a specialized center of the WHO regional office for the Americas, the Pan American Health Organization (PAHO). Recognizing that an important condition for the development of health is universal, equitable and cost-effective access to scientific and technical information in medicine and the health sciences, BIREME aims to promote the regional capacity for collaboration to through open access to data and research on medicine and the health sciences. Throughout its history, BIREME's technical operation has been motivated by the principles of decentralized networking, local capacity building, cooperative product development, and elaboration of common methodologies(BIREME, 1998;BIREME, 2008;Bireme, 2011).

Such cooperative projects linked to the INFOMED Portal include the Cuban VHL[4]and the Virtual University[5] offering online training in medicine and the health sciences. Since 1994, the Cuban National Library of Medicine (CNLM)[6] has collaborated with BIREME to develop the Collective Catalogue of Periodical Publications on the Health Sciences (SeCiMed).[7] In 1998 when the regional VHL was created, the CNLM was converted into a network coordinating center– including 815 libraries and information centers - charged with compiling the Cuban medical bibliography for the regional LiLaCS project led by BIREME.[8] The CNLM played a critical role in the transition to new media for information dissemination to both real and virtual library users.

The Cuban VHL has grown to include more than 50 online Spanish-language journals in medicine and public health. These publications have been formally certified according to standards[9] set by the Cuban Ministry of Science, Technology and the Environment(CITMA, 1994). In 2001, Cuba joined the SciELO Network, and adopted the SciELO methodology(Packer, 2007).[10] The SciELO network serves to promote selected Cuban journals in the international scientific information flow through network access, search tools, and article indexing(Cañedo Andalia et al., 2010). The Cuban VHL links information and research from the Latin American region as well as international scientific research and accounts of medical experiences in developing countries. More than 25 countries of the Latin American region have appropriated models, methods and open source tools to create national virtual libraries connected to the regional network managed by BIREME.[11]

Although English is the international language of science, other languages are essential to the culture and context of health care systems. The Virtual Health Library (VHL) linking BIREME and INFOMED embody an institutional commitment to Spanish and Portuguese languages and context while maintaining linkages to English and French language resources. Shared Spanish and Portugese languages as well as the

---

[4] Cuban Virtual Health Library at
   http://www.bvscuba.sld.cu/html/es/home.html
[5] Virtual University at http://www.uvs.sld.cu/
[6] CNLM website at http://www.sld.cu/sitios/bmn/
[7] SeCiMed website at http://bmn.sld.cu/secimed/msrc/secimed_home.php
[8] See an account of the history of the CNLM at
   http://www.sld.cu/sitios/bmn/temas.php?idv=2381
[9] These journal quality standards include national registration and accreditation by an appropriately formed national commission. Article evaluation must be completed by qualified referees and certified journals must include content of at least 60% original scientific research.
[10] SciELO Cuba website - http://scielo.sld.cu/scielo.php
[11] http://regional.bvsalud.org/php/bvsnet.php?lang=en&list=countries

values of open source systems contribute to growth and self-organization of BIREME and INFOMED. This commitment is especially critical to the interests of Cuban scientists and practitioners as they adopt medical innovation from scientific communities of the developed world and identify topics of common concern for international collaboration(Meneghini *et al.*, 2006;Meneghini & Packer, 2007).

The Cuban Virtual University for the Health Sciences (UVS) was founded by the Ministry of Public Health in 1998 to improve continuing post graduate medical training for more than one hundred thousand Cuban health care professionals and to offer an international center for postgraduate education in medicine and related disciplines(Lalas Perea *et al.*, 2000;Ramírez Machado *et al.*, 2002). This institution links the Cuban health care information and publication infrastructure with Cuban institutions for higher education as well as supercourses with Cuban[12] and international content such as *Epidemiology, the Internet, and Global Health*[13] hosted by the University of Pittsburgh. In 2004, a learning environment, the Virtual Classroom was created and in 2005, migrated to open-source Moodle, a scalable course management system also used in the Virtual Campus for Public Health.

In 2006 the Cuban Virtual University adopted Plone, an open-source content management system[14] to extend university community participation through open courses, event management, and a repository for learning resources. (Díaz Martínez *et al.*, 2010) The collaborative environment for website development fosters service decentralization, user participation, and integration of technology, management and pedagogy. (Jardines Méndez, 2006a;Jardines Méndez, 2006b;Zacca González G. *et al.*, 2008) Members of Cuban university communities including professors and other users collaborate to create and publish content made available through the network. Essential components of the Virtual University are the Virtual Classroom, the Interactive Clinic, the Repository for documents of interest, and the network through which courses are offered. The Virtual Classroom supports medical training and education[15] while the Interactive Clinic provides a forum for discussion on diagnostics and case studies.[16] The Repository is an electronic archive of documents such as courses, conference presentations and scientific articles made available to the university community. Courses may be offered through the network for medical education credit using the Moodle interface, or content may be made available for autonomous learning according to the MIT open courseware model.[17]

Associated with the Virtual University is the Cuban Virtual Campus for Public Health (VCPH)[18] linked to the Latin American infrastructures created by PAHO.[19] This virtual infrastructure now links the VCPH in 11 countries of the region. This

---

[12] Cuban Super Course site at http://supercurso.sld.cu/

[13] Supercourse-Epidemiology, the Internet, and Global Health, University of Pittsburgh:
    http://www.pitt.edu/~super1/

[14] www.plone.org

[15] Virtual Classroom - http://aulauvs.sld.cu/

[16] Interactive Clinic - http://www.uvs.sld.cu/clinica

[17] http://mit.ocw.universia.net/ and the associated Universaria at
    http://www.universia.net/#noticias

[18] Cuban Virtual Campus at http://cuba.campusvirtualsp.org/

[19] http://regional.bvsalud.org/php/bvsnet.php?lang=en&list=countries

interactive community replicates the model of the regional VCPH in national health information systems, and connects Cuban institutions in health sciences research and education including the School of Public Health,[20] the Pedro Kourí Tropical Medicine Institute,[21] the Institute for Hygiene, Epidemiology and Microbiology,[22] the Occupational Health Institute,[23] and the Center for Development of Pharmacoepidemiology.[24] Like the Cuban Virtual University, the VCPH promotes communities of practice through a collaborative environment for creating content, sharing and developing resources throughout the national network. These shared tools and infrastructures create synergies among local, national and regional health information systems.

INFOMED also offers networked infrastructures serving evidence-based practice of medical specialties including participation in clinical trials(Reveiz *et al.*, 2011). The methodology for creation of the Paediatric Surgery National Network (Red Nacional de Cirugía Pediátrica –RENACIP) - the first such specialized network in.

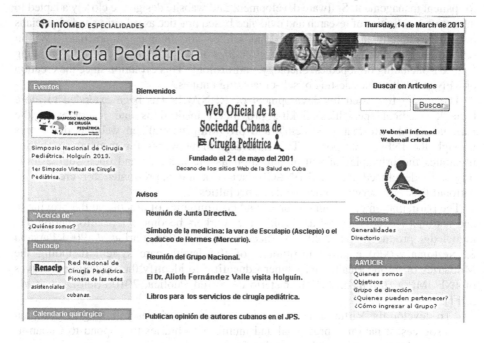

Fig. 3. The RENACIP Portal at http://www.sld.cu/sitios/renacip/(accessed 15-3-2013)

Cuba - demonstrates how human resources and technology are integrated in the Cuban model(Séror, 2006a). The institution to lead the network, the Paediatric Teaching Hospital *"Octavio de la Concepción de la Pedraja"* of Holguín, was

[20] http://www.ensap.sld.cu/
[21] http://www.ipk.sld.cu/indice1.htm
[22] http://www.inhem.sld.cu/
[23] http://www.sld.cu/sitios/insat/index.php
[24] http://www.cdf.sld.cu/

designated by the Cuban Ministry of Public Health in 2001 (Trinchet Soler & Pedrianes Vigo, 2004;Trinchet Soler, 2006). During the initial phase, the local hospital network was developed to integrate the practice of other specialties essentialto paediatric surgery, including radiology, endocrinology, and neurophysiology. The national network began with identification of experts in three regions of the country for consultation in complex cases. A discussion list was used as a tool to scale up the specialized health information system from the hospital to the national level for improved decision making, allocation of resources, and more efficient care. Figure 3 shows a screenshot of the RENACIP Portal.

Consistent with the principles of evidence-based medicine, the specialists of the national RENACIP network have identified best practice protocols through professional meetings and virtual consultation. These protocols are available to health care practitioners on the Internet[25] (Díaz Mastellari, 1999-2006). Other features of RENACIP include a portal,[26] a virtual library collection of scientific publications, and software tools for patient management. Software development and website design are closely adapted to the network activities of research and evidence based practice as scientists and physicians participate directly in website design and related communities of practice.[27] Within RENACIP, groups associated with subspecialties in paediatric surgery are also being formed – including orthopedics, oncology, and urology. This evolution since the creation of RENACIP illustrates nesting of self-organizing entities.

The model first used for development of RENACIP has been extended to more than 45 medical specialties, linking provincial institutions and resources to the national health information system[28] and providing centralized web-based services through the INFOMED portal. The extension of networks for medical specialties illustrates the principles of self-organization as the methods and open source tools originally developed for the RENACIP network are appropriated for creation of national networks serving other medical specialties.

The participation of human resources and communities of practice at the provincial and national levels is critical as health care workers become active information and knowledge producers Since 2002 a process of consultation (Earl et al., 2001;Persaud & Nestman, 2006) engages institutions of the health care system including the Ministries of Public Health and Higher Education to identify the strategic objectives of INFOMED (Infomed, 2011;Ministerio de Salud Pública, 2010;PrietoDíaz et al., 2011):

- To develop the Virtual Library as an interactive work space linking institutional resources of national, provincial and municipal libraries to respond to Cuban as well as international health care priorities.

---

[25] See the RENACIP best practice protocols at
http://www.sld.cu/galerias/doc/sitios/renacip/gbpc_aprobadas.d
oc and http://www.sld.cu/sitios/renacip/temas.php?idv=4415
[26] See the RENACIP Portal at http://www.sld.cu/sitios/renacip/
[27] See ProyectoWeb, the Cuban web design community at
http://www.proyectoweb.info/
[28] See the list of specialized networks at
http://www.sld.cu/verpost.php?blog=http://articulos.sld.cu/edi
torhome/&post_id=5257&tipo=1&opc_mostrar=2_&n=z

- To build technical, organizational and human resource infrastructures for sustainable institutional growth in information services.
- To promote publication of Cuban research in the health sciences and related disciplines for access by national and international scientific communities.
- To improve the technological and methodological infrastructures of the Virtual University serving a health education network.
- To create a system-wide health information intranet linking the Center for Health Information Sciences and networks of provincial institutions.
- To continue to develop the Cuban research base in the field of health information sciences and medical informatics.
- To foster integration of INFOMED with other national and international health information networks and infrastructures.
- To develop methodologies and protocols for continuous and systematic evaluation and control of INFOMED's performance.(Cañedo Andalia & López Espinosa, 2009;Cañedo Andalia, 2009)

These objectives guide concurrent processes of local system empowerment, centralized coordination and control through INFOMED, and growing integration of Cuban and regional infrastructures - the Virtual Library led by BIREME and the Virtual Campus for Public Health founded by PAHO. The emergence of these regional institutions has transformed the knowledge ecology of BIREME. Of particular importance for integration of regional and national health information systems is the coherence between system design and the social medicine values underpinning these infrastructures - including universal health care, open access to health information, and focus on collective social and environmental dimensions of health.

INFOMED effectively mediates a dual market system designed to protect these internal social values while creating links to external global markets beyond national boundaries. Strong research and innovation within the Cuban system contributes to productive evaluation, adaptation and integration of regional infrastructures as well as use of research results and evidence from external sources in Cuban health care.

4   Discussion and Conclusions

The embedded case analysis through the lens of complexity theory offers an understanding of the Cuban national strategy for development of virtual infrastructures supporting health care services and research. The historical evolution of both the regional and national virtual infrastructures suggests that the founding commitment to the Latin American ideological tradition of social medicine – as expressed in Cuban legislation for public health - has shaped development of both INFOMED and BIREME, and made possible the effective integration of health information networks at the regional and national levels of analysis. These systems reflect the critical importance of traditional local institutions in coordinating the transition from paper media to the open access publication model embodied in the Cuban Virtual Health Library and the regional VHL. The Cuban Virtual University has also made possible effective linkage with the VCPH. The co-evolution of regional and national health information systems including virtual libraries and universities demonstrates how open source software systems, standards and methodologies for development of infrastructure offered at the regional level are appropriated at the national level to support local scientific capacity embodied in communities of practice for education and knowledge creation. This process effectively illustrates the dynamics of nested complex systems adapting to their environment and self-organizing in INFOMED and other national health information systems.

These complex dynamics are particularly evident in the way methodologies including SciELO - associated with the regional BIREME VHL - are appropriated for development of the Cuban VHL. The same process is identified in replication of VCPH collaborative spaces for virtual classrooms, document repositories, and wikis within the Cuban VCPH and Virtual University. This process of appropriation is facilitated by the shared ideology of open source software development and open access to health information and research. The collaborative spaces of the Virtual University, the Virtual Campus for Public Health and the Virtual Library integrate the open flow of health information with the creative dynamics of scientific and professional communities of practice. Situated learning in this context also challenges the linear model of research, development, learning and practice, where researchers and practitioners are mutually engaged(Edwards, 2001;McDonald & Viehbeck, 2007).

While in other developing countries, virtual infrastructures for health care services are often designed to compensate for the lack of trained health care professionals; in the Cuban context, a high concentration of qualified multi-skilled human resources is a distinctive feature of the system. Throughout INFOMED, webmasters are often practicing physicians and scientists contributing their efforts according to a model similar to that for collaboration in open source software development. The Cuban experience suggests that this model may be useful for medical research, development and education supported by the culture of open source software communities(Benkler, 2003;Committee for Economic Development (CED), 2006;Lanzara & Morner, 2003;Maurer et al., 2004;Schweik & Semenov, 2003).

The Cuban strategy for development of INFOMED and associated virtual infrastructures for health information, education, research and service delivery is thus founded on coherency among a strong national socialist ideology, shared culture including language and literacy, universal and free access to health care, open access to health information and research in the health sciences, as well as open source software, tools and methodologies to build infrastructures, products and services. Consistent with the view of a complex system as both an open and closed, INFOMED offers a strong centralized planning process and tools for development of networks and websites-essential for network membership and system growth. The development of the methodology for creation of RENACIP illustrates a successful strategy subsequently applied to extend the model to a growing number of medical specialties with networks on a national scale. This example also reveals application of the RENACIP model to develop subspecialties within paediatric surgery.

Strategies identified in this study for development of virtual infrastructures and a national health information system are unique to the Cuban context and their transferablility to other systems requires careful evaluation of contextual factors in other developing countries as well as the industrialized world. The social medicine model promotes centralized planning and public investment in every aspect of the health care system, including health information technology and virtual infrastructures. The single payer system effectively reduces the administrative burden in the health care sector. Market dynamics and transactions pose obstacles to the free flow of information and the ease of collaboration among medical scientists, technologists and practitioners – as seen in a case comparison of the U.K. NHS and the U.S. Kaiser Permanente (Séror, 2002). Social, cultural and ideological diversity challenge the success of these strategies – as observed in the Indian national case. (Séror, 2011).

Future research efforts should focus on innovative methodologies as well as theory development for the study of large scale health information systems. Particular attention needs to focus on coevolution and integration of ideological models for social medicine and capitalist market models of national health care systems. Embedded case studies will be also useful for understanding system dynamics between national and regional levels as well as the respective roles of virtual infrastructures and communities of practice in creation of health information and knowledge. Programs of comparative case studies across regional and national systems are essential to understanding of ideology, culture and technology as determinants of sustainable global system configuration.

References

Albert, K.M.: Open Access: Implications for Scholarly Publishing and Medical Libraries. Journal of the Medical Library Association 94, 253–262 (2006)

Alliance for Health Policy and Systems Research: Strengthening Health Systems: The Role and Promise of Policy and Systems Research (2004)

Amaro, N.: Models of Development and Globalization in Cuba. ASCE, Cuba in Transition 10, 277–287 (2000)

Anonymous: An Open-Source Shot in the Arm? The Economist, (2004)

AsambleaNacionaldelPoderPopular de la República de Cuba: Ley N° 41. Ley De La SaludPública (1983)

Barrett, M., Fryatt, B., Walsham, G., et al.: Building Bridges between Local and Global Knowledge: New Ways of Working at the World Health Organisation. Knowledge Management for Development Journal 1, 31–46 (2005)

Benkler, Y.: Freedom in the Commons, Towards a Political Economy of Information. Duke Law Journal 52 (2003)

Benkler, Y.: Coase'sPenguin,Or Linux and the Nature of the Firm. Yale Law Journal 112, 369 (2002)

Benkler, Y.: The Battle Over the Institutional Ecosystem in the Digital Environment. Communications of the ACM 44, 84–90 (2001)

Bennett, A., Elman, C.: Complex Causal Relations and Case Study Methods: The Example of Path Dependence. Political Analysis 14, 250–267 (2006)

Bireme: VHL Guide (2011),
   http://guiabvs2011.Bvsalud.org/en/presentation/

BIREME: Access to Information Sources in Virtual Health Library-VHL (2008)

BIREME: Towards the Virtual Health Library (1998)

Byrne, D.: Working within a Complexity Frame of Reference- the Potential of 'Integrated Methods' for Understanding Transformation in Complex Social Systems (2009)

Campion, E.W., Morrissey, S.: A Different Model — Medical Care in Cuba. N. Engl. J. Med. 368, 297–299 (2013)

CañedoAndalia, R.: Para Comprender y Tratar El EscasoEmpleo De Los Recursos De Información Disponibles VíaInfomed Se Necesita Una PerspectivaMultidisciplinar. ACIMED 19 (2009)

CañedoAndalia,   R.,   López   Espinosa,   J.A.:   Infomed: Las AdversidadesDespiertanPotencialidadesDormidas De La Red. ACIMED 19 (2009)

CañedoAndalia, R., Pérez Machín, M., Guzmán Sánchez, M.V., et al.: Aproximaciones a La Visibilidad De La Ciencia y La ProducciónCientífica De Cuba En El Sector De La Salud. ACIMED 21 (2010)

Capote, D.G.: Surgimiento y Evolución De La Política De Ciencia y Tecnología En Cuba (1959-1995) (1996)

CITMA: Resolucion no. 59/2003 (1994)

Cockerill, M.: The Economics of Open Access Publishing. Information Services & Use 26, 151–157 (2006)

Coiera, E.: Guide to health informatics, 2nd edn. Hodder Arnold, London (2003)

Collier, D., Mahoney, J.: Insights and Pitfalls: Selection Bias in Qualitative Research. World Polit 49, 56–91 (1996)

Committee for Economic Development (CED): Open Standards, Open Source, and Open Innovation: Harnessing the Benefits of Openness (2006)

Dagnino, G.B.: Complex Systems as Key Drivers for the Emergence of a Resource- and Capability-Based Interorganizational Network. E:CO 6, 61–68 (2004)

Davis, K., Schoen, C., Stremikis, K.: Mirror, Mirror on the Wall: How the Performance of the U.S. Health Care System Compares Internationally 2010 Update. Commonwealth Fund (2010)

DíazMartínez, A.G., Abreu García, M.T., Vega Vázquez, H., et al.: Congreso: Nuevo Producto De Plone Para GestionarUnEvento Virtual. ACIMED 21 (2010)

DíazMastellari, M.: Guías De BuenasPrácticasClínicas En CirugíaPediátrica (1999-2006)

Earl, S., Carden, F., Smutylo, T.: Outcome Mapping: Building Learning and Reflection into Development Programs. IDRC (2001)

Ebener, S., Khan, A., Shademani, R., et al.: Knowledge Mapping as a Technique to Support Knowledge Translation. Bulletin of the World Health Organization 84, 636–642 (2006)

Edwards, K.: Epistemic Communities, Situated Learning and Open Source Software Development (2001)

Egbu, C., et.al.: Knowledge Mapping and Bringing about Change for the Sustainable Urban Environment (2006)

Hannan, M.: Ecologies of Organizations: Diversity and Identity. Journal of Economic Perspectives 19, 51–70 (2005)

Infomed: Acercade infomed (2011)

Jardines Méndez, J.B.: Campus Virtual De SaludPública: El ModeloEstratégico. Reunión de Trabajodel Campus Virtual de Salud (2006a)

Jardines Méndez, J.B.: Educación En Red: MuchoMás Que Educación a Distancia: Experiencia De Las UniversidadesMédicasCubanas. EducaciónMédica Superior, 20 (2006b)

Kannampallil, T.G., Schauer, G.F., Cohen, T., et al.: Considering Complexity in Healthcare Systems. J. Biomed. Inform. 44, 943–947 (2011)

Keck, C.W., Reed, G.A.: The Curious Case of Cuba. American Journal of Public Health 102, e13–e20 (2012)

Lalas Perea, R., Borroto Cruz, R., Hernández Fernández, A.: Universidad Sin Fronteras: Mito o Realidad? RevistaCubana de EducaciónMédica Superior 14, 26–35 (2000)

Lanzara, G.: &Morner, M.: The Knowledge Ecology of Open-Source Software Projects (2003)

Lavis, J., Lomas, J., Hamid, M., et al.: Assessing Country-Level Efforts to Link Research to Action. Bulletin of the World Health Organization 84, 620–628 (2006)

Maurer, S., Rai, A., Sali, A.: Finding Cures for Tropical Diseases: Is Open Source an Answer. PLoS Medicine 1, 180–183 (2004)

McDonald, P.W., Viehbeck, S.: From Evidence-Based Practice Making to Practice-Based Evidence Making: Creating Communities of (Research) and Practice. Health Promotion Practice 8, 140–144 (2007)

Meneghini, R., Mugnaini, R., Packer, A.: International Versus National Oriented Brazilian Scientific Journals: A Scientometric Analysis Based on SciELO and JCR-ISI Databases. Scientometrics 69, 529–538 (2006)

Meneghini, R., Packer, A.: Is there Science Beyond English? EMBO Reports 8, 112–116 (2007)

Ministerio de SaludPública: TransformacionesNecesarias En El Sistema De SaludPública (2010)

Morrison, K.: Searching for Causality in the Wrong Places. International Journal of Social Research Methodology 15, 15–30 (2012)

Morrison, K.: Educational Philosophy and the Challenge of Complexity Theory. In: Mason, M. (ed.) Complexity Theory and the Philosophy of Education, vol. 2, pp. 16–31. Wiley-Blackwell, Chichester (2008)

Mueller, M.: Info-Communism? Ownership and Freedom in the Digital Economy. First Monday 13 (2008)

Ofori-Adjei, D., Antes, G., Tharyan, P., et al.: Have Online International Medical Journals made Local Journals Obsolete? PLoS Medicine 3, e359 (2006)

Packer, A.: SciELO as a Model for Scientific Communication in Developing Countries: Origins, Evolution, Current Status, Management and Perspectives of the SciELO Network of Open Access Collections of Ibero-America Journals (2007)

Packer, A.: The Virtual Health Library and the Remodeling of the Health Scientific and Technical Information Flow in Latin America and the Caribbean (2000)

Persaud, D., Nestman, L.: The Utilization of Systematic Outcome Mapping to Improve Performance Management in Health Care. Health Services Management Research 19, 264–276 (2006)

PrietoDíaz, V., Quiñones La Rosa, I., RamírezDurán, G., et al.: Impacto De Las Tecnologías De La Información y Las Comunicaciones En La Educación y NuevosParadigmas Del EnfoqueEducativo. EducaciónMédica Superior 25, 95–102 (2011)

Ramírez Machado, S., RizoRodríguez, R., BodeMarín, A.: Plan Capacitante Para Desarrollar La Universidad Virtual De Salud En El Instituto Superior De CienciasMédicas De Santiago De Cuba. MEDISAN 6, 53–59 (2002)

Reimers, K., Johnston, R., Klein, S.: The Difficulty of Studying Inter-Organisational IS Phenomena on Large Scales: Critical Reflections on a Research Journey. Electronic Markets 20, 229–240 (2010)

Reveiz, L., Saenz, C., Murasaki, R.T., et al.: Avances y Retos En El Registro De EnsayosClínicos En América Latina y El Caribe. RevistaPeruana de Medicina Experimental y SaludPública 28, 676–681 (2011)

Robey, D., Boudreau, M.: Accounting for the Contradictory Organizational Consequences of Information Technology: Theoretical Directions and Methodological Implications. Information Systems Research 10, 167–185 (1999)

Rodríguez Pérez, J., Urra González, P.: AtenciónPrimaria En La RedElectrónica De Información De Salud. RevistaCubana de Medicina General Integral 12, 81–86 (1996)

Rodriguez Pina, R.A., Guerra Avila, E.: MapasConceptuales y Geo-Referencias En Productos y Servicios De InteligenciaEmpresarial. ACIMED 17 (2008)

Ruffini, M.: Using E-Maps to Organize and Navigate Online Content. Educause Quarterly 31, 56–61 (2008)

Scacchi, W., et al.: Towards a Science of Open Source Systems (2010)

Schweik, C., Semenov, A.: The Institutional Design of Open Source Programming: Implications for Addressing Complex Public Policy and Management Problems. First Monday 8 (2003)

Séror, A.: Virtual Health Care Infrastructures: Markets and Hierarchies. In: Proceedings of the 24th International Symposium on Computer-Based Medical Systems, pp. 1–6 (2011)

Séror, A.: Collaboration for Research and Education in Health Care: The Latin American and Caribbean Health Sciences System (BIREME). In: 25th International Symposium on Computer-Based Medical Systems (CBMS), pp. 1–6 (2012)

Séror, A.: Design of Virtual Infrastructures for Public and Private Services: The Indian Health Care System. In: 44th Hawaii International Conference System Sciences (HICSS), pp. 1–9 (2011)

Séror, A.: A Case Analysis of INFOMED: The Cuban National Health Care Telecommunications Network and Portal. Journal of Medical Internet Research 8, e1 (2006a)

Séror, A.: Donor Contributions to National Health Care Systems: The Role of Virtual Infrastructures in Uganda (2006b)

Séror, A.: Internet Infrastructures and Health Care Systems: A Qualitative Comparative Analysis on Networks and Markets in the British National Health Service and Kaiser Permanente. Journal of Medical Internet Research 4 (2002)

Séror, A., FachArteaga, J.: Telecommunications Technology Transfer and the Development of Institutional Infrastructure: The Case of Cuba. Telecommunications Policy 24, 203–221 (2000)

Thrift, N.: Re-Animating the Place of Thought: Transformations of Spatial and Temporal Description. In: The Twenty-First Century. International Workshop on Communities of Practice (2006)

TrinchetSoler, R.M.: El Éxito De Una Red. ACIMED 14 (2006)

Trinchet Soler, R.M., Pedrianes Vigo, M.: Origen, EstadoActual y Perspectivas De La RedNacional De CirugíaPediátrica. ACIMED 12 (2004)

Trist, E.: A Concept of Organizational Ecology. Australian Journal of Management 2, 161–171 (1977)

Urra González, P.: Las Redes De Computadoras Al Servicio De La BibliotecologíaMédica: INFOMED, Una ExperienciaCubana. ACIMED 3, 6–14 (1995)

Vidal Ledo, M.C., Febles Rodríguez, P., Estrada Sentí, C.V.: MapasConceptuales. EducaciónMédica Superior 21 (2007)

Willinsky, J.: The access principle: The case for open access to research and scholarship. Digital Libraries and Electronic Publishing, MIT Press, Boston (2006)

World Health Organization: World Health Statistics (2011)

Yin, R.: Case study research: Design and methods. 4. Sage, London (2009)

Yin, R.: Enhancing the Quality of Case Studies in Health Services Research. Health Services Research 34, 1209–1224 (1999)

Zacca González, G., Diego Olite, F., López Espinosa, J.A.: Universidad Virtual De Salud: Una Nueva Etapa. ACIMED 17 (2008)

Understanding ISD and Innovation through the Lens of Fragmentation

Michel Thomsen and Maria Åkesson

Halmstad University
Sweden
{michel.thomsen,maria.akesson}@hh.se

Abstract. Information systems development (ISD) and innovation is a complex and challenging endeavor. In this paper we inquire into the process of ISD and innovation to shed light on the ambiguous nature of such processes. This was done in an interpretive study of 10 governmental ISD projects where 14 interviews with key persons were conducted. In addition 11 interviews with senior IT consultants were conducted. Based on this study we propose an analytical lens to understand ISD and innovation. This lens is based on a metaphor grounded in the empirical material. This metaphor, *fragmentation*, mediates a deeper understanding of ISD and innovation regarding three aspects of complexity: knowledge, culture and discourse, and time and space.

Keywords: ISD, Innovation, Process ambiguity, Knowledge fragmentation.

1   Introduction

Ever since IT artifacts became strategic resources in organizational practices, information systems development (ISD) and innovation has been a challenging endeavor. As a consequence, there are seemingly never ending reports of projects not delivering on time, to budget or scope. Given this erratic practice, there are reasons to challenge our assumptions and theoretical understanding of ISD and innovation.

Digital technology has progressed to support many aspects of human life including social activities (Yoo, 2010). Our field is widening to untraditional settings, where ISD can make a difference that matters (Walsham, 2012). For example, information technology and IS research has an important role for environmental sustainability (see e.g. Elliot, 2011; Watson et al., 2010). Widened and global settings, bringing with it societal complexity gives rise to new challenges for ISD – ISD is increasingly engaging in emergent design domains and emergent design solutions.

In this paper, we refer to ISD coping with emergent design domains and emergent design solutions as ISD and innovation. Innovation is a term that widely refers to an outcome perceived as new, whether it is an idea, object, or process, as well as to the process of creating this newness (Slappendel, 1996). Digital innovation refers to innovations enabled by digital technology (Yoo et al., 2009). The newness may also be a recombination of old solutions changing established domains in such a way that it is new to the people involved (Van de Ven, 1986).

Y.K. Dwivedi et al. (Eds.): TDIT 2013, IFIP AICT 402, pp. 467–480, 2013.

We conclude that ISD and innovation is an increasingly complex and challenging endeavor. The question we address in this paper is; *How can the ambiguity of ISD and innovation be understood and gestalted?* We inquire into this and propose an analytical lens to understand the nature of ISD and innovation processes. This lens is based on a metaphor grounded in our analysis of 10 public sector projects, and interviews with senior IT consultants. Our aim is to contribute to the understanding of success and failure of ISD and innovation.

The paper proceeds as follows. First we present literature on ISD and innovation followed by a description of the research design. Thereafter we present the empirical accounts and the metaphor of fragmentation. The paper is concluded with a discussion on the findings.

2   Background on ISD and Innovation

For decades we have been guided by a variety of design ideals when developing IT artifacts. These ideals are reflected in different ISD paradigms. Hirschheim et al. (1995) identify seven generations of traditional approaches ranging from formal and structured approaches, through socio-technical, to emancipatory approaches. ISD is an ever-changing practice. Over time new models, methods, techniques, and tools have been introduced to support development processes. For example, agile development has emerged as an evolutionary approach (Abrahamsson et al., 2002; Highsmith and Cockburn, 2001). This evolution leads to new generations of approaches. These generations have been classified according to inherent structures and their paradigmatically rooted assumptions (Iivari et al., 1999).

In structured and formal approaches design domains and design solutions are considered as well established. One underlying assumption or logic underpinning traditional approaches is that systems development is a coherent and rational process in established domains, and thus can be managed to have quality, be predictable and productive (see e.g. Paulk et al., 1993; Herbsleb et al., 1997; Aaen et al., 2001; Mathiassen et al., 2007). A dominant theoretical foundation of traditional approaches is grounded in an ideal, prescribing solutions to be well organized, efficient, reliable, and esthetically pleasing.

In traditional approaches, system requirements are regarded fundamental for successful ISD. Requirements engineering is a well established line of research in IS, reaching back to when ISD became an academic subject. Much focus was put on meeting complex requirements (Larman and Basili, 2003), which among other things resulted in numerous techniques for requirement documentation. Later, from the 70´s, experimental techniques and iterative approaches were introduced. Ever since then, new techniques to identify, specify, prioritize, etc. have been suggested, as well as new approaches to risk and complexity management in ISD (see e.g. Mathiassen, et al., 2007; Taylor et al., 2012).

There is extensive literature in IS recognizing that ISD and innovation has emergent properties. Orlikowski (1996) propose an alternative perspective of organizational change related to ISD as emergent from situated actions. This perspective acknowledges that actions can be intentional, initiated improvisations to meet contextual circumstances or inadvertent slippage. Truex and Baskerville (1998) outline a theory of emergence in ISD. They suggest that there are underlying structures, which can, if they are uncovered be of guidance in ISD and recognizes change and flexibility and requirements as emergent. Truex et al. (1999) propose that organizations can be regarded as emergent rather than stable. In emergent organizations, social features (e.g. culture, meaning, social relationships, decision processes) are continuously emerging, not following any predefined pattern. These features are a result of constant negotiations, redefining the organization. Given this emergent nature of design domains and design outcomes, Truex et al. (1999) suggest a continuous redevelopment perspective on ISD.

The emergent nature of design domains is accompanied with emergent properties of ISD and innovation (Aydin et al., 2005). There are unpredictable factors that have implications for ISD that need to be continuously managed. Truex et al. (2000) describe ISD as a result of a myriad of activities that emerge more or less independently. The ISD and innovation process is described as disconnected and fragmented, and as a sequence of activities determined by emergent events. ISD and innovation has also been described as culturally differentiated, temporal and spatial, having restricting implications for knowledge sharing (Bresnen et al., 2003). These ambiguities of ISD have also been highlighted in research on project risk management (see e.g. Taylor et al., 2012). In this research ISD projects are described as having a number of dimensions linked to project risks such as uncertainty, incomplete information and complexity. Taylor et al. (2012) conclude that research findings can only be utilized in practice if they are transformed to cope with these dimensions.

In recent literature on digital innovation, processes are recognized as networked spanning organizational boundaries, and traditional industry boundaries (Yoo et al., 2012). Process coordination and control is distributed, and the nature of knowledge resources is heterogeneous (Yoo et al., 2009). Adding to the complexity is the conflicting goals of co-opetition in digital innovation (Vanhaverbeke and Cloodt, 2006). This results in highly dynamic processes, characterized not only by technical complexity, but also complex social processes within the associated networks (Van de Ven et al., 2008). Yet, the ambiguity of IDS and innovation has been recognized to be of value. In a study on digital innovation projects, Austin et al. (2012) found that accidents such as breakage, malfunction, movement outside of intention, and accepted chain of logic can be of value to achieve novel design outcomes.

Drawing on the literature review, we suggest that ISD and innovation can be regarded as ambiguous (see fig. 1). Design solutions can be established and thereby possible to prescribe with requirements, such as a replicated standard solution. However, design solutions can also be emergent, and thereby not possible to foresee or plan for in advance. This is the case with, for example, a not yet existing novel solution. Design domains can be established with well-known needs, for example a standardized governmental practice. Design domains can also be emergent, meaning that problems and needs are unknown or rather evolving, and thereby impossible or even undesirable to pre-define. This could for example be the case in novel practices or organizational environments under rapid and radical change.

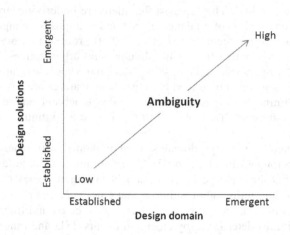

Fig. 1. ISD and innovation ambiguity

ISD of established design solutions, in established design domains, we argue is less ambiguous, while ISD of emergent solutions in emergent design domains is highly ambiguous. This argument has implications for how ISD project success and failure can be understood. With an understanding of the process as stable, predictable and thereby manageable it seems reasonable to deem projects as failures when not delivering according to budget, schedule, and scope expectations (see e.g. Sauser et al., 2009). This would be the case for ISD of established solutions in established design domains. However, understanding the process as highly ambiguous, with emergent properties not predictable and definable, the conventional assessments of delivering according to budget, schedule, and scope expectations can be inequitable.

3   Research Design

In this research we studied 10 cases of ISD projects in the Swedish public sector, and IT consultants´ experiences from public sector projects.

In the 10 public sector projects the main goal was to develop novel, tailored, or fully developed (IEEE 1062 1998) systems. The systems were all realized with aid of external IT consultants, and aimed at supporting governmental core operations. The projects lasted a minimum of 6 months, and the budgets ranged from half a million to several hundred million SEK. They were initiated around the Millennium and the last project was finalized by 2011. 8 of the 10 projects were finalized, one was abandoned and one was absorbed by a following ISD initiative. The majority of the projects can be regarded as failures in terms of not delivering on budget, schedule, or to scope expectations. In more than one case, systems lacked functions that were added post implementation. Documentation and testing were in some cases not completed. However, as mentioned above, 8 governmental organizations got their new and tailored systems implemented, even though the projects exceeded budgets or schedule.

The projects were studied through interviews with key project members employed by the governmental organizations and in leading positions such as project leaders, department managers, and senior consultant. Interviewees were selected with initial assistance of each governmental organization, suggesting individuals with deep insight into the projects. In sum, 14 key project members were interviewed. The interviews were semi-structured and lasted approximately 1.5 hours. Topics guiding the interviews were background information about the interviewee, project details, interviewee´s role in the project and cooperation, project organization, scope and outcome. The interviews also inquired into the interviewees' project experiences, accounts for problems and challenges as well as lessons learned in the projects.

In order to get external consultants´ perspective on and experience from governmental ISD projects, interviews with 11 IT consultants were conducted. The consultants were selected by the aid of management in three major IT consultant firms. Management was asked to selectively choose senior consultants with relevant experiences. Nine of the consultants were interviewed in groups by three, and two were interviewed individually. The group interviews lasted 1.5 to 2 hours and, the individual interviews 1 to 1.5 hours. The interviews were guided by the following topics: consultant roles in governmental projects, cooperation, common and reoccurring problems in ISD projects, experiences and important learnings. In total, 25 people were interviewed. All interviews were recorded with informed consent, transcribed, summarized and sent back to the interviewees for confirmation.

This research was guided by Klein and Myers (1999) principles for hermeneutic research. We initiated the analysis by organizing the empirical material according to the themes informing the inquiry into the process of ISD and innovation. The material was then interpreted to understand the ambiguity of ISD and innovation. The interpretation was done iteratively to seek patterns arising from the material as a whole. This resulted in three conceptualized themes (Walsham, 2006): *knowledge, culture and discourse* and, *time and space*. These conceptualized themes opened for a re-interpretation of the empirical material that we chose to represent in a metaphor, *fragmentation*. Metaphors are important tools for how we interpret, understand and act upon reality (Morgan, 1998; Morgan, 1980), and are powerful to help us understand complex phenomena (Lackoff and Johnson, 1980). In research, metaphors are also useful in exploration, analysis and interpretation of empirical material and for theory construction (Inns and Jones, 1996). Walsham (1993) uses the metaphors culture and political system in order to widen perspectives on development and implementation of information systems.

4   Empirical Accounts

In this section we establish the rationale for the proposed metaphor. The quotes illustrate common patterns in the empirical material – accounts of knowledge fragmentation related to culture and discourse, and to time and space.

4.1   Knowledge

ISD and innovation is knowledge intensive. On the subject of knowledge the interviewees described the challenges of satisfying the needs for knowledge on different subject areas. They also described that knowledge and competence is spread on several persons, and on different organizational levels within and outside of the government. When identifying knowledge and competence needs in a project, a holistic view was emphasized. One interviewee described it as follows:

> One has to consider the whole process, It is not enough to have a god business lawyer, it is not enough to have a good requirement specification, it is not enough to have a committed project leader, it is not enough to have the technical competence, and it is not enough to hire a competent consultant.

Further, the knowledge need concerning the specific governmental application area was emphasized. One interviewee put it like this:

> Apart from knowing what you want to develop, which data to store, which output and the effects for the customer, you must also master the rules for the governmental operation.... You also need to know the organization if you as we did, also change the organization.

Another theme that appeared in the interviews was the need to match knowledge and competence to decide if a suggested design solution was feasible or not, as illustrated by this quote:

> As a manager of operations you are not able to decide whether a suggested design solution is feasible or not. You know the conditions related to your field of competence and for example clarify what rules that might change during the process and how that affects the coming system. ... That in turn requires that you have sufficient dialogue with the IT people so that they can help one understand and explain what the consultants are speaking about.

Even if knowledge needs seemed to be clear in the beginning of projects, they changed when projects were confronted with problems. One interviewee described this as:

> It was very vulnerable because they were programming continuously. We also exchanged consultants a few times, with more adequate programming skills. The consultants thought they were doing the right things, and we thought they were on track. However, after a while when we tested it became apparent that we all were wrong about the correctness of calculations.

One of the experienced consultants described how the complexity of knowledge needs in ISD is increasing:

> 25 years ago you knew everything after 2-3 years in IT business. Today, you only manage to keep up and stay competent in a niched area, so you have to cooperate with a lot of other people to be able to accomplish things. Reality is so much more complex today.... there are hundreds of things you need to know, and if you don't have support for that you will miss out of things and make mistakes, that's just the way it is.

Regarding different types of knowledge, the interviewees described the need for a blend between practical, theoretical, and social skills and knowledge. Interviewees made statements relating to explicit knowledge (regulations, rules etc.), individual knowledge (e.g. personal insights), conditional knowledge (e.g. knowing when to make a decision), relational knowledge (e.g. knowing who can help), and procedural knowledge (e.g. on project management).

As illustrated, quotes reflect the need for knowledge in different areas, and the need for different types of knowledge. One consultant claimed that:

> *As a customer you cannot know everything, but you have to know where to get help and what is needed, and be able to take it in.*

For example, social or relational knowledge is needed for the identification and involvement of people with essential knowledge on different subject areas:

> *Anita, the project leader, managed to recruit skilled people working in different areas. Some from our head office with competence on general operations, some from our regional offices, the end users, and our own specialists holding specific knowledge required for the system.*

Interviewees stressed the need for social skills and ability to coordinate. One governmental official described this as:

> *In most projects there are relationships to two and maybe three stakeholders that needs to be coordinated. They can be for example an external consultant, an internal IT department, and governmental officials. Somebody needs to have the competence to manage and coordinate these different stakeholders. Such a person has to be flexible and responsive, and must really be know some about each area, and also be a skilled negotiator between the involved stakeholders.*

Another example is externalizing tacit knowledge on governmental operations important to design solutions according to expectations and needs. One consultant described it as:

> *The problem is that it is very difficult to describe what is in the head of the managers, and then design it. It is really all that is in their head that they actually want.*

A final example of need for different types of knowledge is exemplified is the need for explicit knowledge related to the specific design domain. One governmental official gave the following example:

> *I have to know the European regulations for this government to be able to sort and clear out what to include in the system. I must be able to organize that in order to show the consultants what rules that could be of value and can be built into the system.*

The quotes illustrate that ISD and innovation span over several and different knowledge areas, for example, knowledge on requirement specifications and competence to communicate operational needs, and to describe operations and existing IT systems. Some other examples are knowledge to formulate project goals, ability to express specific domain knowledge, knowledge on project management, legal requirements, and on being a competent negotiator.

4.2   Culture and Discourse

Regarding culture and discourse, interviewees described that lack of understanding of different cultures and differing vocabularies caused problems in the projects. One example of a cultural collision that one interviewee described was between seniors from the internal IT department and external consultants in one of the projects:

> Young people between 25 and 30 were supposed to discuss and solve problems together with the COBOL-people in their 50´s and 60´s. None of them understood each other, and there I was in the middle trying to over bridge the gap.

Another example of a cultural collision leading to miscommunication was between department staff and consultants as described by one interviewee:

> It was quite an irritated situation here for about 6 months before we got things to work. The governmental department staff reacted on the consultant being to technically orient in the dialogues. I think so too, but after a while I understood that it was his way of communicating. To understand that we speak different languages was an important insight for me. However, at the department they thought he was difficult to deal with. For example, when something went wrong in the system, he started to draw tables and stuff to explain, but the department staff was totally uninterested, they did not understand.

Differing vocabularies between stakeholders and the ability to deal with that in ISD was another distinct theme in the interviews. One interviewee described how there is a risk of misconceptions if this is not dealt with.

> It is always an advantage in the relation between people, clients and consultants, if you have the same vocabulary. When we sit and talk there might be words that mean one thing for us, and another for somebody else, that is, we use the same word for different things. Since I have a broad education I realize this. I sometime think that this guy is probably talking about this and not that. He is not talking about the same thing as I, and then you realize hey, now we are talking about different things, even though we use the same words.

Incomprehensible vocabulary was portrayed by one governmental official in terms of:

> *There is a certain jargon. Sometimes I had to stress, hey now you are talking to me you know... It was Greek to me when they were talking about their packages, tables and whatever they talk about. The system models are really designed for someone who knows a lot about systems development.*

These quotes illustrate that interviewees talked about cultural gaps and clashes, language barriers, disruptive jargon, lack of mutual understanding, misconceptions, unfamiliar work practices, etc. To sum it up, the majority of interviewees expressed that differences in culture and discourse is problematic.

4.3   Time and Space

Regarding time and space, a common pattern in the interviews was that the coordination of time between the project and everyday business was challenging. One interviewee said that this was the most pressing about participating in the project. The interviewee gave the following advice on the subject:

> *One advice is to make sure your closest manager realizes how much time your engagement in the project will take, and make sure that you are given that time to do it. That is what I think has been most pressing. I have spent hundreds of hours on this project during these years, but these hours have never been part of any plan.*

Another interviewee described the dilemma as follows:

> *This was one of the first really large projects we started and we really did not have the time required to do it. It is always difficult to allocate time when you are in the middle of every day operations.*

During the time a project is ongoing, unexpected things happen. This has implications for how the project proceeds. One interviewee told a story about how key people left the project, and the consequences it had for the project.

> *We started with a small project organization where I was project leader with four department staff. After a while they quit, one by one. In the end, there was only me and the consultant left, and then we had come so far in the project that it was no use trying to recruit someone else. So it was very heavy. I was in a situation where I had to manage business as usual full time as well as to run this project. There was no one with IT skills in those days, and thus no understanding for this taking time.*

Time pressure was also a source for communication problems in the projects. One interviewee expressed the difficulty of finding time to communicate with people not engaged in the process.

> *The time pressure sometimes made I difficult to find time to inform about project progression, and to find time to discuss with other colleagues not directly engaged in the project.*

The majority of interviewees stated that they wished more time for dialogue and inte-raction, and that the governmental organizations would have allocated more time for those engaged in the projects.

Another distinct theme in the interview material was the distribution of knowledge and competence between locations. This was considered to have consequences for the availability of resources when needed, as illustrated by this quote:

> *The consultancy firm we hired was taken over by a competitor, and consul-tants were exchanged, and that really did not make things better you know.*

Another example related to time and space is that experiences from one project, had implications for the project at hand. This was exemplified as follows by one of the interviewees:

> *We had difficulties cooperating because the consultant had worked with the tax authorities, and I think he made many parallels from that experience. Sometimes I had to remind him that now you are in this government and you cannot transfer things just like that.*

One of the consultants shared the following reflection on IT projects from a general point of view:

> *IT projects is like everything else in society. It is not like you can state in the beginning how things are going to be and decide how it is going to be. It is not like you will never make mistakes along the way. It is constantly under change. We work in a changing world, we learn, we learn to be attentive to problems. We work with people, some people structure their thoughts in cer-tain ways, others in other ways. You design something and some think the design is good. A new person starts and says it not possible to use.*

In sum, the quotes illustrate how people described aspects of time and space. Inter-viewees described how people were occupied with other things, spread on different locations, moved around, were exchanged, not having access to competence, being under time pressure etc. Experiences developed over time, in other spaces, was also a theme that interviewees talked about having implications for the ISD and innovation process.

5   The Metaphor of Fragmentation

In gestalting our interpretations we propose the metaphor of *fragmentation*. Fragmen-tation embraces three conceptual themes identified in the empirical material: *know-ledge, culture and discourse* and, *time and space*. We acknowledge that knowledge, culture and discourse, time and space are interdependent phenomena, but for the sake of clarity of our interpretations we treat them separately.

The analysis of the empirical material led us to three notable interpretations concerning knowledge:

- the need for knowledge and competence on different subject areas, and the need for different types of knowledge
- client respectively consultant incapacity to span over all relevant knowledge domains
- knowledge and competence specialized and inherent in one or a few key persons, knowledge and competence split between several persons, inherent in people in different locations, and on different organizational levels within as well as outside the organizations

To sum it up; we identified design domains and situations dependent on a blend of skills, capabilities, explicit knowledge including tacit knowing. The latter created by and inherent in the individual, in contrast to (social) knowledge created by and inherent in ISD-project members collective actions (see e.g. Alavi and Leidner, 2001).

The aim here is not to penetrate or to discuss categorization or labeling of knowledge, it is merely to illustrate that ISD and innovation requires complex and multifaceted knowledge and competence that challenges interorganizational and organizational systems.

The analysis of the empirical material led us to three notable interpretations concerning culture and discourse, and three interpretations concerning time and space.

Our interpretations concerning culture and discourse point out:

- cultural clashes and discursive gaps,
- communication breakdowns,
- asymmetries of knowledge and diverging expectations.

Our interpretations concerning time and space reflect:

- project members having a hard time to keep up with project tasks and their every day work
- project members, consultants and competent colleagues that were too busy to aid when problems emerged, or competent people that were moved to solve non project specific problems in other locations,
- knowledge spread over time and space, and thereby not activated in projects problem solving.

Our study portrays ISD and innovation as temporal, spatial and culturally differentiated. The study also point out that the knowledge required in ISD and innovation is multifaceted, heterogeneous and too complex to hold for an individual, possibly even for an organization (compare e.g. Bresnen et al., 2003; Yoo et al., 2009). The empirically grounded metaphor – *fragmentation* – captures critical characteristics of ISD and innovation. Moreover, the metaphor mediates an understanding of three sources of complexity and ambiguity: knowledge, culture and discourse and time and space. We believe *fragmentation* to be useful as an analytical lens to understand the nature of ISD and innovation.

6   Discussion and Conclusions

The overall aim of this paper is to contribute to the understanding of success and failure of ISD and innovation. In particular, this research contributes to our understanding of the nature of such processes. While many studies have focused on for example software process improvement, requirement engineering, critical success factors, heuristics or best practices, limited research has been devoted to frameworks (see e.g. Sauser et al., 2009) that provide us with deeper understanding of ISD and innovation. In this paper we propose the metaphor of fragmentation as an analytical lens to understand the nature of ISD and innovation processes. The metaphor provides a tool to interpret, understand and act upon process ambiguity.

In this paper we argue that processes in emergent design domains aiming at emergent design solutions are highly ambiguous. This implies that conventional assessments of delivering according to budget, schedule, and scope expectations can be misleading. If we recognize ISD and innovation processes as fragmented, we need to explore other dimensions of assessments; assessment dimension that are not based on the dominant logic that processes and design outcomes are predictable, rational and standardizable between design domains. Alternative or complementary dimensions of assessments could for example be more focused on the innovativeness of design solutions and implications in the design domain. This being said, we of course recognize that there are limits to how much resources that organizations are willing to risk and spend on ISD and innovation.

If we accept the gestalt of ISD and innovation as of nature fragmented, it has implications for ISD practice. Firstly, it is of significance for how we design and evaluate ISD models, methods, techniques and tools. Secondly, it is of significance for how we contextualize these to emergent design domains. It seems reasonable that we need approaches that on one hand can reduce destructive fragmentation, and on the other hand enhance valuable ditto to reach emergent design outcomes (see e.g. Austin et al., 2012). The latter is important to reflect on, given a future where ISD and innovation is widening into emergent design domains and emergent design solutions. In this paper we have argued that this direction is accompanied with increased process ambiguity. In our future research, we aim to investigate the explanatory capacity of the metaphor on novel digital innovation initiatives in public transport and health sectors.

References

Aaen, I., Arent, J., Mathiassen, L., Ngwenyama, O.: A conceptual MAP of software process improvement. Scandinavian Journal of Information Systems 13, 81–102 (2001)

Abrahamsson, P., Salo, O., Ronkainen, J., Warsta, J.: Agile Software Development Methods: Review and Analysis. VTT Electronics, VTT Publikation 478 (2002)

Alavi, M., Leidner, D.E.: Knowledge Management and Knowledge Management Systems: Conceptual Foundations and Research Issues. MIS Quarterly 25(1), 107–136 (2001)

Austin, R.D., Devin, L., Sullivan, E.E.: Supporting Valuable Unpredictability in the Creative Process Organization. Science 23(5), 1505–1522 (2012)

Aydin, M.N., Harmsen, F., Slooten van, K., Stegwee, R.A.: On the Adaptation of An Agile Information Systems Development Method. Journal of Database Management Special issue on Agile Analysis, Design, and Implementation 16(4), 20–24 (2005)

Bresnen, M., Edelman, L., Newell, S., Scarbrough, H., Swan, J.: Social practices and the management of knowledge in project environments. International, Journal of Project Management 21(3), 157–166 (2003)

Elliot, S.: Transdisciplinary perspectives on environmental sustainability: a resource base and framework for it-enabled business transformation. MIS Quarterly 35(1), 197–236 (2011)

Herbsleb, J., Zubrow, D., Goldenson, D., Hayes, W., Paulk, M.C.: Software quality and the capability maturity model. Communications of the ACM 40(6), 31–40 (1997)

Highsmith, J., Cockburn, A.: Agile software development – the business of innovation. Computer 34(9), 120–127 (2001)

Hirschheim, R., Klein, H., Lyytinen, K.: Information Systems Development and Data Modeling: Conceptual and Philosophical. Foundations. Cambridge University Press, UK (1995)

Iivari, J.: Information systems development as knowledge work: The body of systems development process knowledge. In: Kawaguchi, E., Kangassalo, H., Hamid, I.A., Jaakkola, H. (eds.) Proceedings of the 9th European-Japanese Conference on Information Modelling and Knowledge Bases, pp. 55–71. Iwate Prefectural University, Morioka (1999)

Inns, D.E., Jones, P.J.: Metaphor in organization theory: Following in the footsteps of the poet? I. In: Grant, D., Oswick, C. (eds.) Metaphor and Organizations, pp. 110–126. SAGE, London (1996)

Klein, H.K., Myers, M.D.: A set of principles for conducting and evaluating interpretive field studies in information systems. MIS Quarterly 23(1), 67–93 (1999)

Lakoff, G., Johnson, M.: Metaphors we live by. University of Chicago Press, Chicago (1980)

Larman, C., Basili, V.: Iterative and incremental development: A brief history. I: Computer 36(6), 47–56 (2003)

Mathiassen, L., Saarinen, T., Tuunanen, T., Rossi, M.: A contingency model for requirements development. I: Journal of the AIS 8(11), 569–597 (2007)

Morgan, G.: Paradigms, metaphors and puzzle solving in organization theory. Administrative Science Quarterly 25, 605–622 (1980)

Morgan, G.: An afterword: Is there anything more to be said about metaphors? In: Grant, D., Oswick, C. (eds.) Metaphor and Organization, pp. 227–240. Sage, London (1996)

Orlikowski, W.J.: Improvising Organizational Transformation Over Time: A Situated Change Perspective. I: Information Systems Research (7), 63–92 (1996)

Sauser, B.J., Reilly, R.R., Shenhar, A.J.: Why projects fail? How contingency theory can provide new insights. International Journal of Project Management 27(7), 665–679 (2009)

Paulk, M.C., Curtis, B., Chrissis, M.B.: Capability Maturity Model for Software v. 1.1. Technical Report, CMU/SEI-93-TR-024. Software Engineering Institute, Pittsburgh, PA (1993)

Slappendel, C.: Perspectives on Innovation in Organizations. Organization Studies 17(1), 107–129 (1996)

Taylor, H., Artman, E., Woelfer, J.P.: Information Technology Projekt Risk Management: Bridging the Gap Between Research and Practice. Journal of Information Technology 27, 17–34 (2012)

Truex, D., Baskerville, R.: Deep Structure or Emergence Theory:Contrasting Theoretical Foundations for Information SystemsDevelopment. Information Systems Journal 8, 99–118 (1998)

Truex, D., Baskerville, R., Klein, H.: Growing Systems in Emergent Organizations. I: Communications of the ACM (42), 117–123 (1999)

Truex, D., Baskerville, R., Travis, J.: Amethodical systems development: the deferred meaning of systems development methods. Accounting, Management & Information Technology 10, 53–79 (2000)

Van de Ven, A.H.: Central Problems in the Management of Innovation. Management Science 32(5), 590–607 (1986)

Van de Ven, A.H., Polley, D., Garud, R., Venkatraman, S.: The innovation journey. Oxford University Press, New York (2008)

Vanhaverbeke, W., Cloodt, M.: Open Innovation in Value Networks. In: Chesbrough, H., Vanhaverbeke, W., West, J. (eds.) Open Innovation: Researching a New Paradigm, pp. 258–281. Oxford University Press, Oxford (2006)

Walsham, G.: Are we making a better world with ICTs? Reflections on a future agenda for the IS field. JIT 27(2), 87–93 (2012)

Walsham, G.: Doing interpretative research. European Journal of Information Systems 15, 320–330 (2006)

Walsham, G.: Reading the organization: metaphors and information Management. Journal of Information Systems 3, 33–46 (1993)

Watson, R.T., Boudreau, M.-C., Chen, A.J.W.: Information Systems and environmentally sustainable development: Energy Informatics and new directions for the IS community. MIS Quarterly 34(1), 23–38 (2010)

Yoo, Y., Lyytinen, K., Boland, R.J.: Innovation in the Digital Era: Digitization and Four Classes of Innovation Networks. Working Paper, Temple University (2009)

Yoo, Y., Boland, R.J., Lyytinen, K., Majchrzak, A.: Organizing for Innovation in the Digitized World. Organization Science 23(5), 1398–1408 (2012)

Yoo, Y.: Computing in everyday life: A call for research on experiential computing. MIS Quarterly 34(2), 213–231 (2010)

IT Innovation Squeeze: Propositions
and a Methodology for Deciding
to Continue or Decommission Legacy Systems

G.R. Gangadharan[1], Eleonora J. Kuiper[2],
Marijn Janssen[3], and Paul Oude Luttighuis[4]

[1] IDRBT, Hyderabad, India
grgangadharan@idrbt.ac.in
[2] Belastingdienst, Apeldoorn, Netherlands
ej.kuiper@belastingdienst.nl
[3] Delft University of Technology, Delft, Netherlands
M.F.W.H.A.Janssen@tudelft.nl
[4] Novay, Enschede, Netherlands
paul.oudeluttighuis@novay.nl

Abstract. Organizations have been confronted with fast moving developments in the Information Technology (IT) sector over the past decades. Many new technological paradigms have emerged and left a landscape of legacy in which more and more money is spent on maintaining this landscape at the expense of innovating. Especially where business requirements put time pressure on the evolution of the IT landscape the decision whether to continue and maintain legacy systems or to decommission legacy systems in time has become a huge challenge. We formulate a set of propositions influencing the decision to decommission or continue legacy systems. This set of propositions is derived from literature and interviews with high level managers of organizations. Software characteristics, development methods, dependency of systems, lock-in, system complexity, new technologies and system ownership influence the decision whether to decommission or to maintain a system. We conclude this paper by proposing a methodology that helps organizations in finding the right balance between discontinuing and maintaining legacy systems.

1   Introduction

As systems are more and more connected with each other, both inside and outside organizations, they become more dependent on each other. The more dependencies, the more difficult these systems can be replaced. Application portfolio management is a means to manage the system landscape (Jeffery and Leliveld, 2004, McFarlan, 1981, Hamilton, 1999). Information technology portfolio management is the management of IT as a portfolio of assets similar to a financial portfolio (Jeffery and Leliveld, 2004). In a portfolio management approach decisions on whether to invest in IT and to decommission systems are made. Portfolios often contain an overview of existing systems and the budget spend on it. The control and maintenance of these

Y.K. Dwivedi et al. (Eds.): TDIT 2013, IFIP AICT 402, pp. 481–494, 2013.

existing legacy systems take away a significant and increasing portion of the total information technology (IT) budget. There is a continuous increase in spending on controlling and maintaining legacy systems since the 1960s and organizations are focusing less on IT innovation. All activities not related to the control and maintenance of the existing IT landscape are referred to as IT innovation in this paper. As such we take a very broad view on IT innovation, as it includes all activities related to the change of the existing IT-landscape. Our focus is on budget, but also without any budget innovation can be accomplished. Although we acknowledge this, this factor is not taken into account in this study. IT innovation can cover a broad range of activities and can take many forms including making business processes into automated IT functions, developing applications that open new markets, or implementing desktop virtualization. Some organizations spend up to 80% of their IT budget on keeping legacy systems running, leaving only 20% for innovation (Glass, 2006). If this trend is not reversed there might be hardly any budget available for innovating and developing new IT. This phenomenon is termed the *IT innovation squeeze*, since innovation is squeezed out by the existing IT landscape (Gangadharan, Kuiper and Oude Luttighuis, 2010).

According to Hillenius (2006) a pension company spent about 75% of its IT budget on maintenance as follows. Half of the total amount was spent on maintenance of the hardware and network infrastructure. Keeping applications running took another quarter. New projects and adapting the IT to new rules and regulations required the remaining quarter. A United States university reported that the cost of software maintenance of its ERP system was increasing 50% per year and the maintenance costs of its CISCO systems increased 12% to 15% per year (Lowe, 2009). Jones (2007) estimated the yearly maintenance cost prospects for software projects for the first five years of maintenance ahead, related to the development costs. He reported an average 860 USD maintenance costs per 1,000 USD development costs per year, as well as a worst case, in which 1,116 USD maintenance costs were required per 1,200 USD development costs per year. The maintenance costs increased at a rate of 20% per year, yielding ever worse figures when the time horizon extended beyond five years. Other studies demonstrated the increase of the relative costs of software maintenance over the years. See Table 1 for figures over the years 1980 – 2000.

Table 1. Gradual increase of relative software maintenance costs

Study	Relative software maintenance costs
Erikh (2000)	> 90%
Eastwood (1993)	75%
Port (1988)	60-70%
Lientz and Swanson (1980)	> 50%

All these figures indicate a tendency that over the years an increasing percentage of budgets is spent on controlling and maintaining existing IT. So far we have not found organizations in literature or in practice with a decreasing percentage of budget, spent on existing IT. If the maintenance activity of existing systems continues to outpace new software development on contemporary platforms, eventually no resources will be left to develop new systems, thereby causing a legacy crisis in organizations

(Iyer, 2008). IT budget imbalance between maintenance and innovation is skewed heavily towards maintenance in environments dominated by large legacy systems. This imbalance is often cited as one of the main limitations in freeing-up resources to take a fresh approach to the question of applications agility, which is the capability to rapidly and efficiently adapt applications to change (Tsang, 2002, Gordon, 2004, Heydebreck et al., 2000).

A legacy system is an information system that is built in the past using technology of that time, and that continues to be used, even though the technology has been succeeded by newer technology (Linthicum, 1999). We will use the term existing IT to denote information systems (IS) and information technology (IT) systems, present in the organization's IS/IT landscape, and new IT for IS and IT systems, that are to be procured, sourced or developed in-house. Changes to one part of these existing systems inevitably involve changes to other components. These systems are often maintained because it is too risky to replace them (Bisbal, Lawless, Wu, and Grimson, 1999) and new software development projects are often expensive and risky (Yeo, 2002).

Maintenance and decommissioning of existing systems become a huge problem where business requirements put pressure on the evolution of organization's IS/IT landscape. To provide insight into this issue, we will analyze propositions that influence decommissioning and maintenance of existing systems in this paper.

The salient contributions of this paper are as follows.

- Propositions that influence decommissioning and maintenance of existing IT systems in organizations are identified based on literature study and interviews conducted.
- A methodology, by which the balance between existing and new IT can be measured, describing the governance of existing and new IT systems in organizations, is presented. This methodology contributes to the theory on portfolio management, see for instance (Blume, 1970).

The remainder of this paper is organized as follows. In section 2, we provide the research methodology. In section 3 we describe the findings from literature that influence the decision to decommission or maintain, and we illustrate these propositions with statements from interviews. Section 4 addresses the way to measure the imbalance between existing systems and to-be new systems and proposes a methodology to govern these systems, followed by concluding remarks in section 5.

2   Research Methodology

Propositions influencing maintenance were identified using literature research. As the fields of software maintenance research and organizational economics research exist for decades and a lot of research is still going on, we had a considerable amount of literature for our research questions. We have extensively searched using multiple relevant keywords in various internet resources including IEEE, ACM, Elsevier, and Springer repositories. New articles are also discovered from the bibliographies of relevant publications, and by searching who references a particular relevant publication. Then, we have shortlisted the literature that we considered useful to form our propositions. As literature often mentions these propositions but did not explain them in detail we opted from organizing discussions with five domain experts and conducting twenty face-to-face interviews with high level managers of large IT user organizations. Thus we have applied triangulation (Denzin, 2006) by using literature and interviews with experts and practitioners. The domain experts were selected based on their experiences in the field of maintenance and decommissioning of legacy systems and technology management. Their inputs and suggestions helped us to further refine the propositions. The organizations interviewed include the following. three government organizations, one energy company, one consultancy firm, one pension fund company, two banks, and two insurance companies. These organizations typically have a large IT center to serve the business needs. In total twenty interviewees were interviewed representing ten different organizations.

The interviews were semi-structured using an interview protocol. Each interview took between one to two hours. In the interview protocol the following elements were addressed: introduction, current practices related to costs and benefits of IT, decision-making on decommissioning, the role of architecture, budget spending, the requirements for managing the IT portfolio, and improvement mechanisms for having a healthy balance between existing systems and to-be proposed systems. The interview questionnaire is given in the appendix. Transcripts were made of all the interviews. The interview reports were validated with the interviewees by sending the report to the interviewees and asking them for comments. Then the reports were updated and archived.

Overall we followed the deductive approach by defining propositions from the literature and we followed an inductive approach by verifying these propositions using the semi-structured interviews.

3   Influencing Propositions on Maintenance and Decommission of Existing Systems: Theory and Practice

In this section, we present propositions (P1 – P7), influencing the decommission and maintenance of legacy systems as found in literature. By conducting interviews, we were able to relate these propositions to the practice in large IT user organizations. We used interviews to refine the propositions and selected statements from the interview reports as illustrations for some of the propositions found in literature.

P1—Software Characteristics Affect System Maintenance

There has been a great deal of speculation about what makes a software system more difficult to maintain. System size, system age, number of input/output data items, application type, programming language, and degree of structure were the characteristics that make system maintenance difficult (Martin and McClure, 1983).

Larger systems require more maintenance effort than smaller systems, because of a lengthier learning curve associated with larger systems, and larger systems are more complex in terms of the variety of functions they performed. Furthermore errors and code, that required changing, are more difficult to find in larger systems.

The length of the source code is the main determinant of total cost during maintenance as well as initial development. For example, a 10% change in a module of 200 lines of code is often more expensive than a 20% change in a module of 100 lines of code (Van Vliet, 2000). There were an estimated 120 billion lines of source code in legacy systems being maintained in 1990 (Ulrich, 1990). According to (Sommerville, 2000), this amount of code doubled (250 billion lines) in 2000.

In general, programs written in high-level languages are easier to understand and to modify than their lower level counterparts. Some programming languages, such as Java, are independent of the operating system, making it easier to adapt the program to changes in its hardware and software environment.

Applying software engineering design principles, such as information hiding and encapsulation, make software easier to maintain. Adopting loose coupling, high cohesion, and fewer internal dependencies facilitate constant change and revision even during development (Parnas, 2011). An illustration for proposition P1: *"Built with data-driven programming languages, generally it is not possible or difficult to extract business content from existing legacy systems"*. The architecture of such existing systems prohibits the design of new solutions to monitor business processes.

P2—Different System Development Methods Imply Different Maintenance Efforts

Maintenance is heavily impacted by the methods used to develop a system (Erdil et al., 2003). Iterative development requires maintenance at every cycle when a working system is being developed. This avoids bugs in the systems. Agile development methodologies tend not to favor extensive documentation, thus complicating maintenance at a later stage. However, agile methodologies signify corrective and perfective maintenance (Cohen, Lindvall and Costa, 2003).

In component-based software development, system developers do not have access to the source code. Hence, maintenance and evolution of the component are controlled by a third party. In a case study (Pree, 1997) it was found that a few changes (12%) on a single component increased the reuse cost by 55% compared to the development of the particular component built from scratch. Reuse may have saved time, but may have also increased the risk of corruption or unreliability due to interactions, making the maintenance process more difficult. A catalogue of the different components had to be kept, and the developers and maintainers needed a good understanding of the different interfaces and the intricacies of the system.

An illustration for proposition P2: *"With their interfaces written with rigid functionality, legacy systems cause business silos"*, suggesting that organizations reap higher returns when they reuse existing software components and data. Without adequate interface linking systems, reusability is inhibited. The process behind the existing legacy systems could be exposed as well defined and wrapped as services. Existing legacy systems could be redesigned using services based on service oriented computing concepts. Integration techniques including presentation integration, business logic integration, and data integration extend the life of legacy systems.

P3—The Risk of Decommission Increases When the Dependency of Systems Increases

Dependencies between system modules play a major role in maintenance. This is due to the fact that changes propagate through dependencies. When a system module is modified, it is possible that other modules dependent on this module will also need to be modified (Ohlsson et al., 1999). The likelihood of a change affecting other modules increases with the number of dependencies a module has. As systems grow more complex and large, the significance of dependency management grows as well (Guo, 2002).

Impact analysis involves the tracing through any relationships defined on an artifact and identifies the targets of the relationships. This impact analysis results in a list of dependencies that the given artifact depends on. From the perspective of requirements engineering, dependencies on goal, service, condition, time, task, infrastructure, and use are identified (Khan, Greenwood, Gracia and Rashid, 2008). From the business perspective, portfolio dependency, contractual dependency, and change, risk and compliance dependency are crucial for system maintenance (Wegener, 2007). It is very important to explore the interrelationships among existing systems and to analyze the impact of the systems that are to be decommissioned on other systems. One comment of an interviewee illustrates proposition P3: *"Legacy systems are added with new features as required by an organization. New modules are designed to be interconnected with other systems of the organization"*. This statement explicitly shows that legacy systems become difficult to maintain and decommission due to their dependencies with other systems.

P4—Lock-Ins Increase the Risk of Decommission

Various forms of lock-in by vendors, based on knowledge, contract, and technology, may have made organizational systems dependent on a particular set of vendors or proprietary technologies. Traditional software and component contracts or licenses deny the rights to access future versions by consumers. Most organizations feel that running unsupportable software and hardware systems cost more to maintain than to replace (Cohen, Lindvall and Costa, 2003).

Many organizations prefer to adopt single vendor software and infrastructure (Kauffman and Tsai, 2009). Then their decommissioning becomes heavily dependent on the vendor's product release strategy. Although this causes problems during decommissioning, organizations do not prefer to adopt multiple vendor-based solutions as this increases the number of contracts and maintenance costs.

The effect of lock-ins on the balance between existing and new IT may go either way. Organizations may be forced by vendors to decommission systems because product releases are not supported any more, or the organizations may opt for expensive maintenance contracts for products, which are no longer officially supported by the vendor. An illustration for proposition P4: *"Suppliers enforce renewal and phase out."* This interview statement indicates that once an organization is in a lock-in situation, the organization may be forced to decommission due to the product release strategy of the suppliers. Forced decommission may increase the risk of decommission, because the organization might not be ready to decommission due to other priorities and limited resources.

P5—The More Complex the System, the Higher the Risk of Decommission

As of 2007 the software industry uses some 600 different programming languages and about 120 kinds of software applications (Jones, 2007). Software applications are built using 26 different development methods that include at least 35 different activities. The software industry faces 24 kinds of complexity and performed 23 different kinds of maintenance activities. The plethora of choices and alternatives in software systems enable one to select whatever may fit the situation at hand. However, these approaches make different silos of systems in an organization and make maintenance complex at later stages.

An empirical survey (Banker, Datar, Kemerer and Zweig, 1993) reports that the high level of software complexity accounts for 25% maintenance costs or more than 17% of total life cycle costs. A study of twenty projects by Reifer, Basili, Boehm and Clark (2003) reports that maintenance costs and complexity increase exponentially as the number of packages increased in a components-based system.

Most organizations already have a complex IT environment. As the costs and risks associated with decommisioning these systems are usually high (Aversano, Canfora, Cimitile and De Lucia, 2001), organizations opt for adding new systems instead.

An illustration for proposition P5 is the following interview statement: *"Logically projects with a high business value and a low risk get a higher priority. "*This statement indicated that some organizations tended to avoid risks, and would only accept risk when the business value was high. For many decommissioning projects, however, the business value was not well known by business managers. When risks were high and business values unclear, decommissioning was avoided.

P6—The Rapid Emergence of New Technologies Makes Systems Obsolete Early

As new technologies emerge very fast, systems turn obsolete early. Because it is unclear how long new technologies will remain, it is hard to claim that adopting new technologies lowers maintenance costs in the future. Castro-Leon, He, Chang and Peiravi (2009) suggest that costs can be managed through aggressive "treadmill" of technology adoption, but this did not fix the general uptrend. Not many organizations are willing or even capable of sustaining this technology innovation schedule. Those organizations, which could not maintain a high speed of decommissioning, ended up with a higher balance between existing and new IT.

A large number of comments were made showing the support for P6 and its importance. *"When something new is introduced you would need to ask the business the question: What will you replace and what is the added value to the organization?"*. Another interviewee commented *"Decisions on rationalizing the portfolio are not just for the IT department, but must be taken in a broader context. Because no extra functionality is delivered, and because of the focus on going concern, the business is not always convinced of the usefulness of rationalizing. "* and

"It proves to be very difficult for the business to say goodbye to systems, since decommissioning also costs money. "

All three statements indicate that the interaction between business and IT is often not sufficient for effective decommissioning. Both business and IT people were often more focused on new functionality and technology rather than on decommissioning existing functionality. The fact that decommissioning of IT systems first requires investments before it saves costs, is sometimes sufficient to prevent decommissioning of systems. One interviewee provided a suggestion for dealing with this.*"In our organization we work with the principle: When something new comes, something else has to go. Earlier we used a ratio that for each new application three existing applications had to be decommissioned, unless the business could convince us to act otherwise."* Using this principle this organization managed to cut down the application portfolio from 3000 applications to 600 over a period of 4½ year. This organization managed the balance between existing and new IT successfully without application or project portfolio management, just by using some simple rules that the business could understand, and by moving along with existing drivers for change in the organization.

P7—Ownership Impacts Decommission

An organization builds systems in-house if these involve confidential business logic and data processing operations that are considered to be of core value to an organization, or when systems on the market do not address the requirements (Cullen, Seddon and Willcocks, 2005). With some kinds of sourcing patterns and contracts, an organization can completely own a system even if it is not developed in-house (Cullen and Willcocks, 2003). Although the organization has ownership over these systems, one of the costly problems is supporting the legacy software and applications. If the system was developed in-house, the organization should have supporting staff for the system. If the supporting staff was not available, at least the organization should have enough documentation to support it, now or in the future (Marwaha, Patil and Tinaihar, 2006).

Experiences in a large organization with many legacy systems suggest that systems, owned by an organization, may remain operational longer than originally planned. In some cases ownership of a system hampers its change. Sometimes owners tend to prefer maintenance over change.

"The business decides on decommissioning of IS/IT, because the systems are theirs. Cost and business value are estimated together with the business, and the business tells the story in the IT governance board. But in practice very little is decommissioned, amongst other things because that requires investments. As a consequence license costs are rising." This quotation shows that ownership plays a crucial role in decision making on decommissioning of systems. When the owner understands the consequences of late decommissioning, like expensive maintenance and support contracts, higher license costs and functional problems for users, the owner is likely to be more active in decommissioning of IS/IT systems, provided that budget was available to invest in decommissioning.   Despite the importance, none of the interviewees stated that their organization was actively governing the balance between budget spend on controlling and maintaining existing IT and money spend on acquiring new IT. Most organizations were taking measures such as portfolio management and creating transparency in budget spending and the related decisions. Portfolio management was often used to determine which projects should be done and which projects should not be done. It did not include mastering the balance between existing and new IT.

4   Methodology for Governing Existing and New Systems

Once an imbalance between existing and new IT is present, organizations may want to improve the balance to ensure that sufficient budget will be assigned to new development and innovation. The normative question remains: What is a healthy balance? There seems to be little evidence on what constitutes a healthy balance in attention and resources between introducing new and maintaining existing systems based on our research described earlier. The healthiness may depend on the nature of the organization at hand, its state of development, maturity of the technology at hand, and other factors.

We propose a methodology by which the balance between existing and new IT can be measured. This methodology can be integrated with existing portfolio management methods. The idea is to make visible what the ratio between existing and new systems is to create awareness and to let the stakeholders determine what the ratio should be according to their insights. Based on the proposition discussed in the previous section directions for improvement can be determined. As existing systems become legacy this should be a continuous activity and the process is started again. The following sections describe:

1. *Defining and measuring* the balance using an innovation indicator to describe the organization's IT landscape and innovation capability;
2. *Shifting* the balance by using measures related to the factors;
3. *Keeping* the balance by deploying adequate IT management and governance processes.

Defining and Measuring the Balance

Once an organization has analyzed its mission, identified by its stakeholders, and defined its goals, it needs a way to measure progress toward those goals (Reh, 2012). In this paper, we define an *innovation indicator* which is the ratio of budget percentage for existing legacy systems and budget percentage for new IT systems, to govern the balance between existing and new IT in an organization at the strategic level. So in (Glass, 2006) an illustration of this indicator is that if 80 % existing IT and 20 % is new IT then this indicator is $80/20 = 4$.

The higher the value of the innovation indicator, the less space there is for innovation of IT (new IT). The ratio between existing and new IT can be used as an indicator for making decisions on decommissioning and maintenance of existing and new IT and for governance purposes of innovation.

Choosing a fraction as the indicator makes clear how serious the situation becomes when the balance is skewed heavily towards existing IT. Then the value of the innovation indicator moves to infinity, suggesting that innovation is squeezed out entirely. In such a situation the organization may not be able to maintain existing systems due to expensive maintenance contracts for out-of-date IT. Organizations need to establish what they consider to be a healthy value for this innovation indicator. For instance an innovative organization may strive after a value of 1, whereas a trend-following organization may strive after a value of 3 for the innovation indicator.

Shifting the Balance

Even if the role of IT in an organization or its operating model provide some reason for relatively high maintenance costs, any organization would favor to lower its maintenance costs, as the released budget can be subsequently used for IT innovation. The propositions presented in section 3 provided the basis for defining strategies and measures, which favor a healthy balance between existing and new IT. In Table 2, an overview of strategies and measures to improve the balance between existing and new IT are shown which are based on industry practices obtained from the interviews and literature review.

Table 2. Measures to improve the balance between existing and new IT related to propositions

Propositions	Improvements
P1. Software characteristics	• Prevent systems from becoming too large and complex. • Use high level languages. • Apply software engineering principles.
P2. Development methods	• Select and use development methods with a view on the impact on maintenance and decommissioning of systems.
P3. Dependency of systems	• Aim at loose coupling between systems and services. • If a system has more dependencies, wrapping may provide a solution.
P4. Lock-ins	• Use open standards where available.
P5. System complexity	• Restrict the size of systems. • Keep a minimum level of granularity of control over the IS/IT landscape.
P6. New technologies	• Assess the stability of new technologies and delay introduction when needed.
P7. Ownership of systems	• Make business owners aware of the costs and risks of late decommissioning.

Keeping the Balance

Organizations need to monitor the balance and take appropriate measures if needed. In our interviews three type of measures were identified that can add to an organization's capability of balancing existing and new IT in its IT budget:

• *Making budget allocation decisions persistent and consistent across the entire life cycle.* Total Cost of Ownership (David, Schuff and St. Louis, 2002) is a well-known approach using this principle. But also servitization (Turner, Budgen and Brereton, 2003) may bring along this persistence, as services tend to involve explicit service contracts, with life-time costs included in the contract prize. Setting such prices requires the service providers to look ahead and think about maintenance and decommissioning beforehand.

• *Explicit IT portfolio management.* This makes transparency between the project portfolio and the way budget is spent. Portfolio management may use the distinction between maintenance and innovation projects. Additionally, it may impose policies, restrictions and roles to the balance. Such rules should be grounded in a solid understanding of the role of IT in the organization and the organization's operating model.

* *Enterprise architecture management.* The management of enterprise architecture may help rationalizing IT budget decisions (Ross, Weill and Robertson, 2006). Especially where extensive interdependencies across many systems and services deprive an organization of the courage to decide to change or decommission systems and services, enterprise architecture provides clarity and prevents a maintenance cost-raising spiral.

Once an imbalance between existing and new IT is present, organizations may want to improve to allow for sufficient innovation. There seems to be little evidence on what constitutes a healthy balance in attention and resources between introducing new and maintaining existing systems. The healthiness may depend on the nature of the organization at hand, its state of development, maturity of the technology at hand, and other factors. A healthy balance could be determined at the strategic level of the organization. Once the innovation indicator is used, benchmarking with other organizations can help further to establish the desired value.

5   Concluding Remarks

Theory and practice show that there is a gradual increase in maintenance costs over the years, rising to 90% of the budget in some exceptional cases. The inability to manage the IT portfolio results in the innovation squeeze, in which increasing portions of the budget are spent on existing legacy systems and thus cannot be spend on innovation. Some large IT user organizations with many legacy systems are faced with the problem of an imbalance between existing and the need for adopting new IT. Their CIOs find themselves in a position where they require more budget every year for IT because projects take longer and cost more than originally anticipated, and the existing IT landscape is consuming an ever increasing percentage of the budget.

Using literature and interviews seven propositions were derived suggesting that software characteristics, development methods, dependency of systems, lock-in, system complexity, new technologies and system ownership influence the decision whether to decommission or to maintain a system. The balance between existing and new IT in an organization can be improved by making use of the seven propositions to determine the influences and then select the most effective measures.

Our interview results indicated that the balance between existing and new IT was not effectively mastered in most of the organizations interviewed. We developed a methodology that recommends CIOs and CFOs to start a discussion where they establish what they find a healthy balance between existing and new IT for their organization based on an innovation indicator. They can use this innovation squeeze indicator to find out what the current value is, and to discuss what the future value should be. This should help to initiate a process to analyze what the main influences are on the balance between existing and new IT in their organization and to ensure that the balance between control, maintenance and innovation is maintained. We did not use this methodology in practice and recommend to evaluate its value in further research.

More research is necessary on decommission strategies to prevent that organizations become trapped by the maintenance costs of existing IT and can hardly innovate. More research is necessary to test the methodology and the use of the innovation indicator to govern the balance between new and existing systems described in this paper.

Acknowledgement. This work resulted from the ArchiValue project, in which the Dutch Tax and Customs Administration collaborates with Novay, BiZZdesign, and APG.

References

Aversano, L., Canfora, G., Cimitile, A., De Lucia, A.: Migrating Legacy Systems to the Web: An Experience Report. In: Proceedings of the Fifth European Conference on Software Maintenance and Reengineering, Lisbon, Portugal, March 14-16, pp. 148–157 (2001)

Banker, R., Datar, S., Kemerer, C., Zweig, D.: Software Complexity and Maintenance Costs. Communications of the ACM 36(11), 81–94 (1993)

Bisbal, J., Lawless, D., Wu, B., Grimson, J.: Legacy Information Systems: Issues and Directions. IEEE Software 16(5), 103–111 (1999)

Blume, M.E.: Portfolio Theory: A Step Towards Its Practical Application. The Journal of Business 43(2), 152–173 (1970)

Castro-Leon, E., He, J., Chang, M., Peiravi, P.: The Economics of Service Orientation (2009), http://www.infoq.com/articles/intel-services-economics (November 24 , 2011)

Cohen, D., Lindvall, M., Costa, P.: Agile Software Development. Data and Analysis Center for Software (DACS), New York (2003)

Cullen, S., Seddon, P., Willcocks, L.: Managing Outsourcing: The Lifecycle Imperative. MIS Quarterly Executive 4(1), 225–246 (2005)

Cullen, S., Willcocks, L.: Intelligent IT Outsourcing. Butterworth Heinemann, Oxford (2003)

David, J.S., Schuff, D., Louis, R.: Managing your total IT cost of ownership. Communications of the ACM 45(1), 101–106 (2002)

Denzin, N.: Sociological Methods: A Sourcebook. Aldine Transaction (2006)

Erdil, K., Finn, E., Keating, K., Meattle, J., Park, S., Yoon, D.: Software Maintenance as Part of the Software Life Cycle. Technical report, Department of Computer Science, UFTS University (2003)

Erikh, L.: Leveraging legacy system dollars for e-business. IEEE IT Professional, 17–23 (May-June 2000)

Eastwood, A.: Firm fires shots at legacy systems. Computing Canada 19(2), 17 (1993)

Gangadharan, G.R., Kuiper, N., Oude Luttighuis, P.: Balancing Old and New in IT Budgets. Novay Technical Report (2010), https://doc.novay.nl/dsweb/Get/Document-114641 (October 2012)

Glass, R.L.: Software Conflict 2.0: The Art and Science of Software Engineering. Developer Books, Atlanta (2006)

Gordon, R.J.: Five Puzzles in the Behavior of Productivity, Investment, and Innovation. NBER Working Paper No. 10660 (2004)

Guo, J.: Using Category Theory to Model Software Component Dependencies. In: Proceedings of the Ninth Annual IEEE International Conference and Workshop on the Engineering of Computer-Based Systems, Sweden, pp. 185–192 (2002)

Hamilton, D.: Linking stategic information systems concepts to practice: System integration at the portfolio level. Journal of Information Technology 14, 69–82 (1999)

Heydebreck, P., Klofsten, M., Maier, J.: Innovation support for new technology-based firms: the Swedish Teknopol approach. Journal of R&D Management 30(1), 89–100 (2000)

Taking the measure of IT. The Economist (March, 2006)

Iyer, V.N.: Legacy Modernization. Technical Report. Infosys, India (2008)

Jeffery, M., Leliveld, I.: Best Practices in IT Portfolio Management. MIT SLoan Management Review 45(3), 41–49 (2004)

Jones, C.: Estimating Software Costs. McGraw Hill, New York (2007)

Kantner, L., Shrover, R., Rosenbaum, S.: Structured Heuristic Evaluation of Online Documentation. In: Proceedings of the IEEE International Professional Communication Conference, Portland, Oregon, September 17-20, pp. 331–342 (2002)

Kauffman, R.J., Tsai, J.Y.: When is it Beneficial for a Firm to Pursue a Unified Procurement Strategy for Enterprise Software Solutions? In: Proceedings of the 42nd HICSS, Big Island, Hawaii, January 5-8, pp. 1–10 (2009)

Lientz, B., Swanson, E.B.: Software Maintenance Management. Addison-Wesley, Boston (1980)

Linthicum, D.: Enterprise Application Integration. Addison-Wesley, MA (1999)

Lowe, S.: Software Maintenance Pricing – Fair or Out of Control? (2009), http://blogs.techrepublic.com/tech-manager/?p=956 (November 24, 2011)

Martin, J., McClure, C.: Software Maintenance: The Problem and Its Solutions. Prentice Hall, Englewood Cliffs (1983)

Marwaha, S., Patil, S., Tinaikar, R.: The Next Generation of In-house Software Development. McKinsey Report (2006)

McFarlan, F.W.: Portfolio Approach to Information Systems. Harvard Business Review 59, 142–150 (1981)

Ohlsson, M.C., von Mayrhauser, A., McGuire, B., Wohlin, C.: Code Decay Analysis of Legacy Software through Successive Releases. In: Proceedings of the IEEE Aerospace Conference, USA, pp. 69–81 (1999)

Parnas, D.: Software Engineering - Missing in Action: A Personal Perspective. IEEE Computer 44(10), 54–58 (2011)

Port, O.: The software trap – automate or else. Business Week 3051(9), 142–154 (1988)

Pree, W.: Component-Based Software Development – A New Paradigm in Software Engineering? Software Concepts and Tools 18(4), 169–174 (1997)

Reh, F.J.: Key Performance Indicators – How an organization defines and measures progress towards its goals, http://management.about.com/cs/generalmanagement/a/keyperfindic.htm (March 20, 2012)

Reifer, D.J., Basili, V.R., Boehm, B.W., Clark, B.: Eight Lessons Learned during COTS-Based Systems Maintenance. IEEE Software 20(5), 94–96 (2003)

Ross, J., Weill, P., Robertson, D.: Enterprise Architecture as Strategy: Creating Foundation for Business Execution. Harvard Business School Press, Boston (2006)

Sommerville, I.: Software Engineering. Addison-Wesley, Boston (2000)

Tsang, A.H.C.: Strategic dimensions of maintenance management. Journal of Quality in Maintenance Engineering 8(1), 7–39 (2002)

Turner, M., Budgen, D., Brereton, P.: Turning Software into a Service. IEEE Computer, 38–44 (October 2003)

Ulrich, W.: The Evolutionary Growth of Software Engineering and the Decade Ahead. American Programmer 3(10), 12–20 (1990)

Van Vliet, H.: Software Engineering: Principles and Practices, 2nd edn. John Wiley and Sons, West Sussex (2000)

Yeo, K.T.: Critical failure factors in information systems projects. International Journal of Project Management 20, 241–246 (2002)

Appendix: Interview Questionnaire

1. Do you have a record of budget details for existing IT projects and projects that are planned in the near future (new IT) in your organization?
2. Do you discuss the expenses for existing IT and new IT projects?
3. How are costs allocated? How are benefits attributed?
4. In what terms is the value of IT defined and quantified?
5. How do you quantify the value/benefits of IT systems versus expenses?
6. Are there also other ways (e.g. Balanced Score Card, Information Economics, Multi criteria, economic indicators such as TCO, ROI, etc. ...) used? Why are these ways (no longer) used?
7. What are your experiences with the present approach? Explain with examples.
8. In what manner do the cost benefit calculations for investment decisions change new IT proposals? Are there any risks associated with cost / benefit weighted?
9. How do you estimate cost benefit calculations for managing IT project portfolio?
10. How is it decided to decommission or replace IT?
11. Are decisions, prioritization rings and business cases evaluated at a later time?
12. Could you please indicate what percentage (approximately) of the budget will be devoted to experiments - development of new IT - maintenance - phasing?
13. Could you please indicate which percentages (approximately) of the budget are spent on experiments - development of new IT – maintenance - decommissioning?
14. How will you focus on the weaknesses of existing IT: to remedy, or is it to future business opportunities?
15. How is your business value driven: by physical, or intellectual resources?
16. Is your business model influenced by new technology or not?
17. Do you see whether IT outsourcing is a threat to your operations, or is outsourcing establishing a balance between IT insourcing and outsourcing?
18. What are the criteria that you will use for valuing IT? Do you use a rigid criterion or multiple criteria to estimate the value of IT?
19. In what way would you like to manage your IT portfolio?
20. How would you decide to invest in experiments, IT development, maintenance, and decommissioning?

Learning from Failure: Myths and Misguided Assumptions about IS Disciplinary Knowledge

Tor J. Larsen[1,*] and Linda Levine[2]

[1] BI Norwegian Business School, Oslo, Norway
[2] Independent Researcher Consultant, Pittsburgh, Pennsylvania, USA
Tor.J.Larsen@BI.NO, llherself@gmail.com

"The division of men's intellectual lives and activities into distinct disciplines is easy to recognize as fact. But it is less easy to explain... How, for instance, are such disciplines to be classified and defined? Here verbal definitions will hardly help."

--Stephen Toulmin, *Human Understanding*

Abstract. Many different methods have been used to understand the field of information systems, including classification, citation, and exploration of genres and lines of discourse. This paper discusses an approach based on the concept of a *family of fields,* where IS has greater proximity to some fields than to others. Our approach was inspired by field theory and discourse communities as a means to explain the diffusion of scientific research. The family of fields concept proved not to be viable but yielded important lessons for the study of IS and its relationship with other scientific fields. We found that (1) fields are not so easily defined, (2) borrowing of ideas across disciplines is not linear, (3) the concept of a reference discipline is obscured, and (4) we need to ask, what are the requirements for a discipline among the social sciences.

Keywords: failure, scientific disciplines, disciplinary knowledge, reference disciplines, information systems, sociology of scientific knowledge.

Prologue

To begin, it is unusual to provide a prologue, however, this research does require some stage setting. There are a number of things that we believed to be true when we first set out, in 1997, to explore the identity and dynamics of the field of information systems (IS). We were concerned with information technology and its role in the knowledge economy, especially the pace of change, and the extent to which we were or weren't living in unusual or accelerated times. We speculated that each era most likely saw itself as unique and important--where the contributions, struggles, and the experiences of its people were unlike that of any other. At the time we took several assumptions about IS for granted. These included that:

---

* The Authors are listed in alphabetical order, but have contributed equally to the article.

Y.K. Dwivedi et al. (Eds.): TDIT 2013, IFIP AICT 402, pp. 495–509, 2013.
© IFIP International Federation for Information Processing 2013

- the field of IS can be understood by looking at IS only,
- IS is in a pre-paradigmatic state,
- given time IS will succeed in developing a dominant paradigm, with ruling theory and this would be a prerequisite for becoming a mature field   (i.e., we would come to have a core),
- theory is the key to understanding, and is also a bridge to reaching practitioners,
- there is evidence of a cumulative research tradition, and
- because technologies are always changing, old insights are no longer relevant.

Over time, through the processes of conducting a number of studies on the identity and dynamics of the field of IS, we have come to view the above assumptions to be myths, or else reflections of wishful thinking.   Our present understanding centers around the following observations, that:

- in order to understand the body of knowledge that makes up IS, it is necessary to investigate working knowledge in other disciplines, and the sociology of scientific knowledge,
- the maturation of the discipline is mixed up with an innovation bias for technology, creating cloudiness and confusion,
- technologies place value on the "new," whereas disciplinary knowledge is about what endures, and
- there may be evidence of a cumulative research tradition in sub-fields of IS (e.g., TAM, GDSS), as yet unknown and largely unresearched.

We explored many different approaches to understanding the field, and met with success using classification methods (Larsen and Levine 2005), citation analysis (Larsen and Levine 2008), and exploration of genres and lines of discourse (Larsen and Levine 2007). We also had high hope for the approach that we used here on *family of fields*.   This was inspired by field theory and discourse communities (Latour 1988, Shaw 1990, Pfeffer 1993, Toulmin 2003) as a means to explain the diffusion of scientific research. The family of fields approach proved not to be viable but yielded important lessons that contributed to our journey. Here is our story.

1   Introduction

IS researchers hold wide ranging views on the makeup of IS and other fields. Some have observed that IS research is cited in many scientific fields (see, for example, Backhouse, Liebenau, and Land 1991; Truex and Baskerville 1998; Davis 2000). Under the category of reference discipline (for IS), Vessey, Ramesh, and Glass (2002) include: cognitive psychology, social and behavioral science, computer science, economics, information systems, management, management science, and others. Holsapple, Johnson, Manakyan, and Tanner (1994) distinguish between academic journals and practitioner publications in the area of business computing systems. They further divide academic journals into "business-managerial orientation, computer science-engineering orientation, and general-social sciences orientation" (p. 74). Pfeffers and Ya (2003) distinguish between journals in IS and in allied disciplines. These subdisciplines are seen as making up IS or serving as reference disciplines for IS. Harzing (2012) identifies sixteen subject areas that make up the business domain, of which MIS-KM is one. Her comprehensive list of journals in the business school domain numbers 933. The Association of Business Schools (2011) defines 22 subject fields and lists 821 journals in the field of business. Finally, Taylor, Dillon and Wingen (2010) argue that IS is composed of six sub fields, including: inter-business systems, IS strategy, Internet applications miscellany, IS thematic miscellany, qualitative methods thematic miscellany, and group work & decision support.

Baskerville and Myers (2002) claim that IS has become a reference discipline for other fields. They base this on a three stage model where (1) initially IS imports theories, methods and results from other fields, (2) IS builds content internally, and (3) IS exports its theories, methods and results to other fields. In stage three, IS has become a reference discipline.

To investigate claims that (a) IS has matured and is now a reference discipline for other fields (Baskerville and Myers 2002) and (b) in the tradition of the sociology of science[1] , IS is borrowing from and lending to other fields, we tried to define and operationalize the construct of "referencing disciplines." In other words, how are the processes of maturation--of borrowing, building, and exporting ideas--made visible and how can this phenomenon be systematically verified? Thus, we were interested in developing a robust way to talk about the disciplines that referenced IS and how IS was coming to be referenced by these other fields. We believed that the range of other disciplines and their diversity were important. To explore this, we created a framework based on the concept of *family of fields* and we used this framework as a tool for a deductive analysis of journals from IS and other fields. Hence our research questions are:

> What are the relationships among fields relative to IS? Does the family of fields concept elucidate these relationships and can scientific journals be mapped to a family of fields?

The paper proceeds with our conceptual model and research design, method, discussion, and conclusion.

2   Conceptual Model and Research Design

Our formulation of the concept of family of fields was made up of four parts. First, recall that *reference disciplines* (Baskerville and Myers 2002) is used in a general manner; thus, we reviewed uses of the term. Second, we explored the relationships among various scientific disciplines, recognizing that some appeared closer to IS than others. We thought that the metaphor of the *family* could effectively illustrate close and distant relationships. For example, siblings are closer than cousins; and first

---

[1] How is a body of scientific knowledge constituted and matured? Some researchers have referred to this transformation as the sociology of scientific knowledge (Crane 1972; Lodahl and Gordon 1972; Toulmin 1972; Ben-David and Sullivan 1975; Cole 1983; Pfeffer 1993). This is the investigation of science as a social activity, particularly dealing "with the social conditions and effects of science and with the social structures and processes of scientific activity" (Ben-David and Sullivan 1975, p. 203).

cousins are closer than 2nd cousins. This metaphor offered a vehicle to grapple with IS and its reference disciplines.

We considered a broad distinction between IS and *all* other scientific disciplines lumped together under the heading of Supporting Fields. This corresponds to Pfeffers and Ya's (2003) distinction between journals in IS and in allied disciplines. However, we felt that this differentiation was too crude. For example, most would agree that a field such as software engineering is closer to IS than marketing. This line of thinking led us to distinguish between (1) IS, (2) Related Fields, e.g. software engineering, and (3) Supporting Fields, e.g. marketing. But how sharp is the distinction between IS and Related Fields? To illustrate, we realize that many (U.S.) universities organize decision sciences (DS) and IS in a single department. DS journals publish IS articles and IS journals publish DS findings. Despite the overlap, some maintain that DS is separate from IS. In the family of fields framework, DS and IS are close relatives.

Third, we speculated that Supporting Fields might include disciplines (i.e., marketing) that were connected to IS but more distant than Related Fields. Fourth, and finally, we defined the umbrella term of Wider Fields for those disciplines outside the business school domain – e.g., civil engineering, agriculture, and psychology. Obviously, these differentiations between IS and DS, Related Fields, Supporting Fields, and Wider Fields are imperfect but provide a starting point. Figure 1, below, depicts these categories of referencing fields and their proximity to IS.

IS – Decision sciences – Related fields – Supporting fields – Wider fields

Fig. 1. Categories of referencing fields and their proximity to IS

3   Method

The exploration of family of fields is part of our larger study of IS, focusing on citation analysis and citation patterns of exemplar articles in IS and other scientific fields (Larsen and Levine 2008). Our investigations employ a set of exemplar IS articles since, according to Ritzer (1975), an exemplar is one of the primary components of a paradigm. Kuhn (1970) defines exemplars as "concrete problem-solutions" that can be found in a range of sources including laboratories, examinations, texts, and periodical literature (p. 187). Exemplars are illustrative of important contributions in the field of IS. Consequently, in creating our dataset, we employed three steps: (1) we defined a portfolio of exemplar IS articles, (2) we identified any articles which cited to these exemplars, (3) we coded journals (containing articles citing to the exemplars) into the family of fields scheme. These steps are described below.

3.1   Step 1: Defining a Portfolio of Exemplar IS Articles

We employed two approaches for compiling our list of exemplar IS articles: (1) award winning articles, and (2) evaluation by peers. First, our sample of award winning articles was drawn from *MIS Quarterly* "articles of the year" and Society for Information

Management (SIM) competition-winner articles. For the period 1993-1999, *MISQ* named eight articles of the year. For the period 1994-2000, five SIM competition articles were named. Henceforth, these are referred to as "award articles." Second, we reflected that peers might have their personal IS research article favorites. We identified 17 peers who were well known in the community. These were senior scholars, professors from across the globe, who were recognized for their achievements. At the time, an AIS World senior scholars' list (or a basket of journals) did not exist (ICIS 2010 program guide, p. 26). Our 17 peers were contacted by email and asked to nominate their "top four" classic, seminal, or influential articles in the field of IS. After one email reminder, 15 had responded, providing us with 23 "peer-nominated articles" (see Appendix A for details.) None of the award articles were peer nominated. We refer to the grand total of 36 articles as "exemplar articles" – consisting of the two categories of award articles (13) and peer-nominated articles (23).

3.2   Step 2: Locating the Journals Citing our 36 IS Exemplar Articles

We looked at the 36 exemplar articles and where they were cited in other (articles in) journals. The social sciences citation index in the Thomson Reuters ISI Web of Knowledge was used for this purpose; it is the dominant, authoritative source for scientific research. In all, 418 journals were identified as having articles citing one or more of the 36 exemplar articles.

3.3   Step 3: Coding Journals into Families of Fields

The final step in our data preparation was the allocation of each of the 418 journals (citing the 36 exemplars) into one of the five Families of IS, DS, Related Fields, Supporting Fields, or Wider Fields. We performed separate coding and then joint reliability checks. The process of coding journals required three meetings. In coding, we recognized the need to account for combinations, i.e., IS and DS, etc. We allocated each of the 418 journals to one of the five Families of Fields (see Figure 1) or one of the ten combinations. Meetings were scheduled at least a week apart to allow for reflection.

4   Discussion

In our analysis, we reached a large degree of agreement on journals classified as "Pure IS journals" as in Walstrom and Hardgrave (2001) or "IS research journals" as in Pfeffers and Ya (2003). However, other journals were not so easily classified in their relationship to IS. Examples of journals we view as being a combination of two families are *Communications of the ACM* and *Management Science* – as we see it, belonging to both IS and Related Fields (and within Related Fields, to the sub-fields of computer science and operations research, respectively). We interpret *International Journal of Electronic Commerce* as belonging to IS and Supporting Fields (marketing). Clearly, this analysis involves interpretation. In several cases, we were unfamiliar with a particular journal and struggled with journal names that were ambiguous. The creation and use of coding schemes like ours involve judgment calls, which are open to debate.

We looked for representations of knowledge networks to assist with our coding of journals and their relationships to IS. Baskerville and Myers' (2002) conceptual model of knowledge networks shows IS as a disciplinary node (see figure 2 below).

They do not define what makes these nodes recognizable, but refer in passing to key people, events attended, and core journals. But questions remain: how can we talk about the IS community and others? Is there a "them" and an "us," or is this distinction a red herring? They succeed with an impressionistic representation of IS and the surrounding "other" disciplines. But the clouds they draw around these entities are indeed cloud-like—simply assuming that disciplinary borders exist, without providing any sharp distinctions or definitions.

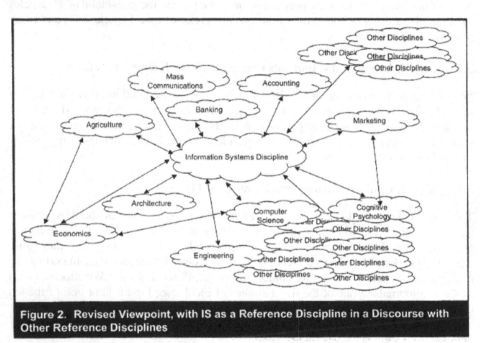

Figure 2. Revised Viewpoint, with IS as a Reference Discipline in a Discourse with Other Reference Disciplines

Fig. 2. From Richard L. Baskerville and Michael D. Myers, "Information Systems as a Reference Discipline," *MIS Quarterly* (26:1), 2002, p. 8. Copyright © 2002, Regents of the University of Minnesota. Reprinted by permission.

Our exploration of family of fields and combinations proved equally problematic. Most journal were coded outside of IS and into multiple categories. This resulted in blurred distinctions. Appendix B illustrates the messiness that we tried to contend with in the development of our coding scheme. We were also unable to make claims about specific familial relationships--disciplines were associated rather than connected in a precise manner. Thus, we were unable to come any closer than Baskerville and Myers (2002) in their characterization of IS as a "reference discipline in a discourse with other reference disciplines" (figure 2, p. 8). Due to our increasing concerns about blurred interpretation and unwieldy complexity, we concluded that the family of fields concept was not viable to pursue. Among the preconditions for a family of fields concept is a degree of agreement on subject areas and journal lists. This does not exist, for example, see Association of Business Schools (2011) and Harzing (2012). Nonetheless, we remain convinced that some fields have a closer relationship to IS than others. A deep understanding of proximity among fields also requires further investigation of detailed content, as proximity most likely derives from (a) similar topics or topics under the same umbrella, (b) domain, (c) shared theory, (d) common methods, and (e) common underlying technology.

How, otherwise, might the landscape be depicted? Diagrams differ in their granularity and composition, as well as their underlying theory. If we focus on the sociology of scientific knowledge, specifically the hierarchy of the sciences, we can illustrate the disciplines in closest proximity to IS. Cole (1983) employed Auguste Comte's hypothesis of the hierarchy of the sciences, which maintains "that the sciences progress through ordained stages of development at quite different rates.... The hierarchy of the sciences described not only the complexity of the phenomena studied by the different sciences but also their stage of intellectual development" (p. 112). Cole refined the hierarchy and developed six salient characteristics: theory development, quantification, cognitive consensus, predictability, rate of obsolescence, and rate of growth. This hierarchy distinguishes between the physical and social sciences, and the in/ability to make verifiable predictions. Figure 3, below, illustrates these two dimensions in our representation of IS and related (sibling) fields.

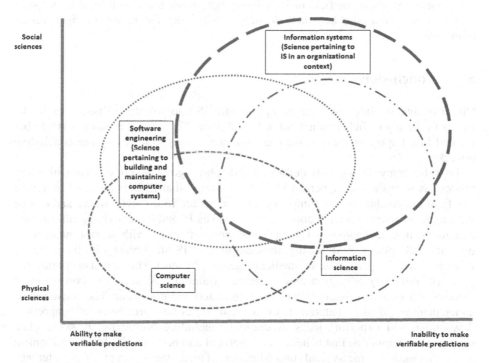

Fig. 3. Information Systems in proximity to sibling fields (adapted from Cole 1983)

This view shows four sibling fields which include their own distinct theories, focii, and research areas. Yet they also exhibit a high degree of overlap and no sharp borders. Similarly, Polites & Watson (2009) find overlap among the areas of computer science, information systems, management--professional, operations research, and multiple/unclassified (see their Figure 2, p. 607). Additionally, we acknowledge the physical sciences' concern with predictability and the social sciences' concern with human activity in organizational settings (description and interpretation). This representation depicts the transactions and exchanges among disciplines, which is also in line with Toulmin's thinking on human understanding and intellectual authority. He states: "By its very nature, the problem of human understanding – the problem of recognizing the basis of intellectual authority – cannot be encompassed within any single technique or discipline. For the very boundaries between different academic disciplines are themselves a consequence of the current divisions of intellectual authority, and the justice of those divisions is itself one of the chief questions to be faced afresh" (Toulmin 1972, p. 7).

Few IS researchers have tackled the topic of disciplinary knowledge but aspects of the evolution of the field of IS have been touched upon (King and Lyytinen 2004; Lyytinen and King 2004; Gregor 2006; Taylor, Dillon, and Wingen 2010; Hirscheim and Klein 2012). Davis (2000) comments on the history of the field, noting that two views have predominated, on: (1) observed systems and organizational functions, and (2) underlying concepts and deep-structure information phenomena. For the most part, discussion about the field of IS is lively but preoccupied with local issues such as the nature of a core and the role of diversity, and the matter of rigor versus relevance.

5   Conclusions

Our investigation into the relationships among IS and reference disciplines in the form of a family of fields turned out to be a failure. The approach was not viable but yielded four important lessons. We present these lessons followed by our concluding remarks.

First, fields are not so easily defined, and display a great deal of overlap with fuzzy borders as is evident in Appendix C. We discovered that IS is being used in almost any field imaginable, because information systems are in use everywhere and can be the subject of research in any domain. This makes IS and its underlying information communication technology (ICT) a broad area of study with a vast number of opinions and options. Additionally, the discipline of IS often blurs with the issues of ICT in context (e.g., agriculture, medicine, geography, etc). This can also confuse the goals of university education and vocational training. Second, the borrowing of theories and ideas across disciplines is complicated and not linear. The conventional understanding of the maturation of a field describes processes of importing, developing, and exporting ideas. Maturation, including borrowing, is not a clear sequence but rather one that is iterative, reciprocal and networked. Idea development and refinement is messy and unpredictable. Third, the concept of a reference discipline is obscured and even exploded. The term is commonly used and a convenient one but on examination it proved simplistic and not very meaningful. Any discipline can be a reference discipline for IS. Consequently, the term has no specific or special meaning. If we are going to continue to use the term "reference discipline" we would be wise to reexamine it closely and define it more usefully. Fourth, we need to ask: what are the requirements for a discipline, one among the social sciences? Rather than focusing continuously on the content and core of IS, we should pause to define and discuss the criteria for constituting a discipline.

More broadly, some aspects of the diversity and uncertainty that we perceive in IS, may be functions of a larger loss of order and unity, emanating from aging, brittle models of academic institutions. These eroding forms govern our current understanding of disciplines and the university itself—the *house* of learning for *bodies* of knowledge. Reinventing the university and disciplinary knowledge challenges us to look at organizations as ecosystems, rather than as edifices. By doing so, we open the door to seeing the university institution, not as a massive file cabinet or catalogue of content, but through alternative metaphors for networks and systems of systems.

IS is not alone in reexamining its identity and value as a field, within the university, and in relation to industry practice. In addition to fractures in the discipline of Sociology, similar concerns have been expressed by researchers in Organizational Communication (Corman and Poole 2000, as noted in Ashcraft 2001), Organization Science (Rynes, Bartunek, and Daft 2001) and Information Science (Monarch 2000; Ellis, Allen and Wilson 1999). Other signs of disciplines under stress, such as competing for funding and recognition in the university environment, translate into a plethora of applied R&D institutes, including inter-disciplinary centers of an overlapping nature.

We introduced this study by acknowledging our early observations some of which we now see as myths or faulty assumptions. This change of heart occurred over time as we conducted a number of studies on the identity and dynamics of the field of IS, including the present one on family of fields. To make progress in understanding our field, we believe it is necessary to investigate the workings of other disciplines and the sociology of scientific knowledge. We must do this keeping in mind that the maturation of the discipline is clouded by an innovation bias for ICT. IS is a hybrid field built upon technology breakthroughs, "silver bullets", enduring knowledge, and capabilities from the social, engineering, and physical sciences. The first step in making progress is reckoning with this complexity and the challenge it poses.

Epilogue

The end of the research on family of fields is not the end of the story. Taking time for reflection, we were left with standard citation material-- our exemplars and who cites to them. We persisted in asking: what kind of distinctions among scientific fields could be made? How can you identify an IS journal? And, could we reframe our research so that it contributed to an understanding of how knowledge evolves in interaction between IS and other fields? We stepped back to pose the most basic and fundamental question: what constitutes a field? This reassessment opened the door to bodies of literature well outside of IS--to field theory and philosophy of science. We are still grappling with this question. Given the complexity of categorizing fields, perhaps the only workable distinction that can be sustained is a coarse one between IS, related, and other fields.

The research tradition on the sociology of scientific knowledge holds promise to enrich our theorizing about IS in a holistic manner, rather than in isolation. The IS exemplar articles and citation analysis can be used as a lens and method for an operational investigation into the sociology of scientific knowledge, as applied to IS (Larsen and Levine, forthcoming). Theorizing from this vantage point allows comparisons with the workings of other disciplines and potential insight into how changes in theory and method unfold over time.

References

Ashcraft, K.L.: Book Review. In: Corman, S.R., Poole, M.S. (eds.) Perspectives on Organizational Communication: Finding Common Ground. Guilford Press, New York (2000); Academy of Management Review, 26(4), 666–668 (2000)

Association of Business Schools, Academic Journal Quality Guide, Version 4 (2011), http://www.associationofbusinessschools.org/ (last accessed on February 8, 2013)

Backhouse, J., Liebenau, J., Land, F.: On the Discipline of Information Systems. Information Systems Journal 1(1), 19–27 (1991)

Baskerville, R.L., Meyers, M.D.: Information Systems as a Reference Discipline. MIS Quarterly 26(1), 1–14 (2002)

Ben-David, J., Sullivan, T.: Sociology of Science. Annual Review of Sociology 1(1), 203–222 (1975)

Cole, S.: The Hierarchy of Sciences? American Journal of Sociology 89(1), 111–139 (1983)

Corman, S.R., Poole, M.S.: Perspectives on Organizational Communication: Finding Common Ground. Guilford Press, New York (2000)

Crane, D.: Invisible Colleges: Diffusion of Knowledge in Scientific Communities. University of Chicago Press, Chicago (1972)

Davis, G.B.: Information Systems Conceptual Foundations: Looking Backward and Forward. In: Proceedings of the IFIP WG8.2 Working Conference on The Socialand Organizational Perspectiveon Researchand Practicein Information Technology, Aalborg, Denmark, June 9-11, pp. 61–82. Kluwer Academic Publishers, Boston (2000)

Ellis, D., Allen, D., Wilson, T.: Information Science and Information Systems: Conjunct Subjects Disjunct Disciplines. Journal of the American Society for Information Science 50(12), 1095–1107 (1999)

Gregor, S.: The Nature of Theory in Information Systems. MIS Quarterly 30(3), 611–642 (2006)

Harzing, A.-W.: Journal Quality List, 47th edn. (August 27, 2012), http://www.harzing.com/download/jql_journal.pdf; Compiled and edited by Professor Anne-WilHarzing

Hirscheim, K.: A Glorious and Not-So-Short History of the Information Systems Field. Journal of the Association for Information Systems 13(4), 188–235 (2012)

Holsapple, C.W., Johnson, L.E., Manakyan, H., Tanner, J.: Business Computing Research Journals: A Normalized Citation Analysis. Journal of Management Information Systems 11(1), 131–140 (1994)

ICIS (2010), Program Guide at, http://c.ymcdn.com/sites/start.aisnet.org/resource/resmgr/ICIS_Insider/ICIS_2010_Program_Guide.pdf?hhSearchTerms=senior+and+scholar+and+consortium

King, J.L., Lyytinen, K.: Reach and Grasp. MIS Quarterly 28(4), 539–551 (2004)

Kuhn, T.S.: The Structure of Scientific Revolutions, 2nd edn. The University of Chicago Press, Chicago (1970)

Larsen, T.J., Levine, L.: Searching for Management Information Systems: Coherence and Change in the Discipline. Information Systems Journal 15(4), 357–381 (2005)

Larsen, T.J., Levine, L.: The Identity, Dynamics, and Diffusion of MIS. In: McMaster, T., Wastell, D., Ferneley, E., DeGross, J.I. (eds.) Organizational Dynamics of Technology-Based Innovation: Diversifying the Research Agenda, IFIP TC 8 WG 8.6 International Working Conference, June 14-16, pp. 163–177. Springer Science + Business Media, Manchester (2007)

Larsen, T.J., Levine, L.: Citation Patterns in MIS: An Analysis of Exemplar Articles. In: León, G., Bernardos, A., Casar, J.R., Kautz, K., DeGross, J.I. (eds.) Open IT-Based Innovation: Moving Towards Cooperative IT Transfer and Knowledge Diffusion, IFIP TC8 WG8.6 International Working Conference, Madrid, Spain, October 22-24, pp. 23–38. Springer, New York (2008)

Latour, B.: Science in Action: How to Follow Scientists and Engineers Through Society. Harvard University Press, Boston (1988)

Lodahl, J.B., Gordon, G.: The Structure of Scientific Fields and the Functioning of University Graduate Departments. American Sociological Reviewvol 37(1), 57–72 (1972)

Lyytinen, K., King, J.L.: Nothing at the Center?: Academic Legitimacy in the Information Systems Field. Journl of the Association for Information Systems 5(6), 220–246 (2004)

Monarch, I.: Information Science and Information Systems: Converging or Diverging? In: Proceedings of the 28th Annual Conference of the Canadian Association for Information (2000), http://www.slis.ualberta.ca/cais2000/monarch.htm

Pfeffer, J.: Barriers to the Advance of Organizational Science: Paradigm Development as a Dependent Variable. Academy of Management Review 18(4), 599–620 (1993)

Pfeffers, K., Ya, T.: Identifying and Evaluating the Universe of Outlets for Information Systems Research: Ranking the Journals. The Journal of Information Technology Theory and Application (JITTA) 5(1), 63–84 (2003)

Polites, G.L., Watson, R.T.: Using Social Network Analysis to Analyze Relationships Among IS Journals. Journal of the Association for Information Systems 10(8), 595–636 (2009)

Ritzer, G.: Sociology: A Multiple Paradigm Science. The American Sociologist 10, 156–167 (1975)

Rynes, S.L., Bartunek, J.M., Daft, R.L.: Across the Great Divide: Knowledge Creation and Transfer Between Practitioners and Academics. Academy of Management Journal 44(2), 340–355 (2001)

Shaw, M.: Prospects for an Engineering Discipline of Software. IEEE Software, 15–24 (November 1990)

Taylor, H., Dillon, S., Wingen, M.: Focus and Diversity in Information Systems Research: Meeting the Dual Demands of a Healthy Applied Discipline. MIS Quarterly 4(4), 647–667 (2010)

Toulmin, S.E.: Human Understanding: the Collective Use and Evolution of Concepts. Princeton University Press, Princeton (1972)

Toulmin, S.E.: The Uses of Argument. Cambridge University Press, Cambridge (2003) (updated edition)

Truex, D.P., Baskerville, R.: Deep Structure or Emergence Theory: Contrasting Theoretical Foundations for Information Systems Development. Information Systems Journal 8(2), 99–118 (1998)

Vessey, I., Ramesh, V., Glass, R.L.: Research in Information Systems: An Empirical Study of Diversity in the Discipline and Its Journals. Journal of Management Information Systems 19(2), 129–174 (2002)

Walstom, K.A., Hardgrave, B.C.: Forums for Information Systems Scholars: III. Information & Management 39, 117–124 (2001)

Appendix A: List of Exemplar MIS Articles in Our Sample

MIS Quarterly, Article of the Year

[1] Klein, H.K. and Myers, M.D. (1999) "A Set of Principles for Conducting and Evaluating Interpretive Field Studies in Information Systems," *MIS Quarterly*, vol 23(1), March, pp. 67-94.

[2] Kumar, K., van Dissel, H.G., and Belli, P. (1998) "The Merchant of Prato – Revisited. Toward a Third Rationality of Information Systems," *MIS Quarterly*, vol 22(2), June, pp. 199-226.

[3] Ngwenyama, O.K. and Lee, A.S. (1997) "Communication Richness in Electronic Mail: Critical Social Theory and the Contextuality of Meaning," *MIS Quarterly*, vol 21(2), June, pp. 145-167.

[4] Hitt, L.M. and Brynfolfsson, E. (1996) "Productivity, Business Profitability, and Consumer Surplus: Three Different Measures of Information Technology Value," *MIS Quarterly*, vol 20(2), June, pp. 121-142.

[5] Mukhopadhyay, T., Kekre, S., and Kalathur, S. (1995) "Business Value of Information Technology: A Study of Electronic Data Interchange," *MIS Quarterly*, vol 19(2), June, pp. 137-156.

[6] Leidner, D.E. and Jarvenpaa, S. L. (1995) "The Use of Information Technology to Enhance Management School Education: A Theoretical View," *MIS Quarterly*, vol 19(3), September, pp. 265-281.

[7] Hess, C.M. and Kemerer, C.F. (1994). "Computerized Loan Origination Systems: An Industry Case Study of the Electronic Markets Hypothesis," *MIS Quarterly*, vol 18(3), September, pp. 251-274.

[8] Orlikowski, W. (1993) "Case Tools as Organizational Change: Investigating Incremental and Radical Changes in Systems Development," *MIS Quarterly*, vol 17(3), September, pp. 309-340.

MIS Quarterly, SIM Best Article

[9] Cooper, B.L., Watson, H.J., and Goodhue, D.L. (2000) "Data Warehousing Supports Corporate Strategy at First American Corporation," *MIS Quarterly*, 24(4), 547-567.

[10] Roepke, R.P. (2000) "Aligning the IT Human Resource with Business Vision: The Leadership Initiative at 3M," *MIS Quarterly*, vol 24(2), June, pp. 327-343.

[11] El Sawy, O.A., Malhotra, A., Gosain, S., and Young, K.M. (1999) "IT-Intensive Value Innovation in the Electronic Economy: Insight from Marshall Industries," *MIS Quarterly*, vol 23(3), September, pp. 305-334.

[12] Cross, J., Earl, M.J., and Sampler, J.L. (1997) "Transformation of the IT Function at British Petroleum," *MIS Quarterly*, vol 21(4), December, pp. 401-423.

[13] Caron, J.R (1994) "Business Reengineering at CIGNA Corporation," *MIS Quarterly*, vol 18(3), September, pp. 233-250.

Peer Nominated Articles

[14] Markus, L. and Robey, D. (1988) "Information Technology and Organizational Change: Causal Structure in Theory and Research," *Management Science*, vol 34, pp. 583-598.

[15] DeLone, W. and McLean, E. (1992) "Information Systems Success: The Quest for the Dependent Variable," *Information Systems Research*, vol 3(1), March, pp. 60-95.

[16] Hirscheim, R. and Klein, H. (1989) "Four Paradigms of Information Systems Development," *Communication of the ACM*, vol 32(10), pp. 1199-1216.

[17] Hammer, M. (1990) "Reengineering Work: Don't Automate, Obliterate," *Harvard Business Review*, vol 68(4), July-August, pp. 104-112.

[18] Henderson, J.C. and Venkatraman, N. (1993) "Strategic Alignment: Leveraging Information Technology for Transforming Organizations," *IBM Systems Journal*, vol 32(1), pp. 4-16.

[19] Myers, M.D. (1997) "Qualitative Research in Information Systems," *MIS Quarterly*, vol 21(2), June, pp. 241-242.

[20] Brancheau, J.C. and Wetherbe, J.C. (1987) "Key Issues in Information Systems Management," *MIS Quarterly*, vol 11(1), March, pp.23-45.

[21] Goodhue, D. and Wybo, M.D. (1992) "The Impact of Data Integration on the Cost and Benefits of Information Systems," *MIS Quarterly*, vol 16(3), September, pp. 293-311.

[22] Ives, B. and Jarvenpaa, S.L. (1991) "Applications of Global Information Technology – Key Issues for Management," *MIS Quarterly*, Vol. 15(1), March, pp. 33-49.

[23] Malone, T.W., Yates, J., and Benjamin, R.I. (1987) "Electronic Markets and Electronic Hierarchies," *Communications of the ACM*, vol 30(6), June, pp. 484-497.

[24] Lee, A.S. (1989) "A Scientific Methodology for MIS Case Studies," *MIS Quarterly*, vol 13(1), March, pp. 33-50.

[25] Daft, R.L. and Lengel, R.H. (1986) "Organizational Information Requirements: Media Richness and Structural Design," *Management Science*, vol 32(5), May, pp. 554-571.

[26] DeSanctis, G. and Gallupe, R.B. (1987) "A Foundation for the Study of Group Decision Support Systems," *Management Science*, vol 33(5), May, pp. 589-609.

[27] Sprague, R.H. (1980) "A Framework for the Development of Decision Support Systems," *MIS Quarterly*, vol 4(4), December, pp. 1-26.

[28] Dickson, G.W., Senn, J.A., and Chervany, N.L. (1977) "Research in Management Information Systems: The Minnesota Experiments," *Management Science*, 23(9), 913-923.

[29] Ives, B., Hamilton, S., and Davis, G.B. (1980) "A Framework for Research in Computer-based Management Information Systems," *Management Science*, vol 26(9), pp. 910-934.

[30] Boland, R.J., Jr. (1984) "Sense-making of Accounting Data as a Technique of Organizational Diagnosis," *Management Science*, vol 30(7), pp. 868-882.

[31] Hirscheim, R., Klein, H.K., and Lyytinen, K. (1996) "Exploring the Intellectual Structures of Information Systems Development: A Social Action Theoretical Analysis," *Accounting, Management and Information*, vol 6(1/2), pp. 1-64.

[32] Orlikowski, W.J. and Baroudi, J.J. (1991) "Studying Information Technology in Organizations: Research Approaches and Assumptions," *Information Systems Research*, vol 2(1), pp. 1-28.

[33] Avergou, C., Siemer, J., and Bjørn-Andersen, N. (1999) "The Academic Field of Information Systems in Europe," *European Journal of Information Systems*, 8(2), 136-153.

[34] Markus, L. (1983) "Power, Politics and MIS Implementation," *Communications of the ACM*, vol 26(6), June, pp. 430-444.

[35] Bostrom, R.P. and Heinen, J.S. (1977) "MIS Problems and Failures: A Socio-Technical Perspective Part I: Causes," *MIS Quarterly*, vol 1(3), September, pp. 17-32.

[36] Davis, G. (1982) "Strategies for Information Requirements Determination," IBM Systems Journal, vol 21(1), pp. 4-30.

[37*] Checkland, P.B. and Scholes, J. (1999) *Soft Systems Methodology in Action*. Chichester, England: John Wiley & Sons Ltd.

Notes: * = the nomination is a book, hence not found in the social citation index and excluded from the analysis.

Appendix B: Coding Scheme

Coding for Decision Sciences and Wider Fields are not included because coding scheme was abandoned at the stage documented below.

I	= Clearly an IS journal presenting key issues
I-A	= Most probably or nearly clearly a IS journal but declaring a special interes area, for example application, specific technology, etc.
I-D	= IS journal within the domain of systems development
I-S	= Clearly a IS journal but declaring a special interest area, for example strategy However, the focus in on managerial issues!
I-I	= IS journal, focus is on individual, work related issues, etc.

R-A	= Related area, various topics, areas, or domains
R-E	= Related area; Expert systems, artificial intelligence, or similar
R-K	= Related area, Knowledge & new economy
R-L	= Related area, e-learning, e-teaching, library sciences, etc.
R-T	= Related area; computer science and computer technology
R-W	= Related area; wider environment, society, etc.

S	= Supporting field and of general nature
S-A	= Supporting field, various application domains.
S-B	= Supporting field, international or global business
S-C	= Supporting field, communication
S-F	= Supporting field, finance, accounting or similar
S-G	= Supporting field, group related issues
S-H	= Supporting field, health care, hospital, etc.
S-I	= Supporting field, individual level, for example psychology
S-L	= Supporting field, managerial and leadership issues
S-M	= Supporting field, marketing
S-P	= Supporting field, manufacturing
S-S	= Supporting field, systems thinking or other modeling approaches
S-U	= Supporting field but unclear what type
S-W	= Supporting field, wider environment, society, etc,

H	= Hybrid journal, in the sense that it's primary dedication is not IS per ce but allows relatively frequently IS type publications. Examples are in particular Management Science and Organization Science.

H-P   = Hybrid, but probably of a practitioner type.
H-T   = Hybrid, but mixed with computer science

Notes: I= Field of Information Systems, R=Related Fields, S=Supporting Fields, W=Wider Fields, H=Hybrid Field.

Appendix C: Random Sample of Journals in Supporting and Wider Fields and their ISI Subject Categories

Journal title	ISI SC1	ISI SC2	ISI SC3	ISI SC4	ISI SC5
ACTA Psychologica	Psychology	Experimental			
Annals of Tourism Research	Hospitality	Leisure	Sport	Tourism	
British J. of Mgmt	Business	Management			
Communication Theory	Communication				
Environment and Planning B-Planning & Design	Environmental studies				
Geographical Review	Geography				
Hospital & Health Services Administration	Health policy	Services			
Industrial & Labor Relations Review	Industrial relations	Labor			
Intern. J. of Industrial Ergonomics	Ergonomics				
Intern. J. of Service Industry Management	Management				
J. of Business Ethics	Business				
J. of Documentation	Information science	Library science			
J. of International Business Studies	Business	Management			
J. of Operations Management	Management				
J. of Rural Health	Health policy	Services	Public	Environmental	Occupational health
J. of the Theory of Social Behaviour	Psychology	Social			
Library Quarterly	Information science	Library science			
Medical Care Research and Review	Health policy	Services			
Organization	Management				
Preventive Medicine	Public	Environmental	Occupational health		
Public Administration	Public administration				
Research on Language and Social Interaction	Communication	Linguistics	Psychology	Social	
Social Networks	Anthropology	Sociology			
Systemic Practice and Action Based Research	Management				
Total Quality Management	Management				
Western J. of Communication	Communication				

Key: Subject category (SC)

From Research to Practical Application: Knowledge Transfer Planning and Execution in Outsourcing

Sabine Madsen[1], Keld Bødker[1], and Thomas Tøth[2]

[1] Roskilde University, Department of Communication,
Business and Information Technologies, Universitetsvej 1, DK-4000 Roskilde, Denmark
{sabinem,keldb}@ruc.dk
[2] Copenhagen Business School, Department of Intercultural Communication and Management,
Porcelænshaven 18A. DK-2000, Frederiksberg C, Denmark
tto.ikl@cbs.dk

Abstract. Despite an abundance of literature about knowledge and outsourcing the theoretical concepts and research findings are not immediately applicable in practice. In this paper we present the *insights* and the *effort* used to find a way to support knowledge transfer in outsourcing. More specifically, we aim to support operational managers responsible for outsourced IT activities in carrying out the concrete task of knowledge transfer planning and execution. We report from a longitudinal project conducted in a major financial company headquartered in Denmark and an offshore development center located in India. We identify the three main knowledge transfer challenges experienced by the case company. The identified challenges inform the design of a systematic five-step approach to the company's knowledge transfer. Our main contribution is to illustrate how extant research can be applied to understand and solve a particular company's knowledge transfer challenges in a way that fits with the company culture.

Keywords: outsourcing, offshoring, knowledge transfer, IT development and maintenance, engaged scholarship.

1   Introduction

Research shows and companies know that it takes time before employees who are newcomers to an organization, or to a specific department, job, or project achieve the same level of productivity as their colleagues (Rollag et al., 2005). Similarly, it is recognized that to get newcomers up to speed, they have to be introduced to and learn about their tasks and the particular context in which they are to perform these tasks (ibid.). Many companies handle this challenge through formal introduction programs, and subsequent on-the-job training, where experienced colleagues show the newcomers the robes. Moreover, much knowledge transfer takes place informally and ad hoc through co-presence and socialization (Nonaka, 1991; 1994; Nonaka and Takeuchi, 1995). However, when it comes to outsourcing of activities to another company, the lack of co-location and opportunities for spontaneous interaction mean

Y.K. Dwivedi et al. (Eds.): TDIT 2013, IFIP AICT 402, pp. 510–524, 2013.
© IFIP International Federation for Information Processing 2013

that knowledge transfer between employees from the two companies does not happen as easily, if at all (Carmel and Agarwal, 2001; Kotlarsky and Oshri, 2005; Oshri et al., 2008). In case of outsourcing to offshore destinations this is further complicated (ibid.). In this paper, we discuss knowledge transfer in such a situation based on a longitudinal case study.

The project took place in Danske Bank – a major financial company operating in northern Europe. Danske Bank has operational experience with a dedicated offshore development center (ODC) in India since 2005. Five hundred Indian associates work in different IT development projects and in various system management areas in close cooperation with employees from the company situated in Denmark. To enable this, initial training programs have been set up. Following the initial training program, the Danish managers who are responsible for outsourced IT activities have to ensure that further knowledge transfer about the domain and/or the activities takes place. This means that they have to figure out what kind of knowledge the Indian associates need and how to transfer it. Geographical distance and cultural differences add to the complexity of this task. In addition, for most of these managers an explicit focus on knowledge transfer is still a new and somewhat unknown area, for which they have had no formal training.

In this paper, we address the research question: *How can a systematic approach help managers establish and execute a knowledge transfer plan that overcomes the challenges of knowledge transfer in offshore outsourcing of IT related activities?* Further we wish to illustrate the efforts it takes to move insights from research into practice. As such, the target audience of this paper is researchers and middle/operational managers who are interested in understanding and solving knowledge transfer challenges in outsourcing in practice - by drawing on and grounding their work in the already existing literature and theoretical concepts about knowledge and outsourcing.

The paper is structured as follows. In Section 2 we review relevant literature and identify the theoretical concepts and understandings that have shaped our research, and in section 3 we describe our research approach. Section 4 presents the case company, its outsourcing arrangement, and experienced knowledge transfer challenges. Based on an understanding of these challenges, in Section 5, we propose a systematic five-step approach to the case company's knowledge transfer. In section 6 we discuss the advantages and disadvantages of the suggested approach. The discussion is structured around a framework that emphasizes the instrumental, aesthetic and symbolic dimensions of artifacts (Vilnai-Yavetz and Rafaeli, 2006). Lastly, in the conclusion we present a short summary of our research.

2   Background

Knowledge is a multifaceted phenomenon that has been researched at the individual and at organizational level, and as something that is inherent to action, necessary for interaction, and embedded in routines, processes, and artifacts.

A number of key concepts have significantly shaped the knowledge management field and the understanding of knowledge as a complex phenomenon. A good example of this is the well-known distinction between explicit and tacit knowledge

(Polanyi, 1962; 1966). In line with this distinction, knowledge is conceived as acquired by an individual as he or she identifies, interprets, and internalizes theoretical or practical knowledge (Pries-Heje, 2004; Myers, 1996), either by hearing about a topic or by doing something. The acquired knowledge is unique to the individual because the information and experience is filtered through and "added" to the stock of knowledge that the individual already possesses. This knowledge can be used to get the work done (to a large extent by making use of tacit knowledge), and it can be articulated and codified for the benefit of others. As individual knowledge can be verbalized and (re-) used by others (Markus, 2001), different types of knowledge processes, e.g., knowledge creation, sharing, transfer, etc. as well as mechanisms that support these processes have also dominated the knowledge management discourse (see for example Nonaka and Takeuchi, 1995).

In this paper, we draw on these key concepts regarding different types of knowledge, knowledge processes, and mechanisms as our theoretical backdrop and vocabulary for understanding what knowledge is, and how it might be transferred. However, the definitions, discussions, and normative prescriptions found in the knowledge management literature are relatively abstract and philosophical in nature. Thus, even though much research about different types of knowledge and knowledge transfer mechanisms exists, there is still quite some distance to travel from the theoretical understanding and recommendations to the concrete task of establishing and executing a knowledge transfer plan for a distributed work environment.

Studies of distributed work have highlighted the impact of geographical distance and the importance of common ground, coupling of work, collaboration readiness and collaboration technology readiness, see for example (Olson and Olson, 2000). Moreover, virtual-teams research has studied the challenges concerning the creation and maintenance of trust, mutual liking and shared meaning as well as the management of conflicts in teams where members work together across time, space and culture (Bjørn and Ngwenyama, 2009; Hinds and Bailey, 2003; Hinds and Mortensen, 2005; Jarvenpaa and Leidner, 1999). Also, in the outsourcing literature the problems and influence of geographical distance, cultural differences, the onshore staff's motivation for engaging in cross-cultural interaction, and the offshore unit's lack of domain knowledge, etc. have received considerable attention (Beck et al., 2008; Carmel and Agarwal, 2002; Gregory et al., 2009). We draw on this literature to understand and support the way managers at the operational level in the company handle the knowledge transfer challenge they face.

In particular we build on the notion of common ground (Kraut et al., 2002; Olson and Olson, 2000). All communication and collaboration rest on a foundation of information, which the interaction partners have in common and which they are aware that they share (ibid.). In some situations, there is already much common ground prior to interaction because people are members of the same group or work environment, belong to the same national culture, have witnessed or experienced the same events, etc. At the same time, and partly due to the dynamic nature of everyday life, people always have to establish common ground during the particular interaction. According to the principle of 'least collaborative effort', people will try to create grounding for their interaction with as little effort as possible and, therefore, people will often prefer to interact in person rather than through written media (Kraut et al., 2002).

3   Research Approach

In this work we adopt an applied approach. As such, we draw on and contribute to the existing body of knowledge with an illustration of how theoretical insights about knowledge and knowledge transfer as well as an understanding of the practical challenges of knowledge transfer in outsourcing can be applied to design a systematic approach that supports managers at the operational level in carrying out the concrete task of knowledge transfer planning and execution.

This piece of research has been conducted as part of a long-term collaboration with Danske Bank as part of a larger research project called SourceIT[1]. An engaged research approach has been applied to ensure production of research knowledge that is concrete and relevant for practical problem solving (Van de Ven, 2007). The research team consisted of people from both academia and industry, more specifically two academics and one practitioner from the company. The research team worked closely together to develop an empirically grounded and shared understanding of the knowledge transfer challenges in outsourcing and how they might be overcome.

Our research activities have been structured into four phases. In the first phase, the two academics spent three weeks in India in March 2009 to study the operational aspects of the outsourcing arrangement. This led to a more focused study of how to understand and support knowledge transfer, involving the practitioner from summer 2009 onwards. The practitioner was at this point in time on a 6 month posting in India and was, among other things, charged with the task of improving the company's way of conducting knowledge transfer. In the second phase, the aim was to understand the challenges of knowledge transfer in outsourcing. Over the course of a two month time period, a literature study of the knowledge management and distributed work/outsourcing literature was conducted and the results here of, delineated in overview tables and text, were jointly discussed and compared with the company's experiences. The discussions were documented in *a project log*, containing our emerging understandings of the knowledge transfer challenges as well as ideas for how to overcome them. In the third phase, the results from phase two (i.e. the documents and shared understanding) informed the first conceptual design of a multi-step knowledge transfer model. In the fourth phase, the knowledge transfer model gradually evolved into the conceptual design of a systematic five-step, tool supported approach to knowledge transfer. Table 1 provides an overview of the four phases and our research activities.

As Table 1 shows the information and results reported below are the product of a number of iterations between data collection at various empirical sites, analysis of empirical data, comparison of literature and practice, and presentations for the people involved in the activities studied, people with managerial positions in Danske Bank, as well as for the other companies and academic researchers in the SourceIT research project.

---

[1] The SourceIT research project lasted 3½ years (from 2008 – to mid 2011) and involved one academic institution, three large companies, and a consultancy company that specializes in dissemination of research knowledge to the broader public.

Table 1. Research phases and activities

Phases	Activities	Who and when
1.Building common ground	Field study at the ODC in India: 18 interviews and observation	The two academics, three weeks, Mar 2009
	A short-term posting at the ODC in India	The practitioner, six months, Mar–Oct 2009
2. Understanding the challenges of KT	Literature study: Knowledge management; KT in outsourcing	The research team, two months, Jul–Aug 2009
	Joint conversations about the results of the literature study and their "fit" with and manifestation in practice; documented in a project log	
3. Conceptualizing a multi-step model to KT	Informed by the results from phase two, a multi-step model for overcoming the challenges of KT was developed	The research team, two months, Sept–Oct 2009
4. Receiving feedback and refining the approach	Workshop: Presentation of KT model to the SourceIT project participants	The research team and the academics and practitioners in the SourceIT research project, Nov 2009
	Workshop: Presentation of a systematic five-step, tool supported approach to the SourceIT project participants	The research team and the academics and practitioners in the SourceIT research project, May 2010
	Presentation of the KT approach to another company with a different outsourcing arrangement to inquire about the approach's broader usefulness	The research team and three employees involved in outsourcing, Jun 2010
	Two interviews to follow-up on Danske Bank's challenges and experiences with KT	The research team and two Liaison Officers working with KT, Jun and Aug 2010 respectively

4   Knowledge Transfer Challenges in Case Company

Danske Bank's outsourcing arrangement is organized as an Offshore Development Centre (ODC) in Bangalore, India. The ODC is a facility owned by an Indian vendor, but dedicated to Danske Bank. The ODC is located in four adjacent buildings that bear the Danish company name. Only the employees who are working for Danske Bank have access to these buildings, and they work on the same technical platform as the Danish employees. Five Danes, i.e. one manager and four Liaison Officers (LOs), are posted in India to oversee the daily operations.

The chosen strategy is such that approximately 500 Indians employed by the Indian vendor are 'hired' from the Indian company into the ODC. These Indian associates are considered a pool of resources to be allocated to IT development projects and/or system management areas, just like other IT employees in Danske Bank[2]. Also, many Indian resources are allocated to tasks onshore (i.e. in Denmark). A typical onshore stay lasts from two to four months. Many activities are jointly performed by Danish employees and Indian associates, regardless of whether people are co-located or collaborate virtually. In other words, a cooperative outsourcing strategy (Dibbern et al., 2004) has been implemented. In this outsourcing arrangement, knowledge transfer is very important as the establishment of common ground is crucial for efficient and smooth collaboration between the Danish employees and the Indian associates.

The knowledge transfer that takes place is essentially twofold. First, it is the obligation of the Indian vendor to hire staff with the appropriate technical skills and train them in the Danske Bank's organization, processes, and tools as well as to provide general cultural training about Denmark and the Danish work culture. In this paper, we do not focus on this initial training. Rather, we are occupied with the subsequent knowledge transfer that has to occur to provide Indian associates with the specific knowledge they need to function in the team they are assigned to. The Danish manager of the team is responsible for this knowledge transfer – which fits well with Markus's (2001) definition of 'classical' knowledge transfer to expertise-seeking novices.

With regard to the latter knowledge transfer three major types of challenges have been identified. These challenges are elaborated below.

4.1   Knowledge Types and Needs

All people know more than they are consciously aware of (Polanyi, 1962). In other words, people possess much tacit knowledge and therefore take many things for granted, also when transferring knowledge. Second, people have different backgrounds and levels of expertise, and thus, different knowledge (transfer) needs when assigned to similar tasks.

A simple, yet illustrative example of the challenge of tacit knowledge in the case company concerns the Danish mortgage system. Most Danish employees know that a mortgage in Denmark is a loan with the currency of up to thirty years whether it is a fixed rate mortgage or another kind of mortgage. So, in Denmark, the maximum currency is regarded somewhat as a constant. However, in India there is no such thing as a formalized maximum currency. Consequently, if the Danish maximum currency is

---

[2] An example of an IT development project that was carried out by a team consisting of both Danish and Indian employees was the re-launch of Danske Bank's web bank application, while the company's IT systems for HRM (salary payment, staffing, competence development, etc.) is an example of a system management area that is maintained (i.e. operational problems) and further enhanced (i.e. new functionality) by a team consisting of both Danes and Indians.

left out of the knowledge transfer there is a risk that the Indian associates will work on the assumption that the mortgage system in Denmark is equivalent to the Indian mortgage system. There are of course an endless number of similar examples of what is so common for the Danish employees that they forget that it may not be just as common for the Indian knowledge recipients, and vice versa.

Another issue that employees of Danske Bank often face is the question of how much the Indians know prior to knowledge transfer. The Indians have different backgrounds and levels of expertise. This inhibits a clear-cut definition of what type of knowledge to transfer and how - as the needs vary from person to person.

4.2   Physical Distance

In line with prior research (see e.g., Olson and Olson, 2000), the experience in Danske Bank is that knowledge transfer is best done when the Indian associates are invited for an onshore stay of two to four months. Knowledge transfer happens more or less automatically when people are in close physical proximity (Kraut et al., 2002). People simply go to each other´s desks and ask for help as the need arises. This fluent pattern of interaction is also exercised by onshore Indian associates. Thus, co-location of Danish employees and Indian associates means that knowledge transfer needs can be handled with low effort through "a quick chat", i.e., in a way where it does not feel like knowledge transfer.

However, there are many occasions in which an initial onshore stay is not possible for a variety of reasons. In these cases, the employees tend to use emails as the primary means of communication (for similar results see Oshri et al., 2008). From the viewpoint of the Danish employees, knowledge transfer hereby becomes a very time-consuming affair because the experience is that a written answer takes time to produce and because an answer might trigger follow-up questions. Furthermore, the Indian associates have on many occasions expressed that they feel they are burdening the Danish employees when asking (too many) questions. At the same time, a significant number of the Danish employees are not entirely comfortable with other types of communication technologies. Moreover, the available video conferencing rooms with possibilities for shared desktops, etc. are not used unless located very close to the workspace.

4.3   Incentives and Priorities

Successful knowledge transfer over distance requires that the employees have an incentive to engage in this activity (Gregory et al., 2009; Lin, 2007; Markus, 2001; Olson and Olson, 2000). However, in the busy environment of Danske Bank's IT department, the Danish employees are inclined to focus their effort on what is immediately beneficial for their own work and on what gets rewarded by their local managers, namely the daily tasks and knowledge sharing with colleagues at the same location.

Moreover, at the outset of collaborating on an IT development project or in a system management area, there are clear knowledge asymmetries. Thus, in the beginning the Danish employees have knowledge that the Indian associates need. However, there are not necessarily any immediate benefits for the Danish employees in sharing their knowledge. In addition, it is difficult to assess the value of the time spent on answering emails and engaging in other knowledge transfer activities. Therefore, the Danish employees' motivation to do so can be quite low. Yet, in line with Heeks et al.'s (2001) findings about global software outsourcing, the experience in the company is that when the Danish employees and the Indian associates have physically met and got to know each other, email exchanges work much better. The reason is presumably that knowledge about each other as persons makes it easier for the interaction partners to know what kind of information to include in the emails (Kraut et al., 2002; Olson and Olson, 2000) and because people are more willing to help someone they have met, know, and like (Clark and Mills, 1993; Haytko, 2004).

Table 2 summarizes the experienced knowledge transfer challenges.

Table 2. Experienced challenges with knowledge transfer

Type of challenge	KT challenge	A systematic approach to KT should help the manager:
Knowledge types and needs	Tacit knowledge. Knowledge needs vary from person to person.	Identify and include (tacit) knowledge that would otherwise be forgotten. Identify the real needs of the knowledge recipient(s).
Physical distance	The Danish employees consider knowledge transfer time-consuming due to the number of questions asked via email. The Indians associates feel that they are burdening the Danish employees with (too many) questions/emails.	Identify the knowledge needs that have to be met to reduce the number of questions from the Indian to the Danish employees. Identify a variety of relevant knowledge transfer mechanisms.
Incentives and Priorities	The Danish employees focus their efforts on progressing with their daily work in accordance with management priorities.	Plan for and make the effort and effect of knowledge transfer transparent.

5   A Five-Step Approach to Knowledge Transfer

In this section we present a systematic, tool supported approach to knowledge transfer. The approach has been developed in responds to the challenges described above. The aim of the approach is to help the Danish managers' plan and carry out knowledge transfer to Indian associates who are newcomers to a particular IT development project or system management area.

The tool is more specifically thought of as a spreadsheet solution. The Danish employees in the company are very familiar with this type of software functionality and they use it for many tasks. Moreover, several of Danske Bank's existing outsourcing assessment and decision-tools, e.g., for making tactical decisions about which IT projects and system management areas to outsource, have been implemented as spreadsheet applications (see, e.g., Jørgensen et al., 2011).

The suggested approach consists of five steps (see Table 3). In step one a gap analysis lays the foundation for the subsequent knowledge transfer planning and execution. Thus, the Danish manager first decides what the desired or required level of knowledge is. Subsequently, the manager obtains information about the Indian associates' actual level of knowledge (via CVs and dialogue with LOs). On this basis, an assessment of the gap between the desired and the current knowledge level is made. The outcome of the analysis is an identification of the gaps that are the most severe and which therefore should be selected as the most important areas for knowledge transfer.

The tool supports the gap analysis in the following way. A number of predetermined categories (business domain, IT, process, task, and organization) and questions within each category help the manager consider what type of knowledge is particularly important for the given project/system management area. Thus, for each question, the manager sets the desired level of knowledge by using a predefined scale. Then, for each question, each Indian associate's current knowledge level is scored using the same scale. The predetermined categories, questions, and scales play an important role in ensuring that both explicit and tacit knowledge needs are addressed. The result is presented as a gap between the desired and the current level of knowledge for each question (in numbers) as well as for each category (in a diagram). The biggest deviations are highlighted so that the manager gets an overview of where the major gaps are by quickly viewing the results for each associate. Based on this analysis of the knowledge gaps, the manager actively chooses the areas for knowledge transfer. The selected focus areas are automatically moved to a new sheet that will eventually become the knowledge transfer plan.

Next identification of knowledge transfer mechanisms is included as a separate step to ensure that it is given due consideration. Thus, for each focus area a list of relevant knowledge transfer mechanisms is provided, and based on this list the manager chooses the mechanisms that s/he prefers. In this way, the tool supports the manager in realizing that there are many knowledge transfer mechanisms (such as class room training, documentation of previously undocumented IT systems and work flows, and mentoring and buddy arrangements to name but a few) and that several mechanisms might be able to address the same knowledge transfer need.

Following the selection of relevant knowledge transfer mechanisms a detailed knowledge transfer plan is made. For each selected knowledge area and transfer mechanism, a Danish employee responsible for the execution of the knowledge transfer is assigned, the Indian participants are named, and time estimates for preparation and execution, as well as room and technology requirements are outlined. In this way the tool supports the planning activity by providing the fields that ensure that the project/system manager considers the most important aspects, including some that are easily overlooked in a busy environment, such as preparation time and resource requirements. The resulting knowledge transfer plan allows for an overview of the effort that the knowledge transfer demands.

Then the knowledge transfer plan is carried out in practice, without support from the knowledge transfer tool. However, evaluation data in the form of the participants' subjective satisfaction and perceived value can be collected and stored in the spreadsheet. Moreover, the experienced challenges (see Table 2) indicate that it is important for the managers to follow-up on the effect of the knowledge transfer initiatives on two measures: productivity and the number of question–answer emails exchanges between the Indian and the Danish employees.

Table 3. The knowledge transfer approach

Step	Action	Tool support
1	**Identify knowledge gaps** • Identify the desired knowledge level. • Assess the Indian associates' current knowledge level. • Analyze the gaps between the desired and the current level, and select the most critical ones as focus areas for knowledge transfer.	• A range of predetermined categories and questions help the manager consider what type of knowledge is particularly important for the given project/system management area. • For each question, each Indian associate's current knowledge level is scored on a scale. • The result is presented as a gap between the desired and the current level of knowledge for each question as well as for each category. The biggest deviations are highlighted. • The focus areas for knowledge transfer are actively chosen and automatically moved to a new sheet that will eventually become the knowledge transfer plan.
2	**Identify knowledge transfer mechanisms** • For each of the selected focus areas, knowledge transfer mechanisms are considered and chosen.	• In the knowledge transfer plan, the knowledge transfer mechanism(s) for each focus area has to be chosen. For inspiration, a list of knowledge transfer mechanisms is provided.
3	**Establish the knowledge transfer plan** • A detailed knowledge transfer plan is made.	• When the knowledge transfer mechanisms have been chosen, the other fields for knowledge transfer planning are activated. • For each knowledge transfer mechanism, it is outlined: who is responsible, who participates, estimated time for preparation, estimated time for execution, room and/or technology requirements, deadline etc.
4	**Execute the knowledge transfer plan** • Intermediates carry out the knowledge transfer. An intermediate may be either a knowledgeable person from the Danish organization or an experienced team member from the ODC.	• The knowledge transfer plan is carried out without support from the KT tool.

Table 3. (*continued*)

5	**Evaluate the effect of the knowledge transfer** • Collect, store, and use data about the effect of the knowledge transfer.	• No specific method for data collection is prescribed, but data about effects can be stored and spreadsheet functionality used for analysis.

6   Discussion

Artifacts are not just neutral objects. Instead they are constructed based on the knowledge and cultural and contextual understandings of the designers and they shape and are shaped by the situated actions of the users (Masino and Zamarian, 2003; Orlikowski, 1992, 2007). In this research we have used an understanding of extant literature as well as of the case company and its experienced challenges to suggest an artifact, namely a systematic tool supported 5-step approach to the case company's knowledge transfer. The purpose of the approach is to ensure that the planning and execution of knowledge transfer takes place in a systematic way. Moreover, through the use of a spreadsheet application, the purpose is to prompt the Danish managers to consider the distinction between explicit and tacit knowledge, to recognize that many types of relevant knowledge transfer mechanisms exist, and to conduct detailed knowledge transfer planning. In this way, the suggested approach is goal-oriented, normative, and 'mechanistic' in nature. What might the advantages and disadvantages of such an approach to knowledge transfer be?

Vilnai-Yavetz and Rafaeli (2006) propose that in order to achieve a comprehensive understanding of what artifacts are and do in organizations they should be considered according to three dimensions: instrumentality, aesthetics and symbolism. Instrumentality refers to the fact that people and organizations have tasks and goals to accomplish and an artifact can be evaluated according to whether it helps or hinders the accomplishment of these tasks and goals. Aesthetics refers to the sensory experience an artifact elicits. It has for example long been recognized that the 'look and feel' of products, such as IT systems, mobile phones, computers, etc. have a huge impact on their success (take Apple products as an example). Symbolism refers to the meanings and associations that are created in the minds of the users, and it therefore concerns the message an artifact sends.

From an instrumental perspective the suggested knowledge transfer approach facilitates goal achievement by guiding the manager through the five steps, presenting possible options in a clear and sequential way in a spreadsheet application. However, the suggested approach and use of the supporting spreadsheet application does not in itself guarantee successful knowledge transfer as there are many other factors that influence the outcome, such as, e.g., how the knowledge transfer is actually prepared and carried out by the Danish employees and the extent to which the knowledge is/can be acquired by the Indian associates. The Danish manager should therefore give due consideration to these and other practicalities in step four and five. Additionally, the company is focused on achieving process maturity and adhering to the CMMI framework for software development. The tool supported approach to knowledge transfer helps satisfy the three sub-goals associated with goal 2 'Provide Necessary Training' in the CMMI process area named 'Organizational Training' (Chrissis et al, 2011).

From an aesthetic perspective we have chosen to implement the suggested approach as a spreadsheet solution. In so doing, the knowledge transfer approach obtains the 'look and feel' of the way the Danish managers normally work and it caters to theirs' and the broader company culture's preference for rational decisions, numbers, and plans. Thus, a key design decision has been to 'ride with the waves' of the organizational culture. Another key design goal is to prompt, and even provoke the Danish managers into broadening their understanding of what they and their Danish employees know and how this knowledge might be transferred to the Indian associates. However, by choosing to implement the knowledge transfer approach in a way that resembles the way the managers normally work there is a risk this broader understanding might not be achieved. Especially if the spreadsheet application is used in an unreflective way to quickly produce a knowledge transfer plan. This indicates that the Danish managers should be given a theoretical introduction to what knowledge and knowledge transfer is, as well as practical information about how to use the suggested knowledge transfer approach.

From a symbolic perspective the knowledge transfer approach has been designed to fit the company culture and the way work gets done in the case company. The advantage here of, i.e. of providing tool support that facilitates rational planning, is that knowledge transfer gets legitimized as "real work". In other words, it gets recognized that it takes time to plan, prepare and conduct knowledge transfer and therefore that (top) management has to sanction and provide work hours for it. However, with this approach there is a risk that knowledge transfer will be perceived to be primarily about planning and less about execution. To counter this, step three in the suggested approach and spreadsheet application 'forces' the manager to make a detailed plan, with names, dates, resource requirements etc. However, use of the approach and application does not guarantee that the knowledge transfer plan will be carried out. It is for example not uncommon in the case company that suddenly emerging system maintenance issues, new politically implemented laws (e.g., concerning mortgages, pensions), etc. take priority over planned initiatives with longer term benefits. Thus, while the approach can help create awareness about knowledge transfer as a distinct, necessary and resource demanding activity, the awareness will only be turned into action if (top) management prioritizes it regardless of the immediate operational circumstances.

In summary the approach reduces the complexity of knowledge transfer planning by structuring the work in a way that is familiar for the Danish managers. This in turn helps legitimize the task by communicating that knowledge transfer is an activity in its own right and by making it clear what the task consists of. However, it is also clear from the above that even with a systematic and quite normative approach (that covers predetermined steps, categories, and questions that have to be adhered to) the actual use situation still offers much room for autonomy. Thus, managers can chose to forgo the fact that the spreadsheet application is intended to make them reflect, and they can instead rush through the planning activity. Moreover, even when a well-thought out and detailed knowledge transfer plan is made it still has to be executed. Here, however, the suggested knowledge transfer approach does not offer any direct support and in addition contextual factors and practical aspects might create barriers for the execution of the plan. We conclude that the tool supported approach is very useful for knowledge transfer planning, but additional support might be needed with regard to execution.

7   Conclusion

Based on our long-term engagement with an offshore outsourcing arrangement between an Indian IT vendor and a Danish financial company, we identify three main types of knowledge transfer challenges, as seen from the client side. The challenges relate to different knowledge types and needs; physical distance; and the Danes' incentives and priorities for taking time to engage in knowledge transfer. The challenges indicate that a pro-active and management initiated approach to knowledge transfer could be useful.

We suggest a systematic tool supported approach that covers five separate steps: (1) The manager identifies the knowledge gaps that are the most important to address. (2) Then, the manager selects appropriate knowledge transfer mechanisms. (3) The manager makes a detailed knowledge transfer plan. (4) The knowledge transfer plan is carried out. (5) Lastly, the effect of the knowledge transfer is evaluated.

Workshop tests indicate that the suggested approach is able to help the Danish manager conduct detailed knowledge transfer planning that overcomes the identified knowledge transfer challenges. However, due to the 'messy' nature of daily life at the operational level, the execution of the knowledge transfer plan can still be subject to a number of contextual and practical barriers and managerial reprioritizations. In other words, the existence of a plan does not guarantee its successful execution, and as the company starts to work more systematically with knowledge transfer new challenges related to practical implementation of the knowledge transfer plan will arise and have to be overcome.

On a meta-level a key finding of this research is that it takes substantial work, i.e. literature study, empirical research, design considerations, and trial-and-error implementation, to 'translate' existing theoretical insights about different types of knowledge and knowledge transfer mechanisms to the practical realm. As such our main contribution is to demonstrate (1) how theoretical concepts can be used to inform the analysis of a particular company's outsourcing setup and experienced knowledge transfer challenges and (2) how the achieved understanding can serve as the foundation for designing a practical approach to knowledge transfer planning and execution that fits with and borrows legitimacy from the company culture.

We believe that similar work, and effort, is needed in all companies that wish to implement a knowledge transfer approach that overcomes the challenges associated with their specific outsourcing setup. However, we also believe that the three identified knowledge transfer challenges that pertain to this case as well as the five steps in the suggested knowledge transfer approach are a relevant inspiration and starting point for other companies.

References

Beck, R., Gregory, R., Prifling, M.: Cultural intelligence and project management interplay IT offshore outsourcing projects. In: Proceedings of the 29th International Conference on Information Systems, Paris, France, December 14-17 (2008)

Bjørn, P., Ngwenyama, O.: Virtual team collaboration: Building shared meaning, resolving breakdowns and creating translucence. Information Systems Journal 19, 227–253 (2009)

Carmel, E., Agarwal, R.S.: Tactical approaches for alleviating distance in global software development. IEEE Software, 22–29 (March/April 2001)

Carmel, E., Agarwal, R.S.: The maturation of offshore sourcing of information technology work. MIS Quarterly Executive 1(2), 65–77 (2002)

Clark, M., Mills, J.: The difference between communal and exchange relationships: What it is and is not. Personality and Social Psychology Bulletin 19, 684 (1993)

Dibbern, J., Goles, T., Hirschheim, R., Jayatilaka, B.: Information systems outsourcing: A survey and analysis of the literature. Database for Advances in Information Systems 35(4), 6–102 (2004)

Chrissis, M., Konrad, M., Shrum, S.: CMMI for Development (2011)

Haytko, D.: Firm-to-firm and interpersonal relationships: Perspectives from advertising agency account managers. Journal of the Academy of Marketing Science 32, 312–328 (2004)

Heeks, R., Krishna, S., Nicholson, B., Sahay, S.: Synching or Sinking: Global software outsourcing relationships. IEEE Software, 54–60 (March/Apil 2001)

Hinds, P.J., Bailey, D.E.: Out of Sight, Out of Sync: Understanding Conflict in Distributed Teams. Organization Science 14(6), 615–632 (2003)

Hinds, P.J., Mortensen, M.: Understanding conflict in geographically distributed teams: the moderating effects of shared identify, shared context, and spontaneous communication. Organization Science 16(3), 290–307 (2005)

Gregory, R., Prifling, M., Beck, R.: The role of cultural intelligence for the emergence of negotiated culture in IT offshore outsourcing projects. Information Technology & People 22(3), 223–241 (2009)

Jarvenpaa, S.L., Leidner, D.E.: Communication and trust in global virtual teams. Organization Science 10(6), 791–815 (1999)

Jørgensen, C., Korsaa, M., Olesen, A.B.: Decision support tool for tactical sourcing. In: Hertzum, M., Jørgensen, C. (eds.) Balancing Sourcing and Innovation in Information Systems Development, Tapir Academic Publishers, Trondheim (2011)

Kotlarsky, J., Oshri, I.: Social ties, knowledge sharing and successful collaboration in globally distributed system development projects. European Journal of Information Systems 14, 37–48 (2005)

Kraut, R.E., Fussel, S.R., Brennan, S.E., Siegel, J.: Understanding effects of proximity on collaboration: Implications for technologies to support remote collaborative work. In: Hinds, P.J., Kiesler, S. (eds.) Distributed Work, pp. 137–162. MIT Press, Cambridge (2002)

Lin, H.-F.: Effects of extrinsic and intrinsic motivation on employee knowledge sharing intentions. Journal of Information Science 33(2), 135–149 (2007)

Markus, M.L.: Toward a theory of knowledge reuse: Types of knowledge reuse situations and factors in reuse success. Journal of Management Information Systems 18(1), 57–93 (2001)

Masino, G., Zamarian, M.: Information technology artefacts as structuring devices in organizations: Design, appropriation and use issues. Interacting with Computers 15, 693–707 (2003)

Myers, P.S.: Knowledge management and organizational design: An introduction. In: Myers, P.S. (ed.) Knowledge Management and Organizational Design, pp. 1–6. Butterworth-Heinemann, Boston (1996)

Nonaka, I.: The knowledge-creating company. Harvard Business Review, 96–104 (1991)

Nonaka, I.: A dynamic theory of organizational knowledge creation. Organization Science 5(1), 14–37 (1994)

Nonaka, I., Takeuchi: The Knowledge Creating Company. How Japanese Companies Create the Dynamics of Innovation. Oxford University Press (1995)

Olson, G., Olson, J.S.: Distance Matters. Human Computer Interaction 15, 139–178 (2000)

Orlikowski, W.J.: The duality of technology: Rethinking the concept of technology in organizations. Organization Science 3(3), 398–427 (1992)

Orlikowski, W.J.: Sociomaterial practices: Exploring technology at work. Organization Studies 28(9), 1435–1448 (2007)

Oshri, I., Kotlarsky, J., Willcocks, L.: Socialization in a global context: Lessons from dispersed teams. In: Panteli, N., Chiasson, M. (eds.) Exploring Virtuality within and Beyond Organizations: Social, Global and Local Dimensions, pp. 21–54. Palgrave Macmillan, N.Y. (2008)

Oshri, I., van Fenema, P., Kotlarsky, J.: Knowledge transfer in globally distributed teams: The role of transactive memory. Information Systems Journal 18, 593–616 (2008)

Polanyi, M.: Personal Knowledge: Toward a Post-critical Philosophy. Harper Torchbooks, New York (1962)

Polanyi, M.: The Tacit Dimension. Anchor Day Books, New York (1966)

Pries-Heje, J.: Managing Knowledge in IT Projects. The IFCAI Journal of Knowledge Management 4, 49–62 (2004)

Rollag, K., Parise, S., Cross, R.: Getting new hires up to speed quickly. MIT Sloan Management Review 46(2), 35–41 (2005)

Van de Ven, A.H.: Engaged Schorlarship, A guide for Organizational and Social Research. Oxford University Press, NY (2007)

Vilnai-Yavetz, I., Rafaeli, A.: Managing artifacts to avoid artifact myopia. In: Rafaeli, A., Pratt, M.G. (eds.) Artifacts and Organizations, Beyond Mere Symbolism. Lawrence Erlbaum Associates, Mahwah (2006)

Yin, R.K.: Case Study Research: Design and Methods. Sage Publications, Newbury Park (1994)

A Guide to Selecting Theory
to Underpin Information Systems Studies

Sharol Sibongile Mkhomazi[1] and Tiko Iyamu[2]

[1] Tshwane University of Technology, Department of Informatics, Pretoria, South Africa
mkhomaziss@tut.ac.za
[2] Namibia University of Science and Technology,
Department of Business Computing, Windhoek, Namibia
connectvilla@gmail.com

Abstract. Empirically or experimental, in every research, methodology (method, approach and technique) are employed. The methodology guides the study from the beginning to the end. What is even more important is how the researcher views and deduces the outcome through his or her analytical lens. Information systems studies are increasingly challenging, primarily because of human interactions with computing. This is mainly due to the fact that human beings are unpredictable, which has impact and influence on how systems are developed, implemented and used.

In the last two decades, researchers of information systems (IS) have begun to employ socio-technical theories (lenses) in their studies. This includes younger and aspiring researchers who strive to understand the importance, as well as the application of the lenses in information systems studies. Selecting appropriate theory to underpin a study is therefore critical, primarily because it shapes and defines the results.

In this article, the factors which influence and determine the selection of theories in IS studies are examined. The aim was not to compare theories that are used to underpin IS studies, rather to understand how the socio-technical theories could provide a systematic method for data analysis in the field. The article also highlights some underpinning theories used in IS studies and their usefulness to researchers seeking to identify a theoretical basis for their arguments.

Keywords: Information systems, Research Methodology, Underpinning Theory.

1 Introduction

Information systems (IS) discipline is an aspect of computing that continue to involve more of social context in its development and implementation (Avison & Elliot, 2005). The discipline inculcates sociology of events into computing. The social context in IS makes it more interestingly challenging, whether in the development or implementation stages, including, in the areas of research. Research in IS are carried out primarily to investigate and understand what events happened; why the events

Y.K. Dwivedi et al. (Eds.): TDIT 2013, IFIP AICT 402, pp. 525–537, 2013.

happened; how did the events happened; and the impact and influence of events in the development, implementation, and use of IS in various environments.

Information systems research is a practical approach to professional inquiry in any social situations and it has become focal in recent times (Agarwal & Lucas, 2005). IS research has expanded significantly and adopted the use of socio-technical theories (Gregor, 2006), many of which are drawn from other disciplines such as sociology. IS research are considered and argued to be practical due to the fact that events are studied in their natural settings, whether through qualitative, quantitative or both methods.

Until recently, fifteen years to be precise, data analysis in IS studies were carried out, using mainly the interpretative approach (Walsham, 1995). This approach by itself is a challenge as it does not have a formula, and it is not guided by distinct views and boundaries (Lawrence, 2010). The argument could be attributed to the fact that people (researchers) often have different opinions and interpretations. Hence, it is useful and critically important to underpin a study with a, or combination of theories. The socio-technical theories are aimed to underpin IS research, meaning it provide guidance from the data collection to empirical data analysis.

However, selecting a theory or combination of theories which is considered to be appropriate to underpin a study is never an easy task by itself. This is a difficult challenge which IS researchers are currently faced with. Many IS researchers are challenged with selecting a theory to underpin their studies. The challenge could be could be attributed to the fact that the theories such as Structuration Theory (ST), Actor Network Theory (ANT), Activity Theory (AT) and Contingency Theory (CT) are not of IS field.

Another critical challenge is that some aspects of the theories could be seen to overlap. The aim of this article is not to compare theories that could be employed in IS research but rather to assist researchers to understand the importance of selecting appropriate theories, and how they could provide a systematic method in data analysis in their studies.

Based on the focus of this article, as stated above, it is important to highlight the role of methodology in IS research. Research methodology encompasses methods, techniques and approaches through which data is collected and analysed. The type of data collected determines the analysis technique that is chosen. The analysis of data provides the end result of the research.

2   The Role of Research Methodology

The research methodology consists of methods, techniques and approaches, which provide guidance to research in many fields including IS. According to Zikmund (2003), research methodology is a master plan specifying the methods and procedures for collecting and analysing the needed information. In the same line of argument, Mouton (2001) emphasised that research methodology focuses on the research process and the kind of tools and procedures to be used in achieving the objectives of the study.

In order to achieve the objectives of any research study, a methodology is required. Empirical (or experimental) research methodology comprises a class of methods, techniques and approaches in terms of which empirical observations or data are collected in order to answer specific research questions. The empirical research methods are divided into two categories, namely, quantitative and qualitative research methods. According to De Vos, Strydom, Fouche and Delport (2002) quantitative and qualitative research methods are the two well-known and recognised approaches in IS research. The two methods are not in contrast, rather, they complement each another.

Qualitative study is concerned with non-statistical methods. It enable researchers to study social and cultural phenomena Myers (2009). The qualitative research method allows study to be carried out in their natural settings, attempting to make sense of, or interpret phenomena in terms of the meanings people bring to them (Denzin & Lincoln, 2005). The interpretative nature of a qualitative research study uncovers and describes the actual meanings that people use in real settings (Olivier, 2009). In this article, interpretative is aimed at producing an understanding of the context of IS studies, whereby IS influences and is influenced by its context (Walsham, 1993). The qualitative approach takes social context into considerations in the construction, whether technical and cultural aspects of IS study. It acknowledges that, although IS have a strong technological component, they are implemented and used by people within social context (Modol, 2007).

Alternative to qualitative is the quantitative research method which is aimed to enable researchers to study, also natural phenomena, to measure the social world objectively, as well as to predict and understand human behaviour. De Vos et al (2002) described quantitative method as an inquiry into a social or human problem, based on the testing of a theory composed of variables, measured with numbers and analysed with statistical procedures in order to determine whether the predictive generalisations of the theory hold true. In quantitative, interpretation of numbers is often seen as strong evidence of how a phenomena work or did not work. Based on this premises, it is argued that it is difficult to underpin a numerical data with a theory. This article therefore focuses on selection of theories that underpin qualitative studies.

The role of research methodology is critical as it defines the engineering components of a study through which the objectives are achieved. The methodology defines research attributes such as "What" (strategy), "Where" (design), and "How" a study is carried out. The methodology starts with what type of data and materials are to be collected:

a. What - The type of data and materials to be collected in order to achieve the objectives of the study is strategic in nature. The strategy is fulfilled, through qualitative, quantitative or both methods.

b. Where: This is the design of the study. It determines the entity to be studied, using methods such as the Case Study.

c. How: The "How" attribute defines the techniques or techniques which are employed in the data collection. Data is collected based on the strategy (What) and design (Where) as briefly described above. Analysis is carried out on the collected data. How the analysis is done remain vital and critical stage of any study.

d. Why: On each of the research methodological steps which are employed in a study, there has to be justifications (WHY). The justification helps to understand the flow and relationship amongst the methods, techniques and approaches. Otherwise, it could be regarded as falsified or lacking bases.

Without a methodology, it will be difficult or impossible to carry out studies which are of rigor, complex or comprehensive in nature. Also, methodology helps to answer questions such as where, when and how the study was conducted, as briefly described above.

Another important factor of the roles of research methodology is the sequence in which the selected methods, techniques and approaches are employed in a study. The importance of this factor is based on the fact that certain actions or events depend on each other. For example, the objectives of a study must be articulated before a decision on whether the study would be qualitative, quantitative or both are reached. Similarly, the qualitative-ness of the study determines the theory that underpins the study. Otherwise, according to Jabar (2009), researchers may not recognise the systematic approach that is provided by theory, in specific steps, during data analysis. Bottom-line is that the selection of methods, techniques and how they are applied depend on the aims and objectives of the study, as well as the nature of the phenomenon under investigation.

3   Underpinning Theory

As already mentioned earlier in this article, in the recent years, IS studies employ socio-technical theories to guide their studies. The use of the theories to underpin studies is mainly in the areas of qualitative interpretive research. This is primarily because of the interplay between technical and non-technical factors which are involved in the field of IS. Underpinning theories are referred to, by Gregor (2002) as theories for understanding social context in IS studies. The theories are intended to explain "how" and "why" things happen in the way that they do.

The theory which underpins a study is often viewed as a lens. In Orlikowski (2000), the word "lens" is used in the sense of assessment, where certain features are focused upon and emerge, and where the rest of the picture falls into the background. Lenses are used as an analytical tool to aid interpretation and analysis of data in research. The analysis of the data determines and shapes the results of the study. The analysis of data is fundamental to any study. Hence, the tool (theory) used in the analysis is deemed critical. How data is collected and analysed is within the frame of the theory which underpin the study.

One of the significance factors of underpinning theories is that they encompass both technical and social contexts within phenomena under study. A theory which underpins a study is characteristically relied upon for rationales such as:

*   To help exhume the dependence and relationships which exist among actors within an environment.
*   Provides guidance in the interpretation of empirical data which was gathered over time and within a context.

- Creates awareness of social events, processes and activities which takes place in the development, implementation and practice of information technology and systems.
- Reduces the gap of assumptions and prediction of actions within a context.

The use of socio-technical theory to underpin a study could be viewed as the heart (core) of a research. As shown in Figure 1, the strategy (qualitative in this case) of the research determines the theory which underpin; and the theory helps to shape the result of the research, through its understanding of the socio-technical contexts that are involved.

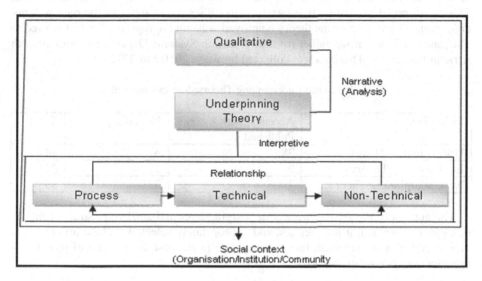

Fig. 1. Research Strategic Approach

As illustrated in figure 1, qualitative research leads itself to narrative description. In this context, narrative is the process of organising the data in units. Roberts (2002) points out that in the process of data analysis it becomes evident that parts of the narrative are not drawn randomly but selected thematically. The data is interpretively analysed using theory, to understand the relationship that exist amongst the core or primary components, which are often Process, Technical and Non-technical. The interpretive analysis of data happens within socio-technical contexts.

The theory which underpins a study is potentially to help find the factors that make a difference either in the development or implementation, or both of information systems in organisations. The aim is to gain better understanding of the socio-technical dynamics in organisations, institutions and how people interact with the systems, so as to solve current or emerging problems. The notion of socio-technical systems is not new. It emerged in the 1950's that through the interaction between people and technology in the course of innovation, socio-technical context do exist (Trist, 1981).

Theories which underpin a study do not predict the outcome of that study. Rather, it enhances our understanding of a situation, and through it, explanation is offered on why things happen in the way that they do. The theories make significant contributions to IS research through it's theorises of IS/IT artefacts, particularly from socio-technical perspectives.

4   The Use of Underpinning Theory: Success and Failure

In recent years, reviewers for conferences and journals draw more attentions and emphasis on how results and conclusions are reached in articles. Without underpinning theories, many articles, particularly those based on qualitative data, look speculative or artificial. As a result, for many research articles are not accepted for publication. This is attributed to, mainly two factors: it is either the analysis of the data was not underpinned by theory, or the theory employed was not appropriate. Table 1 is used to illustrate the data that we gather from Information Systems Department from a South African University. This data was collected between 2010 and 2012.

Table 1. The use Underpinning Theory: Success and Failure

IS Studies	Accepted and Published	Not Accepted	Total
Underpinning Theory	38	6	44
Inappropriate Theory	9	18	27
No Underpinning Theory	7	32	39

The authors of the articles were both postgraduates and academia. Some of the articles were rewritten, using theories, and appropriately selected. These articles were then accepted and published, thus making significant case for the use of theories in information systems studies.

5   Underpinning Theory and IS Studies

Theories from sociology discipline has been used by many scholars to underpin a wide range of studies in IS field. Based on the analysis, using socio-technical theories, studies have had theoretical, practical and methodological contributions to the IS field over the years. Some of the theories include Activity Theory, Actor Network Theory, Contingency Theory, Diffusion of Innovation Theory, Grounded Theory and Structuration Theory. Over the years, the use of the theories in IS studies continue to develop.

Activity Theory

Activity Theory (AT) focuses on human interaction with events and activities within a social context. According to Parks (2000), the theory's investigation of human interaction with others through an activity, forms basic unit of analysis for understanding human behaviour. The theory describes an activity as the way a subject (either an individual or a group) moves towards an object with the purpose of achieving certain results or certain objectives. Some of its advantages are that it supports analysis of the dialectic interactions between people; and the ways technologies shapes and are shaped by human activities.

For more than a decade, AT has been a recognised, and arguably know as a theory for enhancing design practices in Computer Supported Collaborative Work (CSCW) and related fields of Human-Computer Interaction (HCI) (Redmiles, 2002). Kuutti (1999) employed AT in a study, to investigate individuals and social transformation in IS development projects; and Demiraslan and Usleul (2008) used AT to examine the integration of technology into Turkish schools.

Actor Network Theory

Actor Network Theory (ANT) is mainly concern with actors within a heterogeneous network. In ANT, actor is either human or non-human, which seek to make a difference. According to Shin, Choo and Beom (2010), ANT attempt to address power relationship during technology development. As a result of its premises, ANT is often employed to understand why and how technological solutions are created as a carrier of a network of technical and social relations.

ANT has been of IS acceptance for many years (Monteiro & Hanseth, 1996). The acceptance has led to its use in many studies, such as: the role of standards in innovation and diffusion of broadband mobile service (Yoo, Lyytinen & Yang, 2005); local actors build broadband infrastructure (Skogseid & Hanseth, 2005); information infrastructure and rural innovation systems (Skogseid, 2007); and socio-technical dynamics in the development of next generation mobile network (Shin et al., 2010).

Contingency Theory

Contingency Theory (CT) focuses on situational or environmental factors that influence leadership (Fiedler, 1967). It is an approach to the study of organisational behaviour in which explanations are given as to how contingent factors such as technology, culture and external environment influence the design and function of the environment. The theory claims that there is no single best way to design organisational structure that is effective in some situations, and may not be successful in others (Fiedler, 1967).

Similar to other socio-technical theories discussed herewith, the CT has been applied in many IS studies such as Tinaikar and Flor, (1995); Barki, Rivard. and Talbot (2001); Mathiassen and Sørensen (2007).

Diffusion of Innovation Theory

Diffusion of Innovation (DOI) is the process by which an innovation is communicated through certain channels over time among the members of a social system (Rogers, 1995). The theory seeks to explain how innovations are undertaken by population within a context. DOI is aimed at making voluntary decisions to accept or reject an innovation which is based on the benefits that they expect to accrue from their own independent use of technology.

The theory has also been applied and adopted in numerous ways. For examples: Blake, Neuendorf and Valdisseri (2005) applied the theory in a study which attempted to tailor new websites for online shopping; Bharati and Chandhury (2006) employed the DOI to understand the current status of technology adoption; Hsu, Lu and Hsu (2007) used the theory in their investigation of consumer adoption of internet mobile messaging services (MMS).

Grounded Theory

Grounded theory develops theory that is grounded in a systematic data gathering and analysis (Jabar, 2009). The theory develops during the research process itself, and is a product of continuous interplay between analysis and data collection (Glaser & Strauss, 1967). The process involves using multiple stages of data collection and the refinement and interrelationship of categories of information (Strauss & Corbin, 1998).

Grounded theory has been used in IS studies in real-life contexts, particularly when the boundaries between the phenomenon and its contexts were not seen as being clear, nor were they thought to be clearly defined between the practices of ICT and the organisation. The theory has been applied in IS studies by researchers such as (Orlikowski, 1993) where GT was used to investigate incremental and radical changes in systems development. Hansen and Kautz (2005) used GT to examine how system developers use information systems development methodologies in practice. The GT has proven to be useful in developing context-based, process-oriented descriptions and explanations of information systems phenomena (Goulielmos, 2004).

Structuration Theory

Structuration Theory (ST) focuses on agent and structure. The theory is concerned with the relationship and interaction between agents and structure. In ST, agents are both technical and non-technical, and structure is rules and resources. According to Iyamu and Roode, (2010), *the word 'structure' must not be confused with its obvious connotation of organisational hierarchy in the English language.* ST aimed to understand the interplay within social practices across time and space (Giddens, 1984). The action of agent and structure depend on each other, and are produce and reproduce overtime, which is as a result of duality.

The duality of structure consists of three dimensions: Structure, Modality and Interaction. Each of the dimensions contains fundamental elements, Modalities (interpretive schemes, resources and norms); Structure (signification, domination and legitimation); and Interaction (communication, power and sanction). Interaction between agents and structure takes place through the duality of structure, and the interactions produce and reproduce action overtime and space.

6   Guide to Selecting Underpinning Theories

This section provide guide for IS researchers in their zeal and quest to selecting theories for their studies. In providing such guidance, the challenges that are often encountered are hereby examined. This is to avoid continuously getting into the pitfall. IS research have drawn on a variety of disciplines including social studies through which underpinning theories act as lenses to explain the phenomenon. IS researchers are interested in different theories to underpin their studies. This is primarily to deepen and gain better understanding of the empirical data through analysis.

As discussed in the Underpinning Theory section, theories are significant to IS studies. Theories underpin studies with the primary intention to diffuse the rigor, and examine the socio-technical contexts. Hence the selection of appropriate theory is critical. Otherwise, it could add complexity to the study. However, selection of a theory or combination of theories to underpin a study has never been easy. This could be attributed to many factors such as:

a.   Understanding – as mentioned earlier in the article, majority of the theories which are used in IS field originated from sociology discipline. This makes it challenging for IS researchers, in understanding their contexts and focuses.

b.   Knowledge – some IS researcher are knowledgeable about a theory. This group of researchers attempt to make use of the particular theory in all the research types that they conduct.

c.   Application – many IS researchers (students included) have difficulty on how to apply the social-technical theories in their studies. Experience has shown that even those IS researchers who seem to understand some of the theories, have a challenge in the application.

d.   Differentiation – some of the social theories have lots of similarities on their focuses and coverage. Actor network Theory (ANT) and Structuration Theory (ST) are good examples. ANT and ST focuses on Human and non-human actors, and technical and non-technical agents, respectively. The focal points of both theories are on Power relationship, and Negotiation of interest within a system.

The emergence of social-technical theories to underpin IS studies have made research more interesting or challenging, depending on the perspective of your fence. The challenge has become very prevalence, and it impacts the space of research activities in IS. This lead to a question that has now become popular amongst IS researchers (students in particular): "what theory can I make use of in my study?" To answer such question, the choice of a theory to underpin an IS study is based on the research objectives, primarily. As such, the objectives must be well articulated and understood. Understanding of the influences and drivers of the objectives is imperative. Also important is having a good understanding of the research problem statement.

When selecting a theory, the researcher need to map the theory to the research objectives and decide which one of the existing theories is suitable for the study. The implication is huge when appropriate theory for the study is not selected. This could result to gaps and disjoint in the findings, thereby hampering the outcome of the research.

The choice of a theory could be subjective. Walsham (2006) offer some tips to researchers in the process of selecting a theory or theories to underpin their studies:

- Do not fix on one theory and then read nothing else
- Do not leave theory generation to the end of your study

- Do not dismiss a theory's value until you have read about it in some depth
- Do read widely on different theories as this will offer a broader basis on which theory to choose

There is no specific formula for selecting a theory or combination of theories. What are important and helpful are assimilation of the research objectives, and a good understanding of some theories. Understanding of different theories helps the researcher to make appropriate decision.

6.1   Understanding the Theories

Table 2 below presents a guide for possible selection of theories to underpin IS studies. The Table consist of the most popular theories that have been used in the IS studies in the last ten years. For each of the theories, a descriptive insight and tenets are provided. The description and tenets are considered as the influencing factors in the selection of the theories for IS studies.

Table 2. Guide to selecting theories

Theory	Description	Tenets
Structuration Theory	Interpretive, narrative, multi-dimensional	Social context, power relationship, technical, non-technical, process oriented.
Actor Network Theory	Iterative, Interpretive, narrative	Power relation, varies interests, human, non-human, networks, process oriented.
Technology Acceptance Model	Interpretative, narrative	Assumption, Presumption, Human, predictive, Technology, Systems
Contingency Theory	Interpretative, narrative	Social context, process oriented, cultural, human, intents
Activity Theory	Interpretative, narrative	Social context, agents relationship, division of labour, process oriented,
Diffusion of Innovation	Interpretative, narrative	Social context, process oriented.
Grounded Theory	Iterative, Interpretative	Social context, process oriented, cultural

An obvious fact is that the objectives and scope of studies differ in sizes, some are broader than others. In such instances, multiple theories could be required in order to gain full coverage of the data analysis. Also, the theories have the potential to help develop methodological frameworks which are based on a logical appropriation of its tenets and consistent (Avison, Wood-Harper, Vidgen and Wood, 2002). The tenets play a vital role in guiding the analysis of the data.

There should not be conflict or contradiction in combined use of theories in IS studies. The aim is often not to compare or contrast the theories when they are applied complementarily in a study. According to Iyamu and Roode (2010), the aim is to highlight their importance and complementary usefulness in the research.

In terms of complementarily use of theories, the Moment of translation from the perspective of ANT and duality of structure from the perspective of ST as lenses is good example. The duality of structure could be used to analyse the processes through which legitimating structures evolve and are reconstituted by actions of actors within a system. While Moment of translation could examine how people and objects together operate within a network in heterogeneous processes of translation and negotiations.

ST has also been combined with AT in some IS studies. Hussain, Taylor and Flynn (2004), applied ST and AT complementarily in their study, which resulted to the development of legitimation activity model (LAM). Widjaja and Balbo (2005) employed both ST and AT to understand human activity in the larger social context.

7   Conclusion

The number of social-technical theories is growing, so is their use IS studies. The use of theories to underpin studies bring a fresh perspectives into IS research. IS research is gradually becoming more dynamic rather than the traditional stagnant approaches, which are of the direct interpretive of data and statistical methods.

However, the use of the social-technical theories could be detrimental if they are not understood or appropriately selected, and applied. This article presents the importance and implication of understanding the theories before selection; and a guide on the influence and how a theories or theories could be selected to underpin IS studies. These are the primary contributions of the article.

References

Agarwal, R., Lucas, H.C.: The Information Systems Identity Crisis: Focusing on High-Visibility and High-Impact Research. MIS Quarterly 29(3), 381–398 (2005)

Avison, D., Elliot, S.: Scoping the discipline of Information Systems. In: Avi-son, D.E., Pries-Heje, J. (eds.) Research in Information Systems: A Handbook for Research Supervisors and their Students (2005)

Avison, D.E., Wood-Harper, A.T., Vidgen, R., Wood, J.R.G.: A Further Explora-tion into Information Systems Development: The Evolution of Multiview2. Information Technology and People 11(2), 124–139 (2002)

Barki, H., Rivard, S., Talbot, J.: An integrative contingency model of software project risk management. Journal of Management Information System 17(4), 37–69 (2001)

Bharati, P., Chandhury, A.: Current status of technology adoption: Micro, small and medium manufacturing firms in Boston. Communications of the ACM 49(10), 88–93 (2006)

Blake, B.F., Neuendorf, K.A., Valdisseri, C.M.: Tailoring new websites to appeal to those most likely to shop online. Technovation 25(10), 1205–1214 (2005)

De Vos, A.S., Strydom, H., Fouche, C.B., Delport, C.S.L.: Research at Grass Roots: For the social sciences and human service professions. Van Schaik, Pretoria (2002)

Demiraslan, Y., Usleul, Y.: ICT integration in Turkish schools: Using activity theory to study issues and contradictions. Australasian Journal of Educational Technology 24(4), 458–474 (2008)

Denzin, N.K., Lincoln, Y.S.: The SAGE handbook of qualitative research, 3rd edn. Sage Publications, London (2005)

Fiedler, F.E.: A theory of leadership effectiveness. McGraw-Hill, New York (1967); Gregor, S.: The Nature of Theory in Information Systems. MIS Quarterly 30(3), 611-642 (2006)

Giddens, A.: The Constitution of society: Outline of the theory of Structuration. University of California Press, Berkely (1984)

Glaser, B.G., Strauss, A.L.: The Discovery of Grounded Theory. Aldine press, Chicago (1967)

Goulielmos, M.: Systems development approach: transcending methodology. Information Systems Journal 14, 363–386 (2004)

Gregor, S.: A theory of theories in Information Systems. In: Gregor, S., Hart, D. (eds.) Information Systems Foundations: Building the Theoretical Base, pp. 1–20. Australian Univeristy, Cnberra (2002)

Hansen, B., Kautz, K.: Grounded Theory Applied – Studying Information Systems Development Methodologies in Practice. Paper Presented in the Proceedings of the 38th Hawaii International Conference on System Sciences. IEEE (2005)

Hsu, C.L., Lu, H.P., Hsu, H.H.: Adoption of the mobile internet on empirical study of multimedia message service (MMS), OMEGA. International Journal of Management Science 35(6), 715–726 (2007)

Hussain, Z., Taylor, A., Flynn, D.: A case study of the process of achieving legitimation in information systems development. Journal of Information Science 30(5), 408–417 (2004)

Iyamu, T., Roode, D.: The Use of Structuration Theory and Actor Network Theory for Analysis: Case Study of a Financial Institution. International Journal of Actornetwork Theory and Technological Innovation 2(1), 1–17 (2010)

Jabar, M.A.: An investigation into methods and concepts of qualitative research in Information Systems research. Computer and Information Science Journal 2(4), 47–54 (2009)

Kuutti, K.: Activity Theory, transformation of work, and information systems design. In: Engeström, Y., Miettinen, R., Punamäki-Gitai, R.L. (eds.) Perspectives on Activity Theory, pp. 360–376. Cambridge University Press, New York (1999)

Lawrence, J.: The factors that influence adoption and usage decision in SMEs: Evalu-ating interpretive case study research in information systems. The Electronic Journal of Business Research Methods 8(1), 51–62 (2010)

Mathiassen, L., Sørensen, C.: A theory of organizational information service, Working paper series (2007)

Modol, J.R.: Exploring the standardisation and intergration in the implementation of Industry interorganisational Information Systems: A Case Study in the Seaport of Barcelona (2007)

Monteiro, E., Hanseth, O.: Social Shaping of Information Infrastructure. In: Orlikowski, W.J., Walsham, G., Jones, M., De Gross, J.I. (eds.) Information Technology and Changes in Organisational Work. Chapman and Hall, London (1996)

Mouton, J.: How to succeed in your master's and doctoral studies: a South African guide and resource book. Van Schaik, Pretoria (2001)

Myers, M.D.: Qualitative research in Business & Management. Sage Publication, London (2009)

Olivier, M.S.: Information Technology research: A practical guide for Computer Science and Informatics, 3rd edn. Van Schaik, Pretoria (2009)

Orlikowski, W.J.: Case tools as organisational change: Investigating incremental and radical changes in Systems Development. MIS Quaterly 17(3), 309–340 (1993)

Orlikowski, W.J.: Using technology and constituting structures: a practice lens for studying technology in organisations. Organisational Science 11(4), 404–428 (2000)

Parks, S.: Same task, different activities: Issues of investment, identity and use of strategy. TESL Canada Journal 17(2), 64–88 (2000)

Redmiles, D.: Introduction to the special issue on activity theory and the practice of design. Computer Supported Cooperative Work 11(1), 1–11 (2002)

Roberts, C.: Biography research. Open University Press, Buckingham (2002)

Rogers, E.M.: Diffusion of Innovations. The Free Press, New York (1995)

Shin, D.H., Choo, H., Beom, K.: Socio-technical dynamics in the development of Next Generation Mobile Networks Moments of Translation Processes of Beyond 3G. Technological Forecasting and Social Change 75(9), 1406–1415 (2010)

Skogseid, I.: Information infrastructure and rural innovation systems: A study of the dynamics of local adaptation of ICT. University of Olso, Norway (2007)

Skogseid, I., Hanseth, O.: Local actors build broadband infrastructure. Paper presented in the Proceedings of the 13th European Conference on Information Systems, ECIS 2005, 1697–1708 (2005)

Strauss, A., Corbin, J.: Basics of qualitative research: Grounded theory procedures and techniques. Sage Publication, Newbury (1998)

Tinaikar, R., Flor, P.R.: Towards a contingency theory of control in information systems development projects. Producão 5(1), 5–22 (1995)

Trist, E.: The evolution of socio-technical systems: A conceptual framework and an action research program. Issues in the Quality of Working Life 2 (1981)

Walsham, G.: Interpreting Information Systems in Organisations. John Wiley & Sons, Chichester (1993)

Walsham, G.: Interpretive case studies in IS research: Nature and Method. European Journal of Information Systems, 74–81 (1995)

Walsham, G.: Doing interpretative research. European Journal of Information Systems 15(3), 320–330 (2006)

Widjaja, I., Balbo, S.: Structuration of Activity: a view on human activity. Paper Presented at the Proceedings of OZCHI 2005 of the 17th Australia Conference on Computer-Human Interaction: Citizens Online: Consideration for Today and the Future, Australia (2005)

Yoo, Y., Lyytinen, K., Yang, H.: The role of standards in innovation and diffusion of broadband mobile services: The case of South Korea. The Journal of Strategic Information Systems 14(3), 323–353 (2005)

Zikmund, W.G.: Business research methods, 7th edn. Thompson South Western, Ohio (2003)

Organizational Assimilation of Technology in a Sunrise Industry – A Story of Successes and Failures

Ravi A. Rao and Rahul De'

Indian Institute of Management, Bangalore, India
ravi.rao10@iimb.ernet.in, rahul@iimb.ernot.in

Abstract. The study analyzes the contextual factors impacting technology assimilation in an environment that is characterized by macro-economic changes, rapid technological innovations, emerging industry practices and shifting organizational contexts. Stones' strong structuration theory (SST), a refinement of Giddens' structuration theory, is used as the theoretical lens for studying the technology assimilation process. SST is used to analyze the structuration process at the micro-level and its impact on the structures at the meso/macro-level. In addition, actor network theory (ANT) is used to analyze the role of heterogeneous actors in altering the structures as the actor network adapts to the technological innovations and changing contexts.

Keywords: Structuration theory, Actor network theory, Technology diffusion, Technology assimilation.

1   Introduction

Studies of technology in organizations can be classified into two broad streams of research. The first stream adopts the ontological stance of discrete entities; the primary mechanism of diffusion being the moderation effect or technology impact; the methodology being variance-based studies; and the key concepts studied being technological imperatives or contingency models (Orlikowski & Scott, 2008). Most of the early diffusion studies fall into such a positivist stream of research and attempt to understand the relation between technology and organizational context, and its impact on the innovation diffusion process. The second stream of research adopts an ontological stance that assumes technology and organizations being part of a mutually dependent ensemble; the primary mechanism of diffusion being the interaction effect of technology with the organizational context and human actors; the methodology being process-based studies; and the key concepts being the duality of technology with technology viewed as both a physical and a social object (Orlikowski & Scott, 2008). A majority of the studies that fall into this stream of research focus on the interplay of technology and organization / human actors and the resultant impact on technology and organizational structures.

While technology impact in organizations has attracted research approaches from both of these paradigms, technology adoption and diffusion studies has largely remained positivist in nature. Fichman (Fichman, 2000) points out the limitations of the

Y.K. Dwivedi et al. (Eds.): TDIT 2013, IFIP AICT 402, pp. 538–554, 2013.

positivist stream of research in studying the later stages of technology assimilation involving formal adoption and full-scale deployment. In this paper, we attempt to contribute to the technology assimilation literature by conducting a processual study of such a phenomenon using a non-positivist paradigm. We conducted a single-case descriptive study (Yin, 2009) of an organization adopting technology while establishing itself in the emerging organized retail sector in India and as new technological innovations are introduced into this market.

2   Theoretical Background

We provide here a brief review of structuration theory and its application to the study of Information Systems (IS). We then outline the limitation of this theory for analyzing technology diffusion and propose a combination of Strong structuration theory (SST) with Actor Network theory (ANT) as the theoretical framework.

2.1   Structuration Theory and Diffusion Studies

Giddens' theory of structuration (Giddens, 1984) has been extensively used in IS research as a meta-theory for studying the interaction of technology with organizations. Structuration is defined as "the knowledgeable actions of human agents [that] discursively and recursively form the set of rules, practices and routines which, over time and space constitutes [..a] structure" (Rose, 1998). Giddens proposes that structure and agency are mutually constitutive and that social phenomena are a product of both. He also introduces the notion of duality of structures described through three components: structure (signification, domination, and legitimation), modality (interpretive schemes, facility, and norms) and interaction (communication, power, and sanctions). IS research that adopts structuration theory can be seen to fall into two categories: Technology structuration (Orlikowski, 1992) and Adaptive Structuration (DeSanctis & Poole, 1994).

While structuration theory is an appropriate lens for studying later stages of assimilation (Fichman, 2000), it is also constrained by some of its limitations. First, structuration theory being a meta-theory does not lend itself well to empirical studies (Stones, 1996) and can at best be considered only as an analytical or sensitizing device (Giddens, 1984). Secondly, studies using structuration theory do not consider the evolution of technology itself over time - an added dimension that makes the structure-agency duality three dimensional and non-linear (Greenhalgh & Stones, 2010). Thirdly, the assumption of relatively homogeneous actors poses a challenge when the scope of the study includes groups of heterogeneous actors. While these limitations have not posed serious threats to micro-level adoption studies, they form a major hindrance for a meso/macro level study, such as ours. In the next section, we outline the use of Strong Structuration theory (SST) and integrate it with Actor Network theory (ANT) to address these challenges.

2.2   Strong Structuration Theory

Strong structuration theory (SST) is an adaptation of structuration theory developed by Stones (Stones, 2005). SST adapts structuration theory for empirical work by introducing ontology-in-situ as "observing structures and action by agents in everyday occurrences of a conjuncture (a critical combination of events or occurrences)" (Greenhalgh & Stones, 2010). SST develops a quadripartite model for studying structuration using four components (Fig.1):

1) External-structures: comprising of acknowledged or unacknowledged (by the agent-in-focus) conditions of actions that lead to intended or unintended consequences through independent causal influences or irresistible external influences (Jack & Kholeif, 2007).
2) Internal-structures: representing agent's general-disposition that she draws upon and her conjuncturally-specific knowledge through the role or the position occupied by her (Stones, 2005). SST also adopts Cohen's notion of position-practices, a set of structures and practices that a positional incumbent can do (Cohen, 1989),
3) Active-agency: constituting the actions taken by the agent-in-focus drawn either routinely or strategically from their internal structures (Greenhalgh & Stones, 2010).
4) Outcomes: that are the intended or unintended consequences as a result of active-agency and leading to the external and internal structures being either preserved or changed (Jack & Kholeif, 2007).

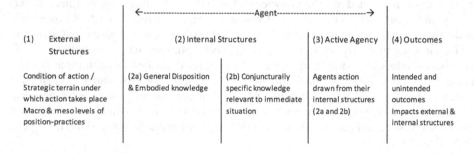

Fig. 1. Quadripartite model of SST - adapted from (Greenhalgh & Stones, 2010)

In brief, SST suggests that agents bring in generic capabilities through their internal disposition and specific knowledge. This capability determines how they are expected to act in a conjuncture and the possible outcome of their actions. However, how these agents will actually act in a particular situation depends on a host of other factors that cannot be determined in advance: such as the constraints imposed by external structures and the actions of other agents holding different position-practices. The analytic framework provided by SST is through the quadripartite model that allows the study of the structuration phenomena at a meso-macro level, across multiple conjunctures and involving multiple sets of agents-in-focus. The SST framework, however, does not address the technology dimension explicitly which limits its applicability for diffusion studies.

2.3   Strong Structuration and Actor Networks

Diffusion theories are often criticized of assuming that technologies once established as best-practices will effectively spread through the population (Briers & Chua, 2001). Actor network theory (ANT) on the other hand views the success or failure of technology as a social accomplishment of human actors and non-human elements (Latour, 1987) and advocates that such heterogeneous networks are inherently dynamic and unstable. Stability is achieved through the process of translation that occurs through the four stages of a) problematization (issue causing instability is identified), b) interessement (other actors agree to the issue being a problem), b) enrollment (main actors are assigned roles and form alliances), and d) mobilization (actor network is extended beyond the initial group) (Callon, 1986). With stability, actor networks become "black-boxes" achieving a high degree of irreversibility and having material inscriptions, and with actors and actants assuming taken-for-granted status (Walsham & Sahay, 1999).

Rose (1998) points out that Giddens' structuration theory does not address the technology dimensions and suggests the need for a careful combination of diverse theories in order to apply structuration to the IS discipline. A specific example of such a combination of theories is a study of GIS implementation in India (Walsham & Sahay, 1999) that combines structuration theory (as a sensitizing device) and ANT (as an empirical tool). Considering the gap in SST's analytical framework and the strength of ANT as a lens for studying technology driven changes, Greenhalgh and Stones (2010) suggest integrating these two theories. They do so by including technical actants into their list of agents-in-focus and expanding the concept of active agency to include actions taken by both actors and actants in a socio-technical network. Secondly, they expand the definition of internal structures by incorporating ANT's notion of material inscriptions in technology. Thus the internal structures, which per SST include human agents general disposition and conjuncturally-specific knowledge, is enhanced to include technology's material properties, socio-cultural inscriptions and the conjuncturally-specific functionality of these technologies (Greenhalgh & Stones, 2010). The resulting conceptual model developed by them is depicted in Fig 2.

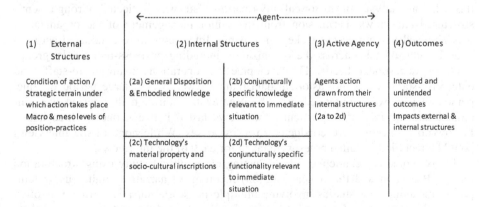

Fig. 2. SST with technology dimension - adapted from (Greenhalgh & Stones, 2010)

In summary, Greenhalgh and Stones adoption of SST for studying socio-technical phenomena include a network of position-practices that comprises of both human actors and technologies. Active agency involves the use of specific technology by human actors in any given conjuncture. These actions are influenced by external as well as internal forces. External forces are exerted through independent institutional, political, economic, and technological structures and forms the external conditions of actions. Internal structures is embodied both by human and technological agents. Actions by human agents are influenced by their general disposition and conjuncturally specific knowledge while technologies influence actions through their material inscriptions and conjuncturally specific functionality. Human agents, influenced by these internal and external conditions of actions, either use the technology faithfully or unfaithfully, or refuse to use the technology altogether. Such actions, in turn, reproduce or change the social structures. This recursive relationship between structures, agency and technology is played at the micro level in the short-run and is visible at the meso-macro level over a longer time scale.

3   Theoretical Framework and Method

Following our arguments in the previous section on the challenges of conducting a technology assimilation study and the applicability of an integrated SST and ANT lens for conducting such a study, we adopt the guidelines provided by Greenhalgh and Stones as outlined in Fig 3.

The analysis of the active agency is conducted across the heterogeneous set of actors participating in each conjuncture. The modified structures arising as a result of the outcome of each of these conjunctures is then used as an input to the subsequent conjunctures. Our attempt is to conduct a recursive analysis comprising of micro-meso level actions in each of the conjunctures and then integrate the analysis across conjunctures to understand the relationships being played out at meso-macro level over longer time duration.

We follow a case-study based approach for conducting our empirical analysis (Yin, 2009). The study was conducted at the end of the technology diffusion process through an analysis of historical information that was collected through semi-structured interviews. Permission from the senior management of the organization was obtained to gain access to key informants. Interviews were conducted across a wide breadth of roles across the organization including business-unit heads, group-CIO, IT department heads, IT development / operations team, store-staff, and enterprise-staff. Since the historical data required was over a large period of time, personnel who were employed with the organization through this period were included into the mix of respondents. Interviews lasted between one to three hours. Follow-up interview were conducted in a few cases. While none of the interviews could be recorded, detailed notes were taken for each of the interviews.

To overcome the challenges of conducting an empirical study using structuration theory, Pozzebon and Pinsonneault (2005) recommend narrative studies using temporal bracketing. For studies involving multiple phases, a narrative strategy is often used as the primary analysis tool: for preparing the chronology and sequence of phases, and to establish the links between them (Langley, 1999). In our study too, we adopt a narrative strategy approach considering the need to first determine the different phases of adoption and then to interpret the links between the different clusters of actors and the technologies across these phases.

1. Identify the various phases or conjunctures over which the organization undertakes the assimilation of technology. For each of these conjunctures, conduct the structuration study using the quadripartite model for analysis.

2. Determine the prevailing political, economic, technological and institutional context that form the external conditions of actions impacting the conjunctures.

3. Identify the socio-technical network comprising of agents and technologies

   (a) For each of the agents in focus

       i. Analyze their position-practices

       ii. Evaluate the agents general disposition

       iii. Evaluate the agents conjuncturally-specific knowledge including the understanding of the external structures, other agent's world view, technology's material property, its inscribed structures, and the functionality relevant to the situation

       iv. Identify the key relationships that the agent has with other agents and technologies

       v. Determine active-agency - the set of practices drawn on her general dispositions, conjuncturally-specific knowledge, and technological properties

   (b) For each of the technology in focus

       i. Analyze its material properties and the inscribed socio-cultural structures

       ii. Determine the functions in use and how the inscribed structures enable, influence, or constrain active agency

   (c) Determine the extent of the stability of the socio-technical network

4. Analyze the outcomes of the actions

   (a) Determine the intended and unintended consequences

   (b) The feedback of these consequences on the position-practices

   (c) The significance of these consequences to other actors in the network

   (d) The role of technology in producing these outcomes

   (e) The implications of these consequences

Fig. 3. Theoretical Framework

4   Organization's Tryst with Technology

In this section, we present a brief report on the organization and its process of technology assimilation.

4.1   Organization and Its Strategic Terrain

The organization (pseudonym Alpha) is a leading multi-format retailer in India. Alpha started as a textile manufacturing company and entered into the retail business circa.1995 during the post-liberalization phase of the Indian economy when modern retail in India was still at its infancy (Sengupta, 2008). With a buoyant economy, the Indian consumer was increasing her spending and modern retail promised immense potential (Srivastava, 2008).

Internationally, retail can be considered as a mature industry with established business practices and information technologies. Most Indian retail firms partnered with international retailers as technology partners with an objective of bringing these business practices and technologies to India. However, Indian retailers were not able to adopt these international practices owing to country-specific challenges, such as: lack of qualified retail personnel, inefficient supply-chains, a weak IT eco-system, lack of understanding of consumer buying behavior, idiosyncrasies of the Indian consumer, and the requirements of India-specific formats (Dash & Chandy, 2009). In addition, functionality required to handle Maximum Retail Price (MRP) which legally prohibits retailers from charging customers above the MRP was not addressed by most international retail software systems. During this period, India also had an established and burgeoning IT services industry. Confident about the availability of qualified IT personnel, retailers unable to adopt international systems chose to develop their own IT systems.

India is known to be a nation of shopkeepers with a proliferation of unorganized retailers (Kachru, 2011). The supply-chain ecosystem in India is tuned to delivering goods to such a vastly distributed network (Dholakia, Dholakia, & Chattopadhyay, 2012) with manufacturers led by the FMCG sector having established last-mile logistics capabilities (Sengupta, 2008). With last-mile distribution costs being built into their pricing, manufacturers were unwilling to part with extra margins. While multi-store retailers in India intended to set-up their own centralized warehouse and distribution channels to gain supply-chain efficiencies, they usually started operations leveraging the direct-store-delivery facilities provided by FMCG manufacturers.

4.2   Technology Adoption at Alpha

In accordance with the prevailing practices, Alpha also chose to develop its own IT systems and implemented a product called Retailer Enterprise Management (REM) during the years 1999-2000. REM functioned both as an enterprise management system as well as the store front-end and point-of-sale (POS) system. Alpha used REM as the sole IS for more than half a decade before adopting SAP to run their enterprise systems. The roll-out of SAP happened during 2006-2009 with REM continuing as the store POS system. The REM system was finally retired and the POS function migrated to a Wincor TP-Linux system by 2010-2011.

The adoption of technology at Alpha can be classified into the following phases or conjunctures: a) Conjuncture-1: conceptualization and initial adoption of REM; b) Conjuncture-2: rapid growth in scale of Alpha's business and associated changes to REM; c) Conjuncture-3: implementation of SAP; and d) Conjuncture-4: retirement of REM and the implementation of Wincor. The primary actors and the technologies participating in these conjunctures are as outlined in Fig.4.

Founder directors
Position-practice:
    Highest authority in decision making
    Key influencer for technology strategy
Internal Structures:
    General disposition of Indianness and
    Entrepreneurship
    Belief in developing home-grown IT
    systems
    Store manager as entrepreneur
	Business leaders
	Position-practice:
	    Department head s constituting senior
	    management
	    Provides functional road map for IS
	Internal Structures:
	    Limited knowledge of internationally
	    established retail practices
	    Exposure to store operations but not
	    enterprise functionalities

IT leaders
Position-practice:
    CIO and IT department heads
    Drives technology strategy
Internal Structures:
    Limited knowledge of internationally
    established retail practices
    Confident on in-house IT capabilities
	Store Manager
	Position-practice:
	    Responsible for running the retail store
	    Key user of the IT systems
	Internal Structures:
	    Trading mindset: maximizing short term
	    benefits
	    Entrepreneurial attitude
	    Uniquely positioned to understand the
	    consumer pulse

IT team
Position-practice:
    IT development systems operation
Internal Structures:
    Aspires to work for large IT service
    providers Eager to perform
	Enterprise staff (head-office / regional office)
	Position-practice:
	    Non-store functions such as B&M, F&A,
	    Warehouse, Marketing etc.
	Internal Structures:
	    New to organized retail, key to learn

Fig. 4. Actors with their position-practices and internal structures

Conjuncture 1: The Making of REM and Its Initial Adoption

The initial version of the IT system emerged as an in-house developed system catering to a largely store-focused functionality. Front-end promotion management emerged as a key functionality. Being a discount merchandiser, enticing consumers with attractive offers was a preferred way of selling. The store managers would assess the consumers' shopping needs and respond with impromptu promotions by modifying the selling price through back-end updates to the database. In addition, the checkout personnel were often allowed the use of "manager's password", an open-access provision that allowed them to alter selling price to overcome any incorrect system updates.

Indian consumer's demands are often thought to be complex, comprising of many unique parts based on cultural and linguistic identities (Bijapurkar, 2009). Alpha's background as an apparel manufacturer meant a superior capability in apparel merchandising. However, with diversification into multi-brand retailing, Alpha faced an acute shortage of category management capabilities in non-apparel merchandises. During such a time, store managers showed leadership in understanding the consumer needs and recommended appropriate merchandises. This resulted in selective enterprise functionalities such as master-data-management (MDM) and merchandise-receipt functions being built as store functionality.

Further, the result of adopting direct-store-delivery practices led to inventory discrepancies such as duplicate SKUs (stock-keeping-units), SKUs without bar-code, multiple MRPs, or `SKU not found' (physical inventory not entered in system). The impact of such data discrepancies led to billing errors, long check-out lines, and products billed at higher than MRP (a legal offense). To overcome these issues, store staff often used to resort to practices such as those of manual billing, price-overrides, and manual data correction.

The technology in focus during this conjuncture is the REM software. The material property of this software can be summarized as being: highly malleable and customizable, and as a store-specific IT system with additional enterprise functionality. The socio-cultural structures inscribed into this technology can be seen as comprising of a) promotion functionality: reinforces the belief of discount merchandising; b) manager's password: stood for the power and dominance of the store manager and the open access nature of the IT system; and c) manual billing: representing the suspect IT ecosystem.

The end of this conjuncture is marked by a rapid increase in store sales and the emergence of the store manager as the central agent in this growth. With the increasing demand of stores on IT maintenance activities, the store IT team size gradually increased and a dual reporting structure emerged.

Conjuncture 2: Rapid Business Growth and the Need for an Enterprise Systems

The unfolding of this conjuncture occurred during 2001-2005 and was marked by a few key changes in the external conditions. Firstly, ERP systems such as SAP and Retek were making inroads into India. Secondly, retailers were now trying to establish centralized warehouses to achieve supply chain efficiencies and better margins (Srivastava, 2008). Thirdly, there was a growing expectation of a policy change allowing foreign direct investment in retail (Mukherjee & Patel, 2006). This created urgency among Indian retailers to achieve scale before the entry of foreign retailers.

With the increase in number of stores, centralized enterprise roles such as master data management (MDM), buying and merchandising (B&M), receipts and distribution, and marketing functions were gaining importance. The distributed nature of the REM system warranted the creation of a new business-intelligence (BI) function for consolidating data across the stores. The entry of this new system highlighted masterdata and inventory related issues residing in the existing system, such as the inability to consolidate data across stores due to duplicate SKU codes. Further, REM lacked an archival functionality leading to ever increasing database sizes and associated performance issues. Severe performance issues were often addressed by adding memory/ processing power and suspending back-end functions during peak business hours. Such ad hoc measures had a cascading effect with further delays in inventory receipts leading to further inventory issues. Data discrepancies, performance issues and inefficiencies arising out of these escalated the need for an enterprise-wide system.

The executive management team took proactive steps to strengthen the IT leadership by inducting new actors. The new IT management advocated the need for replacing the enterprise functionality of REM by ERP systems. The POS functionality of REM was however thought to be suitable for business operations. The removal of enterprise functionality from the store was not seen, by the organization in general and the store managers in specific, as downgrading the responsibilities of the store manager. Instead, it was seen as releasing the bandwidth of the store manager to be productively used in increasing store sales.

Conjuncture 3: REM as a POS System

Conjuncture-3 unfolded during 2005-2009 with the roll-out of SAP across the business units. During this time, organized retail was establishing itself as a mature industry with several retailers adopting international practices including centralized warehousing and distribution, space management, and category management. This duration also saw the advancement of POS technology with integrated cash-registers, bill printers, barcode scanners, weighing machines and software.

The SAP system brought along with it internationally accepted practices. The enterprise staff, so far constrained by the limited functionality offered by REM, adopted SAP without much resistance. However, several functionalities in the new SAP system were in contradiction to the way they were implemented in REM. For example, the industry practice for promotions management was to have centralized promotions with the responsibility of defining and setting of the promotions residing with the B&M team. However, at Alpha, the store managers were given the right to decide on promotions. This conflict was addressed by allowing the B&M team create header level promotions (broad guidelines on the type of sales promotion per category/brand), with the actual execution of these promotions (i.e. decision on specific SKUs to be included under the header) being executed on the REM POS system by individual stores. Since the final control remained with the store managers, the header level promotion guidelines were often not followed faithfully and the stores resorted to floating their own promotions. This led to three significant consequences: a) Alpha noticed a considerable leakage in the revenue margins due to unauthorized promotions; b) led to instances of pilferage due to the open-access control of REM, and c) non-standardization of promotions across stores leading to discontent among the customers.

In addition to these functional issues, Alpha also faced certain technical challenges with the REM system. The POS terminals deployed at Alpha were essentially a combination of a desktop computer connected with peripherals (barcode scanner and printer) and running on Windows OS. The rapid scale-up in the number of stores meant that Alpha had not only to invest in the desktops and peripherals, but also had to buy licenses for Windows and Progress database (required for installing REM). This resulted in a growing need to adopt newer POS technologies such as those that ran on Linux, which offered the promise of not only providing an integrated system but also of being cost efficient.

Enterprise staff, so far constrained by the limitations of the REM system, found the SAP system that was inscribed with industry best practices as an enabler in meeting the demands of a fast maturing industry. However, as noted above, many of these inscriptions were in direct contradiction with those of the REM system. With the implementation of SAP, Alpha reinforced its IT leadership team with key personnel experienced in managing international retail-IT products. The new leadership convinced the directors and other business heads on the need to retire REM and adopt an international POS product. This conjuncture ends with a decision to replace REM by Wincor POS system.

Conjuncture 4: Wincor and Organizational Change

The new IT heads, drawing from their past experience in implementing Wincor on a SAP system, provided the necessary expertise in driving this program. A phased implementation approach was adopted. In contrast to the SAP implementation, the roll-out of POS solution was expected to have a much greater impact on the life at the store. The impact on the checkout staff was expected to be minimal with net positive benefits given the lesser steps to billing, speedier checkout, faster response time, graphic touch-screen and other "friendly" features. However, it was anticipated that the store managers would resist the new system as the removal of access to key functionalities would impact their entrepreneurial empowerment.

Recognizing these challenges, Alpha decided to launch an organizational-change initiative as part of the introduction of the new POS system. The concept of a "Store Kartha" or the "head of the family" was introduced to reposition the store manager. This can be seen as an attempt to reconfigure the store manager's positioning as an overall leader of the store. The introduction of the new POS system was also managed as a cultural activity: marking a new beginning with new philosophy, new machines, new software, and launched with a "pooja" (worship for prosperity).

The issue of managing promotions in the new system was critical to success. The first challenge was the resistance expected by the store manager due to loss of control. This was addressed by positioning the change in responsibility as merely transferring a routine job (of creating promotion codes) from the store to the back-office. The management realized that the issue with the store exercising promotions (once considered as a key strength) was due to the ad hoc nature in which it was being performed that was resulting in margin impacts. Shifting the activity to the back-office would lead to the dual advantage of making promotion management as a centralized activity and also incorporate feedback from stores. The need to plan promotions in advance was portrayed as a valid and reasonable constraint imposed by the system. A second issue faced was the limited promotion functionality offered by SAP as compared to the earlier REM system. This limitation was expected to make the task of setting promotions more difficult. A dedicated promotion-managed team was set-up to ensure that promotions were planned in advance, feedback sought from the stores and implemented in the SAP system.

Pilot implementation of Wincor faced a series of challenges including store resistance and data transfer issues between SAP and Wincor. Once these issues were resolved, the implementation was rolled out in one region, then to all regions under a format and subsequently to all the formats.

5   Analysis Using Strong Structuration and Actor Networks

We now interpret the data from the case using concepts from SST and ANT to demonstrate the act of structuration as the organization adopts and assimilates technologies. Table 1 provides a summary of the analysis.

Conjuncture 1

The broad strategic terrain under which Alpha initiated its technology adoption involved the infancy of organized retail in India with the supply-chain predominantly catering to the unorganized markets (Mukherjee & Patel, 2006). While India's economy was experiencing post-liberalization benefits and India was emerging as a global

IT provider, the organized retail industry in India was still in its infancy with no mature practices and not yet ready to accept international retail software.

At a micro-level, we notice the actions of the founders and the senior management, driven by their general disposition (Indianness) and their understanding of the strategic terrain (inappropriate international products), leading to the adoption of in-house IT systems. We notice the impact of these actions on the position-practices resulting in the emergence of the store manager as the key agent-in-focus. We also notice how these micro-level actions resulted in REM evolving as a distributed system incorporating enterprise functionality. Workaround functions (such as manual overrides, back-end updates etc.) emerged for cases where the technology and agency were not aligned. Practices such as promotions, manual overrides, and back-end updates got inscribed into the IT systems. Over time, these inscriptions assumed a taken-for-granted status and became a way of functioning for the organization. At the end of the conjuncture, the actor network under study gained stability and led to a rapid increase in business.

Table 1. Quadripartite elements of SST as applicable to our study

Quadripartitie Elements	Conjuncture 1	Conjuncture 2	Conjuncture 3	Conjuncture 4
External Structure	- Organized retail not an established industry - Opening-up of Indian Economy - India as a global IT provider	- International ERP products entering Indian markets - Imminent entry of FDI in Retail	- Maturing of organized retail practices - Entry of new generation POS hardware / software	- No change
General Disposition	- Indianness and Entrepreneurship	- No change	- Entry of global actors to IT leadership team	- No change
Conjuncturally specific knowledge	- Apparel retailer - Lack of multi-format retail expertise - Discount merchandiser	- No change	- Organizational scaling needs enterprise management skills	- Global IT leaders with past experience in similar environment - Successful SAP implementation leading to trust in international products
Material property and Social Inscriptions	- Malleable software	- Open access - Runtime promotions	- Retail best practices incorporated in SAP - No changes in REM's inscriptions - Conflict between these two sets of inscriptions	- Opposing inscriptions between REM and Wincor systems - Wincor requiring design time changes, not as malleable

Table 1. (*continued*)

| Conjuncturally specific functionality | - Manual billing
- Promotions management
- Enterprise functions at store | - Consolidation across stores
- Conflict between front-end and back-end functions
- Need for BI functionality
- Scalability and performance issues | - Promotions in SAP executed unfaithfully at the stores
- Manual billing leading to inventory issues
- Incorrect promotions leading to loss of margins | - Integrated POS functionality with touch-screen features
- Faster checkout processing time
- Limited promotions functionality |

Conjuncture 2

In this conjuncture we notice a significant change in the strategic terrain: including the acceptance of ERP products by the Indian retailers, the opening up of the Indian economy, and the impending policy change. At a micro-level, we notice technological limitations leading to the addition of a BI system to the actor network. In ANT terminology, the punctualized state that REM achieved in conjuncture-1 gets broken with the introduction of the BI system. The addition of the BI functionality exposed the deficiencies of the underlying components of REM including POS, MDM and Inventory systems leading to a breakdown of the network.

The IT department heads, influenced by the strategic terrain (need for scaling-up and entry of ERP) and drawing from their conjuncturally specific knowledge (altered actor network), advocate the use of ERP systems. This results in the translation of the actor network with the inclusion of a new technology (SAP) and associated actors (enhanced enterprise roles). We also notice that the REM POS system, with its sets of allies and inscriptions, continued to be reasonably frozen.

Conjuncture 3

Conjuncture-3 unfolded over a period of four years and saw some incremental changes in the strategic terrain with the entry of new generation POS systems. We also notice the polarization of the actor network into two parts: one centered on SAP incorporating enterprise actors; and the other centered on REM including the store actors. This leads to an altered position-practice: with the enterprise staff supported by a superior technology feeling empowered; and the slightly compromised position-practice of the store manager who had to relinquish control of several activities.

The conflict between the inscriptions of the two technological actants also surfaces in this conjuncture. The resulting agency actions lead to the final break-down of the REM system. The failure of the integration layer between REM and SAP, and the escalating licensing costs leads to further breakdown of the actor network. The REM POS system that had thus far achieved a status of being an immutable mobile is now exposed to reveal its functional and technical components.

With SAP system in place, the IT leadership team was strengthened by new global actors who brought with them significantly different disposition and knowledge. The agency initiated by these global players, drawn from their internal structures, their understanding of the modified strategic terrain, and the internal structures of other actors, led to active problematizing of the POS functionality. Enterprise staff and business leaders were then enrolled into this process, leading to the decision to replace the REM systems with a new generation POS system.

Conjuncture 4

There are no additional changes to the broad strategic terrain witnessed in this conjuncture. However, this conjuncture witnessed a series of micro-level actions leading to irreversible change to the IT landscape at Alpha. The Wincor system came with functionality that inscribed internationally established practices, several of which were complete opposites to those of REM. Thus, while the Wincor system was seen to be aligned with the SAP network and its allied actors, it potentially faced resistance from the store managers and was seen as denting the entrepreneurial spirit enjoyed by them.

Ensuring the stability of the new actor network required the alignment of the store managers with the Wincor system. The internal structures of the store managers are seen to be driven by their disposition of entrepreneurship and their dominant position reinforced over several years. The acceptance of Wincor system by the store manager required a significant change to their internal structures. This was achieved by launching an organizational change initiative. The process of introducing the Wincor network was achieved by virtually re-launching the store, introducing the "Store Kartha" philosophy and performing "Pooja" (a religious ceremony). These incidents can be seen as an active agency to alter the general disposition of the store staff.

Thus, the outcome of conjucture-4 can be summarized as re-establishing a stable actor network and an altered position-practice of both the enterprise and the store staff. This conjuncture is marked by agency carried out by various actors: ranging from the role of the leadership team to alter the disposition of the store staff, re-launching of the stores, role of global actors in introducing new technology actants with aligned inscriptions, and the process of aligning the technology's function-in-use to those of the actors needs.

6   Discussions and Conclusions

In this paper, we have attempted to study the technology adoption by an organization as it establishes itself in the emerging retail industry in India. Our choice of retail industry provides us a context of an industry that has internationally established practices and mature technologies, but is still evolving in the Indian context. We notice that the adoption of technology by the organization is not just the implementation of mature technologies, but instead is a process through which the organization "discovers" these technologies and adapts to it. Our study elaborates the interplay of heterogeneous actors, evolving organizational contexts and technologies during the adoption process.

The primary contribution of our study is to demonstrate the applicability of macro-level structuration process in the study of technology adoption. Past IS researchers using structuration analysis have focused on micro-level phenomena such as the study of Case tools (Orlikowski, 1992), Lotus Notes (Karsten, 1995), and Decision Support systems (DeSanctis & Poole, 1994); or to explain adaptations to the development process such as the study of global virtual teams (Maznevski & Chudoba, 2000) and adaptation to agile methodologies (Cao, Kannan, Peng, & Balasubramaniam, 2009). In our study, we demonstrate the impact of micro-level structuration process between technology and human actors unfolding in an organizational and industrial context, and translating into a macro-level impact on the technology assimilation process.

Structuration theory is limited in its usefulness for conducting macro-level studies. Our study demonstrates the value of strong structuration theory and actor network theory, in combination, for conducting macro-level studies involving information technology. We have extended the original work by Stones (2005) and Greenhalgh and Stones (2010), by drawing on additional ANT concepts to explain the agency actions arising out of technology change and the subsequent impact of actor networks on organizational structures.

Our study also indicates that the technology assimilation process is more than just awareness, adoption, and deployment of technologies. It is an ongoing process occurring over an extended period of time and involves a series of successes and failures. The process we elaborated is similar to Gersick's punctuated equilibrium model (Gersick, 1991) which views change as long periods of stability (with incremental change) and brief periods of revolutionary change. Past IS researchers have used the concepts of punctuated equilibrium to understand problems of system-development (Newman & Robey, 1992), virtual teams (Jarvenpaa, Shaw, & Staples, 2004), adoption of new technologies (Loch & Huberman, 1999), technology-led organizational transformation (Orlikowski, 1996), to name a few. Our study contributes to this literature to establish the usefulness of the punctuated equilibrium model to a macro-level technology adoption process within an organization.

As an implications for practice, our study points to the constant need for realigning technology with organization needs as is evident from the actor networks toggling between stability and instability. Our study suggests that a successful technology at a given moment of time may outlive its utility in the future. Such failures may be as a result of the misalignment of technology with other contextual factors. The process of realignment may need a multitude of activities such as incorporating new technologies (adding actants), reinforcing leadership (adding new actors), launching organizational change initiatives (altering disposition of key actors), and realigning roles & responsibilities (altering position-practices).

We adopted a grounded theory approach to our study. We developed the theoretical basis during the process of understanding the phenomena, similar to past contextual studies such as those of Walsham and Sahay (1999). The choice of SST was decided upon only during the analysis phases, and the conjunctures were determined by logically grouping the events based on the technology-in-use. This study would benefit by adopting qualitative coding techniques (Miles & Huberman, 1994; Strauss & Corbin, 1990) that could aid in triangulating the boundaries of the conjunctures. We hope to address this as an extension to this study.

The extent to which we can generalize the research findings is a possible limitation of our study. A proposed extension to our study is to include additional cases that involve organizations that have undertaken different paths of technology adoption under similar contexts. This could be done through a theoretical sampling of additional organizations in the retail industry in India, or by including cases from other emerging industries having similar contexts.

References

Bijapurkar, R.: We are like that only: Understanding the logic of consumer India. Portfolio Penguin (2009)

Briers, M., Chua, W.F.: The role of actor-networks and boundary objects in management accounting change: a field study of an implementation of activity-based costing. Accounting, Organizations and Society 26(3), 237–269 (2001)

Callon, M.: Some elements of a sociology of translation: Domestication of the scallops and the fisherman of St. Briene Bay. In: J. Law, Power, Action and Belief A New Sociology. Routledge, London (1986)

Cao, L., Kannan, M., Peng, X., Balasubramaniam, R.: A framework for adapting agile development methodologies. European Journal of Information Systems 18, 332–342 (2009)

Cohen, I.: Structuration Theory: Anthony Giddens and the Structuration of Social Life. Macmillan, London (1989)

Dash, M., Chandy, S.: A study on the challenges and opportunities faced by organized retail players in Bangalore. Available at SSRN 1435218 (2009)

DeSanctis, G., Poole, M.: Capturing the complexity in advanced technology use: adaptive structuration theory. Organization Science 2(5), 121–147 (1994)

Dholakia, N., Dholakia, R.R., Chattopadhyay, A.: India's Emerging Retail Systems Coexistence of Tradition and Modernity. Journal of Macromarketing 32(3), 252–265 (2012)

Fichman, R.G.: The diffusion and assimilation of information technology innovations. In: Framing the Domains of IT Management: Projecting the Future Through the Past, pp. 105–128 (2000)

Gersick, C.J.: Revolutionary change theories: A multilevel exploration of the punctuated equilibrium paradigm. Academy of Management Review 16(1), 10–36 (1991)

Giddens, A.: The Constitution of Society: Outline of the Theory of Structure. University of California Press, Berkeley (1984)

Greenhalgh, T., Stones, R.: Theorising big IT programmes in healthcare: strong structuration theory meets actor-network theory. Social Science & Medicine 70(9), 1285–1294 (2010)

Jack, L., Kholeif, A.: Introducing strong structuration theory for informing qualitative case studies in organization, management and accounting research. Qualitative Research in Organizations and Management: An International Journal 2(3), 208–225 (2007)

Jarvenpaa, S., Shaw, T., Staples, D.: Toward Contextualized Theories of Trust: The Role of Trust in Global Virtual Teams. Information Systems Research 15(3), 250–267 (2004)

Kachru, U.: India Land of a Billion Entrepreneurs. Pearson Education India (2011)

Karsten, H.: It's like everyone working round the same desk:' organizational readings of Notes. Scandinavian Journal of Information Systems 7(1), 7–34 (1995)

Langley, A.: Strategies for theorizing from process data. The Academy of Management Review 24(4), 691–711 (1999)

Latour, B.: Science in action: How to follow scientists and engineers through society. Harvard University Press (1987)

Loch, C., Huberman, B.: A Punctuated Equilibrium Model of Technology Diffusion. Management Science 45(2), 160–177 (1999)

Maznevski, M., Chudoba, K.: Bridging space over time: Global Virtual Team Dynamics and Effectiveness. Organization Science 11(5), 473–492 (2000)

Miles, M., Huberman, A.: Qualitative Data Analysis: An expanded sourcebook. Sage, Thousand Oaks (1994)

Mukherjee, A., Patel, N.: FDI in Retail Sector: INDIA: A Report by ICRIER and Ministry of Consumer Affairs, Government of India. Academic Foundation (2006)

Newman, M., Robey, D.: A Social Process Model of User-Analyst Relationships. MIS Quarterly 16(2), 249–266 (1992)

Orlikowski, W.J.: The Duality of Technology: Rethinking the Concept of Technology in Organizations. Organization Science 3(3), 398–427 (1992)

Orlikowski, W.J.: Improvising organizational transformation over time: A situated change perspective. Information Systems Research 7(1), 63–92 (1996)

Orlikowski, W.J., Scott, S.V.: Sociomateriality: Challenging the separation of technology, work and organization. The Academy of Management Annals 2, 433–474 (2008)

Pozzebon, M., Pinsonneault, A.: Challenges in conducting empirical work using structuration theory: Learning from IT research. Organization Studies 26(9), 1353–1376 (2005)

Rose, J.: Evaluating the contribution of structuration theory to the information systems discipline. In: 6th European Conference on Information Systems, Granada (1998)

Sengupta, A.: Emergence of modern Indian retail: an historical perspective. International Journal of Retail & Distribution Management 36(9), 689–700 (2008)

Srivastava, R.K.: Changing retail scene in India. International Journal of Retail & Distribution Management 36(9), 714–721 (2008)

Stones, R.: Sociological Reasoning: Towards a Past-Modern Sociology. Macmillan, London (1996)

Stones, R.: Structuration theory. Palgrave-Macmillan, Basingstoke (2005)

Strauss, A., Corbin, J.: Basics of Qualitative Research: Grounded Theory Procedures and Techniques. Sage, Newbury Park (1990)

Walsham, G., Sahay, S.: GIS for District-Level Administration in India: Problems and Opportunities. MIS Quarterly 23(1), 39–65 (1999)

Yin, R.: Case Study Research: Design and Methods, vol. 3. Sage, Thousand Oaks (2009)

Improving Human Cognitive Processing by Applying Accessibility Standards for Information and Communication Technology

Daryoush Daniel Vaziri and Argang Ghadiri

Bonn-Rhine-Sieg University of Applied Sciences, Sankt Augustin, Germany
{daryoush.vaziri,argang.ghadiri}@h-brs.de

Abstract. This article concerns with human-computer-interaction (HCI) from a neuroscientific perspective. The motivation for this perspective is the demographic transition, which shifts population structures of industrial nations. The authors will explain consequences of the demographic transition in terms of HCI and establish a hypothesis for these research activities. To evaluate this hypothesis the authors develop an approach, which combines different disciplines. This approach examines the effects of IT-accessibility on human cognitive processing. Therefore, required methodologies and instruments will be explained, discussed and selected. Possible effects of IT-accessibility on human cognitive processing will be illustrated with an acknowledged cognition model. The result of this article will be a concept, which enables the measurement of IT-accessibility impacts on human cognitive processing.

Keywords: Information systems, Accessibility, Neuroscience, Usability, Cognitive processing.

1 Introduction

Practically no enterprise relinquishes the application of information systems today. The major goal is to support business processes to increase efficiency and productivity. However, due to the commoditization of information technology, the pure deployment of these systems is no longer a competitive advantage (Carr, 2003). Productivity and efficiency are significantly determined by the capabilities of users to interact with applied information systems to achieve specific goals. The design and development of information systems therefore need to focus on human behavior and capabilities. Figure 1 depicts an ideal-typical goal attainment process that is supported by an information system.

Steps 1 to 4 in figure 1 will be normally reiterated. At the end of each iteration the processed data output (step 3) should inform the system user about the achieved progress. The user will interpret (step 4) this information to plan and execute the next activity. After a certain amount of iterations the system user should attain the goal in step 6. If the user is not able to attain the goal after a certain amount of iterations, the process will be aborted by the user. Depending on task complexity step 4 might be

Y.K. Dwivedi et al. (Eds.): TDIT 2013, IFIP AICT 402, pp. 555–565, 2013.

skipped. The time, needed to achieve the goal, decreases with the amount of interferences during this process. Interferences can be for example, loading times, system failures, operating problems, perception problems or comprehension problems.

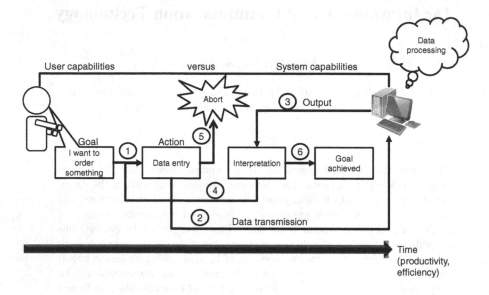

Fig. 1. Goal attainment process

2   Background

The demographic transition of industrialized nations leads to a declining and at the same time ageing population (Lutz et al., 2011). While the amount of young people aged 15-24 stagnates respectively declines, the amount of people aged 60 or over increases significantly (United Nations, 2010). In addition, increased life expectancies and the intergenerational contract demands employees to retire at a later date (Sanderson et al., 2010; Leon, 2011). Referring to these facts, the authors identified three consequences, which will affect the design and development of information systems.

Consequence 1: A higher susceptibility to disorders or injuries related to computer work has to be anticipated. A study conducted in 2001 revealed injuries and disabilities induced by computer work. The mean age of the study participants was 38.5 years (Pascarelli et al., 2001).

Consequence 2: Enterprises will need additional human capital sources to compensate the lack of young personnel. To date, enterprises do not sufficiently concern with the integration of people with impairments or disabilities. In 2003 approximately 45 Mio people of the declared working age population either had a disability or an enduring health problem (Eurostat, 2003). According to the demographic alterations, this figure is likely to increase within the next decades, as elderly people are more susceptible to impairments and disabilities (WHO, 2011).

Consequence 3: Susceptibility to mental disorders induced by computer-related stress factors will increase. Kessler et al. examined that 26.2% of the US population have mental disorders, including anxiety, mood etc. (Kessler et al., 2005). Also in Europe, Wittchen et al. investigated in an extensive study that almost 165 Mio Europeans suffer from brain disorders e.g. depression, anxiety, insomnia or dementia every year (Wittchen et al., 2010). The World Health Organization anticipates an increase of mental and neuropsychiatric disorders of 15% per year (WHO, 2001).

These alterations will affect the capabilities of system users and therefore change the requirements of employees and customers. As elderly and disabled people will constitute a bigger proportion of the overall population, enterprises need to adapt their ICT to different user capabilities to ensure productivity and profit. This adaptation requires developers to apply new methodologies and instruments to derive more detailed user requirements.

3   Hypotheses

The authors assume a correlation between the accessible design of ICT and human cognitive processing. For their research activities they establish following hypotheses in table 1:

Table 1. Hypotheses

Hypothesis	Description
H1	*Accessible ICT does not affect the time a user requires to achieve a specific goal.*
H2	*Accessible ICT does not increase the satisfaction of a user.*
H3	*The user's cognitive strain does not increase with the time required to achieve a specific goal.*
H4	*The user's cognitive strain is not dependent on the user's satisfaction.*
H5	*There is no correlation between accessible ICT and human cognitive processing*

Within this article the authors will elaborate an appropriate approach to reject H1-H5. In the context of this research in progress paper, the approach will mainly focus on required methodologies and instruments.

4   Neuro-Accessibility Design

Neuro-Accessibility Design (NAD) embodies the authors attempt to integrate methodologies and instruments of IT-accessibility design and brain research. It provides the opportunity to measure the influence of IT-accessibility criteria on human cognitive processing. The next sections will concern with information on cognitive processing and IT-accessibility.

4.1   Insights of Neuroscience on Cognitive Processing

Cognitive psychology deals with the mental processes which occur when knowledge and experience are gained from an individual's senses. This can be for example the processing of visual or auditory senses (Esgate et al., 2005) when working with an information system. Figure 2 depicts a simplified model of how the human brain handles cognitive processing (Persad et al., 2007).

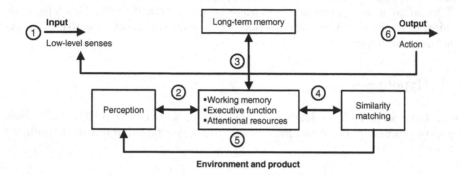

Fig. 2. Simplified model of cognitive processing

As the process of cognition is important for the NAD approach, the authors will briefly explain Persad's cognition model in the following paragraph.

Step 1: The user gets in contact with external stimuli.

Step 2: The perception component analyses and processes the incoming sensory information.

Step 3: The working memory retrieves long-term memories and decides to act on the selected stimuli. The attention resources are directed to focus on the most informative parts of the stimuli and initiate actions and reasoning (Mieczakowski et al., 2010).

Step 4: For matching the selected stimuli with objects of similar physical properties and functional attributes and for grouping them into categories in memory, working memory frequently has to refer to long-term memory (Miller, 1994).

Step 5: If the user has experienced the stimuli before, information about them will probably affect the speed and efficiency of cognitive processing.

Step 6: The user executes an action based upon the previous cognitive processing.

Studies investigated that ageing and certain impairments or disabilities can have significant effects on the elements of cognition. Therefore it is important to understand human cognitive processing and identify methods and instruments which might improve cognitive processing (Rabbitt 1993; Freudenthal, 1999).

Neuroscience, as it is the study of multidisciplinary sciences which analyze the nervous system and its functionalities (Squire et al., 2013), can help to comprehend cognitive processing (Esgate et al., 2005). Studies in the interdisciplinary field of cognitive neuroscience examine the underlying neural mechanisms, which are involved with input, perception, attention, working and long-term memory as well as the transformation of information in correspondent action (McBride and Schmorrow, 2005).

Particularly the brain measurement technique of electroencephalography (EEG) is likely to be of great importance for comprehending the neural processes with regard to cognition (Niedermeyer, 2005). An EEG records the electrical activities in the cerebral cortex. When neurons transfer information, small electrical signals are generated, which can be measured by electrodes (Davidson et al., 2000; Dowling, 2001). These electrical signals represent the neuron's activity and speed which allow the identification of mental states (Sharma et al., 2010). The activities are then further divided into several frequency bands which can be interpreted as shown in table 2 (Sherlin, 2009):

Table 2. Interpretation of EEG frequencies

Frequency	Interpretation
Delta (0.5-4 Hz)	Delta waves primarily occur in states of deep sleep. In addition they may also show slowed cognitive processing, learning difficulties or attention deficits.
Theta (4-8 Hz)	Theta waves can be seen most commonly in states of creativity and spontaneity. This is shown in an increase of theta waves when an individual passes on to drowsiness.
Alpha 1 (8-10 Hz)	Low alpha waves report an unaware state of relaxation with decreased cortical activation. They occur in states where an individual does not focus on surroundings of the environment.
Alpha 2 (10-13 Hz)	High alpha waves appear in a state of vigilance and alertness. They represent awareness of the surroundings but without focusing anything specific.
Beta 1 (13-21 Hz)	Low beta waves are primarily associated with cognitive processing. The cognitive requirements to fulfil a task become obvious by the activation of the cortex.
Beta 2 (21-35 Hz)	High beta waves represent higher states of concentration and cognitive processing and might be a result of cognitive challenges.

These insights provide the opportunity to examine the effects of IT-accessibility on human cognitive processing and therefore will be discussed in Chapter 5.

4.2   IT-Accessibility for Information and Communication Technology

The term "IT-accessibility" stands for the development of systems for users with diverse capabilities. The International Organization for Standardization (ISO) defines IT-accessibility as follows:

"The usability of a product, service, environment or facility by people with the widest range of capabilities." (ISO, 2008).

This definition implies that usability is an essential goal to achieve IT-accessibility not for specific user groups, but all possible user groups, including young, healthy, disabled and elderly people.

For the successful implementation of this goal theory provides detailed guidelines on how to develop accessible IT-systems. The following paragraph will briefly introduce the reader to important accessibility-development principles.

Principle 1: Perception

All content presented within an application must be perceivable for any user. This includes e. g. color contrasts, font sizes and screen reader compatibility.

Principles 2: Operability

The content and its functionalities must be operable by different devices. For example, a visually impaired user is able to navigate through the content by keyboard commands.

Principle 3: Understandability

The structure of the application as well as the content must be easy to understand for the user. For example, abbreviations and foreign words are explained if the user demands it.

Principle 4: Technical openness

An application must be compatible to diverse devices. For example, the content and operation of a website adapts to the accessing device. This device can be e.g. a computer, a smartphone or a tablet.

The aforementioned principles of accessibility are part of the Web Content Accessibility Guidelines 2.0 (WCAG 2.0) published by the World Wide Web Consortium (W3C, 2008). The international organization for standardization approved this guideline as an international standard in the year 2012.

4.3   Influence on Cognitive Processing

In theory there is only little work about individual cognitive aspects of IT-accessibility. Most of the articles and books focus on IT-accessibility criteria that promote people with cognitive disabilities. But none of these examined the influence of IT-accessibility standards on the cognitive processing capability. To evaluate this, the authors imply that a long interval between steps one to six of Persad's model in figure 2 indicates the presence of at least one interfering factor. Interfering factors can be defined as any event that prevents or impedes the user from achieving a goal. For instance, this can be a system failure, distracting elements on the graphical user interface (GUI), low system performance or poor menu structure. These factors induce stress perception by the user and thereby affect human cognitive processing (Shu et al. 2011). In 1984 Craig Brod denoted this kind of stress as "technostress" (Brod, 1984). Technostress can be defined as "any negative impact on attitudes, thoughts, behaviors, or body physiology that is caused either directly or indirectly by technology" (Weil and Rosen, 1997). Figure 3 provides an illustration.

The next section will discuss several instruments to analyze correlations between the utilization of ICT and effects on cognitive processing. These instruments will provide opportunities to measure effects of accessible IT on human cognitive processing. The authors will justify their selection of instruments for future research activities.

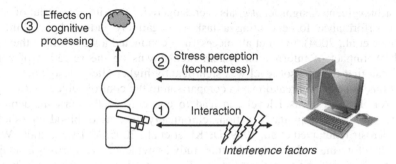

Fig. 3. Interfering factors influence cognitive processing

5   Selection of Methodologies and Instruments

The study of cognitive neuroscience concerns with how cognition and emotion are implemented in the brain. By using EEG, mental events, including all forms of "thinking" or "reasoning", become visible (Penn, 2010).

The electrodes of an EEG record the activities from the cortex and upper layers of the brain where most of the cognitive processes occur. The benefit of using an EEG, compared to e.g. brain imaging techniques, is the real-time recording of brain activities which enables the monitoring of interactions in specific evoked situations. Nevertheless, EEG data only represents one source of data about the cognitive processing. This source is highly dependent on the situation and behavior of the user. Specific factors, which influence the measurement, cannot be clearly identified, such as eye blinking, head movements or muscle movements. This can lead to distorted measurements. Therefore the EEG data should be validated with other sources of information, which help to analyze and interpret the EEG measurement more accurately.

According to this, the attempt to measure the negative effects of technostress on cognitive processing solely with an EEG is insufficient. It is still unclear to which extent stress can be reliably evaluated from the EEG (Seo and Lee, 2010). EEG data can only provide indications for technostress, which have to be validated with additional methods.

As Riedl, Kindermann, Auinger and Javor found in their literature review most studies use questionnaires to investigate origins and impacts of technostress (Riedl et al., 2012). Participants are asked for experienced difficulties when interacting with an information system. The authors doubt that this method can provide reliable data, which can be used to validate EEG measures. Nevertheless, the gathered information about the interaction difficulties could be useful to identify weak spots of the system that refer to specific elements of Persad's cognition model.

Therefore, the investigation of biochemical responses should be taken into consideration to measure technostress. Stress situations induce the secretion of hormones by the human body that includes cortisol, corticosterone, and adrenal catecholamines (Van der Kar et al., 1999). This secretion of cortisol correlates with the repeated exposure to stressful situations. Severe stress leads to a greater increase of cortisol than mild stress (Sherwood, 2010). Typically an increase of cortisol can be expected when

(1) the achievement of significant goals is endangered, (2) a situation is out of control, (3) the performance for executing a task is negatively judged by a third party (Dickerson et al., 2004). Riedl et al. successfully conducted a study where they investigated the impact of information system breakdowns on the secretion of cortisol. They found that the cortisol level was significantly higher after a test subject experienced a random system breakdown in comparison to the control subjects (Riedl et al., 2012). An elevated cortisol level can lead to e.g. chronically burnout, depression, obesity, suppressed immune function, chronically increased blood pressure and atherosclerosis (Melamed et al., 1999; De Kloet et al., 2005; McEwen, 2006; Walker, 2007). Therefore the authors consider this study as evidence that cortisol is an appropriate measurement unit to measure stress. EEG data that indicates stress through a high beta power measurement could be validated, if the corresponding cortisol level is significantly high as well (Seo and Lee, 2010). Numerous body fluids like blood serum, urine, and saliva are suitable to measure cortisol levels (Seo and Lee, 2010). Blood samples for measuring the level of cortisol are associated with greater inter-individual differences than saliva samples (Park et al., 2007). Therefore the authors will prefer saliva samples over blood samples. The comfortable measurement of salivary cortisol suggests that this method could be applied to further studies with justifiable expenditures.

Furthermore, the heart rate variability (HRV) can also be taken into consideration to validate EEG data. HRV represents the variation over time of the period between heartbeats and depends on the heart rate. It describes the ability of the heart to detect and quickly respond to external stimuli and in turn to adapt to new and changing circumstances (Malik, 1996; Acharya et al., 2006). HRV is often combined with other measurement methods like blood pressure, skin temperature etc. to testify certain interpretations in the context of stress measurement (Zhong et al., 2005; Lupien et al., 2006) and emotions (Lupien and Brière, 2000). The consolidation of HRV and EEG data showed that high beta EEG power correlates with increased HRV significantly (Seo and Lee, 2010).

Figure 4 illustrates the authors' selection of instruments that fit the NAD requirements and enable the evaluation of IT-accessibility impacts on cognitive processing.

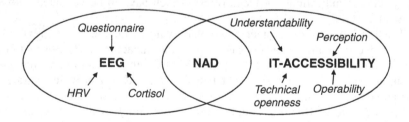

Fig. 4. Selection of instruments

To summarize, the selected instruments for the NAD approach are the principles of accessibility combined with results from EEG records, questionnaires, salivary cortisol measurements and heart rate variability. The latter three instruments are required to validate EEG records that indicate stress. The combination of the instruments, shown in figure 4, provides data on technostress induced by the utilization of information systems and allows the authors to evaluate H3 and H4. To measure the effect of IT-accessibility on cognitive processing, different users and applications have to be tested with these instruments. The comparison of accessible and inaccessible applications will enable the authors to evaluate H1 and H2. The integration and interpretation of all results finally will allow an evaluation of H5 as shown in table 3.

Table 3. Evaluation of H1-H5

Hypotheses	Instruments
H1 / H2	questionnaire, principles of accessibility
H3 / H4	EEG records, salivary cortisol measurements and heart rate variability
H5	questionnaire, principles of accessibility, EEG records, salivary cortisol measurements and heart rate variability

6   Conclusion

This article concerned with consequences for the design of information systems, induced by demographic alterations. The authors hypothesised that there exists a correlation between accessible ICT and human cognitive processing. They established five null hypotheses that need to be evaluated in future research projects. The NAD approach was defined, including instruments and methodologies required for the evaluation of the null hypotheses. In chapter 4.1 and 4.2 the reader was introduced to the basics of human cognitive processing and IT-accessibility. Afterwards this article discussed several instruments needed to evaluate H1-H5. Finally the authors illustrated a bundle of instruments that will be applied in future research projects.

The next step will be the definition of detailed test procedures that will enable an appropriate evaluation of H1-H5. After that the authors will conduct studies and publish the results, to enrich current theory on information systems and neuroscience.

References

Acharya, U.R., Joseph, K.P., Kannathal, N., Lim, C.M., Suri, J.S.: Heart rate variabil-ity: a review. Medical and Biological Engineering and Computing 44(12), 1031–1051 (2006)

Brod, C.: Technostress: The human cost of the computer revolution. Addison-Wesley, Reading (1984)

Carr, N.G.: IT Doesn't Matter. Harvard Business Review 81(5), 5–12 (2003)

Davidson, R.J., Jackson, D.C., Larson, C.L.: Human Electroencephalography. In: Cacioppo, L.G., Tassinary, G.G. (eds.) Handbook of Psychophysiology, vol. 2, pp. 27–52. Cambridge University Press (2000)

De Kloet, R.E., Joels, M., Holsboer, F.: Stress and the brain: from adaption to disease. Nature Reviews Neuroscience 6(6), 463–475 (2005)

Dickerson, S.S., Kemeny, M.E.: Acute stressors and cortisol responses: a theoretical integration and synthesis of laboratory research. Psychological Bulletin 130(3), 355–391 (2004)

Dowling, J.E.: Neurons and Networks, pp. 15–24. Harvard University Press, Harvard (2001)

Esgate, A., Groome, D., Baker, K.L.: An introduction to Applied Cognitive Psychology. Psychology Press, East Sussex (2005)

Eurostat: Employment of Disabled People in Europe in 2002 In: Buhalis, D., Eichhorn, V., Michopoulou, E., Miller, G. (October, 2005), Accessibility Market and Stakeholder analysis - One stop shop for accessible tourism in Europe, University of Surrey, UK, 33 (2003), http://www.accessibletourism.org/resources/ossate_market_anal ysis_public_final.pdf

Freudenthal, A.: The Design of Home Appliances for Young and Old Consumers. Series Ageing and Ergonomics, part 2, PhD Thesis. Delft University Press, The Netherlands (1999)

ISO, International Organization for Standardization: ISO 9241-171, Ergonomics of human-system interaction - Part 171: Guidance on software accessibility (2008)

Kessler, R.C., Chiu, W.T., Demler, O., Walters, E.E.: Prevalence, severity, and co-morbidity of twelve-month DSM-IV disorders in the National Comorbidity Survey Replication (NCS-R). Archives of General Psychiatry 62(6), 617–627 (2005)

Leon, D.A.: Trends in European life expectancy: A salutary view. International Journal of Epidemiology 40(2), 1–7 (2011)

Lupien, S.J.: &Brière, S.: Stress and Memory. In: Fink, G. (ed.) The Encyclopedia of Stress, pp. 721–728. Academic Press, San Diego (2000)

Lupien, S.J., Ouelle-Morin, I., Hupback, A., Walker, D., Tu, M.T., Buss, C.: Beyond the stress concept: Allostatic load—a developmental biological and cognitive perspective. In: Cicchetti, D. (ed.) Handbook Series on Developmental Psychopathology, Wisconsin, pp. 784–809 (2006)

Lutz, W., Butz, W., Castro, M., DasGupta, P., Demeny, P., Ehrlich, I., Giorguli, S., Habte, D., Hayes, A.C., Jiang, L., King, D., Kotte, D., Lees, M., Makinwa-Adebusoye, P., McGranahan, G., Mishra, V., Montgomery, M., Riahi, K., Scherbov, S., Xizhe, P., Yeoh, B.: Demographic challenges for sustainable Development, http://www.iiasa.ac.at/Research/POP/Laxenburg%20Declaration%2 0on%20Population%20and%20Development.html, International Institute for Applied Systems Analysis (IIASA) and Wittgenstein Centre, September 30-October 1 (2011)

Malik, M.: Heart Rate Variability. Annals of NoninvasiveElectrocardiology 1, 151–181 (1996)

McBride, D.K., Schmorrow, D.: Quantifying Human Information Processing. Lexington Books, Oxford (2005)

McEwen, B.S.: Protective and damaging effects of stress mediators: central role of the brain. Dialogues in Clinical Neuroscience 8(4), 367–381 (2006)

Melamed, S., Ugarten, U., Shirom, A., Kahana, L., Lerman, Y., Froom, P.: Chronic burnout, somatic arousal and elevated salivary cortisol levels. Journal of Psychosomatic Research 46(6), 591–598 (1999)

Mieczakowski, A., Langdon, P.M., Clarkson, P.J.: Investigating Designers' Cognitive Representations for Inclusive Interaction Between Products and Users. In: Langdon, P.M., Clarkson, P.J., Robinson, P. (eds.) Designing Inclusive Interactions, pp. 133–144. Springer, London (2010)

Miller, G.A.: The magical number seven, plus or minus two: some limits on our ca-pacity for processing information. Psychological Review 101(2), 343–352 (1994)

Niedermeyer, E., Da Silva, F.L.: Electroencephalography: Basic Principles, Clinical Applications, and Related Fields. Lippincott Williams & Sons, Philadelphia (2005)

Park, S., Kim, D.: Relationship between Physiological Response and Salivary Cortisol Level to Life Stress. Journal of the Ergonomics Society of Korea 26(1), 11–18 (2007)

Pascarelli, E.F., Hsu, Y.P.: Understanding Work-Related Upper Extremity Disorders: Clinical Findings in 485 Computer Users, Musicians, and Others. Journal of Occupational Rehabilitation 11(1), 1–21 (2001)

Penn, D.: Brain Science: In Search of the Emotional Unconscious. In: Van Hammersfeld, M., De Bont, C. (eds.) Market Research Handbook, 5th edn., pp. 481–498. John Wiley & Sons Ltd., West Sussex (2007)

Persad, U., Langdon, P., Clarkson, P.J.: Characterising user capabilities to support inclusive design evaluation. Universal Access in the Information Society 6(1), 119–137 (2007)

Rabbitt, P.: Does it all go together when it goes? The nineteenth Bartlett memorial lecture. The Quarterly Journal of Experimental Psychology 46A, 385–434 (1993)

Riedl, R., Kindermann, H., Auinger, A., Javor, A.: Technostress from a neurobiological perspective-system breakdown increases the stress hormone cortisol, Computer users. Business Information System Engineering (2012)

Sanderson, W., Scherbov, S.: Remeasuring Aging. Science 329(5997), 1278–1288 (2010)

Seo, S.H., Lee, J.T.: Stress and EEG. In: Crisan, M. (ed.) Convergence and Hybrid Information Technologies, pp. 413–426 (2010)

Sharma, J.K., Singh, D., Deepak, K.K., Agrawal, D.P.: Neuromarketing - A peep into customers' minds, PHI learning private limited, New Delhi (2010)

Sherlin, L.H.: Diagnosing and treating brain function through the use of low resolution brain electromagnetic tomography (LORETA). In: Budzynski, T., Budzynski, H.K., Evans, J.R., Abarbanel, A. (eds.) Introduction to Quantitative EEG and Neurofeedback, 2nd edn., Elsevier Inc., Burlington (2009)

Sherwood, L.: Fundamentals of Human Physiology. Brooks Cole (2010)

Shu, Q., Tu, Q., Wang, K.: The Impact of Computer Self-Efficacy and Technology Dependence on Computer-Related Technostress: A Social Cognitive Theory Perspec-tive. International Journal of Human-Computer Interaction 27(10), 923–939 (2011)

Squire, L.R., Berg, D., Bloom, F.E., Du Lac, S., Ghosh, A., Spitzer, N.C.: Fundamen-tals of Neuroscience, 4th edn. Elsevier Inc., Oxford (2013)

United Nations: Population Division of the Department of Economic and Social Af-fairs of the United Nations Secretariat. World Population Prospects (2010 revision) (2010), http://esa.un.org/unpd/wpp/unpp/Panel_profiles.htm

Van der Kar, L.D., Blair, M.L.: Forebrain pathways mediating stress induced hormone secretion. Frontiers in Neuroendocrinology 20, 41–48 (1999)

W3C: Web Content Accessibility Guidelines 2.0 (2008), http://www.w3.org/TR/WCAG/

Walker, B.R.: Glucocorticoids and cardiovascular disease. European Journal of Endocrinology 157(5), 545–559 (2007)

Weil, M.M., Rosen, L.D.: Technostress: coping with technology @work @home @play. Wiley, New York (1997)

Wittchen, H.U., Jacobi, F., Rehm, J., Gustavsson, A., Svensson, M., Jönsson, B., Ole-sen, J., Allgulander, C., Alonso, J., Faravelli, C., Fratiglioni, L., Jennum, P., Lieb, R., Maercker, A., Van Os, J., Preisig, M., Salvador-Carulla, L., Simon, R., Stein-hausen, H.C.: The size and burden of mental disorders and other disorders of the brain in Europe 2010. ECNP/EBC REPORT 2011, European Neuropsychopharmacology 21(9), 655–679 (2010)

World Health Organisation: Worldreport on disability (2011), http://whqlibdoc.who.int/publications/2011/9789240685215_eng.pdf

World Health Organization: Mental Health – A Call for Action by World Health Ministers. In: 54th World Health Assembly, http://www.who.int/mental_health/advocacy/en/Call_for_Action_MoH_Intro.pdf (2011)

Zhong, X., Hilton, H.J., Gates, G.J., Jelic, S., Stern, Y., Bartels, M.N., DeMeersman, R.E., Basner, R.C.: Increased sympathetic and decreased parasympathetic cardio-vascular modulation in normal humans with acute sleep deprivation. Journal of Applied Physiology 98(6), 2024–2032 (2005)

In Praise of Abundance: Why Individuals Matter in Design Science

David Wastell

Nottingham University Business School
Nottingham, UK
david.wastell@nottingham.ac.uk

Abstract. The Platonic quest for universal principles dominates the mainstream of IS research, typically relegating individual differences to the error term as pet theories and derived hypotheses are put to the statistical test. In design science, this neglect of "particulars" is especially egregious as it wastes valuable information about individuals and their interactions with technology. I present a case study of the design of adaptive automation, which shows how critical such information can be when designing complex IT-based systems. The obsession with theory has gone too far, I conclude; it is time to fight back against the tyranny of universals.

Keywords: Universals, particulars, theory, Design Science, Plato, individual differences, unit-treatment additivity.

1 Prologue: The Tyranny of Universals

Dirt is matter out of place – Mary Douglas

Consider the histogram in figure 1, taken from a study presented at the Working Conference of IFIP WG8.6, in Madrid in 2008 (Wastell et al., 2008). The diagram depicts the performance of 45 participants in a design experiment on decision-support tools for the users of complex systems, in this case a domestic heating system. The main dependent variable was energy-efficiency. The experiment compared three conditions: no support (control), a predictive aid and an expert system (in addition to the predictive aid). The means for these three conditions are superimposed on the histogram: control (14.4), predictive aid (17.3) and expert system (17.6); and the ANOVA summary table for the analysis is shown below the graph.

From the ANOVA, the conclusion was drawn that both forms of decision support enhance performance, but that the expert system does not provide additional support above the predictive aid. On the surface, this is a neat, unexceptionable example of design science in action; in its use of ANOVA to examine the effects of an independent variable, it follows to the letter the conventions of the incumbent IS paradigm. But standing back, we may take a more questioning view, not just of this experiment, but of the epistemological settlement in which it reposes. This is my somewhat daunting task in this philippic.

Y.K. Dwivedi et al. (Eds.): TDIT 2013, IFIP AICT 402, pp. 566–578, 2013.

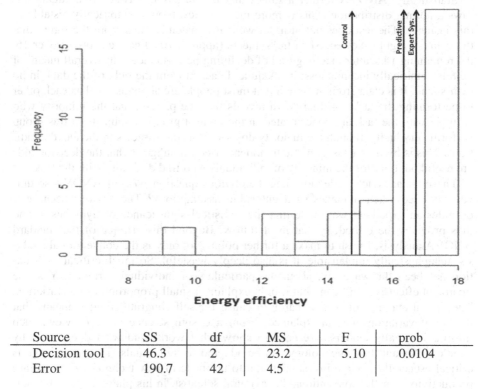

Source	SS	df	MS	F	prob
Decision tool	46.3	2	23.2	5.10	0.0104
Error	190.7	42	4.5		

Fig. 1. Results of experiment on decision aids

My line of attack is primarily ontological, beginning with a "frontal assault" on the assumption of "unit treatment additivity" upon which ANOVA fundamentally depends. This axiom assumes that the response (y_{ij}) of any "experimental unit" (i.e. human subject) i receiving treatment j is simply the sum of the unit's individual unique response (irrespective of the treatment) y_i plus an invariant treatment effect t_j. In other words:

$$y_{ij} = y_i + t_j$$

This seemingly innocuous equation is deeply problematic. For the present experiment it assumes that there is a mathematical abstraction denoted by $y_{i,}$, which corresponds to an individual's intrinsic energy efficiency performance, an in-built measurable property like their height. It further assumes an abstract treatment effect, $t_{j,}$ which is identical for every individual, e.g. that the predictive aid improves everyone's performance by the *same amount* and that this increment is *additive*. Let me re-emphasize, neither y_i or t_j are in the real world, they are metaphysical inventions, ideal types. Exposed and held up to critical examination, they are deeply questionable, if not absurd. In what sense is the quality of "energy efficiency" meaningful as some constant, intrinsic attribute of an individual? Why should all subjects respond to the same treatment by the same amount? Why is the operation additive; why not some other mathematical form, multiplicative for instance? Why not, indeed!

Statistically, ANOVA further assumes that the variation between individuals follows a normal distribution. This is more metaphysics, though empirically testable in this instance. The test does not turn out well: it is patently clear from the figure that the data are highly skewed. 31 of the subjects (approx. 70%) gain a score of over 16, the remaining 14 scatter in a long trail of declining performance. The overall mean[1] of 15.8 is empirically meaningless; it sits quite detached from the bulk of the data, in no man's land. It is clear from the graph that most people are about as good as each other in performing the task. Drilling down reveals the true picture, that the minority who struggle with the task are concentrated in the control group. 5 subjects in this group perform very badly, though the majority do as well as the subjects in the aided conditions. This is by no means a simple treatment effect. It suggests that the decision aids are useful but only for the minority of individuals who find difficulty with the task.

These metaphysical reflections beg the obvious question. Why is ANOVA so universally used when it makes such untenable assumptions? The answer: because it provides an expedient way of testing the statistical significance of hypotheses, and thus provides the orthodoxy that most follow. Beyond this critique of the standard ANOVA analysis, I wish to make a further point. Not only is the conventional analysis metaphysically implausible, it is also deeply wasteful. So much critical information has been thrown away, about the particulars of individual variation. Yes, the treatment effect is significant, but it only explains a small proportion of the variation. The partial eta ($\eta2$) of 19.5 is hardly a cause for self-congratulation; it means that 80.5% of variation goes unexplained. From a design science point of view, such information really matters. We need to know what works and what does not, why people differ and how technology can be adapted to individuals. This knowledge is critical especially if large investments are to be made in new technology to increase productivity. For the conventional behavioural scientist, in his platonic quest for universal laws, we can understand why particulars are a nuisance, to be consigned to the dustbin of the error term. But for the design scientist, particulars and universals should be of at least equal priority. That is the argument of this paper, to celebrate the ideographic over the nomothetic, and the heuristic over the hypothetico-deductive. I shall use my recent research on adaptive automation to prosecute the case.

2   Case Study – Adaptive Automation

Over recent years, automation has become a salient area of design research (e.g. Parasuraman and Wickens, 2008) as technological advancement has enabled an increasing number of tasks to be completed by machines that were previously the preserve of humans. Automation designs that flexibly adapt to the needs of the human operator have attracted considerable research interest. Adaptive automation (AA) conveys the idea that tasks can be dynamically allocated between the human and the machine according to operational requirements, with changes in task allocation being based on the human operator's current functional state (Inagaki 2003, Kaber and Endsley 2004). Changes in task allocations are often described in terms of a shift in the

---

[1] The mean itself is a dubious metaphysical abstraction, if regarded as the estimated property of an unseen, inferred (and therefore unreal) "population", rather than a simple descriptive way of denoting the mid-point of a group of numbers.

level of automation (LOA), drawing on models of automation as proposed by several authors, most notably the seminal model of Sheridan and Verplank (1978) which distinguishes 10 LOAs, ranging from full manual control (LOA1) to full control by the automatic system (LOA10). The rationale for adaptive automation is the potential for balancing out variations in operator workload and the research literature distinguishes between two main types of adaptive automation: implicit and explicit (Tattersall and Hockey 2008). In the *implicit control mode*, the machine decides which LOA is the most appropriate; in the *explicit mode*, this decision is under the jurisdiction of the human. Overall, when compared to static automation, there seem to be benefits of adaptive automation with regard to operator performance, including reductions in mental workload, although there is a considerable degree of inconsistency in the literature (e.g., Inagaki, 2003; Kaber & Riley, 1999; Sauer, Kao & Wastell, 2012).

The work featured here is drawn from long-term programme of research on adaptable automation involving colleagues at the university of Fribourg, Switzerland. There are three distinctive characteristics of this work: first, that we have used the same computer-based simulation in all the studies; second, its psychophysiological nature; third, that task performance has been assessed under adverse working conditions (created by an external stressor, white noise) as well as the optimal circumstances of the typical laboratory experiment. Four studies have been reported to date. The first experiment compared the benefits of static versus adaptable automation, (Sauer, Nickel and Wastell, 2012); although a *preference* for higher levels of manual control emerged, no advantages were found in terms of performance or mental workload. The second experiment investigated different modes of explicit AA: where the operator was completely free to choose, when a prompt was given, and when a decision was forced (Sauer, Kao, Wastell and Nickel, 2012). No salient differences were found between these different regimes. The third experiment compared two modes of implicit adaptive automation (based on decrements in task performance or the occurrence of high demand events) versus explicit AA, where the operator was free to make the change (Sauer, Kao and Wastell, 2012). The results for performance suggested no clear benefits of any automation mode, although participants with explicit control adopted a more active system management strategy and reported higher levels of self-confidence. In the most recent experiment, the effect of system reliability was assessed (Chavaillaz, Sauer and Wastell, 2012). Three levels of automation reliability was compared: interestingly, although unreliability undermined trust, no effects were found on the actual choice of automation level.

The present study returns to the central issue of paper three, the feasibility of performance-based adaptive automation. This type of AA is based on a comparison between current operator performance and a normative criterion. Although an obvious case can be made for using direct measures of primary task performance to provide this criterion, a strongly advocated alternative is to focus on indirect measures of mental workload, using secondary task methodology. Regarding the latter, models of human performance suggest that performance on secondary tasks is more sensitive to variations in operator workload (Hockey, 1997). This was the approach adopted in that study. It was assumed, on an *a priori* theoretical basis, that this was the optimal approach; but as we have seen, it failed to confer an advantage. Whether such an approach was the best one, or even feasible, was not evaluated empirically. It is therefore difficult to interpret the above null result. Can it be taken to mean that performance-based AA is not beneficial, or does it simply mean that there was a problem with the particular version implemented in that study. Here we explore this issue in depth, using an heuristic, idiographic approach. The data for this investigation will be taken from the high reliability condition of our last experiment (Chavaillaz et al., 2012).

3   Method

A PC-based simulation environment, called AutoCAMS 2.0 (Cabin Air Management System) has been used in all our experiments. AutoCAMS provides a model of a complex process control task, namely the life-support system of a space shuttle. The simulation involves five critical parameters (CO_2, O_2, pressure, temperature, and humidity) reflecting the air quality in the shuttle cabin. When functioning normally, automatic controllers ensure that these parameters remain within a defined target range. When a problem develops, a diagnostic support system is available to provide assistance; it is called AFIRA (Automated Fault Identification and Recovery Agent) and provides five different levels of support, ranging from LOA1 (full manual control) to LOA5, where AFIRA proposes a diagnosis of the fault and an automatic procedure for repairing it.

The main interface is shown in figure 2. Operators have four tasks to accomplish. They are asked to diagnose and fix any system disturbances as fast as possible, and to maintain the stability of the system throughout the experimental session by manual control if necessary. In addition to these two primary tasks, operators had to perform two secondary tasks: a prospective memory task, for which they had to record periodically the current level of the N_2 tank, and an annunciator acknowledgement task, which requires them to click a symbol which appears at irregular intervals (on average about 30 s) to indicate the connection between ground control and the space shuttle.

Thirty-nine participants took part in the original, full study (10 females, 29 males), with an average age of 22.8. The present analysis focused on the 13 subjects in the high reliability condition, in which the automatic systems worked perfectly throughout. Subjects attended the laboratory for two sessions, training and testing, separated by a one-week interval. The testing session lasted approximately 2.5 h (with a 15-min break) and consisted of a sequence of two blocks. Each block was 39 min long and contained five fault scenarios.

4   Results

All control actions performed by the operator and each change in the system are automatically recorded by AutoCAMS for further analyses. The purpose of the present study was to go back to these original log files of individual interactions in order to test the assumption that secondary task performance provides a reliable and effective basis for detecting changes in mental workload. The connection task was used for this purpose as it had shown a greater sensitivity to workload manipulations in the original study (i.e. it showed a stronger effect of fault difficulty); moreover, it required a more frequent response, giving a finer grained level of temporal resolution. MATLAB programmes were written to process these log files to enable the construction of synoptic graphs giving a detailed record of connection task performance across the experimental session. Figure 3 provides an example; the figure also shows the occurrence of 2 faults, when we may presume that mental demands are objectively higher.

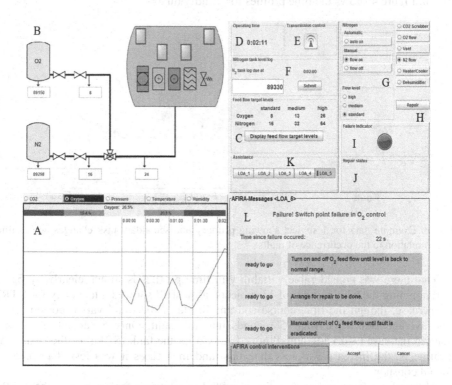

Fig. 2. Main interface of AutoCAMS. Components shown include: (A) history graph for key parameters, (B) functional schema of the cabin (with O_2/N_2 flow meter readings), (C) target levels of flow, (D) system clock, (E) connectivity check icon (secondary task: probe detection), (F) N_2 tank level logging facility (secondary task: prospective memory), (G) manual control panel, (H) repair facility, (I) subsystem failure indicator, (J) repair status (indicates type of repair in progress), (K) control panel of support system, and (L) the support system information display (AFIRA).

For the first analysis, the sensitivity of connection task (CT) reaction time (CTRT) was appraised by examining its temporal profile in response to fault states. For each fault, 3 observation points before the fault and 7 points after fault were extracted. The serial positions (SP) before the fault were designated -2, -1 and 0, and the seven points after the fault, 1 to 7. Note that SP0 indicated the last CT task before the fault began, and SP1, the first CT after its commencement; this was because the CT task and the occurrence of faults was not exactly synchronised. To reduce the effect of outlying values, a logarithmic transformation was carried out, as is customary for reaction time data. Following this, CTRTs for the same serial position were averaged, giving an overall time profile for each participant. Such profiles will show clearly whether CTRT provides a sensitive and reliable indicator of the additional task demands imposed by the fault. If there is a sharply defined increase in CTRT, this suggest it could form the basis for effective performance-based AA; if there is no change in RT, or if it is inconsistent across individuals, this suggests it would not be useful. Figure 4 shows the time profiles for 4 individuals.

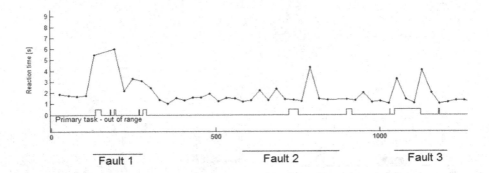

Fig. 3. Example data for 1 subject showing primary and secondary task changes across time and in relation to the occurrence of faults

That there was considerable variability in time profiles is shown clearly by figure 4. Examining the whole group of 13 subjects, almost all showed a tendency for CTRT to increase, though the time course and amplitude of the trend varied considerably. The average peak time was 95 seconds into the fault. Only 5 subjects showed a marked increase (> 0.1 log units) immediately after the fault (SP1); for the remaining 8 subjects, the increase was less than this, and in 4 cases it was less than 0.05, or stayed constant.

Although far from convincing, this provided some *prima facie* evidence that CTRT is responsive to task demands, i.e. to the additional workload putatively associated with fault handling. Whether a reliable detector could be built is another matter. In order to appraise the how well CTRT could perform in this role, a crude "signal detection" analysis was also carried out. A simple algorithm was designed, similar to that deployed in experiment three of our prior work. CTRT values at any instant were compared to the average across the whole experimental session; an anomalous CTRT was held to have occurred when a certain threshold was exceeded based on the standard deviation of CTRT during the baseline period. Two levels of sensitivity were compared: 0.5 and 1 standard deviation from baseline. Three parameters were of interest: the number of Hits, i.e. the detector accurately identified raised workload when a fault was present; the number of False Alarms, i.e. raised workload was detected, but no fault was present; and the number of Misses, i.e. a fault was present, but the detector did not pick up any augmented workload. Two performance indices were derived from these parameters:

Accuracy – Percentage of detections that were correct, i.e. hits/(hits + FAs)
Reliability – Percentage of faults accurately detected , i.e. hits/(hits + misses)

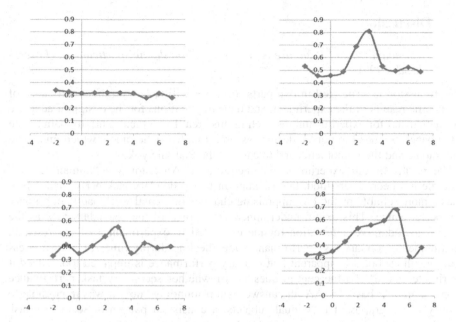

Fig. 4. Time profiles for four representative subjects

Results are shown in table 1. Detection performance is poor. At the 1SD criterion, although accuracy was high (few false alarms), half the faults were missed, producing a reliability of only 50%. Lowering the criterion had the expected effect of reducing the misses and hence increasing reliability, although only to 68%, but at the same time accuracy drastically declined to less than 50%.

As well as secondary task performance, primary task performance was also examined as a potential detector of workload. The following algorithm was used: an abnormal load was inferred when any system parameter (oxygen, pressure, CO2 etc.) was out of its prescribed range for more than 10 seconds. The results for this detector are also shown in the table. It will be seen that this crude approach performed much better in terms of reliability and accuracy. It is notable that the average latency for picking up a change in workload was 50.3 seconds, which also compares favourably with the time profile of the secondary task.

Table 1. Detection performance of the various algorithms averaged across the 13 subjects

Detector	HITS	MISSES	FA	Accuracy	Reliability
1 SD, secondary task	5	5	1.4	77.8%	50%
0.5 SD, secondary task	6.8	3.2	7.2	48.8%	68.3
Primary task	9.5	0.5	1.3	87.9%	95%

5   Discussion

The universals of Plato are tyrants which 'annihilate' particulars.. (Feyera-bend, 1999)

This discussion is structured in two parts; first, we will reflect on the significance of the specific results of the experiment, and their implications for the design of adaptive automation and for experimental research in this area. I will then return to main theme of the paper, the need to pursue design research in a heuristic mode, which mixes the ideographic and the nomothetic, and to cast off the Platonic yoke.

The results of our experiment are unequivocal. An axiomatic "human factors" principle has been discredited, the assumption that secondary task performance provides a more reliable method for appraising changes in mental workload than primary task performance. This axiom underpinned our choice of the secondary task as the basis of the adaptive automation regime evaluated in experiment 3 of our research programme. Secondary task performance does decline during times of known stress (fault handling) but it is apparent that primary performance is impaired too, indeed it deteriorates more[2]. To the central question of whether secondary task performance affords a reliable basis for AA, the answer is a resounding "no". It was impossible to identify in the graphs of individual subjects, a consistent pattern of secondary task degradation. The detector analysis strongly supported this general conclusion, and indeed showed the primary task to provide a mechanism which worked reliably and accurately enough to support a more feasible algorithm. There is a powerful caution-ary tale in this story regarding the limits and seductive lure of theory and the need to challenge dogma. Donald Hebb, in my undergraduate psychology textbook, put it pithily: "theory, like rum, is a good servant and a bad master – this book has em-phazised the importance of theory *and the importance of not believing it*" (Hebb, 1972).

It is clear from the present study that the use of performance-based methods of adaptive automation is problematic. Alternative methods are available, including the use of psychophysiological measures. Heart rate variability (HRV), for instance, tends to decrease when workload increases (Wickens & Hollands, 2000). The advantage of these methods is that they do not pose additional workload for operator to manage. However, the reliability of such methods is yet to be shown and they are costly to deploy. And this brings us to another critical point. What is important in a design context is whether a technology will work in practice. This imposes a much higher level of proof than theoretical research. It is not enough to demonstrate statistical significance, that some feature or manipulation has an effect; after all, the power of an experiment can arbitrarily be increased simply by running more subjects. But an in-tervention which requires 100 subjects before it reveals itself is not an effect which is likely to have any interest in a practical setting. Before making expensive investments in technology, the cost-benefit equation must be favourable; there must be significant

---

[2] In fact, the data of the original experiment show this effect too: two levels of fault difficulty were present; the results showed the effect of novel vs. practised faults was stronger for the primary (F=17.5) than for either secondary task, where a significant effect was only obtained for the connection task (F=4.15).

gains in productivity, sufficient to justify the investment. We wish the majority, if not all, individuals to improve their productivity, a condition nearly met in our opening vignette which showed the value of predictive aids in managing heating systems; a sizeable minority of individuals were performing below par, and the provision of the predictive aid certainly seemed to help, unlike the additional assistance afforded by the expert system.

The goals of what Hevner et al. (2004) call the behavioral science approach to IS research differ significantly from the design science paradigm. For Hevner et al (2004), the aim of "behavioralists" is to develop psychosocial theories which "explain or predict organizational and human phenomena" surrounding the application of technology. Design science, in contrast, seeks to develop a corpus of practically-oriented knowledge through which "the design, implementation, management, and use of information systems can be effectively and efficiently accomplished" (ibid, p. 77). In management science, Van Aken (2005) makes a similar distinction between two forms of research: *Mode 1*, knowledge for the sake of knowledge, aimed at explanation and description; and *Mode 2* which is multidisciplinary and aimed at solving problems. Van Aken goes on to argues for the recasting of management research in the mould of Design Science, rather than conventional explanatory science.

The primary rationale for design experiments, such as the present, is that they generate data from which we can learn to design better. Realistic simulations ("microworlds") like CAMS provide "a valuable tool in the arsenal of design science... for generating realistic behavioral data, testing ideas and developing theory" (Wastell, 1997). But if we are to capitalize fully on this potential, a break with the Platonism of conventional behavioral science is needed. In our search for universals, particulars have been relegated to the error term. Abundance has been conquered (Feyerabend, 1999), but at a price; the wanton waste of important information.

In an early paper using CAMS, I first made the case for the relevance of idiographic analysis in the context of design (Wastell, 1997). The goal of the design experiment, I argued, was heuristic, "theory generating, not theory testing ... to use the rich but controllable environment of the microworld to explore complex behavioural phenomena under quasi-controlled [and] ecologically realistic conditions". The idiographic analysis in that earlier study provided some fascinating insights into the difficulties of controlling a system that was complex enough to present a serious challenge. Some subjects succeeded very well but others manifestly struggled. The weak subjects showed a number of common characteristics: some reacted by withdrawing and adopting too narrow a focus; others responded by taking too much on, throwing themselves into excessive manual control. I likened this dichotomy to the typology of "pathological coping behaviours" (encystment and "thematic vagabonding") observed by another investigator, Dietrich Dörner, with a similar passion for particulars rather than universals. Such an idiographic analysis is not merely an anthropological curiosity; it could have practical value too, suggesting alternative options for implementing adaptive automation. Perhaps a qualitative pattern-matching strategy attuned to detecting symptoms of encystment or vagabonding, might well provide a more effective approach than the measurement of simple quantitative properties of performance. This is something to be explored in future research.

Finally, on a statistical note, it is surely time to give up the black magic of the orthodox ANOVA. There are other ways of testing the null hypothesis, without its dubious ontological and statistical baggage. Testing the null hypothesis simply means evaluating the probability that the difference between the three groups of the heating experiment could have arisen by the chance allocation of subjects to groups. A simple randomisation test would accomplish this[3], without making any statistical or metaphysical assumptions. It provides a direct test of what was operationally done in the experiment – i.e. individuals were actually randomly assigned to three groups and we have compared their average performance. What we want to know is simply whether the performance of the three groups represents a genuine effect. The mean is just one way of characterizing the overall performance of the group, but it is just that, a humble "real world" summary statistic, not a mysterious "population" estimate, hovering spectrally in the background, like Quetelet's *homme type*.

6   Coda: Down with Plato!

I have sat down with the Entities at table,
Eaten with them the meal of ceremony,
And they were stamped with jewels, and intuned God's ordered praises.
But now the Activities hand me to the dancing,
Brown naked bodies lithe and crimson-necklaced,
And tambourines besiege the darkened altars, In what God's honor?

Two Methods – Elizabeth Sewell (1960)

Doing experiments on people is an odd business. Consider for a moment, the experiment from the perspective of the "subject". Answering the call for participation, you turn up at the laboratory. In this "strange situation", you are instructed what to do, but given little more information about why you are really here. You are not told to conform to the norm, but you're expected to carry out the task like everyone else, to behave like *l'homme type*. But (unlike the man at the back of the mob in "The Life of Brian") *you are an individual* and you can only tackle the task in your own way, making sense of what is going on and doing your best. But your individual efforts, however heroic or perfunctory, are of no interest to the experimenter; in his scientific arrogance, only the treatment mean matters, the rest is error, silent error. How very odd is that, you might think – he might at least have asked me what I thought of the experiment. It was about the design of a system, and I had quite a few ideas which might have helped improve it... I did get a lot of training, but I still wasn't sure what to do. But you were not paid to think - you have been infantilized, treated like a guinea pig! But it is the experimenter that wears the motley. Better not to do experiments *on* people; perhaps, better to work with them, with users "as partners and co-producers of design knowledge, rather than passive guinea pigs" (Wastell et al., 2008). In that latter paper, I commented ironically that the current practice of design science, by aping the scientific method, was not itself following well-established precepts of effective design work, e.g. prototyping and user participation. I ended on the

---

[3] Such a test was carried for the present dataset. Interestingly, 10,000 replications generated the equivalent of 65 F values greater than 5.1, i.e. a two-tailed probability of 0.0065. This is actually more significant than the ANOVA result, whilst making no assumption of normality.

chastening thought that, had we worked more collaboratively and iteratively with our users, we may well have produced not only better decision aids (and not spent time and effort on an expert system which users clearly did not like) but more robust theory too.

And a (nearly) final thought. Although my reflections have been directed at the design research, they apply to research in the conventional mode, i.e. behavioural research (Hevner) or mode 1 research, to use Van Aken's terminology. Again, the argument is the same – what a waste of information not to look into particulars to try to understand patterns of individual variation, seduced instead by our Platonic infatuation with universals. Instead of boasting that a significant correlation has been found confirming a cherished hypothesis, we should be more humble. We like to think that a correlation of 0.3, for instance, is impressive. But a correlation of 0.3, means less than 10% of the variation is explained by our hypothesis. Our ignorance (90%) thus exceeds our knowledge by nearly an order of magnitude.

Now the final paragraph in which too much is crammed, but here goes. Any scientific endeavour involves the design of an information system, i.e. a sociotechnical system of people and technology for capturing, processing, and making sense of data. The technology may be very sophisticated, such as the Large Hadron Collider, or mundane, such as a paper-based questionnaire survey. The subject of IS research is IS... so the IS researcher uses IS to study IS; what else was our experiment but an IS. In our perennial angst about the proper subject of our field, some have argued that the technological artifact is what gives IS research its distinctive identity. But this is absurd – it arbitrarily removes from our purview any IS not based on computers! For me the considerations raised in this paper are not esoteric debates about how best to carry on our research[4]; they directly relate to our core business – how best to design an information system. The matter of what technology to use is secondary; epistemology[5] is at the heart of IS, i.e. considerations of the best means of producing valid knowledge about the world. This applies whether the IS has been developed by an IS researcher to study IS; or it has been deployed by an organisation to manage customer relations. Research expertise is, at bottom, IS design expertise. What then are the implications of my argument for the practical business of developing "real world" IS. Actually in the real world, the particular fares better; there is greater concern with understanding individual variation (e.g. customer segmentation in marketing) though again there is the same hierarchy of knowledge, the same Platonic tendency to endow statistics such as means and correlation coefficients with superior prestige, because they are held to reveal general, universal principles. This reverence has got to stop. Surely it is time to leave the ceremonial table, to shake the tambourine and join the naked dancers!

---

[4] And we certainly worry about how to do research: hence the "method wars" which rumble on to this day, amongst those with time on their hands! But because we tend to see these issues as ones of research methodology, rather than IS design, we limit the applicability of our expertise to our research practice, rather than applying it to the design of information systems in general.

[5] Of course, to mention epistemology in the context of management is to risk ridicule as an "other-worldy" egg-head, but there have been noble attempts to raise the standard , most notably Stamper (1985).

References

Feyerabend, P.: The conquest of abundance. University of Chicago Press (1999)

Chavaillaz, A., Sauer, J., Wastell, D.: System reliability, performance and trust in adaptable automation, Submitted for publication to Applied Ergonomics (2012)

Dörner, D.: On the difficulties people have in dealing with complexity. In: Rasmussen, J., et al. (eds.) New Technology and Human Error. Wiley, New York (1987)

Hebb, D.O.: Textbook of Psychology, 3rd edn. Saunders, Saunders (1972)

Hevner, A.R., March, S.T., Park, J., Ram, S.: Design science in information systems research. MIS Quarterly 28(1), 75–105 (2004)

Hockey, R.: Compensatory Control in The Regulation of Human Performance under Stress and High Workload: A Cognitive-Energetical Framework. Biological Psychology 45, 73–93 (1997)

Inagaki, T.: Adaptive Automation: Sharing and trading of control. In: Holl-nagel, E. (ed.) Handbook of Cognitive Task Design, pp. 147–169. Lawrence Erlbaum Associates, London (2003)

Kaber, D.B., Endsley, M.R.: The effects of level of automation and adaptive automation on human performance, situation awareness and workload in a dy-namic control task. Theoretical Issues in Ergonomics Science 5, 113–153 (2004)

Kaber, D.B., Riley, J.M.: Adaptive automation of a dynamic control task based on secondary task workload measurement. International Journal of Cognitive Ergonomics 3, 169–187 (1999)

Parasuraman, R., Wickens, C.D.: Humans: Still vital after all these years of automation. Human Factors 50(3), 511–520 (2008)

Sauer, J., Nickel, P., Wastell, D.: Designing automation for complex work environments under different levels of stress. Applied Ergonomics (2012) (in press)

Sauer, J., Kao, C., Wastell, D.: A comparison of adaptive &adaptable automation under different levels of environmental stress. Ergonomics 55, 1–14 (2012)

Sauer, J., Kao, C.-S., Wastell, D., Nickel, P.: Explicit control of adaptive automation under different levels of environmental stress. Ergonomics 54, 755–766 (2012)

Tattersall, A.J., Hockey, G.R.J.: Demanding work, technology, and human performance. In: Chmiel, N. (ed.) Introduction to Work and Organizational Psychology: A European Perspective, pp. 169–189. Blackwell, Malden Mass (2008)

Sewell, E.: The Orphic Voice: Poetry and Natural History. Routledge and Kegan Paul (1960)

Sheridan, T.B., Verplank, W.L.: Human and computer control of undersea teleoperators. Office of Naval Research, Arlington (1978)

Stamper, R.: Management epistemology: garbage in, garbage out. In: Methlie, L.B., Sprague, R.H. (eds.) Knowledge Representation for Decision Support Systems, pp. 55–77. Springer, Heidelberg (1985)

van Aken, J.E.: Management research as a design science: articulating the research products of mode 2 knowledge production in management. British Journal of Management 16, 19–36 (2005)

Wastell, D.G.: Human-machine dynamics in complex information systems:the "microworld" paradigm as a heuristic tool for developing theory and exploring design issues. Information Systems Journal 6, 245–260 (1997)

Wastell, D.G., Sauer, J., Schmeink, C.: Homeward bound: ecological de-sign of domestic information systems. IFIP Advances in Information and Communication Technology 287, 273–290 (2008)

Wickens, C.D., Hollands, J.G.: Attention, Time-Sharing, and Workload. In: Roberts, N. (ed.) Engineering Psychology and Human Performance, pp. 439–479. Prentice-Hall, Upper Saddle River (2000)

Why Not Let IT Fail? The IT Project Success Paradox

Paul J. Ambrose and David Munro

University of Wisconsin-Whitewater, Whitewater, WI 53190, USA
{ambrosep,munrod}@uww.edu

Abstract. Is a focus on information systems or information technology success a myopic view of evaluating IT success and failure? Are success and failure the opposite ends of a continuum for evaluating IT projects? Conventional measures of success such as meeting cost, time, budgets, and user needs do not address positives that can emerge from failures. We contend that a focus on success and failing to factor the possibility of failure actually hamper IT projects. An organizational mandate that does not allow for failure does not promote risk taking and innovation. It can also foster a project climate fraught with undesirable or unethical behavior and stress among developers, while failing to capture positive lessons that could emerge from IT project failure.

Keywords: IS success evaluation, IT failure, innovation.

1 Introduction

Social and business norms expect success at everything we do - at work, at play, and at home. As a society we remember winners and not losers. We do remember failures, though not in the same positive sense as we glorify successes. It is no different when it comes to evaluating, or setting expectations for IT (Information Technology) projects. Success is mandated explicitly or implicitly by project stakeholders. Perhaps that expectation is justifiable. After all business stakeholders invest time, effort and monetary resources in IT projects and as good stewards of business capital, have a rightful expectation of project success defined by the project meeting its set objectives and goals. But then the focus just on immediate project success could be too narrow a world view, and one can even argue that this could be detrimental especially for the overall or long term success of an organization. After all doesn't the old adage "Failure is the stepping stone for success" seem to encourage not willful actions that precipitate failure but the latitude to make mistakes so that we may learn from such errors and consequently become better? Or become more successful in the long run?

The passion to evaluate IT success in IS (Information Systems) academic research, however elusive that evaluation may be, could be traced to early influences on the discipline that originated in the scientific computing foundations and thoughts. Shannon and Weaver's seminal 1949 work "A Mathematical Theory of Communication" set the stage and standards for information processing with the focus being on the fidelity of information as it moves from the source to destination, and consequently improving technical aspects of communication. At the core of DeLone and

Y.K. Dwivedi et al. (Eds.): TDIT 2013, IFIP AICT 402, pp. 579–582, 2013.

McLean's 1992 and 2003 synthesizing work of past attempts to evaluate IS success we find Shannon and Weaver's thesis on technical communication. DeLone and McLean's IS success constructs and their derivatives continue to play a significant role in the measurement of IT success in IS literature. However it is ironic that a model with theoretical roots in science and engineering is attempting to address a problem that is social sciences in nature. The danger of this approach is that we could be missing behavioral factors that need to be addressed ground up in a theoretical model rather than these factors being grafted on top of a scientific model.

One may wonder why such a deterministic technical approach to evaluation IS/IT project success is being criticized, as after all don't we need a systematic approach to evaluate success? The counter to that argument however is twofold. First the time, size, and cost and effort are difficult to determine at the project initiation stage as IT projects follow the "hurricane" model (Dennis et al, 2009, pg 82) where these parameters can be better estimated only when the project is well underway, just as the actual landing sites of hurricanes are known only after landfall. Second, IT has been a key enabler of business transformation, and IT led transformation projects are inherently high risk, high reward projects where the possibility of failure is implicit and integral to the project. Ignoring failure can lead to not learning from such experiences and set the stage for the same mistakes to be committed again. To dig a bit deeper into this subject, let us consider three specific areas where a focus purely on success and failing to factor the possibility of failure in a positive manner is not desirable for IT projects.

2   Central Arguments

2.1   Success Obsession Hinders Innovation

A holistic approach to developing projects and services that meet a myriad of stakeholder needs could be addressed from the perspective of design thinking. Tim Brown elaborates the core principles behind design thinking to include feasibility (it is functionally possible to deliver the needs using technology), desirability (does the project make sense to users) and viability (can it be a sustainable business model). Further, design thinking espouse an organizational culture that accepts "forgiveness" later than asking for "permission" ahead. This is essential to foster innovation by encouraging risk taking which can also lead to mistakes being made. However if the business mandate is for IT projects to meet time, scope and cost, per traditional project management principles, IT professional are likely to adopt a risk averse strategy that curbs innovation. Current IS/IT success models seem to fail to take this into account.

In addition, developers have a disincentive for being innovative in development approaches, methods or tools when success is determined for the traditional perspective currently being followed. In some cases this reluctance to be innovate is because the benefits are not yet well known and may in fact may not exist. The "let someone else try it first" approach is safer. Furthermore changes due to an innovation that is introduced in a process will introduce new risk factors to the project, thus making it harder to evaluate the risk and trade-offs of doing the innovation, which leads to project managers viewing these innovations as unnecessary risks. Perhaps the biggest reason to discourage them is the very fact that implementing the innovation will take time away from the 'actual project'. For example the learning curve alone will likely take more time on this project then the innovation will provide on this project. It is not surprising that often innovation has to forced top down by upper level management, when most often it would be more effective and cheaper for the organization to have it arise organically from the bottom up.

2.2   Success Obsession Can Foster Unhealthy Stress

Let's start by examining how the stress people feel gets played out. It has to be noted that the stress individual feel about avoiding failure is not uniform and will vary greatly by many factors including their work experience, personality, and factor outside of work to just name a few. However we would be naive to assume that at least some if not most of the individuals on a development effort feel a lot of pressure for a project to succeed, or at least not be the cause of it failing. While the concept of a professional athlete "choking under pressure" has been studied for decades, Sanders and Walia (2012) have shown extended the economic theory that this is not limited to athletes. To quote from their conclusion "Pressure may reduce not only reduce productive output but, more fundamentally, may erode incentives to put forth productive input" While the stress may cause some people to underperform others may leave the organization when their stress levels are too high. As a person's stress from work spills over to their personal lives they are often encouraged by concerned family and friends to consider looking for a less stressful job environment. When this does happen and an individual leaves a project the remaining people on the project are left with more stress from either having to pick up the work of the individual who leaves or in communicating and bringing up to speed the person who replace them. A third way people can deal with stress is to just give up trying to meet what they perceive as unrealistic expectations that are thrust upon them. That is they basically deal with the stress of failure by assuming it is inevitable and hence do what they can but not really wholeheartedly throw themselves into the project.

2.3   Success Obsession Can Motivate Undesired Behavior

Austin (2001) highlights the effect of time pressure on developers where developers were known to take short cuts while dealing with unanticipated project complications, even if these shortcuts are not in the best interest of the project. Austin showcases an example where developers deliberately planted a "bug" in the software that would buy them time to do more work in the project when the project "breaks" during production deployment. So holding down people to hard success measures could encourage them to circumvent boundaries that could be considered as being unethical. This is not an isolated report. Zelazny (2011) reported based on a survey that "software development team members do not consider the internal quality attributes of modifiability, portability, and reusability when considering an information systems development project successful." Considering that the development team members are the people who most benefit from these attributes in their day-to-day work shows the degree in which the area takes back seat in pursuit of success.

3   Conclusion

So where does this all lead to? The bottom line question would be, how do we positively address IT failures as part of IT success evaluation? The motivation is to encourage IT professional to work innovatively and take necessary risks and be proactive contributors on projects. A technical and deterministic view of IS success may not be the right solution to meet that end. Should we then develop a model for IS failure than success?

References

1. Austin, R.D.: The effects of time pressure on quality in software development: An agency model. Information Systems Research 12(2), 195–207 (2001)
2. Brown, T., Katz, B.: Change by design: how design thinking transforms organizations and inspires innovation, 1st edn., viii, 264 p.. Harper Business, New York (2009)
3. DeLone, W.H., McLean, E.R.: Information Systems Success: The Quest for the Dependent Variable. Information Systems Research 3(1), 60–95 (1992)
4. DeLone, W.H., McLean, E.R.: The DeLone and McLean Model of Information Systems Success: A Ten-Year Update. Journal of Management Information Systems 19(4), 9–30 (2003)
5. Dennis, A., Wixom, B.H., Tegarden, D.P.: Systems analysis design, UML version 2.0: an object-oriented approach, 3rd edn., xviii, 581p. Wiley, Hoboken (2009)
6. Sanders, S., Walis, B.: Shirking and 'choking' under incentive-based pressure: A behavioral economic theory of performance production. Economics Letters 116(3), 363–366 (2012)
7. Shannon, C.E., Weaver, W.: The mathematical theory of communication, p. 125. University of Illinois Press, Urbana (1949)
8. Zelazny, L.M.: Toward a Theory of Information System Development Success: Perceptions of Software Development Team Members, June 8. Dissertation, Virginia Polytechnic Institute (2011)

Social Software: Silver Bullet or an Enabler of Competitive Advantage?

Darshan Desai

Berkeley College, New York, USA
dnd@Berkeleycollege.edu

Abstract. According to knowledge based view, firm-specific knowledge is considered to be a foundational source of competitive advantage. However, the recent trend towards social software radically changes the very essence, role, and value of firm-specific knowledge in driving competitive advantage. On one hand, firms are very enthusiastic about the investments in the social software initiatives; on the other hand, the broader strategic impact of these initiatives is not clear yet. This position paper highlights deep-seated problems in applying prominent strategic management theories in the context of social software. To address these problems, drawing on literature on value co-creation and service logic, it describes four ways social software can enable a firm's competitive advantage, and call for more research in this area.

Keywords: Knowledge, social software, competitive advantage.

1   Introduction

For years, strategy scholars have discussed how a firm gains competitive success. However, with the fast paced technological innovations, the concepts and frameworks of the past may no longer work today. For example, in the past, scholars (Kogut and Zander, 1995) have considered tacit and firm-specific knowledge to be fundamental source of competitive advantage. Firms have invested a lot in the knowledge management initiatives that included centrally managed, proprietary knowledge repositories. Today, when the locus of knowledge production is no longer confined within a firm's boundaries, the firm-specific knowledge is no longer sufficient for driving a competitive advantage. Social software supports group interactions, and provides open and inexpensive alternatives for the traditional knowledge management implementations. According to Von Krogh (2012), these social software implementations raise fundamental questions about the very essence and value of the firm-specific knowledge in driving competitive advantage.

With these technological advancements related to social software, today, there has been a profound shift in the roles of firms and customers in the process of knowledge and value co-creation. Empowered with internet and social media, customers have become more connected, informed, and active than ever before. Scholars (Vargo and Lusch, 2004) have well recognized the shift in the role of consumers. Despite the similar shift in the role of a firm, relatively little is known about it. A few scholars

Y.K. Dwivedi et al. (Eds.): TDIT 2013, IFIP AICT 402, pp. 583–586, 2013.

(Von Krogh, 2012; Haefliger, et al, 2011) have provided valuable insights by discussing the role of social software in changing knowledge management and strategic thinking. On one hand, software vendors claim that their social software works like silver bullets that lead to competitive advantages, and, the enthusiasm and investments for these initiatives are on the rise. On the other hand, the broader strategic impacts of these initiatives on competitive advantage are not clear yet.

Social software has potential to empower firms to be more engaged and active; however, it is important to draw on strategic management literature to explore whether and how it enables competitive advantage. This position paper highlights deep-seated problems in applying some of the prominent strategic management theories in the context of social software initiatives. To address these problems, drawing on marketing literature, it suggests four ways social software can enable a firm's competitive advantage and call for more research to extend the dynamic capability view.

2   The Social Software and Strategy Management: Do They Match?

In the strategy literature, resource-based view (Barney, 1991) and knowledge based view (Kogut and Zander, 1995) places the source of competitive advantage at the organizational level. These scholars argue that internal, difficult to transmit and firm-specific knowledge and resources are important sources of a firm's competitive advantage. However, over time, scholars recognized that a firm's internal stock of resources is not sufficient, and the flow of assets and knowledge resources are equally important for driving a competitive advantage. To acknowledge the importance of the flow of assets and external sources of competitive advantage, Teece et al., (1997) extended the resource based view, and presented the dynamic capability approach. According to the dynamic capability approach, when competitive landscapes are shifting, the dynamic capabilities by which managers "integrate, build, reconfigure, internal and external competencies to address rapidly changing environments" become sources of competitive advantage (Teece et al., 1997, p.516). Despite the recognition of the external competencies, due to its roots in resource based view, dynamic capability approach still remains internally focused, and considers enterprise-level dynamic capabilities to be the sources of a competitive advantage.

In these internally focused views, firm's internal value creation is considered to be disconnected from the market, and the customer-firm interface is considered to be a locus of extraction of economic value (Prahalad and Ramaswamy, 2004). Much of these strategy discussions focus on value extraction and capture, not on value co-creation. On the contrary, the social software is the crucial enabler of value co-creation. Social software boosts and facilitates the interaction between employees within and individuals outside the firm, such as members of user communities or customers (Haefliger, et al, 2011). It can enable customers to contribute to the firm's innovation and product development (Franke et al., 2010). It can also facilitate users of technology to organize themselves in communities, and innovate independently of manufacturers (von Hippel, 2007). In this context, to understand the impact of social software, strategy research should broaden the narrow perspective of authoritative decisions about technology adoption and myopic focus of value capture at the enterprise level (Haefliger, et al, 2011). The strategy research should also broaden their perspectives to shift due emphasis to the value co-creation and capability building at the system level.

3   Value Co-creation and Competitive Advantage

Effective leveraging of firm' internal resources and enterprise-level dynamic capabilities for superior delivery of customer value (value-in-exchange) is no longer sufficient for gaining competitive advantage. The prevailing view that the value for customers is embedded in the firms' offerings has been challenged by a view that value for customers emerges in customers' spears as value-in-use. Customers use the market offerings, and collaborate with other users, add other resources (goods, services, and information) and skills held by them, and create value-in-use (Gronroos, 2008). Superior value co-creation built up capabilities at the system level, and enhances the fitness of a firm's business ecosystem that leads to competitive advantage. As shown in Figure-1, most research in the dynamic capability literature focuses on enterprise level dynamic capability as source of competitive advantage. To understand the competitive advantage holistically, it is crucial to explore interactions between enterprise capabilities and fitness of business ecosystem.

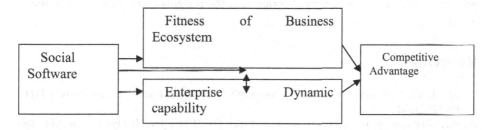

Fig. 1. Impact of Social Software on Competitive Advantage

4   Social Software's Impact: Implications for Future Research

Now to understand the impact of social software on competitive advantage, it is important to explore how it enables value co creation and value capture at the enterprise level and at the system level. Therefore, the impact of social software on competitive advantage can be analyzed in four different ways described in Table-1.

As shown in the analytical framework in Table-1, future research is needed to understand i) whether and how social software enable co-creation of superior value-in-use at the system level, ii) whether and how social software enable sustaining and protecting value-in-use at the system level, iii) whether and how social software enable value orchestration and co-creation at the enterprise level, and iv) whether and how social software enable competitive value capture and capability building at the enterprise level. This type of research that takes strategic approach on social software can generate valuable practical insights that are much needed by the practitioners and managers.

Table 1. Social Software's impact on Competitive advantage

		Competitive Advantage	
		Fitness of business eco system	Enterprise-level dynamic capabilities
Social Software Enablem ent	Value co-creation	Co-creation of superior value-in-use at the system level	Superior value orchestration and co-creation at the enterprise -level
	Value appropriation	Sustaining and protecting value-in-use at the system level	Competitive value capture and capability building at the enterprise level

5   Conclusion

This position paper highlights a key issue in applying prominent strategic management theories in the context of social software. According to this paper, applying the prominent theories to explore the impact of social software may give a myopic view. Prominent strategy management theories generally emphasize value extraction and capture at the enterprise-level more than value co-creation at the system level. On the contrary, the social software is the crucial enabler of value co-creation within a value network. Hence, to holistically understand the impact of social software on competitive advantage, it is important to explore how social software enables value co creation and value capture at the enterprise level and at the system level both. For this exploration, it is important to enrich the internally-focused prominent strategic management theories with the insights about value co-creation at the system level.

References

Barney, J.: Firm resources and sustained competitive advantage. Journal of Management 17(1), 99–120 (1991)

Franke, Nikolaus, Schreier, Martin, Kaiser, Ulrike: The 'I Designed It Myself' effect in mass customization. Management Science 56(1), 125–140 (2010)

Haefliger, S., Monteiro, E., Foray, D., von Krogh, G.: Introduction to Social Software and Strategy. Long Range Planning (2011)

Kogut, B., Zander, U.: Knowledge, market failure and the multinational enterprise: A reply. Journal of International Business Studies, 417–426 (1995)

Prahalad, C.K., Ramaswamy, V.: The Future of Competition: Co-Creating Unique Value with Customers. Harvard Business School Press, Boston (2004)

Teece, D.J., Pisano, G., Shuen, A.: Dynamic capabilities and strategic management. Strategic Management Journal 18(7), 509–533 (1997)

Vargo, S.L., Lusch, R.F.: Evolving to a new dominant logic for marketing. Journal of Marketing 68, 1–17 (2004)

von Hippel, Eric: Horizontal innovation networksdby and for users. Industrial and Corporate Change 16(2), 293–315 (2007)

Von Krogh, G.: How does social software change knowledge management? Toward a strategic research agenda. The Journal of Strategic Information Systems (2012)

A System of Systems Approach
to Managing Emergence in Complex Environments

Igor Hawryszkiewycz

University of Technology, Sydney
Igor.Hawryszkiewycz@uts.edu.au

Abstract. Collaboration now plays an important role in many organizations. Many organizations often see collaboration as a given and provide a myriad of communication tools ranging from e-mail through workspaces to video conferencing. Assumptions are then made that these tools will be used in a productive manner. However, there are now many example of where goals are not achieved through ad-hoc use of technologies as collaboration is often not aligned to business practice, especially to changing business practices. This paper calls for an approach to align technology use to the enterprise practices.

The paper models enterprises as a system of systems where systems are closely integrated through collaborative spaces. These spaces change during system change. The paper provides a set of concepts to describe a system of system and shows how this can be used to align collaboration to the emerging business relationships. The proposed concepts, in contrast to existing methods, place greater emphasis on social structures. They support the idea of a collaborative architecture, which defines the alignment of social collaborative arrangements to business activities through the creation or rearrangement of collaborative spaces. The goal is to get away from traditional approaches in choosing the best pattern based on history, but to encourage design thinking through experimentation at the business structure level. The paper then describes the kinds of tools needed to support modelling based on these concepts.

Keywords: Collaboration, Agility, Modeling, Concepts for collaboration, Living Systems Theory.

1   Introduction

The emerging trend in business and government systems is towards greater networking or what is sometimes called Enterprise 2.0 (McAfee, 2006). Network arrangements often include a number of organizations, who collaborate to jointly co-create products (Cova, 2008) or services. Apart from the trends, current literature does not look at the emergence and change of relationships that occur in networked organizations and their impact on collaboration. Emergence and change has been the characteristic of business practice for many years. Ciborra (1996) describes change at organizational level and develops the concept of a platform. He also identifies a trend to adopt existing patterns in most change decisions in contrast to the trend to design

Y.K. Dwivedi et al. (Eds.): TDIT 2013, IFIP AICT 402, pp. 587–595, 2013.

thinking (Martin, 2009) now emerging in practice. The idea of organization is now going beyond simply business units; it is also going into social communities, which themselves are increasingly seen as organizations. Ibrahim and Ainin (2013) describe the use of ICT in a Malaysian community. (Best, Kumar, 2008) describe how changing client behavior leads to the failure of a community where misalignment between practice and technology grows with changing community practices. In communities, as in many business organizations, there is greater emphasis on social structure (Pralahad and Krishnan, 2008) and collaboration. There are increasing calls (Pisano, Verganti, 2008, Patel, 2012) for a more focused approach to create a collaborative architecture to align collaboration to the business process and avoid failure because of lack of collaboration.

The complexity that characterizes continual business change is here seen in a similar way to Merali (2006). It does not focus on mathematical solutions but ways to manage the continuous change in business relationships. The paper describes the set of modeling concepts that address these issues. The objective of this paper is to develop a model to encourage design thinking in social context by providing a platform, which focuses on collaborative structure within organizations. It brings together ideas from living systems theory (Miller, 1978, Lane and Swanson, 1993) and design thinking as a set of interacting spaces (Brown, 2008). The goal is to align the spaces to the collaboration that best fits the enterprise ways of working. This is in contrast to many current modeling methods, which focus on the technical structure and thus do not address the increasing role of social relationships in business system evolution.

2   Representing a System of Systems

The paper proposes an open systems architecture to provide the semantics for emergence at the system level to define a number of classes of communicating system (Miller, 1978). An enterprise can then modeled in terms of the classes of systems and emergence can be described in terms of changing system structure.

- A group is a small number of people who have a well-defined goal. This may be a sales team, or a software team writing a program, or a temporary focus group working on a proposal. Thus groups usually address one function that requires one or two levels of decision making.
- An organization is something bigger and usually includes a number of groups. It may be a large business unit that develops and sells a financial product. It can include a number of groups as for example a product development group, a marketing group and a client relationship group.
- Organization is a generic term and organizations can include other organizations. Thus a bank can include a number of business financial units. The organizational level differs from the group level in that it has more than two levels of decision making.
- A community is a more loose connection of people. It may for example be a union within an organization. It may be a professional association, or a business group. It may be an association of people formulating a policy.

There are two more detailed levels. An activity is where a group engages in tasks such as to decide how to arrange a software module. A task is then something that is carried out in an activity such as 'develop a program'.

Figure 1 illustrates these concepts with some simple examples of how the different classes of system can be composed into a system of systems. Figure 1 shows a sales group whose goal is to reach a sales target. This group is part of the sales organization that sets the targets. The sales organization is part of a business system that includes the manufacturing and sales organizations. The system of systems is the top-level of the semantics proposed in this paper.

Each of these social systems is described as a lower level set of concepts. These are **roles**, shown by black dots, **artifacts**, shown as disk shapes, and **business activities** shown as ellipses. Links between roles indicate knowledge flows. The sales organization for example has a role sales manager whose responsibility is to 'manage the sales program'. It also has a role 'salesperson' whose responsibility is to make sales. Figure 1 also shows collaborative group between the sales and manufacturing organizations. The concept boundary role boundary role is used to show social interactions across systems

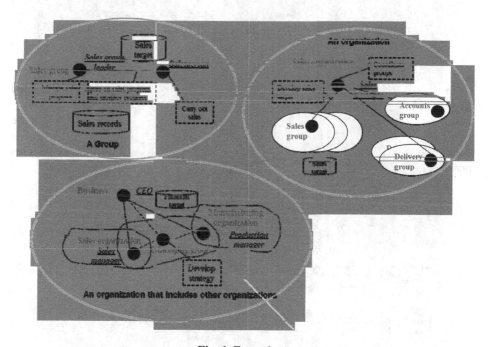

Fig. 1. Examples

An enterprise can also have internal communities, as for example a union, a professional group or a sporting group. All these systems must work together – hence the increasing emphasis on collaboration. There is also emphasis on social networking to support knowledge sharing within and between systems. The systems are now very likely to be **open systems**. That is systems that can respond to unanticipated inputs and can reorganize their activities.

Some readers may see a similarity to context diagrams as each system can be seen as a "process" in structured models. The major difference is that whereas modeling methods such as data flow diagrams focus on process and information flows the concepts here focus on social structures within the system given the more networked environments found in most business systems. There is also a difference in typical representations of organizational structure. Figure 2, for example, illustrates a traditional structure where a business is composed of a sales and manufacturing departments. An alternate representation based on a system of systems is shown in Figure 3.

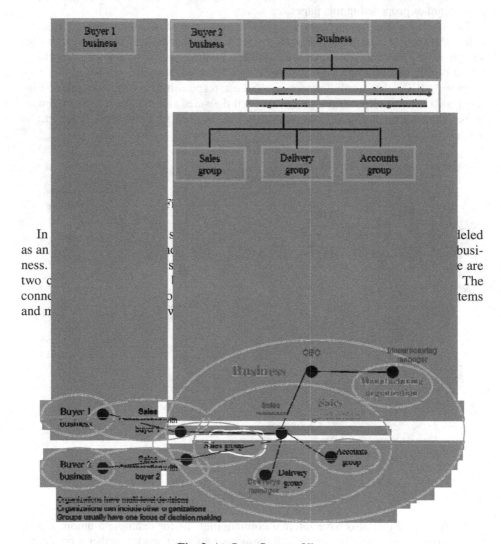

Fig. 3. An Open Systems View

3   Defining Semantics of Change

The premise in this paper is that change is primarily driven through actions of people occupying roles in businesses. It usually commences with some new collaboration that addresses a perceived opportunity. The organization structure thus changes as productive collaborative arrangements are identified and become part of normal operations. Change is modeled in the following steps:

- Change commences with the emergence of new collaborative group nominating boundary roles in each participating system. These become **virtual roles** within a collaborative group,
- Roles in existing systems are assigned to take on the responsibilities of the virtual roles,
- Self-organization takes place by rearranging information flows in line with the new responsibilities.
- Collaborative groups, if found effective can then become new systems that can be combined into the system of systems.

3.1   Example of Change – Emerging Network

Suppose two business managers, as shown in Figure 4, find that they can work together. One has the expertise in product development and outsources product installation to a variety of installers. The other is an expert in delivery and installation. By combining they feel they will add new value to their businesses. Partner A will be able to focus on creating innovative products while partner B will use their contacts to distribute these products.

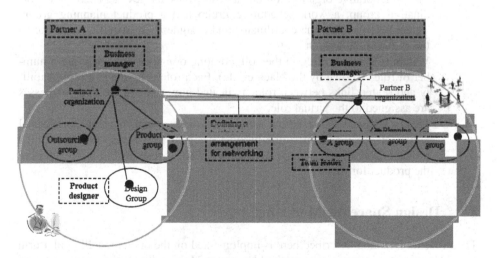

Fig. 4. Starting the Collaboration

In the initial stages the collaboration is simple – an interaction between the managers of two businesses who see some benefit in working together. Once agreement is reached a more sophisticated collaboration is proposed.

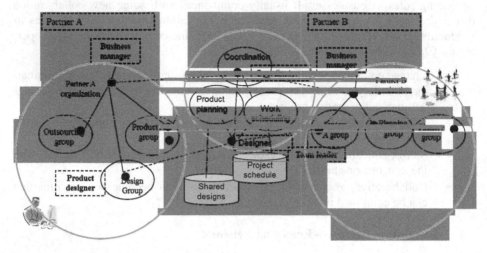

Fig. 5. Communicating Systems – An overall architecture

This, as shown in Figure 5, follows the same steps as the previous example but on a larger scale.

- The two businesses together create a collaborative organization through which they communicate.
- The collaborative organization has its own roles and levels. There is a coordination group, a work scheduling group and a product planning group. There are two roles, the coordinator and designer with specific responsibilities in the collaboration
- Virtual roles are created in the collaborating organization. There are a number of roles (shown by the black circle). Each role is assigned a responsibility and dotted links between roles indicated how roles in the two businesses are assigned to the virtual role.
- People assigned to the virtual roles collaborate in carrying out their formal duties. Hence for example the product designer role is responsible for new product design for partner A whereas the team is responsible for developing the product for partner B.

4   Design Space for Modeling

The modelling method described here is implemented on the open modelling platform at the University of Vienna. The method known as MelCa allows models to be set up from different perspectives and maintains cross references between models as allowed by the open modelling platforms. The modelling concepts used in the model have been described earlier (Hawryszkiewycz, 2005) and support collaboration. The main concepts are a role (shown by a circle, artefact (shown by the disk shape, and activity (shown by the ellipse). New objects can be easily added to the model and rearranged as needed giving the flexibility to use alternate modelling options.

The basic principle used in the model in Figure 6 is to show each system as an aggregation of level in the square box. They must also create a collaborative environment where they can leave together. There is flexibility in rearranging systems, adding new components, and linking systems through collaborative spaces. The tool is highly interactive and supports design experimentation by providing the ability to quickly rearrange systems and collaboration between them. A more detailed application can be found in Yoo (2011).

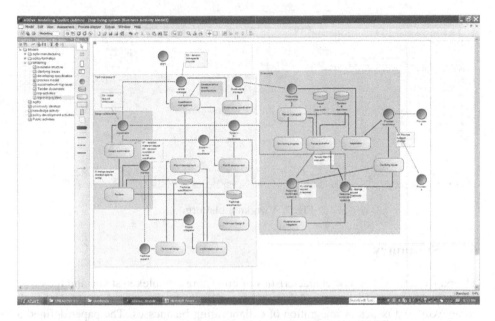

Fig. 6. A representation of business networking using MelCa

5   Implementation Issues – Creating Platforms

Implementations combine objects to create the collaborative systems using adaptable workspaces. An example of a workspace is shown in Figure 8. Beginning with collaboration (Hawryszkiewycz, 2005) which supports the concepts described earlier. Knowledge workers can self-organize their work in a system by creating new roles or artifacts and rearranging responsibilities for working on the artifacts. They should also be able to create interaction spaces to pursue new and evaluate.

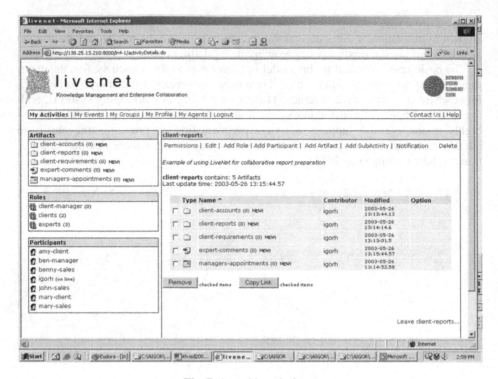

Fig. 7. A working platform

6   Summary

The paper defined the new characteristics of emerging complex systems and the challenges to be met by new methodologies that will help business analysts to deal with complexity and issues of integration of collaborating businesses. The paper defined a set of concepts to manage change using living systems theory (Miller, 1978) as its framework. The paper then identified the kind of tools needed to support the open modelling method and illustrated with an example.

The semantics focused on emergence, self-organization is simply managed by creating collaborative environments as needed. Process integration is also supported through collaborative environments where people assigned to roles that are linked to roles in the collaborative environment. The future work here is to use the semantics to propose services based on social media to quickly adapt social networking to emerging business structures.

References

1. Best, M.L., Kumar, R.: Sustainability Failures of Rural Telecenters: Challenges from Sustainable Access in Rural India (SARI) Project. Information Technologies and Development 4(4), 31–45 (2008)

2. Brown, T.: Design Thinking. Harvard Business Review, 84–93 (June 2008)
3. Camillus, J.C.: Strategy as a Wicked Problem. Harvard Business Review, 99–106 June 2008
4. Ciborra, C.: The Platform Organization: Recombining Strategies, Structures, and Surprises. Organization Science 7(2), 103–118 (1996)
5. Cova, B., Salle, R.: Marketing solutions in accordance with S-D logic: Co-creating value with customer network actors. Industrial Marketing Management 37, 270–277 (2008)
6. Hawryszkiewycz, I.T.: A Metamodel for Modeling Collaborative Systems. Journal of Computer Information Systems XLV(3), 63–72 (2005)
7. Hawryszkiewycz, I.T.: Knowledge Management: Organizing the Knowledge Based Enterprise. Palgrave-Macmillan (2010)
8. Ibrahim, Z., Ainin, S.: Community Technology project in Malaysia: Kodai. Kom. The Journal of Community Informatics 9(1) (2013)
9. Lane, T., Swanson, G.A.: Application of Living Systems Theory to the Study of Management. Organizational Behavior 38(3) (1993)
10. Martin, R.: The Design of Business. Harvard Business Press (2009); Martin, R.L.: The Innovation Catalysts Harvard Business Review, pp.82-88 (2011)
11. McAfee, A.P.: Enterprise 2.0: The Dawn of Emergent Collaboration. MIT Sloan Management Review, 21–28 (2006)
12. Merali, Y., McKelvey, B.: Using Complexity Science to effect a paradigm shift in Information systems for the 21st. century. Journal of Information Technology 21, 211–215 (2006)
13. Miller, J.: Living Systems. McGraw-Hill, New York (1978)
14. Pisano, G.P., Verganti, R.: What Kind of Collaboration is Right for You. Harvard Business Review 83(8), 80–86 (2008)
15. Prahalad, C.K., Krishnan, M.S.: The New Age of Innovation. McGraw-Hill (2008)
16. Yoo, C.-B., Hawryszkiewycz, I.T., Kang, K.-S.: Multi-perspective Framework to Improve the Knowledge Flow. In: Proceedings of the 12th European Conference on Knowledge Management, pp. 988–996 (2011)

Curriculum Design and Delivery for E-Government Knowledge Transfer in a Cross Cultural Environment: The Bangladesh Experience

Ahmed Imran[1], Shirley Gregor[2], and Tim Turner[1]

[1] UNSW Canberra at the Australian Defence Force Academy, Australia
{a.imran,t.turner}@adfa.edu.au
[2] Australian National University, Canberra, Australia
Shirley.gregor@anu.edu.au

Abstract. This paper describes a successful intervention to facilitate the adoption of e-government in a least developed country. The action design research project adopted an unusual approach to facilitating e-government based on earlier grounded research that identified particular underlying inhibitors to adoption. In this case, the need to increase the knowledge of the Bangladeshi public servants to the potential and approaches of e-government was a higher priority than attempting any specific e-government project implementation. A formal education program has been established that is available to all Bangladeshi public servants through institutional training. The project's approach and the lessons learned in its delivery provide a useful framework for other e-government interventions in least developed countries.

Keywords: ICT4D, E-government, Cross culture, Knowledge transfer, Curriculum design.

1   Introduction

In the 21st century's information-intensive economy and society, "knowledge" is considered the most precious commodity, and knowledge transfer initiatives can make significant differences in under privileged societies (Kefela 2010). The e-government capacity building project described here aimed at building knowledge of the benefits of information and communication technology (ICT) for decision making and work practices among public sector leaders. This two year long project involved action design research (ADR) (Iivari and Venable 2009, Sein, Henfridsson et al. 2011) and application of reflective practices (Loughran 2002) in developing an educational curriculum from the ground up. The intervention, with multi-level stakeholders from two countries with different socio-economic and cultural backgrounds, provided rich insights and lessons on cross-cultural design issues, which could be useful for practitioners and researchers working in developing countries. The paper first outlines the project, followed by its rationale and background, discusses the key challenges, lessons learned and implications for the future.

Y.K. Dwivedi et al. (Eds.): TDIT 2013, IFIP AICT 402, pp. 596–604, 2013.
© IFIP International Federation for Information Processing 2013

2   The Project

In 2008, based on existing research work, the first phase of an e-government capacity building project in Bangladesh was launched with the help of the competitive Public Service Linkage Grant (PSLP) from the AusAID (Imran, Gregor et al. 2009). The broad objectives of the project were to improve transparency and efficiency in the public sector in Bangladesh with enhanced benefits to citizens. This activity addressed an important problem area identified through prior research, a lack of fundamental knowledge and awareness of the strategic use and implications of ICT systems for government business processes; a major barrier to e-government adoption in Bangladesh (Imran and Gregor 2010). This lack of knowledge inhibited responses to a range of other barriers such as poor infrastructure, low socio-economic conditions and lack of leadership. Accordingly, a two phase intervention was planned. In 2008, the first phase aimed to: (1) build a long-term strategy for successful e-government adoption, and (2) overcome knowledge barriers by short-burst specially designed training packages for senior decision makers within the public services.

In 2010, the second phase of the intervention was designed building upon the achievements of the initial activity (Imran, Turner et al. 2008) as a next step to institutionalise a more robust knowledge base amongst the public sector officials in Bangladesh. The Bangladesh Public Administration Training Centre (BPATC) was chosen as the counterpart organisation. BPATC delivers training for both new and more senior government officers from all cadres and services of the government, including police, customs and other affiliated organisations. In the past the only ICT-related course at BPATC, "ICT and E-governance", had covered only introductory and basic skills training for ICT and lacked quality and purpose.

To achieve the overarching goal, the activity focused on building a long-term institutional capacity through a well-designed sustainable knowledge building scheme. A techno-centric approach in the past has been the cause of failures of many e-government initiatives in developing countries (Heeks 2003). The approach in our project, in contrast, emphasized 'human-ware' as the precondition or major driver for successful adoption of e-government. Often, managers' lack of motivation, fear of the unknown, resistance to change and negative attitudes are significant obstacles for such innovation (Imran and Gregor 2010).

2.1   Program Purpose

This program was especially designed to give familiarity with the technical and managerial processes required to successfully execute e-government projects and also to highlight the key aspects of successful project management practices in the context of socio-cultural and organisational complexity. The curriculum provides an opportunity to consider real-life experiences through case studies from developed as well as developing countries. The trainee officers are expected to gather clear knowledge of how e-government operates, an understanding of the roles they could be asked to fill, and insight into the combination of managerial, analytic, and technical knowledge they need if they are to handle e-government projects effectively and with confidence.

The program aimed to develop competency in e-government management focusing on three major areas:

- Knowledge of the use ICT and its benefits in e-government in an LDC
- Knowledge of essential ICT systems and technology;
- Knowledge of strategic ICT management.

2.2 Course Design

The course was developed following an outcomes-based approach to learning, where learning objectives are specified for each learning component prior to its development. This approach allows both instructors and students to be aware of what is expected from each other and also to design the assessments. In specifying learning objectives, Bloom's taxonomy of learning objectives (Bloom 1956) that was enhanced by Anderson et al. (Anderson, Krathwohl et al. 2001) was used as the primary guide. This taxonomy has six levels of learning and each level (Remembering, Understanding, Applying, Analysis, Evaluating and Creating) has "action" words associated with it, which indicate the explicit outcomes expected in terms of learning.

One of the underlying objectives of the program was to help the public sector officials to develop their capacity to recognise how they could use e-government to create a positive impact in society. Realizing this objective required a series of reflections from different stakeholders that focused on understanding the broader issue of e-government implementation and the culturally-specific issues of the Bangladesh Public Sector and broader society. These reflections were followed by careful crafting of the course. The course design built on the work in the earlier phase, particularly the short-burst training course, because research has shown that such an approach is effective and relevant in addressing the complexity of embedding innovations in the context of a least developing country (Bangladesh). The curriculum has been designed to harmonise with the counterpart's capabilities and meet priority learning needs of public servants. Training material for use in classroom-based teaching included presentation material, individual, small-group, and whole-group exercises, case studies and review questions (with answers), a short quiz and a long quiz (both with answers), and an instructor's manual (i.e. lesson plan).

3   Project Output/ Deliveries

3.1   The "E-Government Management" Training Package

A full-fledged university standard course (equivalent to a 13 week semester long course in Australian terms) was designed through a series of grounded studies and consultations with the counterpart organisation, tertiary education designers, relevant experts and stakeholders. The primary audience for this course is government officers in developing countries who have some managerial experience (mid-level). Accordingly, the perspectives of practising managers were incorporated in the course. It is expected that participants may come from different fields (such as arts, engineering, science, management) and will have some tertiary education, plus basic IT skills and knowledge (for example, word-processing and email).

3.2   A Text Book on E-Government Management for Developing Countries

A preliminary version of a textbook on e-government in least developed countries (in general, not Bangladesh alone) has been prepared, which follows the format of existing quality texts used in Management of IT courses at the post-graduate level. The final text book is a significant output of the activity as it is the first of its kind for developing countries; consisting of four major parts and sixteen chapters. This text book will be reused by BPATC for ongoing e-government management courses as a main text book and guide to the training.

4   Project Evaluation and Benefits

The project activities included two phases of evaluation, one before the course and one after the course, using a combination of qualitative and quantitative methods. Below is a discussion on the benefits of the course.

4.1   Managers in the Public Sector Who Have Completed the Training Program Have Increased Knowledge of How to Oversee the Use of ICT (E-Government) in the Public Sector

This was the significant outcome and major objective of the activity. Participating officers had increased knowledge and confidence, which was clearly reflected in the evaluation carried out after the course. It was further evident through their initiatives in their workplace after the expiry of the course (Source: Students reflection during certificate award ceremony after six months of the 7th ITEG Course, Date 8th Jan 2012). Some participants played a 'champion' role in initiating actual e-government proposals and projects and some had made policy contributions in their respective organisations which were publicly shared in the certificate award ceremony.

4.2   A High-Quality and Research-Based Training Course on E-Government Management

The newly developed course is a high-quality first of its kind for developing countries that meets the requirements for public sector officials. This paradigm shift has significantly improved the standard, reputation and outcome of the course. The capacity of BPATC was strengthened as it now has a well-designed educational program available for delivery in an area that is essential for the modernization of government.

Before the intervention, staff at BPATC indicated that they see a strong need for developing public sector managers' knowledge of ICT, but they had neither the expertise nor the resources to develop relevant and required curriculum. The offering of the program to train local educators on program delivery as a practical train-the-trainer course has strengthened in-house capacity to run this course after the intervention. Staff at BPATC had the opportunity for personal development by participating in the development and delivery of a leading-edge and innovative program.

Three offerings of the program occurred, with the third offering undertaken by BPATC instructors alone. Each offering received positive ratings by participants on completion of the course. Follow-up interviews with participants after the program showed materials were assimilated and were being applied in practice. According to one participant,

> It changed my vision, it cleared my idea about e-government, now I'm confident and motivated for e-government. It will give me an opportunity to introduce ICT in my organisation (Student feedback, 2nd E-government Management Course, 08 January, 2011).

4.3   A Targeted Textbook for E-Government in Least Developed Countries

Some of the participants of this course were appointed to new positions related to new or existing e-government projects. The textbook, which has been shared amongst many stakeholders, is used as a companion, reference book and for consultation. Use of course material was evident beyond the class room environment.

Follow-up interviews with participants after the program show the textbook is in regular use and is providing assistance in managing e-government projects. According to the Rector of BPATC,

> The experience of the last few years has shown that there is a strong hope in initiating change in officers' through information technology and e-governance. With the knowledge and expertise gained from the course the vision of good governance and true citizen engagement can become a reality. (Message from the Rector, BPATC at Students' Magazine of 2nd E-government Management course, 08 January, 2011)

In addition to the planned output, the project has also contributed in other areas in the form of unanticipated benefits. For example, the application of modern pedagogy, assessment and curriculum design in the course provided much insight and knowledge to the course officials and the instructors who could apply those in other courses within the BPATC. Evidence shows that they are doing this. The project has increased Australia's reputation in Bangladesh through knowledge sharing. Australia's whole-of-government approach to the LDC's development problem in the partner country was well-received. The experience and knowledge from the Australian whole-of-government approach has huge potential in the public sector, with capacity building possible more widely through knowledge transfer.

5   Challenges Faced

5.1   Contextualisation of Contents

One of the greatest challenges was to properly manage the context of the educational material. Many of the concepts and topics used in mature IT organisations in developed countries are difficult to translate or contextualise in the nascent environment of the many developing countries that are at the early stages of IT adoption. Use of terms, which have different connotations in different context and cultures, was particularly noticeable (e.g. speaking of a "business" case when discussing government activity).

Significant attention to these issues was needed to meet cultural norms and customs including the use of particular presentation techniques and the careful use of English language and tone to suit the target audiences in the best possible manner.

Effort was made to sift the important from the unimportant and to pick the right tone for target audiences to avoid burdening them too much with information that was not particularly relevant or was too technical or specific for their use.

5.2   Generating Interest of the Participants

Student participation was the key to success. Maintaining student interest in a newly-developed subject was challenging, particularly as it was addressing an area where they had a self-reported lack of knowledge. Active participation was achieved through good application of pedagogy which included case discussions, projects, video clips, clear power point presentations and relevant contents.

5.3   Addressing the Sustainability Issue

Sustainability was a key element in this activity. The activity and its connection to the 2008 project is a demonstration of commitment to sustainability by the project team and sponsor, something frequently noted by its absence in other international donor initiatives. Research shows many of the e-government initiatives in developing countries fail due to the 'one-off type' and 'techno centric' approaches (Heeks 2003). This activity has addressed those deficiencies, the knowledge of which slowly contributing to the future projects, where citizens will be able to reap the actual benefit.

5.4   Endorsement of the Curriculum

Endorsement of the course and its proper application in replacing the existing offering in the annual training schedule was most challenging. This was also one of the great achievements. Changing curriculum and the name of the course to "E-government Management" through the high-level standing committee of the BPATC was a critical endorsement of the move to a new approach. This outcome was ensured through discussion with the authority concerned in every phase of the design stage.

5.5   Ownership and Maintaining the Interest

A further risk minimization strategy was adopted by keeping the counterpart stakeholders involved in the project at all steps so that a feeling of ownership was developed. It was important to maintain the interest of the stakeholders in the program through regular commitments, communications and timely response and delivery of programs.   A preliminary road test was carried out with the development team and members from the counterpart organisation to carry out a requirement analysis.

5.6   Maintenance of the Integrity of the Program

Over the repeated offerings of the course within the timeframe of the project, there was a tendency to mix in material from other courses within the BPATC program or for modifications to the content to be made by some external instructors to have material that they were more comfortable to teach. However, the project team was diligent to maintain the designed content and delivery so as not to break the integrity of the program, which could have jeopardised the outcomes and overall learning objectives. We tried to make the instructors understand the importance of keeping the program intact, not only to maintain the chronological understanding of the issues but also in attaining external university recognition in future.

5.7   Transfer of Officials

Transfer of officials and instructors who were already trained resulted in the need to train others during the time of the project. These transfers meant duplicated effort that had not been foreseen. However, the effort needed to maintain the base of trained instructors was covered by other contingency plans.

5.8   Political Instability

Instability in the political environment is an inherent problem in many LDCs beyond the control and scope of individual projects. Political instability and unrest often hindered the smooth running of the activity, which also created uncertainty for the future. Because of the political instability, a clear, coherent strategy cannot be maintained within the ICT sector. It seems that every five years a new party comes to power and changes all previous plans and strategies. This is particularly true in complex, leading-edge agenda, such as IT adoption and e-government exploitation.

5.9   Dealing with Bureaucracy

Dealing with bureaucracy and public sector officials in a developing country is always a challenging task, because of the hierarchy and complexities of the procedures involved, especially in implementing an applied research project from overseas. However, this challenge has been met through connections established through one team member's previous working experience in the Bangladesh Government.

5.10   Demanding Time Schedule

Managing the project's schedule and the commitment of all stakeholders to match the BPATC program calendar was also challenging. However, through all-out support and dedication from all involved the project worked out well. The significant time spent on negotiation and correspondences between BPATC and the project team on training, coordination and financial matters at times was extremely demanding.

6   Lessons Learned

Lessons learned from this project will be particularly relevant and useful for e-government interventions in other developing countries. Methodologically, the study provides an example of ADR in an unusual context, an intervention that is aimed at alleviating a situation at a national level. As e-government is frequently aimed at whole-of-government view, or at least cross-government-agency scope, a positive example of supra-organisational intervention is valuable.

The project has also yielded significant outcomes in the area of new knowledge building. Critical reflection has established a number of design principles for a "Sweet

Spot Change (SSC) strategy" (Gregor, Imran et al. 2010) for interventions of this type, with the most important principle being to first identify a "sweet spot", a point of maximum leverage, and then act on it. In e-government, the sweet spot may not be in the immediately expected areas of technology or business processes. Particularly in developing countries, the 'people' element of best practice e-government approaches may be the most challenging, and rewarding area.

The project also demonstrates that e-government in a least developed country is greatly facilitated by the inclusion of a leading participant with a working experience, a well-developed reputation and trust in the context of the public sector environment in the LDC. The 'native' insight was instrumental in addressing the culturally-sensitive challenges and also in capturing the underlying important issues that are often overlooked. Good access and personal liaison with the stakeholders of ICT in the country, some national policy makers, and Government agencies were also important.

Another lesson learned was that good practice guides from other countries (case studies, best practices) can be effective in achieving learning outcomes, when adapted to suit the local context. The experience and formalisations of the Australian Government's experience in e-government, in this case, were an excellent starting point for a properly-contextualised delivery of the concepts of e-government to Bangladeshi public servants. Similarly, having the support of two of Australia's leading universities, with their capable researchers to work as a team, provided the means to deliver proper course development skills-transfer to the BPATC, the peak training agency for Bangladesh's public service.

7   Conclusion

E-government properly implemented offers the potential for substantial benefits to least developed countries, particularly at a whole-of-government level. The project outlined here demonstrates that a thoughtfully conducted project that builds on developed country e-government experience but is sensitive to the cultural and environmental factors present in the least developed recipient country can be very effective.

It was evident from many of the evaluation responses collected after each offering of the course that training of this nature was something new to the participants as it addressed practical issues and needs of the students rather than more conventional 'factory-made' training. Developing and delivering the course was also a rewarding learning experience for the researchers/designers, to be part of such international work aiming to contribute to the societal benefit of a disadvantaged society.

The training package and the text book prepared for Bangladesh address issues and concerns common to other LDCs in the field of e-government. A huge potential exists across many developing countries in the world to benefit from replicating this program with some modification to the country context.

There are a number of potential follow-on activities that can be undertaken based on the success of this activity. For example, offering similar e-government programs and training to other developing countries, expanding and developing longer-term training for the government officers of Bangladesh and elsewhere, and through wider dissemination of the e-government management textbook. Interest shown by other organisations affiliated with civil services, universities and IT industry bodies in other least developed countries is encouraging.

Acknowledgements. The support of a number of organizations is gratefully acknowledged, especially AusAID, the Australian Agency for International Development, which was the primary funding body. Support was also provided by the School of Accounting and Business Information Systems at the Australian National University (ANU) and by the Bangladesh Public Administration Training Centre (BPATC). We also acknowledge the students, faculty members and management of BPATC who were directly and indirectly engaged in developing and improving the curriculum.

References

Anderson, L.W., Krathwohl, D.R., Airasian, P.W., Cruikshank, K.A., Mayer, R.E., Pintrich, P.R., Raths, J., Wittrock, M.C. (eds.): A Taxonomy for Learning, Teaching, and Assessing: A Revision of Bloom's Taxonomy of Educational Objectives. Addison Wesley Longman, Inc., New York (2001)

Bloom, B.S.: Taxonomy of Educational Objectives; The Classification of Educational Goals. Susan Fauer Company (1956)

Gregor, S., Imran, A., Turner, T.: Designing for a 'Sweet Spot' in an Intervention in a Least Developed Country: The Case of e-Government in Bangladesh. In: Proceedings of the Third Annual SIG Globdev Workshop. Association for Information Systems, Special Interest Group on ICT and Global Development, St. Louis, USA (December 2010)

Heeks, R.: Most eGovernment-for-Development Projects Fail: How Can Risks be Reduced? IDPM i-Government working paper no.14. UK, University of Manchester (2003)

Iivari, J., Venable, J.: Action Research and Design Science Research – Seemingly similar but decisively dissimilar. In: 17th European Conference on Information Systems, Verona, Italy (2009)

Imran, A., Gregor, S.: Uncovering the Hidden Issues in e-Government Adoption in a Least Developed Country: The Case of Bangladesh. Journal of Global Information Management 18(2), 30–56 (2010)

Imran, A., Gregor, S., Turner, T.: eGovernment Capacity Building through Knowledge Transfer and Best Practice Development in Bangladesh. In: 10th International Conference on Social Implications of Computers in Developing Countries. IFIP. Dubai School of Governmnet, Dubai (2009)

Imran, A., Turner, T., Gregor, S.: Educate to Innovate – Fast Tracking ICT Management Capabilities Amongst the Key Government Officials for eGovernment Implementation in Bangladesh. In: SIG GlobDev Workshop, Paris, France (2008)

Kefela, G.T.: Knowledge-based economy and society has become a vital commodity to countries. International NGO Journal 5(7), 160–166 (2010)

Loughran, J.: Effective Reflective Practice: In Search of Meaning in Learning about Teaching. Journal of Teacher Education 53(1), 33–43 (2002)

Sein, M.K., Henfridsson, O., Purao, S., Rossi, M., Lindgren, R.: Action Design Research. MIS Quarterly 35(1), 37–56 (2011)

Actor Network Theory
in Interpretative Research Approach

Tiko Iyamu[1], Tefo Sekgweleo[2], and Sharol Sibongile Mkhomazi[3]

[1] Namibia University of Science and Technology,
Department of Business Computing, Windhoek, Namibia
connectvilla@gmail.com
[2] P.O. Box 13121, The Tramshed, Pretoria, South Africa
ts33ci@gmail.com
[3] Tshwane University of Technology, Department of Informatics, Pretoria, South Africa
mkhomaziss@tut.ac.za

Abstract. The main components of information systems include people, process and technology infrastructure. In many studies, these components are often viewed and examined from socio-technical perspectives. This is primarily because of the criticality of human actions. The complexities and the difference which humans bring in the development and implementation of information systems are not getting easier. Hence the increase studies in the field of information systems.

Many approaches such as using the lens of Actor Network Theory (ANT) has been explored to understand the socio-technical factors in the information systems. Although ANT has been employed in many studies, it is of significant important to establishes and clarifies the factors, from the social perspective, which influences the development and implementation of information systems in organisations.

Keywords: Actor Network Theory, Information Systems, Analysis.

1 Introduction

Information systems are considered vital, and some organisations wholly rely on it. Organisations make use of information systems to support their operations, administrations, processes and competitive advantage. The development and implementation of information systems is not as easy as we are meant to belief. Also, even though it is intended to address challenges, it could be by itself challenging to employ. Tan and Tan [1] argued that the development and implementation of information systems is a challenging task to accomplish, in a various ways.

Technology by itself does not make up an information system, they include both human and non-human actors within a networks. The actors own and share various responsibilities in the development and implementation of systems. For example, Business Analysts (BA) is responsible for gathering business requirements and compiling the functional design specification [2].

Y.K. Dwivedi et al. (Eds.): TDIT 2013, IFIP AICT 402, pp. 605–610, 2013.

Both human and non-human actors work together as a collective to deliver information system as requested by the organisation. Chen et al [3] argued that IS consists of technical components, human activities, and describe processes which are used to manage the organisation's activities. Hence it is most appropriate to gain a good understanding of the processes and activities which are involved in the development and implementation of information systems in organisation. This is the ultimate contribution of the lens of Actor Network Theory (ANT), a theory which focuses on human and non-human factors.

ANT is a theory that integrates both human and non-human actors to form or create a network. Wernick [4] stated that irrespective of whether the actor is human or non-human they are both weighed equally as they offer the same contribution to the formed network. The teams, which constitute a network, have different roles, responsibilities, understanding, and interpretation of the same system. ANT describes a heterogeneous network of technical and non-technical as equal interrelated actors that can form a network of actors at any time and space.

2   Information Systems

Information systems discipline is regarded as a very important role in organisations. This is the belief and interpretation of its capability to enable and support organisations to conduct business and develop new opportunities, as well as remaining profitable and competitive [5]. As result, organisations often have a substantial investment in the implementation of information systems.

As depicted in Figure 1 below, the operations in information systems involves many phases. The phrases include both technical and non-technical factors. These factors are not easy to understand, hence a lens such as ANT is required to underpin things in perspective on what, how and why things happen in the way that they do during the development and implementation of information systems in organisations.

As illustrated in Figure 1, through the lens of ANT the roles, activities and processes which are involved in the development and implementation of information systems could be empirically viewed and understood. Some of the phases such as development and implementation are discussed in the next sections.

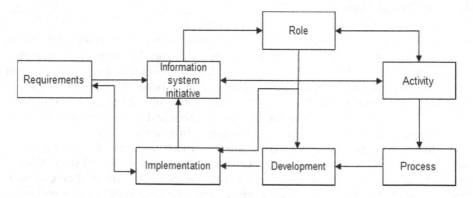

Fig. 1. Operationalisation of Information Systems

Many studies have been conducted in attempts to address the challenges of information systems failure in organisations. Some of the studies, such as Chua [6] vigorously (from different perspectives) argued that information systems failure is caused by many things such as missed schedules, budget overspending, poor planning, the use of unproven technology, organisational changes, and lack of top management involvement.

Some of the factors which are identified as the cause of information systems' failure remain mainly because the rationales (why) behind them have not been appropriately articulated. The social-technical focus of ANT makes the theory appropriate to help investigate the social context, which include the power to make a difference; relationship among the actors, which forms the basis of communication; roles; activities; and processes in the development and implementation of information systems.

i.   Information Systems Development

Information systems are either developed in-house or purchase from the shelves. Companies that choose to develop in-house information systems rely on various approaches to follow. There are tools and techniques available, in conjunction with the methodology to assist in the analysis and design of information systems [7]. However, making use of the appropriate methodologies, tools and techniques does not guarantee successful development or implementation of information systems. According to Chua [6], there are many common factors which influence the failures information systems including lack of user involvement, lack of top management commitment and users rejecting the new system because they feel comfortable with the existing system. In such a case, extra effort to communication, and negotiation, and pursuance is required for the users to show interest.

The activities which are involved in the development phase includes database design and creation, user interface design, application, library and system sources and binary code and the developing and testing of software against the business requirements specification [8]. Each of personnel has their power to negotiate, as well as to make a difference, which is bestowed on the mandate accorded to them.

ii.   Information System Implementation

In the implementation phase, a new system is deployed to production environment, and it is made available to the users, either as an entirely new system or as an upgrade of an existing system. To upgrade or implement a newly developed system, various approaches are followed. Each of the approaches requires interaction, and relationship within the network, which is expected to foster the implementation. Okrent and Vokurka [9] referred to one of the approaches as "big bang". It is described as switch off the old system and instantly moves to the new fully functioning system [10]. Also, there is the pilot approach is usually adopted in multi-department environments. It involves incrementally rolling out the system department. Irrespective of the methodological approach that is employed, the response of the users is often highly a deciding factor.

3   The Lens of Actor Network Theory

Actor network theory (ANT) is social theory that focuses on human and non-human actor, which constitutes networks. The human and non-human components plays vital role in information systems, whether it is in the development or at the implementation stages. Luoma-Aho and Paloviita [11] argued that for an act to occur it is influenced by related or connected factors such as human beings, objects, rules and environment.

Actors within the network have the responsibility of working together as a team with the intention to reach the final goal which is to successfully implement a working information system. Irrespective of whether the actor is human, object or organisation it is equally important to the network. On the understanding of why systems behave in the way that they do allows individuals to provide explanation to other actors, whether in the same network or not.

Many actors are involved in the development, as well as implementation of information systems in organisations. The actors' involvement in the development, and implementation of information systems, inevitably bring about negotiation, in order to reach a common goal in the interest of the organisation. The lens, moments of translation is highly significant from the perspective of ANT, during the process of negotiation. The moments of translation consist of four components, problematisation, interessement, enrolment and mobilisation, and focuses on interaction, negotiation, and transformation of events.

In addition to the four moments of translation, is the obligatory passage point (OPP), which is an entity that is responsible for representing other actors in a way that suits their significance and actions in the world of translation [12]. According to iyamu and Roode [13], ANT does not differentiate human from non-human actors or make division between technical and non technical objects. Thus, ANT brings a different dimension and perspective in viewing the events, processes and activities that are involved in the development and implementation of information systems. The lens of ANT can be used to gain a deeper understanding of how events and activities manifest themselves in the development and implementation of information systems.

4   Information Systems and Actor Network Theory

The development and implementation of information systems involves technical and non-technical factors. The roles of each of the actors are considered important, primarily because their individual action bring a difference, making them more challenging than they portrayed. This could be attributed to the fact that a number of unique skilled personnel, processes and activities are involved, and each of them requires a specific attention. Every individual within a team is assigned tasks which are scheduled to be completed within timeframe. ANT identifies all the personnel involved and objects utilised as actors. Doolin and Lowe [14] argued that actors are regarded as the source of action irrespective of their status whether human or non human.

The main goal of ANT is to create a diverse network which consists of humans and objects with related interests through the moments of translation of the events. The moments of translation involves four stages namely problematisation, interessement, enrolment and mobilization [12]. It is through these stages that diverse networks are formed, and information is shared with those who need it.

The moment of translation explains the roles and responsibilities of actors that are involved in the network. Potts [15] argued that data is translated into information through the extended process of the moment of translation. This encourages actors to share their knowledge with other actors within the network.

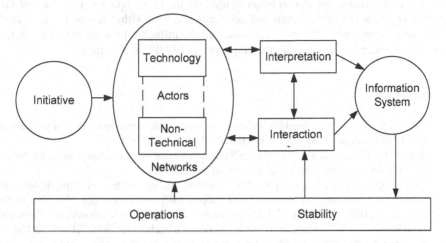

Fig. 2. Social Technical Context in Information Systems

The development and implementation of information systems is a joint effort as it involves multiple participants within social and technical contexts as depict in Figure 3. Participants are also known as actors, they can either be people or technologies [15]. According to Gao [16], the actor network is made up of both human and non-human actors. This network is formed, purposely to accomplish a particular task which in this case is to develop and implement a system.

The interdependency between actors (human and non human) for a common interest and goal within a network, help to provide desired solution to a problematised issue. Currently in business networks, actors are characterised by what they do rather than the positions that they possess. Simply identifying both human and non-human as actor remove individualisation, and foster cooperation and dependence amongst actors within a network.

Technologies are constantly changing for the purpose of making life, processes and activities easier, better, and more flexible. As such, it requires a vibrant network consisting of human and non-human with aligned interest, as opposed to against each other, to comprehend the utilisation of available technologies. Atkinson [17] argued that the use of information systems and technologies plays essential role in solving problems and supporting decision making in various aspects of organisations. This indicates that organisations and individuals are partly, sometimes wholly dependent on technology to function.

5   Conclusion

The development and implementation of information systems is such a challenging and complex task to accomplish in organisations. It requires a diversified number of skills, process and tools that complement each other in a network. Since ANT is unbiased, and equally supports the roles and involvement of both human and non-human actors, it examination is essentially important.

The application of ANT is information systems' studies does not only focus on the creation of networks, but it also helps to identify the roles, technologies and the connection between the two, human and non-human actors within networks. Due to the much interdependency between the actors, and the influential nature of some actors, it is of vital importance to consider the employment of OPP at all times.

References

1. Tan, W.K., Tan, C.H.: Teaching information systems development via process variants. Journal of Information Systems Education 21(2), 159–172 (2010)
2. Avison, D., Fitzgerald, G.: Information Systems Development Methodologies, Techniques & Tools, 4th edn. McGraw-Hill, United Kingdom (2006)
3. Chen, D.Q., Mocker, M., Preston, D.S., Teubner, A.: Information systems strategy: Reconceptualization, measurement, and implications. MIS Quarterly 34(2), 233–259 (2010)
4. Wernick, P., Hall, T., Nehaniv, C.L.: Software evolutionary dynamics modelled as the activity of an actor-network. The Institution of Engineering and Technology 2(4), 321–336 (2008)
5. Bergeron, F., Raymond, L.: Planning of information systems to gain a competitive edge. Journal of Small Business Management 30(1), 21–26 (1992)
6. Chua, A.Y.K.: Exhuming IT projects from their graves: An analysis of eight failure cases and their risk factors. Journal of Computer Information Systems 49(3), 31–39 (2009)
7. Jain, R., Chandrasekaran, A.: Rapid system development (RSD) methodologies: Proposing a selection framework. Engineering Management Journal 21(4), 30–35 (2009)
8. Cervone, H.F.: The system development life cycle and digital library development. International Digital Library Perspectives 23(4), 348–352 (2007)
9. Okrent, M.D., Vokurka, R.J.: Process mapping in successful ERP implementations. Industrial Management & Data Systems 104(8), 637–643 (2004)
10. Capaldo, G., Rippa, P.: A planned-oriented approach for EPR implementation strategy selection. Journal of Enterprise Information Management 22(6), 642–659 (2009)
11. Luoma-Aho, V., Paloviita, A.: Actor-networking stakeholder theory for today's corporate communications. Corporate Communications: An International Journal 15(1), 49–67 (2010)
12. Law, J., Callon, M.: The life and death of an aircraft: a network analysis of technical change. In: Bijker, W.E., Law, J. (eds.) Shaping Technology/Building Society: Studies in Sociotechnical Change, pp. 21–52. MIT Press, Cambridge (1997)
13. Iyamu, T., Roode, D.: The use of structuration theory and actor network theory for analysis: Case study of a financial institution in South Africa. International Journal of Actor Network Theory and Technological Innovation 2(1), 1–26 (2010)
14. Doolin, B., Lowe, A.: To reveal is to critique: actor–network theory and critical information systems research. Journal of Information Technology 17(2), 69–78 (2002)
15. Potts, L.: Using actor network theory to trace and improve multimodal communication design. Technical Communication Quarterly 18(3), 281–301 (2009)
16. Gao, P.: Using actor-network theory to analyse strategy formulation. Information Systems Journal 15(3), 255–275 (2005)
17. Atkinson, C.J.: The multidimensional systemic representation of actor networks: Modelling breast cancer treatment decision-making. In: The Proceedings of the 35th Hawaii International Conference on System Sciences (2002)

Indian IT Industry Firms: Moving towards an Active Innovation Strategy

Rajeev Mukundan and Sam Thomas

India School of Management Studies, CUSAT
{rajeevmukundantampa,sam8570}@gmail.com

Abstract. This paper aims to describe the changing innovation strategies of Indian IT industry firms. Indian firms are responding to global technological discontinuities proactively and faster, compared to the past. Innovations continue to be process driven, however, there is significant focus on non-linear, products & platforms-led growth strategies. There has been an upward shift in R&D/IP emphasis, as empirical data suggests, and emphasis on collaborative innovation. Firms are willing to make riskier investments compared to past. The paper also discusses some of the challenges the players face, as they build the next generation innovations and offerings. Nature of emerging technologies provides further scope for firms to come up with innovative products, services and solutions. Key conclusion is that the innovation strategy of Indian IT industry has changed from 'reactive' to 'active'.

Keywords: Innovation Strategy, Indian IT industry, Open Innovation, Non-Linear Growth.

1 Introduction

The Indian IT industry has been a remarkable success story for the country in the last 2 decades, growing from $150 million in 1990 to $100 billion in size in 2012. The industry has secured its own place in the global map of Information Technology players, comprising product vendors, consulting firms, system integrators, and services providers. This growth has been facilitated by the ability of the industry to continuously move up the outsourcing value chain.

When it was set up, the industry was a disruptive innovation as defined by Clayton Christensen (Christensen, 1997). The offshore business model served an existing customer need, through a different, low-cost based value proposition. However, in recent times, need for non-linear revenue models, changing customer expectations, challenges in talent availability and competitive pressures are forcing the Indian IT firms to shift their innovation strategies.

How do you define innovation strategy? As defined by Dodgson, Gann and Salter, the Innovation Strategy of firms can be categorized into 4 types (figure 1). The Key Research Proposition to be investigated here is that the Indian IT industry is advancing its innovation strategy from 'Reactive' to 'Active' mode.

Y.K. Dwivedi et al. (Eds.): TDIT 2013, IFIP AICT 402, pp. 611–618, 2013.

	Proactive	Active	Reactive	Passive
Objectives	Technology & Market leadership	Not the first to innovate; prepared to follow quickly	Wait and see; Follow a long way behind	Do what is demanded by customers or dominant firms
Type of Innovation	Radical & Incremental	Mainly Incremental	Entirely Incremental	Occasionally incremental
Knowledge Sources	Science; In-house R&D; Collaboration with technology leaders; lead customers	In-house R&D, Collaboration with technology leaders, customers and suppliers	Competitors, customers, purchase of licenses	Customers
Risk acceptance	High risk	Medium-Low risk	Low risk	No risk

Fig. 1. Innovation Strategies - Adopted from (Dodgson, Gann, & Salter, 2008)

2   Innovation Objectives and Type of Innovation

In the early years, the business models of Indian IT firms were primarily dictated by their customer requirements. Innovations were primarily passive and reactive in nature. Customer requirements in of process, productivity and quality improvements influenced the innovation objectives of firms. Consequently, most of the innovations were incremental process improvements. Capabilities to recruit and train large number of engineering graduates, Quality certifications and standards, project management expertise and global delivery model were all examples of such innovation. Dominant firms such as TCS, Infosys and Wipro set the standards, which became de facto practices in the industry. New technology development usually happened in developed markets (primarily the US). Dominant IT firms in India utilized these technological discontinuities to offer services including Application Development and Maintenance, Testing, Systems Integration and Technology Consulting. However, in recent times, there has been a notable shift in the pace of technology diffusion from global majors to Indian firms, as shown below (Fig 2).

As can be seen from recent adoption of emerging technologies (such as Big Data Analytics and Mobility) by Indian firms, the time lag between emergence of a new technology (in a developed market like the US) and development of services/solutions based on the same by Indian IT firms is decreasing. Additionally, smaller Indian IT companies are building solutions of their own, reducing their dependency on the dominant Indian firms for expertise and ideas.

Hence, the Innovation Objectives (quick-to-follow strategy) and the Nature of Innovation (still incremental, primarily) point to an 'Active' stage of Innovation in the Indian IT industry.

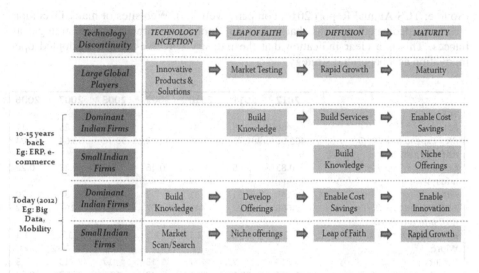

Fig. 2. Quick-to-follow strategy of Indian IT firms (Source: Own Research)

3   Knowledge Sources

Upping the Ante on R&D: Figure 3 below suggests an increase in the R&D intensity of key top players in the industry. TCS and Infosys have significantly increased the number of patents filed in recent times. Firms have publicly stated the need for IP driven growth. An example is the increased focus on products and platforms in the case of some of the larger IT companies.

Collaborative Innovation: The Indian IT firms have a long history of collaborating with industry actors. However, in recent times, the linkages have grown stronger, with more emphasis on leveraging the linkages for innovation. Linkages with customers have evolved from transactional relationships to collaborative partnerships, joint IP creation, joint value discovery and revenue sharing agreements. A case in point is Infosys' strategic relationship with P&G that started in 2007 in achieving business transformation and co-creation of innovation (Source: Infosys Annual Report 2012). Supplier linkages with educational institutions and students (human resources are the key input to IT companies) now incorporate faculty/student training, industry sponsored labs, R&D partnerships & Research sponsorships. IT companies have also forged several strategic partnerships with third party product vendors, which have contributed in technology transfer. For instance a few years back, Wipro launched its ambitious 10x initiative, to train 10000 faculty members across 1500 engineering colleges. The company is involved with more than 1000 schools across the country, and is an active education ecosystem player including periodic meetings and discussions, regular e-mail exchanges, Annual Education Forum, Faculty Workshops, and interactions on the Mission 10x collaborative portal (Source: Wipro Technologies Annual Reports 2008, 2012). TCS has a trademarked co-innovation platform known as COIN for collaborating with several network actors, and also supports (through Research Scholarship) 80 PhD students from about 25 educational institutions

(Source: TCS Annual Report 2012, company web site). Web sites of many IT companies have dedicated sections that talk about Innovation strategies and strategic alliances. This is a clear indication that the industry perceives and has adopted open innovation as a beneficial strategy.

	2012	2011	2010	2009	2008	2007	2006
TCS							
Patents	460	223	87	58	26	25	17
R&D Expenditure (Rs Cr.)	405.06	281.78	77.58	43.92	38.78	33.64	32.04
R&D Intensity (R&D Expenditure/sales) %	0.83	0.75	0.26	0.16	0.2	0.22	0.28
Infosys							
Patents	143	91	31	79	10	38	20
R&D Expenditure (Rs Cr.)	660	527	440	267	201	167	102
R&D Intensity (R&D Expenditure/sales) %	2.1	2.1	2.1	1.3	1.3	1.3	1.1
Wipro							
Patents	15	7	7	13	17	13	3
R&D Expenditure (Rs Cr.)	190.4	165.5	99.3	49	40.5	26.77	20.23
R&D Intensity (R&D Expenditure/sales) %	0.60	0.63	0.43	0.23	0.23	0.19	0.20
HCL Technologies							
Patents	NA	NA	NA	NA	NA	NA	NA
R&D Expenditure (Rs Cr.)	NA	93.16	40.53	40.86	19.44	12.07	4.13
R&D Intensity (R&D Expenditure/sales) %	NA	1.37	0.8	0.87	0.42	0.32	0.14

Fig. 3. R&D and Patenting of Large Indian IT companies (Mukundan & Thomas, 2012)

Hence, the Knowledge Sources of the Indian IT firms (R&D, collaborations) today correspond to an 'Active' Innovation strategy.

4   Risk Acceptance

There are several industry trends that indicate the willingness of Indian IT firms to accept more risks. These include cross-border acquisitions, flexible pricing models (linked to value delivered to clients), and investments in products, platforms & emerging technologies. Barclays, one of the leading global Investment Banks, interacted with several industry experts to compile its 'India Tech Tour Report (2013)'. One of the key findings of this study was increasing willingness of Indian Tech firms to take on more risk on their Balance Sheets (Economictimes.com, 2013).

A report jointly done by consulting firm KPMG and CII (Confederation of Indian Industry) in 2012 elaborates on the emerging trends of the leading Indian IT firms adopting new, 'non-linear' pricing models compared to the traditional Fixed-Price and Time-and-Material models (KPMG/CII, 2012). The non-linear pricing models (outcome, usage, license based) are inherently riskier compared to the traditional pricing models.

Many of the leading firms are making substantial investments in 'Products & Platforms', in an attempt to generate non-linear revenue models. Infosys, in its Annual Report (2012) mentions accelerating growth in products, platforms and solutions, doubling investments in Product Research & Development Center, and strategic acquisitions of domain-specific platforms. TCS Annual Report (2012) discusses elaborately on the firm's investments in platforms, products, Research (in areas such as Green Energy & Social Media), Sponsorship of PhDs, and the Co-Innovation network. An analysis of web sites of TCS, Infosys, Cognizant, HCL Technologies and Wipro Technologies suggests that all 5 companies have invested in the emerging areas of Cloud Computing, Big Data Analytics, Mobility, Knowledge Services and Green IT/Sustainability.

Therefore, it may be concluded that Indian IT firms, in their endeavor to achieve non-linear growth models, have increased the willingness to take calculated risks. It may be argued that the firms have not yet taken bets on radically new, unproven technologies and business models. This 'Medium' level risk-taking willingness corresponds to an 'Active' Innovation strategy.

5   Key Challenges

The industry faces the following challenges.

Leveraging Internal Collaboration & Knowledge: This will be a key challenge for the large and medium sized firms. The pioneering firms have all been in the industry for over 2 decades, and some of them have more than 100000 employees. Past research has highlighted the need for Technology firms to share internal knowledge, and that internal knowledge flows has an inverse relationship with organization size (Serenko, Bontis, & Hardie, 2007). The large IT companies have huge amount of internal knowledge that can be leveraged to create disruptive and breakthrough ideas and innovations. A recent survey done among a sample of IT companies indicated that about 80% of companies identified 'achieving competitive advantage' as the key objective of Knowledge Management (Chaudhuri, 2011). Despite the fact that Indian IT firms have higher awareness and adoption levels of Knowledge Management vis-à-vis other industries (Sanghani, 2008), challenges remain. Internal collaboration challenges include the following: (a) collaboration between various vertical/industry service groups (b) collaboration between vertical and horizontal competency groups (c) and structure and the operating models of the new competency development teams. These collaborations are important, considering the trend of convergence of technologies such as Analytics, Big Data, Mobility and the Cloud (Griffin & Danson, 2012). The large firms could look at limiting the number of employees within a business unit to a certain level, so as to facilitate better knowledge flows (Serenko, Bontis, & Hardie, 2007).

Taking Innovation Capacity to the Next Level: Companies such as 3M, Google and Apple are considered among the most innovative global firms. One of the reasons for their success is their ability to create and sustain unique corporate cultures that foster innovation. Infosys and TCS have made it to the list of top 50 most innovative companies globally, as ranked by Forbes (Forbes, 2012). Most of the scalable innovations in the industry pertain to process improvements. It may be argued that services-driven model that the Indian IT industry follows fosters process excellence than break-through innovations (Deodhar, 2012). The business models of the successful Indian IT companies are based on offshore cost arbitrage, ability to recruit and train thou-sands of skilled employees, program and project management capabilities, quality & productivity benefits offered to customers, and proven global delivery models. Large, successful organizations are built to support repeatable processes that are part of their core business model (Govindarajan & Timble, 2010). Having focused on process-led innovations for several years, the challenge for the large, established IT companies is to create the right organizational culture that would take their innovation capacity to the next level.

Managing the Innovation Process: Innovation process *'consists of an idea that comes from some recognized need that is developed into a concept, followed by inven-tion, and then taken through development, production, and diffusion and adoption by end users'* (Gaynor, 2002). Globally proven models exist for managing the innovation process. Consider IBM, which was issued 6478 patents in 2012 for a variety of inven-tions across technology areas (IBM, 2013). The company topped the list of US Patent recipients in 2012. The company, of course, has a large base of R&D scientists and PhDs. Since 2001, IBM famously introduced the concept of 'Innovation Jams' (colla-borationjam.com platform, which is open to its employees). In 2006, IBM brought a massive 150000 employees and stakeholders together in its Jam platform, to success-fully take several of its technologies to market (Bjelland & Wood, 2008). This is an example of a structured innovation process. In recent years, Indian firms have evolved their innovation processes significantly, as evident from the Innovation literature available on company web sites. The challenge would be to build the right processes that support the non-linear, products & platforms-based strategy.

6   What Is Ahead in the Next Decade?

The president of India declared 2010-2020 as the 'Decade of Innovation' for India (DST, 2010). IT industry players see themselves amongst the drivers of this innova-tion wave. The following trends will influence the innovations in the IT industry, and the direction it will take in the coming years.

Cloud Computing: Cloud computing is disruptive in nature. Global Cloud market is expected to grow from $40.7 billion in 2011 to more than $241 billion by 2020 (InformationWeek, 2011). It levels the playing field to an extent, by providing me-dium and small firms the opportunity to develop and deploy innovative solutions that can be accessed by customers in the global market, at attractive price points. For in-stance, Zoho Corporation, with operations in Chennai, has a suite of award-winning Business/Collaboration/Productivity applications (Source: www.zoho.com) that can be deployed over cloud environment.

Mobility: The proliferation of wireless devices & smart-phones and mobile platforms, along with the emergence of concepts such as Enterprise Mobility, BYOD (Bring Your Own Device), MDM (Mobile Device Management) has revolutionized the Mo-bility space. This provides huge opportunities associated with any General Purpose

Technology Transition (Lalvani, 2012). Innovators have the opportunity to build breakthrough products and solutions, as well as solutions for the bottom-of-the pyramid markets.

Business Analytics & Knowledge Services: It is estimated that Business Analytics market will grow at a CAGR of about 9.8% during 2011-2016, to become a $50 billion market by 2016 (eWeek.com, 2011). Knowledge Process Outsourcing (KPO), which includes Research & Analytics outsourcing, is expected to reach a $17 billion global market by 2014 from $9 billion in 2011, and India is expected to garner 70% share of this (informaticsoutsourcing.com, 2012). Several large IT/BPO services players have already established Business Analytics and Knowledge Services as a value-added offering. However, the niche nature of the business also provides a window of opportunity for the medium/small sized players. Evalueserve with more than 2600 employees and significant presence in India (Source: www.evalueserve.com), Mu Sigma with over 2500 professionals and operations in Bangalore (Source: www.mu-sigma.com) and Amba Research (www.ambaresearch.com) are examples of focused players in this space.

The other emerging areas include Big Data Analytics and Green IT. The opportunity lies in the fact that all these areas offer tremendous innovation potential for firms *of all sizes*.

7   Conclusions

The Indian IT industry is at an inflection point of innovation, as it progresses towards a more 'active' innovation strategy. This is evident from an upward shift in R&D/IP emphasis, adoption of collaborative innovation, faster pace of reacting to technology discontinuities, and willingness to make riskier investments. The next few years will separate the innovation leaders from the rest. Emerging areas such as Cloud Computing and Mobility offer huge opportunities for firms to innovate, where Small and Medium size firms will have an equal opportunity.

This study has the following limitations. Firstly, some of the generalizations are based on analysis of select firms, and not based on empirical analysis. Secondly, the study focuses primarily on the large, established firms. Future work should focus on smaller sized firms and start-up firms to understand trends in innovation within those segments. The study has practical implications, particularly to medium/small sized firms looking to understand the innovation trends being set by the dominant firms. Findings of the study will find utility among academic community interested in the strategies of IT industry firms.

References

From Economictimes.com (March 11, 2013),
    http://articles.economictimes.indiatimes.com/2013-03-
    11/news/37623676_1_investment-bank-business-model-barclays
    (retrieved March 12, 2013)
Arora, P.: Innovation in Indian Firms: Evidence from the Pilot National Innovation Survey. ASCI Journal of Management 41(1), 75–90 (2011)

Bjelland, O.M., Wood, R.C.: An Inside view of IBM's 'Innovation Jam'. MIT Sloan Management Review, 32–40 (2008)

Chaudhuri, S.: Knowledge Management in Indian IT industries. In: 3rd International Conference on Information and Financial Engineering, IPEDR, vol. 12, IACSIT Press, Singapore (2011) © (2011)

Christensen, C.M.: The Innovator's Dilemma: When New Technologies cause great companies to fail. Harvard Business School Press, Boston (1997)

Deodhar, S.: How to Encourage Innovation @ Work, from NextBigWhat (2012), http://www.nextbigwhat.com/how-to-encourage-innovation-work-297/ (retrieved March 12, 2013)

Dodgson, M., Gann, D., Salter, A.: The Management of Technological Innovation. Oxford University Press (2008)

DST. Decade of Innovation (March 2010), from Department of Science & Technology, India, http://www.dst.gov.in/whats_new/press-release10/pib_10-3-2010.htm (retrieved March 13, 2013)

eWeek.com. Business Analytics Market to Reach $50.7B by 2016 on Big Data Hype: IDC (July 2011), http://www.eweek.com/c/a/Enterprise-Applications/Business-Analytic-Market-to-Reach-507B-by-2016-on-Big-Data-Hype-IDC-179369/ (retrieved March 13, 2013)

Forbes. The World's Most Innovative Companies List (September 2012), http://www.forbes.com/innovative-companies/list/ (retrieved March 12, 2013)

Gaynor, G.H.: Innovation by Design: What it Takes to Keep Your Company on the Cutting Edge. AMACOM, American Management Association (2002)

Govindarajan, V., Timble, C.: The Other Side of Innovation: Solving the Execution Challenge. Harvard Business Review Press (2010)

Griffin, J., Danson, F.: Analytics and the Cloud — the Future is Here. Financial Executive, pp. 97–98 (November 2012)

IBM. IBM Tops U.S. Patent List for 20th Consecutive Year (January 2013), http://www-03.ibm.com/press/us/en/pressrelease/40070.wss (retrieved March 13, 2013)

informaticsoutsourcing.com. KPO and the Indian Surge (July 2012), http://informaticsoutsourcing.com/global-outsourcing-services/?p=150 (retrieved March 2013)

InformationWeek. Forrester forecasts USD 241 billion cloud computing market by 2020 (April 2011), http://www.informationweek.in/cloud_computing/11-04-26/forrester_forecasts_usd_241_billion_cloud_computing_market_by_2020.aspx (retrieved March 13, 2013)

KPMG/CII, Non-Linear Models: Driving the next phase of growth for the Indian IT industry (2012)

Lalvani, S.: SMARTPHONE: Smart Opportunity. The Hindu, Survey of the Indian Industry, pp. 182-184 (2012)

Mukundan, R., Thomas, S.: Innovation Strategies of Large Indian IT companies: A study based on the Industry Life Cycle Theory. In: Paradigm Shift in Innovative Business Management, pp. 621–631. CBA Publishers (2012)

Sanghani, P.: Knowledge Management: Inter Industry Comparison in India (2008), http://www.pbfeam2008.bus.qut.edu.au/papers/documents/ParagSanghani_Final.pdf

Serenko, A., Bontis, N., Hardie, T.: Organizational size and knowledge flow: a proposed theoretical link. Journal of Intellectual Capital, 610–627 (2007)

Endless Bad Projects or Evidence-Based Practice?
An Agenda for Action

Briony J. Oates[1], David W. Wainwright[2], and Helen M. Edwards[3]

[1] School of Computing, Teesside University, Middlesbrough, TS1 3BA, United Kingdom
b.j.Oates@tees.ac.uk
[2] Faculty of Engineering and Environment, Northumbria University,
Newcastle upon Tyne, NE2 1XE, United Kingdom
david.wainwright@northumbria.ac.uk
[3] Faculty of Applied Sciences, University of Sunderland,
Sunderland, SR6 0DD, United Kingdom
helen.edwards@sunderland.ac.uk

Abstract. This short position paper promotes the need for more evidence based practice to underpin the successful execution of information systems (IS) projects. This research responds to the high numbers of IS projects that are seen to have failed in terms of either one or many success criteria such as: not meeting original objectives, running over budget, negatively impacting on people, processes or organizations, to name but a few. We advocate the need for the development of a more rigorous evidence base for IS research similar to those used in medicine or more recently in social studies and software engineering. For example, Systematic Literature Reviews (SLRs) and also Meta-Analysis of empirical research studies could be used more extensively within IS to compile more coherent, consistent and referable bodies of evidence and knowledge. We conclude with a 7 point action plan and suggestions for further research.

Keywords: Evidence-Based Practice, Qualitative Research, Systematic Literature Review, Information Systems Failures, Research Methods.

1 Introduction and Background

There have been many information systems (IS) project failures. In the UK, the most detailed analyses of what went wrong tend to be those concerned with public sector IS failures. Taxpayers' money has been wasted, and the existence of the Freedom of Information Act, a Free Press and bodies such as the National Audit Office and the Parliamentary Public Accounts Committee mean that it is hard to conceal the failure, the contributory causes and the amount of money wasted. Commercial and Private Sector failures are much less transparent and visible however, which makes them hard to research, access and gather detailed empirical data. This is often due to powerful corporate interests, strategic and competitive drivers associated with brand, quality and image, and also the ever present threat of litigation and negative impacts on service provision from IT suppliers, vendors and consultants. Examples of documented IS failures include:

Y.K. Dwivedi et al. (Eds.): TDIT 2013, IFIP AICT 402, pp. 619–624, 2013.
© IFIP International Federation for Information Processing 2013

- Student Loans Company. In 2009 a non-departmental public body of the Department for Business, Innovation and Skills took over from local authorities the responsibility for university students' loans & grants. Performance in processing applications and communicating with students was completely unacceptable, for example, in September 2009 (the start of the new academic year) 87% of phone calls went unanswered. Many students waited weeks or months for their financial support and universities had to use their own funds to issue emergency grants and loans (Collins, 2010; National Audit Office, 2010).

- FiReControl System. Part of the UK's fire & rescue service. The project aimed to replace 46 local control rooms with a network of 9 purpose-built regional control centres using a new national IT system to handle calls, mobilise equipment and manage incidents. The project was abandoned in 2010, £469 million having been spent, with no IT system delivered and eight of the nine new regional control centres remaining empty and an estimated £342 million long-term rental costs for the nine control rooms, which the government is locked into until 2033 (Hall, 2011; National Audit Office, 2011).

- Integrated Children's System. The IT system used by social workers and others in local authorities who are concerned with children and families services. It cost £30 million, and is supposed to help social workers record information about children and manage their case loads. Many problems have been reported, including that it does not help achieve the primary goal of child protection, and it was a contributing factor in the death of a baby (Ince and Griffiths, 2011; Wastell, 2011).

- Care Records Systems in the English NHS: As part of the UK government's highly ambitious agenda for transformational change across the National Health Service, the National Programme for Information Technology (NPfIT) launched in 2002 was seen as a central pivot for improving efficiency and effectiveness through the development of electronic patient records and an integrated care records system. Despite a massive investment of over £6.4 billion by March 2011 (NAO, 2011), the programme was effectively cancelled in 2011. Many problems with the programme were reported and many reviews undertaken by the UK government National Audit Office and more recently the Major Projects Agency. Despite the major failings (Currie, 2012) and massive waste of UK taxpayer's money, very few detailed lessons have been learnt, even though concern has been expressed about NHS IT strategy for over a decade (Wainwright and Waring, 2000; Waring and Wainwright, 2013), and no evidence base has been created to differentiate what made certain parts of the programme a success as opposed to high profile and very expensive failures.

2   Evidenced Based Approach

However, despite detailed scrutiny of such failures, the lessons do not appear to be learnt, and the causes of IS failure in one project are repeated in further IS projects:

> "It is deeply depressing that after numerous highly critical PAC [Public Accounts Committee] reports on IT projects in recent years, the same mistakes have occurred once again." (Public Accounts Committee, 2009)

Academic researchers have offered theories that would help predict whether a planned IS project is likely to fail (e.g. Goldfinch, 2007 Heeks, 2003), but again their advice appears to be either ignored or unknown by project clients and developers.

It is our contention that IS project failures will continue to be unacceptably high unless and until the IS profession and its clients adopt an evidence-based practice (EBP) approach, which in turn requires IS researchers to provide them with the necessary evidence to make informed decisions, and IS educators to instil the ethos of EBP in their students.

The concept of EBP was first developed in medicine, in the early 1990's. It was argued that too often clinical practitioners based their decision-making on habit, prejudice, consultant's authority or imperfect knowledge of relevant research. Better treatment decisions would be made if doctors searched the literature for the best available empirical evidence, critically evaluated the study methods to assess the validity of the claimed research findings, and combined this evidence with the values and preferences of their patient (Sackett et al 1996). Evidence-based medicine is now widely taught and practised, and has been called one of the 15 greatest medical milestones since 1840 (Montori and Guyatt 2008). Its scope has now moved beyond informing decisions about clinical treatments, to include the wider management and policy context of healthcare provision, for example, approaches to change organisational culture to improve healthcare performance (Parmelli et al 2011), or strategies for encouraging healthcare professionals to adopt information and communication technologies (Gagnon et al 2009). As evidence-based medicine developed, it was realised that practitioners themselves could not be expected to search for all the available evidence, assess its validity and synthesise the findings of the high-quality studies. Researchers were needed to carry out systematic literature reviews (SLRs) which find, assess and synthesise previous empirical studies, and a knowledge-base was needed to hold the SLRs, which capture the current state of knowledge on treatments, with summaries of the evidence for a non-academic audience. The Cochrane Collaboration (www.cochrane.org) was therefore established, a web-based knowledge-base which includes more than 5000 SLRs (Cochrane Collaboration 2012), with the main findings summarised in a form that practitioners and patients can read.

The idea of EBP has spread to other disciplines, including software engineering (Dybå et al, 2005), social policy (Pawson, 2006), librarianship (Eldredge, 2000) and education (Petty, 2006), and more web-based knowledge-bases have been established, including the Campbell Collaboration (SLRs in education, crime and justice and social welfare: www.campbellcollaboration.org), and one for evidence-based software engineering (www.ebse.org.uk). However, the adaptation and application of EBP, and especially systematic literature reviews for IS research, has not been without critique (Boell & Cezec-Kecmanovic, 2011; Cruzes & Dybå, 2011). This relates to distortions of the techniques from their original purpose, mainly related to the observation that IS can be seen as 'soft' or social science based, whereas medicine or software engineering are seen to be based on 'hard facts' or a greater reliance on exactness and objectivity. There was also a perceived lack of rigour relating to research synthesis, especially of empirical studies. This leads to an over-reliance on processes for literature identification and selection as opposed to placing an emphasis on the interpretation and understanding of the work itself.

Despite these criticisms, which we feel can be overcome, we contend that IS too should explore, develop and perform EBP, so that decision-making about IS strategies, designs, implementations and innovations draws on empirical research findings and previous lessons, rather than gut feeling, current fashion about the latest "silver bullet" or a belief in the "magic" of technology (Wastell, 2011). The EBP paradigm in IS would inform decisions about the design and adoption of new tools, methods, processes or socio-technical systems, because decision-makers would draw on the synthesized findings of empirical research studies into previous use of the tools, methods etc. and integrate this knowledge with their understanding of their local context.

To develop EBP in IS, the following seven-point agenda is proposed:

1. Empirical research into the design and adoption of IS strategies, tools, methods, processes or systems. The IS discipline has a long tradition of empirical research, so this objective is readily achievable.
2. Systematic literature reviews (SLRs). These aim to discover all relevant empirical studies (the evidence) via a transparent and repeatable process, and synthesize their findings. So far, relatively few SLRs have been conducted in IS (Oates, 2011).
3. A web-based knowledge-base. This would contain completed SLRs, with summaries for a non-academic audience. There have been previous proposals for such a knowledge-base to support EBP in IS (Atkins and Louw 2000; Moody 2000; 2003), but nothing tangible has endured. A professional body such as IFIP or AIS could take a lead here.
4. Knowledge transfer of the evidence (the findings of SLRs) to IS practitioners and other stakeholders. Some IS researchers have studied technological innovation diffusion, but translation research and knowledge transfer more generally, from IS researchers to IS practitioners and clients, is not well-developed in IS.
5. EBP in IS education. IS educators need to include EBP in the curriculum studied by our future managers, developers & policy-makers, so that they learn to incorporate empirical evidence into their decision-making, and so that they routinely collect data about their own IS projects, which can be added to the knowledge-base.
6. Evangelists for EBP. There have been some calls for EBP in IS (Atkins and Louw 2000; Baskerville & Myers 2009; Moody 2000; 2003; Oates et al 2012; Wastell, 2011), but more are needed, to raise awareness and lead the movement.
7. Research into EBP. Research is needed into: methods for synthesising previous research in IS which has a plurality of research methods and philosophical paradigms, effective dissemination approaches to help translate research findings into practice, and critical evaluations into the use of EBP in IS to understand the process, benefits and limitations, and to counter any unfounded claims of the evangelists.

3   Conclusions

Our own work presently falls within the action points one and two. In particular, the on-going development of a model-driven method for the systematic literature review of qualitative empirical research (Oates et al, 2012). In terms of our contribution to IS theory, we highlight how this might be used to explore more evidence based practice for the adoption of business process modelling notation (BPMN) methods in organizations. The approach can then be assessed for more generic and practical applicability within IS adoption and diffusion studies. This study was initially based on empirical research and then augmented with supporting evidence from relevant empirical research reported in the literature. The work is continuing and also being developed into a UK based research council proposal where we would aspire to develop a Web-Based knowledge repository; falling within action points three and four.

Following our seven-point agenda would enable the IS discipline to develop an EBP approach, and to assess the strength of our position. We do not assert that EBP is a silver bullet, guaranteed to prevent all future IS project failures. EBP has its critics too (e.g. Wastell, 2005; Boell & Cezec-Kecmanovic, 2011). But we do contend that EBP in IS offers the prospect of decision-making which takes account of previous lessons and experiences, rather than simply repeating the mistakes of the past.

References

Atkins, C., Louw, G.: Reclaiming Knowledge: A Case for Evidence Based Informa-tion Systems. In: Proceedings of ECIS 2000, Paper 28 (2000), http://aisel.aisnet.org/ecis2000/28 (retrieved November 25, 2010)

Baskerville, R.L., Myers, M.D.: Fashion waves in information systems research and practice. MIS Quarterly 33(4), 647–662 (2009)

Boell, S.K., Cezec-Kecmanovic, D.: Are systematic reviews better, less biased and of higher quality? In: Proceedings of the European Conference on Information Systems (ECIS 2011), paper 223 (2011), http://aisel.aisnet.org/ecis2011/223

Cochrane Collaboration 2012. Cochrane Database of Systematic Reviews in numbers (2012), http://www.cochrane.org/cochrane-reviews/cochrane-database-systematic-reviews-numbers (retrieved May 1, 2012)

Cruzes, D.S., Dybå, T.: Research synthesis in software engineering: A tertiary study. Information and Software Technology 53, 440–455 (2011)

Currie, W.: Institutional isomorphism and change: the national programme for IT – 10 years on. Journal of Information Technology 27, 236–248 (2012)

Collins, T.: Over-optimism dogged Student Loans Company's IT-based scheme. Computer Weekly (March 19, 2010)

Eldredge, J.D.: Evidence-based librarianship: an overview. Bulletin of the Medical Library Association 88(4), 289–302 (2000)

Hall, K.: Sifting through the wreckage of the failed £469m FireControl public sector IT project. Computer Weekly (July 11, 2011)

Heeks, R.: Most eGovernment-for-development projects fail: How can risks be reduced? University of Manchester, IDPM Working Papers (2003), http://www.sed.manchester.ac.uk/idpm/research/publications/wp/igovernment/documents/igov_wp14.pdf (accessed October 26, 2012)

Gagnon, M.P., Légaré, F., Labrecque, M., Frémont, P., Pluye, P., Gagnon, J., Car, J., Pagliari, C., Des-martis, M., Turcot, L., Gravel, K.: Interventions for promoting information and communication technologies adoption in healthcare professionals. Cochrane Database of Systematic Reviews 2009 (1), Article number: CD006093 (2009)

Goldfinch, S.: Pessimism, Computer Failure, and Information Systems Development in the Public Sector, pp. 917–929 (September-October 2007)

Ince, D., Griffiths, A.: A Chronicling System for Children's Social Work: Learning from the ICS Failure. British Journal of Social Work, 1–17 (2011)

Moody, D.L.: Building links between IS research and professional practice: Improving the relevance and impact of IS research. In: Weber, R.A., Glasson, B. (eds.) International Conference on Information Systems (ICIS), Brisbane, Australia, December 11-13 (2000)

Moody, D.L.: Using the World Wide Web to Connect Research and Professional Practice: Towards Evidence-Based Practice. Informing Science 6, 31–48 (2003)

Montori, V.M., Guyatt, G.H.: Progress in evidence-based medicine. Journal of the American Medical Association 300(15), 1814–1816 (2008)

National Audit Office. The Customer First Programme: Delivery of student finance (March 2010), http://www.nao.org.uk/publications/0910/student_finance.aspx

National Audit Office. The National Programme for IT in the NHS: an update on the delivery of detailed care records systems (May 2011), http://www.nao.org.uk/publications/1012/npfit.aspx

Oates, B.J.: Evidence-based information systems: A decade later. In: ECIS 2011 Proceedings, Paper 222 (2011), http://aisel.aisnet.org/ecis2011/222 (accessed October 26, 2012)

Oates, B.J., Edwards, H.M., Wainwright, D.: A model-driven method for the syste-matic literature review of qualitative empirical research. In: Proceedings International Conference in Information Systems (ICIS 2012), Orlando, Florida, December 16-19 (2012), http://aisel.aisnet.org/icis2012/proceedings/ResearchMethods/5/

National Audit Office. The failure of the FiReControl project (July 2011), http://www.nao.org.uk/publications/1012/failure_of_firecontrol.aspx

Parmelli, E., Flodgren, G., Schaafsma, M.E., Baillie, N., Beyer, F.R., Eccles, M.P.: The effectiveness of strategies to change organisational culture to improve healthcare performance. Cochrane Database of Systematic Reviews 2011 (1), Article Number: CD008315 (2011)

Pawson, R.: Evidence-based policy. A realist perspective. Sage, London (2006)

Petty, G.: Evidence-based teaching. Nelson Thomas, Cheltenham (2006)

Public Accounts Committee. The National Offender Management Information System (November 2009), http://www.publications.parliament.uk/pa/cm200809/cmselect/cmpubacc/510/51003.htm (accessed October 26, 2012)

Sackett, D.L., Richardson, W.S., Rosenberg, W.: Evidence-based medicine: How to practice and teach EBM. Edinburgh, Churchill Livingstone (1996)

Wainwright, D.W., Waring, T.S.: The Information Management and Technology Strategy of the UK National Health Service: determining progress in the NHS acute hospital sector. International Journal of Public Sector Management 13(3), 241–259 (2000)

Waring, T.S., Wainwright, D.W.: The Information Management and Technology Strategy of the UK National Health Service: Quo Vadis? In: Proceedings for the UK Academy for Information Systems 2013 Conference, Worcester College, Oxford University, March 18-20 (2013)

Wastell, D.G.: Enabling partnership work in crime reduction: Tales from the trenches of evidence-based policy. Evidence and Policy (1), 305–333 (2005)

Wastell, D.G.: Managers as Designers in the Public Services – Beyond Technomagic. Triarchy Press, Axminster (2011)

Participatory Approach versus Bureaucratic 'Pressure': The Case of Health Information Systems Programme

C.R. Ranjini

Centre for Public Policy,
Indian Institute of Management Bangalore, India
ranjini.cr@gmail.com

Abstract. Implementation of Information Systems in Public Healthcare in India has been a very complex undertaking. Participation of the end-users during design and implementation is important. Participation within bureaucratic settings poses unique challenges, due to hierarchical, centralized, authoritarian and formalistic practices. Even where State agencies have experimented to bring in imaginative changes, participation have not been voluntary, but have been enforced. This short paper attempts to analyse less know and less understood aspect of participatory approach entangled within bureaucratic systems. This paper attempts to analyse the issues around participation in order to identify two key areas: [1] How to encourage public sector employees to participate during design, development and implementation of IS? [2] How can public sector institutions encourage effective participation? Discourses on Participatory Approach is drawn upon to analyse the case of Health Information Systems Programme.

Keywords: Health Information Systems [HIS], Participation, Public Healthcare, Design, Implementation.

1 Introduction

Information and Communication Technologies [ICTs] offer tremendous potential to improve and transform many facets of public healthcare delivery. Yet the reality of ICT projects most often does not match the general optimism surrounding the grand notion of bringing about transformations through the introduction of technology. There are various reports of 'total', 'partial', 'sustainability', and 'replication' failures [Heeks, 2000a]. Projects fail due to 'design-actuality' or 'design-reality' [Heeks, 2003a] gaps, or lack of commitment on the part of the political leadership and public managers [Bhatnagar, 2000].

While Health Information Systems are being actively introduced by international agencies, national and local governments as a part of various health reform efforts, what is often found is that the focus of such efforts is primarily on the means (computerization) rather than the ends, or what needs to be achieved (i.e., strengthening information support for health management) [Ranjini & Sahay: 2006]. Over the years, research has emphasized that the critical issues to be addressed in the implementation of information systems are social and organisational, not solely technical

Y.K. Dwivedi et al. (Eds.): TDIT 2013, IFIP AICT 402, pp. 625–632, 2013.

[Anderson & Aydin, 1997, Walsham, 1993]. Institutionally, HIS in developing countries are situated in rather centralized structures [Braa *et al*, 2001, Braa, Heywood & Shung King, 1997] in which local use of information is not encouraged [Opit, 1987].

This article seeks to examine the relationship among participatory practices during the design and implementation of HIS and that of bureaucratic practices, with a view to analyze the potential role of ICTs in furthering the e-governance agenda and how it can be achieved in practice. This question is analyzed based on an examination of the literature around participatory approach in order to identify what makes it problematic to achieve participation in public sector institutions and what can be done about it.

2   Participatory Approach

Participation of people, end-users and more importantly by beneficiaries/stakeholders themselves has been emphasized during the design and use of ICT projects. Participation is considered a key issue not only for understanding existing capabilities but also for developing new ones among different users [Quraishy and Gregory, 2005]. In Information Systems, participatory design [Kuhn. S & Muller. M.J, 1993] has been emphasized to duly consider the social context in which the system is to be embedded [Avgerou, 2002], potentially contributing to better designed systems. In Scandinavia, the collective resource approach [Ehn & Kyng, 1987] emphasized union empowerment, not merely to oppose induction of new technologies [including ICTs], but also to develop innovative ways in which technology could be harnessed in the workplace to further workers' interests through democratic participation [ibid]. Mumford, E [2006a] developed a system design methodology, that she called ETHICS (Effective Technical and Human Implementation of Computer-based Systems) to help design a system primarily from the perspective of the user(s) and advocates that it is paramount that they work closely with developers to specify socio-technical requirements. Users be allowed to change work practices and organizational structures so as to enable the smooth transition of the new system. Participative design is seen as being consultative, democratic and responsible in nature, thus fitting with the ethical stance that individuals have an inherent right to take part in changes that take place within their own work situation.

3   Case Study: Health Information Systems Programme

The Health Information Systems Programme [HISP] is a global research and development network initiated in 1994 by researchers in the Department of Informatics, University of Oslo, in collaboration with universities and health authorities in South Africa. The stated goals of HISP [Braa *et al*, 2004] are to develop an open source, not-for-profit District-based Health Information Software [DHIS], strengthen health information management at district and community levels, assist in local analysis and use of data, conduct training programmes, standardize primary healthcare data and maximize end-user participation. Most distinctively, HISP is committed to a bottom-up design and system development approach to support decentralised health management.

In India, HISP was started in December 2000 in Andhra Pradesh. HISP India sought to strengthen information practices within the primary healthcare sector, with the larger aim of improving processes of healthcare delivery for the rural community. The HISP in Andhra Pradesh had the following key aims:

1. To develop a district-focused computer-based health information system;
2. To develop capacity for information management among staff at various levels of the health system; and
3. To integrate the health information system with other ongoing e-governance initiatives in the State.

3.1   Pilot Phase

Kuppam, in Chittoor district of Andhra Pradesh was chosen by HISP as a locale offering adequate infrastructural and government support, and also because the area is relatively small. During situational analysis, the HISP team undertook a study of the reporting processes and analysed the existing technological and physical infrastructure. The situational analysis found that health assistants went out into the communities served by their sub-centres and collected data on several health programmes, including some programmes that had long been discontinued by the department! The quality of data was poor and all the data were recorded manually in different registers for different health programmes. Together, these registers contained about 1,500 data elements, all of which were collected by the health assistants and entered manually week after week, month after month. The Health Supervisor at each health centre compiled aggregate reports from the registers obtained from all the health assistants of the sub-centres under the health centre and sent these reports, numbering about 25, to the District Office every month. Each District Office, in turn, aggregated the reports from all the health centres into district reports and sent them to the State office in Hyderabad, called the office of the Commissioner of Family Welfare.

HISP began its activities by rationalizing and constructing Minimum Data Sets for the sub-centres and health centres. It adopted a participatory approach involving health assistants and staff at the health centres and district office during the construction of these minimum data sets [Puri *et al*, 2004]. The data sets were subsequently discussed with the Commissioner of Family Welfare, and this effort was aligned with similar efforts at streamlining data sets undertaken by the office of the Commissioner. This was followed by customization of the district health information software package that was originally developed in South Africa to suit the local needs of the health staff in Andhra Pradesh. The software package allowed entry, validation and analysis of routine data of the health service rendered [monthly, quarterly and annually], semi-permanent data [population estimates, equipment, and personnel numbers] and survey data. Routine and analysis reports were customized. The HISP software also enabled automatic generation of reports. Computers were installed in six health centres and the minimum data sets and the database were then set up there. Health assistants began to enter the data and generate reports.

HISP trainers were involved in implementing the project. Training health centre staff was an important aspect of the implementation process, and HISP team offered both on-site and off-site training. The content of the training included practical sessions on how to use the software application and generate analysis reports, and lectures on the use of information for local action.

3.2   Expansion Phase

After the pilot phase, the project was extended to 37 health centres in Madanapally, Andhra Pradesh, thus taking the project to 46 health centres in all. In Madanapally, however, a different approach – a hub strategy – was adopted, with one computer serving a cluster of health centres. Twelve health centres with adequate physical infrastructure and facilities were selected as hubs. Trainers were stationed in the twelve hubs. They trained the staff from three or four nearby health centres. The hubs became the location for their regular data entry work and report generation.

Simultaneously, HISP also created a computerised health database for Chittoor district. The database was put together at the district office by manually entering health data from all 84 health centres in Chittoor district into DHIS. A team member did this at the end of each month. HISP also began to integrate routine data with maps, using Geographical Information Systems. The aim was to provide spatially-based information on the health status of the district; for example, with regard to the prevalence of diseases in certain regions. The HISP team was later involved in developing a web interface, and in translating the interface into Telugu, the local language.

4   Participation versus 'Pressure'

With reference to above described case study the author attempts to analyse participation from two standpoints: [1] How to encourage public sector employees to participate during design, development and implementation of IS? [2] what is the role of institutions in enabling effective participation.

Influenced by the Scandinavian discourse of Participatory Approach, the HISP focused not just on the development of DHIS, but also involved health workers, doctors and other health staff during the design, development and implementation of the HISP. Participation of the health staff and assistants was essential for HISP as it had adopted an approach committed to bringing about changes from the grassroots level, at sub-centres and health centres. However, in order to introduce new ways of working and change the existing practices at the sub-centres and health centres, participation of the health staff had to be facilitated by the district and State officials. Only when they received instructions from their higher officials did the staff at the health centres and sub-centres participate in these activities. When I asked Prof Sundeep Sahay, who had initiated the HISP programme in Andhra Pradesh, to what extent the health assistants had participated in the design of HISP software and how the health staff had participated in the implementation, he said:

> It has been very different from the way it has been done in Scandinavia... It is not that they, health assistants have said they want the system. We have gone with the system. We have gone to Kuppam because the Chief Minister asked us to go to Kuppam. In that sense, the decisions were taken very much from the top.

However, he added that health assistants participated during the system development process and particularly during the creation of the minimum data sets. Health assistants regularly collected about 1,500 data elements for different health programmes. The HISP team adopted a participatory approach, involving health assistants, to rationalise the data set. This effort resulted in eliminating redundancies and construction of a minimum data set with about 400 elements [Ranjini & Sahay, 2006]. Prof Sahay explained:

> During the creation of the minimum data sets we got together all the forms and data items from sub-centres and health centres and gave them to the health assistants and asked them to use this form to collect the data. Then the next month, the HISP team went and saw what data had been collected and what problems they have had. This process was repeated three or four times. Then we had a workshop. There were some 70-80 people. We created small heterogeneous groups of doctors and health assistants. We gave them the forms we had re-designed and asked them to comment on them. We got lots of comments on that day. Then we sat with the district officer in the evening. We went through all the suggestions people had made and the district officer gave his comments on what should be accepted and what should not. Then we created new set of forms and I went to Hyderabad [the State capital] with that. ... The Commissioner then made more changes... It was quite an interactive process at different levels. From health assistants to... the Commissioner.

Achieving local participation, although not impossible, is extremely difficult in practice, particularly in a bureaucratic organisation such as the Family Welfare Department. This is because work activities within government organisations are tied to rigid hierarchical structures, strong adherence to complicated rules, procedures and norms, differential power relations and frequent delays. Besides these institutional constraints, there is also corruption. This environment undermines local innovation based on the reflection and learning.

A recurring theme that emerged during my discussion with trainers was that of 'pressure'. HISP trainers felt that to initiate these changes at the grassroots, a push from the top was necessary. Attempts to institutionalise these new systems resulted in putting pressure on the end-users to participate and to learn. Quraishy and Gregory [2005] recall that during the initial stages of HISP: "A majority of health staff, mostly women and those working at the community level, attended the training programme... they participated in the training programme because there was pressure from their immediate superiors, the District Manager and Health Officer at the district and the Special Officer at the constituency level." HISP trainers also admitted that health assistants attended classes only because of the pressure from the Special Officer. The HISP trainers saw the strategy of applying pressure as necessary for sustaining the project. One trainer said: "The project will be successful only if there is pressure from higher authorities. Only if it is made compulsory will the whole exercise be useful." Higher authorities had to be involved in encouraging as well as enforcing participation of health assistants during the development of the system as well as during its adoption into use. However, one doctor was critical of HISP's approach and commented: "They brought in a lot of pressure from higher officers. There was pressure from the Special Officer. Out of fear they (health assistants) have learnt computers. That has added to our stress."

That is, unless there was pressure from the higher officials to regularly enter data or to generate computerised reports or to attend computer training, the health assistants, supervisors and doctors did not participate in the project. There was pressure also because it was the then Chief Minister's political constituency and the performance and implementation of projects were regularly monitored. To a certain extent health assistants did yield to these pressures and began data entry. However, supervisors and doctors resisted these kinds of pressures during the stage of data collation and report generation. A system developer said that the supervisors and doctors resisted using the HISP system to generate health reports [Ranjini.C.R: 2007]. He commented:

> I think the direction has to come directly from the top to generate these [computerized] reports. Until then it won't happen. Now a trainer is going, and because of him everyone is entering data. Everything must be institutionalised. Only then health staff will generate the reports.

Puri *et al* [2004:48] in a paper on user participation in HISP's Andhra project write:

> The course of health informatics in India has been strongly influenced by differential power relations arising from rigid hierarchical structures and strong bureaucracy. In starkly different historical, political and social contexts such as India, participatory processes will not arise naturally as a result of democratic aspirations or reasoned argumentation, as may be the assumption in formal workplace settings of Western countries like Scandinavia or the UK. Paradoxically, however, participatory processes often need to be initiated by government officials in-charge, rather than these emerging idealistically from grassroots as a bottom-up process... and then be gradually nurtured over time.

In such a scenario, How can public sector institutions encourage effective participation? Mumford [2006a] advocates: "Participation can take many forms but at the lower levels it is increasingly concerned with the relationship between individuals and their work environment. It must be stressed, however, that if employees are to be able to exercise some control over this then they need opportunity, confidence and competence and methods for achieving this need careful thought. One prerequisite for a participatory community... is the development of some shared values and objectives concerning participation." But an approach primarily focused on building grassroot level participation, without the permission from the top, would arguably end in a failure in the Indian context [Braa & Sahay, 2012].

In the case of HISP, the Family Welfare Department could have individually as well as collectively encouraged participation both through in-house training activities, during monthly meetings as well as official visits by officers. Internet and mobile technology can be innovately harnessed to enroll participation of staff, even in remote area. It can be suggested that participation at different levels is necessary and that it should be ongoing during implementation leading to instituitonalisation. Institutionalisation can be seen as necessary for the sustainability of information systems. Silva and Backhouse [1997:390] characterise stabilisation of an information system as institutionalisation: "Information systems become institutionalised when they are no longer considered as innovations, but as unnoticed and unremarkable tools that people take for granted in doing their work." That is, use of analytical reports or schedules or reporting through health information systems can be possible in practice only if it is institutionalised over time through official procedures and practices. Institutionalisation, arguably becomes a necessity for sustaining information systems, but the challenge is to involve the health staff by encouraging participation, rather than coercion.

5   Conclusion

One of the main reasons for the failure of HISP in Andhra Pradesh was that top bureaucracy was only partially involved in this initiative. Even today, most of public sector e-governance projects, initiated by different government departments do not encourage individual and collective participation by heterogeneous groups of employees. In bureaucratic settings, neither top-down nor bottom-up approaches succeed. There need to be an integrated participation effort, where-in both officials at the top and staff at the bottom of the hierarchy are enrolled. Continuous participation from a heterogeneous group has to be attempted, not through pressure and coercion, instead by facilitating 'genuine' participation. For Simonsen and Robertson (2012) 'genuine' participation, refers to the fundamental transcendence of the users' role *from* being merely informants *to* being legitimate and acknowledged participants in the design process. Further, this role is established – for example – when users are not just answering questions in an interview about their point of view or knowledge of a particular issue, but are asked to step up, take the pen in hand, stand in front of the large whiteboard together with fellow colleagues and designers, and participate in drawing and sketching how the work process unfolds as seen from their perspective. This is a big challenge both for leaders and employees in public sector.

References

Anderson, J.G., And Aydin, C.E.: Evaluating The Impact Of Health Care Information Systems. International Journal of Technology Assessment in Health Care 13(2), 380–393 (1997)

Avgerou, C.: Information systems and global diversity. Oxford University Press, New York (2002)

Avgerou, C., And Walsham, G.: Introduction: IT in Developing Countries in Information Technology In Context. In: Studies from the Perspective of Developing Countries. Aldershot, Ashgate (2000)

Braa, J., et al.: A Study Of The Actual And Potential Usage Of Information And Communication Technology at District And Provincial Levels In Mozambique With A Focus On The Health Sector. Electronic Journal In Information Systems For Developing Countries 5(2), 1–29 (2001)

Braa, J., Heywood, A., Shung King, M.: District Level Information Systems: Two Cases From South Africa. Methods Of Information In Medicine 36(2), 115–121 (1997)

Braa, J., Monteiro, E., Sahay, S.: Networks of Action: Sustainable Health Information Systems Across Developing Countries. Management Information Systems Quarterly 28(3) (2004)

Braa, J., Sahay, S.: Integrated Health Information Architecture, Power to the Users. Matrix Publishers, New Delhi (2012)

Beck, E.E.: On Participatory Design in Scandinavian Computing Research. Department of Informatics, University of Oslo (2001)

Bhatnagar, S.C.: Information Technology in Development Communication: Key Issues. In: Bhatnagar, S.C., Schware, R. (eds.) Information & Communication Technology in Development Communication: Cases from India, pp. 17–31. Sage Publications India Pvt Ltd., New Delhi (2000)

Ehn, P., Kyng, M.: The Collective Resource Approach to Systems Design. In: Bjerknes, G., Ehn, P., Kyng, M. (eds.) Computers and Democracy–A Scandinavian Challenge, pp. 17–57. Avebury, Aldershot (1987)

Heeks, R.: Information Technology, Information Systems and Public Sector Accountability. In: Avgerou, C., Walsham, G. (eds.) Information Technology In Context. Studies From The Perspective Of Developing Countries. Ashgate, Aldershot (2000a)

Heeks, R.: Most E-government-For-Development Projects Fail: How Can Risks Be Reduced. IDPM I-Government Working Paper No.14 (2003a)

Kappelman, L., McLean, E.: The Respective Roles of User Participation and User Involvement in Information System Implementation Success. In: DeGroass, J.L., Benbasat, I., DeSanctis, G., Beath, C.M. (eds.) Proceedings of the Twelfth International Conference on Information Systems, New York, pp. 339–349 (1991)

Kling, W, S.: The Web of Computing: Computer technology as social organization. In: Yovits, M.C. (ed.) Advances in Computers, vol. 21, pp. 1–90 (1982)

Kuhn, S., Muller, M.J.: Participatory Design. Communications of the ACM 36(4), 24–28 (1993)

Mumford, E.: Designing Human Systems for New Technology - The ETHICS Method, Manchester Business School, Manchester, U.K (1983)

Mumford, E.: The Ethics Method (2006a), http://www.enid.u-net.com/index.htm (last visited March 14, 2013)

Opit, L.J.: How Should Information On Healthcare Be Generated And Used? World Health Forum (8), 409–438 (1987)

Puri, S.K., Byrne, E., Leopoldo, J., Quraishi, Z.B.: Contextuality Of Participation In IS Design: A Developing Country Perspective. In: Paper Presented At The Participatory Design Conference, Toronto, Canada (2004)

Quraishy, Z., Gregory, J.: Implications Of (Non) Participation Of Users In Implementation Of The Health Information System Project (HISP) In Andhra Pradesh: Practical Experiences. In: Proceedings Of The 8th International Working Conference of IFIP WG 9.4, Enhancing Human Resource Development Through ICT, Abuja (2005)

Ranjini, Sahay: Computer-Based Health Information Systems - Projects for Computerization or Health Management?: Empirical Experiences from India. In: Gascó-Hernández, M., Equiza-López, F., Acevedo-Ruiz, M. (eds.) Information Communication Technologies and Human Development: Opportunities and Challenges, Idea Group Inc. (2006)

Ranjini, C.R.: Towards Building and Implementing Public Health Information Infrastructures: An Ethnographic Study in India, unpublished PhD dissertation, Department of Sociology, Lancaster University (2007)

Silva, L., Backhouse, J.: Becoming Part of The Furniture: The Institutionalization Of Information Systems. In: Lee, A.S., Liebenau, J., Degross, J.I. (eds.) Information Systems And Qualitative Research, pp. 389–413. Chapman and Hall, London (1997)

Simonsen, J., Robertson, T. (eds.): Routledge International Handbook of Participatory Design. Routledge, New York (2012)

Walsham, G.: Interpreting Information Systems in Organizations. John Wiley and Sons Ltd., Chichester (1993)

Using the Lens of "Social Construction of Technology" to Understand the Design and Implementation of Aadhaar (UID) Project

Lewin Sivamalai

Indian Institute of Management, Bangalore, India
lewin.sivamalai08@iimb.ernet.in

Abstract. Extant Research on e-government projects has shown that multiple stakeholders are at play always, each with their own divergent interests. And many a time, differences in stakeholder expectations from a project has resulted in projects failing or being abandoned after initial usage. Social Construction of Technology (SCOT) studies look at the development history of a technology in order to understand how that particular technology has evolved, based on the interpretations of various stakeholders involved. This short paper looks at the Aadhaar project (Unique Identification Project) of India through a constructivist lens and tries to present the current understanding of the Aadhaar project, as seen by the various stakeholders, using publicly available data.

Keywords: Social Construction of Technology, Aadhaar, E-government, Stakeholders.

1   Introduction – Building E-Government Systems

Building a e-government system involves multiple stakeholders which can be classified as both demand side (the citizen users or even the businesses and government officials) and supply side (primarily the stakeholders responsible to conceiving, funding, implementing and maintain the systems) and it is important to have a framework that looks at both sides to determine the design or outcome of the system (De, 2005). The field of e-government research has seen a lot of growth over the past few years but research has largely been restricted to analyzing the impact of e-government and ICT4D projects and scholars have worked on philosophical and methodological issues related to that narrow aspect of e-government research (Heeks & Bailur, 2007) . The studies so far mainly look at post implementation scenarios. So the researchers tend to emphasize on collecting data from the end users or the demand side. Hence a study which looks at the supply side and the decisions taken during the design, development and implementation of an e-government project would add key insights to the field of ICT4D related to how an e-government system evolves over time.

Currently Aadhaar (or the Unique ID project) project in India is in the news for its ambition of generating an unique Identity Number(ID) for each and every resident of the country. The main purpose, as claimed by the UIDAI, is to enable a number and

Y.K. Dwivedi et al. (Eds.): TDIT 2013, IFIP AICT 402, pp. 633–638, 2013.

an accompanying set of biometric details which will sufficiently prove the identity of a person. And the grander aim is to integrate this ID into systems and processes that facilitate the delivery of government services to Indian residents.

Since various stakeholders will have different intentions for promoting or impeding the implementation of such systems, the design of the e-government system will be influenced by the dominant stakeholders (e.g: some authorities would prefer that the e-government system aids centralized decision making it order to take some powers away from the regional authorities.) (De, 2005)

Such a situation reinforces the notion that e-government systems can be inherently political and this argument has also been emphasized by scholars who have argued that any technology can be inherently political and each technology has to be seen in its historical and social context, in order to understand its evolution better (Winner, 1985). And the role of politics can be more significant in cases where a particular technology enables a user to interact with the State for his regular needs.

It would be of interest to scholars, practitioners and policy makers if studies could include research on whether the user perception of these systems are influenced by some decisions taken during the design of the system itself. There are a lot of decisions to be made when a e-government system is to be implemented: identifying a need; conceptualizing a solution; convincing stakeholders that there is a problem and there is solution for it too; putting together a team; getting the requirements ready; making a detailed design; then testing the project and then taking this to implementation; taking feedback and acting on them. Now all this requires multiple decisions to be made at various levels and it is important to understand how these decisions are made and how all this impacts this future use of the system. The user perception varies also depends a lot on how the system has been designed. The involvement of multiple stakeholders, each having their own perception of technology, results in ontological differences between stakeholders on the nature and purpose of a technology and thus a consensus need to emerge, over time, on what the meaning of technology is and how it evolves and eventually accepted by all stakeholders. (Bijker E. W., 2010) . SCOT studies (Social Construction of technology) attempt to address the above concern.

2   Social Construction of Technology

Social construction of Technology or Constructivist studies are based on the premise that any system evolves over time due intervention by various social actors and so the historical and social shaping of this system has to be considered to determine how a system is perceived by the users (Bijker & Pinch, 1984). The proponents of social shaping of technology argue that social and political relations, either directly or indirectly, shape the way technologies evolve (MacKenzie & Wajcman, 1985) and using this background, it would be interesting to study the design, implementation and evolution of e-government systems.

For e.g. The SCOT framework which is used to study the evolution of bicycles (Bijker & Pinch, 1984), first looks at the various social groups which try to define the problem (for e.g. deciding on how the bicycle is to be designed). After identifying the relevant social groups, an Empirical program of relativism (EPOR) was adopted by Bijker and Pinch(1984), to study how the 'idea' of the bicycle evolved over the years, due to multiple interpretations by the relevant social groups and they suggested the following stages of changes in technology:

Stage 1: This is the stage where the various relevant social groups interpret the technological artifact and the problems it tries to address, in ways they see appropriate to their social setting. This is the stage of interpretive flexibility.

Stage 2: Consensus stage: After multiple iterations on what a particular technology means, the groups try to arrive at a consensus on what the problem is.

Stage 3: The Closure stage – Once a common ground has been established on the 'state' of the problem, this is the stage where the technological solution to the problem is implemented in a larger social context.

So the SCOT framework necessarily takes into account on how multiple groups, each having its own perceptions of a problem or technology, arrive at a common understanding of the problem at hand.

Thus, the SCOT framework depends on the existence of multiple stakeholders and interplay of ideas between them. This calls for a more multidisciplinary approach to decide on the future path of science and technology as suggested in the paper on "Technologies of humility" (Jasanoff, 2003) , where the author refers to setting up of environments and processes where experts from multiple fields will interact to create science and technology that can go towards betterment of society. The papers also points out that progress should not be decided by Politics(policy) alone or by scientists alone but that they all should work together along with the public and produce work of good quality and adhere to ethics. The underlying notion is that is it not possible to predict the outcome of an event but if experts and users to interact, many antecedents and   consequents of a change in technology can be debated upon.

In another paper which looks at how some commonly used artifacts have been designed, interpreted and used (Latour, 1992), the author suggests that no system can be artificially intelligent and hence there has to be a human actor to take calls. And thus, the strength and weaknesses of a system may be correlated to the strengths and weaknesses of the human actor. This paper draws some ideas from Structuration theory where agency influences structure and structure influences agency. The term 'Agency' is broad enough to include human and non-human actors. This again emphasizes that technology can only aid a human process but not solve every problem. Here is a statement from the paper that further emphasizes this view: *"It is not that society and social relations invade the certainty of science or the efficiency of machines. It is that society itself is to be rethought from top to bottom once we add to it the facts and artifacts that make up large sections of our social ties"* (Latour, 1992). The author explains that the missing link is that we tend look at things in black and white due to which we miss the shades of grey where a part of the non-human actors manifest in human actors and vice versa.

Another example of studying the evolution in the design and production of a technological artifact, through the SCOT framework, is the design of cars (Kline & Pinch, 1996) in the United States. Initially the car was resisted and seen in a very negative light in rural America but later various groups like manufacturers, the male and female users, new business entrepreneurs etc, each tailored the car for their own purposes. This serves as a very good example on how the technological artifact was interpreted in multiple ways and it exposed many new interpretations of an artifact and finally closure was reached upon agreeing to use different vehicles for different purposes, rather than using the same car for multiple purposes. (Kline & Pinch, 1996).

In another seminal paper, relevant to SCOT, the author looks at how politics plays a role in technological development (Winner, 1985). The author brings forward two aspects of politics in technology: One which is explicitly political (which seeks to exclude or include certain stakeholders directly during planning and implementation) and one which is implicitly political (e.g. - solar power can decentralize power generation whereas building nuclear power plants transfers more power to the government in electricity generation). The author sums up his paper saying *"To understand which technologies and which contexts are important to us, and why, is an enterprise that must involve both, the study of specific technical systems and their history as well as a thorough grasp of the concepts and controversies of political theory."* (Winner, 1985)

Based on the above SCOT studies, to apply the SCOT framework to study an e-government system, the following characteristics should be seen in the development of the system:

- Existence of multiple stakeholders, each having a different expectation from the system
- A situation where there is no consensus on what or how the system has to deliver
- Possible complications caused by the forces of 'politics'.

It would be relevant to apply this framework to any system which is a work-in-Progress, because from an academic point of view, one can see how the system is built and how the differences between stakeholders are resolved and this can contribute to the theory of design and development of e-government systems. And from a practitioner perspective, application of this framework offers a check point where in the practitioners and policy makers can review the progress and make changes to keep development on track. And since the Aadhaar project is at an earlier stage of implementation and pilot tests, this project is an ideal candidate to be subject to SCOT studies.

3   Possible Example of Looking at an Evolving ICT4D System: Aadhaar (UID) Project

The Aadhaar(Unique ID) Project is being implemented in India, the purpose of which is to create a unique Identity for all Indian residents[1]. The Unique Identification Authority of India (UIDAI) site clearly states that this card will be just be a proof of Identify but not a proof of citizenship or entitlement to any facility[2].

The unique ID project was launched by the UPA government as it hoped that creating a large registry would help it in implementing many schemes – MNREGS, PDS, Health schemes etc as evident from the documents on the UIDAI site. So the govern-

---

[1] "Aadhaar is a 12 digit individual identification number issued by the Unique Identification Authority of India on behalf of the Government of India[1]."
    http://uidai.gov.in/what-is-aadhaar-number.html
[2] http://uidai.gov.in/what-is-aadhaar-number.html

ment created a Core Team, headed by Mr. Nandan Nilenkani, and through an executive order, and entrusted them with the responsibility of delivering this project.

There are four clear groups who have different ideas about Aadhaar. The primary group is The Government of India (The United Progressive Alliance Government headed by the Congress party) which flagged off this project and is projecting this initiave as the basis of solutions to some of India's critical social issues. Then there is the UIDAI team itself, headed by Mr. Nandan Nilekani, which states that Aadhaar is just an ID proof which can lead to potential benefits, if leveraged properly by the public and private service providers. Finally, there are the residents at whom this project is targeted. Some of the questions that arise are - Do the residents know what they are signing up for? Have they been involved in any of the decision making process? Is there a feedback mechanism which helps in the review of the implementation process?

So the citizens believe that Aadhaar will make many facilities available to them. The Government thinks the Aadhaar would help in the implementation of its social schemes. The UIDAI itself states that this is only an ID proof and if this ID proof helps anyone to get some facilities then it would have served its purpose. Now these three contrasting situations would only lead to a big 'cycle of confusion' as each of these stakeholders have no clue where this project is heading. And this could lead to negative consequences as far as e-government projects are concerned. After the Aadhaar numbers have been generated, it is up to the various other systems like the banking systems, Public Distribution System, Oil and Marketing companies(LPG distribution) etc. to make use of the Aadhaar database. This adds a new dimension to the above questions as to how the how the ecosystem can be enabled. So the agencies looking to use the Aadhaar numbers will now become a relevant social group.

Table 1. Summary of relevant social groups

Relevant social group	View point of the group	Contradictory views	Resolution point
The Government at the Centre	Aadhaar is being projected as a solution to many of India's key challenges	India's problems is an amalgamation of socio-economic issues. Not just a technical one.	Aadhaar to be used as a tool. Not a 'solve-all'.
UIDAI Team	Aadhaar is just an ID. The emphasis is on technology.	The various pilot studies indicate other multiple forces at play other than just technology.	The UIDAI's duty is not clearly defined to the public
Public	Aadhaar can solve problems. Seen as a novel thing. A symbol of hope	Talk about Aadhaar not being a "proper ID card". Aadhaar seen as another card like ration card. Seen as an entitlement.	Clarifying the link between India's problems and the issue of a lack of identity.
The Aadhaar ecosystem stakeholders.	The PDS shop owners perceive this as a loss. Not willing to go into details. Perhaps due to stringent monitoring.	The users do not see it as a hassle but in some cases the issue of Identity make people lose benefits. These are people from the Economically weaker sections. Issues are deeper than identity.	How are some systems doing well without Aadhaar (like the PDS systems in some states).

As indicated in the above table (based on the author's field notes), there seems to be multiple perceptions about the Aadhaar project and each social group seems to view the system from its own context. So it will be interesting to observe how the various differences of opinions are sorted out and make this a successful initiative.

4   Conclusion – Does SCOT Offer Answers?

Using Social Construction of Technology to study an ongoing project (like the Aadhaar project) can help the various stakeholders to reach a consensus on what the current problems and help them work towards an effective solution. And these problems can be addressed at the design stage itself.

Now the any design decision taken should be analyzed using questions on the following lines: Will this decision favour a particular stakeholder? Is this design inclusive or is it exclusive for certain type of users? Is this design sustainable or does it have a short term political motive? Can we draw inspiration from history or from other examples around the world, as to what the probable impacts of these design decisions are?

So a SCOT study on finding the set of stakeholders, who use interpretive flexibility to look at an artifact and the final terms of closure they agree upon, is a good framework to apply to the UID project. Given that there are multiple stakeholders in such studies, the SCOT framework can reveal interesting explanations and solutions for the challenges identified.

Acknowledgement. The author would like to thank Prof. Rahul De, Prof. Rajendra Bandi and Prof. Sourav Mukherji for their inputs on this area of research. The author is also grateful to the constructive comments through the IFIP WG 8.6 review process of this short paper.

References

Bijker, E.W.: How is technology made? - That is the question! Cambridge Journal of Economics 34, 63–76 (2010)

Bijker, W., Pinch, T.: The social construction of facts and artefacts: or how the sociology of science and the sociology of technology might benefit each other. Social Studies of Science 14, 399–441 (1984)

De', R.: E-Government Systems in Developing Countries: Stakeholders and Conflict. In: Wimmer, M.A., Traunmüller, R., Grönlund, Å., Andersen, K.V. (eds.) EGOV 2005. LNCS, vol. 3591, pp. 26–37. Springer, Heidelberg (2005)

Jasanoff, S.: Technologies of humility: Citizen participation in governing science. Minerva 41, 223–244 (2003)

Kline, R., Pinch, T.: Users as agents of technological change: the social construction of the automobile in the rural United States. Technology and Culture 37(4), 763–795 (1996)

Latour, B.: Where are the missing masses? The sociology of a few mundane artifacts. In: Bijker, W.E., Law, J. (eds.) Shaping Technology/Building Society: Studies in Sociotechnical Change, pp. 225–258. MIT Press, Cambridge (1992)

MacKenzie, D., Wajcman, J.: Introductory Essay. In: MacKenzie, D., Wajcman, J. (eds.) The Social Shaping of Technology, pp. 2–25. Open Univeristy Press, Birmingham (1985)

Winner, L.: Do artifacts have politics. In: MacKenzie, D., Wajcman, J. (eds.) The Social Shaping of Technology, pp. 165–172. Open Univerisity Press (1985)

Heeks, R., Bailur, S.: Analyzing e-government research: Perspectives, philosophies, theories, methods, and practice. Government Information Quarterly 24, 243–365 (2007)

Quality Improvements for Ensuring e-Retailing Success in India: Constructs and Frameworks

Marya Wani, Vishnupriya Raghavan, Dolphy M. Abraham,
and Madhumita G. Majumder

Alliance School of Business, Alliance University, Bangalore, India
{malikmarya,vishnupriyaraghavan}@gmail.com
{dolphy.abraham,madhumita.gm}@alliance.edu.in

Abstract. This extended abstract presents a review of various constructs and evaluation frameworks proposed in the literature for e-Retailers. Our study shows that the existing frameworks apply to either the technical or the non-technical elements of an e-Retailing site and not *both* of them. Therefore, a comprehensive framework covering all aspects of quality is what is required. Furthermore, for the long run sustenance and growth of e-Retailing, it is necessary to focus on the service provided and not only the technical aspects. In the Indian context, where e-Retailing is beginning to enter a rapid growth phase, evaluation methods and metrics which are appropriate are necessary. Our extended abstract highlights the key issues that will help define these constructs.

1 Introduction

e-Retailing has grown as a service sector globally. The e-Retailing market stood at $198.8 billion in 2011 in the United States, and €200.52 billion in Europe (Center for Retail Research, 2012). e-Retailing in India has started to gain momentum. The industry stood at a valuation of $948.6 million in 2011 and is expected to reach $260 billion by the year 2025 (First Data, 2011).

Quality improvement in e-Retailing can ensure a robust growth of the sector and encourage standardization and improvement of overall business practices. For evaluating the measurement of quality improvements a broad approach suggested by Practical Software and Systems Management (Statz, 2005) is employed to understand the comprehensiveness of the constructs and frameworks available in literature.

Practical Software and Systems Management (Statz, 2005) identified four major areas of quality improvement derived from the balanced score card approach. These areas are:

- Financial (F): That deal with financial goals from the project.
- Customer Satisfaction (CS): The satisfaction for both internal and external customers is important. These relate to things like mean time to failure, response time, price/performance etc.
- Internal Business Processes (IBP): These goals relate to practices and methods for product and service development, management of people in the organization etc.

Y.K. Dwivedi et al. (Eds.): TDIT 2013, IFIP AICT 402, pp. 639–643, 2013.

•   Learning and Growth (L&G): This relates to people related capabilities of the organization like technical skills of staff, staff growth in terms of numbers, domain knowledge, morale and turnover.

Table 1. Important measures for e-Retailing quality improvement

Author(s) & Year	Major Areas	Existing Measures	Suggested Measures
Baty & Lee (1995)	CS, IBP, F	Wide reach, multimedia, better market functionality, information availability, shopping agents , better search, reduced transaction costs	Semantic representation, advanced navigation and product comparability features
Hawkins, Mansell, & Steinmueller (1999)	IBP, F	Provision of wider product basket (complementary) e.g. linking cash to smart cards	Customer perception issues, develop and harness virtual communities, disintermediation to re-intermediation
Srivastava & Mock (1999)	CS	Trust, business practices, transaction integrity, information protection, legal environment	Trust should be incorporated as an essential construct
Casati & Shan (2000)	IBP	Different vendors like SAP, ATG, Oracle	Integrated platform for a seamless process like Enterprise Application Interface (EAI)
Rust & Kannan (2003)	CS,IBP, F	Strategic, cost reduction, supply chain efficiency, brand equity	Revenue expansion, information flows, customer profitability, customization
Van der Merwe & Bekker (2003)	CS,IBP	Design, content, navigation, reliability	Conversion of buyers decision making process into technical aspects
Croom & Johnston (2003)	CS, IBP, L&G	Cost efficiency, process conformance, internal customer satisfaction	Greater awareness of and importance to internal customer satisfaction
Burt & Sparks(2003)	CS,IBP, F	Cost reduction, low inventory, branding	ROI is not very clear for traditional retailers
Desai, Richards & Desai (2003)	CS, IBP	Trust, process efficiency	Employment of EDI, and other standards that can iron out deficiencies causing trust issues
Klischewski & Wetzel, (2003)	CS, IBP	XML based representation	customer orientation

Keeping the above framework in mind, we focus on measures for e-Retailing service quality improvement as suggested by researchers over the years. Table 1 and 2 provide a list of measures employed in various studies to evaluate an e-Retailer's quality. Table 1 lists important constructs and Table 2 lists important frameworks identified by researchers. The last column of table 1 i.e. 'suggested measures' lists the measures that the researchers have suggested for future investigation.

It can be observed from Tables 1 and 2 (column 2) which lists the areas covered by the study in terms of the four suggested dimensions, that most of the measures focus on three aspects of quality improvement i.e., customer satisfaction, financial and internal business processes and learning and growth has been mostly ignored.

Table 2. Major frameworks for e-Retailing quality improvement

Author(s) & Year	Major Areas	Title of Framework	Measures Employed
Bressolles (2006)	CS, IBP	NetQual	Ease of site use, design, reliability, security
Chiou, Lin & Perng (2010)	CS, IBP, F	4PsC	Place, product, price, promotion and customer relation.
Yoo & Donthu (2001)	CS, IBP	Sitequal	Ease of use, design, speed of order processing, security of financial information
Barnes & Vidgen (2003)	CS, IBP	Webqual	Usability, quality of information, quality of interaction
Wolfinbarger & Gilly (2003)	CS, IBP	E TailQ	Site design, customer service, reliability, security, privacy.
Parasuraman, Zeithaml & Malhotra (2005)	CS, IBP, F	E S Qual/ E RecSQual	Efficiency, fulfillment, system availability and privacy. E RecS Qual is a measure for non-frequent customers

2   e-Retailing in the Development Context

According to A. T. Kearney (2012), India's retail sector ranks 5th in the world based on the global retail development index. This growth in e-Retailing is fuelled by increased broadband connectivity, rising living standards, busy lifestyle and traffic, much wider product range, and convenient processes. As the industry matures it would require quality improvement to keep up with the rising customer expectations and maturing industry standards. Indian e-Retailers can greatly benefit from studies on e-Retailing available from developed countries. Most e-Commerce research in India is based on adoption factors and employs qualitative measures without empirical analysis (Vaithianathan, 2010). e-Retailers like flipkart.com and snapdeal.com have benefited by following the business models and best practices of established e-Retailers like amazon.com and groupon.com.

Few researchers have addressed the e-Retailing quality dimensions in developing countries which can be applied to the Indian context. For example studies have focused on core service dimensions (Malhotra et al, 2004); system availability and fulfillment (Kim and Kim, 2010); e-Commerce infrastructure (Okoli and Mbarika, 2003); strategic alliance and innovative business strategies (Li and Chang, 2004); cultural adaptation (Zahedi & Bansal, 2011; Singh & Matsuo, 2004). Researchers suggest that developing countries have typical issues like infrastructure, technology acceptance etc. (Malhotra et al, 2004) and hence require different quality dimensions.

3   Conclusion and Future Research Opportunities

This research provides a list of measures for evaluating e-Retailing quality. It highlights the need for a comprehensive framework that encompasses the major aspects of e-Retailing quality i.e., customer service, financial, internal business processes, and learning and growth. However, this paper suffers from the limitation in that it lacks a proposed framework and an empirical analysis.

As e-Retailers expand their markets across the globe future research on e-Retailing quality improvements must also include country specific issues. Extensive studies are required to examine if country-specific websites reflect national cultural values (Zahedi & Bansal, 2011). Future research should focus on development of an evaluation framework for e-Retailing quality improvement that addresses technical, non-technical and country specific issues.

References

1. Kearney, A.T. (2012), `http://www.atkearney.com/consumer-products-retail/global-retail-development-index`
2. Barnes, S.J., Vidgen, R.T.: An Integrative Approach to the Assessment of E-Commerce Quality. Journal of Electronic Commerce Research 3(3), 114–127 (2003)
3. Baty, J.B., Lee, R.M.: Intershop: Enhancing the Vendor/Customer Dialectic in Electronic Shopping. Journal of Management Information Systems, 9–31 (1995)
4. Bressolles, G.: La Qualite de Service Electronique: NetQual. Proposition d'uneechelle de Mesure Appliqué Aux Sites Marchands et Effets Moderateurs. Rescherche et Applications en Marketing 21(3), 19–45 (2006)
5. Burt, S., Sparks, L.: E-commerce and the Retail Process: A Review. Journal of Retailing and Consumer Services 10(5), 275–286 (2003)
6. Casati, F., Shan, M.C.: Process Automation as the Foundation for E-Business. In: Proceedings of the 2000 International Conference on Very Large Databases, Cairo, Egypt, pp. 688–691 (2000)
7. Centre for Retail Research (2012), `http://www.retailresearch.org/onlineretailing.php`
8. Chiou, W.C., Lin, C.C., Perng, C.: A Strategic Framework for Website Evaluation Based on a Review of the Literature from 1995–2006. Information & Management 47(5), 282–290 (2010)
9. Croom, S., Johnston, R.: E-Service: Enhancing Internal Customer Service through E-Procurement. International Journal of Service Industry Management 14(5), 539–555 (2003)
10. Desai, M.S., Richards, T.C., Desai, K.J.: E-commerce Policies and Customer Privacy. Information Management & Computer Security 11(1), 19–27 (2003)
11. First Data Corp, How E-commerce can Improve the Customer Experience and Increase Revenues? Report (2011), `http://www.firstdata.com/downloads/thought-leadership/Ecomm-Paper.pdf`
12. Hawkins, R., Mansell, R., Steinmueller, W.E.: Toward Digital Intermediation in the Information Society. Journal of Economic Issues, 383–391 (1999)
13. Kim, J.H., Kim, C.: E-service Quality Perceptions: A Cross-Cultural Comparison of American and Korean Consumers. Journal of Research in Interactive Marketing 4(3), 257–275 (2010)
14. Klischewski, R., Wetzel, I.: Serviceflow Management for Health Provider Networks. Logistics Information Management 16(3/4), 259–269 (2003)
15. Li, P.P., Chang, S.T.L.: A Holistic Framework of E-Business Strategy: The Case of Haier in China. Journal of Global Information Management 12(2), 44–62 (2004)
16. Malhotra, N.K., Ulgado, F.M., Agarwal, J., Shainesh, G., Wu, L.: Dimensions of Service Quality in Developed and Developing Economies: Multi-Country Cross-Cultural Comparisons. International Marketing Review 22(3), 256–278 (2005)
17. Murtaza, M.B., Shah, J.R.: Developing Efficient Supply Chain Links Using Web Services. Journal of Internet Commerce 3(3), 63 (2004)
18. Okoli, C., Mbarika, V.A.: A Framework for Assessing E-Commerce in Sub-Saharan Africa. Journal of Global Information Technology Management 6(3), 44–66 (2003)

19. Parasuraman, A., Zeithaml, V.A., Malholtra, A.: E-S-QUAL: A Multiple-Item Scale for Assessing Electronic Service Quality. Journal of Service Research 7(3), 213–235 (2005)
20. van der Rian, M., Bekker, J.: A Framework and Methodology for Evaluating E-Commerce Web Sites. Internet Research 13(5), 330–341 (2003)
21. Rust, R.T., Kannan, P.K.: E-service: A New Paradigm for Business in the Electronic Environment. Communications of the ACM 46(6), 36–42 (2003)
22. Schmid, H.A., Rossi, G.: Modeling and Designing Processes in E-Commerce Applications. IEEE Internet Computing 8(1), 19–27 (2004)
23. Singh, N., Matsuo, H.: Measuring Cultural Adaptation on the Web: A Content Analytic Study of US and Japanese Web sites. Journal of Business Research 57(8), 864–872 (2004)
24. Srivastava, R.P., Mock, T.J.: Evidential Reasoning for WebTrust Assurance Services. Journal of Management Information Systems 16(3), 11–32 (1999)
25. Statz, J.: Measurement for Process Improvement. Practical Software and Systems Measurement, Technical paper (2005), http://www.psmsc.com/Downloads/TechnologyPapers/PI_Measurement_v1.0.pdf
26. Vaithianathan, S.: A Review of E-Commerce Literature on India and Research Agenda for the Future. Electron Commerce Research 10(1), 83–97 (2010)
27. Van der Merwe, R., Bekker, J.: A Framework and Methodology for Evaluating E-Commerce Web Sites. Internet Research 13(5), 330–341 (2003)
28. Wolfinbarger, M., Gilly, M.C.: EtailQ: Dimensionalizing, Measuring and Predicting E-tail Quality. Journal of Retailing 79(3), 183–198 (2003)
29. Yoo, B., Donthu, N.: Developing a Scale to Measure Perceived Quality of an Internet Shopping Site (SITEQUAL). Quarterly Journal of Electronic Commerce 2(1), 31–46 (2001)
30. Zahedi, F.M., Bansal, G.: Cultural Signifiers of Web Site Images. Journal of Management Information Systems 28(1), 147–200 (2012)

Innovation in Government Services: The Case of Open Data

Zhenbin Yang and Atreyi Kankanhalli

Department of Information Systems, National University of Singapore, Singapore
{zhenbin,atreyi}@comp.nus.edu.sg

Abstract. Governments are initiating open data initiatives as a new approach where external stakeholders can play an increased role in the innovation of government services. This is unlike previous approaches of e-government service innovation where services are solely initiated and developed by the agencies themselves. However, despite public agencies actively promoting the use of their data by organizing events such as challenge competitions, the response from external stakeholders to leverage government data for innovative activities has been lacking. This raises the question about the reasons inhibiting the interest to innovate using open data. Yet, the existing literature points to a lack of understanding about external stakeholders' willingness to innovate with the data provided. Motivated thus, this paper aims to identify the antecedents of the willingness of external stakeholders to innovate with open data. We propose the use of the case study methodology for this purpose.

Keywords: Open data, eGovernment, open innovation, open government data.

1 Introduction

Since the launch of the first open data portal (data.gov) by the United States government in 2009 to provide a single point of access to data from multiple public agencies, an increasing number of countries have launched similar open data initiatives (e.g., UK, Singapore, Australia, Chile). Open data involves the disclosure of raw data by government agencies that they have collected for public consumption. By leveraging the advancements in ICT and the Internet, government agencies which are commonly viewed as among the largest creators and collectors of data have the potential to share a multitude of information across many domains, e.g., finance, transport, environment (Janssen, 2011). For example, data.gov currently hosts more than 450,000 datasets, up from the 47 datasets when the site was introduced.

Previous studies have emphasized the opportunities afforded by open data (Huijboom and den Broek, 2011). By promoting data openness, governments hope to enhance transparency, public participation, and collaboration (Nam, 2011). Essentially, these initiatives can serve to reduce information asymmetry between public agencies and their external stakeholders for the innovation of government services. Although datasets are in their raw form and may not have much value on their own, public agencies can leverage on businesses and citizens to contribute to the innovation of government services through the reorganizing, repackaging, and synthesizing information from various sources (DiFranzo et al., 2011).

Y.K. Dwivedi et al. (Eds.): TDIT 2013, IFIP AICT 402, pp. 644–651, 2013.
© IFIP International Federation for Information Processing 2013

The role of government agencies in open data initiatives does not lie solely in the release of data. Other than increasing the variety and improving the quality of data made available to the public, there have been concurrent efforts by public agencies to motivate the use of open data for innovation activities by external stakeholders (Lee et al. 2012). A commonly used approach is through challenge competitions, where participants compete to provide the best idea or develop the most useful application with the available data. Winners are awarded prizes or other incentives such as recognition for their effort. For example, an European Union-wide open data competition was held for two months in 2011, which gathered a large number of entries aiming for the prize of 20,000 euros[1].

However, beyond the buzz created through these ad-hoc initiatives and even with the efforts to improve data availability, it appears that the full potential of massive participation and collaboration to achieve innovation in government services has yet to materialize. Unlike the interest from the supply-side, the situation on the demand-side seems to be less positive (Huijboom and Den Broek, 2011). Overall, it appears that there is a lack of external innovators making use of open data. As achieving a critical mass of such innovators is essential for a sustainable initiative, there is a need to understand what influences participation in open data.

1.1   Research Question

Following the increasing pace of open data initiatives globally, researchers are starting to investigate different aspects of this phenomenon in recent years. These include identifying the challenges of implementing open data (Huijboom and Den Broek, 2011; Janssen et al. 2012), key success factors of open data initiatives (European Commission, 2011), principles of open data (e.g., Sunlight Foundation, 2010), and proposing stage models for open data (Kalampokis et al., 2011).

However, most prior research in the area of open data has been either conceptual or practitioner-focused in nature and not based on theoretical foundations. Moreover, the majority of prior studies were conducted from the perspective of government agencies (supply-side), with little focus on external stakeholders (demand-side). Among the exceptions, Kuk and Davies (2011) observed various motivations of innovators participating in open data challenge competitions, but not for open data innovation in general. We contend that despite the potential of using open data to promote co-innovation between government agencies and external stakeholders, there is a lack of understanding of the perceptions of potential and current open data innovators. Specifically, research in open data has not explored what factors influence external stakeholders' decision to develop new applications and services with open data. Motivated thus, this paper seeks to answer the research question: What determines external stakeholders' behaviour to innovate with open data?

1.2   Expected Contributions

This study aims to contribute to research in open data by developing a model to provide insights into the factors that determine the innovation behaviour of external

---

[1] http://opendatachallenge.org/

stakeholders e.g., businesses and citizens. It will examine the effects of different motivators and inhibitors that influence peoples' willingness to innovate with open data. For government agencies, this study is expected to highlight important factors leading to the innovation of new services with open data, and if there are ways that they can help mitigate the barriers faced by their external stakeholders.

2 Background and Previous Studies

In this section, we provide a review of the relevant literature on open data. The search for relevant studies was conducted in several online journal databases (e.g., EBSCO-Host, Science Direct), Google Scholar, and AIS Electronic Library. Terms such as "open data", "open government data", and "government 2.0" were used for the search with a period spanning from 2009 when the initiative first began to 2012. Subsequently, we review the past studies on open innovation and suggest how they apply to the study context.

2.1 Open Data

Open data initiatives involve making data produced or commissioned by government freely usable, reusable, and redistributable by anyone. Government agencies often embrace open data initiatives with the aim of promoting transparency, participation, and co-innovation (Nam, 2011).

In particular, public agencies seek to leverage their external stakeholders e.g., businesses and citizens, to further innovations in the area of electronic service delivery (Davies and Lithwick, 2010). Contributing to this trend is the increasing government recognition of the economic potential of open data. Vickery (2011) suggests that the economic value from the exploitation of open government data surpasses government investments in collecting and disseminating the data. From open data portals users will be able to access datasets generated for application development. In addition, government agencies may post a challenge online for users to solve. Table 1 lists a sample of open data initiatives and innovations developed with open data.

Table 1. Sample of Open Data Initiatives and Innovations

Name	Link	Country	Description
Government initiatives to promote innovation through data openness			
Data.go.kr	data.go.kr	South Korea	Provides services allowing the public to take advantage of the country's variety of public information
Data.gov	data.gov	USA	Allows the public to access datasets that are generated and held by the Federal Government

Table 1. (*continued*)

Data.gov.au	data.gov.au	Australia	Provides an easy way to find, access and reuse public datasets from the Australian Government and state and territory governments
Open Kenya	opendata.go.ke	Kenya	Allows the public to obtain core government development, demographic, statistical and expenditure data available in a useful digital format
Overheid.nl	data.overheid.nl	Netherlands	Allows the public to obtain open government data from the national registry with references to existing open datasets
Portal de Datos Públicos	datos.gob.cl	Chile	Allows the people to have access to information based on which the government makes decisions for public policy
Business or citizen-driven innovations with government-released data			
BUSit London	data.gov.uk/apps/busit-london	UK	Uses London Bus data from Transport for London to plan your multi-leg bus journey in the capital
CrimeReports	www.crimereports.com	USA	Offers a family of affordable, easy-to-use software tools for law enforcement agencies to understand crime trends and share current neighbourhood crime data with the public
Dunny Directories	data.gov.au/apps/dunny-directory/	Australia	A location based mobile application, which provides the ability to easily locate public toilets throughout Australia.

Table 1. (*continued*)

LiveTraffic	www.livetraffic.sg	Singapore	Accesses data from various government sources to provide customized real-time navigation for drivers
Park It DC	www.parkitdc.com	USA	Allows user to check a specific area in the district capital for parking information
ShowNearBy	www.shownearby.com	Singapore	A location-based service delivering business intelligence solutions for Singapore's private, people and public sectors based on public information from the government

Very few studies have examined the open data phenomenon from the demand side. Using a combination of methods including field studies during open data events, survey, archival analysis, and interviews with open data innovators, Kuk and Davies (2011) identified several elements that facilitate and impede the use of open data among innovators. Respondents highlighted that most data provided by government agencies were of poor quality that had little value. Some of these issues relates to bad data formats, data releases that were not timely, or a lack of data granularity. However, despite the poor data quality, innovators were motivated by factors such as a desire for access to specific facts, having direct relevance and appeal to their needs, or the prospects of monetary rewards. Based on interviews with representatives from various ministries in the Netherlands, Janssen et al. (2012) surfaced several other factors inhibiting public use of open data such as the lack of explanation of the meaning of data, and the lack of knowledge to make sense of data.

The release of government data can spur the development of new services by external stakeholders, which is a recent way for governments to engage external parties in open innovation (Rossel et al., 2006).

2.2   Open Innovation

Organizations can perform open service innovation by engaging external stakeholders to contribute in developing new services or enhancing existing services based on ideas they generate or from the problems they encounter (Den Hertog, 2010). The concept of *open innovation* was introduced by Chesbrough (2003) to describe the shift from the closed innovation paradigm to a model where innovation ideas reside both internal and external to an organization. According to the closed innovation paradigm, organizations rely on internal R&D functions for discovery of new business opportunities. They attempt to achieve competitive advantage by utilizing internal knowledge for staying ahead of the competition and raising the barrier to entry for competitors. However, towards the end of the 20th century, the foundations of the closed innovation paradigm started to erode. With the blurring of boundaries between an organization and the environment, the open innovation paradigm has emerged acknowledging the increased porosity of knowledge flow.

Open innovation is defined as the use of purposive inflows and outflows of knowledge to accelerate internal innovation and expand the markets for external use of innovations, respectively (Chesbrough, 2006). With escalating R&D costs and shortening product life cycles, organizations have come to realize that relying on internal innovation would negatively affect their competitive position (Keupp and Gassmann, 2009). Organizations can also benefit from adopting open innovation to achieve economies of scope and scale (Chesbrough, 2011).

Three main strategies can be seen in open innovation (Gassmann and Enkel, 2004). First, open innovation can be achieved with an *inside-out* strategy where firms bring ideas to the market by externalizing knowledge and transferring assets beyond the firm to stimulate external innovation. An example of this approach is the licensing of firms' intellectual property to external parties to gain additional revenue. Second, firms can engage in the *outside-in* strategy where the focus is to reach out to the external environment for acquiring resources such as knowledge. This is often performed with the realization that the abundance of external knowledge should be tapped to develop better products or services instead of relying on internal R&D (Boudreau and Lakhani, 2009). A popular approach here is crowdsourcing, where firms can post challenges online for external knowledge workers to tackle for a reward (Ye et al., 2012). Last, as a hybrid strategy, firms can adopt the *coupled* approach that combines both the outside-in and inside-out strategies to achieve synergy among different parties. This strategy often entails firm-level cooperation for the joint development of knowledge through arrangements such as joint ventures or alliances.

3   Subsequent Work

Although open innovation research has focused on the shift towards this paradigm in the private sector, governments are also getting involved in open innovation initiatives (Assar et al. 2011). However, unlike the private sector that is concerned with profits, the public sector aims to increase the benefits to its stakeholders and improve service delivery. Lee et al. (2012) examined open innovation initiatives in the some of the world's most innovative countries (e.g., USA, Canada, Singapore) and noted that they can either be government-led or community-led. In particular, open data initiatives were classified as government-led and adopting the inside-out open innovation strategy. The release of internal data assets by government agencies allows the leveraging of resources possessed by external stakeholders that agencies may not have in abundance. Open data facilitates open innovation in services because external parties now have access to government data to build useful applications for the public. Therefore, by adopting the open service innovation approach, new or enhanced services developed externally can benefit government agencies and the public alike. Despite the potential, Lee et al. (2012) noted that initiatives using the *inside-out* strategy deserve more investigation, as they have received less research interest. Therefore, in response to this call, this study takes a deeper look into the factors influencing external stakeholders' decision to innovate with open data.

To identify and validate the influential factors, we plan to conduct multiple case studies of open data efforts at public agencies in Singapore. A multiple-case study design is preferred over a single-case study design for obtaining more compelling and robust data (Herriott and Firestone 1983). As an initial guide, we will review the suitability of previously found factors in prior literature of similar areas (e.g., Kuk and Davies, 2011; Janssen et al., 2012). Singapore is chosen for this study because of its leading status in eGovernment. In June 2011, the Singapore government announced data.gov.sg as its first-stop portal to search and access publicly-available data. The portal brings together over 5000 datasets from 50 government ministries and agencies. One of its key aims is to create value by catalysing application development by external parties. We intend to conduct in-depth case studies of such efforts to identify factors influencing participation in innovation activities. This research potentially has significant implications for both eGovernment researchers and practitioners in identifying the motivators and inhibitors of open data innovation.

References

Bommert, B.: Collaborative Innovation in the Public Sector. International Public Management Review 11(1), 15–33 (2010)

Boudreau, K., Lakhani, K.: How to Manage Outside Innovation. MIT Sloan Management Review 50(4), 69–76 (2009)

Chesbrough, H.W.: Open Innovation. In: The New Imperative for Creating and Profiting from Technology. Harvard Business School Press, Boston (2003)

Chesbrough, H.W.: Open Business Models – How to Thrive in a New Competitive Landscape. Harvard Business School Press, Boston (2006)

Chesbrough, H.W.: Open Services Innovation – Rethinking Your Business to Grow and Compete in a New Era. Jossey-Bass, San Francisco (2011)

Davies, A., Lithwick, D.: Government 2.0 and Access to Information: 2. Recent Developments in Proactive Disclosure and Open Data in the United States and Other Countries (Background paper) (2010), http://www.parl.gc.ca/Content/LOP/ResearchPublications/2010-15-e.pdf

Den Hertog, P., Aa, W.V.D., De Jong, M.W.: Capabilities for Managing Service Innovation: Towards a Conceptual Framework. Journal of Service Management 21(4), 490–514 (2010)

Difranzo, D., Graves, A., Erickson, J.S., Ding, L., Michaelis, J., Lebo, T., Patton, E., Williams, G.T., Li, X., Zheng, J.G., Flores, J., McGuinness, D.L., Hendler, J.: The Web is My Backend: Creating Mashups with Linked Open Government Data. In: Wood, D. (ed.) Linking Government Data, pp. 205–219. Springer, New York (2011)

European Commission.: Pricing of Public Sector Information Study: Open Data Portals (E), Final Report (2011), http://ec.europa.eu/information_society/policy/psi/docs/pdfs/report/11_2012/open_data_portals.pdf

Gassmann, O., Enkel, E.: Towards a Theory of Open Innovation: Three Core Process Archetypes. Paper Presented at the R&D Management Conference (2004)

Herriott, R.E., Firestone, W.A.: Multisite Qualitative Policy Research: Optimizing Description and Generalizability. Educational Researcher 12(2), 14–19 (1983)

Huijboom, N., den Broek, T.V.: Open Data: An International Comparison of Strategies. European Journal of ePractice 12, 4–16 (2011)

Janssen, K.: The Influence of the PSI Directive on Open Government Data: An Overview of Recent Developments. Government Information Quarterly 28(4), 446–456 (2011)

Janssen, M., Charalabidis, Y., Zuiderwijk, A.: Benefits, Adoption Barriers and Myths of Open Data and Open Government. Information Systems Management 29(4), 258–268 (2012)

Kalampokis, E., Tambouris, E., Tarabanis, K.: Open Government Data: A Stage Model. In: Janssen, M., Scholl, H.J., Wimmer, M.A., Tan, Y.-h. (eds.) EGOV 2011. LNCS, vol. 6846, pp. 235–246. Springer, Heidelberg (2011)

Keupp, M.M., Gassmann, O.: Determinants and Archetype Users of Open Innovation. R&D Management 39(4), 331–341 (2009)

Kuk, G., Davies, T.: The Roles of Agency and Artifacts in Assembling Open Data Complementarities. Paper Presented at the International Conference on Information Systems, Shanghai (2011)

Lee, S.M., Hwang, T., Choi, D.: Open Innovation in the Public Sector of Leading Countries. Management Decision 50(1), 147–162 (2012)

Nam, T.: New Ends, New Means, but Old Attitudes: Citizens' Views on Open Government and Government 2.0. Paper Presented at the 44th Hawaii International Conference on System Sciences (2011)

Nam, T., Sayogo, D.S.: Government 2.0 Collects the Wisdom of Crowds. Social Informatics, 51–58 (2011)

Rossel, P., Finger, M., Misuraca, G.: Mobile e-Government Options: Between Technology-Driven and User-centric. The Electronic Journal of e-Government 4(2), 79–86 (2006)

Sunlight Foundation.: Ten Principles of Opening Up Government Information (2010), http://assets.sunlightfoundation.com.s3.amazonaws.com/policy/papers/Ten%20Principles%20for%20Opening%20Up%20Government%20Data.pdf

Vickery, G.: Review of Recent Studies on PSI Re-Use and Related Market Developments (2011), http://ec.europa.eu/information_society/policy/psi/docs/pdfs/report/final_version_study_psi.docx

Yc., H., Kankanhalli, A., Yang, Z.: Knowledge Brokering for Open Innovation: A Case Study of Innovation Intermediaries. Paper presented at the International Conference on Information Systems, Orlando (2012)

Information Communication Technology (ICT) for Disabled Persons in Bangladesh: Preliminary Study of Impact/Outcome

Md. Jahangir Alam Zahid[1], Md. Mahfuz Ashraf[2],
Bushra Tahseen Malik[1], and Md. Rakibul Hoque[2]

[1] Brainstorm Bangladesh, Road 28/K, House 08, Banani, Dhaka 1213, Bangladesh
jaz.zahid@gmail.com, bushra@brainstorm-bd.com
[2] Dept. Management Information Systems, University of Dhaka, Bangladesh
mashraf@univdhaka.edu, rakibdu471@gmail.com

Abstract. To meet the need of digital inclusion and to mitigate the digital divide between disable and general people different ICT interventions are implemented in different developing and developed countries. But question arises to what extent these interventions are successful? Are these interventions are successful for creating new hope and confidence among disabled people? In this working paper we have tried to find the impact of these interventions from actual beneficiary perspectives. We have adopted Technology Acceptance Model (TAM) to know about perceived usefulness and perceived easiness from the disabled/visually impaired person's perspective. We found that though Technology has provided initial access to technology and information but the users are facing many challenges to overcome language barriers. Our ongoing study also reveals that social issues/ variables are also important for getting acceptance of ICT interventions for disabled people.

Keywords: ICT, Disabled Persons, Development, Technology Acceptance Model (TAM), Thematic analysis, Bangladesh.

1   Introduction

The concept of Information Communication Technology (ICT) for developing courtiers comes in the 1990s when researchers identified "Digital Divide" as an important factor which is hindering developing countries to get the benefits of ICT interventions (Guillen, 2006; Servon, 2002). From 1990s to till now various researches are undertaken to measure digital divide and gradually various forms of digital divide emerged like divide between developed and developing countries, urban and rural area, rich and poor people, male and female etc (Nations, 2010; Hanimann & Ruedin 2007, Norris, 2001; Mark, 2003). But most of the researchers have ignored one important aspect of digital divide that exist between general people and disabled people. Though few researches are

Y.K. Dwivedi et al. (Eds.): TDIT 2013, IFIP AICT 402, pp. 652–657, 2013.

undertaken regarding the issue but most of them have focused on technological perspective or supply side where they have tried to show how different technological innovations can increase the capability of disabled people (Bigham et al., 2008, Forgrave 2002, MacArthur 2009) which is parallel to thought of medical/individual model (Llewellyn and Hogan, 2000) where disability is regarded "patient" subject either to cure or to ongoing medical care. But today disabled concept is considered from social perspective (Tregaskis, 2002; Barnes and Mercer, 2005) which considers disabled as the "loss or limitations of opportunities that prevents people who have impairments from taking part in the normal life of the community on an equal level with others due to physical and social barriers."- (Cited in Finkelstein and French, 1993). So to consider the demand side i.e. the perception of disabled people regarding existing technology and to get the insight beyond technological perspective we have initiated a research on early 2011 which is still continuing.

In this working paper, we have attempted to investigate a preliminary outcome/impact of ICT interventions for disabled people from actual beneficiary perspective. We have used Technology Acceptance Model (TAM) to understand the outcome/impact of ICT interventions for disabled people in Bangladesh; one of the most densely populated developing countries in the World. Bangladesh is a small developing country with 150 million populations and according to one estimate almost 10 percent of total populations are disabled (BBS 2012).

The research will give an important insight for policymakers about the impact of ICT interventions from developing country as the research is not generalized in nature and has considered local context of Bangladesh. Besides the research is qualitative in nature and based on case study which will make an important contribution by understanding complex context of disabled people and by providing holistic, in-depth investigation (Zaina, 2007). In our research qualitative and case study technique will make significant contribution as in the last 20 years qualitative research has developed new principles to shed light on the complex interrelationships among physical impairment, societal barriers, and public programs (O'Day & Killen 2002).

2   Conceptual Framework of the Study: Technological Acceptance Model (TAM)

Technology Acceptance Model (TAM) (Davis, 1989; Davis, Bagozzi & Warshaw, 1989), originated in the Theory of Reasoned Action (TRA) (Fishbein & Ajzen, 1975), offers a powerful explanation for user acceptance and usage behavior of information technology. According to TAM the use and benefits of a system largely depends on the motivation of actual user which is influenced by external factors and capabilities of a system. The model also says that the motivation of user depends on three factors (Figure-1) (a) Perceived ease of the system (b) Perceived benefits of the system (c) Attitude towards the system. According to Fred Davis (1989), attitude towards the system depends on Perceived ease of the system and Perceived benefits of a system, whereas perceived ease of use is defined as "the degree to which person believes that using a particular system would be free of effort" and Perceived benefits of a system defines the extent to which a person believed that a particular system will develop their life. These then lead to individual behavior intention and actual behavior. It is noted that perceived usefulness possess the strongest predictor of an individual's intention to use an information technology (Adams et al., 1992; Davis, 1989).

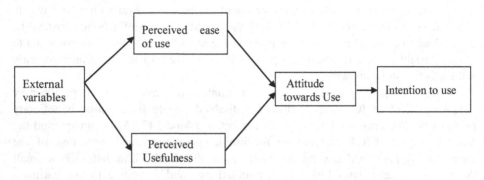

Fig. 1. Technology Acceptance Model (Davis,1989)

TAM also proposes that external factors affect intention and actual use through mediated effects on perceived usefulness and perceived ease of use. For measuring the perceived easiness Davis (1989) developed 10 criteria where focus is given on increasing quality of work, increasing quickness & control, effectiveness and quantity of works. Besides for measuring perceived usefulness Davis (1989) developed 6 criteria where focus is given on improving job performance, easiness and quicker performance. Though the paper enjoyed the benefits of TAM (Technology Acceptance Model) but an important limitation of TAM model is it ignores many external factors like age, education etc (Burton & Hubona,2006).

3   Methodology

This research is exploratory and explanatory studies. A semi structured questionnaire was used to gather the information required for the study. Data was mainly gathered from 25 respondents from different ICT training centers for disable persons, university disable students and disabled job holders. The criteria's for understanding perceived usefulness and easiness are given in table-1.

Table 1. Criteria used in the research to understand perceived usefulness and easiness from the disable persons' perspective

Perceived Usefulness	• *Economic*: To what extent ICT will help them to obtain economic freedom like: obtaining jobs, getting new source of income etc.
	• *Social:* To what extent ICT will help them to get new social identity and respect like: new social network, social identity, perceived importance in family and society.
	• *Knowledge*: To extent ICT will help disabled people to gather knowledge from different sources. like: access to new paper, job circular, study material.
Perceived Easiness	• *Easy & Understandable*: To what extent disabled people believe that existing ICT facility is easy and understandable for them.
	• *Flexibility & Accessibility*: Is the existing facility is flexible enough and are the disabled people can access to all kinds of information sources?
	• *Controllability:* how much control the disabled people have on the existing facility?
	• *Effort:* How much effort, both from physical and time perspective is necessary for using the existing system?

Table 2. Key issues of respondents

Title	Description
Software Used	JAWS (Job access with speech), Skype, AIM
Profession	Masters students and Job holders
Social Status	Middle class and lower middle class family members
Place of living	Origin is Rural Area and now currently living in Capita city for study and Job purpose.
Gender	20 Male and 5 female.

4   Preliminary Findings

In case of perceived usefulness, most respondents believe that ICT or ICT training has increased their capability to compete in the increasingly complex technological work place as highlighted in another study by Hasselbring & William (2000). According to respondents access and training to ICT has helped them to prepare draft, upload CV, searching jobs etc. But at the same time respondents are quite uncertain about their future job as most of the corporate bodies are still reluctant to recruit them. It is noteworthy of mentioning that corporate bodies are not confident about the capability of the Visual Impaired Person (VIP) persons (Frix & Pal, 2010).

Our preliminary findings revealed that most of VIP persons either get the profession of teaching in computer learning center or in others jobs where little application of computer required. According to respondents though ICT has given them access in different application programs but in case of complex program like graphics design they are not doing well. These has raised the concern of further digital divide between disabled and competent people as competent people will adopt more easily with complex software programs and their capacity will enhance at an increasing rate than that of disabled people (Doh & Stough 2010).

In case of knowledge perspective most of the respondents think that ICT has helped them to increase their knowledge by providing access to online based paper, study materials etc. Besides it has helped them to transfer recorded class lecture in computer and listen that with flexibility. Finally in case of social perspective most respondents believe that ICT has given them new social identity and reduce dependency in community, family and workplace.

In case of perceived easiness most respondents are satisfied with the existing platform for flexibility and controllability, however, local content is relatively limited. Hence they are unable to understand different computer training sessions in their own language. Another challenge identified by our participant was poor sound system of existing software/application.

5   Conclusion and Future Work

This working paper has attempted to find an early outcome or impact of ICT interventions for disabled in a developing country: Bangladesh by considering the actual beneficiary perspective. It considered the perception of disabled people looking at the social, economic, knowledge context as these issues are important in development research. We emphasized the study of particularization in the local context than generalization while understand the users perceptions. Our preliminary field data identified different themes through the lens of TAM. One of the major limitation of this study is we has to select literate disable person which actually represents very low proportionate of the entire disable population size in Bangladesh. In future, we will consider other forms of disabled people which may give a holistic view for ICT-enabled disable persons' benefit to the policymakers, NGO workers, academicians and researchers. We are also interested to evaluate how disabled people are adopting with changing technology and to what extent they are competent. In theoretical consideration, we are also interested to extend TAM considering the various social issues of the disable people. Further research will take more holistic view of disabled people with developed framework to generate new indicators for evaluating the ability of various kinds' disabled people to cope with changing technology and demands.

We conclude this working paper raising an important policy issue i.e. to what extent the policymakers, regulatory agencies and website builders are aware about disabled people, how much emphasize they have given to disabled people. This has again reemphasized our focus i.e. changing social attitude regarding disabled people.

References

Adams, D.A., Nelson, R.R., Todd, P.A.: Perceived Usefulness, Ease of Use, and Usage of Information Technology: A Replication. MIS Quarterly 16(2), 227–247 (1992)

Barnes, C., Mercer, G.: Disability, Work and Welfare: challenging the social exclusion of disabled people. Work Employment and Society 19(3), 527–545 (2005)

BBS, Bangladesh Bureau of Statistics, Government of Bangladesh (2012)

Bigham, J.P., Prince, C.M., Ladner, R.E.: WebAnywhere: a screen reader on-the-go. In: Proceedings of the 2008 International Cross-Disciplinary Conference on Web Accessibility (W4A), pp. 73–82. ACM, Beijing (2008)

Burton-Jones, A., Hubona, G.S.: The mediation of external variables in the technology acceptance model. Information & Management 43(6), 706–717 (2006)

Doh, S., Stough, R.R.: Analysis of the Impact of the Perceived Usefulness of ICT on the Digital Divide between Disabled and Non-disabled People in South Korea. International Review of Public Administration (IRPA) 14(3), 53–70 (2010)

Davis, F.D.: Perceived Usefulness, Perceived Ease Of Use, and User Acceptance of Information Technology. MIS Quarterly 13, 983–1003 (1989)

Davis, F.D., Bagozzi, R.P., Warshaw, P.R.: User Acceptance of Computer Technology: A Comparison of Two Theoretical Models. Management Science 35(8), 982–1003 (1989)

Finkelstein, V., French, S.: Towards a Psychology of Disability. In: Swain, J., Finkelstein, V., French, S., Oliver, M. (eds.) Disabling Barriers – Enabling Environments. Sage Publications, London (1993)

Fishbein, M., Ajzen, I.: Belief, Attitude, Intention and Behavior: An Introduction to Theory and Rresearch. Addison-Wesley, Reading (1975)

Forgrave, K.E.: Assistive technology: empowering students with learning disabilities. Clearing House 75, 122–126 (2002)

Frix, M., Pal, J.: A question of visibility: A rights-based look at ICT centers for persons with disabilities in Latin America. In: Proceeding of ICTD 2010 (2010)

Guillen, M.F.: Explaining the Global Digital Divide. Social Forces 84, 681–708 (2006)

Hanimann, T., Ruedin, E.: Digitale Gräben oder Digitale Brücken? Chancen und Risiken für Schwellenländer, http://eprints.rclis.org/11455/ (accessed)

Hasselbring, T., Williams-Glasser, C.: Use of Computer Technology to Help People with Special Needs. Children and Computer Technology 10(2), 102–122 (2000)

Llewellyn, A., Hogan, K.: The Use and Abuse of Models of Disability. Disability and Society 15(1), 157–165 (2000)

MacArthur, C.: Reflections on research on writing and technology for struggling writers. Learning Disabilities Research & Practice 24(2), 93–103 (2009)

Warschauer, M.: Excellent Technology and Social Inclusion: Rethinking the Digital Divide. MIT Press, Cambridge (2003)

Nations, U. (ed.): United Nations E-Government Survey 2010 (2010)

Norris, P.: The Digital Divide: Civic Engagement. In: Information Poverty & the Internet Worldwide, Cambridge Uni Press, Cambridge (2001)

O'Day, B., Killeen, M.: Research on the lives of persons with disabilities: The emerging importance of qualitative research methodologies. Journal of Disability Policy Studies 13, 9–15 (2002b)

Servon, L.J.: Bridging the Digital Divide: Technology, Community, and Public Policy. Blackwell, Oxford (2002)

Tregaskis, C.: Social Model Theory: the story so far... Disability and Society 17(4), 457–470 (2002)

Zainal, Z.: Case study as a research method. Jurnal Kemanusiaan bil. 9 (2007), http://eprints.utm.my/8221/1/ZZainal2007-Case_study_as_a_Research.pdf (accessed on 21)

Organization Culture Dimensions
as Antecedents of Internet Technology Adoption

Subhasish Dasgupta[1] and Babita Gupta[2]

[1] George Washington University, 2115 G Street, NW, Suite 515, Washington, DC 20052, USA
dasgupta@gwu.edu
[2] California State University Monterey Bay, 100 Campus Center, Seaside, CA 93955, USA
bgupta@csumb.edu

Keywords: Organizational Culture, Technology Use, UTAUT, India.

1   Introduction

In recent years, growth of the Internet and the World Wide Web has had an impact on the way local, state, and national governments work. In this research, we examine the factors that influence adoption of Internet technology in a government organization in India using an integrated model, the Unified Theory of Acceptance and Use of Technology (UTAUT) model (Venkatesh, Morris, Davis, and Davis, 2003). This research examines organizational culture as an important antecedent to the UTAUT to evaluate user acceptance of Internet technology in a governmental organization.

2   Research Model

Based on reviewed literature on research into adoption of Internet technology in a governmental organization in a developing country, and on models that are used to understand user acceptance and use of information and communication technology; we present the model for Internet technology use, the UTAUT model (Venkatesh, Thong and Xu, 2012; Gupta, Dasgupta, and Gupta, 2008; Stafford, Stafford, and Schkade, 2004; Taylor, 2004; Venkatesh, et al., 2003). The UTAUT identified seven factors that influence use of information technology (Venkatesh, et al., 2003): performance expectancy, effort expectancy, and attitude toward using technology, social influence, facilitating conditions, self-efficacy, and anxiety. Performance expectancy is the degree to which an individual believes that using the system will help her to attain gains in job performance. Effort expectancy is the degree of ease associated with the use of the system. Social influence is the degree to which an individual perceives that important others believe she should use the new system. Facilitating conditions refer to the degree to which an individual believes that an organizational and technical infrastructure exists to support use of the system. Recent studies also suggest that the adoption and use of a new technology in an organization might be influenced by organizational culture (Venkatesh and Zhang, 2010; Karahanna, Evaristo,

Y.K. Dwivedi et al. (Eds.): TDIT 2013, IFIP AICT 402, pp. 658–662, 2013.
© IFIP International Federation for Information Processing 2013

and Srite, 2005). Schein (1992) defined organizational culture as a pattern of shared set of basic assumptions that a group learned as it solved its problems of external adaptation and internal integration.

In this study we propose organizational culture is an important antecedent to the UTAUT (Venkatesh, et al., 2003). It is important to note that only four of the seven UTAUT factors listed above are represented in the model. The reason is that some of the factors identified above are not expected to impact the intention to use the system. In our study, the intention to use refers to the extent to which individuals would like to use Internet technology in a governmental organization. Gender, experience, age and voluntariness of use were identified as moderating variables in the original UTAUT; we have controlled for age, experience and voluntariness, and therefore, removed them from the model.

In this paper we use Denison and Mishra's (1995) model for understanding organizational culture. Denison and Mishra's (1995) model emphasizes cultural traits and values associated with effectiveness and identified four traits of organizational culture: involvement, consistency, adaptability, and mission. Involvement refers to the extent of participation in the organization. More the involvement of an individual within an organization, greater is the sense of ownership and responsibility. Consistency provides an implicit control system based on internalized values within the organization. It represents the degree of normative integration. Adaptability is a reflection of the norms and beliefs in the organization and provides the capacity for internal change in response to external conditions. Mission trait provides purpose and meaning and long-term vision. We use these four traits, involvement, consistency, adaptability and mission as constructs for organizational culture.

There have been a few studies in the information system literature that have used Denison and Mishra's model. Ahmad (2012) case study of e-government use in Egypt demonstrates that inherent cultural values and beliefs in the organization are critical to e-government adoption of and implementation of new technologies. Cerne, Jaklic, Skerlavaj, Aydinlik, and Polat (2012) argue that innovative firms with strong cultures have employees that tend to have similar beliefs and behavior patterns as identified by Denison and Misra (1995). Fey and Denison (2003) applied the Denison and Misra (1995) framework to compare cultures of Russian and America firms arguing that "organization culture is embedded in and shaped by national culture (pp 687)". In this study, we examined the use of Internet technologies in a government agency in a developing country. We believe that these individual traits will impact an individual's perception of the ease of use and usefulness of the Internet. That is, we propose that organizational culture is an antecedent to the UTAUT. We use the terms Internet technology and system interchangeably in this paper.

3   Methodology

3.1   Sample and Data Collection

This study is aimed at understanding how employees in a government organization, Wildlife Institute of India (WII), use Internet technologies, and how can the acceptance and use of these technologies be enhanced equitably across government organizations. Wildlife Institute of India (WII) was established in 1986 as a non-profit autonomous Institute of the Ministry of Environment and Forests, Government of India. WII's mandate is to provide research, training and advisory services in wildlife management and nature conservation to officers in various Indian government services and to sensitize people at various strata for nature conservation.

For this study, authors designed the survey and then conducted a pilot study with 5 employees in a department at another government organization in India to test the design efficacy of the survey. Pilot study did not suggest any major changes to the survey research questions except for some minor changes to language in a few questions. After finalizing the research questions, a survey was conducted at WII in India by distributing paper-based surveys to employees over several days. Out of the 110 surveys that were distributed, a total of 102 completed surveys were returned with a return rate of almost 93%. One of the reasons for these high surveys return rate was that one of the authors was able to spend several weeks at the government agency.

3.2   Results and Discussion

We analysed data using multiple regression analysis. Our results show that organizational culture influences information technology adoption. The adaptability and mission cultural traits have a significant impact on performance expectancy. While mission has a positive influence on performance expectancy, adaptability has a negative impact. Only mission has a positive impact on effort expectancy. Involvement and mission cultural traits influence social influence. The only cultural trait that has an effect on facilitating conditions is consistency. In short, our results show that organizational culture affects Internet technology adoption.

According to our results adaptability and mission cultural traits influence performance expectancy. Adaptability is a reflection of the norms and beliefs in the organization and provides the capacity for internal change in response to external conditions. Mission trait provides purpose and meaning and long-term vision. These two components of the culture are related since they are a reflection of the long-term vision of the organization and flexibility the organization has to attain this vision. Effort expectancy is only influenced by the mission cultural trait. This seems intuitive since the mission of an organization helps in focussing effort to achieve certain common objectives.

Involvement and mission cultural traits affect social influence. Social influence is the degree to which an individual perceives that important others believe she should use the new system. Involvement refers to the extent of participation in the organization. More the involvement of an individual within an organization, greater is the sense of ownership and responsibility. Since involvement refers to the degree of participation, it seems likely that someone with high involvement will consider what others want and feel important. Therefore, this individual will use the system. The consistency cultural trait impacts facilitating conditions. Consistency provides an implicit control system based on internalized values within the organization. It represents the degree of normative integration. Facilitating conditions refer to the degree to which an individual believes that an organizational and technical infrastructure exists to support use of the system. An organization that exhibits higher consistency cultural trait is likely to have a consistent organizational and technical infrastructure in place to support system use. This is confirmed by the results.

We also found support for the traditional UTAUT - performance expectancy, effort expectancy and social influence impact the behavioral intention to use the system. Facilitating conditions also positively influence usage. But, we did not find a relationship between intention to use and actual use. One of the reasons for this could be the fact that Internet technology was already implemented in the organization when we conducted this study. Intention to use is relevant in situations where the technology is very new and the users have not used it, which was not the case here. We also did not find that gender had any significant effect in the model, i.e., there is no difference in the acceptance and use of the Internet technologies among men and women in the organization. Considering all the results, we can say that the UTAUT, which was primarily proposed and tested in a developed country, can also explain information technology acceptance in a developing country such as India.

Overall our results show that organizational culture is an antecedent to the technology acceptance, and UTAUT is a valid model that can explain the acceptance of internet technology in a government organization in a developing country.

4   Conclusion

Our results show that organizational culture has an impact on individual acceptance and use of Internet technology in a government agency in developing country. This implies that organizational culture should be carefully managed for the successful adoption and diffusion of Internet and other technologies. Moreover, greater emphasis should be placed on increasing the capacity for change if the organizational culture promotes stability. Change management techniques may be used to help organizations handle change better.

We believe that we have made a valuable contribution to the literature in the area of cultural research in information systems. We recommend additional research in governmental and non-governmental organizations in different countries for further inquiry into the acceptance and use of Internet technologies.

References

Ahmed, S.R.: Barriers to E-government implementation and usage in Egypt. Journal of American Academy of Business 18(1), 185–197 (2012)

Cerne, M., Jaklic, M., Skerlavaj, M., Aydinlik, A.U., Polat, D.D.: Organizational learning culture and innovativeness in Turkish firms. Journal of Management and Organization 18(2), 193–219 (2012)

Denison, D.R., Mishra, A.K.: Toward a Theory of Organizational Culture and Effectiveness. Organization Science 6(2), 204–223 (1995)

Fey, C.F., Denison, R.D.: Organizational culture and effectiveness: Can American theory be applied in Russia? Organization Science 14(6), 686–706 (2003)

Gupta, B., Dasgupta, S., Gupta, A.: Adoption of ICT in a Government Organization in a Developing Country: An Empirical Study. Journal of Strategic Information Systems, Special Issue on E-government 17(2), 140–154 (2008)

Karahanna, E., Evaristo, J.R., Srite, M.: Levels of Culture and Individual Behavior: An Integrative Perspective. Journal of Global Information Management 13(2), 1–20 (2005)

Schein, E.H.: Organizational Culture and Leadership. Jossey-Bass, San Francisco (1992)

Stafford, T.F., Stafford, M.R., Schkade, L.L.: Determining Uses and Gratifications for the Internet. Decision Sciences 35(2), 259–288 (2004)

Taylor, D.S.: Technology Acceptance: Increasing New Technology Use by Applying the Right Messages. Performance Improvement 43(9), 21–26 (2004)

Venkatesh, V., Morris, M.G., Davis, G.B., Davis, F.D.: User Acceptance of Information Technology: Toward a Unified View. MIS Quarterly 27(3), 425–478 (2003)

Venkatesh, V., Thong, J., Xu, X.: Consumer Acceptance and Use of Information Technology: Extending the Unified Theory of Acceptance and Use of Technology. MIS Quarterly 36(1), 157–178 (2012)

Venkatesh, V., Zhang, X.: Unified Theory of Acceptance and Use of Technology: U.S. Vs. China. Journal of Global Information Technology Management 13(1), 5–27 (2010)

Facilitators and Inhibitors
in the Assimilation of Complex Information Systems

Anand Jeyaraj

Wright State University, Dayton, Ohio, USA
anand.jeyaraj@wright.edu

Abstract. Complex information systems may be viewed as systems that cut across functional boundaries within an organization and even organizational boundaries. These include enterprise resource planning (ERP) systems, supply chain management (SCM) systems, customer relationship management (CRM) systems, product lifecycle management (PLM) systems and business-to-business (B2B) systems. Such systems pose significant knowledge barriers for assimilation, require coordination with internal and external actors, and entail reengineering of both cross-functional and inter-organizational business processes. Moreover, organizations progress through various stages of assimilation such as initiation, experimentation, implementation, and routinization in assimilating complex systems.

An often-overlooked consideration when dealing with such systems is that organizations may not completely assimilate them and even abandon them midway through the assimilation process. Such stories are well-documented in the popular press (e.g., failed projects, cancelled contracts) but generally do not provide insightful explanations of the accompanying assimilation process. However, there is not much evidence in prior empirical literature as to how assimilation processes came together in real-world organizations or the differences in the assimilation processes between organizations that succeeded or failed when dealing with complex information systems.

Conceptualizing assimilation as a process by which organizations move from the initiation through the routinization stages, this research strives to uncover *facilitators* that enable an organization to move to the next stage and *inhibitors* that may force organizations to stay in the current stage or completely abandon the assimilation process. Employing a multiple case-study approach involving both successful and failed projects of different complex systems with data provided by key informants, this research aims to uncover usable knowledge for researchers and practitioners.

Keywords: Complex information systems, assimilation, stages, facilitators, inhibitors.

1 Introduction

Complex information systems include enterprise resource planning (ERP) systems, supply chain management (SCM) systems, customer relationship management (CRM)

Y.K. Dwivedi et al. (Eds.): TDIT 2013, IFIP AICT 402, pp. 663–666, 2013.
© IFIP International Federation for Information Processing 2013

systems, product lifecycle management (PLM) systems, and business-to-business (B2B) systems (e.g. Wang et al. 2008). Such complex information systems may cut across functional boundaries within an organization or even organizational boundaries, pose significant knowledge barriers for assimilation, take considerable time for implementation, need coordination between internal and external actors of the organization, and require reengineering of cross-functional and inter-organizational business processes (Attewell 1992; Fichman and Kemerer 1999; Gallivan 2001; Roberts et al. 2012). Often times, organizations enlist the assistance of external consultants or other professionals to ensure the successful implementation and deployment of such complex information systems.

When dealing with complex information systems, organizations may not completely assimilate or routinize them and sometimes even abandon them midway through the assimilation process. Such stories are well-documented in the popular press (e.g., failed projects, cancelled contracts, abandoned implementations). Consider, for example, two high-profile cases. The United Kingdom government scrapped a £12 billion National Program for IT in 2011 that was aimed at providing electronic health records for citizens after having been in the works for more about 10 years (PCWorld 2011). The United States Air Force terminated the Expeditionary Combat Support System (ECSS) with its provider after more than 7 years of effort and costs totaling more than $1 billion (IEEE Spectrum 2012). However, insightful explanations of the accompanying assimilation process in such implementations are often missing—which are crucial for understanding why projects succeed or fail.

Conceptualizing assimilation as a process by which organizations move through various stages from initiation through routinization, this research strives to explain how and why the implementation of complex information systems may become unqualified successes or spectacular failures. Moreover, this research aims to uncover *facilitators* that enable an organization to move to the next stage in the assimilation process and *inhibitors* that may force organizations to remain in the current stage or even completely abandon the assimilation process.

2   Assimilation

Assimilation may be defined as the process by which organizations identify, adopt, and routinize complex information systems for their operations. Ettlie and Vellenga (1979) described six different stages of assimilation: awareness, interest, evaluation, trial, adoption, and implementation. Fichman and Kemerer (1997) and Fichman (2001) proposed six stages of assimilation: awareness, interest, evaluation/ trial, commitment, limited deployment, and general deployment—the evaluation and trial stages were combined into a single stage, while the implementation stage was split into the limited deployment and general deployment stages. Kwon and Zmud (1987), Cooper and Zmud (1990), and Gallivan (2001) argued for six stages of assimilation as well: initiation, adoption, adaptation, acceptance, routinization, and infusion. Rogers (1995) introduced five different stages of assimilation for organizations: agenda-setting, matching, redefining/ restructuring, clarifying, and routinizing.

Figure 1 identifies the assimilation stages employed in this study, which have been formulated based on descriptions of assimilation in prior literature. These stages are designed to accommodate organizational activities from the early phases when the organization may evaluate its needs or identify opportunities for complex information systems to the late phases when the organization may routinize the usage of complex information systems for various business processes.

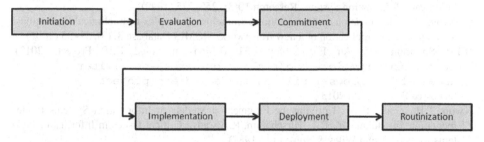

Fig. 1. Assimilation stages

3   Methods

This research employs a multiple case-study approach to examine the assimilation process at organizations that dealt with complex information systems. Multiple key informants knowledgeable of the organizations' assimilation activities are targeted for discussion. The interviews with key informants are semi-structured in that they deal with a specific set of broad questions on an interview guide but allow the informants to describe the assimilation process in as much detail as they possibly can in their own words consistent with how the process transpired within the organization. The interview guide includes questions that may elicit responses on how the organization initiated its journey with complex information systems, the sequence of activities that may have taken the organization through evaluation, commitment, commitment, implementation and deployment stages, and how it routinized the usage of complex information systems within its boundaries. The data analysis will involve two phases: a) a within-case analyses that illuminates the specific assimilation process within the organization and b) a cross-case analysis that identifies patterns in the assimilation processes across organizations. The combination of within-case and cross-case analyses would enable the extraction of facilitators and inhibitors that drive the assimilation of complex information systems by organizations. The research would provide usable knowledge on assimilation of complex information systems for both researchers and practitioners.

References

Attewell, P.: Technology diffusion and organizational learning: The case of business computing. Organization Science 3(1), 1–19 (1992)

Cooper, R.B., Zmud, R.W.: Information Technology Implementation Research: A Technological Diffusion Approach. Management Science 36(2), 123–139 (1990)

Ettlie, J.E., Vellenga, D.B.: The Adoption Time Period for Some Transportation Innovations. Management Science 25(5), 429–443 (1979)

Fichman, R.G.: The Role of Aggregation in the Measurement of IT-Related Organizational Innovation, MIS Quarterly 25(4) (2001)

Fichman, R.G., Kemerer, C.F.: The Assimilation of Software Process Innovations: An Organizational Learning Perspective. Management Science 43(1), 1345–1363 (1997)

Fichman, R.G., Kemerer, C.F.: The illusory diffusion of innovation: An examination of assimilation gaps. Information Systems Research 10(3), 255–275 (1999)

Gallivan, M.J.: Organizational adoption and assimilation of complex technological innovations: development and application of a new framework. SIGMIS Database 32(3), 51–85 (2001)

IEEE Spectrum. US Air Force blows $1 Billion on failed ERP Project (2012), http://spectrum.ieee.org/riskfactor/aerospace/military/ us-air-force-blows-1-billion-on-failed-erp-project, (accessed February 25, 2013)

Kwon, T.H., Zmud, R.W.: Unifying the Fragmented Models of Information Systems Implementation. In: Boland Jr., R.J., Hirschheim, R.A. (eds.) Critical Issues in Information Systems Research. John Wiley & Sons, Ltd. (1987)

PCWorld. 10 biggest ERP software failures of 2011(2011), http://www.pcworld.com/article/246647/10_biggest_erp_software _failures_of_2011.html (accessed February 25, 2013)

Wang, W., Hsieh, J.J.P., Butler, J.E., Hsu, S.: Innovate with complex information technologies: A theoretical model and empirical examination. Journal of Computer Information Systems 49(1), 27–36 (2008)

Roberts, N., Galluch, P.S., Dinger, M., Grover, V.: Absorptive Capacity and Information Systems Research: Review, Synthesis, and Directions for Future Research. MIS Quarterly 36(2), 625–648 (2012)

Rogers, E.M.: Diffusion of Innovations. The Free Press, New York (1995)

Virtual Worlds as Platforms
for Digital Entrepreneurship:
The Role of Internal Governance and the Rule of Law

Anuragini Shirish[1], Shalini Chandra[2], and Shirish C. Srivastava[3]

[1] CERDI (Center for Studies and Research in Law of the Intangible),
Faculté Jean Monnet, Université Paris-Sud 11
anuragini.tandalam@u-psud.fr
[2] S P Jain School of Global Management, Singapore
shalini.chandra@spjain.org
[3] Department of Operations Management and Information Technology, HEC, Paris
srivastava@hec.fr

Abstract. Based on the principles of 'rule of law' this research-in-progress paper theorizes the key role of internal governance procedures within virtual worlds for promoting digital entrepreneurship. By fostering adequate trust, internal governance procedures within VWs, provide the requisite amount of certainty, transparency, predictability and legitimacy to the transactions carried out within the VWs. In summary, this research proposes a plausible framework for conceptualizing the adoption and diffusion of VWs as a platform for digital entrepreneurship.

Keywords: Virtual Worlds, Rule of Law, Trust, IT Adoption, IT Diffusion, Internal Governance, Digital Entrepreneurship.

Research Agenda

Virtual Worlds (VWs) are fast emerging as attractive platforms for creating and conducting innovative business. Unlike traditional Internet based tools (such as e-commerce), which serve only as a medium for transaction and collaboration, VWs provide a comprehensive environment which could be leveraged for creating novel digital products and services. Analogous to real-world entrepreneurs, the emerging breed of digital entrepreneurs is looking to leverage the VW platform for producing and selling digital products and services within the VW. However, the potential adoption and diffusion of VWs among digital entrepreneurs appears be relatively less due to several reasons. One of the prime concerns limiting its entrepreneurial use is the fact that internal governance within VWs is seldom transparent, clear and predictable. The providers of VW often purport to have absolute discretion on the exercise of their powers to refuse user's interests/rights both under contract and property law. The basic and important questions that concern any digital entrepreneur are thus left vague and unanswered, leading to lack of trust in wanting to adopt VWs for entrepreneurial activities.

Y.K. Dwivedi et al. (Eds.): TDIT 2013, IFIP AICT 402, pp. 667–668, 2013.
© IFIP International Federation for Information Processing 2013

Grounding the current study in the 'theory of the rule of law', and 'literature on virtual trust' we propose that similar to 'real world', digital entrepreneurs require predictable, legitimate and transparent internal governance procedures within the VW. It is well established in the real world that for fostering economic activity it is necessary to have the governance of persons (real or fictitious), based on the basic principles of the rule of law. The rule of law generally requires that the governing agencies announce and follow pre-negotiated procedures so that the expectations of the governor and the governed are clear, predictable and transparent. It is also well established that in societies where the rule of law is strong, economic development is progressive (Tamanaha, 2004). Moreover, rule of law becomes significant as a business enabler when virtual commerce expands (Balkin, 2004). In this research-in-progress poster paper, we propose a framework for conceptualizing the adoption and diffusion of VWs as a platform for digital entrepreneurship. We also suggest a plausible methodology for testing the formulated hypotheses.

References

Tamanaha, B.Z.: On the rule of law: History, politics, theory, p. 119. Cambridge University Press (2004)
Balkin, J.M.: Virtual Liberty: Freedom to Design and Freedom to Play in Virtual Worlds. Virginia Law Review 90(8), 2043–2098 (2004)

Author Index

Abraham, Dolphy M.   639
Åkesson, Maria   467
Alam, M. Shahanoor   359
Alexander, Martin   164
Amar, A.D.   39
Ambrose, Paul J.   579
Antony, George V.   73
Ashraf, Md. Mahfuz   652

Baskerville, Richard   279
Bhat, Jyoti M.   343
Bødker, Keld   510
Brooks, Laurence   136, 359
Bunker, Deborah   21

Casey, Rebecca   164
Cecez-Kecmanovic, Dubravka   1
Chandra, Shalini   667
Chen, Hsin   136
Coakes, Elayne   39

Damsgaard, Jan   261
Dasgupta, Subhasish   658
De', Rahul   105, 538
Desai, Darshan   583
Deschoolmeester, Dirk   57
Devos, Jan   57
Dijkshoorn, Andres   391
Dwivedi, Yogesh K.   73, 203, 240

Edwards, Helen M.   619
Elbanna, Amany   89
El-Haddadeh, Ramzi   436

Gangadharan, G.R.   481
Gardner, Lesley   151
Gerostergioudis, Georgios   136
Ghadiri, Argang   555
Granados, Maria L.   39
Gregor, Shirley   596
Gunupudi, Laxmi   105
Gupta, Babita   658

Haque, Akhlaque   375
Hawryszkiewycz, Igor   587

Homburg, Vincent   391
Hoque, Md. Rakibul   652
Hossain, Mohammad Alamgir   184

Imran, Ahmed   596
Irani, Zahir   436
Iyamu, Tiko   525, 605

Janssen, Marijn   121, 481
Jeyaraj, Anand   663

Kameswari, V.L.V.   407
Kankanhalli, Atreyi   644
Kapoor, Kawaljeet   203
Kartik, Muktha   73
Kautz, Karlheinz   1
Klein, Richard   221
Krishnan, Satish   420
Kuiper, Eleonora J.   481

Lal, Banita   73
Landeweerd, Marcel   221
Larsen, Tor J.   495
Lee, Habin   436
Levine, Linda   21, 495
Lim, John   420
Linderoth, Henrik C.J.   89
Luttighuis, Paul Oude   481

Madsen, Sabine   510
Majumder, Madhumita G.   639
Malik, Bushra Tahseen   652
Mantode, Kamna L.   375
Marath, Bhasi   326
Michaelson, Rosa   295
Miller, Siân   73
Mkhomazi, Sharol Sibongile   525, 605
Molnar, Andreea   436
Mukundan, Rajeev   611
Munro, David   579
Myers, Michael D.   151

Oates, Briony J.   619

Papazafeiropoulou, Anastasia   136
Persson, John Stouby   310
Pries-Heje, Jan   279

Quaddus, Mohammed   184

Raghavan, Vishnupriya   639
Rana, Nripendra P.   240
Ranjini, C.R.   625
Rao, Ravi A.   538
Ravichandran, Karthik   73

Sekgweleo, Tefo   605
Séror, Ann   451
Shirish, Anuragini   667
Sivamalai, Lewin   633
Spil, Ton   221
Srinivasan, Nikhil   261
Srivastava, Shirish C.   667

Teo, Thompson S.H.   420
Thomas, Sam   326, 611

Thomsen, Michel   467
Tøth, Thomas   510
Turner, Tim   596

Vaidya, Ranjan   151
van der Voort, Haiko   121
Van Landeghem, Hendrik   57
van Veenstra, Anne Fleur   121
Vaziri, Daryoush Daniel   555

Wainwright, David W.   619
Wani, Marya   639
Waring, Teresa   164
Wastell, David   566
Weerakkody, Vishanth   436
Williams, Michael D.   73, 203, 240
Woody, Carol   21

Yang, Zhenbin   644

Zahid, Md. Jahangir Alam   652

Printed in the United States
By Bookmasters